THE HOME OWNERS'
COMPLETE
Garden Handbook

THE HOME OWNERS'
COMPLETE
Garden Handbook

By JOHN HAYES MELADY

Illustrated by EVA MELADY

Grosset & Dunlap *Publishers*

NEW YORK

ISBN: 0-448-01578-1
1977 PRINTING

PRINTED IN THE UNITED STATES OF AMERICA

Contents

BOOK I

Flowers

BOOK II

Vegetables

BOOK III

Lawns

BOOK IV

Fruits

BOOK V

Landscaping

INTRODUCTION

IT HAS BECOME increasingly popular over the years to turn for relaxation and pleasure to spectator activities. We watch television,
we go to the movies and to ball games, and we listen to the radio.
But there is one pastime that is more fun to indulge in actively
—and that is gardening.

Oddly enough, or perhaps because there has been such a tendency to passive relaxation, more and more people are turning to
gardening—not only those who live in the country and in small
towns but the many who are daily moving into the great new
housing developments that are springing up all over the country.
And wherever we have a plot of ground, we cannot resist doing
something with it, whether it is to plant flowers to enjoy from
spring to fall, to produce a crop of vegetables to feed the family
and save money, to grow a lush emerald lawn, or even to plunge
into the complicated but fascinating world of landscaping.

Most of us begin by buying a book about one side of gardening
—a flower book, for instance—but soon we are intent upon developing a green thumb in all directions. And before we know it we
are encumbered with more books than seeds. Not only do these
many books duplicate each other to some extent but they provide

an immense reference problem for the poor gardener who is faced with, possibly, a strange new insect and doesn't know which book holds the cure. How much happier to begin with a book that has everything you will need to know as your interests in gardening expand.

Here is that book. Written by an expert in the field, this is a compendium of authoritative, detailed information on everything the beginning or experienced gardener needs to know about planting, soil, fertilizers and plant foods, insects and diseases, and the many flowers, vegetables, trees and shrubs that may be used to enhance the charm of his home. Conveniently separated into five sections devoted to each of the principal aspects of gardening —flowers, vegetables, lawns, fruit trees and landscaping—THE HOME OWNERS' COMPLETE GARDEN HANDBOOK allows you to apply yourself to a single field while at the same time having information on all the others at your fingertips in one book. Each section is completely independent of the others, yet they can all be used interdependently in making any kind of garden. To help you find your way you will find a comprehensive index right at hand at the beginning of each section.

In addition there are hundreds of detailed line drawings of the many flowers and other plants, as well as charts of sowing times, flower colors, and crop expectancy, and graphic garden plans.

THE HOME OWNERS' COMPLETE GARDEN HANDBOOK has been compiled from five successful previously published garden books, and we feel that any gardener, young or old, novice or veteran, will find it as indispensable to his success in tilling the soil as his hoe.

BOOK I
Flowers

Index

The Flowers of Spring

"For, lo! the winter is past, the rain is over and gone; the flowers appear on the earth; the time of the singing of birds is come, and the voice of the turtle is heard in our land." SONG OF SOLOMON xi. 12.

THE FLOWERS THAT BLOOM IN THE SPRING, TRA LA

A CHARMING SPOT I often visit is the Neighbors' garden; quick to recognize that a garden-owner is the best type of citizen, the community respects the Neighbors. Small enough to be very personal, the garden is tended by its owners; they love every plant in it, and sometimes they feel that the plants know them in return. Within its hedges you find friendliness, contentment and quiet. Cars are passing near by, but you fail to notice them. Willingly the junior members of the family assume their share of the lighter tasks, their young friends come to work with them and the atmosphere is jolly and peaceful.

One of the first flowers to greet us in the Neighbors' garden is the crocus: modest, bright little blooms peep from the lawn or from the borders of flower beds, where bulbs were planted last October. Blue, lavender, white and gold were the colors used.

Other bulbs were put in then, and as a result the yard is now a riot of the red, pink, gold, orange and white of early-flowering tulips, followed by the giant late-flowering Darwin and breeder tulips, mostly 30-inch giants. The owners also planted yellow and white daffodils amid their shrubs, and in front of them blue grape hyacinths. In a flower bed they put sweetly perfumed Dutch hyacinths, some pure white, others in every hue of blue, pink, red, lavender and yellow. The white star of Bethlehem is here, the blue mertensia, spotted fritillarias, white and blue scillas, handsome tall crown-imperials, and blue and white chionodoxas. There are little purple pasque-flowers; and later, but still in spring, there will be the chaste white lily-of-the-valley, the dwarf crested iris, and the taller English and Dutch varieties of iris, mostly blue and yellow.

Not much effort was needed for this gay pageant. The Neighbors merely dug holes in the earth and slipped the bulbs in. Now, but a few months later, these are glorious flowers, and most of them will appear every future spring for years to come if weeds are kept away and roots of shrubs do not compete with them overmuch for food and moisture.

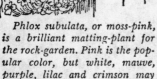

Phlox subulata, or moss-pink, is a brilliant matting-plant for the rock-garden. Pink is the popular color, but white, mauve, purple, lilac and crimson may also be used.

There is a rock garden here, skillfully made to look as though Nature, and not the Neighbors, built it. Dwarf-growing perennial plants were set in it last autumn, and already lots of them are blooming: yellow and red columbines, perennial candytufts and moss-pinks; forget-me-nots and primulas down near the fish pool. In the shady corner of the rock garden are blue violets and violas. Roots of these were purchased last fall; they also will flower every spring for years.

Roots of some hardy perennials were set out half a year ago; they all were put in one area to form a perennial border, the shortest in front, the tallest in the rear, each spaced with enough room to allow it to expand; the spring bloomers are already greeting us, and others will follow in summer and autumn. Because a new perennial border looks a little sparse at first, the Neighbors will dibble in some marigolds, petunias and other annuals to fill the spaces between the perennial plants for the first year. Some of the best spring-blooming hardy perennials can be selected with the help of the later pages in this book, including the fleurs-de-lis in their yellows, pinks, purples and white; the taller oriental iris, with their large delicately veined flowers; blue

Siberian iris; peonies with their large red, pink or white flower-bombs; charming bleeding-hearts and painted daisies.

Flower beds which the Neighbors are planting will provide a blaze of color all summer. Some plants were bought from the florist, and others were grown in the house from seeds. One bed has red geraniums in the center and blue lobelia around the edge; another has home-sown tall and dwarf marigolds; purchased fuchsias are in another, surrounded by own-grown petunias.

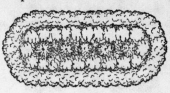

A typical flower-bed. Color is the first consideration; height is the next. Put the tallest in center, and use dwarf plants for the edging. A bed is usually viewed from all sides.

Last August, seeds of pansies and English daisies were sown in the garden, transplanted to rows, and transferred to beds this April; looking right at you, as pansies seem to do, there are no two alike. Canterbury bells and sweet williams are two other biennials sown last year which are now getting ready to flower.

We get an early splash of color when the forsythia bushes turn to gold; their flowers appear ahead of the leaves, as do those of the redbud. Those charming lilac-pink and rose-pink bushes we see are probably Japanese cherries or flowering almonds. A host of other shrubs are beginning to be covered with blossom: azalea, beauty-bush, flowering crab, flowering quince, dogwood, hawthorn, lilac, magnolia, mountain laurel, pussywillow, weigela, and the fragrant viburnum carlesii.

Forsythia blooms in early spring ahead of the leaves, making most American suburban areas bright with gold.

The Neighbors and their friends are set for a season of beauty.

WORK SHEET FOR SPRING

What is your latitude? Your height above the sea? These dates apply to average conditions in latitude 40 and at 200 feet above sea-level.

It is suggested that, in spring, for every two degrees south of the 40th parallel, you plant one week earlier.

Also for every two degrees north of the 40th parallel you plant one week later. Further, for every 1000 ft. elevation you plant one week later.

Planting a rose. (1) A large hole is dug. (2) Sheep manure, bonemeal and compost are put in.

Planting a rose. (3) The plant-foods are mixed with the bottom and sides. (4) A pyramid of soil, un-mixed with plant-foods, is placed in the center.

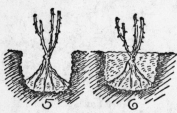

Planting a rose. (5) Rose is placed in position on the pyramid; roots are arranged naturally. (6) The hole is filled with garden soil, firmed with the shoe, and flooded with water.

Annual gaillardia
Annual larkspur
Lavatera
Linum
Mignonette

MARCH 20 TO JUNE 20

March 20 to 31

Plant young trees and shrubs. Sow sweet peas outdoors.

April 1 to 15

Plant roses. Plant hardy perennials. Set out pansies and English daisies, Canterbury bells, foxgloves, hollyhocks and sweet williams. Plant begonia tubers in pots indoors. Pinch salvias.

April 16 to 30

Plant gladiolus; make repeat plantings every two weeks to July 15. Remove coverings of leaves from perennials. Plant lily bulbs and lily-of-the-valley. Prune roses; spray or dust them with fungicides and insecticides; repeat every 10 days through the season.

Prune away dead branches from shrubs. Burn shrub- and rose-prunings. Add raked-up leaves to the compost-heap.

Sow seeds outdoors of

Calliopsis
Annual candytuft
Annual chrysanthemum
Cornflower
Four o'clock

Morning glory
Pinks
Annual poppies
Strawflower
Annual sunflower

May 1 to 31

Remove side-buds from peonies and roses. Set out seedlings of annuals after the 15th. Transplant Japanese anemones, chrysanthemums, perennial asters. Shear off withering flowers of daffodils, hyacinths, tulips, and other flowering bulbs. Shear off fading pansy blooms. Plant outdoors roots of begonia, calla, canna, dahlia, elephant's ear, glory lily, tigridia and tuberose. Side-dress perennial plants, biennials and shrubs with 5–10–5 fertilizer; rake in.

Sow seeds outdoors of the following:

Balsam	Cypress vine	Nasturtium
Cardinal climber	Dimorphotheca	Portulaca
Castor bean	Eschscholtzia	Salpiglossis
Celosia	Euphorbia	Star of Texas
Annual coneflower	Ice-plant	Swan River daisy

Set house plants amid shrubs for the summer. Stand the pot on a flat stone at the bottom of a hole, to discourage earthworms from entering; pot's rim should be level with the surface.

(1) *Disbudding carnations, leaving one to develop into a large flower.* (2) *Disbudding single dahlias, for one large bloom.*

from below the point where the choice variety was grafted onto wild stock.

Shrubs that may be reproduced by inducing cuttings to take root may be worked on now.

Spray or dust hollyhock, delphinium and snapdragon with Bordeaux mixture to control rust, blight and wilt. Set water lilies in the pond. Sow seeds of hardy perennials. Pinch chrysanthemums to induce compact bushy plants.

June 1 to 20

Prune spring-blooming shrubs like lilac and forsythia, after they have flowered.

Remove side-buds from carnations and dahlias.

Shear off the blossoms of all shrubs as they commence to wither.

Prune away growths from all shrubs that develop below ground. Chances are that these growths are

A tropical water-lily. One of the day-bloomers, it closes in overcast weather.

CHAPTER 2

Summertime Flowers

"Roses red and violets blew,
And all the sweetest flowres,
That in the forrest grew."
EDMUND SPENSER.

WHEN WE LOOKED in at the Neighbors' garden in spring we saw a brilliant display of flowers, and many more plants were showing buds ready to burst into bloom. Summer has arrived, and on our next visit to the garden we find it to be an even greater riot of color.

June is the month of roses, and here they are in their deep reds, pinks, coppery-yellows and white; most of the bush roses here are everblooming or hybrid-tea varieties, and they are sweetly perfumed as well as beautiful. There are a few ramontant or June-only-flowering kinds with their rich hues; these have little perfume, but we are grateful for their large size. Hedges are here too of floribunda roses, which have crop following crop of rather smaller blooms until late autumn stops them. There are rustic arches in this rose garden, and on them are climbing varieties. Around the plot are a number of cedar posts 6 feet apart, each supporting a climbing rose; and other climbers are fastened to a heavy wire cable running from post to post. Two paths cross in this rose plot, and at their crossing are eight standard or tree roses; the Neighbors are willing to take the trouble to protect them against winter's cold.

Stately lilies are here. In June Madonna, coral and umbellatum are in bloom; in July the Canadian, Henry's, panther, royal and Turk's cap are flowering; in August the gorgeous goldband, hardy Easter, Philippinense, oriental orchid and tiger lilies are filling the air with their fragrance. Madonna lilies were planted in September. Bulbs of the others were put in last October, or as

A good way to fence a flower-garden. Climbing roses are attached to strong posts and are tied to wire cable leading from one post to the next.

late as April. They will remain undisturbed from summer to summer.

Coming into bloom are the white or golden callas, six-foot high modern dahlias, gladiolus in every conceivable color combination, the remarkable glory lily, the striped and spotted tiger-

Left, Philippinense, a hardy Easter lily; center, the goldband auratum; right, the tiger lily.

flower, and the white sweetly fragrant tuberose—all these from bulbs planted in early May, and which will be dug up when frost kills the top growth, the bulbs being stored over winter. The Neighbors plant these tender bulbs in a border along with annual flowers, much like the perennial border, but in the latter are plants which frost does not kill and which come up smiling every year. In the annual border, along with the bulbs that have to be planted annually, they put flowers from seeds which have to be sown every year, like the annual poinsettia, California poppy, scarlet flax, flower of the Incas, nasturtium, four-o'clock, ice-

17

plant, painted tongue, annual phlox, pinks, poppy, snow-in-summer, star of Texas, sunflower, sun-plant, Swan River daisy, scabious and tree-mallow. They plant them according to their color preferences, and especially in regard to their height, the tallest in back, the dwarf ones in front.

The Neighbors like fresh flowers in the house every day, and they grow some kinds especially for this purpose. Because it is the simplest way to cultivate them and the most convenient for gathering them every evening, they grow them in rows just as one would grow vegetables, in straight lines two feet apart. They sow seeds thinly and pull out individuals where they crowd, or they set out plants from boxes or pots, of the following:

Aster	Cornflower	Pot marigold
Candytuft	Annual gaillardia	Strawflower
Annual carnation	Larkspur	Sweet sultan
Celosia	Cape marigold	Tickseed
Annual chrysanthemum	African marigold	Verbena

We saw the Neighbors planting flower beds in spring. As the weeks go by other opportunities for flower beds show up, and they may use one or another of the following combinations: balsam, edged with blue ageratum; cockscomb, with begonias; cosmos with gomphrena; heliotrope with mignonette; nicotiana with salvia; snapdragon with midget zinnia; cleome with ten-week stock; cannas and zinnias, with sweet alyssum.

Scarlet-runner beans are often grown solely for the decorative value of their red flowers; they climb 7 feet.

They take every opportunity to use climbing plants. Clinging to a 5-foot hedge of tree branches are fragrant, many-colored sweetpeas; also balloon vine, cardinal climber, cobaea, cypress vine, moon-flower, morning glory, tall nasturtium, scarlet-runner beans and passion-flower. Along the wire fence enclosing the drying-yard have been planted the perennial climbers, bittersweet, clematis, honeysuckle, hyacinth-bean and trumpet-vine. Some wire has been strung in front of the porch, and the Neighbors sit in the privacy of the large leaves of Dutchman's pipe. Over the garage doors a trellis has been erected, and on it are a blue and white wisteria.

In the rock garden, many dwarf plants are in bloom; among them are the following:

Carpathian bellflower	Golden-knee	Mother of thyme
Coral bells	Ground ivy	Dwarf perennial pinks
Coral lily	Houseleek	Stonecrop
Stemless gentian	Johnnie-jump-up	Miniature verbena

In the perennial border the color symphony is now made up of:

Anchusa	Iceland poppy
Aster Frikarti	Loosestrife
Balloon-flower	Marshmallow
Beard-tongue	Monkshood
Bee-balm	Montbretia
Blanket-flower	Oriental iris
Blazing star	Oriental poppy
Boltonia	Ox-eye
Cardinal-flower	Plantain-lilies
Coneflower	Red-hot-poker
Cupid's dart	Rose campion
Delphinium	Shasta daisy
False dragonhead	Speedwell
Fleabane	Spiraea
Garden phlox	Tickseed
Hemerocallis	Transvaal daisy

Change the position of your delphiniums every second year. Feed them occasionally small amounts of 5–10–5 fertilizer, and spray with a fungicide every ten days.

And the following biennials are in flower: Canterbury bells, evening primrose, foxglove, hollyhock, and sweet william.

In the pond garden, water lilies are blooming—the tropical day-bloomers in bright weather, the night-bloomers when it is cloudy. Lotus is pushing cream or pink flowers above the water, and the water-hyacinth is bright with blue.

Many of the shrubs are now the happy feeding grounds of the butterflies and hummingbirds. Some outstanding ones blooming in early summer and midsummer are abelia, bean-tree, butterfly-

Leaves of the elephant's ear are often four feet long and 2½ feet wide. Plant the roots for a striking semi-tropical effect.

bush, crape myrtle, deutzia, white and blue hydrangeas, mock orange, rhododendron, rose of sharon and swamp honeysuckle.

Among the foliage plants, three are always striking, used to fill odd corners and give a semi-tropical appearance: the castor-bean, grown from spring-sown seeds; elephant's ear and fancy-leaved caladium, bulbs of both being set out after May 15 and dug up for winter storage in October.

WORK SHEET FOR SUMMER
JUNE 21 TO SEPTEMBER 22

June 21 to 30
Mulch all your bushes, which means spread a 3-inch layer of screened compost on the soil around their roots. Use a 1½-inch layer of humus or peatmoss if the compost is not ready.

July 1 to 31
Dig up and transplant oriental poppies.
Sow seeds of Canterbury bells, evening primrose, foxglove, hollyhock and sweet william for bloom next year. Prune away all but two main stems of dahlias. Make last plantings of gladiolus.

August 1 to 31
Sow seeds of pansies, forget-me-nots, English daisies, violets and violas around the 1st for bloom next year.
Shear off fading flowers of phlox.
Remove side-buds of dahlias for larger blooms.

September 1 to 22
Transplant pansies, forget-me-nots, English daisies, hollyhocks, violets and violas around the 15th. Put them where you expect them to flower next spring. If the space is occupied by other plants, set them in nursery rows and put them in their flowering positions in early April.
Renovate the perennial border. Dig up plants that are spreading overmuch, or that are too tall or too short. Spread rotted horse manure, cow manure, new or old, or humus, compost or peatmoss; also sheep manure and bonemeal. Fork these under, rake, and replant the divisions

Two popular biennials to sow in summer to bloom next spring: pansies and double English daisies.

into which you have cut your perennials; put tall or dwarf ones into more favorable positions. Increase the border's interest by purchasing varieties that are new to you, or in colors that appeal to you.

Bulbs of the madonna lily are grown in Europe; they should be planted as soon as they arrive— in late summer or early autumn.

Get your order in early for madonna lilies, and plant them as soon as you get them; they must develop a rosette of leaves before winter sets in, for normal blooms next year.

CHAPTER 3

Autumn Flowers

FLOWERS THAT BLOOM IN THE FALL
SEPTEMBER 23 TO DECEMBER 21

THE NEIGHBORS' GARDEN down the road is brilliant in September; these folk have always been on the look-out for new hues in hardy chrysanthemums—yellow, pink, red, bronze, purple and white. And they are fond of the modern kinds with flowers that begin as

Double and single garden chrysanthemums; modern sorts bloom from late August to frost.

early as August, to get bigger and better every week until November frosts stop the show. Michaelmas daisies are with them, adding their own tones of rose, pink, blue and white. They also have a number of Japanese windflowers with their pink, rose, crimson, mauve and white flowers. Elsewhere in the perennial

22

border are violet-blue mistflowers, and in back of all the 10-foot spires of the Yucca or Adam's needle.

Climbers are festooning every fence and trellis. Noteworthy are the white-flowered virgin's bower, so sweetly perfumed; the quaint shapes, markings and colors of ornamental gourds; and the orange-red fruits of the bittersweet.

The bittersweet is collected in autumn for winter decoration. It may be planted successfully in open woodland.

Many bushes and trees are maturing their berries which are so attractive and so interesting to the wild birds. These include a barberry hedge, scarlet-fruited thorn, the wahoo or burning bush, holly, winterberry, buckthorn, firethorn, mountain ash and cranberry bush—delightful to the catbirds, chickadees, snowbirds, sparrows, woodpeckers, and many another of "God's poor."

One of the last plants to bloom in autumn, when the bush is otherwise bare, is the curious witch hazel, with its yellow-brown blooms. And the Neighbors are gathering the red fruits of the Chinese lantern for room decoration.

WORK SHEET FOR THE FALL

What is your latitude? Your height above the sea? These dates apply to conditions in latitude 40 and at 200 feet above sea-level.

It is suggested that, in autumn, for every two degrees south of the 40th parallel, you plant one week later.

Also for every two degrees north of the 40th parallel you plant one week earlier. Further, for every 1000 ft. elevation you plant an additional week earlier.

SEPTEMBER 23 TO DECEMBER 21

September 23 to 30

Plant lily bulbs. Any that may not be available for autumn planting place in a cool cellar when they arrive and put in around April 1. You leave these in the ground for a number of years, so mark their position with 12-inch dowel sticks, to avoid disturbing them.

Other "bulbs" that may be set in the autumn and left in for years, are chionodoxa, spring-flowering crocus, cypripedium, Dutch, English and Spanish iris, dicentra, winter aconite, fritillaria, dog's-tooth violets, eremurus, crown imperial, lily-of-the-valley, mertensia, star of Bethlehem, ranunculus, scilla, sparaxis, trillium; and especially daffodils, tulips, and Dutch hyacinths.

Protecting a rose over winter. Soil is not hoed up.

October 1 to 31

After the first killing frost, hill roses with a 12-inch pyramid of dirt, obtained from elsewhere in the garden; do not hoe it up to the plants from around them.

Roses may be planted, now or in early April.

Dry and shellac your ornamental gourds.

Sow seeds outdoors of poppies, larkspur, calendula, and sweet peas.

In pots of soil, in bowls of moist peatmoss, or in bowls of small stones, plant polyanthus narcissi, daffodils, Dutch, French or Roman hyacinths, and lily-of-the-valley. In pots of soil plant amaryllis, begonia, calla, freesia, Easter lily, and oxalis. Set hyacinth bulbs in water.

Room-gardening. Hyacinths grow in water kept half-inch below the bulb—lift it carefully when you add more. Daffodils in peatmoss.

Dig gladiolus, dahlias, and other spring-planted "bulbs."

Dig up and plant in a cold-frame the more tender perennials, including snapdragons.

November 1 to 30

Clean up the garden. Don't burn leaves unless they are diseased or bug-infested; put them on your compost heap along with healthy weeds.

Mulch with compost, humus, peatmoss or leaves the more tender of your bulbs—anemone, cypripedium, dog's-tooth violets, ranunculus. If your garden is exposed, wind-swept and extra cold, you might well mulch tulips, daffodils and hyacinths also.

December 1 to 21

Put the garden to bed. Clean and repair tools.

CHAPTER 4

Winter Flowers

"Shed no tear—O shed no tear!
The flower will bloom another year.
Weep no more—O weep no more!
Young buds sleep in the root's white core."
JOHN KEATS.

DECEMBER 22 TO MARCH 19

IN A SHELTERED CORNER, a spell of mild weather will probably let us see the modest little white snowdrop blooming outdoors, some yellow winter aconites, or one or two of the 2½-inch greenish-white flowers of the Christmas rose. The Neighbors planted bulbs of snowdrops and roots of aconites and Christmas rose in October. There are plenty of hints that the garden is wakening from its winter sleep, but there will be few flowers outdoors until April, when there will be plenty if we planted bulbs or set out roots last year.

When the Neighbors were setting bulbs outdoors in the autumn for their spring display they took time out to plant some Dutch hyacinths in pots, Roman hyacinths also. They planted Easter lilies too, one bulb to a 5-inch pot; also callas, freesias, begonias and oxalis, some roots of lily-of-the-valley, and quite a few daffodils and early-flowering tulips. Some Chinese sacred, paper-white, and golden sun narcissus were planted at the same time; but these three kinds are in china bowls of pebbles. All the bowls and pots were placed in the dark, probably the coolest part of the cellar, and were kept moist; they were looked at once a week and watered if they showed they needed moisture. As they began to grow they were brought upstairs and placed near windows;

and now they are in bud or in blossom, so they have their own-grown flowers in winter.

All winter the Neighbors' house is gay with the dried flowers of helichrysum, honesty, gomphrena, statice, and other everlastings. They were gathered in last summer's garden.

In September the Neighbors did something else to have flowers in the home in winter. They carefully dug up some geranium plants, some sweet alyssum, annual carnations, fuchsias, helio-trope, marigold, nicotiana, petunia, salvia, and bush-basil from the herb corner. They also took half-grown seedlings found in the garden and put them in pots, standing them in a half-shaded spot; pruning and pinching them to make them develop into shapely, stocky plants. In late October they brought them into the house, where many of them are flowering gaily in the sunniest windows.

Every so often the Neighbors take a trip to the florist and buy some of his plants; if possible, they get those which have buds on them but are not actually flowering, for they want the plants to develop their flowers after they get them. There are a lot of good ones to select from, but they always have some of the following:

African violet   Cigar-plant
Azalea   Jerusalem cherry
Begonia   Poinsettia

Jerusalem cherry is a type of pepper; grown for its decorative round scarlet fruits which are not edible; but they remain a long while on the plant.

In late autumn the Neighbors sow seeds of balsam, lobelia and sweet alyssum, trans-planting them four inches apart into large pots, giving them all the light the room af-fords. They also put in some grapefruit or orange pips to give pretty green pot-plants; and they buy an ounce of timothy grass seeds and sow it fairly thickly on the soil of their ready to bloom pot-plants to give a lawn effect. They cut off the top inch of several carrots and stand them in half an inch of water, to furnish fernlike plants. They cut the stem of a globe artichoke to make it stand level in a saucer of water, so it can open into a large purple sunflower. And they stick wooden match stalks into a shapely sweet potato, suspend it in a vase with one end in water to produce a pleasing vine.

And in late February they go into the garden and cut an armful of branches of forsythia. They select branches with the biggest buds on them, place them in water in the house, and they bloom in March.

WORK SHEET FOR WINTER

What is your latitude? Your height above the sea?

These dates apply to average conditions in latitude 40 and at 200 feet above sea level.

It is suggested that, in winter, for every two degrees south of the 40th parallel, you move forward the dates given, by one week.

Also for every two degrees north of the 40th parallel you move back the dates by one week. Further, for every 1000 ft. elevation you move them back an additional week.

DECEMBER 22 TO MARCH 19

December 22 to 31

Send for seed and nursery catalogues.

January 1 to 31

Plan your garden. Order seeds, bulbs, plants, bushes and trees.

Plant bulbs of amaryllis to grow indoors; make last plantings of narcissus bulbs in pots.

Purchase flowering plants for indoors. Replant into larger pots when you get them. Repot old house plants; keep fading leaves clipped off.

Bring pots of narcissus, daffodils, hyacinths and other bulbs out of the dark as they show commencing growth; put them in a light window and turn them daily, to induce an upright growth.

Outdoors, spray shrubs, climbers and trees with Scalecide.

February 1 to February 28 or 29

Sow seeds of ipomoea bona-nox, blue edging lobelias, salvia and verbena in boxes or pots; sow sweetpeas one inch apart in pots with a 9-inch branch in the center for them to start climbing upon. Later, thin sweetpeas to 2 inches apart and thin other plantlets to 1 inch apart. Those which you had thinned to one inch should be transplanted into flats or pots later, where they should stand 2 inches apart also.

Bright blue is the color of this lobelia. Best to sow seeds in late winter indoors and to transplant in May.

From the garden cut branches of forsythia, dogwood, lilac, magnolia, mountain laurel or weigela. Place them in water indoors.

March 1 to 19

If you own a frame, make it into a hot-bed if you can get manure; or purchase an electric soil-heater. Or merely use it as a cold-frame. Put the boxes or pots of seedlings in the hot-bed, but keep them in the house for a while if you merely have a cold-frame.

Sow seeds indoors of:

Ageratum	Cockscomb	Petunia
China asters	Bedding dahlias	Snapdragon
Annual carnations	Heliotrope	Zinnia

Also sow cobaea, but in small pots, two seeds to a pot; later thin to one.

Sow all except cobaea in large pots or boxes; thin as they crowd, and when 2 inches high transplant into other pots or flats 2 inches apart. The above nine are the most important. Here are additional ones:

Sweet alyssum	Marigolds	Scabious
Calendula	Nicotiana	Ten-week stock
Cleome	Phlox, annual	Sweet sultan
Cosmos	Salpiglossis	Tithonia

Also mignonette. This does not like being transplanted; so put a pinch of seed in each of a number of small pots. Later thin to two plants per pot, and set out, keeping the ball of soil intact.

The above 22 annual flowers may be sown outdoors in early May, but the plants will never be so large, nor will they bloom so early.

Pinching plants to make them more shapely. Principle is the same as pruning, but the thumb-nail is sufficient on the soft tissues.

Prune hydrangea and spiraea.

Pinch the main leader of your salvias growing indoors; pinch side branches also. This to produce bushy plants.

Dig up, divide and replant roots of perennial sunflower, phlox and chrysanthemum. But set the chrysanthemums in a new spot.

CHAPTER 5

Sowing Seeds and Setting Seedlings

*"Be patient, O be patient! Put your ear against the
  earth;
Listen there how noiselessly the germ o' the seed has
  birth;
How noiselessly and gently it upheaves its little way
Till it parts the scarcely broken ground,
  and the blade stands up in day."*

WILLIAM JAMES LINTON.

STARTING SEEDS INDOORS

A GOOD MIXTURE in which to sow seeds is two parts of fresh surface soil from the garden to one part each of washed coarse sand or Vermiculite, if preferred, and of humus or compost.

Boxes or flats should be porous enough to permit drainage;
bore holes in them if necessary.
Pots and boxes should be
washed clean. Put crocks or
broken pieces of flowerpots over
holes to prevent loss of soil, and
fill them level with the top with
the soil mixture, shaken down
but not pressed.

In the boxes make shallow
dents 2 inches apart, parallel
with the shorter sides, with a
ruler; dribble seeds in this, aim-

2 PAILS 1 PAIL 1 PAIL
GARDEN HUMUS COARSE
SOIL   OR   WASHED
        COMPOST SAND

*Good soil-mixture for seed sow-
ing. Transplant into a similar mixture, but add a little sheep manure
and bonemeal to it. Note that plant-
foods are not added to the mixture
at first.*

ing to get them about three to the inch. For very small seeds like petunia or nicotiana make only a slight dent in the soil.

29

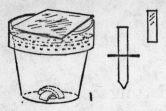

Sowing seeds in pots. (1) Scatter thinly, and barely cover them; press the surface lightly with the base of a wine-glass. After watering, lay a glass or card partly over the pot to reduce evaporation, yet allow for ventilation. Cut wood-label in half, write name and date and push into soil below pot's rim.

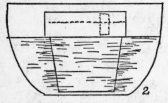

Watering. Merely stand the pot in deep water long enough thoroughly to moisten the soil. Water should not be deep enough to flow over rim of pot.

Avoid crowding; remove any seedlings which touch.

Scatter seeds on the surface of the pots, again about ⅓ inch apart. If you are short of pots, cut a wooden plant label, and press it lengthwise and edgewise into the dirt, dividing the pot into two or more compartments. Write the variety and sowing date on a 2-inch piece of plant label and insert at the end of the row or against the rim of the pot.

When seeds are in place, take a sifter from the kitchen and shake enough soil to no more than hide the seeds. With the flat bottom of a wine glass press the soil firm, so it now will be ½ inch below the edges of the box or rim of the pot.

Stand boxes and pots in water for fifteen minutes; water should be deep, but not deep enough to run over the edge onto the soil. After this you can again stand them in water when they need moisture, or they can be sprinkled with a can having a very fine rose-nozzle. It is a good plan to cut a piece of burlap the shape of the box or pot and to sprinkle through it before the plants appear.

Cover boxes and pots with glass, card or paper to discourage evaporation, but not entirely over them; leave an inch gap for ventilation. Discard this cover and the burlap when the seedlings come through. Pull out with tweezers all seedlings that crowd, and turn the containers every day so the plants do not lean towards the light.

When four or more leaves have developed, transplant 2 inches apart into other boxes or pots, making certain the roots go downwards their full length or as deep as the box will permit.

Transfer the plants to the garden when the weather becomes warm.

SETTING OUT SEEDLINGS

(1) With a trowel make a hole deeper and wider than is necessary. (2) Clip off one half of each of the larger leaves, but do not cut the growing point. (3) Quarter-fill the hole with water. (4) Place the plant in the hole, taking care that the plant will be the same depth in the garden that it was in the pot or box. Be sure the roots go down and are not doubled on themselves or twisted. (5) Lightly push the mud up to the roots.

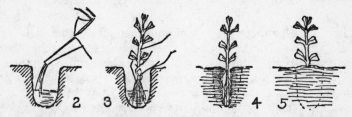

Transplanting seedlings. (1) Cut off half of each leaf; don't injure growing tip. (2) Pour water into the hole. (3) Place seedling in position. (4) Push some of the mud against the roots. (5) An hour later push against the plant the remainder of the soil, now partly dry. Firm the soil around the plant by pressing down with the fingers.

(6) Leave for an hour, when most of the water will have drained away. (7) Push all the soil into contact with the roots with the trowel. (8) Press lightly down with the hand, leaving a one-inch depression around the plant. (9) Fill this depression with water on each of the two following days.

Best time to transplant is around sunset. If the weather is hot, shade the seedlings for three days with inverted flowerpots, empty boxes, or shingles placed on the sunny side of the plants.

CHAPTER 6

Hardy Herbaceous Perennials

"God sent flowers to beautify
The earth and cheer man's careful mood;
And he is happiest who has power
To gather wisdom from a flower,
And wake his heart in every hour
To pleasant gratitude."

MARY HOWITT.

THESE LIVE for three years or more—some for decades. A few remain approximately the same size season after season; others grow and spread very rapidly. Every few years these expanding plants should be dug up, and the clumps cut into two, three, or more smaller divisions and replanted—in another part of the border if possible. Cutting is normally done with a spade held vertically, in spring or fall; the divisions must be complete, each consisting of a part of the crown or top, down through to include the roots belonging to the portion.

Plants may be purchased and set in the ground in spring or fall. As you will see from the descriptions, many may be obtained by sowing seeds in early summer, the resulting seedlings thinned or transplanted to give them ample room to grow, and finally placed in the border. Sometimes two or more years must pass before flowers are obtained.

A good way to prepare the soil of a perennial border is to spread ½ pound per square foot of pulverized sheep manure, ¼ pound per square foot of bonemeal; if compost is available spread a 1-inch layer of it, or use the same amount of humus. Dig the border the depth of a spade, rake smooth, and set out your plants:

taller ones in back, shorter ones in front, 2-foot or 3-foot ones in the middle distance.

During the period from April to September weeds must be kept away by pulling them and by hoeing; and the soil should be kept loose by the constant use of a small rake. About four times in a season, before raking, whiten the surface of the ground with 5–10–5 fertilizer. Shear off all flowers as they wither to encourage more flowers and to give each plant a longer period of effectiveness.

See the notes on beds and borders elsewhere in this book. You will find it easy to place the plants, because their height is given here. Average distance apart is one foot; taller or spreading types at wider intervals, dwarf ones slightly closer together.

A newly planted border will be sparse, and perhaps disappointing the first year. To fill bare spots temporarily, before the perennials are able fully to occupy their allotted space, sow seeds or set out plants of annuals.

Aconitum napellus. *Monkshood.* Beautiful blue helmet-shaped flowers in long spikes on 4-foot plants from midsummer until November. Tolerates partial shade and does best in soil with plenty of organic matter in it; use compost or humus. A poisonous subject; do not grow it near the vegetable garden where a root may be dug up and confused with horseradish, parsnip or similar vegetables.

* **Æthionema warleyense.** *Rock-daphne; stone-cress.* Pink flowers in May and June, resembling those of a miniature daphne, are borne on a spreading plant. Likes a sandy soil and a sunny location. Grows 4 to 6 inches high.

Agrostemma coronaria. *Rose-campion; mullein-pink; dusty-miller.* This 2½-foot plant has woolly leaves and stems, with inch-wide 5-petal flowers of bright crimson, effective from June to September. You may also meet it under the name of *lychnis coronaria.*

Alyssum saxatile, the golden-rain; a spreading perennial, smothered with yellow bloom in spring.

* **Ajuga reptans.** *Bugle-weed.* The leaves of this useful spreading plant are bronze-green. Tolerant of shade, growing in sun also, it is good for the rock garden, and an ideal ground cover. It is slightly under 1 foot, and the flowers are blue; there is a white form if you wish.

* Varieties suitable for planting in a rock garden.

* Alyssum saxatile. *Madwort; basket of gold; golden rain.* RECOMMENDED. This yellow-flowered perennial should not be confused with the white or lavender annual alyssums. About a foot high and trailing, it is covered with flowers from April to June. Plant it in the rock garden, in walls, and use it as an edging for sunny borders.

Anchusa azurea. *Alkanet; bugloss.* Striking hairy-leaved plant, growing to 4 feet, and with large bright blue flowers in summer and autumn. May be grown from seeds sown in summer, or by dividing the roots.

Wind-flowers are a feature of the garden every autumn until stopped by frost.

Anemone japonica. *Windflower.* Growing either in sun or partial shade, windflowers make a charming picture from early September to late October. Height 3 feet, and the blooms, which are 3 inches across, are purple, red, pink or white.

* Anemone pulsatilla. *Pasque-flower.* This pretty little 9-inch plant, native of the prairies, is the state flower of North Dakota. Solitary mauve or blue flowers, bell-shaped and 2½ inches across, appear before the leaves in April and May. Blooms are covered with silky hairs and have yellow stamens.

Anthemis tinctoria. *Golden marguerite.* Scented foliage and yellow daisylike flowers, 2 inches across, from July to September. Good cut-flowers for room decoration. It grows 3 feet high.

Two-color blooms are usual with the columbine. The long spurs also are an interesting feature.

Aquilegia. *Columbine.* RECOMMENDED. Old-fashioned border plants of great charm. Graceful, long-spurred flowers, often two-colored and on long stems, are at their best in May and June. Excellent for cutting.

A. caerulea, with blue and white blooms, is the state flower of Colorado. 3 feet tall.

* A. canadensis, the American columbine, is one of our best native plants; flowers are yellow, or yellow and red. Although 2½ feet tall, it is appropriate to include in a rock garden.

* Arabis albida. *Wall-cress.* Makes a fine display in a rock garden or as an edging; valuable in dry-wall gardening. Spreading gray tufts carry spikes of white blossoms in April and May. 1 foot high.

* Varieties suitable for planting in a rock garden.

* **Arenaria montana.** *Sandwort.* Another subject for walls and rock gardens. Mats of leaves about 4 inches thick have white flowers in early spring.

* **Armeria.** *Statice armeria. Sea-pink; thrift.* Useful tufted plants, 12 inches tall, with reedlike leaves and ball-shaped flower heads, 1 inch across, pink, purple or white, in July and August. Pretty, rugged little semi-everlasting, the blooms remain a good while in winter bouquets for room decoration.

Artemisia. Aromatic plants mostly grown in the herb garden for medicinal and flavoring purposes. Included are:

A. abrotanum. Old man; southernwood. Perfumed plant, 4 feet high, with finely divided leaves that mix well in floral bouquets.

A. frigida. Fringed wormwood. Narrow silvery leaves. 1½ feet.

A. stelleriana. Old woman; dusty miller; beach wormwood. White woolly foliage with small yellow flower heads on a 2½-foot plant.

Beach wormwood or old-woman is an aromatic herb that can be used as an edging if you pinch it to keep it dwarf. Leaves are gray-green.

A. vulgaris. Mugwort. Fragrant foliage plant, 3½ feet high, also with yellow flower heads.

Other artemisias are *tarragon, absinth* and *sage-brush* of the western plains; the latter is the state flower of Nevada.

Asclepias tuberosa. *Butterfly weed; pleurisy root; orange milkweed.* One of our native wild plants, with showy orange clusters in July and August. Height 2½ feet.

Mugwort is a fragrant herb that at one time was a household remedy. It has yellow flowers.

Aster (*Starwort*) **Novae angliae,** the *New England Michaelmas daisy,* RECOMMENDED, growing 5 feet; and **Aster Novi-belgii,** the *New York Michaelmas daisy,* RECOMMENDED, 3 feet high, are the originals from which many white, pink and blue named varieties have come, like Harrington's pink; Mt. Rainier, white; red cloud; little boy blue. They give a wealth of bloom in September and October, are splendid for borders and woodland plantings, thriving almost anywhere. They grow readily from seeds, but to perpetuate certain colors it is desirable to divide the clumps or to grow them from cuttings.

* Varieties suitable for planting in a rock garden.

Aster, Wartburg star. RECOMMENDED. An early-flowering lavender-blue variety, blooming in May and June. It grows 3 feet high.

Aster frikarti. RECOMMENDED. A charming blue 2-foot variety; flowers are large and borne from August to October.

Hardy perennial asters are invaluable for an autumn display of white, pink and lilac-blue.

Aster hybridus luteus. A compact plant, 2 feet high, it has small yellow flowers July through September.

* Some *dwarf hybrid asters,* around a foot high, can be obtained to put in the rock garden.

Astilbe rosea. (*Spiræa*) Fine summer-flowering plant with graceful fernlike leaves and plumes of small flowers. It likes rich damp soil. The light pink Peach Blossom, and the darker pink Queen Alexandra, are especially good. Fanal is a handsome red kind. All grow around 2½ feet.

* **Aubrieta deltoides.** *False wall-cress.* Rock-garden plants, 8 inches high, forming mats bearing purple or lilac blooms in spring and early summer.

Bee-balm flowers are scarlet. The 3-ft. plant is fragrant.

Bee-balm. *Monarda didyma. Oswego tea; horse mint; bergamot.* RECOMMENDED. A 3-foot fragrant herbaceous bush with clusters of 2-inch long scarlet flowers in July. White, pink, and dark red kinds are also obtainable.

Boltonia. *Bolton's starwort.* These 6-foot plants have flowers that look like white or lilac-pink Michaelmas daisies, but they are at their best in August. This is a wild American plant found on the prairies.

Campanula. *Bellflower.* In this family are some beautiful subjects for the perennial border and the rock garden:

* Varieties suitable for planting in a rock garden.

* *C. carpatica. Carpathian bellflower.* A compact foot-high plant with large blue or white flowers in July.

* *C. garganica.* Trailing little 6-inch gem with deep blue starry blossoms in July.

C. medium. The *Canterbury bell.* Included in the list of biennials.

C. persicifolia. The *peach-leaved bellflower.* RECOMMENDED. In June, on stately 3-foot bushes are charming bells, 1½ inches in diameter, bright blue, lavender-blue or white, according to the variety selected.

Centaurea montana. *Mountain bluet.* Typically the flower heads are blue-violet and 3 inches across, produced in July through September on plants that grow 2 feet high.

* **Cerastium Tomentosum.** *Snow-in-summer.* A 9-inch high creeping plant with whitish leaves, covered with rather large white flowers in June and July.

Chelone (*Pentstemon*) **barbatus.** *Turtlehead.* The plant grows to 5 feet, and produces long panicles of small two-lipped flowers in August that are coral-red. One of the perennials readily grown from seeds.

Chrysanthemum. There are several varieties of this plant, the most popular group comprising the hardy perennial class known as *"Mums."* Best started by purchasing roots in the spring, and your stock may be increased by dividing clumps and rooting cuttings. Included are the Korean; if seeds of these are sown in early spring they will provide flowering plants by the following September. The remarkable range of color in these autumn-blooming subjects is well brought out by listing some modern varieties. The following are double: Charles, yellow; Chippewa, wine-color; Dean Ladd, orange; Glacier, white; Morning Glow, shell-pink; Welcome, purple. In large single sorts: Pipestone, bronze; Redwing, red; Waterlily, white. RECOMMENDED.

All the above are large-flowering sorts. Also good to include in a chrysanthemum planting are the small buttonlike or *pompon* kinds like Mandalay, orange-bronze; Harbor Lights, yellow; Irene, white. The height of all these varies from 1½ to 2½ feet.

* *Cushion chrysanthemums* are striking dwarf moundlike kinds, covered with blossoms from August on; the color range is white, pink, red, bronze and yellow. They are good for the rock garden.

Among other good chrysanthemums are the *Shasta daisy, C. maximum,* flowering in June and July; the *Paris daisy, C. frutescens,* large white with a yellow center, and a favorite for window-box planting; the *Japanese daisy, C. nipponicum,* a shrubby 2½-foot plant with very large single white flowers, sometimes 3 inches in diameter; *C. balsamita* is the favorite sweet-smelling *Costmary* or alecost, frequently planted in the herb garden.

* Varieties suitable for planting in a rock garden.

Chrysanthemums should be mulched over the winter with a 2-inch layer of compost or 4 inches of leaves. Some gardeners like to dig them up early every spring, dividing the plants when they are over-large, planting the divisions or replanting the clumps in another section of the garden, possibly no more than a couple of feet away.

* Chrysogonum virginianum. *Golden knee; golden star.* One of our natives, this is a spreading plant that may make a mat 9 inches thick. It is an excellent ground cover for either sun or part-shade in rich woodland soil. It has bright yellow flower heads, 1½ inches across, from April to July.

Coneflower. *Echinacea or Rudbeckia.* Grows 4 feet high and has bright daisy-like flowers, 3 inches in diameter, that vary from purple to near-white, from July to October; the centers usually are dark brown and cone-shaped. Easily grown almost anywhere in full sun and good for cut-flower purposes. The related *black-eyed Susan* is a smaller native plant frequently met in the fields. It is the state flower of Maryland, and a favorite with wild-flower gatherers.

Long stems of the perennial coreopsis make it an ideal yellow cut-flower that is easy to grow.

Coreopsis. *Tickseed.* Old-fashioned border plants around 3 feet high, with yellow flowers in July and August. A good cut-flower, and seen in many a perennial border.

* Creeping Jenny. *Creeping Charlie. Lysimachia nummularia.* A ground-hugging creeping plant, running several feet. With its small yellow flowers it is a good rock-garden plant or ground cover.

Cynoglossum nervosum. *Hound's tongue.* Growing up to 2½ feet, with skeins of brilliant gentian-blue flowers in July.

* Daphne cneorum. *Garland flower.* Dwarf evergreen shrub with clusters of bright pink fragrant flowers in May, and again in September. It prefers a sandy, peaty soil. Growing up to 12 inches, it is a good rock-garden subject.

Delphinium elatum. *Perennial larkspur.* Mostly over 6 feet, these striking plants produce magnificent closely crowded flower spikes in July and August. By cutting the foliage to within 6 inches of the ground, a second crop of smaller blooms may be had in autumn. A new variety is the *giant Pacific,* larger, with enormous flowers, and resistant to disease. Various hues of blue and violet, with white, are seen.

This disease or blight is so widespread in the warmer sections of the U. S. that many gardeners grow this plant as a biennial, sowing seeds

* Varieties suitable for planting in a rock garden.

in a cold-frame in late summer and discarding the plants after they have flowered in the following year. Preferring cool conditions, the delphinium has less disease in New England and Canada and grows to greater perfection there. *D. belladonna* and *D. bellamosum* are forms of the *"garland" larkspur,* also blue and also tall. Their flowers are less crowded on the stem.

D. grandiflorum or chinense is a dwarfer variety, averaging 2½ feet, and deep blue. All bloom in July and August.

See also the larkspur described among annual flowers.

Dianthus. *Pinks*

* D. Allwoodii is a perennial hybrid in a great variety of colors; dwarf plants, mostly under 12 inches.

* D. deltoides. Maiden pink. A dwarf matting plant, though the white, pink or red flowers often are on 12-inch stems, well above the foliage. A good rock-garden subject, flowering in June and July.

* D. knappii. Sixteen inches high; it is unusual in that the ¾-inch flowers are yellow and odorless. Blooms in July.

* D. plumarius. Grass pink. Up to 18 inches high, but a spreading plant; very fragrant blossoms in a variety of colors and markings; this is a parent of many of the garden pinks, some double, that are offered in great variety, such as Her Majesty, Loveliness, Highland hybrids, and sweet Wivelsfield.

* New blue dianthus, actually, lavender, is a charming subject, usually blooming from July to September. Called the *blue sweet william,* it is readily grown from seeds.

Most dianthus are quick, flowering in a few months after late winter seed sowing or rooting cuttings. They act like annuals or biennials, but are true perennials, blooming in summer and autumn.

D. barbatus. Sweet william. Described under biennials.

D. chinensis and *D. heddewigii* are two *Chinese pinks,* described under annuals.

D. caryophyllus. Clove pink; carnation. This sweetly perfumed plant shows great variation. One form is

The skeins of rose-pink hearts of the dicentra make their welcome appearance every spring.

the florists' carnation, treated under greenhouse plants; close to it is the hardy garden clove carnation.

Dicentra (or *Dielytra*) spectabilis. *Bleeding-heart; seal-flower.* RECOM-

* Varieties suitable for planting in a rock garden.

MENDED. Familiar garden plant, 2½ feet high, with graceful racimes of heart-shaped, rose-pink flowers in mid-spring.

D. exemia is one of our native woodland plants. Growing 18 inches high, with fernlike leaves, it has bunches of small reddish pink flowers in April. Plant it in the wild garden in partial shade. Bountiful is an improvement; blooming in both spring and autumn with some scattered flowers in summer.

Dictamnus fraxinella. *Dittany; gas-plant; burning bush.* Strongly perfumed white, purple or rose flowers on a 3-foot plant; leaves also are fragrant. It is claimed that in hot, dry weather the gas in the vicinity of the plant will ignite. Blooms in summer.

Doronicum. *Leopard's bane.* Yellow daisylike flowers, sometimes 3 inches across, on 3-foot plants in June. Good for cutting, it will thrive in sun or partial shade.

Echinops sphaerocephalus. *Globe thistle.* Plants grow 5 feet, have white-green foliage and 2-inch-diameter metallic-blue and green spherical *everlasting* blooms in July. Good for the back of the perennial border.

* **Edelweiss.** *Leontopodium alpinum. Gnaphalium.* One of the *everlasting* plants. Tufted creeping rock-garden subject with white-woolly foliage and white flowers in June. Grows in clefts high in the Alps, and many an enthusiast risks his life to obtain it, despite the fact that it grows readily from seeds sown in spring.

Eupatorium Coelestinum. *Mistflower; boneset; thoroughwort; hardy ageratum.* Three-foot plant with hairy leaves and clusters of blue-violet daisylike blossoms in August and September. A good subject to plant near a pond, and excellent for cut-flower purposes. Near relatives are the giant 10-foot *E. purpureum* or *Joe Pye weed; E. perfoliatum, common boneset,* 5-foot old-time remedy for ague and fevers; *E. urticaefolium,* 4 feet, *the white snakeroot.* They bloom in July and August.

Ferns. These often answer the question, what shall we plant in the shady corner? Hardy maidenhair, the lady fern, spleenwort, and polypodium are some good hardy ones you can select.

Funkia (*or Hosta*). *Plantain-lily.* Easily grown, shade-tolerant bushy plants with shining leaves, parallel-veined, blooming in July and August.

F. caerulea. Blue plantain-lily. Three feet high, the flowers are lavender-purple. RECOMMENDED.

F. japonica (lancifolia). Narrow-leaved plantain-lily. Two feet high; flowers are pale lavender. A form has variegated leaves.

F. plantaginea. Fragrant plantain-lily. Two and one-half feet. The white flowers are sweetly scented.

* Varieties suitable for planting in a rock garden.

40

Gaillardia aristata. *Blanket-flower.* Grows 3 feet high, with bright yellow daisylike flowers, sometimes 4 inches across, from July to October. Excellent for cut-bloom and garden decoration.

* **Gentiana acaulis.** *Stemless gentian.* Good rock-garden subject for the cooler parts of the country, especially for placing around the margins of a pool, for it likes moist land and semi-shade. Only 4 inches high, it has dark blue flowers in summer and fall.

Gerbera jamesoni. *Transvaal daisy; Barberton daisy.* This will survive northern winters only if the soil over the roots has a coating of 3 inches of leaves or compost. It grows 18 inches high and has flame-orange daisylike blooms 4 to 5 inches in diameter. Other pastel hues of red, cerise, salmon, orange and yellow, also white, can be purchased. Wonderful cut-flower, and good for the central parts of the U. S. Flowers from July through September.

Geum. *Avens.* Grows 2 feet high and has 2½-inch semi-double blooms from July through September. Excellent cut-flower. Good varieties are Fire Opal, orange-scarlet; Princess Juliana, orange; Wilton Ruby, red; Lady Stratheden, yellow. RECOMMENDED.

Gypsophila paniculata. *Baby's breath.* The mistlike white flowers, ready in July, are much used for mixing with bouquets. The plant grows 3 feet high. RECOMMENDED.

* *G. repens,* a prostrate type, growing to 6 inches, is planted in the rock garden. White or pinkish flowers in July.

Helenium autumnale. *Sneezeweed.* Five-foot plants for the back of the border, with 2-inch daisy blooms in August and September; excellent for cut-flower purposes. The variety Riverton beauty is light yellow; Riverton gem is striped with red. Center of the daisy is yellow.

* **Helianthemum nummularium.** *Sun-roses.* They like sun and dry limestone soil; so add lime at planting time and side-dress with lime every season. Height 12 inches. Flowers are an inch in diameter; and yellow, white, copper, rose or lilac; double forms can be obtained. Good rock-garden plant that grows readily from seeds.

Helianthus. *Sunflower.* In addition to the well-known annual sunflower, described elsewhere, we have many tall-growing perennial kinds. They are useful for the back of the border or for screening outbuildings; valuable, also, for cut-flower purposes.

H. decapetalus. Thinleaf sunflower. Five feet high and yellow; a double form exists.

H. giganteus. Giant sunflower. Grows to 12 feet.

H. scaberrimus. Stiff sunflower. Grows 8 feet.

Flowers of the above three are 3 inches in diameter. All are yellow.

Heliopsis. *North American ox-eye; hardy zinnia.* Four-foot plants,

* Varieties suitable for planting in a rock garden.

41

with 3-inch all-yellow flowers, some sorts being double, in June through August. Cut the growth back after flowering for a second crop of blooms from September on.

Helleborus niger. *Christmas rose.* Growing 18 inches high, the leaves are shaped like a hand with seven outstretched fingers. Greenish-white or purplish flowers, $2\frac{1}{2}$ inches across, appear in late winter. Needs deep rich soil and partial shade. Several seasons must elapse before they bloom profusely. Quite unlike the rose as we know it.

You can have yellow and gold day-lilies, maroon, wine-color or purple, if you plant a modern mixture. Early kinds start in May; late ones continue the display through August.

Hemerocallis. *Day-lily.* A root-matting plant, valuable for holding sloping banks against erosion; good also for the perennial border and for edging driveways. About 3 feet high, bright flowers are borne from late May through July into August. Three modern mixtures are important: Sunshine, all light hues, yellows, and gold; Jacob Murray series, all darker colors, maroons, mahogany, and bi-color flowers; Francis Marion series, reds, wines, and purples. RECOMMENDED.

Hesperis. *Rocket; dame's violet.* Three-foot plants with showy spikes of fragrant lilac flowers, sometimes white; in early summer. An excellent cut-flower.

*Heuchera sanguinea. *Coral bells; alum root.* From a compact tuft of leaves, slender graceful sprays of $\frac{1}{4}$-inch red bells grow to 2 feet in July and August. Place it in the front of the perennial border or towards the rear of the rock garden. White, pink or dark crimson are other hues to be had. As a cut-flower, coral bells are good to mix with bouquets.

Hyssop, a 12-inch decorative herb for edging, is an everlasting. Useful also for flavoring in the kitchen, and used in old-time medicine.

Hibiscus moscheutos. *Rose mallow.* Shrubby species, with large scarlet blooms, are a part of the scene in the tropics, and some kinds will grow in northern gardens, this being one of them. On 4-foot plants the large pink or white blooms may be 7 inches

* Varieties suitable for planting in a rock garden.

in diameter; they cover the bush in August. Does best in moist land.

Hollyhocks are treated among the hardy biennials.

*Hyssop. *Hyssopus officinalis.* Ornamental subject for the herb garden, and decorative enough for the perennial border or rockery. It grows 12 inches high and has spikes of ½-inch blue flowers; white types are obtainable.

Iberis. *Candytuft.* Two evergreen foot-high kinds are valuable for edging the perennial border, setting into the rock garden, and for dry-wall planting; they bloom in May and June. They are multiplied by division of the roots, and they may readily be grown from seeds:

* *I. gibraltarica. Gibraltar candytuft.* Plant has clusters of lilac blossoms.

* *I. sempervirens.* The blooms are white.

The candytuft with various colored flowers is described among the annual flowers.

A nursery catalogue will show you what a wide color-range there is in the easily-grown bearded iris or fleur-de-lis.

Incarvillea delavayi. Plants are 2½ feet high; flowers are 3 inches, rose-purple with a yellow tube, looking like gloxinias. They appear from June through August.

Iris vulgaris. *Bearded or German iris; flag; fleur-de-lis.* The 2-foot high plants bear flowers in mid-June that have an extraordinary range of color. Following are among good named sorts: Gudrun, white; Royal Splendor, purple; Alta California, yellow; Ambassadeur, rosy-lilac and purple; Goblin, ox-blood; Queen Catherine, pale blue. RECOMMENDED.

Iris kaempferi. *Japanese iris.* Growing 2½ feet high and blooming in early July, these have very large and charming flowers, many as delightfully pencilled as to suggest an old oriental

Iris kaempferi is an accommodating perennial; it thrives in moist soil as well as in dry; both in sun and partial shade.

drawing. Improved sorts include: Elbrus, double lavender; Light-in-the-opal, double orchid-pink; Mahogany, velvety maroon; White Giant, white with yellow markings; Ruby King, crimson; Blue Queen, deep blue, veined with yellow. These grow in any kind of soil, but do especially well where it is moist. RECOMMENDED.

* Varieties suitable for planting in a rock garden.

43

Iris Siberica. *Siberian iris.* The graceful narrow flowers can be sky-blue, violet, or white, appearing in June. Height 3 feet. RECOMMENDED.

* Iris cristata. *Crested iris.* A 6-inch midget, with large amethyst-blue flowers and a touch of gold, appearing in May. One of our native wild plants that are ideal for the rock garden.

Lavender. *Lavendula vera.* Aromatic plant, ordinarily found in the herb garden, but its bluish *everlasting* flowers in June are decorative enough for the perennial border. The scent may not be so powerful in plants grown from seeds; it is better to use divisions of, or cuttings taken from, especially perfumed plants. Grows 2½ feet high, and a white form is available.

Lavender-cotton. *Santolina incana.* Growing 2 feet high, this feath-ery-leaved aromatic plant, with small globular yellow flowers, is almost evergreen and is used as an edging and sometimes for carpet-bedding. Normally the foliage is gray, but an all-green-leaved type can be procured. Propagation is by means of cuttings taken in spring from plants wintered in a cold-frame, or in autumn.

Liatris pycnostachya. *Blazing star; gayfeather; snakeroot.* A 5-foot plant with grassy leaves and dense bold spikes, 18 inches long, of purple flowers, from July through September. One of our native wild plants that grows well in back of the perennial border.

Lilies. These should be included in every perennial planting, and * *lilium tenuifolium* is good for the rock garden. See the section on lilies and lily-of-the-valley.

The many-flow-ered or polyphyllus lupine blooms in June and July, likes part-shade and not over-rich soil with no added lime.

Linum perenne. *Flax or linseed.* Growing 2½ feet high, it has narrow leaves and 1-inch azure-blue flowers from June through fall.

L. flavum. *Golden flax.* Leaves are broad in this 2-foot variety, and the flowers are yellow. Blooms all summer.

Lobelia cardinalis. *Cardinal flower; indian pink; indian paintbrush.* Striking 3- to 4-foot native American wild plant of pond sides and marsh. Grows in semi-shade; red flowers in July and August.

Lupinus polyphyllus. *Lupine.* One of our native wild plants found on the west coast, growing 5 feet high and giving us long spikes of bloom from June through September. Typically violet-blue, rose, red, and white types are available. Unusual in that it is one of the pea-flower

* Varieties suitable for planting in a rock garden.

plants that appears to dislike lime in the soil; it will grow in semi-shade.

A splendid English selection of large flowers in a striking range of new colors is found in the *Russell lupines.*

Lychnis chalcedonica. *Maltese cross; Jerusalem cross; scarlet lightning.* A somewhat hairy 3-foot plant with heads of scarlet flowers in June and July.

* **Lychnis viscaria.** *Catchfly.* A tuft of grassy leaves produces 18-inch stems on which are clusters of red, pink, or white flowers in May and June.

Lythrum salicaria. *Loosestrife.* Sprays of flowers are purple, pink, or cerise, carried by 3-foot-high plants in August through October.

* **Mazus reptans.** Creeping carpeting plant, spreading by means of underground stems; about 3 inches high, it has small white or blue flowers with yellow centers. Fine for the rock garden and the crevices of walks and garden steps.

Meconopsis baileyi. *Tibetan poppies.* Five-foot plants with bluish-green leaves and 2-inch purple-blue flowers in July. Fine subject for the rear of the perennial border.

* **Myosotis palustris.** *Forget-me-not.* RECOMMENDED. Eight inches high, it is covered from June through September with bright blue flowers, having yellow, pink, or white eyes. Forget-me-not is the state flower of Alaska.

* **Nepeta mussini.** *Ground ivy.* The 18-inch branching plant has long racimes of blue flowers, with dark spots, in May and June. They should be cut back after flowering to develop a compact growth.

Pachysandra terminalis. *Japanese spurge.* Growing 10 inches high, this is a glossy evergreen plant. It has green-white flowers in May, but they may escape you, because they are not at all conspicuous. It is an ideal ground cover in shady locations, planted 9 to 12 inches apart. Slips readily become rooted in midsummer. It is possible to obtain a variegated type, the leaves edged with white. Pachysandra is a satisfactory house plant when grown in pots, and bowls of the leaves are good for room decoration.

Remove side-buds of the peony, to develop blooms of maximum size. Ants like them, but they do little harm.

Peony. RECOMMENDED. Among our most popular perennials, growing 3 feet high and flowering in early June. Give them deeply prepared, rich soil and set them either in spring or fall. See that the point where

* Varieties suitable for planting in a rock garden.

the purple stems leave the root is no more than 1½ inches beneath the surface. Peonies that refuse to bloom frequently behave that way because they are too deep. Dig these barren plants up after other peonies have finished blooming, and re-set them. Cutting off the dried foliage and banking it over the roots will insure their carrying readily over the winter. Nip off side-buds in spring, allowing only one bloom to a branch, and you will get large ones.

Some good varieties of double herbaceous peonies are Kelway's Glorious, large white; Karl Rosenfield, rich crimson; Germaine Bigot, light pink; Primevere, yellow and white.

The tree peony is a 6-foot shrub with a great variety of named kinds, European and Japanese. The plants are quite expensive.

The garden phlox (decussata) likes to be given water during a spell of dry weather.

Phlox decussata. *Garden phlox.* RECOMMENDED. Mostly growing to 3 feet, the following are among the good varieties: A. L. Schlageter, scarlet; Mary Louise, white; Prime Minister, white with red eye; Catherine, lavender; Eva Foerster, salmon with light eye. All flower in July and August.

* *Phlox divaricata. The blue phlox.* RECOMMENDED. Growing 15 inches high, it is a mass of fragrant blue-violet blooms in May.

* *Phlox subulata. Ground pink; moss pink; mountain pink.* RECOMMENDED. Four-inch-high, mat-forming, rock-garden plant, and for covering sunny banks. Flowering in May; white, mauve, purple, lilac, crimson, and deep pink are the colors you can obtain.

Phlox suffruticosa. RECOMMENDED. Also 3 feet, and in various colors, blooming two weeks earlier than garden phlox. A good variety is white Miss Lingard, large and flowering in June.

Physalis alkekengi. *Chinese lantern; winter cherry.* Everlasting plant, growing 2 feet high, with small white flowers; these are followed by red fruits enclosed in a red inflated calyx about 2 inches long. Readily grown from seeds, fruiting same year if they are got in early.

Physostegia virginiana. *False dragonhead.* The plant grows 4 feet high, with 8-inch spikes of purple-pink flowers in July. White and lilac types can be had. An American native that spreads and lives long.

Platycodon grandiflorum. *Balloon flower; Japanese bellflower.* The plant is 2½ feet high with bell flowers of deep blue in June and July.

* Varieties suitable for planting in a rock garden.

46

A white type, also an autumn-flowering kind, can be purchased.

* **Plumbago larpentae.** *Leadwort.* A spreading foot-high plant, which develops a mound smothered with ½-inch deep blue flowers in August through October.

Plume poppy. *Macleaya (Bocconia) cordata. Tree celandine.* Mammoth gray-green 6-foot plant with foot-long leaves and panicles of small cream-colored flowers in August. A striking plant for the rear of the perennial border.

* **Polemonium reptans.** *Jacob's ladder.* Creeping foot-high plant with light blue bell-shaped flowers in June. One of our native wild plants. Good for the front of the perennial border and for the rock garden.

Poppies. *Papaver*

Iceland poppy. *Papaver nudicaule.* RECOMMENDED. Bright green fernlike foliage is 12 inches high, and from it in May and June issue slender stalks bearing yellow, white, orange or reddish flowers 3 inches in diameter; sometimes double.

Oriental poppy. *Papaver orientale.* RECOMMENDED. The hairy plant grows to 4 feet and has enormous 6-inch glowing scarlet flowers in

Blooms of the oriental poppy often are 6 inches in diameter; flaming scarlet is the usual color.

June and July, with black at the base of the petals; orange, white and pink varieties are also available—double types too. A vivid and striking plant for the center of the perennial border.

Primula. *Primrose*

Hardy types do best in a moist, partly shaded situation; a good place for them is around the pool; dwarf kinds are ideal growing in the rock garden. Among the best are:

P. beesiana. Two feet high. Purple flowers each with a yellow eye, in early summer.

P. bulleyana. One-inch yellow flowers in June on a 2½-foot plant.

* *P. denticulata.* Ten inches high. Globular heads of lavender flowers in April and May. A white type is offered.

* *P. elatior. Oxlip; polyanthus.* Eight-inch plants have 1-inch yellow flowers in clusters. Other colors are available.

P. japonica. Two-foot vigorous plants have clusters of copper-red, crimson, purple, pink, or white flowers in June and July; florets are 1 inch in diameter.

* Varieties suitable for planting in a rock garden.

P. sikkimensis. Two-foot plants have groups of 1-inch yellow flowers in late May.

* *P. veris (officinalis). English cowslip.* Ground-hugging plants have a group of fragrant yellow flowers atop 8-inch stems.

* *P. vulgaris. English primrose.* Small 6-inch plants have 1½-inch light yellow flowers in spring. Purple and blue varieties also.

Pyrethrum. *Chrysanthemum coccineum. Painted lady.* RECOMMENDED. Gay 2-foot high plants for the front of the perennial border. Good daisy flowers in June and July, red, pink, lilac or white; also double forms. A splendid cut-flower.

Salvia azurea. *Meadow sage.* Four feet high, this is a useful bushy perennial, with sprays of blue flowers in September.

S. farinacea. Mealycup sage. Bush 2½-feet high, with whitish hairy leaves and skeins of flowers from July through September. These are powdery violet-blue or white. These two and *S. scleria,* or *clary,* are often treated as annuals.

* **Saponaria ocymoides.** *Soapwort.* A trailing plant, 9 inches high, with loose heads of pink and purple flowers from May to August. A white form is obtainable. Good for the rock garden. The wild whitish-pink *bouncing bet* of the wayside is a related plant.

Scabiosa caucasica. *Mourning bride; pincushion flower.* Growing 2½ feet high, the rather flat flower-heads are 3 inches across and usually lavender-blue. Needs a rich and slightly alkaline soil. The long stems make it good for cutting. Hybrids of the Isaac House strain are excellent; they are assorted hues of lilac, mauve, and white.

* **Securigera coronilla.** A trailing plant, less than 12 inches high, with a profusion of golden pea-shaped flowers in July and August. Readily grown from seeds sown in spring.

Sedum spectabile. *Live-forever.* A bushy plant, 1½ feet tall, with bluish green fleshy leaves and clusters of small pink flowers in August to October. White and crimson-flowered types may be had.

Sedum. *Stonecrop*

Creeping plants for the rock garden and for dry-wall planting:

* *S. acre.* Bright yellow flowers in July and August.

* *S. capablanca.* Blue-green rosette leaf clusters, and bright yellow flowers in spring. A new arrival from Europe.

* *S. lydium.* White flowers in June and July.

* *S. middendorffianum.* Tufted 9-inch matting plant with yellow flowers in July and August. Leaves become reddish-purple in the fall.

* *S. sieboldii.* Has small pink flowers in August and September.

* **Sempervivum tectorum.** *Houseleek; live-forever.* The well-known

* Varieties suitable for planting in a rock garden.

hen-and-chickens or *old-man-and-woman,* with rosettes of fleshy leaves, which are colored at the base and are sometimes covered with a white cobwebby material. Little plantlets grow from the parent plants. Small flowers are pink. Height 3 inches.

Sidalcea malvaeflora. *Checkerbloom.* Grows 2 feet high, and has sprays of inch-long pink flowers in August, something like hollyhock blooms. A purple type may be had.

*Silene schafta.** *Moss-campion; autumn catchfly.* A compact matlike plant, 6 inches high. Stems bear one or two pink or purple flowers in October. A good subject for the rock garden.

Statice (*Limonium*) perezii. *Sea-lavender.* May be used as a dainty addition to bouquets, for the blue-and-yellow flowers are small. Blooms in August; height 20 inches. Dried, it is a desirable *everlasting.* There are some varieties of statice that grow quickly from seeds. They are described among annuals under the heading *Sea-lavender.*

Stokesia. *Cornflower aster.* The 2-foot plant bears handsome, silvery lavender-blue, cornflower-like blossoms in heads that may be 5 inches across in July through September. A good plant for the perennial border and excellent for cutting. The roots should be given the protection of a mulch of leaves or compost over winter.

*Teucrium chamaedrys.** *Germander.* Foot-high spreading plant, with glossy green foliage and sprays of pink or red-purple flowers in August; good for edging and for the rock garden.

Thalictrum majus. *Meadow-rue.* Foliage is suggestive of the maidenhair fern, with sprays of small green-yellow flowers in August. A group of the plants is attractive in the middle distance of the perennial border. Grows 4 feet high.

T. dipterocarpum. Growing 2½ feet high, it has sprays of violet-mauve flowers with prominent yellow stamens. A good cut-flower.

Thermopsis Caroliniana. Five-foot plant with sprays of large yellow pea-shaped flowers in July.

*Thymus serpyllum.** *Mother-of-thyme; creeping thyme.* Trailing aromatic herb, 4 inches high, used in the kitchen, but especially valuable as an edging, for planting in the rock garden, in walls, and particularly between the stones of a patio or walk; treading on the plants brings out their fragrance. A good ground cover on a sunny bank. The small flowers are bright lilac-purple in

Mother-of-thyme is a fragrant herb that may be planted between the stones of a terrace.

* Varieties suitable for planting in a rock garden.

49

June and July. Now an American wild plant: It came to us from Europe.

Tritoma (*Kniphofia*) **uvaria.** *Red-hot-poker; flame-flower; torch-lily.* RECOMMENDED. The 3-foot leaves are grasslike, and above them are produced the 10-inch spikes of crowded flowers, usually scarlet on top, those beneath yellow. Blooms from July through September. Not strictly hardy in the northern states; give a winter covering of leaves.

Trollius europaeus. *Globe-flower.* Three feet high, the plant has yellow buttercup-like flowers all summer, from May through August; they may be 3 inches in diameter.

Valeriana officinalis. *Valerian; garden heliotrope; heal-all.* Growing to 4 feet, the sprays of fragrant flowers are white, pink, crimson, or lavender and are borne in June and July. Long known for its medicinal qualities.

Veronica. *Speedwell*

V. incana. Whitish-green 2-foot plant, with 6-inch skeins of blue flowers in July and August; a pink form can be purchased.

V. maritima. Two-feet high with dense spikes of lilac flowers in July.

V. spicata. Grows 1½ feet high, with close sprays of blue, pink, or white flowers in July through September.

* **Vinca minor.** *Periwinkle; old maid; running myrtle.* Trailing evergreen, 6 inches high, much used as a ground cover for shaded areas. Flowers are 2 inches across and usually lilac-blue, though white and purple can be had; also double-flowered and variegated-leaved forms.

* **Viola cornuta.** *Horned pansy; tufted pansy.* Height 9 inches. Like pansies, but the flowers generally are less strongly marked and they are less sensitive to hot weather, often blooming through spring and summer. Cut them back and get a second crop of blooms in fall. Some good varieties are Jersey Gem, violet; Arkwright Ruby, red; Blue Perfection, blue; Chantryland, apricot; Lutea splendens, yellow.

* **V. odorata.** *Sweet violet.* Give them cool, moist, but well-drained soil, in a not-too-shady position. For early flowers, place straw over, around, and between them through the winter; or carry them over in frames. Good varieties are Royal Robe, deep violet-blue; Rosine, dark rose-pink; Snow Queen, white. They bloom in spring, with a smaller crop of flowers in the autumn. The violet is the state flower of Illinois, New Jersey, Rhode Island, and Wisconsin.

V. tricolor. Pansy. *See hardy biennials.*

Yucca filamentosa. *Adam's needle.* RECOMMENDED. Wide lance-shaped 2½-foot leaves are evergreen, with long curly threads on the margins and tips. In late summer an 8-foot spike grows, and on it are 2-inch cream-white flowers. This is the state flower of New Mexico.

* Varieties suitable for planting in a rock garden.

CHAPTER 7

Autumn-Planting Bulbs

"When Spring unlocks the flowers to paint the laughing soil." REGINALD HEBER.

WHEN IS A BULB NOT A BULB

WE PLANT the bulbs of tulips in the autumn. They are swollen, fleshy underground buds, in which the plant has stored a supply of food, largely in the form of starch, to give it an easy start after it has rested through winter. During this dormant period, bulbs can be dried, cleaned, often shipped halfway round the world, sold, and planted. Hyacinths, daffodils, lilies, and garden onions are also bulbs; small young bulbs are bulblets. Similar resting portions of other plants may be tubers, as in the potato, some begonias, and the dahlia; others are corms, as in the crocus and gladiolus. Young corms are cormels. Spanish, English, and Dutch iris have bulbs, but the bearded iris, oriental iris, and canna have subterranean or on-the-surface creeping stems called rhizomes or rootstocks.

In the horticultural trade it is usual to group bulbs, tubers, corms, and rhizomes together and to call them all bulbs. We have largely followed this method because of its simplicity, though it may not be strictly correct.

THE BULBS YOU PLANT IN THE FALL

The first heavy frost spoils our summer garden, and is the sign that daffodil- and tulip-planting time has arrived.

We pull up the weeds and clear away the rubbish; all that is clean we put on the compost heap. Plant remains that are infested with insects or disease we dry and burn. If time and energy are forthcoming, the spots where bulbs are to be planted are best dusted with 5 pounds of bonemeal per 100 square feet and pulverized sheep manure at 10 pounds per 100 square feet; if compost is ready, a 1-inch layer can also be spread. The area would then be spaded; and on the dug surface a repeat dressing of bone-meal, sheep manure, and compost would be given, and the whole raked smooth.

The manuring, digging, manuring and raking could be omitted, but the chances are that your flowers will not be so good or last as many years. In this case you would merely hoe out the weeds and rake smooth. It is well to treat the land generously, however, for we are planting for future years: provided the land is not filled with roots of trees, shrubs or hedges, these hardy bulbous flowers will reappear spring after spring. These are the bulbs you might well plant:

Miniature daffodils are at home in the rock-garden; they are good pot-plants also.

Daffodils look best when a mixture of varieties is planted in an open space near shrubs.

DAFFODILS

RECOMMENDED. Dig holes with a trowel and put one in each. The base of the bulbs have the remains of roots; the top usually tapers to a blunt point. There is no difficulty in planting them top up and base down, though no great harm will be done if they are planted the wrong way; they will still flower. Place them so that the soil above the top is twice the size of the bulb measured from base to tip, which means large bulbs are covered 6 inches or more, smaller ones covered 4 or 5 inches. Large bulbs may stand 12 inches apart, smaller ones closer, from 11 to as near as 6 inches. Daffodils look best planted informally, especially between shrubs or peonies. One favorite scheme, especially in a large garden, is to set them in open woodland to look as though Nature herself has planted them; the process is termed naturalizing. Allow two or three bulbs to the square foot; using mixed varieties, drop the bulbs carelessly and plant each exactly where it falls, avoiding straight lines and even spacing.

Daffodils are normally 15 inches tall and are either yellow, cream, white, or yellow-and-white flowered. The center of the bloom is called the trumpet: some have large trumpets, others have medium or small ones, and some have double flowers. Here are some good kinds:

Large trumpets: King Alfred, all yellow; Spring Glory, yellow trumpet, the perianth, which surrounds the trumpet, white; Beersheba, all white. Shorter trumpets or cups: Lucienne, with a creamy perianth and a deep yellow cup edged with orange; Firetail, creamy white with a flat cup, frilled and scarlet. Very short cups: Actaea, one of the scented *pheasant-eye* daffodils, white with the yellow cup rimmed with scarlet.

All the above have one flower to a stem, but in the *poetaz* daffodils we have several pheasant-eye blooms on one stem, a good one being Laurens Koster. The poeticus and poetaz varieties are sweetly perfumed.

Some double daffodils that make excellent cut-flowers are Twink, yellow and orange, and Cheerfulness, a double all-white poetaz kind.

* There are some pretty *miniature daffodils,* less than half the usual height and good for planting in the rock garden; among good ones are triandrus albus, or angel's tears, cyclamineus or cyclamen-flowered, bulbocodium or hoop-petticoat daffodil.

All daffodils may be grown in pots or bowls of gravel or peat-moss in the home or greenhouse; varieties with large bulbs are preferred.

Sweet-scented *jonquils* are a kind of daffodil, but the leaves are rounded in section or rushlike, and several of the deep yellow flowers may be on one stem.

All the foregoing are hardy and will stand winter cold out-

* These bulbs are suitable for planting in the rock garden.

53

doors in any part of the United States. But the *polyanthus narcissi* are tender. With several flowers on a stem, they are favorite indoor plants. The beautiful flowers are fragrant, and three varieties are used: paperwhite, which often flowers eight weeks after planting; golden sun, with all-yellow flowers; Chinese sacred, white perianth and yellow cup.

Tulips. Lower row, early-flowering varieties, blooming in April. Top row, darwin and breeder tulips, blooming in May.

TULIPS

In these we get almost every color except true blue. The *early kinds* (RECOMMENDED) bloom in April in the middle Atlantic states and grow 12 to 14 inches high. Good single kinds are keizerskroon, red and yellow; bel ami, rosy pink; general de Wet, golden-orange. Fine double ones are peach blossom, pink; schoonoord, cream-white; tea rose, yellow and pink.

The parrot tulip has fringed petals, usually with several colors in the flower, and invariably some stripes of green. Blooms are so large that the stems cannot support them without stakes.

Most popular are the Darwin and breeder tulips (both RECOMMENDED), 30 inches or more high and blooming in May, including city of Haarlem, dazzling vermilion; Clara Butt, rose-pink; glacier, ivory-white; golden age, yellow; insurpassable, orchid-lavender; the bishop, deep violet. All are good *Darwins.*

Outstanding *breeders* are dillenburg, salmon-orange and bronze; Louis XIV, purple and gold; tantalus, yellow and slate-violet; Indian chief, reddish mahogany.

Parrot tulips have large, deeply cut and fringed flowers. Rec-OMMENDED. By all means, plant fantasy, rose-pink; blue parrot, bluish heliotrope; red champion, carmine; sunshine, gold; black parrot, dark purple. Tie each to a thin plant stick, for often the stems are weak and unable to support the mammoth flowers, in which usually there are streaks of green. Parrot tulips average around 2 feet high.

Tulips have been grown for centuries, during which patient Dutch growers have developed a great variety of color combinations. The *wild tulips* which have been used as parents to make our modern varieties are still collected, mostly around the shores of the Mediterranean and the middle East. These unimproved wild types are offered by dealers as botanical or species tulips; among interesting ones are: * tulipa acuminata, the yellow-red rat-railed tulip; * clusiana, the white and red striped lady tulip, like peppermint candy; * eichleri, large deep scarlet flower; * kaufmanniana, yellow and carmine; praestans, hairy plant with light red flowers; viridiflora, green flower streaked with yellow.

Tulips are planted 6 to 9 inches apart and are covered with soil as thick as three times the size of the bulb from base to tip. They grow well in pots; the foot-high early kinds are preferred. Taller ones need five thin canes set close to the rim of the pot; tie rows of twine from cane to cane to form a supporting fence.

DUTCH HYACINTHS

RECOMMENDED. These make good formal beds, set in circles, curves or straight lines. Red, white, and blue varieties can be planted to represent the U. S. flag; yellow and pink kinds can also be obtained, all growing about a foot high. Plant them 6 to 9 inches apart and cover them with 6 inches of soil.

Planted outdoors, hyacinths provide a perfumed corner, with all the colors of the rainbow.

They grow well in pots indoors, and for this purpose specially large bulbs are used, as also for the quicker *French or Roman hyacinths,* with a less crowded flower stalk. All hyacinths are sweetly

* These bulbs are suitable for planting in the rock garden.

perfumed. Dutch hyacinths are so large and the flowers so close together on the stem that they are often mistakenly called double hyacinths; but kinds exist in which each bell is an actual double flower. They are most suitable for growing indoors.

OTHER AUTUMN PLANTING BULBS

* **Grape Hyacinths.** *Muscari botryoides.* RECOMMENDED. Growing 9 inches to a foot in height, these charming plants have a long period of effectiveness. They are in bloom when the daffodils flower and they continue until the late-flowering tulips are over. The closely packed blooms are ball-shaped and an intense blue; a white form can be planted, and the feather hyacinth, *Muscari plumosum,* has finely fringed flowers.

* **Aconite, winter.** *Eranthis hyemalis.* With the snowdrop, these are among the first flowers to appear outside in late winter. Only 8 inches high, the obscure little flowers are golden. Plant 3 inches deep.

Bluebell, Virginia. *Mertensia virginica.* It grows 2 feet high and has clusters of purple and blue flowers in spring; both colors in the same cluster. Striking when planted with daffodils and yellow tulips.

* **Chionodoxa.** *Glory of the Snow.* Pretty dwarf plants with blue and white bell-shaped flowers. They look good amid shrubbery in front of daffodils.

Spring-flowering crocus may be used to edge a flower-bed; or for a charming effect they may be dibbled into the lawn.

* **Crocus.** RECOMMENDED. They are bright, 8-inch, cheerful flowers, often used as an edging to beds of early tulips or hyacinths. Another attractive way to plant them is to scatter them carelessly, about four to the square foot, on portions of the lawn that run up into corners in the shrubbery. Exactly where each one drops, plant it 4 inches deep in the turf, using a narrow trowel. In the spring, the part of the lawn in which crocus is planted is allowed to grow longer than the other grass, by delaying spring mowing by about three weeks. The yellow, white, blue, and striped flowers amid the grass look particularly well.

Crocus do not last so long as other bulbs, usually disappearing after the third season—sooner if squirrels and chipmunks find them.

Crown-imperial. *Fritillaria imperialis.* In spring the 4-foot-high stems are topped with a whorl of leaves and a cluster of lily-flowers that are

* These bulbs are suitable for planting in the rock garden.

56

red, yellow, or purple-brown. A very permanent plant, unusual and interesting, but with an unpleasant odor. Plant the large bulb 5 inches deep.

Eremurus. *Desert candle; foxtail lily.* Mostly 3 feet high, the plants have spikes of yellow, pink, or white bell-shaped flowers. Groups of three or more should be planted in the perennial border and given a covering of leaves or compost over winter.

Erythronium. *Adder's tongue.* Suitable for shaded spots, these are native woodland plants, blooming in spring.

* E. americanum. Foot-high plants with spotted leaves and lily-shaped flowers, white, pink, or yellow-and-pink.

* E. dens-canis. Dog's-tooth violet. The 6-inch plants have pink or purple flowers.

Guinea-hen Flower. *Checkered lily or snake's head. Fritillaria mileagris.* Plants are 18 inches high and have 3-inch nodding flowers that are spotted, checkered, and veined. Basic colors are purple, maroon, or white. Plant 4 inches deep.

Iris. *Spanish, English and Dutch iris,* all about 2 feet high, are bulbous and make interesting blue, white, or yellow subjects in an iris border, where they bloom in May or June. Other iris varieties are treated in the hardy perennial section; they may well be planted along with the bulbous kinds.

* Lady Slipper. *Moccasin flower. Cypripedium acaule.* These wild American orchids may be planted in damp woodland spots. Set them 4 inches deep. The plant is 10 inches high, and the flowers pink or greenish.

Scilla *or* **Squill.** Three members of this charming family are commonly planted:

S. campanulata. Twenty inches tall, this is known as the *Spanish bluebell;* it has 1-inch bellflowers, some blue and others rose-purple.

* S. nutans. One foot high, skeins of nodding tubular blue bell-shaped flowers. Known as the *English bluebell;* white, pink and near-red varieties are available.

* S. siberica. A 6-inch plant, called the *Siberian bluebell,* has deep blue flowers. There is also a white form.

All these are flowers of the open woodland; plant them 4 inches deep and 4 inches apart.

* Snowdrops. *Galanthus.* RECOMMENDED. Set these little bulbs 4 inches deep and the same distance apart. The plants are 9 inches high and bear nodding green-white flowers very early in spring.

Snowflake. *Leucojum.* Small 9- to 12-inch plants with white flowers tinted with green or red. Plant them 3 inches deep.

* These bulbs are suitable for planting in the rock garden.

L. vernum blooms in early spring; *L. aestivum* in late spring; *L. autumnale* in the fall.

Star of Bethlehem. *Ornithogalum umbellatum.* Foot-high plants have white bell-shaped flowers with green margins. Plant the bulbs 4 inches deep and 4 inches apart.

Since all these bulbs are hardy perennials, one good place for them is the perennial border. Plant them in groups of five bulbs or more and mark where you put them. One way is to make an accurate plan of the border. Another is to insert green-painted half-dowel sticks around each group, 12 inches of the stick being below ground. The idea is that when you make changes in the border you do not dig up the bulbs. The spaces where bulbs are planted may have salvias, asters, or other annuals dibbled in after they have bloomed to grow over the bulbs.

Similarly flower beds containing tulips or hyacinths may be planted every late spring with annuals like marigolds or ageratum. Wait until the leaves of the bulbs have dried and break off; then clean the bed by shallow raking and plant your summer flowers. The bulbs will be deep enough to escape injury from your rake or trowel.

There is little need to dig up your bulbs in the spring.

Hardy bulbs should be planted in the autumn, but if you are delayed for one reason or another you can put them in the ground quite late—even in early January, making holes in frozen land with an axe, if necessary. It is not recommended, but they will grow, usually with smaller flowers the first spring and more normal ones a year later.

* These bulbs are suitable for planting in the rock garden.

CHAPTER 8

Consider the Lilies

*"By cool Siloam's shady rill
How sweet the lily grows!"*
REGINALD HEBER.

LILIES AND LILY-OF-THE-VALLEY

THE FOLLOWING are hardy perennials; plant them in fall or early spring (except *L. candidum*). They are so charming and many are so sweetly perfumed that they may appear difficult to grow, but the ones mentioned here are easy. Most of them like their roots in shadow and their stems in full light—amid shrubs, in the perennial border, or with a ground cover. Spade the land 18 inches deep, work in fertilizer, and plant in groups of three of a kind. It is a good idea to set each on a 1-inch layer of sand to ensure drainage.

With one exception, the lilies here are stem-rooters; they develop roots on the stem above the bulb, in addition to those below it. Candidum is a basal-rooter, depending solely on roots under the bulb; it is overlaid by soil equal to one-half the size of the bulb from base to top. The rest are planted deep enough that the top of the bulb is covered by a thickness of soil three times the size of the bulb.

Most lilies prefer a slightly acid soil, well supplied with organic matter, so dig in compost or leaves. Here again candidum is an exception; it likes the organic matter, but wants a neutral or slightly limy soil.

Auratum. RECOMMENDED. Growing up to 6 feet high. One alone may have twenty or more fragrant flowers, 12 inches across, in August—

white flowers, spotted red, with a yellow band on each petal. Plant 10 inches deep, for it is a stem-rooting variety. *Goldband lily.*

Canadense. *Meadow lily.* Sprays of nodding bell-like orange-yellow blooms, spotted with brown, are borne on 5-foot stems in July. Stem-rooting, plant 7 inches deep.

Candidum. *The madonna lily.* RECOMMENDED. Favorite in old-world gardens, and blooming in June. It is one of the few lilies that likes a neutral soil; one of the few also that should be planted shallow. The one time to plant it is in early autumn, as soon as the bulbs arrive from France, where most are produced. They will commence to grow, developing rosettes of green; these are essential for satisfactory growth the first year, for damage by frost seems to be required. The lilies are in clusters, 3 inches long, white and fragrant.

Davidii. In July showy, nodding, 3-inch long blooms appear. They are cinnabar-scarlet, spotted with black, on a 5-foot stem. Set the bulbs 6 inches deep.

Three brilliant lilies. On the left is the showy; regal in the center, and coral is on the right. The latter is only two feet high and may go in the rock-garden.

Henryi. Husky, 7 to 9 feet high, with apricot-yellow recurved blooms, spotted with brown; often more than twenty on a plant. They appear in July and August.

Longiflorum. Like the Easter lily. For outdoor planting. Has large white trumpets in early August. Often bearing five flowers on a stem, each 7 inches long. Perfectly hardy, it grows 3 to 4 feet high.

Pardalinum. *Leopard lily.* A strong 6-foot stem carries a dozen or more handsome flowers in July, each 4 inches in diameter. The petals are recurved, bright scarlet and yellow, spotted with brown. Set the bulbs 6 to 8 inches deep.

Philippinense. Another August-blooming Easter lily, the flowers continuing until autumn frost. The trumpet is slender and graceful; the plant is 2 to 3 feet high. Pure white tinged with green, and delightfully fragrant. Set the bulbs 4 or 5 inches deep.

Regale. *Regal-lily.* RECOMMENDED. Enormous alabaster trumpets, **6** inches long, fragrant, are suffused with lilac outside and with yellow within. Stem-rooting, the bulbs should be put in 6 or 7 inches deep. The plant grows 5 feet tall and blooms in July.

Speciosum. *Showy, Japanese lily; oriental orchid.* White, spotted and bordered with crimson, with broad recurved petals, blooming in August. One of the best garden lilies, doing well in part shade and lasting many years; it grows 4 feet high.

Superbum. *Turk's cap lily.* It grows 8 feet high, with a cluster of orange-red, turban-shaped blooms, yellow inside and spotted with brown, in July. Plant 6 inches deep in partial shade.

Left, the leopard lily; center, orange-cup, an upright-looking lily; right, the yellow Henryi lily.

*Tenuifolium. *Coral lily.* RECOMMENDED. Small, graceful plant with clusters of nodding, bell-like, recurved coral-red flowers in June. Only 2 feet high, it is good for the rock garden. It likes sunlight, but moist soil. Plant the bulbs 6 inches deep.

Tigrinum. *Tiger-lily.* RECOMMENDED. Showy, spotted, red-orange flowers in August. Growing 6 feet, it thrives in any soil. Plant the bulbs 6 inches deep. A double form is obtainable.

Umbellatum. *Orange cup lily.* The erect flowers are on 2-foot stems and are orange-scarlet, appearing in June. Plant 4 to 6 inches deep in full sunlight.

Warleyense. In July and August the 4-foot stem bears orange-red blooms, measuring 3 inches across, with recurved petals, spotted with brown. The stem is a trifle weak, so attach it to a stake. Plant 8 inches deep.

LILIES FROM SEED

Many kinds can be reproduced in this manner, and mostly they will give you flowers by the third year. Treat them as you would other perennials. Seeds may often be purchased of the following:

* Suitable for planting in the rock garden.

61

candidum, longiflorum, philippinense, regale, and tenuifolium. You may have opportunities to collect seeds from other kinds.

Scales from the bulbs will often produce new plants if stuck into sand in a greenhouse, or even outdoors as soon as the weather becomes warm.

Some lilies develop bulblets, or miniature bulbs, above ground where the leaves join the stem. They may be grown to flowering size, often in three years. Lay the leaves lengthwise in the garden and cover with 2 inches of soil.

Lily-of-the-valley does well in a shaded area, and will persist for many years.

* LILY-OF-THE-VALLEY

RECOMMENDED. Easy to grow, this charming perennial is appreciated for its pure white, fragrant flowers in spring. It is hardy, preferring partial shade and rich soil. Portions of the roots, called "pips," are planted. Very persistent plants, they live for years. Height 9 inches.

It is also good for growing indoors. Planted 2 inches apart in pots of soil, or bowls of damp peatmoss, they will grow and flower in about a month.

* Suitable for planting in the rock garden.

CHAPTER 9

Spring-Planting Bulbs

*"That God once loved a garden
We learn in Holy writ
And seeing gardens in the Spring
I well can credit it."*
WINIFRED MARY LETTS.

NEARLY ALL are tender perennials; northern winters would kill them. So you dig up the bulbs in late autumn, and they remain in a cool but frost-free part of your cellar, garage, or barn. They are replanted the following spring.

Acidanthera murieliae. *Abyssinian sword lily.* Something like the gladiolus, this is an upright 3½-foot plant bearing spikes of wide creamy flowers in late summer, each petal with a splash of pink.

Amaryllis *or* Hippeastrum. Mostly grown in the house or greenhouse as a winter plant. They may also be set outdoors in summer. The 2-foot stems are topped by three or more lily-shaped 6-inch-long trumpets, red, pink, salmon or white, in various combinations and stripings. It is rare to find two alike.

A half-hardy amaryllis, Lycoris squamigera, develops leaves in early summer. They are followed by 2½-foot flower-stems bearing ten or more lily-like lilac-pink trumpets. May remain in the ground all winter south of New England if 4 inches of leaves are spread over the roots.

Veritable jewels of the garden are tuberous begonias. Scarlet, apricot, pink, yellow and white are some of the colors.

Anemone. Poppy-shape flowers, in brilliant hues of blue, white, or scarlet, mostly with a white band near the center. Plant outdoors at the end of April in well-drained soil. A florists' flower mostly for green-house culture. Height 1 foot.

  * Tuberous-rooted begonias. With their brilliant colors they are true jewels of the garden, blooming all summer. On the north side of a building and in other partly shaded spots, they do well. Tubers are an inch or two across and are usually thick and saucer-shaped; plant them either side up. You may set them outdoors 8 inches apart in mid-May, or start them earlier indoors in pots and plant them with the soil intact when the weather gets really warm. A good soil for the pots consists of equal parts sandy topsoil, compost or leafmold, and rotted manure. If either compost or manure are not available, use humus instead; if neither compost nor manure are to be had, use equal parts of sandy earth and humus. Mix bonemeal into either combination, allowing 2 teaspoons for each bulb you plant. Never let the soil in the pots become dry, which means watering once a week, as a rule; when the leaves are above ground, sprinkle them with water through an atomizer or clean sprayer, also once a week. Most tuberous begonias grow about 12 inches high. RECOMMENDED.

Fancy-leaved caladiums. Soft pastel colorings in the foliage make these charming plants for a sheltered position in the garden in summer, or in the greenhouse anytime.

  Caladium *or* **Calocasia esculentum.** *Elephant's ear; taro.* Decorative foliage plants, their large green leaves are often 4 feet long and 2½ feet wide. Plant outdoors from mid-May on. The large cocoanut-like tubers which you plant are eaten in the tropics, mostly in the form of poi.

  Fancy-leaved Caladiums. Valued for their beautifully colored leaves, for outdoor bedding in semi-shaded positions or for growth in the greenhouse. They may be started in pots, and the directions given above for begonias will apply to these also.

Callas may be grown in the garden during summer; in the living-room, sunroom or greenhouse at other times. The golden calla is recommended.

  Callas. *Zantedeschia or Richardia.* Plant in the open border when danger of frost is over. Excellent pot-plants for the green-house or sunny window. Three types are commonly met with:

  Golden calla. Two feet high. Yellow flowers with white spots on the leaves.

  * These are suitable for setting in the rock garden.

* *Pink calla.* A lovely foot-high variety with pink or near-white flowers.

White calla. Two and one-half feet high with flowers which may grow to a length of 10 inches.

Canna. Planted in pots in March or April, they should be kept warm and set out between May 20 and June 10 in the vicinity of New Jersey about 2 feet apart; or dormant roots may be set outside in mid-May. They make splendid centers for flower beds; red, yellow, or pink varieties can be obtained, some with dark brown leaves, most with green. They vary in height from 3 to 10 feet. RECOMMENDED.

Canna likes hot weather. Tall kinds are stately and have a tropical appearance.

Dahlia. Other than the fact that dahlias are highly sensitive to cold, there is little difficulty in growing them. Dig a foot-deep hole, dust in about 1 pound of sheep manure and ½ pound of bonemeal; stir with a spade to mix them with the sides and bottom. Drive in a stout pole to project 5 feet above ground; at its base lay the tuber that you buy and that must have an eye or bud. The tuber, which usually is a

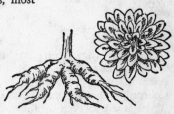

A root or "hand" of the dahlia as you dig it in autumn. Each of the fingers may be planted in spring, provided it possesses a bud or eye. Double dahlia blooms may reach a diameter of 15 inches.

finger cut from a hand-like dahlia root, should be horizontal with the eye 4 inches beneath the surface. Prune away all but two main stems; pinch the tops of these when the third pair of leaves develops; pinch the tips of the main branches when the third pair of leaves on these show. Pinch out all buds except one at the end of each branch.

Most popular dahlias are the *doubles,* with large flowers; large *single* varieties too are valuable for cut-bloom. So are the *miniature* types, smaller bushes and smaller flowers. The ball-like blooms of the *pompon* class are much liked. RECOMMENDED.

In the section dealing with annual flowers the small bedding varieties grown from spring-sown seeds are described.

Gladiolus. A week before the usual date for the last spring frost in your section you may plant the bulbs, or corms to be correct, and after 11 to 14 weeks you get flowers. You plant batches up to mid-July for a succession of bloom. RECOMMENDED.

* These are suitable for setting in the rock garden.

Expect flower-spikes of gladiolus about three months after planting the corms or bulbs.

Getting your corms from a reliable source is important, for they will have been treated against the thrips insect. Taking care not to injure the growing tips, you remove the skins, which you burn. Steep the now bare corms in 2½ ounces of Semesan in one gallon of water, allow to dry, and then plant them, covering the corms 4 inches.

Spray your growing plants every week with 2 teaspoons of tartar emetic and 4 teaspoons of brown sugar in one gallon of water. When you have dug your glads in the autumn and have dried them, break off the withered remains of the old corms from the plump new ones above them. Burn the withered remains and place the new corms in open paper bags. Keep naphthalene flakes in contact with them for a month, using 1 ounce for each 100 corms; then sift out the flakes.

Also when you dig up the corms do two things. First, search the soil for immature corms, called cormels; these you plant next spring and again dig in the fall, when they will have increased in size. Planting them the following spring, a lot will flower. By doing this you should only buy a stock of glads once, except to get some of the newest varieties. Secondly, dry and burn all leaves, stalks, and later the remains of the old bulbs: all to keep thrips under control.

Digging gladiolus. At summer's end the plants are dug, dried and the dead leaves cut off; during winter the withered remains of the old corm are pulled from below the plump new corm. Old corms and dried leaves are burned.

* **Glory lily.** *Gloriosa rothschildiana.* This is a tropical climber that may be planted in the garden after all danger of frost is over. Waxy lilylike blooms are 3 inches across, crimson, banded with gold, reflexed and waved; stamens are prominent and look spidery. Pinch to produce bushy spreading plants for an unusual flower bed.

Gloxinias may be grown in the garden during summer, or in the greenhouse in winter.

* These are suitable for setting in the rock garden.

66

* Gloxinia. *Sinningia speciosa.* Handsome subject normally grown in the greenhouse. You may plant the tuberous roots outdoors in the spring, just as you would begonias, to get wonderful velvety trumpet flowers 3 inches long: purple, red, violet, white, and spotted. It should be given a sunny spot protected against strong winds. Grows around 12 inches high.

Hyacinth, summer. *Galtonia candicans.* Quite unlike the ordinary garden hyacinth, this is a 4-foot pyramid bearing 25 or more large green-white bellflowers. Plant in mid-spring.

Montbretia. *Tritonia crocosmæflora.* A good cut-flower; blooms are golden, orange, yellow, scarlet, or vermilion. Bulbs can be planted outdoors 3 inches deep during April and May. Over the winter they require the protection of leaves or litter if planted in a permanent location south of Long Island. Lift the bulbs in autumn north and east. Height 3 feet.

Ranunculus Asiaticus. *Persian buttercup; turban buttercup.* Giant double and semi-double flowers in orange, red, yellow, and pink. Plant during May. Roots are like bunches of claws; when planting, let the claws point downward. Height 1½ feet.

Tigridia. *Tiger flower; Mexican shellflower.* Growing 2½ feet high, the plant has 6-inch-diameter flowers, lilac, red, or white, spotted yellow and purple. They last only a day, but are promptly followed by others. Plant the bulbs 4 inches deep and 6 inches apart after mid-May in a sunny situation; give them plenty of water.

Tuberose. *Polianthes tuberosa.* RECOMMENDED. Three feet high, the plants bear waxy white flowers, delightfully fragrant and beautiful. Plant in early June, with the top one-third of the bulb above the surface of the soil.

Tuberose; "The sweetest flower for scent that grows."

Of the above group, Anemones, Gloxinias and Ranunculus are sometimes disappointing. Better stick to the varieties that are recommended.

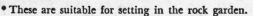

* These are suitable for setting in the rock garden.

CHAPTER 10

Hardy Biennials

"Of all the bonny buds that blow
In bright or cloudy weather,
Of all the flowers that come and go
The whole twelve months together,
This little purple pansy brings
Thoughts of the sweetest, saddest things."
MARY EMILY BRADLEY.

Sow SEEDS in summer; transplant to 12 inches apart. They bloom the following year.

Canterbury Bells. *Campanula.* RECOMMENDED.

C. calycanthema. Cup-and-saucer bells. This sub-variety is the more attractive. The calyx, which surrounds the flower and is green in most varieties, is here colored with the same hue as the bell itself.

Two biennials to sow one year and bloom the next: sweet william and canterbury bells.

C. medium. Growing up to 4 feet high, the plant bears flowers in June and July—white, blue, or pink.

* English Daisy. Bellis perennis. Good for planting in spring with pansies, the plants are 6 inches high, with bright pink or white flowers,

the double forms being the more popular. Stands the winter if given the help of leaves or straw placed between the plants.

Evening Primrose. *Sundrop; Œnothera.* A bushy plant growing up to 4 feet. The yellow flowers are open in the afternoon and close next morning. A good plant for the biennial border. Place it in a sunny position.

Foxglove. *Digitalis purpurea.* A 4-foot high biennial that sometimes lives for several years. In July it has 3-inch tubular blooms on spikes; they are pink, white, purple, or yellow and often are spotted. The plant is tolerant of shade. RECOMMENDED.

Hollyhock. *Althaea rosea.* Grows sometimes 9 feet high. Though it often lives longer than the second year, it is

The foxglove is a biennial, but often lives several years. Best play safe, however, and sow some seeds every summer to be sure of blooms the next.

best to regard it as a biennial. Particularly good for background planting. Pink, red, white, and yellow are the colors you may like to use; there is also a near-black; and you may have either single or double forms. Effective in July and August. RECOMMENDED.

Honesty. *Moonwort; satinpod. Lunaria biennis.* An interesting *everlasting* plant for winter decoration. On 2-foot-high plants purple flowers are followed by round, silvery, paperlike flat seed pods. Sow in June and protect over winter with a 4-inch covering of leaves or compost.

Hollyhocks should be sprayed with Bordeaux mixture to control rust. This is a double-flowering pink kind.

*** Pansies.** *Heartsease. Viola tricolor.* RECOMMENDED. Best sowing date is August 1. Cover the seeds three times their diameter and firm the soil above them; the seed bed should not be allowed to become dry. Transplant to 1 foot apart. Protected during winter in a cold-frame, plants are set out in bloom in April; carried over in winter they flower two weeks later. Height 1 foot.

Specially long-stemmed, large-flowering types are available for greenhouse growing.

Rose-campion. *Mullein-pink; dusty miller. Lychnis coronaria.* A biennial that sometimes lasts several years, or appears to do so through self-sown seed. Growing 3 feet high, the white woolly plant bears bright crimson blossoms in June and July.

Sweet William. *Dianthus barbatus.* RECOMMENDED. Two feet high, these bright old-world garden favorites are indispensable in the garden. They are at their best in June. The flower heads are red, purple, pink, or white, with some charming white-eyed types. Double forms may be had.

Wallflowers. *Cheiranthus cheiri.* Sweet scented and great favorites with European gardeners, they are rarely seen in America and are not too easy to grow. Sow seeds either of the single or double kinds in summer, and in autumn transplant them into a cold-frame; set them out to bloom in early spring. If a frame is not available, place salt-hay and leaves around, between, and over the plants, removing some every day in spring so as to expose them gradually. Rich soil and plenty of moisture are necessary. Height 2 feet.

Hardy herbaceous biennials are usually planted in with the perennials, replacing them every autumn; although some gardeners like to have a special place for them, a biennial border.

CHAPTER 11

The Annuals

"I don't believe the half I hear,
Nor the quarter of what I see!
But I have one faith, sublime and true,
That nothing can shake or slay;
Each spring I firmly believe anew
All the seed catalogues say!"
CAROLYN WELLS.

ANNUAL FLOWERS

THIS LISTING includes those biennials and perennials that may be treated as annuals; that is, they bloom the same summer from seeds sown in spring. Nearly all may be sown outdoors in early May where they are to bloom, or sown earlier indoors and transplanted to the garden when frost is over.

The distance apart is largely governed by the height: thin or set foot-high subjects 9 inches apart; 2-foot plants, 12 inches apart; 3-foot plants, 18 inches from each other; 4-foot plants, 24 inches apart; 5-foot plants, 36 inches apart.

The following do not like being transplanted: *gypsophila, eschscholtzia, larkspur, lupinus, mignonette, nasturtium, poppies, and sweetpeas.* If you start them earlier indoors, sow a few seeds in each of a number of small pots, thin to one plant in each, and set them out with the soil intact. But several sweetpeas may be grown in a large pot, with a twig in the center to support them in their early weeks; the soil may be set out intact, with the twig and seedlings. Or you may purchase a flat holding 40 square, cardboard, 2-inch boxes; filling these with soil and sowing seeds in them allows you to transfer the seedlings without disturbing

71

the soil around their roots. Another scheme is to cut a number of turves from the lawn, turn them dirt side up, and sow seeds; when the seedlings are large enough to be transplanted, cut the sod into squares with a mason's trowel.

A few annuals are slower to grow from seeds than most. With them it is most desirable to sow early indoors, transferring them to the outdoors when the soil is warm; otherwise they may not bloom until towards the end of the summer. Among those that should be sown early, if possible, are: *ageratum, the late asters, brachycome, cigar-plant, late cosmos, heliotrope, lobelia, petunia, ranunculus, salpiglossis, salvia, schizanthus, snapdragon, night-scented stock, tobacco, torenia, verbena, and annual wallflower.*

It is a good plan to go over your flowers several times a week with shears to clip off all flowers that are beginning to fade. If they are permitted to mature their seeds they will cease blooming.

Sorts marked * are suitable for sowing or planting in a rock garden. They are valuable for this purpose to relieve the bare appearance when the rockery is new, before the perennials with which it is planted have grown to their proper size.

For edging a flower-bed, few annuals are as useful as the floss-flower or ageratum; mix with rose-colored ones if you wish.

Carpet of snow is a good name for the white sweet alyssum, and you should plant the violet-hued variety also. Both are fragrant.

Acroclinium (Helipterum). *An everlasting.* Chaffy, double, daisylike flowers in 2-inch clusters are suitable for dried bouquets; 20 inches high. Sow outdoors in late spring; or sow earlier indoors for setting out when warm weather has arrived. Colors are mostly pink and white.

* **Ageratum.** *Floss-flower.* RECOMMENDED. Tassels of clustered daisy-like blooms, for bedding or edging. Best started indoors for transfer to the open in May; for later flowering, sow outdoors in May. Colors are blue, pink, or occasionally white. Dwarf 4-inch kinds are preferred, especially when ageratum is used in carpet-bedding, and

* Varieties suitable for setting in the rock garden.

are kept more compact by light shearing and an occasional pinching.

* Alyssum, sweet. *Madwort.* RECOMMENDED. Popular edging plant for flower beds. Sow in the open in spring where they are to flower and thin or transplant to 6 inches apart. Or start them indoors and transfer them to the garden later. Normally white and about 9 inches high, some strains are as dwarf as 3 inches. A violet-colored variety is especially pleasing; both it and the white types are fragrant. They like lime.

Amaranthus. *Tassel-flower.* Brilliant foliage-plants, some bearing curious flowers, mostly red. Sow seeds outdoors and allow the plants to stand 18 inches or more apart, for they often grow to 3½ feet. Several sub-varieties are obtainable, such as Love-lies-bleeding, Prince's feather, Molten fire, Combustion, Joseph's coat, Sunshine. Good for the annual border, but seldom used for flower beds.

Amaranthus, an easily grown annual with decorative foliage and brilliant flowers; upper leaves sometimes share the color with the flowers, most often red or yellow.

Ammobium alatum. *Winged everlasting.* Yellow daisy-flowers, each surrounded by silver-white bracts, and 2 inches or more across. Of Australian origin, the 3-foot plant is easy to grow; it is a perennial but may be grown as an annual, sowing seeds in spring. If cut before the flowers are fully open they dry white and can be dyed. "Winged" refers to the thin flat shape of the stem.

Arctotis. *African daisy.* The plant has woolly leaves and daisylike flowers, often 3 inches across; they are usually white or light lilac, though other colors have been evolved like coppery-rose, red, crimson, orange, gold, or cream. But these hybrid plants are dwarfer, 12 inches instead of the 2½ feet of *A. grandis*, the original plant.

Asters. *China aster. Callistephus.* RECOMMENDED. They should have an open, sunny position in the garden and they prefer a rich, loamy soil; do not grow them in the same ground two years in succession. Seeds are best started in a sunny window, hot bed, or cold-frame in March and transferred to the garden as soon as danger of frost is gone. May also be sown outdoors in May, though they

Annual asters should be in every garden. Thirty-inch mid-season giants, with flowers 6 inches across, in center; dwarf queen-of-the-market at left; right, single comet aster.

* Varieties suitable for setting in the rock garden.

will flower later. They are prone to be attacked by rust; but all colors are now obtainable in varieties that are highly resistant to this disease. Early dwarf varieties like * Queen of the market (1½ ft.) make showy beds. Taller kinds like Crego or Late-branching (2½ ft.) are good for annual borders or cut-bloom; these may have blooms 5 inches in diameter. Double varieties are mostly used, but single types may be even 6 inches across, and they have a yellow center. Sunshine asters have a center cushion of tubular florets, surrounded by flat guard-florets. Colors are white, scarlet, crimson, blue, purple, and pink.

Baby's Breath, annual. *Gypsophila.* Panicles of flowers about ¼ inch across; mostly white, but light and dark pink forms are seen; largely used in bouquets. Sow directly outdoors, because gypsophila does not transplant readily; and several batches should be sown

These camellia-like flowers on a single main stem of the balsam or lady's slipper give us good bedding plants. Colors are red, pink or white; some flowers have stripes or spots of a deeper color.

through the summer to maintain a continuing supply of this valuable cut-flower. Height 1½ feet.

These pot-marigolds may be apricot, orange or yellow; equally well-known as calendulas, they grow readily in the garden. Florists raise them under glass in winter also.

Balsam. *Lady's slipper. Impatiens balsamina.* Pyramid-shaped plants, 2½ feet high, usually with a single main stem bearing brilliant double flowers shaped like small camellias. White, pink, red, and yellow are the available colors; there are also spotted, blotched, and striped varieties. A new bush-flowering balsam is now offered; instead of having one main stem, these branch at the base to become neat little bushes 18 inches high, covered with double flowers. Both the normal and bush-flowering types are excellent flower-bedding plants.

Brachycome. *Swan River daisy; annual cineraria.* These annual plants from Australia are 1½ feet high and are covered with a profusion of flowers, blue, pink, or white. They make excellent flower-bed edgings and look good towards the front of an annual border. Best started indoors and planted out when warm weather has arrived; they may be sown outdoors, but may not bloom until late summer.

California poppy is the state flower of California. The foot-high plants will grow anywhere in the sun. Sow seeds where they are to flower; don't try transplanting them.

Browallia. *Amethyst.* Beautiful dark blue tubular flowers, each with a white eye, during summer and autumn. They bloom freely as house plants if dug up in the autumn, cut back close to the soil, and planted in pots. Average height is 1 foot or less.

Calendula. *Pot marigold.* RECOMMENDED. Large daisy flowers. Sow outdoors in spring, or earlier indoors and transplant. Also a florists' flower to grow under glass during winter. Height 2 feet. Likes a neutral soil; side-dress with lime occasionally. Colors are various hues of yellow and orange.

California Poppy. *Eschscholtzia.* RECOMMENDED. Easily grown annuals. Sow where you intend them to flower, in full sun, and thin to 12 inches apart, for they do not transplant very well. Various hues may be selected, from white through pale yellow to orange-scarlet; many are fluted and ruffled. Growing up to 12 inches high, they are excellent in flower beds or towards the front of the annual border. Appropriately, it is the state flower of California.

These are blooms of the annual calliopsis: mostly yellow, with brown markings. On foot-high plants, they are good cut-flowers, pleasingly fragrant.

Calliopsis. *Golden wave.* Long-stalked flowers are mostly yellow and daisylike; the center is tufted, and the ray-florets are wide, fluted, and frequently notched on the margin. They average about 3 feet high. This is one of the few annuals that does not last the entire season; a second batch of seeds should be sown in June for an autumn crop of flowers.

Candytuft. *Iberis.* RECOMMENDED. Showy plants with bright carmine, crimson, lavender, pink, or white flowers in clusters, appearing two

Candytuft, a useful 10-inch edging annual, with crimson, pink, lavender, carmine or white flowers. There is also a variety that is twice the height, in white only. All are scented.

* Varieties suitable for setting in the rock garden.

75

months after sowing seeds; for flower beds or the annual border. Sow indoors in April and thin to 9 inches. Sow also in July for a fall crop of flowers. The plants normally grow to 10 inches, but the giant rocket candytuft reaches 15 inches and comes in white only.

Iberis gibraltarica and *I. sempervirens* are almost evergreens; they are perennials and are described in that section.

Carnations, annual. RECOMMENDED. These are types of marguerite carnations, which are perennials but behave satisfactorily as annuals. Pinching the

Annual carnations are not so large as those you see in the florist store, but they are as varied in color and have as wonderful a fragrance. No difficulty in growing them from seeds.

tops of the leading stems and tips of the branches once a month will produce bushy plants, and removing all buds but the terminal ones on each stem or shoot will develop perfect blooms about one-half the size of the ones sold by florists and as sweetly perfumed. Colors are red, pink, white, and yellow; the average height 2 feet. The state flower of Ohio.

Castor-bean. *Palma Christi. Ricinus communis.* Tender foliage plants. Sow outdoors in late spring; if started indoors, take small pots and plant two beans in each; thin to one plant per pot and set out when the weather becomes warm. Among the several forms available are: Africanus, with large green leaves; borboniensis, red stems and gray leaves; cambodgensis, dark red; macrocarpus, purple-red; sanguineus is a blood-red; Zanzibarensis, green with white veins. All make fine tropical-looking groups; some grow 10 feet high. Castor oil is pressed from the curious seeds.

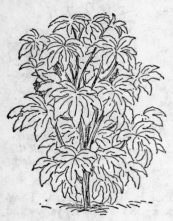

A quick-growing plant, imparting a tropical appearance to the garden, is the giant castorbean.

Catananche cœrulea. *Cupid's dart.* A perennial, but it flowers the first year from seeds. It has 2-inch, daisylike, *everlasting* blue flowers. Grows 2 feet high. A white and blue-and-white form are available.

Celosia. Striking flowers, mostly red and yellow, but sometimes purplish, salmon, or orange. There are two popular types, the *cockscomb,*

Scarlet cockscombs are striking bedding-plants. They grow two feet high.

offered as *C. cristata,* in which the blossoms are compressed into a tight mass; and the more feathery type, offered as *C. plumosa,* Chinese woolflower, or childsii. They are good flower-bed subjects, growing 2 feet high. *Everlastings*—they may be dried for winter bouquets.

Centaurea cyanus. *Bluebonnet, cornflower, bluebottle, bachelor's button.* RECOMMENDED. Should be sown outdoors in April and at intervals later for a succession of bloom. Maroon, pink, red, and white are the colors you may choose, as well as the bright blue, which is the state flower of Texas and is a favorite with folk of German ancestry. Plants grow 2 feet high: let them stand 12 inches apart.

C. americana. *Basket-flower.* Rose, lavender, or white blooms are sometimes 4 inches in diameter. Growing to 4 feet, this is a striking plant for the annual border.

C. moschata. *Sweet sultan. Everlasting.* Sweet-scented fluffy flowers. Sow for succession from May to July. Grows 2½ feet high. Yellow, white, purple, red, pink, and lilac are the colors.

Single and double cornflowers are liked by everyone. White, red, pink, maroon and blue are the colors available, but blue is the most popular.

Centaureas do not transplant readily; if you start them early indoors put a pinch of seeds each into small pots, thin to one plant, and then set out with the soil intact around the roots. All centaureas are excellent cut-flowers.

Two centaureas that may be treated as annuals, although they actually are perennials, are the *dusty millers.* Their white-green woolly foliage contrasts well with other plants and they are used for edging flower beds. They are:

The sweet-sultan has fluffy sweet-scented flowers and grows 2½ feet high.

C. candidissima. Leaves lanced and silvery.

C. gymnocarpa. Fernlike leaves. It grows wild on the island of Capri.

Chrysanthemums, annual. Showy daisylike flowers, which are useful for cut-bloom, are produced from July through October. They are very different from the perennial chrysanthemums with which we are more familiar.

C. carinatum. Tricolor chrysanthemum. Blooms are 2 inches across and white, red, or purple; the eye of the daisy is purple, and a ring surrounds it of some color different from the rest of the flower. Height 3 feet.

You may not recognize these as chrysanthemums, but that's what they are, the annual chrysanthemum carinatum.

C. coronarium. Garland chrysanthemum; crown daisy. The flowers are yellow. In Chinese cookery the young shoots are eaten under the name of shungiku or chop suey greens. Height 3 feet.

C. segetum. Corn marigold. These 18-inch plants have clusters of medium-size flowers which are yellow to near-white. Northern Star is a good variety.

* **Cigar-Plant.** *Cuphea.* Pretty half-hardy plants for beds or growing in baskets or window boxes. They are covered with small long tubular blooms which appear twelve weeks after seeding. Bright red, they have a black ring at the end and white tips—quite suggestive of the ash of a lighted cigar. They are usually started indoors and set out when the weather is warm. Height 1 foot.

Clarkia. This has showy flowers in leafy spikes—white, pink, or red-purple, single or double—for the annual border; useful greenhouse plant, too, and a good cut-flower. Average height 2 feet.

Coneflower, annual. *Rudbeckia.* This is an American wild flower, which you know as the *black-eyed-Susan* or yellow daisy and which has been improved by cultivation to give us larger flowers. Colors range from primrose to mahogany. Height 3 feet.

Cosmos. Recommended. One of the most charming of our garden flowers and of great value for cut-bloom. Tall (4 ft.) and dwarf (2½ ft.) types can be used, quick-growing and slow-growing. They are mostly like single daisies, but in the crested type the yellow center is replaced by a cushion of florets, white, pink or red, matching the rest of the flower. Yellow or *golden cosmos* is a distinct sort and defi-

Cosmos. Single at left; crested in center; golden cosmos at right. All are excellent for the garden, and for cut-bloom.

* Varieties suitable for setting in the rock garden.

nitely should be included in your planting, the new kind, Fiesta, especially. Cosmos likes a neutral soil; side-dress with lime occasionally.

Cynoglossum. *Chinese forget-me-not; hound's tongue.* A somewhat

Dahlias from seeds grow only 2 feet high. But just like big dahlias they develop tubers, which you can plant the following year if you wish.

weedy plant, but a valuable cut-flower when blue, always scarce, is called for. It looks like myosotis and is perfumed. Height 20 inches.

Dahlias from seeds. RECOMMENDED. These are tender perennials, but you may treat them as annuals. An ideal source of cut-bloom, the plants make excellent flower beds and borders. Sow in March indoors and plant out later, or sow outdoors in May and you may expect blossoms in three

months. They grow about 2 feet tall, but need no staking, as do large dahlias. Flowers are in pastel hues of yellow, orange, apricot, pink, red, and many another. In the autumn, dig, dry, and store the small tubers which will have developed during the summer, and replant them the following spring. They like a neutral soil; side-dress with lime occasionally.

Datura cornucopia. *Trumpet-flower.* Akin to the Jimson weed of the Southwest, from which the drug stramonium is obtained, the fragrant trumpet-flowers are 8 inches long by 5 inches across; white inside and purplish out-

Dimophotheca or cape-marigold comes to us from South Africa and has orange-colored daisy-blooms.

side. The plant grows 4½ feet high.

Dimorphotheca. *Cape-marigold.* Bright daisylike flowers, the 2-foot plants doing especially well in full sun. The typical color is orange, but hybrids are obtainable from white, through yellow to salmon. RECOMMENDED: a good flower-bed or annual-border subject. Good for cut-bloom also.

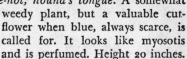

Euphorbia variegata, a green-and-white-leaved annual that is called snow-on-the-mountain.

Euphorbia. *Spurge; wolf's milk.* Unusual plants, allied to poinsettia and rubber plants, with sticky milky sap or

79

latex in the stems and leaves. A showy subject for the annual border.

E. heterophylla. Annual poinsettia; Mexican fire-plant. Bushes are 2½ feet high, with smooth, glossy orange-scarlet upper leaves.

E. variegata. Snow-on-the-mountain. The leaves are marked with white. Height 2 feet.

Do not chew on the leaves of these plants.

Four o'clock. *Mirabilis jalapa. Marvel-of-Peru.* Bushes bearing red, yellow or white flowers, often striped and spotted, which open in the afternoon or earlier in cloudy weather. Grows 2½ feet high. A good subject for the annual border.

Gilia. A 2-foot plant with feathery foliage and 1-inch flower heads, which make good cut-blooms. Lilac-blue is the predominating color, but various other pastel hues are to be had.

Four o'clocks open in cloudy weather or at the end of a bright day. Two-foot high annuals that are easy to grow.

Globe amaranth. *Gomphrena.* RECOMMENDED. A good bedding-plant with brightly-colored *everlasting* flowers resembling clover heads, which may be dried for winter decoration. Purple, red, pink, and white are the colors you may select. Average height is 1½ feet.

Godetia. *Farewell-to-spring.* Showy flowers varying from white through pink to lilac-crimson in leafy racemes; many have a spot of darker color; open in daylight, they close at night. Splendid for bedding and a good pot-plant. Height 2 feet.

Helichrysum. *Straw-flower.* RECOMMENDED. Valuable *everlastings.* Bright yellow, orange, pink, red, purple, or white flowers, double and chaffy, make a fine display in the annual border, and their cheerful effect is continued through winter, for they retain their color perfectly when dried. They grow 2½ feet high.

Heliotrope. *Cherry-pie.* Sweetly perfumed plant for summer bedding or for growing in the greenhouse. Violet, purple, or white varieties may be used. Seeds can be sown outdoors in May, but it is better to start them indoors in late winter for planting out when the weather becomes warm. Height 2 feet.

Ice-plant is so-called because it is covered with blisters containing water, giving it a frosted look.

Hunnemannia. *Mexican tulip poppy; Santa Barbara poppy; golden-cup.* Sow in late winter in small pots; thin to one plant to a pot and transfer to the garden later with the soil intact—they dislike transplanting. Flowers are canary-yellow and 3 inches across. Give it a sunny position and plenty of room; it grows 2 feet high.

* **Ice-plant.** *Mesembryanthemum crystallinum.* Dwarf spreading plant with small pink-white flowers. The foliage glistens because it is covered with watery pustules. Valuable as an edging for hot, dry flower beds or for sunny spots in the rock garden. Height 8 inches.

The color is scarlet of this impatiens, which is a satisfactory flower-bed annual.

Impatiens. *Touch-me-not; snapweed.* Good bedding annual and a satisfactory plant for the greenhouse. Profuse and continuously blooming. The flowers are about 1½ inches across. Scarlet is their usual color, but carmine, white, and pink varieties are found. A tender plant, very sensitive to frost. Average height 2 feet. (*See also* Balsam.)

Kingfisher Daisy. *Felicia bergeriana. Blue marguerite.* Sky-blue daisylike flowers with yellow centers are 1½ inches in diameter; may be grown outdoors in summer or under glass at other times of the year. Height 2 feet.

Kochia. *Summer cypress; Mexican firebush; belvedere.* Reaches about 3 feet. A pyramidlike bush, grown entirely for its foliage, which looks like an evergreen shrub with feathery, light green leaves, changing to purple-red in September. Can be planted for a formal effect, like lining a driveway or path; and some should be in the annual border.

* **Lantana.** A bedding and greenhouse plant. The flowers are in flattish heads of orange, white, rose, or red. The colors change as the flowers get older, so a flower head may be made up of two or more tints. It is a trailing plant and needs an occasional pinching to keep it neat. Under favorable conditions it will run 3 feet.

Kochia, grown for its foliage, which changes from green to purple-red in autumn.

Larkspur, annual. Easy to grow; sow seeds in April and you have flowers in July. Also sow in September and in November for the following year. Larkspurs make handsome beds or annual borders, are effective among shrubs, and are invaluable for cut-bloom. They may grow up to 5 feet high; the colors obtainable include

* Varieties suitable for setting in the rock garden.

blue, carmine, lavender, lilac, pink, purple, violet, and white. They dislike being transplanted; best to sow the seeds where you want the plants to grow. RECOMMENDED.

Lavatera. *Tree-mallow.* The plant is covered with large, cup-shaped pink or white flowers and grows about 2 feet high. A good subject for the annual border.

Linaria. *Toadflax.* Compact 2-foot plants that bear large flowers in rose, yellow, pink, lavender, carmine, red, violet, salmon, and white. Good for bedding or growing in pots.

* **Linum coccineum.** Flax. Showy plant with brilliant scarlet flowers. Averages around 12 inches high.

* **Lobelia.** Much used for edging or bedding. Some pendulant types are good for window boxes and hanging baskets. RECOMMENDED. Preferably sown indoors during winter and set outdoors 6 inches apart; you could sow them outdoors in spring, but they will bloom much later. Blue is the most-used color, though violet and white are also favorites. Average height is 1 foot or less.

There are no difficulties in growing the annual larkspur; sow seeds in spring, and give the plants plenty of room.

Because the blue flowers mostly are hiding behind the leaves, nigella is variously known as love-in-a-mist or devil-in-the-bush.

Love-in-a-mist. *Nigella; fennel-flower.* An easily-grown 2-foot annual with cup-shaped light blue or white flowers partly hidden by lacelike foliage. The double type, Miss Jekyll, is popular. Nigella does not transplant readily; sow seeds outdoors in early spring. And since it does not bloom all summer, sow a second batch of seeds six weeks after the first to insure a succession of bloom.

Lupinus. *Lupine.* For beds, cutflowers, or greenhouse growing. Handsome branching plants have six or eight large flower spikes to a plant. Their average height is 3 feet; white and various hues of blue are usual.

Malope grandiflora. Large hibiscus-like flowers 3 inches across on 2½-foot plants. Rose, purple, and white are the colors.

African and * French marigolds. RECOMMENDED. Very easy to grow.

* Varieties suitable for setting in the rock garden.

Push groups of three seeds just under the surface at intervals of 12 inches after frost has gone in spring; thin to one plant from each group. Or sow indoors in March and set out in May. Both kinds are wild plants in Mexico, not Africa or France, strange as it may appear. Usually the so-called Africans are larger plants, up to 4 feet, with large one-color blooms. The * French mostly are smaller, around 15 inches and often two-colored —yellow and red. Plant-breeders have worked hard on marigolds in recent years, producing new varieties with larger

Yellow African marigold at left is usually tall. Yellow-and-red French marigold at right is dwarf. They are ideal flower-bed subjects.

flowers, while the odor of the leaves, objectionable to some, has been made more pleasant. And they now have a variety especially for growing in a greenhouse, winter-flowering marigolds.

* Mathiola bicornis. *Evening-scented stock.* A straggling foot-high weedy plant with scattered dull purple-lilac flowers, which remain closed during the day; when they open at night, however, they emit an intense fragrance.

Matricaria. *False chamomile; feverfew.* Half-hardy perennial treated as an annual, with white daisylike flowers; for cutting or bedding. Height 15 inches.

Mignonette flowers are green, but the stamens in some are yellow, red in others. All are very fragrant. Sow several batches of seed to have mignonette all season. They resent being transplanted.

* Mignonette. *Reseda.* RECOMMENDED. Well-known sweet-scented flowers for beds or annual borders. At home everywhere, either in the greenhouse, garden, or as cut-bloom. Sow in spring where they are to flower. If you wish to have earlier bloom, fill some pots with soil and sow a few seeds in each; thin to one plant per pot and set out with the dirt ball intact, for they resent being transplanted in the usual way. Make two additional seedings outdoors, one in late spring and another in early summer, to give you a succession of blossoms all summer. Height 15 inches.

Nasturtium. *Tropæolum.* RECOMMENDED. Unexcelled for ease of culture, duration of bloom, and brilliant color. All they need is a sunny position, doing almost as well in poor as in good soil. Sow directly where they are to grow,

* Varieties suitable for setting in the rock garden.

as they do not like being transplanted. Two types are popular nowadays: the *dwarf or globe,* about 12 inches high, and the *gleam,* which is a 3-foot trailing plant. Both have double sweet-scented blooms. Older types are unscented and have single flowers, the *tall* being a 10-foot climber. Colors of nasturtiums include gold, mahogany, orange, ruby, salmon, and scarlet. Flowers and leaves can be added to salads, and the green unripe seeds may be pickled in vinegar.

Dwarf globe and trailing gleam nasturtiums are double and sweet-scented. Spray with Black-leaf 40 as soon as you see black aphids on the plants.

*Nemesia. Flowers are short tubes with broad flattened lips. All are brilliant, and a good mixture will include crimson, orange, purple, rose, scarlet, white, and yellow. Splendid bedding and rock-garden plants averaging 12 inches high.

Nemesia is a brilliant little foot-high annual. It grows wild in South Africa.

*Nemophila. *Baby-blue-eyes.* Prostrate plant about 6 inches high, with bright, sky-blue, bell-shaped blossoms. A white variety can be had. Set it as an edging in the annual border or to fill blanks in the rock garden. Your cat will like to doze on this fragile plant.

*Nierembergia. *Cup-flower.* A perennial that may be treated as an annual. The matlike plant is 6 inches high, with deep violet-blue flowers 1¼ inches across. Good for the rock garden or as an edging.

*Nolana. *Chilean bellflower.* Prostrate foot-high bedding plant, it has deep blue flowers on 6-inch stems. Also a good pot-plant for the sunny rock garden or the greenhouse.

Pentstemon. *Beard-tongue.* Perennial which is treated as an annual. Attractive 2-foot plant producing sprays of bright-colored tubular flowers. Good for bedding. Give it the same culture as salvia, sowing seed in March, and it will be effective the same summer. Colors available are carmine, cherry, lilac, purple, red, and rose.

Petunia. RECOMMENDED. Perhaps the most useful annual flower. Ideal for beds, porch boxes or window boxes. May be sown outdoors in May, but flowers will be late. Better sow indoors in March or April to get larger and finer flowers earlier. Especially attractive are the balcony types; their spreading habit enables them to festoon over window boxes,

* Varieties suitable for setting in the rock garden.

Petunia types: left, single balcony; ruffled in center; right, double. First two are best for outdoor growing.

porches, and walls. Their flowers are 3 inches across. Dwarf bedding types grow 9 to 12 inches; try Fire Chief, an intense red in this group; normal bedding varieties are 18 inches. Colors include white, pink, red, purple, violet, blue, and (rarely) yellow.

Giant single-fringed petunias, with 4-inch blooms, make good flower beds; a new variety for 1952 is one of these—Ballerina, a soft glowing Salmon. But the *double petunias,* beautiful as they are, are not recommended for planting in the garden; the blooms are so heavy that each stem needs the support of a plant stick. Excellent for the greenhouse, however.

* Phacelia. *California bluebell.* Intense blue flowers are produced all summer. Charming little edging plant about 10 inches tall.

The bright cheerful phlox, one of the few annuals that should be watered in dry weather. One, too, that does not bloom all summer; make a second sowing for an autumn show.

Phlox, annual. RECOMMENDED. Brilliant free-flowering bedding plants 15 inches high. Sow outdoors in May, or earlier indoors. Make two additional sowings, one in late spring and another in summer, to insure a succession of the heavy trusses of 1-inch blooms. The annual phlox needs moist, but well-drained, rich soil. Colors include pink, red, rose, salmon, white, and yellow.

Pinks. *Dianthus.* Some of them are biennials that bloom quickly the first year from seeds. Among these are *D. chinensis,* with double flowers, mostly red, pink or white, in a variety of combinations and fantastic in shape; *D. heddewigii,* the double-fringed pink, ranging from rose to red; striking, tufted, jewel-like plants. Both these are 18 inches high or less. They like a neutral soil;

* Varieties suitable for setting in the rock garden.

side-dress with lime occasionally.

Poppies, annual. *Papaver rhoeas.*
Sow in spring; make a second sowing
in July and a third in the fall to
bloom the following year; do so sparingly, thinning the plants to 9 inches
apart, where they are to flower. Poppies do not transplant well; and do
not remain in flower all summer, so
the second sowing is necessary to insure a succession of bloom. The

*Two pleasing annual pinks: dian-
thus chinensis at left, dianthus
Heddewigii at right.*

graceful *shirley or ghost poppies* are
RECOMMENDED as highly satisfactory; they like a neutral soil, so side-
dress with lime occasionally. Colors
are pink, white, apricot, and gray-
blue. Height 2½ feet.

* Portulaca. *Sun-plant; purslane,
rose-moss.* RECOMMENDED. They are
6-inch-high plants with narrow
fleshy leaves and 1-inch flowers,
which open only in fine weather. As
bright as candies in a bottle. Scatter
the seeds very sparingly in a sunny

*Shirley or ghost poppies should be
sown where you want them to
flower, because they resent being
transplanted.*

place and thin to 6 to 8 inches apart.
Good for edging or for the rock
garden, provided the place is sunny.
Double or single sorts may be sown.
Colors are white, yellow, pink, and
crimson.

Queen Anne's Lace. *Didiscus
coerulea.* An upright plant about 2
feet high with flat umbrella-shaped
flower heads. The blooms of the
wild carrots of the fields are some-

*Flowers of the Queen Anne's lace
are charming lavender-blue.*

times called by this name; it does suggest the shape of didiscus flowers,
but not their charming sky-blue color.

* Ranunculus. *Buttercup.* A perennial which may be grown as an
annual, blooming the same year. The large-flowering tecolote hybrids
are good to use; the large flowers come in a brilliant mixture of
reds, yellows, and oranges; singles, semi-doubles, and doubles. The
plants reach a height of 12 inches; place them towards the front of the

* Varieties suitable for setting in the rock garden.

86

The painted-tongue or salpiglossis is so variable a plant that seldom are two alike. The veining seen in the illustration is the source of much of the flower's charm.

annual border or in the rock garden.

Salpiglossis. *Painted-tongue.* RECOMMENDED. Best start the seeds indoors and transplant later, for it takes longer to grow than some. You will get good blooms in late summer if you sow seeds of this 30-inch plant outdoors in May. Lily-like, funnel-shaped flowers are veined in colors that vary from those of the flower itself. One of the most striking annuals you can grow; excellent for the annual border and for cut-bloom. You would see more salpiglossis in the florists' stores if the stems were not sticky— a disadvantage to the dealer that does not affect you. Colors are crimson, primrose, violet, blue-and-gold, brown-and-gold, purple-and-gold, rose-and-gold, scarlet-and-gold, blue-and-silver.

Salvia. *Sage.* RECOMMENDED. The scarlet salvias are familiar bedding plants, covered with bloom throughout the summer. Best to sow seeds in February or March indoors; pinch out the leading stems and tips of the branches every two weeks to develop bushy plants. Set them out when the weather is warm. Average height is 2 feet. They are somewhat slow, and if you wait and sow seeds outdoors, it may be the end of summer before you get flowers.

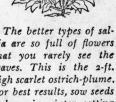

The better types of salvia are so full of flowers that you rarely see the leaves. This is the 2-ft. high scarlet ostrich-plume. For best results, sow seeds indoors in winter, setting out the plants when warm weather has arrived.

Blue or white *farinacea salvias, the mealy-cup sages,* are 3-foot perennials that may be treated as annuals. Also the *clary, Salvia sclarea,* an interesting 2½-foot plant in which both the flowers and the topmost leaves are colored blue.

Another type, the *blue sage, Salvia patens,* is a beautiful tender garden or greenhouse plant, growing 2 feet high with flowers 2 inches long.

In the herb garden we grow the sage used in stuffing the turkey; it is *Salvia officinalis.*

* **Sanvitalia procumbens.** A trailing plant, useful in beds, edges of borders, or in the rock garden; and the showy, double, yellow flowers

* Varieties suitable for setting in the rock garden.

are good for cutting. May grow 6 inches high. Give it a sunny position.

Scabious, sweet. *Scabiosa. Mourning bride; pincushion flower.* REC-OMMENDED. These beautiful annuals grow about 2 feet high and bloom from July to frost. As a flower for cutting they are very popular and are equally so for annual borders or beds. Colors are white, pink, rose, rosy-lilac, scarlet, blue, purple-black, mauve, and yellow.

Schizanthus. *Butterfly-flower.* Pretty odd-shaped, notched, and spotted flowers are often 1¼ inches across; they look like small butterflies. Of easy culture outdoors, it is best started in the

Schizanthus grows about 4 feet high, and is covered with charming butterfly-like flowers.

house, because it is a little slow; and sowing seeds outdoors will give you only a few weeks of bloom at the end of summer. Favorite as a greenhouse plant, growing 3 feet high. Mostly the blooms are white, spotted with rose and darker hues, and the plants usually are covered with them.

Sea Lavender. *Limonium sinuata and L. suworowi. Sea-pink.* The dainty cloudlike flower heads make the annual border interesting; use them as cut-flowers to lighten bouquets. They blend well with other *everlastings* for winter decoration. You often come across masses of them growing wild in marshes near the sea. Height 1½ to 2 feet. Colors are blue, mauve, pink, and white.

* **Sensitive-plant.** *Mimosa pudica.* Modest little individuals, eventually growing to 2 feet, with small heads of lavender flowers. It is a plant curiosity: touch a leaf lightly with the finger; immediately the leaflets close and the leaf droops flat to the ground. Half-an-hour later it slowly returns, none the worse, to its normal position.

Snapdragons. *Antirrhinum.* RECOMMENDED. Plants of simple culture, with hooded flowers on long spikes. Excellent for beds and the annual border; and ideal for cutting. They are perennials, but are treated as annuals. Sow indoors in late winter and set out in

Antirrhinums are half-hardy perennials, but you treat them as annuals. Sow in the open in May, or indoors in March and transplant them.

spring. Or sow outdoors in spring, but do not expect your display until the end of summer; they take longer to grow than some plants.

* Varieties suitable for setting in the rock garden.

The rust disease was once a handicap in growing snapdragons, but the following three types in a great variety of colors are now obtainable in rust-resistant strains: *tall* (3 ft.), *intermediate* (1½ ft.), and *dwarf* (9 ins.). Thus, an effective bed of snapdragons alone can be planned. Colors include cherry, copper, crimson, gold, orange, pink, red, scarlet, terracotta, yellow, and white; many have two-color blooms.

Greenhouse snapdragons are of special interest to commercial gardeners, who use colors that are popular at the moment. Under glass,

The large stamens of the cleome give the flower a spidery look.

monthly sowings are often made, beginning in July.

Blues and near-blues are about the only colors one cannot get in snapdragons.

Spider-flower. *Cleome.* RECOMMENDED. Excellent for the middle-distance of an annual border or to line a driveway. Light, airy flowers of pleasing salmon-pink, changing to white as they mature, and fragrant; the stamens look like spider legs. Grows 3 to 4 feet high.

Stock, ten-week. *Mathiola incana.* Fragrant and showy plants of simple culture. Set them in the annual border or flower bed or grow them in the greenhouse. For outdoor blooming it is best to sow early indoors and transplant in May; though you should obtain quite good results by sowing outdoors in spring. An old gardener's trick is to keep for one's self the smaller and weaker seedlings, and generously to give away the stronger ones. Puny plants usually produce double flowers, the stronger ones are often single. The giant imperial strain is a good one, blooming continuously through the summer. Plants are 2 to 2½ feet high. Colors are blue, lavender, pink, purple, red, yellow, and white.

Giant imperial stocks reach 2½ feet in height; the doubles with highly fragrant flowers, are preferred. Advisable to sow in late winter indoors, and to use—not discard —the weaker seedlings.

Sunflower. *Helianthus.* Mostly tall, majestic and striking plants, they bear big daisylike blooms; the single kinds mostly have a large brown center disk. Sow in almost any soil, but in full sun. The common sunflower or polly-seed may reach 12 feet, and the bloom may exceed a foot in diameter. Tall double and dwarf double kinds are seen; and some with more or less reddish color in the rays. They like a neutral soil; side-dress with lime occasionally.

So-called red sunflowers are usually yellow with some red markings; not so large as the ordinary sunflower, but equally easy to grow.

Sweet Peas. *Lathyrus odoratus.* Rich soil and sowing very early in spring are essential for good results; some gardeners even sow at the end of autumn, so the seeds may get the

Sweet peas are ideal 9 ft. climbers for the cooler latitudes, especially New England and parts of California; often they do not thrive in warmer sections.

earliest possible start in spring. Dig under a 2-inch layer of compost, rotted manure, or humus, ½ pound to the square foot of pulverized sheep manure and ¼ pound to the square foot of bone-meal. Sow seeds 2 inches apart and cover them 1 inch; thin the resulting plants to 8 inches apart. A 6-foot hedge of tree branches, fencing, or twine on sticks should be provided for their support. Flood the soil with water in dry weather and cover the ground around them with compost, manure, or garden trash in the hot weeks to keep the roots cool. They like the climate of New England, the northern states, the Canadian maritime provinces, and parts of California. Only limited plantings are advised elsewhere. They grow to 9 feet. Almost every hue except true yellow can be had.

Special quick-growing strains are available for greenhouse culture; these are also used in the southern states where they do well as a winter crop.

Tithonia Speciosa. *Mexican sunflower; flower-of-the-Incas.* RECOMMENDED. Shrublike plant growing 6 feet high; the orange daisylike flowers are 3 or 4 inches in diameter and are good for cutting. *Torch* is a new tithonia that

Flower of the Incas is the romantic popular name of the giant tithonia. In this new type, named Torch, the large flower is grenadine-red.

90

Evening-scented tobacco is one of the most fragrant annuals you can grow. Seeds are dust-size; watch that they are not covered with soil too thickly.

Torenia fournieri, a foot-high annual with beautiful blue flowers, each with a yellow center.

reaches only 4 feet, and the flowers are grenadine-red. Set tithonia towards the rear of the annual border.

Tobacco, evening-scented. *Nicotiana affinis.* Easily grown annuals, often 4 feet high, with broad leaves and spikes of narrow trumpet-flowers opening to broad lips, 3 inches across. Usually white and strongly perfumed, but crimson and pink varieties, often less fragrant, may also be had. Takes rather longer than most to develop; best started indoors in late winter and planted out when the weather is really warm.

* Torenia fournieri. A fine annual for cut-bloom, for planting in hanging baskets, in rock gardens, annual borders, and flower beds. Blossoms are sky-blue with yellow centers. Growing a foot high and slightly creeping, it likes some shade and plenty of moisture.

* Verbena. RECOMMENDED. Mostly creeping annuals with clusters of showy flowers. Sow outside in May, but better results will be obtained by sowing indoors in late winter and planting out in spring. Space them a foot apart. The flowers are very brilliant; many are blue, pink, white, red or crimson, often with cream or white eyes. May grow to 1½ feet.

* Vinca. *Madagascar periwinkle; old maid.* Begins blooming in August from seeds sown in May. White, pink, or white-with-pink-eyes are the colors; and they may be had in July if seeds are sown indoors in March and transplanted. Grows to 1 foot.

* Virginian Stock. *Malcolm stock.* Gay in the period between spring and summer flowers. Half-inch blooms have fresh, bright colors, mostly lilac and reddish to white. Height 9 inches.

Viscaria. The plants are compact and bushy and bloom so freely as to be entirely covered with white, purple, pink, or red ½-inch flowers, resembling single wild roses in miniature. Height about 1½ feet.

Wallflower, annual. The typical wallflower is a biennial, but some

* Varieties suitable for setting in the rock garden.

91

special strains will bloom in summer if seeds are sown indoors in March. They need cool soil, so only try them in the northern states and New England; give them semi-shade, and water when necessary. Two feet.

Wallflower, Siberian. *Cheiranthus allionii.* A 2-foot-high perennial which may be treated as an annual, flowering the same year when seeds are sown early. Or regard it as a biennial, sowing in September to bloom in spring. The flowers are orange.

Xeranthemum. *Immortelle.* Easily grown annual reaching 3 feet; the pink, lavender, purple, or white daisylike flowers are 1½ inches in diameter. A good *everlasting*.

Zinnia. *Youth-and-old-age.* RECOMMENDED. Most popular annual grown in North America, because it thrives in our hot summers. Seeds may be sown in a sunny window and transplanted, or sown later in the open ground. You may select 3-foot-high kinds with mammoth dahlia-like blooms. Introduced for 1952 is the new assortment, Persian Carped. Double globular flowers are yellow, orange, red, crimson, maroon and pink. Or you may like the fantasy type, which is shaggy, waved, and frilled. Separate colors may be sown—scarlet, white, orange, pink, or violet—to make designed flower beds.

This is a giant zinnia of the dahlia-flowered type. Three-foot plants have six-inch diameter blooms. But foot-high kinds with miniature flowers can also be had.

* *Midget* types (12 ins.) for edging the bed can be used. These and the * *Liliput* kinds (12 ins.), with soft pastel hues, are good cut-flowers.

* Varieties suitable for setting in the rock garden.

NOTE

Tables for Perennials, Biennials, Bulbs, and Annuals follow on pages 93–105 to help you decide on the kind, height and color of the flowers you want to grow.

THE POPULAR FLOWERS

Their Height, Color and Effective Period

This will help you plan your garden. *Sorts in heavy type are specially recommended. Varieties marked * are suitable for the rock-garden.*

Subjects grown solely for their foliage are omitted.

LEADING HARDY HERBACEOUS PERENNIALS

	Average height in inches	Colors							Blooming period					
		White; near white	Pink	Red	Orange and yellow	Lavender, mauve, or purple	Blue	Multi-colored flowers	Apr.	May	June	July	Aug.	Sept.
Aconitum napellus	48						x					x	x	x
* Aethionema warleyense	5		x							x	x			
Agrostemma coronaria	30			x						x	x	x		
* Ajuga reptans	10					x				x	x			
* Alyssum saxatile	12	x			x				x	x				
Anchusa azurea	48						x				x	x		
Anemone japonica	36	x	x			x							x	x
* Anemone pulsatilla	9				x	x			x	x				
Anthemis tinctoria	36				x						x	x	x	x
* Aquilegia	30–36	x	x	x		x	x	x		x	x	x		
* Arabis albida	12	x							x	x	x			
* Arenaria montana	4	x								x	x			
* Armeria	12	x	x			x				x	x	x		
Asclepias tuberosa	30				x							x	x	
Aster novae-angliae	60	x	x	x		x	x						x	x
Aster novi-belgii	36	x	x	x		x	x						x	x
Aster, Wartburg Star	36	x					x			x				x
Aster frikarti	24						x				x	x	x	x

LEADING HARDY HERBACEOUS PERENNIALS (Continued)

	Average height in inches	Colors							Blooming period					
		White; near white	Pink	Red	Orange and yellow	Lavender, mauve or purple	Blue	Multi-colored flowers	Apr.	May	June	July	Aug.	Sept.
Aster hybridus luteus	24				X								X	X
* Aster, dwarf hybrids	12	X	X			X							X	X
Astilbe rosea	30		X	X							X			
* Aubretia deltoides	8	X				X			X	X				
Bee-balm	36	X		X								X		
Boltonia	72	X	X										X	X
* Campanula carpatica	12	X					X				X	X		
* Campanula gargarica	6	X					X				X	X		
Campanula persicifolia	36					X	X			X	X			
Centaurea montana	24	X				X				X	X			
* Cerastium tomentosum	9	X		X					X	X				
Chelone barbatus	60											X	X	
Chrysanthemum, autumn "Mums"	24	X	X	X	X	X							X	X
* Chrysanthemum, cushion types	12	X	X	X	X								X	X
Chrysanthemum, Shasta daisy	24	X			X						X	X		
Chrysanthemum balsamita	30	X										X		
Chrysanthemum nipponicum	30				X								X	
* Chrysogonum virginianum	9	X			X				X	X	X			
Coneflower	48				X	X					X	X	X	
* Coreopsis	36				X						X	X	X	X
* Creeping Jenny	4				X							X	X	
Cynoglossum nervosum	30						X			X	X			

94

* Daphne cneorum	12
Delphinium elatum	72
Delphinium belladonna	60
Delphinium bellamosum	60
Delphinium grandiflorum	30
* Dianthus allwoodii	12
Dianthus caryophyllus	24
* Dianthus deltoides	12
* Dianthus Knappii	16
* Dianthus plumarius	18
* Dianthus, new blue	12
Dicentra spectabilis	30
Dicentra eximia	18
Dictamnus fraxinella	36
Doronicum	36
Echinops	60
* Edelweiss	4
Eupatorium	36
Funkia caerulea	36
Funkia japonica	24
Funkia plantaginea	30
Gaillardia aristata	36
* Gentiana acaulis	4
Gerbera jamesoni	18
Geum	24
Gypsophila paniculata	36
* Gypsophila repens	6
Helenium autumnale	60
* Helianthemum nummularium	12

LEADING HARDY HERBACEOUS PERENNIALS (Continued)

	Average height in inches	Colors							Blooming period					
		White; near white	Pink	Red	Orange and yellow	Lavender, mauve or purple	Blue	Multi-colored flowers	Apr.	May	June	July	Aug.	Sept.
Helianthus decapetalus	60				x								x	x
Helianthus giganteus	140				x								x	x
Helianthus scaberrimus	90				x							x	x	x
Heliopsis	48	x			x						x	x	x	x
Helleborus niger	18	x							x					
Hemerocallis	36	x		x	x						x	x		
Hesperis	36	x	x			x					x	x		
*Heuchera sanguinea	24	x	x	x							x	x	x	
*Hibiscus moscheutos	48	x	x									x	x	x
*Hyssop	12	x				x						x	x	
*Iberis gibraltarica	12	x				x			x	x	x			
*Iberis sempervirens	12	x	x						x	x	x			
*Incarvillea delavayi	30		x			x			x		x			
*Iris cristata	6	x				x				x				
Iris kaempferi	30	x	x	x		x		x			x	x		
Iris siberica	36	x		x		x	x	x		x	x			
Iris vulgaris	24	x		x		x	x			x	x			
Lavender	30	x				x					x			
Liatris pycnostachya	60					x							x	x
Linum flavum	24				x						x	x	x	x
Linum perenne	30						x				x	x	x	x
Lobelia cardinalis	40			x								x	x	x
Lupinus polyphyllus	50	x		x		x	x			x	x	x		x

Plant	No.
Lychnis chalcedonica	36
* Lychnis viscaria	18
Lythrum salicaria	36
* Mazus reptans	3
Meconopsis baileyi	60
* Myosotis palustris	8
* Nepeta mussini	18
Peony	36
Phlox decussata	36
* Phlox divaricata	15
* Phlox subulata	4
Phlox suffruticosa	36
Physalis alkekengi	24
Physostegia virginiana	48
Platycodon grandiflorum	30
Plumbago larpentae	12
Plume poppy	72
* Polemonium reptans	12
* Poppy, nudicaule	12
Poppy, oriental	48
Primula beesiana	24
Primula bulleyana	30
* Primula denticulata	10
* Primula elatior	8
Primula japonica	24
Primula sikkimensis	24
* Primula veris	8
* Primula vulgaris	6
Pyrethrum	24
Salvia azurea	48
Salvia farinacea	30
* Saponaria ocymoides	9

LEADING HARDY HERBACEOUS PERENNIALS (Continued)

	Average height in inches	Colors							Blooming period					
		White; near white	Pink	Red	Orange and yellow	Lavender, Mauve, or purple	Blue	Multi-colored flowers	Apr.	May	June	July	Aug.	Sept.
Scabiosa caucasica	30	x				x	x					x	x	x
* Securigera coronilla	10				x						x	x	x	
* Sedum spectabile	18	x		x								x	x	x
* Sedum acre	9				x						x	x	x	
* Sedum lydium	9	x		x							x	x	x	
* Sedum middendorffianum	9				x						x	x	x	
* Sedum sieboldii	9											x	x	x
* Sempervivum tectorum	3	x	x			x					x	x	x	
Sidalcea malvaeflora	24	x	x			x						x	x	
* Silene schafta	6	x	x			x						x	x	
Statice perezii	20							x			x	x	x	x
Stokesia	24					x					x	x	x	x
* Teucrium chamaedrys	12	x	x			x					x	x	x	
Thalictrum diptericarpum	30					x					x	x	x	
Thalictrum majus	48				x						x	x		
Thermopsis caroliniana	60				x						x	x		
* Thymus serpyllum	4					x					x	x		
Tritoma uvaria	36		x	x				x			x	x	x	x
Trollius europaeus	36		x		x					x	x	x		
Valeriana officinalis	48	x	x			x					x	x	x	
Veronica incana	24	x					x				x	x	x	
Veronica maritima	24	x	x			x					x	x	x	x
Veronica spicata	18	x				x	x				x	x	x	x
* Vinca minor	6	x							x	x	x			
* Viola cornuta	9	x	x			x			x	x	x	x	x	x
* Viola odorata	9	x	x			x			x	x	x	x	x	x
Yucca filamentosa	100	x									x	x		x

Six Leaders; 20 of almost equal importance. Kinds in heavy type are recommended. * Rock-garden varieties.

	Average height in inches	Colors							Blooming period					
		White; near white	Pink	Red	Orange and yellow	Lavender, mauve, or purple	Blue	Multi-colored flowers	Apr.	May	June	July	Aug.	Sept.
Daffodils	15	x			x				x	x				
Tulips, early flowering	12	x	x	x	x	x		x	x	x				
Tulips, darwin and breeder	30	x	x	x	x	x		x	x	x				
Tulips, parrot	18	x	x	x	x	x		x		x	x			
Hyacinths, dutch	12	x	x				x		x	x				
*Hyacinths, grape	10	x					x		x	x				
*Aconite, winter	8				x				x	x				
*Bluebell, Virginia	24						x		x	x				
*Chionodoxa	8	x					x		x	x				
*Crocus	6	x			x	x	x		x	x				
Crown Imperial	48			x	x					x				
Eremurus	36	x	x		x					x	x			
*Erythronium americanum	12				x				x	x				
*Erythronium dens-canis	6	x	x			x			x	x				
Guinea-hen flower	18	x		x		x			x	x				
Iris, Dutch	24	x			x	x		x		x	x			
Iris, English and Spanish	18				x	x		x			x	x		
*Lady slipper	12		x			x				x				
Scilla campanulata	20	x	x			x	x		x	x				
*Scilla nutans	12	x	x				x		x	x				
*Scilla siberica	6	x					x		x	x				
*Snowdrop	12	x							x	x				
*Snowflake, aestivum	10	x								x				
*Snowflake, autumnale	10	x												x
*Snowflake, vernum	10	x							x					
Star of Bethlehem	12	x								x				

FIFTEEN GORGEOUS LILIES; AND LILY-OF-THE-VALLEY

Plant them in spring or fall. Kinds in heavy type are specially recommended. Varieties marked * are suitable for the rock-garden.

	Average height in inches	Colors							Blooming period					
		White; near white	Pink	Red	Orange and yellow	Lavender, mauve, or purple	Blue	Multi-colored flowers	Apr.	May	June	July	Aug.	Sept.
Lilium candidum	40	x									x			
auratum	60	x						x				x		
canadense	45			x	x						x	x		
davidii	60	x		x	x							x	x	
henryi	90													x
longiflorum	45	x		x				x				x		
pardalinum	65			x								x		
philippinense	35	x						x				x		x
regale	60	x		x				x x			x			
speciosum	45	x		x				x					x	
superbum	90			x								x		
* tenuifolium	24			x	x					x	x			
tigrinum	70			x	x							x	x	
umbellatum	24			x	x					x	x			
warleyense	45											x	x	
* **Lily-of-the-valley**	9	x								x				

100

EIGHTEEN COLORFUL SPRING-PLANTED BULBS

These should be in every garden; dig them up in fall. Kinds in heavy type are specially recommended. Subjects grown solely for their foliage are omitted. Varieties marked * are suitable for the rock-garden.

	Average height in inches	Colors							Blooming period					
		White; near white	Pink	Red	Orange and yellow	Lavender, mauve, or purple	Blue	Multi-colored flowers	Apr.	May	June	July	Aug.	Sept.
Acidanthera	40	x											x	x
Amaryllis, hippeastrum	24	x	x	x								x	x	
Amaryllis, Lycoris squamigera	30	x	x									x	x	
Anemone	12						x				x	x		
*Begonia	12	x		x	x	x					x	x	x	x
Calla, golden	24	x		x	x							x	x	x
*Calla, pink	12	x	x									x		
Calla, white	30	x									x		x	
Canna	36 to 120	x	x	x	x	x		x			x	x	x	x
Dahlia	72	x	x	x	x	x		x			x	x	x	x
Gladiolus	36	x	x	x	x	x		x			x	x	x	x
*Glory lily	Pinch to 24			x	x	x		x			x	x	x	x
*Gloxinia	12	x		x		x	x	x			x	x	x	x
Hyacinth, summer	48	x									x	x	x	x
Montbretia	36			x	x						x	x	x	x
Ranunculus	18		x	x	x						x	x	x	x
Tigridia	30	x				x		x			x	x	x	
Tuberose	36	x											x	x

TEN INVALUABLE HARDY BIENNIALS

Sow in summer to flower the following year. Kinds in heavy type are specially recommended. Varieties marked * are suitable for the rock-garden.

	Average height in inches	Colors							Blooming period					
		White; near white	Pink	Red	Orange and yellow	Lavender, mauve, or purple	Blue	Multi-colored flowers	Apr.	May	June	July	Aug.	Sept.
Canterbury bells	48	x	x				x				x			
*Daisy, English	6	x	x	x						x	x			
Evening primrose	48	x	x		x						x	x		
Foxglove	48	x			x	x					x	x		
Hollyhock	100	x	x		x	x						x	x	x
Honesty	24	x				x				x	x			
*Pansies	12				x	x		x	x	x	x			
Rose-campion	36	x	x	x				x		x	x			
Sweet william	24		x	x		x				x	x			
Wallflowers	24	x			x					x	x			

102

OUTSTANDING ANNUALS

With some biennials and perennials treated as Annuals. Heavy type sorts are specially recommended. Subjects grown solely for their foliage are omitted. Varieties marked * are suitable for the rock-garden. Most annuals bloom from July to frost, but many will commence flowering earlier when sown indoors in late winter.

	Average height in inches	Colors						
		White; near-white	Pink	Red	Orange and yellow	Lavender, mauve, or purple	Blue	Multi-colored flowers
Acroclinium	20	x	x					
* Ageratum	4 to 6	x	x			x	x	
* Alyssum, sweet	3 to 9	x				x		
Amaranthus	40			x	x			
Ammobium alatum	36				x			
Arctotis	12 to 30	x		x	x	x		
Asters, China	18 to 30	x	x	x		x		
Baby's breath, annual	18	x	x					
Balsam	18 to 30	x	x	x	x			
Brachycome	18	x	x			x	x	
* Browallia	10					x		
Calendula	24				x			
California poppy	12	x			x			
Calliopsis	36				x			
* Candytuft, bedding types	10	x	x	x		x		
Candytuft, rocket types	15	x						
Carnation, annual	24	x	x	x	x			
Catananche cœrulea	24	x						
Celosia	24			x	x			
Centaurea americana	48	x	x			x		
Centaurea cyanus	24	x	x	x		x	x	
Centaurea moschata	30	x	x	x	x	x		
Chrysanthemum carinatum	36	x		x		x		x
Chrysanthemum coronarium	36				x			
Chrysanthemum segetum	18	x			x			
* Cigar-plant	12			x				x
Clarkia	24	x	x	x				
Coneflower, annual	36			x	x			
Cosmos	30 to 48	x	x	x				
Cosmos, yellow types	24				x			
Cynoglossum	20					x	x	
Dahlias from seeds	24		x	x	x			
Datura cornucopia	54	x						

	Average height in inches	Colors						
		White; near-white	Pink	Red	Orange and yellow	Lavender, mauve, or purple	Blue	Multi-colored flowers
Dimorphotheca	24	x	x		x			
Euphorbia heterophylla	30			x				
Euphorbia variegata	24	x						
Four-o'clock	30	x		x	x			
Gilia	24		x			x		
Globe amaranth	18	x	x	x		x		
Godetia	24	x	x			x		
Helichrysum	30	x	x	x	x	x		
Heliotrope	24	x				x		
Hunnemannia	24				x			
* Ice-plant	8		x					
Impatiens	24	x	x	x				
Kingfisher daisy	24						x	
* Lantana	36	x	x	x	x			x
Larkspur, annual	60	x	x	x		x	x	
Lavatera	24	x	x					
Linaria	24	x	x	x	x	x		
* Linum	12			x				
* **Lobelia**	12	x				x	x	
Love-in-a-mist	24	x					x	
Lupinus	36	x				x	x	
Malope grandiflora	30	x	x			x		
Marigold, African	48				x			
Marigold, French	15			x	x			x
* Mathiola bicornis	12					x		
Matricaria	15	x						
* **Mignonette**	15			x	x			
* **Nasturtium, dwarf globe**	12			x	x			
Nasturtium, gleam	36			x	x			
Nasturtium, tall	120			x	x			
* Nemesia	12	x	x	x	x	x		
* Nemophila	6	x					x	
* Nierembergia	6					x		
* Nolana	12						x	
Pentstemon	24		x	x		x		
Petunia	9 to 18	x	x	x		x	x	

	Average height in inches	Colors						
		White; near-white	Pink	Red	Orange and yellow	Lavender, mauve, or purple	Blue	Multi-colored flowers
* Phacelia	10						x	
Phlox, annual	15	x	x	x	x			
Pink, chinensis	18	x	x	x				x
Pink, heddewigii	18	x	x	x				x
Poppy, annual	30	x	x		x	x		
* **Portulaca**	6	x	x	x	x			
Queen Anne's lace	24						x	
* Ranunculus	12			x	x			
Salpiglossis	30		x	x	x	x	x	x
Salvia, clary	30					x		
Salvia, scarlet	24			x				
Salvia farinacea	36	x				x		
Salvia patens	24						x	
* Sanvitalia procumbens	6				x			
Scabious, Sweet	24	x	x	x	x	x	x	
Schizanthus	36	x	x					x
Sea lavender	24	x	x			x		
* Sensitive-plant	24					x		
Snapdragons	9 to 36	x	x	x	x			x
Spider-flower	40	x	x					
Stock, ten-week	24 to 30	x	x	x	x	x		
Sunflowers, annual	25 to 144				x			
Sweetpeas	108	x	x	x		x		x
Tithonia	72			x	x			
Tobacco, night-scented	48	x	x	x				
* Torenia fournieri	12						x	
* **Verbena**	18	x	x	x		x	x	x
* **Vinca**	12	x	x					x
* **Virginian stock**	9	x	x	x		x		
Viscaria	18	x	x	x		x		
Wallflower, annual	24			x	x			
Wallflower, siberian	24				x			
Xeranthemum	36	x	x			x		
Zinnia, tall varieties	36	x	x	x	x	x		
* **Zinnia, midget varieties**	12	y	x	x	x	x		x

CHAPTER 12

Climbing Plants

"I'd leave all the hurry, the noise, and the fray,
For a house full of books, and a garden of flowers."
ANDREW LANG.

CLIMBING HERBACEOUS PERENNIALS

THESE ARE HERBACEOUS; once planted, in autumn the tops will die down and then you clear the dead stems away. But the roots persist, and the vines reappear next spring to cover again the fence or trellis. Best to start with a purchase of roots; though seeds may be sown of Kenilworth ivy, passion flower and perennial sweet-peas.

Kenilworth ivy or creeping-sailor is a 3-ft. perennial climber with blue flowers; but sometimes they are white or pink.

Kenilworth Ivy. *Mother of thousands; creeping sailor. Cymbalaria muralis.* This has many very small flowers, usually blue though white and pink types can be obtained. Specially good for trailing over a bank, because it develops roots on its creeping stems, which trail about 3 feet.

Kudzu Vine. *Pueraria thunbergiana.* The purple flowers are fragrant. Stems trail as much as 50 feet. A native of south China and the islands of the Pacific, it needs help to carry it over our northern winters; cover the soil above the roots

The passion-flower will grow 20 feet in a season. Mostly the curious flowers are blue, and in them may be seen several implements associated with the story of the Crucifixion.

with 3 inches of leaves or compost in December.

Madeira Vine. *Climbing mignonette.* Fleshy oval leaves, and racemes of feathery, fragrant white flowers in summer and autumn. Protect with litter in winter south of Long Island.

Passion Flower. *Passiflora cærulea.* The flowers show the crown-of-thorns, nails, hammers, and other attributes of the Christian belief. They are blue, white and blue, all white. Climbing up to 20 feet, it is hardy only in the South, but if covered around the roots with a 4-inch layer of leaves or compost, it may be carried over the winter in the central sections of the United States.

Perennial Sweetpea. *Lathyrus latifolius.* Perfectly hardy, this climbs to 9 feet and has pink, white, purple, or red blooms. They serve as good cut-flowers for room decoration.

Lathyrus latifolius, the hardy perennial sweet-pea, climbs to 9 feet and furnishes good cut-flowers. Pink, white, purple or red are the colors. Unlike the annual kind, it grows most any-where.

WOODY PERENNIAL CLIMBERS

For growing up walls or on a permanent trellis or fence, these are highly satisfactory. Plant them either in spring or autumn.

Shrubby Bittersweet. *Waxwork. Celastrus scandens. Everlasting.* This is our native climbing plant of the woods, whose orange-red berry clusters are offered to us along the wayside for winter decorations. Yellow flowers precede the berries. A good plant to set amid semi-wild conditions, especially to ramble over stone fences and tree-stumps.

Some clematis. Left, a small-flowering type; center, a double large-flowering one; right, the fragrant paniculata.

Clematis. *Virgin's bower.* In the average garden, three groups are met with. First, there is the *large-flowered Jackmani* type, with blooms often 6 inches across; named varieties may be purple, red, pink, or white; some are double. They climb around 10 feet.

The second familiar group are tougher plants with *small and often brilliant flowers,* including *crispa,* with urn-shaped purple flowers, also 10 feet; *Texensis* with small brilliant scarlet flowers, climbing only 6 feet; Montana, light pink, climbing to 20 feet.

The third is *clematis paniculata,* a very woody climber growing to 30 feet, with white blossoms in autumn, which are pleasantly fragrant.

Dutchman's pipe is valued for its large leaves. A valuable woody perennial climber.

Dutchman's Pipe. *Aristolochia durior.* Flowers are yellowish-green with a U-shaped tube 3 inches long. The valuable feature is the foliage: large heart-shaped leaves arrange themselves like shingles on a roof. Install some upright cords 12 inches apart from the porch floor to the eaves, and every summer the dense leafy screen will give you complete privacy.

Honeysuckle. *Lonicera japonica.* Hardy climbers permanently hide fences, stumps and trellis; good for covering sloping banks because it is semi-evergreen. Two good kinds are *halliana,* with white and yellow flowers, and *goldflame,* with yellow and carmine blooms.

Ivies are valuable for covering walls.

English ivy and the slower-growing *euonymus radicans* will cling to brickwork and to the mortar between the stones of a wall.

Boston ivy will attach itself to

Honeysuckles are useful woody perennial climbers, and the easiest to grow. Plant them, and they fend for themselves, trailing over the ground if they have nothing upon which to climb.

these and to stucco and wood, and may eventually reach the top of the average home.

The *Virginia creeper, American ivy or woodbine,* is not self-clinging, but will trail over stone fences and travel over a wire fence or similar support.

Silver Lace-vine. *China fleecevine. Polygonum auberti.* A native of Tibet, it will travel 25 feet or more with the support of a wire or trellis. In late summer it has sprays of perfumed white flowers.

Trumpet Vine. *Campsis radicans.* Striking husky climber with 3-inch trumpet blooms. You can select a variety with either yellow or deep orange colors.

Wisteria. Given deep, rich soil and wires or trellis on which to twine, it will grow 15 to 20 feet in a season. Watch to see if the soft young stems work their way around a rain pipe. Next season the stem will be hard and strong, and in a few years its expansion may pull your pipe from the wall. Pinch it off while pinching is easy. Hanging tassels of beautiful pea-flowers appear in late spring, either blue or white, with an additional one or two during the rest of the summer.

Sometimes a wisteria will hesitate to bloom; then ruthless pruning may be the answer, cutting out all thin young stems, retaining the older thicker ones. Also, dig down under the plant to see if a thick taproot goes straight down; it should be sawed through. Roots that slope outwards and downwards may remain.

Trumpet vine is a very permanent woody climber growing 25 feet or more; yellow or orange trumpets are 3 inches long. Roots need a protective cover over winter in the north and east.

Wisteria is a self-twining climber. Give it a trellis, and it will work its own way up. Blue is the favorite color, but white is also beautiful.

CLIMBING ANNUALS

These are easily grown plants that will quickly cover a wire fence, veranda, trellis, arbor, or tree stump. The treatment of all is the same: sow in early May where they are to grow, placing the

Balloon Vine. *Heart seed; love-in-a-puff. Cardiospermum halicacabum.* Will grow to 10 feet. Tiny white flowers are followed by curious three-angled inflated hollow balls.

seeds about 3 inches apart and covering them three times their diameter; thin the resulting plants so they stand 9 to 12 inches apart. Or sow the seeds earlier indoors and plant them outdoors when the weather is warm. Cup-and-saucer vine is best sown quite early in small pots, thinning to one plant to a pot and setting them out with the soil intact. All do best in full sun.

Black-eyed Susan. *Thunbergia alata. Clock-vine.* It climbs about 4 feet, and has cream, white, or buff tubular flowers, each with a dark throat.

Cardinal Climber. *Star-glory. Quamoclit sloteri.* Will climb to 15 feet under favorable conditions. Flowers are 2 inches long, crimson with a white throat.

Canary-bird Vine. *Tropaeolum canariensis.* A quick-growing annual vine with small yellow nasturtium-like blooms. Climbs to 5 feet.

Cup-and-Saucer Vine. *Cobaea scandens.* Climbs to 25 feet. Flowers are like canterbury bells, 2 inches long, and violet-purple. May be sown outdoors in May, but best to sow indoors in small pots in March.

Cypress Vine. *Quamoclit pennata.* Will grow to 20 feet, with fern-like foliage and scarlet or white flowers that are 1½ inches long.

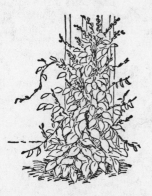

Hyacinth Bean. *Dolichos lablab.* Grows to 8 feet and has pea-shaped blossoms which may be purple or white. In flower from July to fall.

Ipomœa or morning glory climbs 12 feet. Heavenly blue is the popular variety; its blooms are 4 inches in diameter.

You sow seeds of ornamental gourds every late spring. Mostly inedible, their interest is in the unusual shapes and curious markings of the fruits.

The Japanese hop is an annual liked for its foliage and growing 25 feet; to obtain hops you should plant, not this, but humulus lupulus, a perennial, and insist on female plants.

Ipomoea. *Morning glory.* **Called** this because its blooms open in the morning and close shortly past noon. *Heavenly Blue* is the most popular variety; the white *Pearly Gates* and the red *Scarlett O'Hara* together are a close second.

The white moonflower, *Calonyction aculeatum,* is an allied plant; it acts in reverse, with the blooms open at night and on cloudy afternoons.

Ornamental Gourds. They will climb a trellis or fence. The curious fruits have various quaint markings, mostly yellow and green, striped and spotted; and the queer shape of one may suggest a club, others a dipper, bottle, apple, egg, spoon, or pear. Let the gourds dry thoroughly; then give them a coat of shellac, and they will serve for colorful winter decorations.

One of the ornamental gourds is the *luffa,* the fruits of which may be 2 feet long. In the tropics these are allowed to decay in water until only fibers remain; they are used as vegetable sponges or made into hats or inner soles for shoes. A well-established small industry in some Central American countries, but now suffering from the competition of woven plastics for these purposes.

Hop, Japanese. *Humulus japonicus. Oriental hop.* Its leaves are its source of attractiveness, because it does not produce true hops. However, a variety with variegated leaves exists. Either kind will climb to 25 feet, preferring a 45-degree angle, and both are good for shutting out unsightly buildings or screening the porch.

Wild Cucumber. *Echinocystis lobata.* Climbs to 20 feet and may escape to be a bad weed. Small white flowers in skeins are followed by 1½-

inch, spiny, quaint, cucumberlike fruits.

Nasturtiums, *Tropæolum majus,* are good climbers, the old-time tall kinds especially. An allied variety, *Tropæolum tuberosum,* may be used in the Southern sections of the U. S. The small yellow flowers have red spurs; underground are large tubers which may be eaten.

Climbing nasturtiums will travel 10 feet; these are the old-time single sorts in brilliant combinations of yellow and red. See the annuals section.

Sweetpeas may also be used in the north and New England. (Both nasturtiums and sweetpeas are described under annuals.)

Scarlet Runner Bean. A popular vegetable in European gardening; sometimes grown in America for decoration. It climbs to 7 feet, and its red flowers are highly decorative.

Although the green pods are stringy and have to be "topped and tailed" before going into the pot, their flavor is considered superior to our regular garden snap-beans.

CHAPTER 13

Beautiful Roses! Fragrant Roses!

"Baby said
When she smelt the rose,
'Oh! What a pity
I've only one nose!'"
LAURA ELIZABETH RICHARDS.

ROSES
Hardy Woody Perennials

ROSES DO NOT need clay land, as frequently claimed; they will thrive in almost any kind of soil provided it is well drained. If it happens to be clay, a layer of stones or gravel 2 feet below the surface takes care of the drainage of an average rosebed. It is best to plant roses in 3- or 4-foot-wide beds reserved exclusively for them, so they can receive regular care. A good spacing is 2 feet in all directions for everblooming or hybrid-tea varieties, 2½ feet for hybrid-perpetuals, 3 feet for floribunda, rugosa, wichuriana, and hugonis varieties.

Plant in spring in the extreme north, spring or fall elsewhere. Dig a hole overlarge to hold the roots, put in about 3 trowelsful of sheep manure, 1½ trowelsful of bonemeal, about a pailful of screened compost if you have a heap; with a garden fork mix all with the soil of the bottom and sides. Put a spadeful of plain soil in the center of the hole to form a small hill on which the roots of the rose will be stood, arranging them naturally downwards and outwards. Note the mark of the soil in the nursery on the lower stem; place the plant so that this mark will be 2 inches under the surface. Be sure the roots do not tangle or twist around each other or cross in such a way that, as they increase in size,

114

they might strangle one another. If you notice any bruised or fractured roots, prune just above the damage. Return the soil, tread lightly with the shoe, and leave a depression around the bush which you can fill with water daily for a week; after which hoeing and raking will gradually fill it up.

Pruning a rose. Cut suckers from below the surface; remove dead branches.

Spring has arrived, and you break down the earth pyramids which have protected your plants. You are now ready for spring pruning. With your hybrid-

Bush looks like this.

teas and hybrid-perpetuals winter has killed much of the growth that was not covered by the mound of soil. These and any other dead branches are cut away. If the plant consists of more than five stems, prune out all over five; also take out any that crowd, even if doing so leaves less than five. Shorten each branch until it has two, three, or more buds, leaving the topmost bud one which faces away from the center. Also cut below ground any growth other than the main plant.

Do a similar pruning job to a tree rose, which is merely a bush that has been attached by budding to the top of a 3½-foot stem. Regard the stem as the soil; your bush on the stem should look the same as one in the ground.

Cut one inch above the second, third or fourth bud, whichever points outward, away from the plant's center.

Small-flowered, bunch-flowered climbers are pruned after blooming is over, in summer, by removing old spent canes down to the ground, but leaving the younger stems and the branches on them untouched. Old canes of large-flowered climbers are cut out. Then all the branches are cut to within 2 inches of the parent stem or cane. The tops of climbing roses, as a rule, are not cut.

Floribunda, hugonis, rugosa, and wichuriana roses are only pruned if the stems are over numerous, when the oldest may be cut to the ground. All dead branches are cut away when seen.

Most roses are offered budded to strong-growing wild plants, and the wild plants are often rosa multiflora or rugosa. The manetti rose, *rosa chinensis,* is also much used. Budding is a form of grafting whereby a bud from a scarce variety is planted onto the

stem, just above the roots, of the wild plant. This is to make a bush; when the bud is planted on the wild stem 3½ feet from the ground we get a standard or tree rose.

If you take cuttings from your roses you will have "own-root" roses; some gardeners prefer these. Others like budded roses, and either will give you good blooms.

Hybrid-tea or ever-blooming roses withstand winter's cold if soil is added around them to enclose them within an earthen pyramid. Mostly they are highly fragrant.

Hybrid-tea roses, referred to as H.T.'s or everblooming roses, are not quite so resistant to cold as are the hybrid-perpetual roses, called H.P.'s or remontant roses, but they thrive as far north as southern Ontario and are at home in the central sections of the United States. A few varieties are very double, but often they are somewhat sparse; an H.T. rose with 50 petals is considered full; many new varieties have around 25 or 30. Nearly all are sweetly perfumed. They produce crop after crop of blooms from June until frost.

Hundreds of good varieties are available. As splendid as any are Crimson Diamond, velvety crimson, 35 to 40 petals; Kaiserin Auguste Viktoria, snow-white, 100 petals; the novelty of the year 1952, Fred Howard, a glorious yellow; Peace, cream-gold and pink, 45 petals; Talisman, red, orange, pink and yellow, 25 petals. All are fragrant.

Typical hybrid-perpetual or remontant rose. Large blooms, mostly very double, are borne in June, with a possible additional few in autumn.

Hybrid-perpetual or remontant roses bloom strongly in June. Usually they give a second smaller crop of flowers in late summer. This second crop is the only claim this class has to the word perpetual. Their blooms are very large, often with 100 petals; but some are without fragrance. Frau Karl Druschki, white; Paul Neyron, dark pink; Hugh Dickson, crimson-scarlet, are among the good ones.

Tree or standard roses are for planting amid bush roses, where they stand head-and-shoulders above their companions, or in the perennial border. Many H.T.'s and a few H.P.'s may be had in this form. Keeping them over winter in the north is a problem. They may be dug up and buried, or heeled in under a shed, to be replanted the following spring; in mild latitudes we merely fix straw among the branches and tie it around the stems.

A tree-rose or standard-rose is a normal bush budded onto a 3½-ft. stem. In the north, carrying them over winter is not easy.

To carry bush roses safely through a northern winter, we place earth around them to form a sort of pyramid, with the plant in the center. Do not hoe soil up to them, but bring fresh soil from elsewhere in the garden.

Multiflora climbing rose at left. One of the newer large-flowered climbing roses at right.

Climbing roses may be trained over an arch, draped around posts, or festooned on wire from one post to another. Planted on steep slopes and pegged down, they hold the soil against erosion. Mostly they are of the multiflora type, with clusters of five-petaled flowers in brilliant colors; some are semi-double, and almost all are June-blooming. Typical are Dr. W. Van Fleet, flesh-pink; Paul's Climber, scarlet; Easlea's Golden Rambler, patent No. 114, yellow and orange. Some fully double large-blooming types are becoming available, with ever-blooming characters: New Dawn, flesh-pink, and Mme. Gregoire Staechelin, pink and crimson.

Floribunda roses are shrubs in bloom from June to frost. The older kinds had mostly small flowers, but some are now almost as

At left, floribunda roses, which bloom all season. Rosa rugosa, with 4-inch diameter flowers, at right.

large as the more familiar types of roses. They are excellent for lining driveways, for hedges, or for planting along with other shrubs. World's Fair, and Pinocchio, are outstanding; the first is velvety scarlet, the latter gold, salmon and pink.

The hugonis rose is very hardy. Flowers are two inches in diameter, yellow and borne in June.

The hugonis rose is from north China and very hardy. This is a graceful shrub with single yellow flowers; it may grow 8 feet high.

Rosa rugosa is often planted in with other shrubs. It grows 6 feet, is resistant to cold and has red, white, pink, or purple single or double flowers, sometimes 4 inches in diameter.

The wichuriana or memorial rose is a trailing shrub, useful for covering banks. It has single white blooms which are scented.

Miniature or thimble roses are a pleasing addition to a rose garden. Edge a flower bed with them or plant them in a children's garden. Six to nine inches tall, the semi-double blooms are dime-size. Pixie and Tom Thumb, patent No. 169, are good midgets in this group.

Rosa wichuriana, the memorial rose, has 2-inch white flowers, which are fragrant. Thimble serves as a vase for miniature roses.

CHAPTER 14

Flowering Shrubs and Trees

"The kiss of the sun for pardon,
The song of the birds for mirth,
One is nearer God's heart in a garden
Than anywhere else. on earth."
DOROTHY FRANCES BLOMFIELD GURNEY.

FLOWERING SHRUBS AND TREES YOU SHOULD HAVE

YOUR GARDEN will be made lovelier by their presence as each blooms in its appointed season, with a wealth of color and often of fragrance. At the end of winter you may cut branches of the earlier kinds to bring into the house and put into vases to bloom while the garden outside is still in its winter sleep.

Carolina Allspice *or* Sweet-shrub. *Calycanthus floridus.* Growing up to 8 feet, with dark red-brown, 2-inch scented flowers.

Flowering Almond. *Prunus triloba.* Fragrant dainty flowers cover the bush in early May, ahead of the leaves. Normally they are light pink, but white forms may be had. May grow to 10 feet or more, but with early summer pruning it may be kept to a size in keeping with its surroundings.

AZALEAS

Mostly evergreens, these are covered with bloom in spring, the *Japanese* kinds being mostly crimson-scarlet. The varieties Hinodegiri and Kurume are commonly planted, as is the *Indian azalea,* a 6-foot plant with pink flowers. The Japanese grow to 3 feet high and get bushier every year. Orange-yellow flowers are the characteristic of *A. calendulaceum. A. mucronatum* is a 6-foot white-flowering kind, and *A. luteum* is a 10-foot giant with fragrant yellow blooms. Mostly these will not survive the winter in our northernmost states, except on the seaboard.

Our native *A. nudiflorum* or *pinxter flower* can be found in the woods from Maine to Florida. It is not evergreen, but drops its leaves in autumn, and its light pink flowers appear ahead of them in spring.

Azaleas do best in a sandy or gravelly soil containing compost or peatmoss.

Beauty Bush. *Kolkwitzia amabilis.* A charming bush from China. The bell-shaped flowers, each

Pinxter-flower, azalea nudiflorum, is one of our native American shrubs which drops its leaves in autumn, producing its pink flowers in spring, ahead of the new foliage.

The beauty-bush has lovely pink flowers in May and June. A dwarf shrub, it rarely exceeds 6 feet.

light pink with a yellow throat, are borne in May and June. Reaches a height of 5 feet.

Butterfly Bush. *Summer lilac. Buddleia variabilis.* Originally from China and with fragrant lilac flowers; lavender-pink, rose-purple, rose-lilac, dark purple, mauve, white, and near-red are colors now obtainable. May grow as high as 15 feet. For the first few years it may behave as a herbaceous perennial, dying down to the ground in fall, before it becomes more shrublike, and it may retain its herbaceous habit permanently in the north. Butterfly bush is well named, for it does attract butterflies. Plant it if your son is a budding entomologist. It is quite hardy and is good for the northern United States, but some patience is necessary with it, for some years may elapse before flowers are seen.

Catalpa. *Indian bean. Catalpa speciosa.* Large-leaved avenue tree with brown-spotted, white bell-flowers in late spring; these are in 6-inch skeins and are followed by 12-inch flat pods. Height at maturity, 100 feet.

Butterfly-bush or buddleia is sometimes called the summer lilac. The fragrant flowers attract butterflies.

Chaste-tree. *Monk's pepper-tree. Vitex agnus-castus.* The flower spikes of this handsome 10-foot shrub are lavender, although you may select a white kind. In the north it is well to spread a 3-inch coat of dried leaves or compost on the soil over the roots during winter.

Japanese cherries are the trees which thousands travel to the national capital in spring to see. Plant some in your own garden.

Japanese Cherries. You can dupli-cate the annual display of cherry blos-soms which thousands travel to Washton annually to see. You purchase varieties of *Prunus serrulata,* a good double one being kwanzan. It may reach a height of 30 feet or more.

Clethra alnifolia rosea. A rare pink form of the Pepperbush. 5 ft. high, it will thrive in sun or shade, in damp soil.

Flowering Crab. *Malus ionensis.* Many of the crabs are developed from our native crab apple of the prairies. Improvement has been along two lines —size, color, and beauty of the flowers, and decorative qualities of the little apples. These are rarely edible, but some are used in making crab-apple jelly. One popular kind is Bechtel's crab, which grows into a handsome 30-foot tree.

Deutzia gracilis. Bushes may grow 6 feet high and have clusters of white flowers in June. A variety with golden leaves may be obtained.

Dogwood. *Cornus florida.* One of our most beautiful native trees, it grows in the woods from Maine to Texas and attains a height of 35 feet, flowering in spring. The pink variety is striking, as is the white, and trees with double flow-ers are occasionally found. The scarlet fruits in autumn are attrac-tive. The Siberian Dogwood, *Cor-nus alba,* is a 10 ft. shrub with red branches; its clusters of small flow-ers, however, may be disappointing.

Our native dogwood, with white or pink flowers, brightens the Ameri-can woodland scene in late spring from Maine to Texas.

Forsythia Suspensa. *Golden bells.* This is one of the most widely planted shrubs; it is covered with bright golden flowers in earliest spring before the leaves appear. Gather branches in winter to flower in the house. The new Lynwood Gold is the brightest and best to date.

Holly. *Ilex opaca.* The spiny-leaved evergreen tree so much in de-mand for Christmas decorations. Mostly the berries are red, though there is a yellow-berried variety. Height when full grown, 50 feet.

Horsechestnut. *Aesculus hippocastanum.* Splendid flowering shade tree. The white-flowering variety may attain 100 feet, and the red about 75 feet.

HYDRANGEAS

Blue Hydrangea. H. macrophylla. For the most charming hue the land should be acid and at planting time ½ pound of aluminum sulphate should be mixed with each bushel of soil. Dressing annually with ½ pound of the same chemical per 5 square feet and raking it under will usually maintain the blue color. May grow to 10 feet.

Buy your plant from a reliable nursery, and stress that you want a *blue* hydrangea. Otherwise there may be some confusion and you may possibly get one with white or pink flowers.

The blue hydrangea likes an acid, moist soil. To maintain its deep blue color small amounts of aluminum sulphate are worked into the land from time to time.

Hills of Snow. H. arborescens grandiflora. Has 6-inch clusters of small pure-white flowers in June and July, and grows to 10 feet.

Paniculata Hydrangea. H. paniculata. May grow to 30 feet; 12-inch clusters of white flowers, which change to purple at the end of summer. Partly *everlasting,* they are used for winter decoration in the home.

Hills of snow and the paniculata hydrangea are easy to grow, and are always effective. They like a rich but well-drained soil, and should be pruned in very early spring.

Hydrangea paniculata blooms from summer to fall. The flowerheads are sometimes used as everlastings for room-decoration.

Hypericum, Hidcote variety. A low shrub, 3 feet high. All summer it is covered with bright yellow cup-flowers that are fragrant.

Laburnum. *Golden chain; bean tree. Cytisus laburnum.* Imagine 6-inch hanging clusters of wisteria-shaped flowers, but bright yellow, in June, on a shapely tree which may grow to 25 feet. Pods in autumn contain the beans. Do not allow the children to eat them, for they are somewhat poisonous.

Lilac. *Syringa vulgaris.* Perhaps the easiest shrub to grow, it stands city conditions and partial shade. Flowers are in beautiful fragrant clusters, and purple, white, blue, purplish-red, and violet are the colors

Much loved for their fragrance, lilacs are the most accommodating shrubs you can plant, thriving almost anywhere.

obtainable. The *French* types have larger flowers, often double; the varieties Charles X, Ludwig Spaeth, Le Gaulois and Madame Abel Chatenay are especially fine. Prune lilacs just after the flowering period —ruthlessly if they hesitate to bloom. Take away all weak or young twigs, as well as new growth from around the plant; dig under for a taproot growing straight down into the subsoil, and saw through it if one is found.

MAGNOLIA

M. soulangeana. Growing 25 feet or more, the tree has smooth gray bark like a beech tree. Before the leaves appear in early spring, the flowers cover the tree. These are often 6 inches across, white inside and purple outside; others may be striped rosy-red, others again pure white.

M. stellata. This has star-shaped attractive white flowers, 3 inches in diameter. The tree is little more than half the height of *M. soulangeana,*

The magnolia blooms in spring ahead of the leaves. The cone-like fruit or center of the flower is much liked by squirrels and birds.

The mock-orange or philadelphus will thrive in any part of the garden, including partial shade. It is sweetly fragrant.

but its blooms are fragrant.

Mock-orange. *Philadelphus coronarius.* A shrub growing to 10 feet, covered in late spring with very fragrant cream-white flowers. Some double kinds can be obtained. Prune after flowering.

Mountain Ash. *Sorbus americana.* Handsome 30-foot avenue tree. In late summer it is covered with clusters of scarlet rowanberries. Birds like them, and they may be made into preserves. So cold-resistant that it stands Canada's winter.

Mountain Laurel. *Calico bush. Kalmia latifolia.* Few sights are

123

more beautiful than a New England wooded hillside when these clusters of pink-tinted, white, 1-inch jewel-flowers are opening in early June. The evergreen bushes may grow to 8 feet high and will tolerate shade but not a clay or limestone soil; so dig out a larger hole than the roots require, and plant in a mixture of sandy soil with which one-third its bulk of compost or peatmoss is mixed. Use aluminum

Mountain-laurel, our charming native flowering evergreen, and known as calico-bush.

sulphate as suggested under hydrangeas.

Pussywillow. *Salix discolor.* A small tree or large bush common to the New England swamps and river banks. Its catkins swell and develop in March, and are regarded as one of the early indications of approaching spring.

Flowering Quince. *Japanese quince. Chaenomeles lagenaria.* A 10-foot bush with spiny branches and 2-inch brilliant scarlet flowers in early spring. This is grown only for ornament; the fruits are of little value.

Catkins of the pussy-willow are an early sign of spring. Good for a damp area; suitable for placing in moist soil near a pond.

RHODODENDRONS

Plant them in pockets of sandy soil, mixed with compost and peatmoss. They flower in June.

R. carolinianum. Rose-purple flowers; some are found with white flowers. It is 6 feet high and is native to North Carolina.

R. catawbiense. Mountain rose bay. A native evergreen shrub from open woodland in the mountains of Pennsylvania and Virginia. Growing up to 20 feet, it has either lilac-purple or white flowers.

R. ponticum. A dwarfer plant, native of the Mediterranean basin, 10 feet high, with purple flowers spotted with brown.

These, with sorts from the Himalayas, China, and Japan, are the parents of the many hybrids with large and brilliant flowers that are offered by nursery concerns. Plant them along driveways and in semi-shade, where large evergreens are appropriate.

Rose of Sharon. *Shrub althaea. Hibiscus syriacus.* A popular shrub because it is very resistant to cold and because it blooms from summer to fall—a period when few shrubs are in flower. It may grow up to 12 feet, and the pink, white, or purple flowers, sometimes double, look like the individual florets of the hollyhock.

The fine white-flowered shrub, spiraea Van Houttei, may grow 6 feet high.

are bright carmine-crimson.

S. vanhouttei. Bridal wreath. Growing up to 6 feet, the graceful arching twigs are covered with bunches of small white flowers in June.

Tulip Tree. *Liriodendron tulipifera.* The 2-inch flowers are greenish-yellow and orange. It may grow to a height of 200 feet and is the whitewood of the carpenter.

Snowberry. *Waxberry. Symphoricarpos albus.* Dwarf shrub, growing not over 4 feet, with small, pink, bell-shaped flowers. The interesting feature is the berry, which is white.

SPIRAEA

S. bumalda. Only 2 feet high, it produces flat clusters of pink or white flowers in July and August. In the variety *Anthony Waterer*, they

Oriental snowball, viburnum plicatum, is covered with balls of white flowers in May.

VIBURNUM

Viburnum Carlesii matures at 5 or 6 feet. Large clusters of white waxy flowers in spring are delightfully fragrant.

Easily grown shrubs that are markedly resistant to cold. The fruits or haws are attractive to birds in winter.

V. plicatum. Japanese Snowball. This 10-foot shrub has rounded ball-shaped heads of 1-inch pure white flowers in May and June, followed by fruits that are first red, turning black.

V. tomentosum. Tomentosum means hairy, describing the under side of the leaves. Growing 10 feet high. Flowers are in clusters on long stalks, dazzling white and produced in May and June. Red fruits, later turning black.

V. carlesii. Fragrant viburnum. Growing 5 feet, this shrub has dense clusters, 3 inches across, of waxy white fragrant flowers in early spring. Berries are black.

V. carlcephalum. The finest shrub in a decade. Six feet high. Fragrant white flower clusters sometimes are six inches across. New hybrid from Europe.

Weigela. Growing up to 10 feet, this is a particularly hardy shrub, though in the northernmost states it is well to have a 4-inch layer of compost or dead leaves on the soil over the roots in winter. Trumpet-shaped flowers in late spring are rose-pink; there also are white varieties. Does best in full sun. Prune as soon as the flowering period is over, and later in the year prune the longer branches to encourage an occasional additional flower in autumn.

Weigela has large red trumpet-shape flowers in early summer. Prune after flowering; not in spring.

WHEN SHRUBS AND ROSES ARRIVE

Heel-in shrubs if they come when you are not ready to plant them. Dig a trench, stand the shrubs upright in it, closer than if you were planting them; shovel dirt onto the roots and water them if rain does not occur. They will keep well for several weeks and probably will take root better than if you had planted them on arrival.

Should shrubs or roses reach you in a condition that causes you to think they have become too dry to grow, dig a shallow trench and lay them in it and cover them with earth, roots and tops. Dig

them up and plant them two weeks later; probably they will have become swollen to a normal condition, will take root when you plant them, and will thrive.

A "B and B" shrub.

B. & B. SHRUBS

You may have plants offered to you "B. & B.," which means balled and burlapped. The roots have the original soil around them, retained with a piece of burlap. They cost more than shrubs with bare roots, but they suffer less in transportation and planting.

CHAPTER 15

Hedges and Ground Covers

*"To me the meanest flower that blows can give
Thoughts that do often lie too deep for tears."*
WILLIAM WORDSWORTH.

HEDGES

To frame your property, ensure privacy, and discourage trespassing, make a windbreak for more tender plants.

Barberry. Wear stout leather gloves, for the tiny thorns are painful and hard to extract from the skin. One foot apart is the usual spacing, and the *red-leaved type* is more pleasing than the green; the new Crimson Pygmy is an acquisition. A spreading plant only 8 inches high. Autumn fruits of the barberry are scarlet, and birds enjoy them.

Beech makes a thick screen when pruned annually to the required height. Set the plants 2 feet apart.

Caragana or pea-shrub makes a good hedge. The spines require that the planter and pruner wear leather gloves. Set them 1½ feet apart.

Crataegus. The various thorns, especially Paul's scarlet, make a fierce thorny hedge, planted at 2-foot intervals.

Lilacs make good flowering hedges, and **Rosa Rugosa** is also used.

Mixed Hedges. The golden-leaved privet looks good planted along with the green. One plant in five or ten of some of the flowering shrubs is satisfactory in a privet hedge; despite clipping, they will flower. For this purpose, forsythia, lilac, flowering quince, rose of sharon and floribunda roses may be used.

Privet. Very quick-growing plants. They may be pruned and sheared to any height; uncut, the California or the common privets will reach 15 feet for a perfect screen. One good way to plant a privet hedge is to dig a trench 1 foot deep and 2 feet wide, rake in 1 pound of pulverized sheep manure and ½ pound of bonemeal to the running foot; set the plants in two rows 1 foot apart and 1 foot from each other, the blanks in one row opposite the bushes in the other. For real effectiveness, run a three-wire fence down the middle. Note that this method of planting calls for two plants per foot. A kind with golden leaves can be obtained.

EVERGREEN HEDGE PLANTS

Taxus *or* **Yew.** Often clipped to neat flat sides and a flat top, for a formal hedge near the residence.

Boxwood. From Long Island south, a hedge of the slow-growing buxus sempervirens is valued for its perfume; perhaps also on account of its high initial cost.

Arborvitae, Cypress, Hemlock and Spruce may be used; for a formal effect they need several shearings and prunings a year. If not kept under control, overcrowding will necessitate the removal of every second tree in future years; perhaps repeating again until our hedge becomes a line of trees. Two such rows of trees with a path or road between is called an *allée* by landscape architects, and when the tops come together they are called *pleached allées*.

Another unusual term is the *haha*. It is a scheme for protecting the property without obstructing the view. Some owners of acreage dislike the confining appearance of fences and hedges, yet they wish to keep animals in the spaces allotted to them. So they dig out a wide depression, and along the bottom erect their hedge, which is not visible until you come to it. The combined double row of privet, with wires between, is very suitable for a *haha*. The modern zoological park, with wide sheer-walled ditches or fences hidden from your sight to give you a view of dangerous animals seemingly roaming at will, is a development of the idea.

GROUND COVERS

We find from experience that in some places flowers and shrubs cannot be grown; some of the causes may be extra-dense shadow, winter snow sliding from the roof, unusual wear at certain seasons, or shallow soil over foundations. Or we try sowing grass seeds and fail to get turf. So we turn to *ground covers* to hide the soil. A border planted with lily bulbs and carpeted with a ground cover fills the requirements of most lilies—their leaves in light and their roots in shade. Edging with ground covers is an excellent treatment for a driveway.

Among the best ground covers for areas in shadow are:

Creeping jenny, ground ivy, mazus reptans, sedums, funkia or plantain lily. Plant them 18 inches apart.

English ivy, 3 feet apart.

Euonymus radicans, spaced at 2 feet.

Pachysandra, or oriental spurge. It stands sun also. Plant the roots 9 inches apart.

Lily of the valley, vinca or periwinkle, violets. Set them 12 inches.

For sunny spots, use the following:

Chrysogonum or golden star, lavender-cotton, mother-of-thyme; all at 12-inch spacing.

Honeysuckle planted at 2-foot intervals.

Flower Borders and Flower Beds. Rock Gardens and Pond Gardens. The Artistry of Carpet-Bedding. The Herb Garden.

"A Garden is a lovesome thing, God wot!
Rose plot,
Fringed pool,
Ferned grot—
The veriest school
Of peace; and yet the fool
Contends that God is not—
Not God! in Gardens! when the eve is cool?
Nay, but I have a sign:
'Tis very sure God walks in mine."

THOMAS EDWARD BROWN.

BORDERS AND BEDS

A TYPICAL BORDER is from 5 to 15 feet wide and as long as is convenient; the front is frequently wavy in outline, and often flowering shrubs are at the back. Borders usually are viewed from one side; beds often are viewed from all sides. Flowers are planted in a border in relation to both their height, with the tallest in back, and their color. Some gardeners like a mixture of colors; others prefer one color in one section, a different color in another—blue to suggest distance and make a garden appear larger than it is, red to suggest friendly hospitality; white flowers in one place, pink in another.

Note that in gardening we do not use the word border to describe something planted around other flowers. We employ the term edging for this. The difference between a bed and a border is also one of symmetry. In a border we have the dwarfer varieties in front, but the whole effect is one of pleasing naturalness. In a bed we are more formal: lines are often geometric in character, and around the circle, oval, or rectangle we usually have an edging of dwarf plants like lobelia or alyssum.

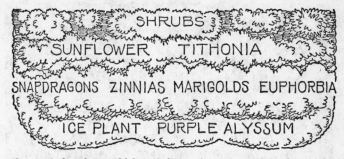

Some of the plants which may be set in an annual border. Spring-planted bulbs are often placed here also, gladiolus, summer hyacinth, begonia and the like.

Most of the plants in an annual border bloom all summer until frost, especially if fading flowers are kept sheared off. But in a perennial border nearly all are effective for but a short while, so the season of bloom is a further consideration here. Some owners like a perennial border divided into three blooming seasons: one section showing color in spring, another in summer, the third in autumn. The non-blooming parts might have a few flowers at the time, but generally would be green. Folk who plan to be away every summer often plant two sections, one effective in spring, the other in autumn.

Another scheme is to select plants so that every third one is in bloom at one time, methodically planting spring sorts alongside summer and autumn sorts, so that flowers are spotted throughout the border. Still another arrangement is to have one section with spring- and late summer-flowering plants side by side, and in another section, early summer and late autumn plants together.

The table in chapter 12, summarizing the information given

under each perennial, will help you quickly to work out your own plan.

THE ROCK GARDEN

This is an attempt to reproduce on a small scale a rocky slope, moraine, miniature mountain, or cliff. In its design five points may well be kept in mind:

Perennial borders may have foxglove, hollyhock and other biennials *set in with the perennials. Autumn-planted bulbs also go in, like lilies, tulips and grape hyacinths; they are true perennials. Many gardeners like to plant to a color-scheme; you can readily work out a plan to suit your ideas with the help of the tables in chapter 12.*

1. It should have a reason, such as to occupy the space between two levels or between two sections of the garden.

2. It should look natural.

3. Plants in it should consist of those suitable for the situation, the rock-loving or alpine plants. Highly developed garden flowers are frowned upon, except for filling temporarily bare spaces when the garden is young.

4. Paths, trails, and flat stepping stones should provide easy access to every part for planting and weeding, the latter being one of the continuing demands of a rock garden.

5. Pockets of soil between and under the rocks should be as large as possible, and well enriched with manure, bonemeal and compost.

Rock-garden plants are hardy perennials, although some dwarf annuals may be used in addition for the first year, when the permanent plants are not fully developed. The perennials, bulbs, and annuals that may be used are marked * in the lists in this book.

An old stone wall may be used as a rock garden. Spaces between the rocks may be filled with rich soil and in these pockets the roots of suitable plants would be inserted. Suitable for this so-called dry-wall gardening are *alyssum saxatile, arabis, aubretia, erinus, heuchera, iberis, edelweiss, phlox subulata, saxifrage, hen-and-chickens, sedum,* and many others.

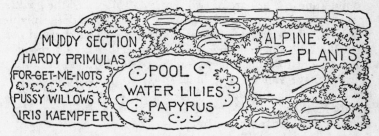

*The rock-garden should look as though Nature herself constructed it ages ago. The dozens of dwarf plants which may have a place in it are marked * in the chapters 6 to 12.*

If the situation warrants, a stream may be diverted through the rock garden, or an artificial one devised to furnish a series of waterfalls leading to a pond in which aquatic plants may be grown, along with suitable bog plants near the water level.

A pleasing extension of the rock-garden idea is the growing of plants in pockets intentionally left for the purpose in the construction of garden steps. *Alyssum saxatile, germander, sedum and thrift* are among the plants which may be used.

Another variation is the filling of spaces purposely provided in the stone floor of a terrace. Two subjects are highly suitable for this purpose, *mazus reptans* and *mother-of-thyme;* treading on them does little harm.

AQUATIC PLANTS

You have a pond, possibly a still pool along a stream. In the mud at the bottom you may plant one or more **Hardy Water Lilies.** Since they should be in water about 2 feet deep, mound up the bottom if the water is much deeper. Once established, they become a permanent source of beauty; they may remain all winter under the ice. If the bottom is concrete, plant each root in a 9-inch-deep box, using ordinary garden soil and stand them on the bottom. Splendid white, yellow, or pink flowering varieties can be obtained.

But you may want larger flowers, with a wider range of color; so you have some **Tropical Water Lilies,** which are planted around June 1. They are of two types: day-bloomers, the flowers opening with the sun and closing at evening; and the night-bloomers, whose flowers open at the close of day and remain so until the following morning. In cloudy weather the latter sometimes are open through the twenty-four hours. All are beautiful; you can have violet kinds, blue, pink, or white. None in this group may remain in the water all winter in the north; lift them in fall, let them dry and keep them in a cool but frost-free garage or cellar until the following June.

You have no pool? Then grow them in tubs of water. In pool or tub, fish are desirable to control mosquito larvae.

Lotus. Handsome 6-foot plants with large shield-shaped leaves and big flowers, followed by flat-topped fruits. Soil should be rich and covered with 6 to 10 inches of water. Set the tubers at an angle, so that the tip is barely covered with soil.

Planting may be in the mud of the bottom or in pots of garden soil standing on the bottom. Dig the roots or take up the pots in autumn,

The striking flower and perforated receptacle or fruit of the lotus.

allow to dry, and store in a frost-free place over winter. The botanical name of the plant is *nelumbium.*

Egyptian Paper Plant. *Cyperus papyrus.* Plant this in the mud just under the surface, to grow up to 8 feet high. Thin strips of the pith were hammered together into sheets to provide the papyri which archeologists unearth in the East. Lift the roots for the winter.

Water Hyacinth. *Eichhornia crassipes.* A few of these make the pool or tub interesting; small ball-shaped green plants have each a few leaves. Floating freely, their feathery roots get all they need from the water alone. In summer they have yellow-spotted violet-blue flowers.

Along the edges of a pond, the following will thrive and look appropriate:

Hardy aster	Lobelia cardinalis
Marsh marigold	Forget-me-not
Gentian	Hardy primula
Hemerocallis or day-lily	Sarracenia or pitcher-plant
Oriental iris	Hardy ferns

Pussywillows may also form a background to the picture.

CARPET-BEDDING

This type of gardening calls for the highest horticultural skill. Ingenious designs and patterns are worked out by the planter, usually of a geometric character, introducing straight and curved lines, panels, circles, part-circles, ovals, spirals, or stars. Sometimes letters are worked out, perhaps the word "Welcome" or the name of a church or the town; for carpet-bedding is suitable for displays near buildings and in city parks.

Mostly the color of the foliage of various dwarf plants is more depended upon for effect than are flowers. Contrasts in these colors and planting with extreme accuracy and so close that the soil is entirely hidden are the important features, together with constant trimming.

Plants frequently used for this effect include:

PERENNIALS

Mostly grown from cuttings or root divisions, made in late summer. Alternanthera. Varieties with red, golden or red-and-yellow spotted leaves are much used.

Echeveria	Sempervivum or houseleek
Lavender-cotton	Mother-of-thyme

ANNUALS

From seeds sown in winter in a greenhouse.

Ageratum, dwarf blue or white	Begonia semperflorens or gracilis
Alyssum, white or lilac	Centaurea gymnocarpa

Cigar-plant
Coleus
Golden feather
Heliotrope

Lantana
Lobelia, dwarf blue or white
Phlox drummondi
Portulaca

Catnip is a wooly whitish herb used for seasoning. Your pet cat would enjoy some plants in the garden.

Costmary or alecost is a fragrant herb that may be dried and used for scenting linen.

THE HERB GARDEN

Midway in interest between flowers and vegetables are the various herbs. Often planted in intricate designs, they were given much attention in olden times, when they provided the homemaker of medieval Europe with her salad ingredients, her condi-

Woodruff, a fragrant herb, useful as an edging plant for partial shade.

Rosemary for remembrance. Herb used for seasoning, and its fragrant dried leaves may be added to potpourri.

ments when spices from the Indies were scarce and expensive, her perfumes, and her household remedies when the herbalist was the druggist of the day. They were used to preserve food, to ward off disease, drive away insects, and banish unpleasant odors.

Their value in the modern garden is chiefly for their perfume

Pot marjoram. An old-time herb that makes a good edging; the fragrant leaves may be added to potpourri.

Sweet marjoram. A seasoning herb, the leaves of which may be added to salads; dried they can be added to potpourri.

Lemon- or bergamot-mint. Fragrant sweet herb needing moist, rich soil.

Left, peppermint; center, wooly mint; right, pennyroyal. All wonderfully fragrant, green or dried.

Summer savory. 18-inch annual herb that is claimed to impart a meat-like flavor to vegetarian dishes.

One of the scented geraniums.

and their use as edging plants; there is also some sentiment associated with them. Plants that once were important herbs and are used by gardeners today are described in this book among the perennials, biennials, or annuals; or they are illustrated here. They include:

Aconite	Bee-balm	Boneset	Calendula
Catnip	Costmary	Cowslip	Datura
Digitalis	Dittany	Germander	Hop
Hyssop	Lavender	Lavender-cotton	Mints
Marjoram, pot	Marjoram, sweet	Pennyroyal	Pansy
Rosemary	Sage	Saponaria	Savory
Mother-of-thyme	Valerian	Woodruff	Wormwoods

There are a number of other herbs, not described or illustrated, which would be desirable if you aim for a more complete herb garden. Seeds of some of the annuals and biennials would be obtainable from the larger supply houses, and nurseries would have roots of most of the perennials. These additional herbs are:

Annuals and biennials

Angelica, *Archangelica officinalis*
Basil, *Ocymum basilicum*
Fenugreek, *Trigonella fœnum græcum*
Scurvy grass, *Cochlearia officinalis*

Anise, *Pimpinella anisum*
Bene, *Sesamum orientale*
Safflower, *Carthamus tinctorius*

Perennials

Balm, *Melissa officinalis*
Chamomile, *Anthemis nobilis*
Feverfew, *Chrysanthemum parthenium*
Lemon verbena, *Aloysia citriodora*
Rue, *Ruta graveolens*

Betony, *Stachys officinalis*
Elecampane, *Inula helenium*
Horehound, *Marrubium*
Lovage, *Levisticum officinale*
Tansy, *Tenacetum vulgare*

CHAPTER 17

The Greenhouse. Basket Plants

"If winter comes, can Spring be far behind?"
PERCY BYSSHE SHELLEY.

IF YOU OWN A GREENHOUSE . . .

HERE ARE SOME of the purposes for which you will use it.

Rooting Cuttings. Over the heating pipes you will have a bench or a box filled with moist coarse sand, which has been thoroughly washed with a hose to remove any traces of earth. In it you will insert portions of the stems of hundreds of kinds of plants, for the development of roots. Among others, you will be able to produce new plants of coleus, geraniums, fuchsias, begonias, carnations, gloxinias, poinsettias, and many shrubs and hedge plants. Root-formation can be hastened by coating the lower portion of the cutting with one of the hormones offered for the purpose. Vermiculite, a coarse-ground mica rock may be mixed with the sand, or used instead of it. Cuttings root well in it.

Young Plants for the Garden. The greenhouse is the best place to start plants from seeds. An ideal arrangement is when these young plants can be placed in a cold-frame for a few weeks to bridge the period between time spent in the warm greenhouse and the outdoor garden. These few weeks in the frame are said to be for "hardening off."

Unusual Plants can be kept there. The hundreds of varieties of cactus. Some of the less exacting orchids. The insectivorous plants, that quaint group that needs insect food to supplement the nourishment the roots gain from the soil—nepenthes or pitcher-plant from Malaya, our native sarracenia, the dionaea or fly-trap from the Carolinas, the lowly drosera or sundew that captures midges, from the woods of New England to Florida.

Winter Flowers. The major interest in a greenhouse is that you may grow plants out of their normal season, and your gardening can be carried on the year round. Following are some of the plants that normally are grown under glass; an average minimum night temperature of 50 degrees may be aimed for; varieties marked † would be given space in the warmer part of the structure.

Anemone. The rough slablike tubers of St. Brigid and similar types are usually planted in the autumn.

Antirrhinum. *Snapdragon.* Special greenhouse varieties, in the colors that appeal to you, are used.

Read all you can about these orchids before starting to grow them in the greenhouse: their culture is exacting. Left, odontoglossum; center, cattleya; right, cypripedium.

More orchids difficult to grow. Left, cœlogyne; center, oncidium; right, vanda.

Asparagus. *A. plumosus* and *A. sprengeri.* Give these climbers the support of vertical wires. Their foliage is valuable for mixing in bouquets. Seeds are sown or roots divided in March.

†**Begonia.** *B. semperflorens* and *B. gracilis.* Seeds are sown or cuttings rooted in winter; the plants should be protected from direct sun.

†*Ornamental-leaved begonias* are usually grown from the leaves. Cross-cuts are made here and there along the main veins, and the leaf is laid on the sand, cut side down, and kept in contact with it by placing a few stones on the leaf. Or the stem of the leaf is stuck in the sand of the cutting-box.

†*Tuberous begonias.* Seeds may be sown in February to produce tu-

† These require more heat than the others; set them in the warmer parts of the greenhouse.

bers for planting a year later. The young plants may be set outdoors during summer if you wish.

† **Caladium.** *Fancy-leaved types.* The foliage is red, pink, white or green, striped with color. Plant roots in pots in February.

You need a greenhouse to grow the large-pouched calceolaria.

† **Calceolaria.** *Slipperwort.* Pot-plants with large pouch-shaped flowers, mostly yellow or reddish, spotted with brown. Seed is sown in early summer, the plants successively transferred into larger pots until they flower in late winter in the 6- or 7-inch size.

Calendula. Normally grown outdoors, but extensively cultivated under glass as a florists' annual. Sow seeds in late autumn.

Carnation. The greenhouse kinds are made from cuttings rooted in late winter. Many gardeners like to have them planted outdoors all summer and bring them into the greenhouse in autumn, where they flower all winter.

Chrysanthemum. You may sow either the branching kinds, akin to the hardy perennial chrysanthemums of the garden, or the monster florists'

Cinerarias have a wide color-range. The remarkable blues are true, deep and velvet-like; red, white and other colors, also.

sorts, which are made still larger by the skill of the grower in pruning and disbudding.

Cineraria. Seed is sown in summer to furnish late-winter flowering plants. The daisylike blossoms are most brilliant—white, charming blues, pinks, and red-purple.

† **Coleus.** Highly decorative foliage subjects. Seeds are sown in winter, or cuttings may be rooted at any time. Several pinchings are necessary for shapely plants.

Coleus is planted for its beautiful foliage. Sow seeds or root cuttings. Pinch out the flower-stem when it appears.

Cyclamen. Sow seeds in autumn or in very early spring. A corm or bulb develops, which is repotted in August—the corm is kept on the surface, only the root being under the soil. They bloom in late winter. Time may be reduced by purchasing corms from supply houses.

† These require more heat than the others; set them in the warmer parts of the greenhouse.

Daffodils and Narcissi. Batches of the bulbs are planted in boxes or pots successively from October through December.

Ferns are interesting to work with in a shaded corner of the greenhouse. Spores are purchased, dusted sparingly on a mixture of peatmoss, sand, and fine charcoal, and kept moist and under a belljar. Young plants are set in pots of the same soil mixture.

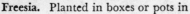

With cyclamen you first grow a tuber or bulb. The leaves and charming flowers develop from this.

Freesia. Planted in boxes or pots in October, they are kept as near the glass as shelving or brackets will allow, an abundance of light being essential.

Fuchsia. Shift into new pots and new soil in February, keep them shaded until summer arrives, then plant out in full sun. For new plants, cuttings are rooted in winter or seeds sown in March.

Geranium. *Pelargonium.* Cuttings are usually rooted in September or October to make flowering plants the following summer. They also grow readily from seed.

Gloriosa. Climbers needing the support of wires. Plant several tubers in a 10-inch pot, or in the bench, during February.

† **Gloxinia.** Seeds are sown in March; cuttings also are easily made, using 2-inch slips. Or young leaves, with their stems, may be inserted in the sand. Mature leaves may be used as cuttings as described under ornamental-leaved begonias. Tubers result, and these may be potted in winter.

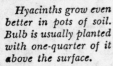

† **Hippeastrum.** *Amaryllis.* This is much grown under glass. See list of spring-planting bulbs.

Iris *reticulata* and *Wedgwood.* Plant bulbs in September for Christmas bloom.

Kalanchoe. Seeds are sown in March, or cuttings rooted in July.

Lilies. Two types of the so-called *longiflorum* or Easter lilies are popular, the *Bermuda harrisi* and the *imperial croft.* Thirteen weeks, more or less according to the temperature, is the usual time needed to bring them into bloom.

Hyacinths grow even better in pots of soil. Bulb is usually planted with one-quarter of it above the surface.

Lilium philippinense and *speciosum* are two varieties, ordinarily planted in the garden, which grow well in the greenhouse.

† These require more heat than the others; set them in the warmer parts of the greenhouse.

Lily-of-the-valley. Portions of the rootstock, called pips, may be planted any time to flower a few weeks later. Use a shady and cooler part of the greenhouse.

Petunia. The double varieties have such large heavy flowers that they need staking, so they are more suitable for greenhouse growing than in the outdoor garden. Seeds may be sown in February, or cuttings may be taken and rooted in May.

The poinsettia, which grows 10 feet high in its native home in tropical America, is a favorite house-plant at Christmas-time. Flowers are small, but the upper leaves are bright red.

† **Poinsettias.** Usually grown from cuttings taken from old plants and rooted in June. After flowering, let them rest in dry pots until April, then water and start them growing to produce branches to cut off and place in the sand. Old plants not used for cuttings may be salvaged. Prune down to the second bud from the base, in April. Repot when growth begins, place in a cold-frame during July and August; then bring into the greenhouse.

Primula. *P. sinensis. Chinese primula.* Sow seeds in February to flower the following winter. Several transplantings terminate in one plant per 5-inch pot. Double kinds are reproduced by division of the roots in March or by rooting cuttings.

P. obconica. Treat as suggested for *P. sinensis.* Some persons, allergic to the plant, acquire a skin rash from contact with obconica.

P. malacoides. Baby or fairy primrose. Growth is the same as for *P. sinensis.*

Schizanthus. *Butterfly flower.* Described among outdoor annuals. For the greenhouse, seeds are sown in late summer.

Shamrock. The small pots sold just before St. Patrick's Day are sown very sparingly with seeds on January 1.

† **Solanum Capsicastrum.** Seeds are sown in February, or cuttings rooted in April.

Stocks. Columnar or one-stem types are used in greenhouses. Seeds are sown in late summer.

The fringed Chinese primula is popular with the greenhouse gardener. Flowers are 1½ inches across.

† Strelitzia. *Bird of paradise flower.* Remarkable yellow and blue blooms on a large 3-foot plant, eventually needing a tub in which to

† These require more heat than the others; set them in the warmer parts of the greenhouse.

grow. Seeds may be sown in spring, or old plants divided in late winter.

Sweet Peas. Special quick-growing, early-flowering varieties are employed for indoor growing. Seeds are usually grown from October through January.

Tritonia. Plant in pots during October.

Tulips. Plant in October through December. Early-flowering types present no difficulty. Darwin and breeder types need staking. Narcissi, daffodils, hyacinths and similar bulbs are potted at the same time. All are kept cool.

Veltheimia. Easily grown bulbs. Plant in pots in October through December.

The baby- or fairy-primrose, primula malacoides, has dainty, charming little flowers one-half inch in diameter, white or various shades of pink.

BASKET PLANTS

The florist will sell you baskets especially for growing these. They are made of open wire-work and are round and open at the top, with three or four long supporting wires. Hang them outdoors in summer, or in the sunroom or greenhouse in winter.

Line them with 2 inches of sphagnum moss and fill with potting-soil. Plant in them trailing geraniums, balcony petunias, pendant types of lobelia, gleam nasturtiums, ageratum, or glory lilies. Schizanthus is a particularly effective basket plant.

Let the basket soak in water for 15 minutes after planting, repeating before it shows signs of becoming dry. Spraying daily with water is a routine process with them.

CHAPTER 18

A Potpourri of Flowers

"And because the breath of flowers is far sweeter in the air (where it comes and goes, like the warbling of music) than in the hand, therefore nothing is more fit for that delight than to know what be the flowers and plants that do best perfume the air." FRANCIS BACON.

WINDOW BOXES

SOME OF THE PLANTS that may be used in these include:

Outside in Summer. Sunny position. Alyssum, lobelia, gleam nasturtiums, kenilworth ivy, balcony petunias or ice-plant. These would be planted along the edge of the boxes. In the center you may use geraniums, tuberous begonias, marigolds or heliotrope. Shady position. Tradescantia, kenilworth ivy, sedum, vinca; these along the edge. In the center, dracaena, ferns, coleus or calla.

Inside in Winter. Daffodils, narcissi, hyacinths, tulips, geranium, fuchsia or lobelia.

Plants for outside window boxes may be set directly into the soil. Inside boxes look well if the plants are kept in their pots, placed in the boxes, with some standing on blocks to bring their tops level. Put moist peatmoss between and over them.

PLANTS FOR SHADE

Here is a list of annuals and perennials, shrubs and climbers that will tolerate day-long shade:

Aconitum	Forget-me-not	Primula
Begonia	Hardy ferns	Vinca
Cardinal-flower	Lady slipper	Viola
Digitalis	Lily-of-the-valley	Violets
English ivy		

Euonymus radicans

Typical window-box planted with marigolds and heliotrope in the center, lobelia along the edge; balcony petunias festooning over the side.

The following should have sun for half the day:

Ajuga	Cornflower	Nicotiana
Azalea	Cynoglossum	Pansy
Balsam	Fuchsia	Petunia
China aster	Gentian	Phlox divaricata
Christmas rose	Godetia	Rhododendron
Clarkia	Lupinus	Snapdragon
Dogwood	Mountain laurel	Witch hazel

Most other flowers like full sun all day, the following especially:

Armeria, calendula, calliopsis or coreopsis, cosmos, dahlia, eschscholtzia, gladiolus, helianthus, marigold, nasturtium, portulaca, zinnia.

PERFUMED PLANTS

For the most intimate part of your garden, the area where you like to place your garden furniture, or in borders surrounding a flagstone terrace. These are the spots where perfume is as important as color when considering your plantings. Following are some of the plants you may use to create the perfumed outdoor living-room:

Annuals

Alyssum	Datura	Mignonette	Pinks
Carnation	Heliotrope	Nasturtium	Snapdragon
Centaurea	Marigold	Nicotiana	Stock
Cynoglossum	Mathiola bicornis	Sweet peas	Petunia

Biennial Wallflower

Spring-planting Bulbs

Lilies: auratum, Philippinense, regale, Lily of the valley, lycoris, Madeira vine tuberose.

Fall-planting Bulbs

Pheasant's eye daffodils, Dutch hyacinths, Jonquils, Lily of the valley. Lilies: Madonna lily, candidum, auratum, Philippinense, regale.

Herbaceous Perennials

Arabis albida	Dianthus	Old man	Valerian
Bee-balm	Mother-of-thyme	Phlox	Violets
Daphne	Lavender	Dictamnus	Yucca

Herbs

In addition to scenting the garden, these may be dried and placed in sachets for placing with the household linen, or in bowls around the home.

Costmary	The various mints	Rosemary	Lemon verbena
Lavender-cotton	Marjoram	Woodruff	Scented geraniums

Climbing Perennial Kudzu vine

Woody Perennial Climbers Clematis paniculata, honeysuckle, silver lace vine.

Shrubs and Trees

Flowering almond	Butterfly bush	Philadelphus
Carolina allspice	Lilac	Viburnum carlesii
Everblooming roses		Rosa wichuriana

Evergreen Boxwood

Some good everlastings for winter decoration indoors. Left, acroclinium; center, celosia plumosa; right, Chinese lantern.

EVERLASTING FLOWERS

Most blooms will wilt or fall apart a few days after they are gathered; but a few may be dried and will retain their shape and color, making excellent floral decorations in the home over the winter. Cut them, and hang the bunches in the garage for a week or two, or until ready to use them. Good everlastings include:

Annuals

Acroclinium	Catananche	Globe amaranth	Sea lavender
Ammobium alatum	Celosia plumosa	Helichrysum	Xeranthemum

147

Biennial Honesty

Herbaceous Perennials
Echinops Edelweiss Lavender Physalis Statice

Woody Perennial Climber Shrubby bittersweet

Shrubs Hydrangea paniculata, Holly

More good everlastings. Left, the edelweiss, sought by alpine climbers; center, globe thistle; right, cupid's dart or catananche.

ORNAMENTAL GRASSES

If you have room, a limited planting of these is worth while. Many are curious, and all are good for dry bouquets. Seeds are offered by leading supply houses.

Everlastings. Ammobium at left; various ornamental grasses in center; globe amaranth at right.

DECORATIVE VEGETABLES

If your garden is small, you may combine beauty with utility and grow some good-looking vegetables among your flowers.

The bright crimson leaves of the rhubarb-chard make a handsome bed, edged with parsley; you can cut for the kitchen all year without marring its effectiveness. The fernlike foliage of carrots always looks well; so do beet leaves. Dandelion is a pretty flower once you forget it is a weed, and it is the healthiest of cooking greens. New Zealand spinach makes a good ground cover in the sun; pick from it as you need. The unicorn-plant or proboscidea is a broad bush 2 feet high, grown for its young seed-pods, which are pickled; it is a handsome plant with 2-inch creamy or red-violet flowers.

Everlastings. Helichrysum at left; honesty in center; right, sea-lavender.

Many of the culinary herbs are decorative, among which are the small-leaved basil, which makes a good pot-plant, chives, lavender, old man, rosemary, winter savory, tansy, and mother-of-thyme.

Everlastings. Left, lavender; center, holly; right, immortelle or xeranthemum.

Avoid growing root vegetables close to hardy perennials, some of the roots of which may be poisonous; when dug, the poisonous monkshood looks quite like horseradish.

FLOWERS FROM THE WILD

You may wish to bring home to your own garden wild plants you meet in your travels. It is well to make sure the plants are not protected by law, as they are in a good many states: for example, the mountain laurel in New England. And ordinary courtesy suggests that you obtain the owner's permission before digging them.

149

CHAPTER 19

The Soil

"I ask not for a larger garden,
But for finer seeds."
RUSSELL HERMAN CONWELL.

SOIL

As a GENERAL RULE, flowering plants are not exacting as to the quality of the soil you grow them in, provided it is topsoil; many, like marigolds, nasturtiums, or zinnias, give more and better blooms in poor land than in rich.

Exceptions are the heavy feeding roses, China asters, begonias, chrysanthemums, delphiniums, dianthus, iris, lilies, pansies, peonies, and phlox. These should have compost, old manure, and bonemeal worked into the soil. Another exception is the perennial border, which should be spaded and well enriched before planting. These heavy-feeding plants and all in the perennial border should be helped by occasional side-dressings of 5–10–5 fertilizer.

If the topsoil on your property has been lost by grading or erosion, you had best set out all your plants in pockets, sowing no seeds direct for two seasons. Dig larger holes than are necessary, fill them with a mixture of soil, sand, and humus or compost, with added sheep manure and bonemeal, and plant your bulbs and plants.

SOIL ACIDITY OR ALKALINITY

Most flowers thrive in a neutral or a slightly acid soil and may be side-dressed with lime occasionally, but the following are among those that seem to prefer definitely acid land. Keep lime away from them:

Aquilegia	Iris kaempferi	Linum, blue
Bee-balm	Lady slipper	Lupinus
Calliopsis and coreopsis	Lilium superbum	Œnothera
Chrysogonum	Lily-of-the-valley	Phlox subulata

Also azalea, dogwood, mountain laurel and rhododendron.

If you are in a limestone region and wish to make your soil acid to accommodate these subjects, dig under peatmoss, hardwood sawdust, and sand; also whiten the soil occasionally with aluminum sulphate, and rake under.

COMPOST

Every garden may well have several heaps placed under trees, where little will grow; on the heaps place all clean weeds, vegetable trimmings, and autumn leaves. Give them a year to decay; then use the material to mix with soil or to cover your more tender biennials and perennials for the winter. Several materials are offered to place on the heap to hasten decomposition and to reduce the time needed from a year to a few months.

SOIL DRAINAGE

Few plants will grow satisfactorily in an area in which water remains over-long and is followed by a sea of mud. There are three ways for you to get rid of the water: (1) If the spot is a depression and is reasonably small, the addition of more soil to turn it from a hollow into a mound may take care of it. (2) Very often the top 5, 10, or 15 feet of soil may stand on a porous vein of gravel or sand. Digging down will disclose such a vein; you then fill the shaft with large rocks, add smaller rocks, and finish with a layer of soil thick enough to grow plants. (3) Dig trenches with a 5 per cent grade to a lower level, for carrying the water away, usually into a brook or ditch. There is no brook or ditch? Then lead the water to a blind well, which is a shaft dug in a dry location, also filled with large rocks, then small rocks and soil. The trenches may have drain-tile laid in them; they are concrete or clay tubes, 12 inches long, placed end-to-end on the bottom, surrounded with gravel, ashes or stones, and the trenches filled to level.

CHAPTER 20

Diseases and Insects

"Show me your garden and I shall tell you what you are." ALFRED AUSTIN.

DISEASES AND INSECT ENEMIES

LIKE ALL OTHER PLANTS, flowers sometimes are attacked by sickness. Maintaining a tidy garden, burning diseased plants, autumn digging rather than spring digging, constant hoeing, changing plants from one part of the garden to another when convenient, avoiding brushing against plants when they are wet with dew or rain, giving plants plenty of room and free air circulation, applying a sufficiency but not an excess of plant food, and spraying or dusting to kill insects, which are flagrant carriers of disease—these are the primary means of avoiding sickness in plants. The secondary and equally important thing is to spray or dust with fungicides: as soon as black spots are seen on roses, yellow-brown patches on hollyhocks and other plants; or mildew appears on any leaves; or there is any departure from the normal color.

For many years the standard remedy for disease has been bordeaux mixture, a combination of copper, sulphur, and lime. It can be purchased ready to use, and the directions on the container can be followed readily. The garden and rose dust, for use also on other flowers, is a good fungicide and insecticide combined. Many gardeners like a three-unit set, containing a fungicide, an insecticide for chewing insects, and one for sucking insects. The idea is that the former may be controlled by poisoning their food; but the latter, feeding on juices within the plant must be killed with a corrosive chemical which will shrivel the insect but not harm the tender growing shoots of the plant; there are not many substances that will do this.

But DX nicotine spray or black-leaf 40 will; they are two good remedies for the crowds of green or black aphids or plant-lice which may be found crowded on nearly all plants at some time or another. Twenty-five per cent D.D.T. will control Japanese beetles, and ¾ per cent rotenone will take care of most others.

Trees, shrubs, bushes, and roses will benefit from two or more sprayings with scalecide during winter, the last spraying immediately before the buds open in spring.

Dusting is quicker, but spraying is more effective. Always keep a hand dust-gun filled, and use it when you are in a hurry. Keep a sprayer clean and ready for use; give a fine mistlike spray and hold it long enough until the leaves drip. Both spraying and dusting give best results when the material reaches under the foliage as well as on it.

If one of your aster plants wilts, dig it up and you may find the roots crowded with gray or green root aphids. Dilute some DX nicotine spray to the strength recommended for use on the leaves; make a depression around the stems of your other asters, cosmos, dahlias, or any other plants that seem to be unthrifty, and soak the roots with the material. (*For control of the thrips insect, see* Gladiolus *in Chapter* 9.)

A collar made from a standard 3″ × 5″ index card wrapped around seedling plants when you set them out is the best way to protect them against cutworm until the stems harden and are less vulnerable to the grub. If you neglect this you may find some plants eaten off at the ground; but if your plants are too numerous to put a collar on each one, spread some poisoned bait on the ground near them; you can buy this. Or you can make your own by mixing 1 teaspoon of lead arsenate, 2½ pounds bran, 1 cup of molasses and 1 pint of water; drop this around. The cutworm bait that you purchase is less likely to be touched by household pets or wild birds. In any case, rake up either of the baits after the second night.

When you sow seeds in boxes or pots, use the seeds very sparingly and never give more water than is needed to keep the soil moist. As the seeds germinate, pull out any seedlings which touch. Over-watering and overcrowding are the chief causes of damping-off, a fungoid condition where the plants collapse at the soil surface, falling over dead. Use fresh soil for each sowing.

CHAPTER 21

A Few Definitions

"There's a lesson in each flower,
A story in each stream and bower;
In every herb on which you tread
Are written words which, rightly read,
Will lead you from each fragrant sod
To hope, to holiness, and God."
ALLAN CUNNINGHAM.

Herbs. Any plant that dies to the ground in autumn and that lacks definite woody stems is an herb. All annuals in the garden and most hardy perennials are herbs. The term is also applied to the medical and aromatic plants that have been grown for centuries, often to furnish the flavorings and condiments for the kitchen. Mostly they are true herbs, but a few, like old man, the thymes, lavender, lemon verbena, and rosemary, are sub-shrubs and not herbs, since woody stems persist with them.

Annuals are herbs which grow from seeds, produce flowers followed by new seeds, and then die—all in one season. There are some plants that do this but are not true annuals; they are actually biennials or perennials, the roots sometimes persisting. But in this book, any plant that will act as an annual, flowering the first year from seed, is listed as an annual. Four o'clock is a perennial that acts as an annual, flowering the first summer from seeds.

Biennials are sown one year to bloom the next, and then to die. Again this behavior is not constant; some turn out to be perennials. Typical biennials are foxgloves, canterbury bells, and hollyhocks. They self-seed, and make you think they are perennials.

Perennials live longer than two years, many for decades, some for generations. Shrubs, trees, and roses are woody perennials. Much of the beauty of our gardens is derived from herbaceous perennials, which live through the years, so far as their roots are concerned, though their tops die every autumn.

Hardy plants are those not killed by winter's cold. It does not mean that the plants are necessarily perennials, though this meaning is applied to the word in error. Many annuals are hardy.

Tender plants are killed by frost. Some are annuals or are treated as annuals; some are perennials which bloom the first year from seeds, like heliotrope, impatiens, or tithonia. These may not be set outdoors until all danger of frost is over. Tender perennials that will not flower the first year from seeds, and whose roots have to be carried over winter indoors include dahlias and begonias.

Half-hardy plants are midway between hardy and tender; they cannot be set outdoors until frost is over for the spring, but they stand some degree of autumn cold. Half-hardy annuals include such varieties as celosia, cynoglossum, petunia, salvia, and zinnia. Perennials in this category are such things as madeira vine, montbretia, torch-lily or gerbera, all of which need a mulch or cover of leaves, compost or manure on the soil in northern winters.

These groups depend very much on the climate in the growing area. Many that are hardy in the middle Atlantic states may not be so farther north; and a lot that will not stand the winter outdoors in the middle Atlantic states will do so in the Carolinas.

> "Go, little book, and wish to all
> Flowers in the garden, meat in the hall,
> A bin of wine, a spice of wit,
> A house with lawns enclosing it,
> A living river by the door,
> A nightingale in the sycamore!"
>   ROBERT LOUIS STEVENSON.

BOOK II

Vegetables

Index

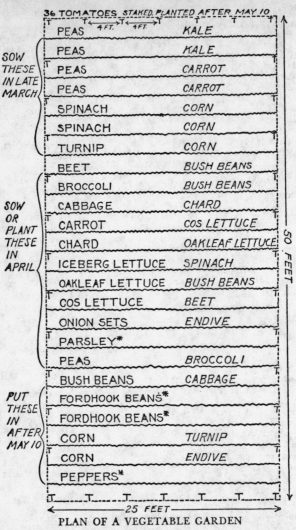

PLAN OF A VEGETABLE GARDEN

Left column in heavier upright lettering indicates first planting; right column in lighter sloping letters shows the follow-up crop. Both run completely across the plot. No second crop follows vegetables marked *, which occupy their row all season. At each letter T you may set a tomato plant.

CHAPTER 1

Planning and Planting the Garden

God Almighty first planted a garden: and indeed, it is the purest of human pleasures.

FRANCIS BACON, 1561–1626

GROWING food is easy. It means effort, but the work need not be hard unless you make it so. Gardening frequently is started by the very young and carried on into old age. The open-air exercise seems to increase one's life-span; though grandpa may become deaf, grandma doesn't see so well, and they both seem to putter instead of working, up they come all summer with onions and tomatoes, beans and carrots, lettuce and corn for the family table, all garden-ripe, full of flavor, more nutritious than any you could buy. They avoid poisonous sprays, so their produce is safe.

Whether your plot is large or small, the effort always is worthwhile, and it will reward you out of all proportion to what you put into it. Despite the criticism of less energetic neighbors, you do save money when you grow your own. The yield from even a modest planting is surprising; it is claimed that 1000 square feet (say 20 by 50 feet) of first-class land, intensively cultivated, can be made to produce all the vegetable food that one person eats in one year, including potatoes.

Some evening hours towards the end of winter may be devoted to planning your effort for the months to come: what you will grow and where you will grow it. You may use a diagram like the one shown, but most likely will make a similar one of your own, adapted to suit the shape and size of your plot. Note a feature that is missing from most similar charts: the first section is occupied by those vegetables that must be planted first, as soon as frost is out of the land, and it is dry. The next portion receives those kinds that can stand cold but do not actually need it. The bottom section is reserved for hot-weather varieties that may only be put in when all frost is over, about May 10 in the Middle Atlantic states. At this time, also, strong 6-ft. canes might be driven in at 4-ft. intervals around the garden and a tomato planted against each.

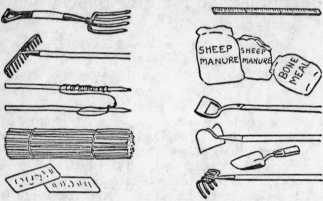

WITH THESE YOU GROW YOUR FIRST VEGETABLES

Reading down they are, (left row) spading fork, rake, garden line, 6 ft. bamboos, old auto license plates, (right row) yardstick, plant-foods, scuffle hoe, garden hoe, trowel and speedy cultivator hoe. Additional tools you will need eventually are listed in chapters 6 and 7.

For starting the work you should assemble the following:

Scuffle hoe, 4-in.	Trowel	50 Bamboo canes, 6 ft.
Garden hoe, 6-in.	Rake, 14-tooth	Yardstick
Cultivator hoe,	Old license plates (2)	200 lbs. Sheep manure
4-prong	50 ft. heavy twine	100 lbs. Bonemeal
Spading fork	Onion sets	Cabbage and broccoli
Seeds		plants

As a rule there will be no need to get the garden plowed, and you don't have to spade it unless you want to. Make the job simple. If the patch had been a garden last year, all you do is rake it clean. If it was a weed-patch last year, many of the dead weeds can be raked out; others you can cut off just below the surface with the scuffle hoe. Some tough roots may have to be forked out, and any young trees will be pried out. In short, clean down to the bare surface the easiest way. Pile the weeds in a heap, perhaps under a tree where little can be grown anyway; these will start your compost-heap, the weeds, leaves and vegetable rubbish decaying into valuable "compost," a blanket of which can be spread around your tomato plants and in the space between rows of vegetables after they have grown too big to let you hoe or rake.

Although the sooner your ground is in production the more you will get out of it, you can take your time, for with a few exceptions it is not overimportant to plant early. But note the exceptions; sow these as soon as you can:

Vegetables that need cold weather

Green peas, Savoy-leaved spinach, white Milan turnip. Also Chinese cabbage and fava beans if you like them. Follow these with:

Vegetables that tolerate cold, but do not actually need it

Early Wonder beet, De Cicco broccoli, Copenhagen market cabbage, Chantenay carrot, Large White chard, Iceberg, Oakleaf and White Cos lettuce, white onion sets, curled parsley and spring radish. Katahdin potatoes if you have the space and the locality is favorable for potatoes.

TRANSPLANTING. *Dig a hole more than large enough, and partly fill it with water. Stand the plant in position and gently squeeze the mud up to the roots. An hour later, press the partly dried soil up to the plant on all sides with a trowel, and press a small depression all around the plant into which water can be flooded two days later. Put on a collar to protect against cutworm. Hoeing will level out the depression.*

Obtain plants of broccoli and cabbage or grow your own; buy onion sets and certified seed potatoes. Sow seeds of the others. Finally, when all danger of frost is over and warm weather has arrived, sow seeds of Longreen bush beans, Fordhook 242 bush lima beans and Spancross corn; Marketer cucumber and Acorn squash if you have the room. Put out young plants of Marglobe tomato, California Wonder pepper; eggplant if you wish to. The plants you will have grown yourself or will buy.

SEEDLINGS MUST NOT BE-COME DRY. *Stand the pot in water for ten minutes every day or so; a larger bowl and deeper water cuts the time in half, but don't let water spill into the pot around the rim.*

If you raise your own broccoli, cabbage, tomato and pepper plants, you may start them indoors, take them to a cold-frame if you have one, and protect them against frost there. Transfer broccoli to the garden when 4 inches high; set out tomato and pepper when all danger of frost is over, around May 10 in the Middle Atlantic states.

You sow cucumber and squash in groups of six or eight seeds, the groups 6 inches in diameter and 5 feet apart. These groups are often referred to as "hills," but they normally are level and are only mounded if the area is wet because of insufficient drainage. You will find it best to plant everything else in lines 2 feet apart, because this lets you hoe the soil between the rows.

Mark the ends of the first row with two canes, and stretch the twine tightly between them. Spread on the ground under the string a ribbon of sheep manure, allowing a trowelful to each 2 feet, and then a ribbon of bonemeal, a trowelful to each 4 feet. Remove the twine and hoe the plant-foods under, using the cultivator-hoe. Merely chop and pull, to turn the surface 3 inches, then smooth the loosened soil with the rake. Replace the cord, and along it make a 2-in. deep groove with an old auto license plate, pushing the upper edge away from you and pulling it towards you to make a V-section furrow, wide at the top. Drop peas into the groove about an inch apart, cover them with soil by drawing the rake lengthwise; firm the soil by lightly pressing with the shoe.

Peas give best results when supplied with something to climb upon, even the dwarf ones. Save tree branches, or clip some from waste land in the vicinity. Stick these into the ground in a line 3 inches from the seed, and on the sunny side if there is any difference. The plants will lean towards the light, growing against the branches. Their tendrils will take hold without any help from you. If branches cannot be obtained, erect a fence of chicken-wire, or drive in some stakes and run coarse twine from one to another 4 inches apart. It's worth-while to bore holes in the posts, attaching the string to the end ones and threading it through the others; let it sag a little to allow for shrinking when it gets wet.

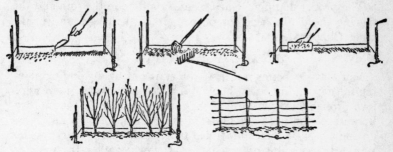

A GOOD WAY TO SOW GREEN PEAS

(1). *Along a stretched string, spread sheep manure and bonemeal.* (2). *Hoe them under; then rake.* (3). *Make a groove with an old auto license-plate; drop seed peas in, and rake along the row to cover them.* (4). *Insert brush for peas to climb.* (5). *Or one of string.*

You arrange for a continuous supply of peas by using kinds that are quick and others that are slow, but you might make a second planting of the slowest kind two weeks later to wind up the pea-picking season. Putting in additional rows of a vegetable every two or three weeks is "succession-cropping," and is routine practice with many crops, especially beans, lettuce or cabbage; but often it does not work with peas, which give their normal yield only when planted very early. Some peas are dwarf and others are taller, so make your fence of branches, chicken-wire or string the proper height to take care of them. Here are four reliable kinds:

First of All. Height 30 inches. Start picking in 55 days
Gradus. 36 inches; 68 days
Laxtonian. 24 inches; 65 days
Potlach. 24 inches; 80 days

No support is required for the other early-seeded crops. Merely mark the rows, stretch cord, spread and cultivate to work in the plant-foods; but make the grooves only ½ in. deep for spinach, turnip or Chinese cabbage seeds; rake and tread lightly as for the peas. Fava beans, which are rarely grown, should be 2 inches deep and 2 inches apart. They and the others will be later "thinned," by which we mean that surplus plants will be removed so that those which remain are the correct distance apart.

The proper depth at which seeds should be in the soil, and the spacing the plants need for proper growth will be found in the table, Chapter 14.

HOEING VERSUS DIGGING

You may get better results if you start out by digging or plowing the garden instead of hoeing, if a wet spring and summer follow; probably worse results if the ensuing weather is hot and dry. Because of the need for haste in the spring, and because mere hoeing works, it is recommended that you hoe in preparation for your first crop. But dig each row after you gather from it and prepare it for a following crop. Do your general digging or plowing as part of your autumn clean-up.

No great harm if you disagree. The diagram is so arranged that you can dig the first 15 feet, put in your cold crops; then resume your digging, sow and plant your beet, onion sets and other cool crops. Take up your digging again for the beans and corn.

To sum up: Clean the land to a bare surface; plant (1) vegetables that need cold, then (2) vegetables that will *tolerate* cold; finally, when frost is over, (3) those that only may be set out when the weather is warm. Full details in the table, Chapter 14. Dig or plow if you wish, but these are best left until later.

At transplanting time, clipping onion seedlings, or cutting off one-half of each of the side leaves of a tomato plant will keep the plants from wilting.

CHAPTER 2

Getting Down to Earth

It is a pleasant employment and profitable to one's pocket, and such an exercise of the body as fits a man for everyday duty which a free citizen may be called upon to perform.

XENOPHON, 430–354 (about) B.C.

OUR land is made up of particles of rock of various sizes, which in the course of centuries have been broken up by frost, wind and rain; often transported many miles by glaciers in bygone ages, by melting snow, rivers and wind in more recent times. These particles, in the form of gravel, sand, silt and clay, form the framework of much of our subsoil.

The difference in these rock fragments is a matter of size. The pieces in gravel are 2 millimeters or larger (a millimeter is about $\frac{2}{5}$ of an inch); sand from 2 millimeters down to $\frac{1}{10}$ of a millimeter; silt about $\frac{1}{16}$ of a millimeter; clay around $\frac{1}{250}$ of a millimeter, and so fine as to be sticky, or have colloidal properties. The addition of lime cements some of the particles into larger ones, making a clay more like a medium-loam: it is said to flocculate it. Lime also tends to bind sandy soils, making them too like a medium-loam.

Few of the plants we use will grow in subsoil, or will grow only poorly. But through the years, first mosses and lichens, then minor weeds, grasses, larger weeds, bushes and, finally, often trees have grown in this subsoil. Gradually the top layer has turned into topsoil, which is the portion which has been influenced by the weather, and in which plant remains have accumulated.

To this residue of past generations of plants has been added the manure of wild animals and birds, the relics of dead animals,

17

insects, insect wings, pollen-dust and leaves. Bacteria, simple forms of animal life, insects and earthworms have broken fragments into simpler forms to become the organic matter in the soil; decaying, the organic matter becomes a source of food for plants of the present generation.

An important effect of organic matter is to absorb moisture and hold it for plants to use between rains. Soil with a high organic content retains water for a longer time than one with a low organic content, and the truck-farmer who works with crops that must be grown rapidly, like lettuce or celery, often grows them on muck land, which has so much organic matter in it and is so moist, that it is black. There is a tendency for organic matter to disappear. This is prevented by digging and hoeing under organic manures, plant remains, weeds and compost.

Average topsoil is rarely black, but usually it is darker in color than the subsoil on which it rests, and topsoil can usually be distinguished by its tint. This is the material in which vegetables grow satisfactorily. When digging, do not go so deep that the lighter subsoil is brought to the surface in any quantity; a trace is helpful, since it shows that your work is thorough; you are turning over the topsoil to its full depth and are even deepening it every time you dig.

Vegetables grow poorly or not at all in subsoil. On some housing projects it is the rule to sell topsoil from the area before building commences. Sometimes, too, subsoil obtained by excavating for the cellar is neatly spread over the plot, covering the topsoil. In either case, gardening will be difficult for a few years until a layer of topsoil has been developed. This you can do by any of the following six methods:

(1). If the topsoil has been covered with subsoil, see if you can bring some of it to the surface by digging.

(2). For the first years select those sorts which are not too particular as to the quality of the soil. These include snap beans, both bush and pole, corn, the vine crops like cucumber and pumpkin; also pepper and tomato. Varieties which are grown in rows should have the organic manures, sheep manure and bonemeal, worked in; and along with them one pound to each running foot of hyper-humus or about a quart of peatmoss. Both are obtainable in garden supply houses. Kinds which are grown in groups or hills would have these same materials worked under, along with some topsoil from elsewhere, if you can get it; perhaps you can scrape a bushel or so from nearby waste land. If rotted horse-manure, or new or rotted cow-manure, can be obtained, use them along with, or instead of, the humus and peatmoss. Grow tomatoes and peppers in pockets; dig a hole 18 inches deep and fill it with one pound each of sheep manure, bonemeal and two pounds of humus or about two quarts of peatmoss mixed with enough nearby topsoil to refill the hole. Tread fairly firm, and then plant.

(3). When your plants are half-grown, scatter some winter rye seeds between the rows and rake them under, allowing 2 pounds or one quart per 250 square feet. You do not hoe any more where you have sown the rye, but after you have picked all your beans, corn, vine-plants, tomatoes or peppers, dig their remains under if they are free of bugs or disease, first cutting them into short lengths with pruning shears; also going under will be the rye, now looking for all the world like a small lawn. Of course, you will put in some follow-up crop if you have any period of growing weather left, consulting the tables for the vegetables to grow.

A more drastic method is to dispense with any vegetables for a season or two in the area, and sow a succession of crops for the sole purpose of digging or plowing them under. Spread fertilizer, say 50 pounds of 5–10–5 per 1000 square feet, and sow rye any time up to December 1, dig or plow June 1, spread more fertilizer and sow soybeans at the same rate as the rye; dig or plow when these are 2 feet high, fertilize and sow buckwheat, again at the same rate. Repeat with rye in October, dig under in spring and either commence gardening or continue the plow-under crops for another season.

(4). When growth is over for the year, spread three inches of leaves over your garden, spade under, spread fertilizer and sow rye at the rates suggested. Rye grows quite well under the snow. When the land is dry in spring, dig or plow it, rake smooth and go ahead with the new year's garden.

19

(5). Save all leaves, potato-peelings, disease-free vegetable-tops and weeds, and place in as large a compost-pile as you can. Usually it takes 18 months for these to decay into a black mould; but if neighbors will not object to a little steam coming from the heap, with sometimes a slight odor, you can hasten decay by using some Adco or Compo as you build the heap. In dry weather it should be well soaked with water.

Spread compost liberally between your rows and around your plants; while the plants are small, hoe as weeds appear in the compost; when vegetables grow too large for you to hoe, let the compost remain, but first sow rye, as suggested in paragraph 3.

(6). Should you heat your home with coke or coal, some of the ashes may be spread on the poor area in a half-inch layer before digging or hoeing. Coke ashes are more helpful than those from coal. A layer of similar thickness may be given to the compost-heap from time to time, along with any horse manure you find, and road-sweepings provided there is no oil in them. If you burn hedge-clippings, prunings or paper, spread the residue on the garden or on the compost-heap. And the ashes from a wood fire in the home are excellent.

If the minute particles which make up the soil's framework, the silt or clay, which is sticky, and the larger particles of sand, are in equal amounts, we have a medium-loam. When the finer pieces predominate we have a clay-loam, with still more we have a clay-soil. With sand slightly in excess we have a sandy-loam, and so much of it that you have difficulty in holding a handful of dry soil because it runs through your fingers, you have a sandy-soil. Clay-soils and clay-loams are said to be heavy or strong; sandy-loams and sandy-soils are termed light or weak soils. The terms apply to the work needed to cultivate them and their ability to produce, not actually to their weight, sandy soils weighing a few pounds more than clays or clay-loams. For land to be fertile it must have a minimum of five per cent in dry weight of organic matter, and when the organic matter is greatly in excess we have muck-land, often a reclaimed and drained marsh area.

Among the popular crops that do well in these six classes of soil are:

Clay-soils and clay-loams: fava beans, broccoli, Brussels sprouts, cabbage, cauliflower, leek, onions, peas and spinach.

Medium-loams: corn, eggplant, endive, kale, kohlrabi, lettuce, parsley, pepper, potato and radish.

Sandy-loams and sandy-soils: asparagus, beans except the fava, beet, the vine-crops, carrot, onion sets, parsnip, peanut, sweet potato, tobacco and turnip.

Muck-land: celery, lettuce and onion.

This does not mean that if your soil is in one class you cannot grow the vegetables in another bracket. The direction in which your garden slopes, the rainfall and general care may balance any handicaps, but the list may help you in selecting your varieties.

So far we have dealt with the structure of the soil. Plants live on chemical salts, which are released gradually by the rock particles, by the organic fragments, and the manures and bonemeal which you add. These have to decay before the roots can dissolve the chemicals, but decay is rapid in warm weather and the plants begin to use them in a week or two. The addition of extra chemicals is taken care of by your side-dressings of fertilizer, which begin to go into the plants in a day or two.

A Sudbury soil-testing kit is a help in indicating if any of the four chief chemicals are short. These four are calcium or lime, nitrogen, phosphorus and potassium; with the average kit comes a list of the elements which each plant needs in major quantity. If calcium is short, 100 pounds of limestone, 50 pounds of hydrated lime or 35 pounds of gypsum may be broadcast every winter on each 1000 square feet, and they may be given in occasional side-dressings during the summer; and gypsum is good to dust on the compost-heap as various materials are added to it. If nitrogen, phosphorus or potassium is inadequate, occasional applications of 5–10–5 fertilizer will usually take care of the shortage; but a marked lack of phosphorus suggests spreading ground phosphate rock or superphosphate along with the original sheep manure and bonemeal dressing. A marked shortage of potassium would be met by using commercial hardwood ashes or scrap tobacco. Any of these four materials would be given at the rate recommended for bonemeal, a trowelful to each 4 feet of row.

The chemical elements described above are referred to as "The Big Four." It has been discovered in recent years that plants need some twenty additional ones, but in such minute amounts that they are referred to as the trace elements; they include magnesium, sulphur, iron, manganese, boron, iodine, zinc, copper, chlorine and some others. Most soils contain the minute quantities needed, certainly those to which manure, sheep manure and compost have been added; but if results are still under par after using the materials suggested in this book, the application of more of these trace elements may be tried. One good way is to dissolve in water some Trace-L, a preparation containing these substances, and pour the solution onto the soil near the roots of your vegetables. But one treatment for any purpose often fails to produce, and several dressings of plant food are usually necessary.

SOME INDICATOR WEEDS

Top row, left, *sheep's sorrel and wild strawberry point to an acid soil. Butter-cup says the land is a moist clay-loam. Right, self-heal, indicates an excess of clay.* Bottom row, left, *devil's paint-brush is a demand for more organic matter; sedges and rushes call for drainage; right, garlic tells that the land is rich.*

Some weeds often indicate the condition of the soil. The halberd-shape leaf of sheep's sorrel tells you that the soil is acid, and calcium is needed, and if the leaves have a red color you may conclude that it needs it badly. Presence of the wild strawberry confirms it. Wild buttercup grows in moist clay-loams. Self-heal indicates that there is too much clay. Devil's paint-brush says the land needs organic matter. Sedges and rushes indicate that drainage is desirable. Wild garlic announces that the ground is rich.

Organic gardening is the modern name for emphasis on the use of compost, manures and desiccated organic substances like pulverized sheep manure, shredded cattle manure or bonemeal, and exclusion of chemical fertilizers. Recognizing the beneficial effect of earthworms, organic gardeners often breed, sell, or buy and plant them. They ingest large total amounts of earth below, absorb what they need and reject the balance on the surface in the form of worm-casts, actually turning a large amount of soil, equal to a thorough spading, over a period of time. In the fall you will notice rosettes of dead leaves scattered over bare soil, where a worm has dragged them to the entrance of his burrow to draw them below. Their holes carry much rain down into the land that might otherwise run off the surface. Organic gardeners bury a few worm colonies here and there to increase this beneficent population.

Earthworms do hardly any damage to growing plants, except those living in flower-pots where they disturb the roots unduly, but they don't feed on them, and their presence in the land should be welcome. Next time you go into the garden at night with a flashlight and see them in their hundreds sliding into their holes on your approach, your surprise at their numbers and their size, possibly your disgust, may well be mixed with gratitude.

To sum up: Rock fragments form the framework of our soil; remains of dead animals and plants determine its moisture-holding ability and its fertility. The weather's action, and the organic matter, distinguish subsoil from topsoil; only in the latter will vegetables grow; then only when food-elements are present. Testing soil and looking at the weeds will tell us if they are. Earthworms are beneficial.

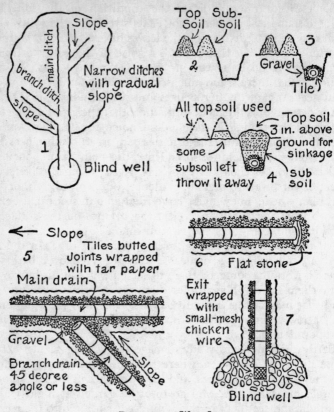

DRAINING A WET SPOT

1. *The spot. Ditches are dug, branches meet at a 45 degree angle; all have a gentle slope.* 2. *The ditch in section; topsoil and subsoil are kept separate.* 3. *Tile is laid and surrounded by gravel.* 4. *Ditches are filled.* 5. *Tiles are butted, joints wrapped with tar paper.* 6. *Start of a drain; flat stone helps keep dirt out.* 7. *Main drain ends in a blind well if there is no lower spot to receive the water.*

CHAPTER 3

Drainage

*The thirsty earth soaks up the rain, and drinks, and
gapes for drink again; the plants suck in the earth,
and are with constant drinking fresh and fair.*

ABRAHAM COWLEY, 1618–1667

You probably have some places in the garden where water stays in
pools long after rain has ceased and that become mud spots. In
them, rushes, sedges, even cattails may be growing.

Few useful plants will grow here—mints, perhaps, or watercress
—until you get rid of this unwanted moisture. Decide on a spot
at a lower level to which you can conduct the water; if no spot
is available, dig a "blind-well," which is merely a deep hole. Fill
it to within two feet of the top with rocks and stones; a layer of
smaller stones or gravel, and some branches, will enable you to
fill to the surface with soil. This will settle in course of time, and
more soil will be needed now and again.

Before filling the blind-well, dig ditches from the wet spots to
it, all having a slight slope or fall to the well, say five or ten per
cent. The ditch might begin at a depth of two feet.

Twelve-inch agricultural drain-tiles can be purchased; these are
tubes of concrete or baked clay with the hole running through
them 4 inches or more in diameter. They are placed end to end
along the bottom of the ditch, the ends touching but not cemented; water finds its way into the tiles through the joints, and
runs to the lower point. Dirt is kept out of the tile by wrapping
each joint with waterproof building paper. Soil is then returned;
subsoil first, then topsoil; but if stones, gravel or ashes are at hand,
they are placed along the pipes ahead of the soil.

Sometimes more than one ditch is necessary; sometimes a ditch has branches running into it, always meeting the main ditch in the direction of the flow and at an angle of 45 degrees. Tile in the branches is carried right up to touch the main tile, and although Y-units can be obtained, the usual method is merely to butt the branch right up to the side of the main tile, using plenty of gravel or ashes at the meeting point. After all, the chief purpose of the tile is to keep the tunnel open, and as much water finds its way around the tile as within the pipe itself.

If the wet spot is a hollow, filling to two inches above grade with extra soil may aid the condition. If extensive areas have to be corrected, consult a book on land drainage for the ideal distance apart of the drains and their depth, whether 20, 25 or 30 feet apart, and whether 2, 2½ or 3 feet is your best starting depth. In clay soils they have to be closer than in loams; and generally the deeper they are the farther apart they may be placed, but the slower is their action in removing water.

Drainage brings much otherwise useless land into production; and in drained land plants usually suffer less for lack of moisture, strange as it may seem.

To sum up: Water must not remain over-long on land; if it does, drain it away.

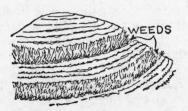

CONTOUR-PLANTING

On steep slopes, the washing down of soil is prevented by growing in plowed bands across the slope. Weed-barriers, four feet wide, are left.

CHAPTER 4

Manure and Chemical Fertilizers

O, mickle is the powerful grace that lies in herbs,
plants, stones, and their true qualities: for naught so
vile that on the earth doth live but to the earth some
special good doth give. WILLIAM SHAKESPEARE, 1564–1616.
Romeo and Juliet. Act 2, scene 3

NATURE's plan seems to be that the living are supported on the dead of the past. Plants growing out of the remains of previous generations of plants and animals, animals living on the plants, and man living on both. Definitely the excreta of animals looms large as a source of plant-food during the ages. We seem to be working in Nature's way when we dig rubbish under, spread compost, and especially when we use the cleanings from the barn, stable and slaughterhouse. Only in the English-speaking countries is the use of human manure frowned upon; almost everywhere else the contents of the privy are highly prized as aids to horticulture. Even in America, some municipalities sell their sewage for plant-food after chemically treating it.

Digging under cow-manure, fresh or old, and horse-manure, preferably old, to condition the land for cultivation is almost as old as gardening itself. And for the largest, finest and best vegetables, other materials are poor substitutes for them. As much as 20 tons to the acre of manure is the farmer's allowance, which means a pound to each square foot, and more can often be used advantageously. If you are preparing land for vegetables, the one best thing to do is to dig manure under, if you can get it.

With horse traction gone, much of the manure has gone too; what the stable-man of years ago would pay you to take away, now costs you real money, if it is obtainable at all. So we have to fall back on the next best substitutes.

If you live within a few miles of the shore you can use seaweed in large quantities; there are some factory by-products that may be had—spent malt or spent hops from the brewery, cottonseed meal, castor pomace, apple pomace from the cider-mill, droppings from poultry houses, residues from the manufacture of certain drugs. The cleanings from a pond-bottom is another possibility. From the stockyards come materials like pulverized sheep manure, shredded cattle manure, dried blood, bonemeal or tankage; cigar factories offer scrap tobacco. Though valuable, most of these fail to possess the bulk of manure, but we have three materials partly to take its place: our own ripened compost, made from leaves, weeds and vegetable trimmings, hyper-humus and peatmoss. Peatmoss is a little difficult to use and does not break up in the land so freely as the other two, unless you can buy shredded peatmoss, which sometimes is available. With compost or hyper-humus, some one or other of the stockyard products, along with such materials from the factories that may be offered from time to time, you are on the way to being almost as well off for manure as grandpa was. Especially if you side-dress with 5–10–5 fertilizer once in a while, and if you occasionally water the roots of your plants with a soluble plant-food.

Nothing has yet been found to take the place of horse-manure for growing mushrooms. But you can plug your lawn or compost-heap with pieces of spawn, and probably get a crop. And you can heat a hot-bed from your electric supply just as satisfactorily as the past generation of gardeners grew their plants from fermenting horse-manure.

CHEMICAL FERTILIZERS

The use of 5–10–5 fertilizer as an occasional stimulant for side-dressing your vegetable rows is suggested throughout this book. But in our judgment its more extended use is not advisable in the home garden, for the reason that manure and its substitutes, and organic plant-foods, are more gradual in their effect and less exhausting to the land.

However, if you can get fertilizers with a high organic-content there is less objection to their use. The analysis of a chemical fertilizer is not over-important, but if you use a different formula than 5–10–5, you may consider that one with a higher nitrogen-content, the first figure, is most helpful to the leaf-crops. One with a high phosphorus-content, the middle figure, encourages seed development, or fruit like muskmelon. One high in potassium, the third figure, is mostly employed in potato-growing.

To sum up: Manure is most helpful to the gardener, but our home-made compost, the stockyard by-products, hyper-humus and peatmoss are good substitutes, with commercial fertilizers; best of the latter have a high organic content.

CHAPTER 5

Lime Sweetens Soil and Feeds Plants

And God said, Behold I have given you every herb
bearing seed, which is upon the face of all the earth,
and every tree, in the which is the fruit of a tree
yielding seed; to you it shall be for meat.

GENESIS, Chapter 1, verse 29

CALCIUM is one of the big four essential elements without which plants cannot live. There may be enough in the soil to support growth, but in most sections in the United States there is not, and gardening and farming are dependent upon frequent applications of it. A heavy powder, it tends to sink into the land, which is why it is even necessary to add lime to soils in regions where the rocks from which the soil is derived are solid limestone or where the soil is standing on lime. Its weight is also the reason why we do not dig lime under: instead we put it on the surface, rake or hoe, and let it make its own way down. Soils lacking it are frequently acid or sour; soils to which much lime has recently been added are often alkaline.

The condition of soil from this angle is frequently described in terms of pH, rated according to Sorensen's scale: pH 7 indicates a neutral soil, figures from 7 down indicate degrees of acidity, those from 7 up show degrees of alkalinity. The pH can be determined easily with a soil-testing kit, but the results should be regarded as an approximate suggestion rather than a precise finding, since materials other than lime may be of an alkaline character, and their presence may interfere with the results that you seek; among alkaline elements are sodium, potassium and magnesium. An excess of one of these may give a high pH rating; yet the land actually may need lime.

Nearly all vegetables prefer a neutral soil, because plants feed through their root-hairs from which exude fluids that are slightly acid and which dissolve the plant-foods. If the soil is already acid, these fluids work less efficiently, or not at all.

BRAMBLES. *Often grow on acid soil, and their presence suggests that periodic dressings with lime will be helpful to garden crops.*

CHICORY. *Has a leaf which is like that of the dandelion, but the flowers are blue. It indicates that there is lime in the soil.*

If the soil has moss on it, or if the weeds indicate acidity—the presence of rushes, sedges, brambles, buttercup and sorrel do—or if it is crusted with the scaly growth of lichens, if many of the weeds have a red color in their leaves, and if you have not applied lime for several years, you may assume that the land needs lime.

You might apply lime every winter, except where you propose to grow potatoes, for newly spread lime is accused of causing mechanical injury to them; so miss the application for once on this land, planting potatoes only where lime was applied 14 months or so previously.

There are several kinds of lime available to you. First is natural limestone rock, or calcium carbonate, occurring here and there in most parts of the United States and Canada. It is ground to a very fine powder to shorten the time in which it becomes available to the plant roots; despite this fine grinding, it is slow to show results on the plants, but its effect is lasting; it is described as ground limestone, lime-rock or pulverized limestone.

Lime-rock may be burned in a slow fire, water and carbonic-acid driven off, and the residue is burned-lime or quick-lime, an ingredient in Portland cement. This is unsuitable for you because of its caustic properties, but when water is poured onto it, it recombines with it to form hydrated lime or slaked-lime, the particles of which are much finer than those of limestone. This may be applied to the soil and is quicker to show results. If the quick-lime is allowed to remain outdoors it recombines with water more slowly, and we have air-slaked lime, quite similar to hydrated lime.

Gypsum is calcium sulphate; when burned it is the familiar plaster of Paris. Sometimes called land-plaster, the application of gypsum is referred to as plastering the land, though the unburned gypsum is used. It adds calcium without changing the acidity or alkalinity of the land.

Marl is a natural mixture of calcium and clay often found under swamps in limestone country. It is a good material to apply to sands or sandy-loams. Bonemeal is an organic source of lime in the form of calcium phosphate.

Actually, plants get much of their calcium from decaying plant remains. Nevertheless, an application of one of the forms of lime is almost always a good thing every year or every second year. It should not be given in excess of the quantities listed below at any one time. In reasonable amounts it is an essential plant-food; in any form it is effective in making other elements available, releasing additional nitrogen, phosphorus or potassium. It has the effect of making both porous and retentive soils loam-like, by cementing tiny fragments into larger particles; in the case of clay it is said to flocculate it.

The usual dressing of pulverized limestone or ground limestone rock is 2 tons per acre; of hydrated lime, 1 ton per acre; of gypsum, 1500 lbs. per acre. These respectively mean 100 lbs., 50 lbs. and 35 lbs. per 1000 square feet. Marl can be used in any reasonable amount up to a dressing one-half inch thick. Winter is a convenient season for applying lime, but in addition it can be dusted on as a side dressing several times in a season, using only enough to whiten the soil, then hoeing or raking it just under the surface.

To sum up: Calcium is an essential plant-food; it helps plants assimilate other elements; it sweetens soil and makes it more loamy. Nearly all soils need it; every late winter you can spread, per 1000 square feet, 100 pounds ground limestone rock, or 50 pounds hydrated lime, or 35 pounds gypsum.

CHAPTER 6

The Tools of Your Trade

Accuse not Nature: she hath done her part;
do thou but thine.   JOHN MILTON, 1608-1674

IN CHAPTER 1 we noted the essential tools you need to start a garden; when you get more completely into the effort you will gradually acquire a complete kit. The suggestion is that your purchases be made without haste. Buying a spade? Then lift up several, and in the store go through the motions of digging; find if the weight is right for you. Is your hand comfortable? Does it balance well?

Like a pair of shoes, be sure that your new spade fits you; in other words, has a good "heft." Buy it right, and it will give you a deal of pleasure through the years. So you will purchase:

A Spade for digging the garden. It should be reasonably light, but be sure the blade does not bend and its top does not cut into your shoe when you press it into the earth. In use, small bites of soil are taken the full depth of the blade, which is

A good spade that fits you is a joy for ever, or almost ever; you even may think it a thing of beauty.

Spading goes easier if you arrange to have one edge of the spade free. Turn each spadeful over.

33

12 inches more or less, so long as this does not exceed the thickness of your topsoil; note the color, and dig shallower if you are bringing up much lighter tinted subsoil. The spadeful is lifted, turned, and the clod is placed to your left if you are right-handed. Try always to dig along the edge of the undug soil, so that one edge of the spade is free; the work goes better if you do. Don't rush; take it easy; go slowly, and every ten minutes rest for five; you'll accomplish more and live longer.

A spade has other uses than digging. Working to a stretched line, you cut turf and keep the edge of your lawn neat with a spade. You divide clumps of artichoke or rhubarb by cutting them with a spade. There are times when you will use the spade like a scuffle-hoe, cutting weeds under the surface. You are unlikely to need it, but if you want to you can purchase a **Transplanting Spade,** with a longer and narrower blade. Very similar is a **Drain Spade,** also narrow, which enables you to dig narrow ditches.

A **Shovel** with a rounded point; efficient for turning compost, piling soil, gravel or sand; if you have only a little of this to do, your spade is sufficient help. Shovels can be purchased with short D-handles, or long handles, 4 feet or more.

A **Trowel** may be regarded as a miniature one-hand shovel. Invaluable for setting out plants; for mixing potting-soil, planting seedlings in pots, and scores of other uses. A special narrow type is the **Transplanting Trowel,** seldom needed in the vegetable garden; but a small **Mason's Trowel** is a great help for thinning vegetable seedlings or for transplanting.

A **Spading Fork** is indispensable. Use it for turning soil in place of the spade, if the latter is too hard a job in clay soil, for digging potatoes, parsnips and other root-crops that are too large to pull out of the soil; for turning over compost or digging out larger weeds. There are two general types, the American with four wide flat tines, the English type with narrow square-section sharp pointed tines.

A **Small Hand-Fork** is an attractive member of a set of garden-tools, but is the least valuable. An occasional use for it is to remove weeds, complete with roots, from against your asparagus and rhubarb plants, and in the herb garden.

A Dibble is usually improvised by sharpening to a point the upper end of a broken fork or spade handle. In soil that is loose after hoeing or digging, a dibble enables you to plant cabbage, broccoli, celery or lettuce. Generally a trowel is preferred.

The Hoe is so important a tool, in daily use, that we have devoted chapter 7 to it.

Rakes. One of their jobs is to cover newly sown seeds in the row, by drawing it lengthwise. They supplement the work of the hoe in maintaining a powdery dust mulch between your plants; often they are superior to the hoe, because a rake is a shallow-acting tool and is less likely to injure roots that are close to the surface. A small rake with all but six teeth hacksawed off should be in daily use. Raking up leaves is often done with a **Spring-Tooth Rake**; this type or a **Bamboo Rake** is good for gathering up general rubbish. Combing pathways and driveways is frequently done with a **Steel Rake**, and one with **Curved Teeth** is self-cleaning to a degree; pushing it forward and pulling it backward you will have little need to lift it.

An Axe is a good tool to have around; one of its uses will be to act as a sledge to drive a piece of half-inch pipe 2 feet into the ground; pull the pipe out and tap in your **Plant Supports**. Use a stepladder for 8-ft. **Bean Poles**. Buy heavy 6-ft. **Bamboo Canes** for tomatoes grown to a single stem, and **Adjusto Plant Supports** for unpruned tomatoes. These are wooden stakes with a wire loop sliding on the stake. **Pipe-Cleaners** obtained in 5-cent packages in the tobacco stores make excellent tyers, much easier than the **Raffia** which for generations has been used for this work. For tomatoes, loop a pipe-cleaner around the cane, twist, then loop it around the stem of the plant.

A Sprayer and a **Duster** are necessary for liquid and dry insecticides and fungicides. A sprayer holding either 2½ gallons or 4 gallons, pumped up before you start out, and the weight carried by the shoulder-strap, is the accepted pattern; you may prefer a 4-gallon **Knapsack-Sprayer**, carried on the back, a constant pressure of 80 pounds being maintained by pumping a lever under your arm. You will supplement these with a small one-quart **Compressed Air Sprayer** for emergency use. All of these types are best filled with plain water when you finish using them for the day, spraying a little to clear the nozzle. Dump the water before using them again, and they should work at once; but if you wash them and put them away empty, the chances are you will have a job unstopping nozzles before you can start. In a large garden you will need sprayers with 15, 50 or more gallons' capacity, the larger ones powered with gasoline. Sprayers must be emptied for winter.

Suppose you have a few minutes before you start for your morning train, and find aphis on your broccoli, beetles on your potatoes or celery-worm on your carrots. You can do a quick first-aid job with a dust; keep your duster filled and use it when you see the necessity. You'll still make your train. When either spraying or dusting, use of a **Respirator** is a worth-while safety measure.

Fertilizer Spreaders. Materials are so easily broadcast by hand —this is one operation that you can conveniently do with gloves on—that the necessity for their use is hard to see. However, some gardeners like them.

A Wheelbarrow, narrow enough to go through your walkways, is always useful.

An Outdoor Water Faucet is desirable. Not for watering your garden, but for washing flower-pots and getting dirt off tools. You need not wipe them when they are constantly used, but dry them thoroughly and paint a film of oil on them when they are put away for the winter. If you use any of your garden tools on a cement job be sure and clean them thoroughly that evening; otherwise you may have difficulty in using them later. **A Watering-Can** with a fine removable nozzle is helpful for seedlings in your frame, and for half-filling holes with water at transplanting time.

Traps for moles—get the Reddick. Have-a-hart traps for rabbits, rats, foxes or woodchucks may be necessary; call your game warden to find out the law applying to these animals. Beetle-traps are not so popular nowadays.

Pruning Shears are needed for general work around the garden, for snipping off the trailing tops of some varieties of beans which sometimes run away to become semi-climbers, cutting trash into small lengths for digging under. Get a good large Snapcut kind, hefty enough for cutting brush and branches for supporting peas.

Plant Labels. Made of flat wood, pointed, and dipped in paint just thick enough to enable your pencil to make a good black mark. The 6-inch size is recommended. Write the variety and date planted, especially for seeds sown in the house; for these, cut the labels in two halves with the shears; insert them in the pot below the rim.

Walls of Concrete or Cinder Blocks can be built on the three sides of a square without cement and laid on the bare ground; this to make a good receptacle for holding compost.

A Sieve for screening compost can be made by tacking smallest mesh chicken-wire to a wooden frame of any convenient size, say 12 inches by 24 inches and 3 inches deep. Better tack a lath down the center to strengthen it. Stand it on a clean garbage-can, put a shovelful of compost in it, shake and put in another shovelful. Use the tailings that won't screen as the base for a new heap. A much larger screen can be made with two legs to support it at an angle of 45 degrees; throw compost at this, then rub it through.

Flower-Pots of clay may be bought or begged until one has a good stock of them. Flower-pots of the ordinary dimensions, azalea pots which are shorter, and bulb pans which are shorter yet, can be used. You would sow cabbage, lettuce and most everything else in 4- or 5-inch pots or pans, and transfer the seedlings into Flats 2 inches apart. When planting-out time comes, the root-filled soil in the flats can be cut into squares with the mason's pointing trowel, and the young plants transferred to the garden with a minimum disturbance to the finer roots. Some growers like to transplant tomatoes, peppers and eggplants individually into 2½- or 3-inch pots. When the young plant is knocked from the pot, the soil is intact, and the plant can be set into place with even less shock.

Flats are boxes usually 12 inches by 18 inches and 3 inches deep. They can be bought, made, or sometimes begged at a fish-market. Holes for drainage are bored in the bottom, pieces of broken flower-pots or flat stones are placed over the holes to hold the soil back. Flats with little square card boxes in them can be procured; you fill the card boxes with soil and put a seedling in each: they make transplanting into the garden very easy.

37

Gloves are recommended. Heavy work and heavy weights are not so serious when a pair of strong gloves is worn. A good source is a store dealing in army surplus goods and work clothes; good thick bramble-proof leather gloves are usually on sale there.

Index Cards measuring 5 inches by 3 inches are good guards against cutworm. Take half a dozen and spindle them into a tight 3 inch roll; now spindle them from the opposite end. Having planted a tomato, roll one of the spindled cards around the stem, and draw a little earth up to it to fix it. By the time the card has become worthless through rain, the tomato stem will have hardened, and cutworms will no longer bother.

Celery-Bleaching Tubes. To develop white lower stems and hearts, earth may be drawn up to the celery plants; this calls for extra washing, and many growers use 10 inch wide planks set close against the rows. In the home garden, several thicknesses of newspapers can be wrapped around each plant, and then the soil banked. Or celery-bleaching tubes may be employed: a sheet of flexible metal is wrapped around the plant; then a heavy waterproof cardboard tube is slipped down over the metal sheet, which is then withdrawn.

A Thermometer with maximum and minimum indicators for the period since the last readings were taken is a useful item. So is a wet-and-dry-bulb thermometer, which will help you determine relative humidity. A third kind, mounted in a pointed wood cover, can be pushed into the sides of a hot-bed or a heap of manure; this is essential when growing mushrooms.

A Pocket-Knife, well honed, is used for pruning away side-branches of tomato plants when growing them to a single stem; also for shortening the foliage when transplanting seedlings.

Left to right: *gardeners' basket, picking, English garden and flower-and-fruit baskets.*

Baskets are desirable for gathering your crops, and **Pails and Garbage Cans** have dozens of uses. So has a large cotton **Drop-Sheet** such as painters use to put over furniture; you rake leaves into it, gather up the corners and carry them to the compost heap. Failing this, bushel baskets or a large galvanized tub will be useful.

An Incinerator is necessary for a tidy garden. Always use it with the lid on for safety; courtesy suggests that you do not burn until the neighbor's laundry has been taken in. A large garbage-can-cover can be kept in place on it to keep the contents dry during rain, and usually it smokes far less if the heap is ignited at the top. Better not burn after dark; some nervous person might call out the fire department.

Several **Tool-Holders** are good in the garage. Be sure you hang rakes and hoes up; leaning them against a wall, business head down, is a fertile cause of knocked heads and ruffled tempers. It is a shock to learn how forceful a blow can be inflicted on oneself by treading on a rake-head.

To sum up: A complete kit of tools may be acquired gradually. They should fit *you*. Care for them well, keep them clean, each in its proper place, and you will use them for years.

Dry and burn diseased or insect infested plants in an incinerator, and most garden troubles will bypass you. Spread the ashes over the garden.

CHAPTER 7

Constant Hoeing Is a "Must"

*Earth is here so kind, that just tickle her with a hoe
and she laughs out a harvest.*

DOUGLAS JERROLD, 1803–1857

As SOON as new seedlings appear above ground, and shortly after setting out plants, the stirring of the surface soil should commence. It is not fully understood why a coating of loose broken soil, called a soil-mulch or dust-mulch, is so beneficial to the plants, but it makes them grow; in periods without rain, hoeing keeps them from wilting for some time, and during this period, hoeing is more effective than sprinkling. Hoeing eliminates all weeds except those right in your vegetable rows, and the pulling of these few is simple when hoeing has been carried out faithfully. Hoeing also helps to keep certain fungoid parasites under control by breaking up the fine thread-like roots or micelia in or on the land. And hoeing destroys many insect enemies; beetle-grubs brought to the surface by hoeing usually die; and cutworms suffer along with other night-working pests.

There are several types of hoes that chop the soil; the draw or garden hoe, the warren hoe with a point for more easily working in clay soils, the nursery hoe for working close to plants in tight places; this is useful for hoeing beets or carrots into small colonies, the colonies being reduced to single plants by hand.

You can get a narrower nursery spade than this if you wish. A pointed Warren hoe. At right is a heavy type for rough work.

In vineyards and especially among sugar-cane in the tropics tough hoes are used; clay land containing heavy roots and stick fragments may justify the employment of one of these heavy tools. A speedy cultivator hoe has three or four sharp straight prongs, and can easily be chopped into most soils; with these, a light hammer-stroke with a slight pull loosens the surface.

Other cultivator hoes have five or more curved prongs, the distance between them in some types being adjustable to fit your spacing; sometimes the center prong can be removed so that you can straddle the plants when your vegetables are small enough to escape damage. They are pulled towards you, leaving a fine powdery surface.

A scuffle-hoe, called the English or Dutch hoe, is built on another principle. You push it forward in a series of jerks. Its blade cuts the soil into small flakes, and it cuts weeds at their roots about an inch under the surface. It gets under spreading vegetables like lettuce or endive. It becomes more useful as you use it and it wears down, because at first you must watch that its sharp corners do not cut the plants: a minor source of crop losses is the vegetable stung with a hoe.

So we have three types of soil-stirring, weed-destroying hoes: those you chop with, those you pull and those you push. There remain the wheel-hoes. Pushed in a series of jerks, the weight of the implement is carried on either one or two wheels, for there are two general types; the one-wheeler travels between the rows, the two-wheeler straddles a row. A lot of thought has been devoted to the design of these machines during the many-years they have been in use, and the ingenuity shown is fascinating. A metal frame is bolted to adjustable handles; and to the frame at various angles and in several positions you attach appropriate implements: blades which work just under the surface—much like a scuffle-hoe—cultivator teeth, a small plow, rakes and even arms to push leaves out of the path of the machine.

If your garden is too large for a hand wheel-hoe you may give thought to a rather similar device, but bigger and powered by a gasoline engine. There are several good makes offered for sale. It is possible to buy extra attachments for some of them, so that

41

in addition to plowing, cultivating, hoeing and raking, you can cut a hay-field or mow a lawn, spray your crops or shovel snow.

Depending upon the make of powered implement you select you may have to change somewhat the distance apart of your rows; so decide on a machine and find out all you can about it, even if you buy it later. Plan your rows to fit the machine, and run the rows parallel to the longer margins of the plot, since every turn-around is wasted space and you need the fewest possible of them.

Theoretically, if vegetable rows run north and south they get the morning sun on their east side and the setting sun on the west. There is little practical value to this, however, and we suggest that longer rows and fewer turns are more important.

In a hand-worked garden, or in a large one that is square or nearly so, the rows might run north and south one year, east and west the next year. In this way a rotation of crops between one year and the next is assured—desirable in every agricultural or horticultural project.

Weeds do not grow in the dark, and recently some publicity has been given to the use of heavy waterproof paper or metal foil to smother weeds between plants and to conserve moisture. The killing of weeds by spraying with chemicals has been written about, also. The hoe will do these equally well, and it is a question whether paper, foil and chemicals have a place in the moderate-size garden. Hoeing goes easily and quickly when it is done often; only when the garden is growing beyond us does hoeing become difficult.

To sum up: Hoeing is perhaps the most important task in the garden; several kinds of hoes are available, each best for a particular job. They should be in use continually.

CHAPTER 8

Trenching or Two-Spit Digging

*If Gentlemen which have little else to doe, would be
ruled by me, I would advise them to spend their spare
time in their Gardens; either in digging, setting,
weeding, or the like, than which there is no better
way in the world to preserve health. If a man want
an Appetite to his Victualls, the smell of the Earth
new turned up, by digging with a Spade will produce
it, and if he be inclined to a Consumption it will recover him.*   WILLIAM COLES, 1657

MANURE, humus or compost, sheep manure and bonemeal are
spread on the surface of the ground to be dug.

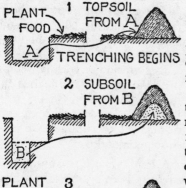

Two-Spit Trenching

(1). The topsoil at the starting point is taken out of a trench
1 foot deep and 2 feet wide; it is
placed in a heap at the farther
end, where the trenching will
finish.

(2). At the bottom of the
trench a second excavation is
made, also 1 foot deep but only
1 foot wide. This is also taken to
the finishing point to make a second heap, this time of subsoil; it
will be one-half the size of the
first heap. We now have an excavation with a step in it.

(3). Some of the manure mixture is spread on the step and on
the bottom.

43

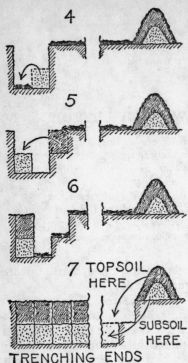

Two-spit trenching in autumn; much work, but often justified by results.

(4). The step is dug and turned over to fill the bottom of the trench.

(5). A 1-foot width of topsoil is dug, turned and put on the top of the newly turned subsoil.

(6). After putting some of the manure mixture on the step and bottom we have diagram No. 6, which is the same as No. 3, but one foot nearer the finish-line.

(7). When we come to the end we put manure mixture on the bottom, and place the smaller heap of subsoil on it. The larger heap of topsoil fills the remaining hole, and the job is done.

The entire garden area has now been thoroughly spaded; we manured and turned the topsoil, and it is still on top; we have manured and turned the subsoil and have kept it at the bottom, where it should be.

By starting out with two steps instead of one, observing the rule to keep the topsoil on top, the upper layer of subsoil next, and the lower layer on the bottom, turning all, we would have performed three-spit digging, which is sometimes done.

To sum up: To get the most out of land it may be manured and turned two or three feet deep, carefully keeping topsoil on top, subsoil at bottom. It is performed by two-spit or three-spit trenching. Ordinary or one-spit digging is treated in chapter 6.

CHAPTER 9

Growing Vegetables in the Cold Season

Yes, in the poor man's garden grow far more than herbs and flowers—kind thoughts, contentment, peace of mind, and joy for weary hours.

MARY HOWITT, 1804–1888

PROTECTING THEM AGAINST FROST IN EARLY SPRING AND LATE AUTUMN

THE logical way to protect a limited number of plants would seem to be to grow them inside a heated home, but almost always the light is inadequate. If you possess a sunroom, you can start your spring seeds very easily, and you can grow a limited supply of herbs, a tomato plant or so up against the glass, and some pulling onions from sets. Without a sunroom there are three handicaps to overcome in house culture: deficient light, over-dry atmosphere, and possible gas-leaks from your cook-stove or heating plant.

It is sometimes difficult to understand that plants are getting less light than they require, especially if you have a window into which the sun streams for hours. But the so-called actinic light, that which affects photographic film, rather than exposure to sun, is mostly the kind to make plants grow; this is light reflected from high clouds and the sky generally, bright but diffused, and next in brightness to the sun itself. Under outdoor conditions this light reaches the plant on all sides in the form of a half-globe. But if you have a pot against a window, your light may be less than that from one quarter of a globe.

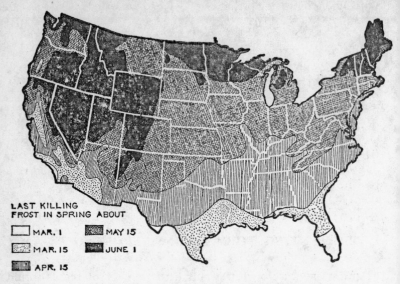

LAST KILLING
FROST IN SPRING ABOUT

☐ MAR. 1   ▨ MAY 15
▨ MAR. 15   ▧ JUNE 1
▥ APR. 15

WHEN SPRING COMES TO THE UNITED STATES.

Other windows in the room may contribute some illumination; but under even favorable conditions the plants get nothing approaching the total amount of light they need. Certain decorative house-plants will tolerate these conditions, because many of them are native to the half-light of the tropical jungle, and they will live for years; but our vegetable plants refuse to spend their lives inside the window of the average living-room. The most we can expect is for our seedlings to spend their first few weeks there; so we may sow our cabbage, lettuce or tomato seeds in the house, and get the young plants outdoors, where they belong, as soon as the temperature permits. First sowings should be made in pots, because when the plants are up they can be turned daily; they will then grow upright instead of bending towards the source of light. You can also place the pots close together, standing them in a shallow pan on a half-inch layer of small charcoal, which you sprinkle daily. Moisture coming from the charcoal, the soil in the pots, and from the plants, will do a lot to offset the normally over-dry atmosphere of our homes in winter.

A good soil-mixture for the pots would be a spadeful each of soil from the garden, of sifted compost and of coarse sand which has been washed with a hose and allowed to dry; with these three spadefuls a cup of limestone or hydrated lime may be mixed. If compost is not yet available, use hyper-humus instead. On half a plant-label write the variety and the date, and push the label down level with the pot's rim. Scatter the seeds thinly on the pot, aiming to get them half-an-inch apart, then sift just enough of the soil mixture to hide the seeds, and press firm with the bottom of a water-glass. Stand the pot in a bowl of water for five minutes, preferably with the water one inch below the pot's rim, drain and stand on your charcoal layer in the window. Keep a sheet of glass or a heavy card two-thirds over the surface of the pot until the young plants come through, then remove it. Instead of sand, you can use the granules of mica sold under the name of Vermiculite with advantage; or mix sand and Vermiculite half-and-half. Moisten all your pots by standing them in water often so that the soil does not become dry—perhaps twice a week, perhaps three times.

Watering seeds through a piece of canvas avoids disturbing them.

Thinning begins as soon as the seedlings are above ground; take a pair of tweezers, and wherever two plants are touching, pull out one of them. Your sheet of glass or card now comes off, but be sure to turn the pots every day.

Earlier than this, in January, sow a few tomato seeds; transplant the seedlings into small pots, again into larger ones if roots appear through the drainage hole at the bottom to tell you that the plant is getting root-bound and needs larger accommodation. If you care to, you can put these plants out of doors in the garden on May 15, with small fruits on them. The object of growing them is to find out about coal-gas or illuminating gas in the home. If they thrive you may be assured that you have no troubles of this kind; if they wilt, do what you can to correct the trouble, fill cracks with iron cement, file doors to make them fit snugly, have a plumber grind your gas-stove taps for a closer fit and look for small leaks. It will be better for you as well as for the plants if you keep the gases out. We use tomato plants for this purpose, because they are most sensitive to gas.

When the young plants are three inches tall they will be ready for wider accommodation, either into larger pots, farther apart, or in the shallow boxes we call flats. These are harder to turn than pots, so put in them the cold-tolerant kinds, the beet, chard, kohlrabi, lettuce, onion, parsley, broccoli, cabbage and cauliflower. These you can put into a cold-frame, protecting the frame with bags and boards if the nights are cold. Put the eggplant, pepper and tomato into larger pots which you will keep in the house, and which you can turn every day.

COLD-FRAME. *Cover it with a mat at night when necessary. To make it into a hot-bed stand it on a heap of fresh horse-manure and leaves, capped with soil. Or install electric heating wires under it.*

The cold-frame containing your flats of hardy types should have compost, manure or earth piled up around it on all sides. Exercising great care, you might stand a lighted watchman's lantern inside should the thermometer drop very low. You can improvise a cold-frame with some of your storm sash taken down ahead of the spring, but you would be well advised to purchase a professional one.

The glass windows or sash of a standard cold-frame are 6 feet long and 3 feet wide; frames can be bought or made to take one sash up to any number, 5 feet 9 inches from front to back, and as long as convenient in multiples of 3 feet. Instead of glass, the plastics Vitapane or Cel-O-glass are much used, translucent weather-resistant fabrics that can be sheared and tacked to wood; watch your lighted lantern with them, however. The **Green Thumb** is a frame for the amateur, well made in more than one size. It is smaller than the standard type and is obtainable in the supply houses, as are standard frames.

An arrangement used for centuries is a **hot-bed**. Merely a cold-frame set on a lightly tamped two-foot thick heap of equal parts of fresh horse-manure and dry autumn leaves, the heap capped with six inches of good soil. The manure and leaves become warm through decomposition, and plants grow especially well in such a hot-bed. If such a bed fails to become heated, a peck of fresh hen manure, dibbled through the soil into the manure, will start it.

An **electric hot-bed heater** is the modern version. Leading a weather-resistant cable from the house to the flexible heating units is simple; the heating wires are buried under the frame.

Sometimes a frame and sash may be adapted to fit against the outside of an open cellar window, a certain amount of heat coming from the cellar; a southern exposure, not shaded by evergreens or buildings, should be selected.

Along the lines of the unheated cold-frame is the French **cloche** or bell-jar under which the market gardeners of Paris grow carrot, lettuce, radish, pulling onions and beans. In so-called French-gardening, manure is spread six inches thick; on top is a 5-inch layer of earth. By working to a scheme of succession-cropping, companion-

LETTUCE. *Growing in soil-covered manure, protected by a cloche.*

ion-cropping and moving the cloches from one spot to another, large crops are produced on surprisingly small areas.

An American cloche made of sheets of glass and a framework

HOTKAPS. *Under their protection seeds may be sown outdoors earlier than normal for the locality.*

of wire is offered, and will produce early crops in a similar way.

Taking your late winter drives in the country you may come across a farm with rows of what look like brown derby hats running across the field. They probably are Hotkaps, made of semi-transparent weatherproof paper, protecting early-sown hills or groups of muskmelon, corn or cucumbers; with these the grower can put out plants or sow seeds three weeks earlier than would normally be safe.

The **sun-heated pit** is the name for what practically is a large cold-frame in which a person may enter and stand upright. The glass is kept near the surface of the ground, but the gardener stands in a trench about 3½ feet deep, the sides being boarded or cemented. Although glass holds back some of the important light-rays, and all glass structures are slightly inefficient from this cause, glass magnifies the sun's heat. Low structures retain this heat more than tall ones, so a sun-heated pit is hot when the sun is shining upon it, and must be ventilated. The sun-heated pit is warmer than it otherwise would be because the trench-bottom

A HEATED GREENHOUSE ENABLES YOU TO GARDEN ALL YEAR

is well below the limit of frozen soil in all but the most severe localities. A lot of seedlings can be raised, or crops produced, in one sun-heated pit.

The heated greenhouse is generally used for the commercial production of seedling plants. Seeds are sown in flats as a rule, thinned, and transferred farther apart to other flats, which are then taken from the greenhouse to a cold-frame after April 1. This shift of plants from a warm greenhouse to an unheated frame is termed hardening-off. When the outside temperature it 60 or more, sash should be open three inches for ventilation by putting a block under the sash, closed when it is less than 60, covered with mats at night when it is 45 degrees or lower. Provision to cover the sun-heated pit during cold nights is also necessary, unless a small coal stove, laundry stove, oil heater or pipes from the home have been installed.

If you grow your own plants in a hot-bed or greenhouse, you can use a square of turf cut from the lawn with a spade; turn it upside-down in a shallow box, and sow seeds sparingly in the dirt side, the sod taking the place of flower-pots. Thin to 2 inches apart. At planting-out time the turf may be cut into small squares with a mason's trowel, each containing a seedling, which can be set out with little check to the plant's growth. Hills of corn, muskmelon, squash or beans can be started this way on a 6-inch square sod, which may be transferred bodily to the garden for an early crop. Better lift the turves in the autumn before freeze-up, lay them on boards outside all winter; bring them indoors to thaw and dry, then sow your seeds.

A conservatory is the same thing as a greenhouse, but usually is more elaborately built; its purpose is to display flowers and shrubs rather than produce plants of vegetables.

USE YOUR FRAME IN THE AUTUMN

You can plant some lettuce or endive in it around September 10 from seeds sown first week in August. At the same time you can sow in the frame beet and carrot. On October 15 you can sow spring radishes in it.

Or put in a late crop of tomatoes. On July 15 sow some tomato seeds in the open; in the meanwhile, cut some flexible tree branches and prune off all side twigs. Cut them of such a length that you can push one end a foot deep in the soil at the front of the frame, and arching them, can push the other end a foot in the soil at the rear of the frame; when the sash is in position, the sticks should nowhere be closer to the glass than 6 inches. Allow three sticks to a standard sash, so they can be 1 foot apart and 6 inches from the frame's sides. On September 1 plant a tomato seedling against each end of the curving sticks; train each plant to a single stem by cutting off side branches, and once a week wire the stems to the sticks with pipe-cleaners. The stems will meet and overlap, but continue with the pipe-cleaners; if a stem gets to within a foot of its companion's root, nip off the top.

You will have to work on the tomatoes with the sash off, so you may not be able strictly to stick to this schedule in cold weather; they must be kept warm.

Bank earth and compost right up to the tops of your frame, and cover with old rugs and boards on cold nights.

Plant the same crops in your sun-heated pit; because it is warmer than a frame, you may sow or plant up to two weeks later if necessary. If you have a stove or steam pipes in it, however, consider it a greenhouse. In either a heated pit or greenhouse you might sow all the following around September 1:

Dwarf snap beans, beet, carrot, endive, lettuce, parsley and radish.

And you may plant tomatoes at the same time.

Should you own an unheated greenhouse you can plant tomatoes up to August 20 from seeds sown outdoors July 1. Better train them to a single stem, and attach them to stout upright canes. And you may sow dwarf snap beans, beet and carrot any time up to September 5, summer radish to September 25, and spring radish to October 10.

To sum up: Seeds can be started in the house in late winter, close to the lightest window. The plants should be transferred to a cold-frame, improvised if necessary, and planted out on the dates given in chapter 14. Frames may extend vegetable growing later into the fall.

CHAPTER 10

Thinning and Weeding

*The life of the husbandman—a life fed by the bounty
of earth and sweetened by the airs of heaven.*

DOUGLAS JERROLD, 1803–1857

IF YOU sow seeds at the rates recommended in the table in chapter 14, the plants will be too close together if all the seeds grow.
Lashing rain may wash some of the seeds away, cutworms, caterpillars and birds may rob you of some of the young plants. As
an insurance, therefore, slightly more seeds are sown than should
be necessary, and often the row, or part of it, has to be thinned—
destroying some of the young plants to leave sufficient room for
those which remain. A narrow nursery hoe or a warren hoe will
prevent part of the back-bending: a row of seedlings may be cut
into a number of tufts with it, and from each tuft the unwanted
extra seedlings are pulled out by hand, to leave each plant the
distance from its neighbor suggested in the tables. The mason's
trowel can also be used for this purpose, but there is some stooping with it.

Some gardeners prefer to work without the narrow hoe; they
bend over a row once a week, pulling out plants which crowd,
until the remainder stand at the proper spacing.

At this time the few weeds which appear in the row are pulled
out also. Hoeing between the rows every week will prevent weeds
appearing elsewhere.

SUN AND SHADE

All vegetables do their best in good light, with full sun on them
for at least half the day. However a few will tolerate a little shade,

53

while others insist on full sunlight. Here are some of the favorite kinds with their preferences:

Vegetables needing full sun: All beans, beet, carrot, corn, eggplant, the vine-crops, peanut, pepper, New Zealand spinach, tobacco, tomato. They all do best in the hot weather of midsummer.

Vegetables which tolerate some shade: Broccoli, asparagus, artichoke, Brussels sprouts, cabbage, celery, endive, kale, onion, parsley, radish, spinach, chard, turnip; also potatoes. These are mostly cool weather crops, growing their best in spring or fall.

SEEDS SHOULD GROW, AND HAVE A PEDIGREE

The seedsman counts out a definite number of seeds and sows them in sterilized soil or on moist blotting-paper; notes those which grow, and arrives at a percentage of germination. Most states require that the germination be printed on the container, with the date on which the tests were completed. Inspectors occasionally check the printed figures, and the supplier is subject to penalties if his figures are incorrect, or the germination is below standard.

The supplying companies are much concerned with damage to their reputation that would arise from selling seeds that are of poor vitality. The odds are that you will garden for many years before you get caught with poor seed if you purchase from reliable companies.

Of even greater importance is strain. Two clutches of eggs may look alike, but one will hatch into pedigree chicks and the other into mixed barnyard fowl, some good and others not so good. The average seed concern is as careful with seeds as a pharmacist is with his drugs; from companies of standing you are likely to get what they say you will—pedigreed plants. To keep check on the quality of their wares, and to find out how good their competitors' seeds are, most suppliers maintain experimental grounds, where every conceivable variety is grown to maturity.

Subject to criticism, however, is the exaggeration that some companies indulge in. They often advertise that they are "Seed merchants and growers," letting you conclude that they grow their own merchandise. A few do, most do not; they do what may be better: they contract ahead of time with skilled farmers for kinds that are best grown in a particular locality: certain onions and beets in Connecticut, peppers and tomatoes in New Jersey, lettuce, corn and beans in the Middle West, peas in western New York, radish, carrot and many another in California—wherever they grow well. They go to France and the Low Countries for many specialties, Britain for some, even to Japan. Superior strains are like the better mousetrap: commercial growers will wear a path to the door of the seedsman who has cabbage that is a week ahead of most, a celery that is nuttier or has fewer strings, spinach that does not readily bolt to flower. This is what pedigree means.

In these respects the requirements of the home-owner may not be the same as those of the commercial grower. The amateur likes beans and peas that mature their crop gradually, so he can go into the garden any time and pick a basketful; he wants to pick and come again. But picking is a heavy expense to the commercial man, so he wants his vegetables to mature quickly and all at once; he must catch the earliest markets to get his best price.

The professional grower wants strains that will ship long distances without damage; stronger skinned tomatoes, for example. This is of little interest to the home-gardener who would prefer thin-skinned tomatoes for slicing and canning. The commercial man likes beets and turnips with short tops because they are cheaper to handle, but the amateur recognizes the outstanding food value of beet-tops and turnip-greens, and likes long leaves. So be guided by the catalogue descriptions.

New-crop seeds are usually of high germination, but one-year and two-year-old seeds of most vegetables are often preferred by experienced gardeners, even if they have to be sown a little heavier. Better produce is claimed for them, and the supplier and his customers have had an opportunity to prove their worth.

To sum up: Unwanted plants must be thinned, so that those which remain have room to grow. Some vegetables will tolerate partial shade. Seeds from responsible suppliers are usually reliable, but commercial strains are not always best for the home garden.

CHAPTER 11

Rotate Your Crops

There is no ancient gentlemen but gardeners.
WILLIAM SHAKESPEARE, 1564–1616. Hamlet. Act 5

SOME vegetables go deep into the soil for their food; they have long roots. Others have short roots. It is good practice to follow a deep-rooted crop with a shallow one in the same land, and vice versa. Good practice too is to follow a leaf crop, like spinach, with a root crop like carrot. This applies both to succession crops within the season and to crops one year with another; don't grow tomatoes in the same place every year. Never follow lettuce with lettuce or beans with beans. Rather follow lettuce with beans, and beans with lettuce. Rotation should be aimed for.

For safety, do not let one crop follow another of the same botanical family in a particular row. There are several reasons: plants in the same family usually draw from the soil the same plant-foods in much the same proportions. They frequently leave in the soil a residue of roots, leaves and juices that are similar.

Many parasites confine their attack to one family; some are found on one race of plants and not on another. The spinach leaf-miner invades all plants of the goosefoot family, and the tomato horn-worm eats other members of the solanaceæ. To present the parasite with a second crop of its favorite host is to encourage it unduly.

Certain one-celled worms, called nematodes, live in the roots of plants; they frequently multiply and attack a new planting of the same family with greater vigor, so that the first crop may be fair but the second crop may fail completely, because of the increase in the nematodes. The kind which live in pea roots, increasing every year, may become so numerous that peas cannot be grown in a district for years, and the locality is said to be pea-sick.

Here is a list of some botanical families, and the better-known vegetables that belong to them:

Aizoaceæ, *Carpet-Weed Family.* New Zealand Spinach.

Chenopodiaceæ, *Goosefoot Family.* Beet, chard, spinach.

Compositæ, *Aster Family.* Globe artichoke, Jerusalem artichoke, cardoon, chamomile, chicory, dandelion, endive, lettuce, salsify, scorzonera, southernwood, tarragon.

Convolvulaceæ, *Morning Glory Family.* Sweet potato.

Cruciferæ, *Mustard Family.* The cross-bearers, because the flowers are in the shape of a cross. This family contains no poisonous members. Broccoli, Brussels sprouts, cabbage, Chinese cabbage, cauliflower, collards, cress, horseradish, kale, kohlrabi, mustard, radish, turnip, rutabaga, seakale, watercress.

Cucurbitaceæ, *Gourd Family.* Citron, cocozelle, cucumber, gherkin, muskmelon, pumpkin, squash, vegetable marrow, zucchini, watermelon.

Fungi. Mushroom.

Gramineæ, *Grass Family.* Corn.

Labiatæ, *Mint Family.* Many of its members contain volatile oils. Balm, basil, catnip, mint, rosemary, sage, savory, thyme.

Leguminosæ, *Pea Family.* All kinds of beans, peas, peanut.

Liliaceæ, *Lily Family.* Asparagus, chives, garlic, leek, onion, shallot.

Malvaceæ, *Mallow Family.* Okra.

Martyniaceæ. Martynia.

Polygonaceæ. *Buckwheat Family.* Rhubarb (stems are good, but leaves are poisonous), sorrel.

Rutaceæ, *Rue Family.* Rue.

Solanaceæ, *Nightshade Family.* Contains many poisonous members. Do not eat the leaves of any of these. Do not eat potato balls or fruits. Do not eat potatoes that have acquired a green color through exposure to light. Eggplant, pepper, physalis, potato, tobacco, tomato.

Umbelliferæ, *Carrot Family.* Contains some poisonous members. Anise, caraway, carrot, celeriac, celery, chervil, coriander, dill, fennel, lovage, marjoram, parsley, parsnip.

Valerianaceæ, *Valerian Family.* Corn salad.

We cannot practice short-term rotation with perennial vegetables and herbs; but eventually an asparagus bed may show signs of exhausting the soil, when a new one may be made elsewhere. Artichokes, Egyptian onions, horseradish, rhubarb and the perennial herbs may well be shifted every few years.

COMPANION-CROPPING and SUCCESSION-CROPPING

We practice companion-cropping if our garden is small and we wish to get the most out of it. The principle is the growing of quick dwarf plants between slower kinds, the speedier ones maturing before the others need the room. Examples are:

Tomatoes planted 3 feet apart on May 15 yield all summer, beginning in 10 weeks. Between each tomato you sow a 1½-ft. row of bush snap beans; you pick beans in nine weeks, and then cut away the plants at the ground.

Peppers at 1½-ft. intervals may have a lettuce planted between each; you eat the lettuce when the peppers commence to fruit.

Sow a row of beets in April, pull out a handful of the seedlings at 2½-ft. intervals on June 1. Put in an eggplant at each gap.

Between the hills or groups of the vine plants are many opportunities for rows of quick early seeded crops. Some seeds of pumpkin or squash may be sown with corn in every third hill.

Working with the tables in this book, many space-saving combinations can be worked out. Make side-dressings of fertilizer every two weeks to allow for the extra work the soil is performing.

Another scheme is to sow more than one kind of seed in the same row and at the same time; the quicker one will yield its crop before the later ones need the space, and the later ones will not be reduced. Examples are:

Two reasons why you should grow beet and radish in the same row: space economy, and a more certain crop. Beet seeds sown alone at top could not crack the soil crust; later sown beet and radish has a perfect stand.

Radish seeds sown in the same groove as beet, or as carrot, leek, onion, parsley, parsnip, salsify or chard. Thus two crops are obtained from the same row.

Instead of two crops, three in one row are possible, such as:

Radish, beet and leek seeds, sown in the same row at the same time.
Spinach seeds, broccoli plants and parsnip seeds.
Onion sets, carrot and salsify seeds

Succession-cropping should be practiced in every garden. It is merely the principle that as soon as one crop has been gathered from a row in which only one kind is planted, the remains are cut into small pieces, sheep manure, compost or hyper-humus and bonemeal are spread and the land spaded; thus burying the remains of the previous crop, and raking smooth. Another crop of a different family is put in at once to succeed it. The tables giving planting dates and time taken to grow may surprise you with the many kinds that may be sown or planted in July, August or September. Succession-cropping is particularly important in the case of dwarf snap beans, cabbage and lettuce, to insure a steady and constant supply of these vegetables.

Planting for Succession. You may have seen this phrase in a garden book. It means that when you sow or set out a vegetable you plant several varieties of it at the time: a quick one, a second not so quick, perhaps another that is very slow. Sown on the same day, you gather First of All peas 55 days later, Gradus peas 68 days later, and Potlach 80 days later. Spancross corn yields in 66 days, Golden Cross Bantam in 88 days, Stowell's Evergreen in 100 days if you sow all three on the same day.

EARLY AND LATE VARIETIES

When the seed catalogues describe early and late varieties they mean quick sorts and slow sorts. Perhaps a little misleading, because it is often good practice to put in an early (meaning quick) sort late. Sown at the same time, Chantenay carrot, early, is ready in 10 weeks, and Danvers, a late sort, takes 13 weeks. For your last planting of carrots on July 15, the quick Chantenay is a good one, even if the catalogues call it early and you plant it late.

To sum up: Get maximum production by putting in a new vegetable as soon as an old one has yielded its crop. Let one vegetable follow another of a different kind. Economize space by growing a quick vegetable alongside a slow one; even plant two or three kinds in the same row. Use more than one variety of a vegetable at planting time, to spread the yield over several weeks. Don't hesitate to sow "early" varieties late.

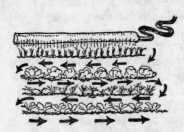

With a sloping garden you can start water at the top and let it take a zigzag path downwards. Here an old section of worn canvas pipe delivers the water.

CHAPTER 12

Growing Prize Specimens

God the first garden made, and the first city Cain.
ABRAHAM COWLEY, 1618–1667. The Garden.

You may want to exhibit your products at local shows, or you merely wish to display superior specimens to your friends. Or you just want to grow the best vegetables you can.

For show purposes, it is important that you find out how long the particular variety takes to grow; play safe, and start one batch a little ahead and another batch a little behind the date you calculate. Prepare the land in late autumn; if possible, "trench" it, two or even three spades deep. Consult chapter 8.

Spray at regular intervals to protect against fungoid and insect attacks. Use dust for any troubles that get through your sprays.

Gather peas and beans in the morning, when wet with dew. Select your other products the evening before the show, and pack carefully; eggplant, peppers, muskmelons, tomatoes, cucumbers and squash should be wrapped in absorbent cotton to avoid injury. Be sure to preserve the thin film of natural wax, called the "bloom," on cucumbers.

Wash roots carefully by soaking and wiping with a cloth, soaking and wiping again. Do not brush them. If the show regulations allow, trim tops off beet, carrot and parsnip. Again if the rules permit, after removing only as much of the outer skin as may be weathered, bend over the top of each large onion, tie with raffia, and cut off the top just below the raffia.

Lay groups of snap beans, carrots, squashes, and similar, on a bed of parsley in plates or dishes, first putting a layer of cotton-batting on the dish. Garnish tomatoes with their own leaves.

Let groups be made up of specimens that are uniform, even sacrificing size if you have to. Let beets and carrots match.

Here are some recipes for producing vegetables that may be striking in size, shape and quality:

Crowbar Culture of Parsnips. In early March, drive a pipe or crowbar six feet deep, or as deep as you can. Circle the top of the pipe to make the hole 3 inches wide at the top; fill with good sandy-loam soil with which you have mixed one part in ten of sheep manure and one part in twenty of bonemeal; tamp it lightly with a bamboo, and pour water into the sandy-loam soil on about three occasions to cause it to settle. On April 1, sow five parsnip seeds on each filled-in hole; thin until only one plant occupies each hole. Cultivate normally, and you should have quite a job digging down completely to get out the straight, clean, whip-thong-end root. Fine specimens of long beet, carrot, rooted parsley, long radish, salsify and scorzonera can be grown similarly, but the holes need not be deeper than two feet.

Underground Watering and Feeding. Prepare the soil two spades deep by "trenching" and dig a hole 18 inches deep. Set any size flowerpot-saucer on the bottom, stand an inverted pot on the saucer, first putting enough stones in the saucer to bring the pot bottom ten inches below the surface. Stand a 12-inch drain-tile on its end on the flower-pot; put two quarts of peatmoss around the pot, and return the soil—subsoil, first, then topsoil, to fill the hole. Place a small flower-pot over the drain-tile to keep dirt out.

In a circle with a 2-ft. radius around the drain-tile, put in four tomato plants, training each to a stake; between them put four peppers. Around other similarly placed tiles plant broccoli, celery, Brussels sprouts, endive or kale. Pour water down the drain-tile in dry weather, and with every second watering give some liquid fertilizer: sheep manure stirred into water and allowed to settle, a solution of Trace-L, or 5–10–5 fertilizer stirred in water and allowed to settle. Thus you water and feed your plants from below, with a constant reserve of moisture around the sunken pot.

Long White Leeks. First dig a 1½ ft. deep trench; fill 6 inches with decayed manure and topsoil in equal parts. Use hyper-humus, compost, sheep manure and bonemeal instead of manure if it cannot be obtained. Transplant individual seedlings 12 inches apart from seed sown indoors March 15. Carefully slip a drain-tile over each leek; place another empty drain-tile alongside. Bank with two inches of soil around each of the tiles; add to it every week until finally earth fills the trench. Meanwhile, treat as suggested above for underground watering and feeding, pouring first water and then dissolved plant-foods through the tile that does not contain the leek.

Extra Large Tomatoes. Prune away side branches, and cut off half the flower-clusters, to limit the number of tomatoes the plant will produce. Pinching out most of the flowers can be practiced with peppers, eggplant, cucumber, muskmelon, squash. Prune side buds of broccoli to give you one fine center head.

To Get Cucumbers of Equal Size. Measure them as they are growing. Two weeks before the show, cut some of the largest ones with a two-inch stem, and stand in jars of water in partial shade. As others grow to a similar size, cut them off and treat similarly. Do the same with squashes, vegetable marrows and eggplants.

Carrots and Beets. If you need room and must dig them before the show, use a spading fork and select the most uniform. Cut off the leaves to allow but 6 inches of the stalks to remain. Replant in nearly dry sand indoors or out. When ready, wash and trim.

Cauliflowers may be cut with a long stem when nearly at their best; cut off part of the leaves, leaving the lower 12 inches, stick in damp sand in a light spot in the garage, and cover the heads only with a layer of wax paper. Trim off the leaves neatly before the show opens.

Above all, follow the show regulations; within the rules, neatness and a good eye for color will be helpful.

To sum up: For outstanding vegetables allow more than enough room, and grow them in deep, rich soil with a constant moisture supply. Fine specimen tomatoes and peppers may be obtained by reducing the number on each plant.

CHAPTER 13

The Salad Greens

A little work in the garden early in the morning, or late in the afternoon, each day, furnishes wholesome exercise besides the joy one gets from watching plants grow. GEORGE R. BRIGGS in "Gardening in the South, 1931

ON THE whole, uncooked fresh vegetables are better for you, because the minerals and vitamins are intact: cooking may dissolve or remove many of them. Make delicious raw salads from the following, all of which you can grow yourself:

Artichoke, globe	Dandelion
Cabbage, green or red	Endive and escarolle
Cabbage, Chinese	Fennel
Cardoon	Lettuce
Carrot	Mustard, white London
Celeriac	Mustard, curled
Celery	Onion
Chervil	Parsley
Chicory from sprouted roots (Witloof)	Pepper
	Radish
Corn salad	Seakale from sprouted roots
Cress, curled	Sorrel
Cress, water	Tomato
Cucumber	Turnip

If you have nasturtiums in the flower garden, put some of the leaves and flowers in salads.

Flavor salads with a little garlic, horseradish and the herbs anise, balm, basil, chervil, chives, lovage, marjoram, mint, tarragon and thyme. Add to the salad greens, left-overs of the following cooked vegetables, first cooling them:

Artichoke, globe	Cocozelle	Rutabaga
Artichoke, Jerusalem	Collards	Salsify
Asparagus	Dandelion	Scorzonera
Beans	Kale	Spinach
Beet	Kohlrabi	Squash
Beet greens	Leek	Swiss chard
Broccoli	Parsnip	Turnips
Brussels sprouts	Peas	Turnip greens
Cabbage	Potato	Vegetable marrow
Cauliflower		Zucchini

HERBS, THE HOME-GROWN CONDIMENTS

A section of the garden will be devoted to the perennial vegetables, asparagus, rhubarb and the like. Alongside would be those herbs that are permanent also, appearing every spring after the first planting. Like the perennial vegetables, these also need little attention beyond side-dressing with fertilizer, and hoeing. However, some of them are spreading plants, the mints in particular; these need to be dug up when they crowd in the rows. Ruthlessly cutting down into the soil with a spade on both sides of the row will keep them in bounds for a time, but eventually each overgrown root should be dug out, cut into smaller sections and the pieces replanted. The important perennial herbs include:

Balm	Anise mint	Rue
Catnip	Lemon mint	Sage
Chives	Peppermint	Winter savory
Lovage	Spearmint	Tarragon
Knotted marjoram	Pennyroyal	Common English thyme
Pot marjoram	Rosemary	French thyme

The average family can use a dozen plants each of chives, spearmint, sage and English thyme, with three each of others in the list.

Near the perennial herbs is a good place to sow seeds every spring of the annual herbs in rows 2 feet apart. The cook gets a deal of help from:

Anise	Caraway	Fennel
Lettuce-leaved basil	Coriander	Summer savory
Sweet basil	Dill	

A fifty-foot row of fennel, twenty-five-foot rows of caraway, coriander and dill would be good, with ten-foot rows of each of the four others.

These are described in the alphabetical list of vegetables and herbs. Many herb leaves are used green in soups and salads. All the plants can be tied into small bunches, cutting them close to the ground when they first show flowers; hang the bunches in the garage to dry, then keep them in jars and boxes. Seeds of anise, caraway, coriander, dill and fennel can be rubbed out from the dry plant-remains and kept in jars.

The most aromatic of the dried herb foliage can be sown up into sachets for scenting linen; bowls of dried herbs in the house will camouflage cooking odors with their fragrance.

Grandmother's favorites, these interesting, attractive and useful plants, were in the gardens of Colonial America. And prior to the time of Columbus, they provided the European homemaker with her salads, condiments, perfumes and remedies. In medieval times much thought was expended on the design of the herb garden, because here amid their perfume, contentment could be found.

THE PERENNIAL VEGETABLES

The kinds shown in the tables in chapter 14 are annuals or are grown as annuals; you sow or plant them every year. If you own your property you might well find room for some at least of the perennial varieties, occasionally spreading old manure or compost on the soil near them, side-dressing with fertilizer in spring and autumn, and hoeing around them every two weeks to prevent weeds choking them. Don't hoe deeper than two inches; hoeing will then have the effect of keeping plants growing steadily, even during spells of dry weather. Hoe only when the soil is dry.

Artichoke, Globe	Egyptian Onions
Artichoke, Jerusalem	Horseradish
Asparagus	Rhubarb

Along with these, put in at least two dozen pick-at-will perennial herbs, selected from the eighteen varieties listed above.

VEGETABLES IN THE FLOWER GARDEN

Some vegetables are attractive enough to plant along with flowers if your space is limited. Carrot and parsley leaves look like ferns, and they make a good edging; so do chives. The red leaves of beet can be built into effective designs; martynia is a handsome plant for the middle distance of a flower border; so is rhubarb, even. Although you have to top-and-tail the beans of scarlet runner, their superior flavor is worth the trouble, and the red blossoms make it a useful climber. The green seeds of nasturtium, picked as the flowers drop, make good "capers" when pickled in vinegar, and nasturtium leaves may be added to salads. Red chard may be planted. Dandelion, disliked as a weed, is a good garden flower. Jerusalem artichoke makes a screen for the back of the border; horseradish also, but be sure you know where you plant it, or you may dig up poisonous roots in mistake for it—aconitum, for instance. Peanuts look good in the front in full sun; also in a sunny spot, sweet potatoes are a good ground cover.

If your vegetable plot is too small for herbs, plant them in ingenious designs in your flower garden; they were grown in quaint patterns in medieval times. The over two dozen varieties listed in this book are those most valuable to the cook; many more are available to you that are more medicinal or fragrant than culinary. These herbs were the main source of drugs in the early days. Again, many of our garden flowers were once used for culinary or medicinal purposes; they can be brought back into the herb garden; among them are anchusa, ajuga, clary, colchicum, cowslip, marigold, matricaria, foxglove, hollyhock, iris and primrose. Books are available on this interesting development of gardening.

To sum up: Salads are healthful, and are easily grown; so are herbs, which should be in every garden. The perennial vegetables should have a section of the garden to themselves. Some vegetables are decorative enough to grow with flowers.

CHAPTER 14

When and How to Plant Vegetables

God made the country, and man made the town.
WILLIAM COWPER, 1731–1800

THE dates given in the following charts are based on conditions in the coastal districts of the Middle Atlantic states, where the annual precipitation is around 40 inches and is well distributed through the year; although in summer, evaporation may exceed rainfall. Hoeing slows evaporation from the soil,* so hoe continually. In this area the average January temperature is 32 degrees, the mean July temperature 74. Lowest temperature is 12 below, highest in summer about 104, all Fahrenheit.

The last severe frost in spring is expected around April 20, and first killing frost may be on October 10, giving a total of 173 frost-free days.

Find the date of the last killing frost in spring for your own locality, and plan your gardening accordingly; best sources of information are the County Agricultural Agent, the nearest office of the U. S. Weather Bureau, or local newspapers.

Sow and plant a week, or two, or three weeks later than suggested if your frost-free period starts a week, or two, or three weeks later; sow and plant earlier if it commences sooner. The map of the climatic zones in Chapter 9 will also help you.

If the year's precipitation, which is the total rain, snow, sleet,

* This statement may be challenged, but in the absence of convincing evidence to the contrary, I prefer to believe it; I find that a dust-mulch, continually stirred, keeps plants alive in dry weather as nothing else will. J. H. M.

hail and dew, is less than 25 inches, again consult your County Agent; he may suggest some crops that will be unprofitable for you to grow. But moisture is affected by contours in the land: in a dry area, valleys may have ample; even in a wet section, hillsides may get too little. Subsoil also affects the condition; rock or retentive clay may hold much water; sands and gravels may let it escape. Seed catalogues will also assist; hesitate before growing crops not offered locally.

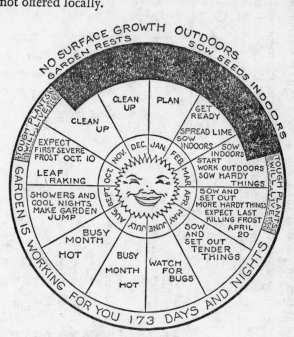

GARDENING THE YEAR ROUND.

VEGETABLE PLANTING TABLES

A. EASY KINDS usually grown in parallel rows, called drills; average distance apart 2 feet.

If your garden is small, you may wish to have double rows of some, the rowlets 6 inches apart. Kinds you may double up are beet, carrot, leek, onion seed and sets, peas, radish, spinach and Swiss chard.

Kind	When to plant See notes in Chapter 15	Seeds needed for 100 feet	Sowing depth ins.	*Distance to thin ins.	Time from planting to harvest weeks
Beans, dwarf snap	May 1 to Aug. 10	1 lb.	2	4	8
" bush lima	May 10 to June 15	2 lbs.	2	6	14
Beet	Mar. 1 indoors for transplanting Apr. 1 to July 15	1 oz.	½	3	9–13
Carrot	Apr. 1 to July 15	1 oz.	½	2½	9–13
Endive or Escarolle	June 15 to Aug. 15 Mar. 1 indoors for transplanting	½ oz.	½	10	11
Kohlrabi	Apr. 1 to Apr. 15 July 15 to Aug. 10	½ oz.	½	4	8–9
Leek	Apr. 1 to May 10	1 oz.	½	6	18
Lettuce and Romaine	Mar. 1 indoors for transplanting Apr. 1 to Aug. 15	½ oz.	½	12	10–12
Mustard, curled	Mar. 25 to Apr. 9 Aug. 1 to Sept. 15	1 oz.	½	6	6–7
Onion seed	Jan. 15 to Mar. 1 indoors for transplanting Apr. 1 to June 10	1 oz.	½	3	12–16
" sets	Apr. 10 to July 10	1½ lbs.	1	2	{Pulling onions 5–7 {Large onions 9–13

	Planting dates	Seed			
Parsley, curled	{ Mar. 1 indoors for transplanting Apr. 1 to June 15 }	⅔ oz.	½	4	10
" rooted	Apr. 1 to July 15	1	½	3	10
Parsnip	Apr. 1 to June 10	½ oz.	½	4	15–18
Peas	Mar. 15 to Apr. 30	1 lb.	2	3	8–12
Potatoes	Apr. 20 to May 31	7–10 lbs.	3	10	14–16
Radish, spring	{ Mar. 15 to June 15 Sept. 1 to Sept. 25 }	1 oz.	½	1	4–5
" summer	June 15 to Aug. 20	1 oz.	½	2½	6
" winter	July 15 to Aug. 15	1 oz.	½	4	8
Salsify	Apr. 15 to June 15	2 ozs.	1	4	15
Spinach	{ Mar. 15 to May 15 Aug. 15 to Sept. 15 }	1 oz.	½	3	7
" New Zealand	May 15 to July 15	2 ozs.	1	5	10
Swiss chard	{ Mar. 1 indoors for transplanting Mar. 25 to July 19 }	1 oz.	½	9	8
Turnip	{ Mar. 25 to May 10 June 25 to July 25 }	⅔ oz.	½	3	9
" Swedish or rutabaga	June 15 to July 15	⅔ oz.	½	6	13

*Observe these distances also when transplanting beets, lettuce, onions, parsley and chard.

B. NOT-SO-EASY ONES or UNUSUAL KINDS sown or planted in parallel rows; average distance apart 2 feet. If your garden is small, you may wish to have double rows of some, the rowlets 6 inches apart. Kinds you may double up on are chervil, corn salad, dandelion, garlic and potato onion.

Kind	When to plant *See notes in Chapter 15*	Seeds needed for 100 feet	Sowing depth ins.	*Distance to thin ins.	Planting to harvest: weeks
Beans, broad or fava	Mar. 15 to Apr. 30	2 lbs.	2	6	11–13
" soy	May 15 to June 15	1 lb.	2	6	12–16
" shell	May 1 to June 20	3/4 lb.	2	5	12
Cabbage, Chinese or celery	{Mar. 25 to Apr. 9} {July 20 to Aug. 10}	1/2 oz.	1/2	6	10
Celeriac	{Apr. 15 to June 15}	2/3 oz.	1/4	6	12
Chervil	{Apr. 1 to May 1} {July 25 to Aug. 10}	2/3 oz.	1/2	4	8
Chicory	Apr. 1 to June 1	1/2 oz.	1/2	6	16
Collards	{Apr. 1 to May 1} {Aug. 15 to Sept. 10}	1 oz.	1/2	6	7–8
Corn salad	{Apr. 1 to May 15} {Aug. 15 to Sept. 15}	2/3 oz.	3/4	4	6
Dandelion	Apr. 1 to July 25	1 oz.	1/2	5	10
Garlic	Apr. 20 to June 10	20 bulbs	1	6	13
Okra or gumbo	May 25 to July 15	1 oz.	1 1/2	12	9
Peanut	May 25 to July 1	1 1/2 lbs.	1	9	13
Potato onion	Apr. 10 to June 10	100 onions	1	12	12
Scorzonera	Apr. 15 to June 15	1 1/2 ozs.	1	4	14
Seakale	Apr. 15 to June 1	1 1/2 ozs.	1	12	2 years
					weeks
Shallots	Apr. 10 to June 10	150 onions	1	9	12

* Observe these distances also when planting garlic, potato onions and shallots.

C. EASY KINDS grown in groups. The groups are called hills, but customarily they are level with the surrounding garden. Groups or hills may be 6 inches in diameter, and the following distances apart in every direction: pole snap beans 3 ft., pole lima beans 3 ft., corn 3 ft., cucumber 4 ft., muskmelon 5 ft., bush squash 5 ft., trailing squash 6 to 8 ft., pumpkin 8 ft.

Kind	When to plant See notes in Chapter 15	Seeds for 25 hills	Depth ins.	Plants in each group or hill after thinning	Planting to harvest weeks
Beans, pole snap	May 1 to July 25	2 ozs.	2	5	11
" pole lima	May 15 to June 10	½ lb.	2	5	15
Corn	Apr. 20 under hotkaps May 1 to July 15	2 ozs.	1	3	11–15
Cucumber	Apr. 20 under hotkaps May 10 to July 15	½ oz.	1	3	9
Muskmelon	Apr. 20 under hotkaps May 15 to June 20	½ oz.	1	3	12–16
Pumpkin	May 15 to June 10	¾ oz.	1	3	15–18
Squash, bush	May 15 to July 9	1 oz.	1	3	10
" trailing	May 15 to June 15	1 oz.	1	3	13–15

D. NOT-SO-EASY ONES or UNUSUAL KINDS grown in groups or hills. Groups are level with rest of garden, 6 inches in diameter, and the following distances apart: citron 8 ft, cocozelle 6 to 8 ft., gherkin 4 ft., watermelon 8 ft., vegetable marrow, 6 ft., zucchini, 6 ft.

Kind	When to plant See notes in Chapter 15	Seed for 25 hills	Depth ins.	Plants in each group or hill after thinning	Planting to harvest weeks
Citron	May 15 to July 9	¾ oz.	1	3	11
Cocozelle	May 15 to July 15	½ oz.	1	3	9
Gherkin	May 10 to July 20	½ oz.	¾	3	9
Watermelon	May 15 to July 1	¾ oz.	1	3	12–14
Vegetable Marrow	May 15 to July 9	½ oz.	1	3	8
Zucchini	May 15 to July 9	1 oz.	1	3	10

Cress, curled Mustard, White London	Indoors, all winter	Scatter seeds thinly, about 6 to the square inch. Press in, don't cover. Shear when 2½ inches high for sandwiches or salads.
	Outdoors, any time	Grow on damp cloth, or in boxes or pots of soil indoors; grow in patches between hills of cucumbers or pumpkin outdoors. Cress is ready in 2½ weeks, mustard in 1½ weeks.

74

E. EASY KINDS usually planted out individually. Protect against cutworm, which see. Buy young plants, or sow seeds indoors in late winter, of broccoli, early cabbage, early cauliflower, eggplant, pepper and tomato. Sow outdoors in spring, Brussels sprouts, late cabbage, late cauliflower and kale.

Kind	Plants from one ounce of seed	When to set out See notes in Chapter 15	Minimum distance apart in 2-ft. rows	Time from planting to harvest
Broccoli	3000	Apr. 20 to July 30	2 feet	8 weeks
Brussels sprouts	3000	June 25 to July 10	2	13
Cabbage	3000	Apr. 20 to Aug. 1	2	13
Cauliflower	3000	Apr. 20 to July 25	2½	9
Eggplant	1000	May 15 to June 15	2½	11
Kale or borecole	3000	July 10 to Aug. 15	2	12
Pepper	1000	May 15 to June 15	1½	10
Tomato	1000	May 15 to July 10	4	10-12

F. NOT-SO-EASY ONES or UNUSUAL KINDS planted out individually. Sow seeds indoors in late winter of cardoon, celery, martynia and tobacco. Sow outdoors in spring and summer additional seeds of celery. Purchase rooted cuttings of sweet potatoes.

Kind	Plants from one ounce of seed	When to set out See notes in Chapter 15	Minimum distance apart in 2-ft. rows	Time from planting to harvest
Cardoon	500	May 10 to June 10	3 feet	16-18 weeks
Celery	3000	{May 1 to June 15 / Aug. 10 to Aug. 25}	½	15-17
Martynia	400	May 25 to June 20	3	10
Sweet Potato	....	June 1 to June 25	2	16
Tobacco	30,000	May 25 to July 15	2½	14
Watercress	Mix quarter-ounce of seed with one quart of sifted earth, roll into inch-size marbles; press marbles into mud of pond or slow stream at water-level.			

WHAT YOU SHOULD GET FROM YOUR GARDEN

There will be a wide variation between one season and another, and between one soil and another. Constant hoeing, weeding and thinning will give you more; poor soil and partial neglect will give you less. Here are average quantities that you may expect:

Kind	From 100 feet of row	From 25 hills. From 25 plants in the case of egg-plant, martynia, and tomato
Beans, snap bush	100 lbs. pods	. . . . . .
" snap pole	. . . . . .	75 lbs. pods
" bush lima	100 lbs. pods	. . . . . .
" pole lima	. . . . . .	75 lbs. pods
" broad or fava	75 lbs. pods	. . . . . .
" soy	100 lbs. pods	. . . . . .
Beet	100 lbs.	. . . . . .
Broccoli	8 bushels	. . . . . .
Brussels sprouts	80 quarts	. . . . . .
Cabbage	40 cabbages	. . . . . .
" Chinese	200 stalks	. . . . . .
Cardoon	35 heads	. . . . . .
Carrot	100 lbs.	. . . . . .
Cauliflower	40 cauliflowers	. . . . . .
Celeriac	100 lbs.	. . . . . .
Celery	200 heads	. . . . . .
Chicory	200 roots	. . . . . .
Citron	. . . . . .	75 citrons
Cocozelle	. . . . . .	200 cocozelles
Collards	12 bushels	. . . . . .
Corn	. . . . . .	150 ears
Cucumber	. . . . . .	300 cucumbers
Eggplant	. . . . . .	125 eggs
Endive or escarolle	125 heads	. . . . . .
Garlic	300 garlics	. . . . . .
Gherkin	. . . . . .	600 gherkins
Kale or borecole	8 bushels	. . . . . .
Kohlrabi	100 lbs.	. . . . . .
Leek	200 leeks	. . . . . .
Lettuce or romaine	100 heads	. . . . . .
Martynia	. . . . . .	100 lbs.
Muskmelon	. . . . . .	125 melons
Mustard, curled	6 bushels	. . . . . .

Kind	From 100 feet of row	From 25 hills. From 25 plants in the case of eggplant, martynia, and tomato
Onion	125 lbs.	......
Parsley	100 bunches	......
Parsnip	150 lbs.	......
Peas	125 lbs. pods	......
Peanut	100 lbs.	......
Pepper	150 lbs.	......
Potato	125 lbs.	......
Sweet potato	100 lbs.	......
Pumpkin	......	75 pumpkins
Radish, spring	100 bunches	......
" summer	75 bunches	......
" winter	75 lbs.	......
Rhubarb	......	150 stalks
Salsify	125 lbs.	......
Shallots	100 lbs.	......
Spinach	8 bushels	......
" New Zealand	4 bushels	......
Squash, bush	......	150 squashes
" trailing	......	175 squashes
" Zucchini	......	250 zucchinis
Swiss chard	10 bushels	......
Tomato	......	275 lbs.
Turnip	100 lbs.	......
" rutabaga	200 lbs.	......
Vegetable marrow	......	150 marrows
Watermelon	......	75 melons

To sum up: Plant hardy vegetables in spring as soon as the ground is frost-free and dry. Plant tender vegetables after danger of frost has passed. Many may be resown during the summer, but have in mind the time needed by them, and when the first frost in your locality is probable. The total produce you can get from even a small garden is surprising.

CHAPTER 15

Growing Vegetables Month by Month

At Christmas I no more desire a rose than wish a snow in May's new-fangled mirth; but like of each thing that in season grows.

WILLIAM SHAKESPEARE, 1564–1616. Love's Labour's Lost. Act 1

THESE dates are based on conditions in the Middle Atlantic states, where the last killing frost is expected about April 20. Delay or advance the dates if the last killing frost in your locality is later or earlier than April 20.

It is suggested that you re-read the introduction to Chapter 14.

JANUARY. The planning month.

Read garden books, the garden page in newspapers of last year, and magazine articles.

Plan the year's work. Write for seed, nursery and hardware catalogues.

Order seeds, roots, fertilizers, insecticides, fungicides and plant labels.

WHITE LONDON MUSTARD. *Here it is growing in a pot for sandwich fillings. Produce cress the same way, but sow the cress a week earlier than mustard.*

Buy tools. Watch your local paper for offerings of manure.

If you have the facilities, plant mushroom spawn in a frost-free barn or outhouse, in beds of fresh horse manure mixed with leaves. Force indoors witloof, rhubarb, asparagus and seakale.

In a sunny window sow boxes of mustard, cress; plant chives, onion-sets and mint in pots or indoor window-boxes.

Around the 15th of the month, make sowings indoors of onion seeds for large bulbs outdoors later; Prizetaker, Valencia or Sweet Spanish are suitable varieties.

FEBRUARY. The get-ready month.

Place old barrels, boxes or bushel baskets over large roots in the garden of rhubarb, witloof, asparagus or seakale; mound first with trash, and then with earth against the sides.

In most localities, up to 100 pounds per 1000 square feet of crushed limestone might be spread with advantage over your garden. Avoid the neighborhood of rhododendrons, azaleas and mountain laurel.

Get lighter-colored sweeter rhubarb ahead of time this way. Try it with asparagus also.

MARCH. Indoor seed-sowing month.

Side-dress asparagus, rhubarb, globe and Jerusalem artichokes, horse-radish, Egyptian onions and sorrel with 5–10–5 fertilizer. Hoe under the surface at month's end when the land has dried. Build a hot-bed. Start a compost-heap.

Commence removing the cover of manure, compost, straw or salt-hay from winter-sown spinach.

1st to 15th. Sow in pots or boxes indoors seeds of beet, broccoli, cabbage, cauliflower, chard, kohlrabi, lettuce and parsley.

Last sowings of large onion seeds indoors may be made.

16th to 30th. Sow in pots or boxes indoors seeds of eggplant, pepper and tomato; martynia and tobacco if you propose to grow them.

Sow in 4-inch pots seeds of New Wonder Bantam corn, for groups to be planted out in May. Pots of green snap beans may also be started. For both use six seeds to a pot; thin to three plants. Or put seeds of corn or beans one inch apart in upturned grass sods; thin the plants to stand 2 inches apart.

As soon as the land is free of frost and is dry, spade under sheep manure, bonemeal, hyper-humus or compost, if you prefer to dig in spring. Spread more of these on the dug surface and rake smooth. Approximate amounts would be 50 lbs. sheep manure, 25 lbs. bonemeal, 250 lbs. hyper-humus or two bushels or more of compost; all per 1000 square feet. On land which was spaded in the autumn and left rough, spread these same materials, and rake smooth. These quantities are for (1) digging under. Use identical quantities before you (2) rake the rough dug-over surface. If you dig in spring, the total would be twice these: one dressing the depth of your spade; the other, your rake's depth.

Dig up parsnip, salsify and scorzonera roots grown last year; store in a cool, dry place, using in the kitchen as needed.

Sow outdoors, provided the soil is dry, early round smooth or dimpled peas, spinach, chard, fava beans and spring radish; Chinese cabbage, curled mustard and turnips.

APRIL. The busy cool month.

1st to 9th. Sow outdoors wrinkled peas, beet, carrot, chard, corn salad, chervil, chicory, collards, dandelion, kohlrabi, leek, lettuce, onion seeds, parsley, parsnip and spring radish.

Make last sowing of the spring of Chinese cabbage and curled mustard.

10th to 15th. Plant onion sets, multiplier onions, potato onions and shallots. Last severe frost may be expected around this date.

Plant globe and Jerusalem artichokes, asparagus, horseradish and rhubarb roots.

Sow outdoors salsify, celeriac, scorzonera, seakale.

16th to 30th. Make last sowings of peas and fava beans.

Set out broccoli, cabbage and cauliflower.

Plant potatoes; plant garlic.

Turnip seeds may still be sown.

Under hotkaps sow corn, cucumber and muskmelon.

MAY. The busy warm month.

1st to 9th. Sow dwarf snap beans, shell beans, pole snap beans and corn.

Sow seeds of annual herbs and watercress.

Plant out early celery; plant herb roots, especially mint.

Make last sowing for the spring of chervil and collards.

10th to 14th. Sow bush lima beans, cucumber and gherkin.

Plant out cardoon.

Make last sowings of leek for the year, last sowing of the spring of turnip.

15th to 24th. Sow New Zealand spinach, soy beans, pole lima beans, muskmelon, pumpkin, squash, citron, cocozelle, watermelon, vegetable marrow and zucchini.

Set out eggplant, pepper and tomato; corn and beans also if you started them indoors.

Make last sowing of the spring of corn salad and spring spinach.

25th. Plant out martynia and tobacco.

31st. Make last planting for the year of potatoes.

Thin all crops; seedlings of beet, kohlrabi, leek, lettuce, mustard, onion, parsley, parsnip and chard may be replanted to fill gaps or to make new rows. Thinnings of most others may be washed and used in the kitchen.

Sow through the month: Snap and pole snap beans, shell beans, beet, carrot, celeriac, celery, chicory, corn, dandelion, lettuce, onion, parsley, parsnip, radish, salsify, scorzonera, seakale, New Zealand spinach, chard. And the following may be planted: onion sets, garlic, potatoes, potato onions, shallots, broccoli, cabbage and cauliflower.

Tomato seeds may be sown outdoors for transplanting, giving a fall crop.

JUNE. A busy hot month.

1st to 9th. Sow okra and peanuts; plant sweet potatoes.
Make last sowing of the year of chicory and seakale.

10th to 14th. Make last sowing of the year of pole lima beans, onion seeds, parsnip and pumpkin.
Make last planting of the year of cardoon, garlic, potato onions, multiplier onions and shallots.

15th to 19th. Sow endive and kale outdoors for transplanting; sow rows of summer radish and rutabaga.
Make last sowing of bush lima beans, celeriac, curled parsley, salsify, scorzonera, soy beans and trailing squash.
Make last seeding until September 1 of spring radish.
Spring planting ends of celery and resumes August 10.
Final planting-out date for eggplant and pepper.

20th to 24th. Make last sowings for the year of shell beans and muskmelon. Last date for planting out martynia.

25th to 30th. Sow turnip for autumn; set out Brussels sprouts. Last date for planting sweet potatoes.
The following may also be sown this month: Dwarf snap beans, beet, carrot, lettuce, New Zealand spinach, chard, dandelion, pole snap beans, corn, cucumber, bush squash, citron, cocozelle, gherkin, watermelon, vegetable marrow and zucchini; also rooting parsley, okra and peanut.
And these may still be set out: onion sets, broccoli, cabbage, cauliflower, tobacco and tomato.

JULY. Another busy hot month.

Spray all vine crops, cucumbers and the like, with bordeaux mixture for fungoid diseases; and dust with ¾ per cent rotenone for squashbugs and other insects.

1st to 9th. Make last sowing for the year of peanuts, bush squash, vegetable marrow, zucchini, watermelon and citron.

10th to 14th. Set out kale plants.

Sow kohlrabi and winter radish for fall.

Make last planting for the year of onion sets and Brussels sprouts.

Last date for setting out tomatoes for a fall crop.

15th to 19th. Make last sowing for the year of beet, carrot, chard, corn, cucumber, cocozelle, gherkin, rutabaga, okra, New Zealand spinach.

Sow a few tomato seeds outdoors if you are going to plant some in your cold-frame.

20th to 24th. Sow Chinese cabbage for an autumn crop.

25th to 31st. Sow chervil.

Last month for planting out tobacco. Broccoli and cabbage plants may still be set out, and the following seeds may still be sown: Dwarf snap beans, endive, kale, lettuce. summer radish and chard (up to 19th).

Last chance for sowing pole snap beans, dandelion and turnip; last chance for planting out cauliflower.

AUGUST. Third hot month; not so busy.

1st to 9th. Sow curled mustard. Last date for planting out cabbage,

Sow a few seeds of lettuce and endive for planting in your cold-frame in the fall.

Plant celery and endive.

10th to 14th. Sow collards and spinach. Last date for sowing dwarf snap beans, kohlrabi, curled mustard, Chinese cabbage and chervil.

15th to 19th. Last day for sowing endive, lettuce and winter radish. Last opportunity to set out kale.

20th to 31st. Make last sowing for the year of summer radish; and the last planting out of celery.

The following seeds may still be sown: spring spinach, collards and corn salad.

SEPTEMBER. The harvest month.

Plant rhubarb, asparagus, perennial herb plants, Egyptian onions; any time this month.

Earth up maturing celery.

If you have a heated greenhouse you may sow in it seeds of: Dwarf snap beans, beet, carrot, endive, lettuce, parsley and radish. And you may plant tomatoes in it.

In a cold-frame, unheated greenhouse or sun-heated pit you may plant seedlings of tomato. Lettuce and endive seedlings may also be planted there, and seeds of beet and carrot sown.

10th. Make last sowing of the year of collards.

15th. Make last sowings of corn salad and spinach.

25th. Make last sowings of spring radish.

OCTOBER. Leaf-raking month.

First killing frost may be expected around the 10th.

Dig beet, carrot, turnip, rutabaga, and other root crops, and store for the winter.

Dig some parsnips, salsify and scorzonera for immediate use; allow the balance to remain in the garden until spring.

Cover rhubarb with manure, compost or leaves.

Rake up all the fallen leaves you can, and build a new compost-heap with them.

Spread on land which has been cropped 50 lbs. of sheep manure, 25 lbs. of bonemeal, 250 lbs. of hyper-humus, or two bushels or more of compost, all per 1000 square feet; dig and leave rough over winter.

15th. Sow spring radish in the cold-frame or sun-heated pit.

NOVEMBER. The clean-up month.

Cut off and burn asparagus foliage. Also burn remains of any other plants that show evidence of disease; put the balance on your compost-heap. Be sure to destroy and not put on the heap any sick or yellowed cabbages, diseased-riddled corn leaves and stems, or continuous trouble may be expected. Let only healthy leaves, weeds and vegetable refuse go into compost.

Smooth some areas of soil, wait for the land to freeze, scatter spinach seeds on the frozen surface, aiming for about two seeds to each inch of row. Cover the seeds with a light dressing, two inches thick, of manure or compost; or a four-inch layer of straw or salt-hay. Spring growth will start early, and when you see it, take away the covering a little at a time, allowing two weeks to remove all.

DECEMBER. Put the garden to bed.

Clean up. A tidy garden is always a good one.

Wash wooden seed flats; wash clay pots.

Repair tools. Wash, sandpaper and paint with oil all metal parts; paint the handles red, yellow or blue, so that you can find them readily when you lay them around in the summer.

VEGETABLES IN THE SOUTH

There are three seasons for planting vegetables in the southern states:

The following should be put in during October and November, with a repeat seeding from February 15 to March 15. They are mostly kinds that will tolerate slight frost:

Cabbage, carrot, cauliflower, celery, collards, kale, lettuce, mustard, onion, parsley, parsnip, peas, potato, radish, salsify, spinach and turnip.

When danger of frost has passed, from March 1 to April 15, depending upon the latitude and height above sea-level, these may be planted:

Snap beans, lima beans, corn, cucumber, muskmelon, squash, eggplant, okra, pepper and tomato.

To sum up:
WINTER. Plan; sow indoors.
EARLY SPRING. Sow and plant the tougher things outdoors.
LATE SPRING. Sow and plant the tender things outdoors.
SUMMER. Crop and replant.
AUTUMN. Final big harvest.

IT'S AS SIMPLE AS THAT

CHAPTER 16

Eat Vegetables for Robust Health

The kindly fruits of the earth.
BOOK OF COMMON PRAYER

THE diet requirements of the average person consists of proteins, fats and carbohydrates; the proportions vary with the preferences of the individual.

The greater part of these can be obtained from your garden, supplemented by dairy-products, eggs, fish and meats. Vegetables supply most of the minerals your body needs. Of the vitamins known at present it seems that five of the six most important are carotene, thiamin, ascorbic acid, riboflavin and nicotinic acid or niacin; you can grow all of them. The other, antirachitic "sunshine" vitamin D, is about the only important one you cannot get from the garden; but you will find plenty of sunshine there.

VEGETABLES THAT SUPPLY PROTEIN—The body-builder

All beans, peas and peanuts; and the leafy vegetables, collards and kale. These supplement the proteins taken in the form of meat, poultry, fish, dairy products and eggs.

VEGETABLES THAT FURNISH FATS—The energy producers

Soy beans, peanuts, dried beans and sweet potatoes. Most garden products have a slimming effect, but in excess these four may tend to increase weight.

VEGETABLES THAT GIVE CARBOHYDRATES—The body-fuels

All beans and peas, potatoes and sweet potatoes, corn and Jerusalem artichokes. These also may increase weight, when used to excess.

THE CALORIES IN VEGETABLES

They are measures of energy, derived from the proteins, carbohydrates and fats. A moderately active person needs from 2500 to 3000 calories, a sedentary one 2200 to 2500 calories. More calories than needed may result in overweight.

High calorie vegetables: All peas and beans, potatoes and sweet potatoes, peanuts and corn.
Medium calorie vegetables: Parsnip and other root vegetables, winter squash, leek and pulling onions, cooked green leafy vegetables.
Low calorie vegetables: The raw green leafy vegetables in salads, tomatoes, summer squash and Chinese cabbage.

The number of calories, and the vitamins, in foods, fresh, cooked or dried, can be found in Handbook No. 8 on the Composition of Foods, 1950, issued by the Bureau of Human Nutrition, U. S. Department of Agriculture, Washington 25, D. C.

THE MINERALS IN VEGETABLES

These chemicals are necessary for its growth and maintenance of health. The most important are calcium, phosphorus and iron.

To absorb calcium and phosphorus, the antirachitic or sunshine vitamin D must be taken with them. This vitamin is almost missing in vegetables; so to benefit from the minerals, a diet to include vitamin D is necessary: butter, milk and cream, eggs, liver and fish-liver oil, salmon and sardines.

VEGETABLES HIGH IN CALCIUM

Necessary for bones and teeth. Prevents excessive bleeding; regulates the muscles and nerves, including those of the heart. Regulates other body functions. Best sources of calcium are the dairy products; following are vegetables furnishing it: The green leafy vegetables, especially turnip greens and spinach, mustard, green salads, baked beans and soy beans.

VEGETABLES HIGH IN PHOSPHORUS

With calcium, this element is necessary for building bones and sound teeth. Found in all parts of the body. Keeps the blood slightly alkaline. The following furnish the most phosphorus: All beans and peas, cooked green vegetables, parsnip and corn.

VEGETABLES HIGH IN IRON

Aids the formation of hemoglobin in blood and muscle; necessary in all growing body cells. Lack of iron results in anemia. The following give us iron: All beans, spinach and other cooked green leaf vegetables, watercress, rutabaga and cucumber.

OTHER CHEMICALS IN TRACE AMOUNTS

Iodine. Only those foods grown near the sea can be depended upon to contain iodine. In the Middle West and around the Great Lakes, the so-called goiter belts, it is desirable to purchase some vegetables brought in from the coast, and to include dulce, Irish moss, sea-fish and shell-fish in the diet, and to use iodized salt. Crushed oyster-shell, as a source of lime in the soil, may have some merit.

Sodium and Chlorine. Sufficient of these are found in most vegetables, and in the table-salt used in cooking.

Copper. In minute quantities this is needed to enable iron to be assimilated. Sufficient is present in nearly all vegetables, notably asparagus, all beans, beet, cooked green leafy vegetables, parsley and peas.

Sulphur. This is in nearly all proteins, and if high-protein foods are used in average amounts, sufficient will be obtained.

ACIDITY AND ALKALINITY

A physician or a dietician should be consulted if you feel that some vegetables are too acid-forming for you. Many of them are not nearly so in their end-results as are meat, fish or cereals. A few vegetables and fruits are even found to be alkaline in their final result.

GROW YOUR OWN VITAMINS

Your garden can be a food factory, and a source of health. Fully ripened vegetables, gathered and eaten immediately, are not only so much better tasting, but they contain more vitamins. Raw vegetables are superior to cooked ones, and in leafy vegetables, green leaves are better than blanched ones.

Carotene, or vitamin A. Known as the eyesight vitamin, because it is believed to help night-blindness. Encourages normal growth and health; claimed to aid resistance to infection. Cooking reduces it but little. The body stores it, ready to be drawn upon as needed; but see that the daily intake is adequate. Following are high in carotene: All the cooked green leafy vegetables, carrots, parsley, pepper, watercress and salads.

Thiamin, or vitamin B$_1$. The digestive vitamin. Stimulates appetite, regulates the nerves and promotes growth. The modern well-rounded diet has almost eliminated the disease beriberi, for which lack of this vitamin was thought to be a cause. Eat some of the following generously every day, for thiamin cannot be stored in the body. Water-soluble, some may be lost in cooking; so boil lightly and use the cooking water in soups, gravies and stews; chill it, and add to the morning tomato-juice. The following furnish thiamin: All beans, peas and peanuts, cooked green leafy vegetables, watercress, endive, tomato, artichokes, asparagus, corn, potato and sweet potato.

Ascorbic Acid, or vitamin C. Helps the gums, builds teeth and bones, helps maintain strong capillary blood-vessels; it prevents scurvy. It is water-soluble; much may be lost in cooking, so boil lightly if at all, and use cooking-water in soups, gravies and stews; chill it and add to the morning tomato-juice. Eat generously of some of these every day, because ascorbic acid cannot be stored in the body. Best sources are raw greens in salads, also the boiled green leafy vegetables, especially turnip greens, mustard and beet greens; asparagus, kohlrabi, parsnip, peppers, tomato, beans and peas.

Riboflavin, vitamin G or B$_2$. Promotes healthy skin and hair. Aids the nervous and digestive systems. Promotes bodily vigor; tends to prolong the prime of life, and increases resistance to certain infections. It is water-soluble: some may be dissolved in the cooking-water, though light rather than heat is the destroying factor; however, boil lightly and use the cooking water in soups, gravies and stews. Chill it and add to the morning tomato-juice. Eat generously the B_2 vegetables every day, because riboflavin cannot be stored in the body. Following are the chief sources: the cooked green leafy vegetables, the salad greens, asparagus, peppers, beans and peas.

Nicotinic Acid or Niacin. This is the pellagra-preventive vitamin, and is sometimes referred to as vitamin PP in consequence. A lack of it causes general weakness, loss of appetite and weight, skin eruptions and mouth-sores. It is water-soluble; some of the vitamin may be lost in cooking, so boil lightly and use the water in soups, gravies and stews; chill it and add to the morning tomato-juice. Eat generously of some of the vegetables containing it every day, as niacin is not stored in the body. Here they are: the boiled green leafy vegetables like spinach and turnip-greens, peas and peanuts, lettuce salad, tomato and carrot.

GROW YOUR OWN SAUCES AND PICKLES

Here is a formula nearly a century old for **Tomato Sauce:** Take half a peck of clean, dry tomatoes from the garden, 3 pints of vinegar, 4 large onions, previously boiled, 2 pounds salt and 1 ounce cayenne pepper. Cut up the fresh tomatoes and the boiled onions, and boil for an hour; beat and strain. Simmer for a further half-hour, adding the vinegar, pepper and salt, and strain again.

Put into clean jars; keep the lids loose for a day, and then seal.

A fifty-year-old recipe for **Mixed Pickle:** Take ½ gallon of vinegar, which you boil and allow to cool, 2 ounces bruised ginger, 2 ounces powdered mustard, 2 ounces salt, 1 ounce whole mustard seeds, ¾ ounce turmeric, ½ ounce ground black pepper, 2 ounces cayenne pepper; along with an assortment of your vegetables.

Take a jar or crock with a tight-fitting lid. In a pint of the vinegar mix the mustard, turmeric, pepper and cayenne; stir until free from lumps and put, with the rest of the vinegar, along with the ginger, salt, mustard seeds, into the crock and stand in the kitchen. Stir every day with a wooden spoon.

As vegetables become ready in the garden, wash them and let them dry; and put them into the pickle. Cut cauliflower into small bunches, cut snap beans, celery, cucumber, onions and peppers into slices. Put in martynia and nasturtium fruits, small gherkins and young radish seed-pods whole.

Drop them into the pickle raw, adding until there is no room for more but the vinegar still shows, always giving a daily stir. When the batch is finished, put into jars, seal and keep 12 months before using.

One way to **Pickle Onions.** Take 2 quarts of vinegar, 4 teaspoons of allspice, 4 of whole black peppers. Peel off enough skin of small pickling onions with the fingers, or use a silver knife, to make them look white and semi-transparent, which means a heavy peeling. Instead of pickling onions you may use sliced larger onions or shallots, sliced or whole.

Put them into dry jars as they are peeled or sliced, and cover them with boiled vinegar which has been allowed to cool. Put in each jar its share of the allspice and peppers; seal, and in two weeks they should be fit for use, and continue for 6 or 7 months.

Secure other good recipes, and use the following from your garden:

Snap beans	Green nasturtium seeds from the flower garden.
Beet (boiled)	Onions
Red cabbage	Peppers
Cauliflower	Green seed-pods from radishes that have bolted
Cucumber	to flower.
Gherkin	Shallots
Kohlrabi, diced	Tomato
Martynia	Turnip and rutabaga, diced
	Watermelon

Flavor with these in moderation:

Dill seeds, garlic, horseradish, mustard seeds, tarragon.

To sum up: Your garden can produce most of the food you need, including proteins, some fats and carbohydrates, with the essential vitamins and minerals. You are likely to get better flavor, and more vitamins, from the vegetables you grow than from those you buy.

CHAPTER 17

Vegetables Commonly Raised in the United States and Canada

WITH THE MORE POPULAR KITCHEN HERBS

*There's rosemary, that's for remembrance; Pray, love,
remember.*

WILLIAM SHAKESPEARE, 1564–1616. Hamlet. Act 4

WHY USE BOTANICAL NAMES?

THE semi-scientific language of the botanist, based on Latin or
Greek, often describes the plant and where it grew originally.
Everyone, all over the world, knows what you mean when you
write *vicia faba*. The common name varies: an American would
call it fava bean; a Spaniard, haba; a German, garten-bohnen; an
Englishman, broad-bean or just bean.

Vicia faba fixes it. If you want to read further about it, its name
is in every reference book, and you will not confuse it with snap-
bean, lima bean or soy bean.

WHY USE THE BOTANICAL ORDER, OR FAMILY NAME?

In this case, leguminosæ. Chiefly because when you select a
plant to grow in land that previously was occupied by another,
it is best to have one of a different family. Let a leguminous plant
be followed, let us say, by one of the compositæ or umbelliferæ.

It emphasizes that many vegetables are related, often wanting
similar soil or culture, often taking food from the soil in the same
proportions, often being attacked by the same bugs or subject to
the same diseases.

Sometimes we learn something from the family name. In this case we are reminded that the seeds of plants in this family contain legumin, a vegetable protein; causing a meal of beans to be as nourishing as one of meat.

ANISE

Pimpinella anisum. *Umbelliferæ.* An easily grown aromatic herb. Sow seed in late April, and thin the plants to stand 6 inches apart. Claimed to aid digestion, it is used in candy-making, cake-making and general cooking; and a few leaves will improve any salad. It grows 16 inches high; with its white flowers it is an attractive addition to the herb garden.

ANISE. *An easily grown annual herb.*

ARTICHOKE

There are two very different plants with this name.

GLOBE ARTICHOKE

Cynara scolymus. *Compositæ.* It grows 5 feet high, and is practically a giant thistle with large purple flowers. Before they open, however, the enormous fleshy buds are cut off to become the artichokes with which we are familiar; they are served raw in salads, or boiled.

GLOBE ARTICHOKE. *A large swollen flowerbud.*

Seed may be sown May 1; set the resulting plants 2 feet by 3 feet apart, and you ought to get some artichokes the following year. In the north it is a good plan to "mulch" them; put a 2½-inch covering of leaves, compost, manure or peatmoss over the roots after the land has frozen; use seaweed if you live near the coast. Your bed should be in production four years.

The plants increase in size, spreading outwards; from those which give you the most or largest artichokes, cut with a spade down to the roots some of the largest pieces of the outer growth, and plant them instead of sowing more seed for new plantings.

Globe artichokes are heavy feeders, needing rich soil, with manure dug in deeply when preparing the land; side-dress with fertilizer, and apply liquid manure to the ground around the plants during summer.

JERUSALEM ARTICHOKE or GIRASOLE

Helianthus tuberosus. *Compositæ.* This is a handsome 10-foot-high perennial yellow sunflower. Tubers that cook like close potatoes are produced in quantity under ground; they contain sugar, and the carbohydrate inulin instead of the starch of potatoes. Plant the tubers as soon as you get them at 2 feet by 2 feet spacing, and dig them as needed, or dig them in autumn and place in boxes of dry sand in the garage, away from frost. Jerusalem artichokes will

JERUSALEM ARTICHOKE. *These have underground tubers that may be dug any time.*

stand a fair amount of shade, if the sunny spots in the garden are filled up, but land filled with tree roots must be avoided. It is a wild plant, found in Canada and the northeast, so should do well in your garden.

ASPARAGUS

Asparagus officinalis. *Liliaceæ.* Mistakenly called sparrow-grass or sparagrass; the professional grower often refers to it as grass. A plot 8 feet by 50 feet will take 200 roots, enough for an average family, and you will have a surplus for canning. In well-manured land, dig trenches 12 inches deep and 2 feet apart; hoe into the bottom of the trench 3 pounds of rotted manure, or one pound of hyper-humus, and ¼ pound of 5–10–5 fertilizer per running foot; along the trench-bottom place a 3-inch ridge of soil that contains no added plant-food; on this ridge set the roots 12 inches apart, straddling

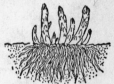

ASPARAGUS. *This should not be gathered until the third spring from planting; but read how a temporary bed helps you conquer your impatience.*

it, with the rootlets festooning both sides. Cover 4 inches, and as the asparagus grows, gradually fill the trench. It tolerates light shade.

Let asparagus grow two full seasons before cutting. But if you are impatient, plant two beds; gather nothing from one until the third year; this is your permanent bed. Gather all you wish from the second, a temporary bed, and which you dig up when you start gathering from the permanent bed. The asparagus we eat are the young stems which show above ground in spring; we cut them two inches below the surface, and get stems 6 inches or longer; the richer the soil the thicker they are. Do not cut all of them; allow three to five of them from each root to grow and develop into stems and leaves.

93

Buy 2- or 3-year-old roots, but you can sow seed if you are willing to wait an extra year, three years in all. One ounce sows 100 feet of drill, and some time in the summer the young plants should be set out 12 inches apart.

Extra large roots are sometimes planted indoors in late winter; or some roots outdoors are covered with boxes or inverted baskets, heaped up first with earth and then with leaves, to give us asparagus ahead of time. Or they may be planted in a hot-bed. Growing plants out of their normal season is termed "forcing."

Asparagus is a healthful food, possessing mild aperient and diuretic properties, the latter meaning it increases the flow of urine.

Asparagus rust comes from a fungous parasite, causing sickly plants. The variety Mary Washington is recommended, because it has a marked resistance to this condition bred into it.

BALM

Melissa officinalis. *Labiatæ.* A perennial aromatic herb growing 1½ feet high. The lemon-scented leaves are added to salads and may be used for flavoring food, vinegars, confections and wines. Balm tea is an old remedy for fevers, asthma and headache. For drying, cut the stems just before the flowers open. Buy roots, and plant them 18 inches apart.

LETTUCE-LEAVED BASIL. *This is the form to grow for the kitchen.*

POT BASIL. *Makes an aromatic plant for a window.*

BASIL or BASILICO

Ocimum basilicum. *Labiatæ.* A 2-foot-high aromatic herb. Annual, it is readily grown from seed sown in mid-spring. Use it for flavoring stews, soups and salads. An infusion makes a skin lotion, and is used internally. Snuff, made by powdering the dry leaves, is a headache remedy.

Bush- or pot-basil is a small form, and lettuce-leaved basil a much larger one, with bigger leaves.

94

BEANS

All are members of the *Leguminosæ* family.

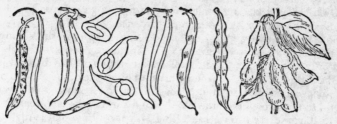

Left, *horticultural bean with red spotted pods; asparagus or yard-long pole bean; dwarf green beans.* In center, *snap beans in section, flat at top,* saddleback *in center,* round *at bottom; dwarf wax beans, old homestead or Kentucky wonder pole bean; a dry-shell bean.* Extreme right, *soy beans.*

DWARF or SNAP BEANS

Phaseolus vulgaris humilis. Both green-pod and wax-pod kinds may be grown, wax-pods being an inviting cream-yellow. Not many years ago they were known as string-beans, and in the kitchen you had to take a bean, cut nearly through the top, tear away the string to the bottom, nearly cut through again, and pull the string up to the point where you started. To top-and-tail beans was a daily nuisance-chore in the kitchen. Breeding has eliminated the strings, and we call them snap beans now; but many believe that their flavor is not quite so good as the old stringy types. Some varieties have pods round in section: like tubes if you cut one in two; these are preferred for canning. Others are flat, others again midway between the two, and are called saddle-back. Here are some good varieties: Green-pods, round and saddle-back: contender, longreen, ranger, stringless black valentine, stringless green-pod, supergreen, tendergreen, top crop, wade and stringless refugee. Last named is best for pickling or canning, as well as for immediate use; but plant it July 25, as it does not do so well when sown early.

Green-pods that are flat: plentiful and streamliner, the latter with white seeds; a surplus can be allowed to ripen on the plants for excellent shell-beans.

Three green beans that are now outdated, but once were very popular, are black valentine, bountiful and refugee 1000 to 1. These all have strings when they are more than half size.

Good wax-pod sorts, all without strings, are: brittle wax, cherokee and puregold, all round or saddle-backs. Early golden wax is one of the finest flat stringless wax beans.

Dwarf snap beans are sometimes grown in a greenhouse or heated frame during winter by professional gardeners.

Sow seed of dwarf snap beans 2 to 3 inches apart in drills about 2 inches deep, the rows 2 feet apart. Hoe frequently between the plants, but only when the land and the plants are dry; each time draw an inch of the soil to both sides of the plants to support them, to keep the pods off the ground and to insure good drainage. Remove plants which crowd so that those in the row finally stand 4 inches asunder. Plant a 10– or 20–ft. row every two weeks starting May 1, continue until August 10.

When gathering beans, separate each pod from the plant with the thumb-nail, and take care not to pull on the plant, or you will injure the smaller roots and stop production.

POLE or CLIMBING SNAP BEANS

They will climb in a spiral around a stout 8-foot pole without any help from you. Erect the poles 3 feet apart, sow 8 beans in a circle around the base of each about May 10; thin to five plants to each pole. One pound plants 200 poles. Here are three good ones: **Old homestead or Kentucky wonder, Phaseolus vulgaris.** Pods are tender, stringless when young, hang in clusters and are a silvery green. Begins to yield in eleven weeks, and thereafter bears continuously. A good deep-freeze kind.

Scarlet runner, Phaseolus coccineus. Good for growing on a pole, and quite the best for climbing up a wire fence, when you allow 2 pounds per 100 running feet. Has a superior flavor to most sorts, but it has to be topped-and-tailed for it has strings. Flowers are bright red.

Yard-Long Asparagus Bean, Vigna sesquipedalis. A curiosity, and yet a good bean. Pods are too feet long, narrow and round.

LIMA BEANS

Sow only after danger of frost is over and the land thoroughly warm. Sow bush or dwarf sorts in rows 2 feet apart and about 2 inches deep with the beans 3 inches apart in the row, eye down, thinning later so the plants stand 6 inches apart. For pole kinds sow about ten to a group and thin to five plants to the pole; poles may be 8 feet long and spaced 3 feet apart. When the stems have reached the top, pinch them and you will

LIMA BEANS.
Plant eye down, but only after the soil is dry and quite warm.

increase the yield. Some gardeners sow under glass and set the plants out May 25; they put pairs of beans in small pots and transfer the young plants with the soil around them intact, later destroying one of the plants. Or they dig some thick turf from an unimportant part of the lawn, turning the sod over and planting in the dirt side. A mason's pointing trowel is used to cut the turf into squares which are set out at planting time, each square containing a bean plant.

Lima beans take almost the whole season to develop. You cannot sow them for succession, except the dwarf variety, Early Giant, which is rapid enough to afford a second planting in June.

One pound of lima beans plants 50 feet of row or 50 poles.

Good varieties are:

Pole limas, Phaseolus limensis: challenger, king of the garden, sunnybrook.

Bush limas, Phaseolus limenanus: early giant, Fordhook 242 (the number is important), and triumph.

All varieties are suitable for deep freezing.

FAVA or BROAD BEANS

Vicia faba. *Leguminosæ.* These differ from American types in that they do best in cool weather; light frost does them no harm, and they must be planted early in deep, rich, clay-loam soil. Spray or dust continuously against aphis and blight.

The favorite variety is English windsor. Heavy pods are produced in pairs with three or four large beans in each. They are tender and delicious. One pound of the seed beans, which look like thick lima beans, will plant 50 feet set four to the foot; reduce the seedlings so that they stand 6 inches apart. If, despite dusting and spraying, the aphis are not controlled, pinch off and burn the tips of the plants where most of them congregate.

FAVA. *The one bean you sow early. Aphids are fond of it; so much so that it is not an easy plant to grow.*

SOY BEANS

Glycine Max. *Leguminosæ.* These are highly nutritious, but they take up a lot of room in the garden and are troublesome to shell. If you like them and have the room, buy seed of an edible variety from a seedsman in your locality; he may recommend the varieties bansai or mendola.

Sow 6 seeds to the foot one inch deep, thin to 2 to the foot. Spray or dust with preparations containing rotenone against the Japanese beetle.

In 12 to 16 weeks cut the plants to the ground and gather the clusters of pods; soak these in boiling water for 5 minutes, and you will then be able to shell them with little difficulty.

BAKED BEANS

Varieties used are pea or navy, white kidney and red kidney, all Phaseolus vulgaris. Their pods are unsuitable for use as snap beans.

When the pods begin to ripen, cut the plants and let them dry on the garage or barn floor; place them in foot-thick layers and beat them unmercifully with a flail, which is a whip with part of the thong a wooden slat. Rake up the dry stems and burn them, sweep up the beans and chaff. Separate these by tossing them and catching them again in a bowl on a windy day or in the current of an electric fan.

Any surplus you may have of other beans may be ripened, dried and flailed in the same way to get dried shell beans.

Lima beans are used in the green shell state, as also are soy beans as a rule. The variety of dwarf snap bean, horticultural, is mostly used this way. This and other snap beans are allowed to ripen to the point where the pod begins to get brownish, but the beans within are still soft, providing a new vegetable to some.

BEET

Beta vulgaris. *Chenopodiaceæ.* Beets are easy to grow, especially in medium-loam or sandy-loam soils. They are uninjured by light frosts. Sow seeds ½ inch deep at two-week intervals from early spring to mid-July; thin to 3 inches between the seedlings. Thinnings may be transplanted elsewhere or may be washed, boiled and served as spinach.

SOME BEETS. Beginning at left: *wonder, Detroit, winter keeper, long red, sugar-beet, and mangel* on the right.

A few seeds of radish sown in the same row with the beets will come through first, breaking any soil-crust, marking clearly the row and showing you where to start hoeing. Pull the radishes when they are mature; your crop of beets will not be reduced by this two-kinds-in-one scheme.

Beets may be kept for winter use in boxes of sand in a cool cellar; or in a pit outdoors, dry, well-drained, lined with hay and ventilated. Another good way to keep them is to pickle them.

Beets are a valuable food, and the leaves or tops are of greater nutritional value than are the roots. There is considerable variation in the shape of beets; reliable varieties include Egyptian, which has a very flat root; wonder, a thick-flat root; crimson globe and Detroit, globe-shaped; winter keeper, a large top-shape kind with mostly green leaves; long red, a long parsnip-shape root—the most economical, but its depth in the land makes you dig each one out with a fork. Sugar-beet, much grown in the Middle West, and one of our main sources of table-sugar, is parsnip-like and yellow. Mangels are very large and coarse beets, some red and others yellow, grown to enormous individual weights as winter food for cattle.

BORECOLE. See Kale.

BROCCOLI

Brassica oleracea italica. *Cruciferæ*. A delicious green vegetable which cooks in 20 minutes, with little unpleasant odor. Sow indoors in March, and plant out 24 inches apart; make several later sowings for a continuing yield, ending with one in late June for autumn.

On this continent we grow mostly the sprouting broccolis, De Cicco, Propageno

Broccoli. *Easy to grow; but watch for cabbage worms and plant lice. See chapter 19.*

or Italian market, delicious types which produce a compact, bluish-green head, called the king sprout; after this is cut, the plants develop side shoots, each bearing a small head. Broccoli-Rape is a similar type, but with smaller and less tight heads. It is good eating and is ready for the kitchen when the first yellow flower appears.

In Europe many related types of broccoli are seen, mostly being like cauliflower but hardier and coarser. One of these sometimes grown in America is the Italian purple, which loses some of its color when boiled and arrives on the table mostly green. This is very like a colored cauliflower and is often listed in the catalogues as such.

BRUSSELS SPROUTS

Brassica oleracea gemmifera. *Cruciferæ.* This splendid vegetable is at its best after first autumn frosts. Buds, like baby cabbages, develop in the angle where each leaf leaves the stem; the sprouts are best cut when they are a little more than one inch through.

When early winter has stopped all growth in the garden, pull up the plants, roots and all, and hang them in the garage; additional sprouts will grow for several weeks.

Sow seeds outdoors in late spring, and set the young plants out 2 feet apart. 30 to 50 plants suffice for an average family.

BRUSSELS SPROUTS. *Best in Indian summer, after frost has chilled them.*

CABBAGE

Brassica oleracea capitata. *Cruciferæ.* Served raw, or not cooked overlong, cabbage is a vegetable food of great value; the outer green leaves are superior to the whitened center; cabbage-juice that is newly squeezed is claimed to be healing and nourishing.

Sow seeds indoors in March, and in the open during April and May. Transplant to 2½ feet apart in the rows. If young plants become stunted, sickly, and eventually die, they probably have yellows: burn them. Don't put them on the compost heap to perpetuate the trouble; and don't plant cabbages in the same part of the garden next season.

SOME CABBAGE TYPES
Cone-shape, red, savoy and ballhead.

The center of the cabbage takes one of three shapes, cone, round, and flat-round or drumhead. Smooth-leaved and crumple-leaved varieties are found in all three types; the latter, called savoys, are similar in flavor, a trifle hardier, and are improved by slight frosts.

Red cabbages also appear in all three shapes; good for pickling, they are just as suitable as other kinds for cole slaw, salads or boiling.

100

When you cut a cabbage in the garden, sever the stem and let a few of the lowest leaves remain; with your knife slash a cross in the stump. From this cross several small green loose cabbages will arise, which will be found even more delectable than the cabbage which has been cut off.

Good cabbage varieties are: golden acre, a small but very good early round sort; Jersey wakefield, a pointed head type; Copenhagen market, an excellent early round cabbage that may grow up to 10 pounds in weight; Danish ballhead, a good round late sort; and yellows-resistant globe. Chieftan savoy is one of the best wrinkled types, and rock is a smooth red one. Early cabbage takes 11 to 13 weeks from seed, savoy and red types 12 to 14 weeks, and late ones 14 to 16 weeks.

If you object to the smell of cooking cabbage, grow the odorless savoy, developed by Cornell University; the odor is less marked.

CABBAGE, CHINESE or CELERY

Brassica pekinensis. *Cruciferæ*. There are two features about this plant: attempt to grow it a little late, and it bolts to flower. Transplant it, and the same thing happens. So sow it in late March or early April, again on July 25, in rows; thin to stand 6 inches apart. Chinese cabbage tastes something like mustard, but the stem is solid, brittle and refreshing, like celery. Wong bok is short, broad and compact; pe-tsai is a tall type; michihli is an improved pe-tsai. A good vegetable, worthy of extended culture.

CHINESE CABBAGE. *It likes the cool weather of spring and autumn. Wong Bok at left, Michihli at right.*

CANTALOUPE. See Muskmelon.

CARAWAY

Carum carvi. *Umbelliferæ*. An annual herb, growing 2 feet, with white flower-clusters something like those of Queen Anne's Lace. When the flower-heads have drooped and the seeds are nearly ripe, cut them and spread on a large sheet; leave for a few days, and then flail out the caraway seeds, for flavoring in the kitchen, for bread- and cake-making. A favorite with German cooks, seed is sown in spring, and the plants thinned to stand at 6-in. distances.

CARAWAY. *An annual herb that is simple to grow.*

101

CARDOON

Cynara cardunculus. *Compositæ.* Five-foot perennial plant grown from seed and transplanted 2 feet by 3 feet apart. Or you may dig the side-growths or suckers in spring, complete with roots; push a spade down their full length to get them. Treat cardoon as though it were a giant celery: three weeks before using tie the

CARDOON. *Giant thistle-like plant that is grown in a manner similar to celery.*

heads together, pile straw against the stems, and pile earth against the straw. Serve raw as a salad, or boiled like asparagus.

CARROT

Daucus carota. *Umbelliferæ.* Palatable and nutritious, either when eaten raw or cooked; well-known source of the eyesight vitamin A, carrot is economical of space in the garden and an easy vegetable to grow. Prefers sandy-loam, but will thrive in almost any soil; radish sown along with carrot helps to break any soil crust caused by pelting rain. Allow one ounce of carrot seed per 100 feet, and thin the resulting carrots to stand 2½ inches apart. So-called early carrots are quick, ready in 9 or 10 weeks; so-called late varieties merely are a little slower, ready in 11 to 13 weeks. It often happens that the slower growing kinds are better than the quick ones.

CARROT TYPES. *Chantenay at left, danvers, long orange, Nantes, with French forcing at the right.*

Section of carrot showing a core. Modern ones are almost coreless.

Carrots show some differences in size and shape. Among quick sorts, French forcing is ball-shape; oxheart is thick and stumpy; chantenay is tapering; Nantes is cylinder-shape. Slower sorts including danvers, imperator, streamliner and tendersweet are blunt-tapering. Intermediate ends in a long point; long orange is more tapering and a foot long.

The color of carrots depends partly on the strain and on the soil in which you grow them, a rich soil generally giving brighter colored roots.

CATNIP or CATMINT

Nepeta cataria. *Labiatæ.* A three-foot perennial sweet herb, with pale velvety leaves and white-purple flowers. Young shoots are used for seasoning; tea was made from it before tea came out of China, which was thought to impart courage. Cats have a strong liking for it. You can sow seeds, or buy plants and set them out 12 inches apart.

CAULIFLOWER. *Snowball cauliflower at left, autumn giant in center; so-called purple cauliflower at right. This usually is a European type of heading broccoli, somewhat coarser than cauliflower but similar, except in color.*

CAULIFLOWER

Brassica oleracea botrytis. *Cruciferæ.* Sow ½ inch deep in March indoors or in a hot-bed and transplant in April. Have the plants 2½ feet apart in rows 2 feet from each other. Rich soil is essential. Outdoors sow the first week in May and transplant in July. When the flower is the size of an egg, tie the leaves together or bend them to form a cover. For wintering under glass sow in September; transplant into a frame; give plenty of air in mild weather, and cover up well when it is cold.

The best seed is produced in Denmark; the favorites are the quick-growing Erfurt or snowball varieties, short stemmed plants with large heads. A slow sort that thrives in certain localities is autumn giant.

CELERIAC

Apium graveolens rapaceum. *Umbelliferæ.* The knob-celery that has a thickened turnip-like edible root. It has white flesh that tastes like celery hearts. Grate it, and serve raw as a salad ingredient, or dice it and serve as a boiled vegetable. Sow one ounce per 150 feet of row; thin to stand 6 inches apart.

CELERIAC. *A kind of celery with a large root (right).*

PASCAL CELERY. *The outer green stringless stalks may also be eaten raw.*

CUTTING CELERY. *Does not develop the heart we associate with celery.*

CELERY

Apium graveolens dulce. *Umbelliferæ*. A valuable anti-scurvy food, low in calories; a fair source of calcium. Sow seed ⅛ inch deep in a cold-frame in March or outside in April or May, and again in July. Transplant to 6 inches apart. Rows often are double, the parallel row-lets 6 inches from each other. Three weeks prior to harvesting, the plants should have boards placed against them, or be wrapped in paper and have earth piled against them 16 inches or more high: this to de-velop a stringless, brittle heart or center. Twice-transplanted seedlings are preferred; each transfer into rich, moisture-holding soil. Use plenty of organic matter. In poor soil they are likely to bolt to flower.

Most popular celery varieties are summer pascal; the extra nutritive green outer leaves are as stringless as the blanched hearts; golden plume, Cornell no. 19 and golden treasure.

For soups, the large Cutting Celery is sometimes grown; this does not develop a heart. For flavoring. celery seed is much used.

CHAMOMILE

Anthemis nobilis. *Compositæ*. A perennial herb. Half a pint of boil-ing water poured on half an ounce of the dried flower-heads and al-lowed to stand 15 minutes, makes the famed chamomile tea, a tonic, febrifuge, sedative and hair-bleach; is emetic in large quantities. Smoked, it is said to relieve asthma. A chamomile poultice helps with toothache. The plant grows 12 inches high; from seed, or roots may be purchased.

CHARD. See Swiss Chard.

CHERVIL

Anthriscus cerefolium. *Umbelliferæ.* An annual herb, the leaves of which can be used like parsley for garnishing, and flavoring soups and salads. Grow it for spring or autumn, as it dislikes hot weather. Sow outdoors, and gather leaves in eight weeks; plants are thinned to 4 inches apart.

Chervil is an important ingredient in the French chef's mixture of Fines Herbes.

CHICORY

Cichorium intybus. *Compositæ.* Sow seeds in spring, and thin the resulting plants to stand 6 inches apart. Roots are lifted in the fall, and planted during the winter in a cellar or under a greenhouse bench in boxes of soil and peatmoss, or of compost, first shortening the roots to the upper 8 inches. Plant so that the roots are 9 inches below the surface. Fill level with sand or manure, through which the white salad appears in about a month. Let the growing shoot push up a 2-inch flat stone which you place over it as soon as you see it; then add a further 2 inches of soil. This makes the stocky, curved, white witloof. Some seed stores offer the parsnip-like roots ready for you to plant indoors.

WITLOOF. *The second growth from roots of chicory, developed in the dark. A popular and costly salad item.*

Roots of chicory are sometimes sliced, roasted and ground to make an ingredient in French coffee.

CHIVES

Allium Schoenoprasum. *Liliaceæ.* Pretty little grass-like plant with rose-purple flowers that can be used as a flower-garden edging plant; it is a variety of onion, and the hollow grass-like leaves are cut with shears into small pieces and used for flavoring salads and cheeses. A few roots of this useful perennial in a window-box is probably the most practical vegetable-garden for the city-dweller. You may grow it from seed, or purchase plants, and when your plants grow too crowded, dig them up and pull into several pieces, each of which you replant ten inches apart. The height is ten inches.

CITRON. See Watermelon.

COCOZELLE. See Vegetable marrow.

COLLARDS

Brassica oleracea acephala. *Cruciferæ.*
These are leafy plants with a large loose head,
which is served boiled and tastes like cabbage.
Sow seeds early in spring and early in autumn. An outstanding source of vitamin C;
good one of A and G; fair source of B_1. High
in calcium and phosphorus. One ounce of
seeds will produce about 3000 plants. Quick;
it takes only 7 weeks from seeds to cutting;
prolific, a 25-ft. row should give you a total of 3 bushels of produce.

COLLARDS. *One of the
quickest crops you can
grow, and full of vita-
mins.*

CORIANDER

Coriandrum sativum. *Umbelliferæ.* The seeds are used in cooking,
candy-making and for flavoring cordials. Oriental culinary recipes call
for it. An annual, growing 2½ feet high. Seeds may be sown in spring,
and the young plants thinned to stand 6 inches apart.

CORN

Zea mays. *Gramineæ.* Within an hour or
two of gathering, corn loses much of its sugar;
day-old corn is definitely inferior. To really
enjoy it, grow your own, and lose no time in
cooking and serving it. Yellow corn is a good
source of vitamin B_1 and an outstanding one
of phosphorus. Two perfect ears from each
plant is a good average yield. It may be gathered daily from July to frost if you plant every
three weeks from May 1 through July 15. It is
a good idea to use more than one kind, further to keep you supplied daily.

Sow in groups or hills 2 or 3 feet apart, the
size of a dinner plate, 6 seeds to each group;
later thin to 3 plants per group. Or sow in rows
1 inch deep, placing the seeds three inches
from one another; later thin the young plants
to stand 12 to 15 inches apart. Allow 2 feet between the rows.

CORN. *Three plants are
usually grown to the hill
or group. Draw earth up
to the roots when culti-
vating.*

The midget sorts, 3½ feet high only, are grown closer: groups 2 feet
apart, and individual plants in rows standing 6 or 8 inches from each

other. One pound sows 200 to 300 groups, or 200 feet of drill; this is for normal varieties—the midgets need more seeds for 200 feet in a straight run, the smaller plants being suitable for closer than usual planting. Hills may be set nearer each other if you wish.

In the production of seed corn each variety must be kept half a mile or more from others, to prevent wind-borne pollen from mixing with it. Grow a black variety in your garden, and see how easily this can happen; your yellow corn ears will be speckled with black grains.

Instead of keeping kinds widely apart, intentional hybrids are made by growing two parent kinds close together. Corn is said to be monœcious: that is, the male flowers and the female flowers are separate, but both are on the one plant. The top or male portion of one parent is pruned off, so that there is only one source of pollen, that from the other parent planted near by. These special hybrid corns are favorites just now and are much planted, because they have been proved to be fine. Good ones: golden midget hybrid flagship,* golden cross bantam,* lincoln, evergreen hybrid, honey cross, marcross and spancross. They yield in 10 to 13 weeks. Good non-hybrid sorts are golden bantam,* wonder bantam, black Mexican, country gentleman and Stowell's evergreen. Varieties marked * are suitable for quick freezing.

CORN SALAD or LAMBS' LETTUCE

Valerianella olitoria. *Valerianaceæ.* A quick-growing annual that is much liked in Europe as a salad plant. One ounce of seed will sow 150 feet of row, and should be put in during early spring or late summer. Latest sowings will usually live well into the winter if kept covered with three inches of leaves; remove them when spring growth begins elsewhere in the garden, and a worth-while spring crop may be ready for you.

CORN SALAD. *A favorite of the European gardener.*

CURLED CRESS or PEPPERGRASS

Lepidium sativum. *Cruciferæ.* Chief use for this is in the seedlings which are good for salads and sandwich fillings. A good house-grown crop: scatter seeds thinly on fine soil and press—do not cover. Will also grow on cloth kept constantly moist. Ready in about 2½ weeks; sow at short intervals for a continuing yield.

WATERCRESS

Nasturtium officinale. Cruciferæ. Mix a small quantity of the seed with a pint of moist soil, or one ounce in 4 quarts; roll into one-inch marbles, and push a marble here and there into the mud just at the water-level of your pond or slow stream. Be sure that the water is not polluted. It may also be cultivated as an ordinary crop if you water it often.

WATERCRESS. *Grow it if you have a sweet-water pond or stream.*

CUCUMBER

Cucumis sativus. Cucurbitaceæ. Sow six seeds in a group or hill the size of a dinner-plate. Hills are flat unless the land is over-moist, when they may be 3 inches above the general level; and they should be at least 4 feet apart each way. Starting on May 10, sow at two-week intervals until mid-July. Thin to three plants per group. Place half a spadeful of soil midway along the length of each branch to induce roots to enter the soil. One ounce seeds 50 groups, 2 pounds an acre; yield in about 9 weeks. Expect 5 cucumbers per plant. Among good modern varieties are: A and C, staysgreen and marketer.

At left, *West India gherkin, which is described in the text on page 110.* Staysgreen cucumber at top, *marketer variety* below. At right, *two greenhouse-grown cucumbers.*

The very long shapely "telegraph" cucumbers, sometimes offered at high prices, are special varieties grown in greenhouses. Their culture is exacting: a mixture of one-third rotted manure and two-thirds loam is used; temperatures are maintained around 80 in summer and 70 in winter. By pinching out branches a single stem is developed, and supported by wires to reach the roof. It is usually necessary to pollinate the female flowers by dusting a male flower onto them.

DANDELION

Taraxacum officinale. Compositæ. Healthful boiled greens and a good salad. One ounce sows about 100 feet of row; thin the plants to stand about 5 inches from each other. The heart may be bleached like endive by tying the leaves together two weeks before using for salad purposes. Some gardeners sow in summer, and cover with leaves or old manure over winter.

A large and erect kind is called the cut-and-come-again dandelion, asparagus chicory or ciccoria catalogna. This kind may well be thinned to stand 8 inches from plant to plant in the row. Dandelion is a good plant to grow and eat, for its minerals and vitamins; in addition, it stimulates the liver.

DILL

Anethum graveolens. *Umbelliferæ*. The leaves are used sparingly in fish dishes, and the seeds are an ingredient in dill pickles. A 2½-ft.-high, easily grown annual; sow seed in spring and thin to six inches. The dry plants may be placed on a clean sheet and flailed or beaten with a long whippy stick.

EGGPLANT

Solanum melongena esculentum. *Solanaceæ*. One ounce of seed will produce about 1000 plants, and eggs should be ready in about 11 weeks after planting out. Sow during March indoors, put out 2½ feet apart in the row when settled warm weather has arrived. It is important that the young plants experience no check in their growth through low temperatures or lack of moisture when indoors. Greenhouse-grown plants, each in a small pot, may be purchased in late May. New York spineless is a good large oval variety, with a deep purple-black skin. Long purple is an elongated fruit. Expect 4 to 8 eggs from each plant.

EGGPLANT. *Very easy to grow; set the plants out only after warm weather has arrived.*

ENDIVE or ESCAROLE

Cichorium endivia. *Compositæ*. An excellent salad vegetable with a pleasing bitter tang, outstanding in vitamin A, good source of vitamin G, with a fair supply of calcium. Most gardeners sow from the middle of June until the fifteenth of August in rows, and thin to 10 inches between the plants. When fully grown, and at a time when the plants are dry, tie the outside leaves over the

BROAD-LEAVED ENDIVE or ESCAROLE. *Sow late to mature in the autumn.*

hearts to blanch them. A very hardy plant; first autumn frosts improve its flavor and texture.

One ounce of seed will sow 200 feet of drill and yield 250 heads; more when thinnings are transplanted, and they will shift very easily. Ready in about 11 weeks after sowing. There are two general types: the curled which have leaves finely cut and crinkled; these are confusedly called chicory in the markets. And the broad-leaved kinds with entire leaves, to which the name escarole is generally limited.

CURLED ENDIVE. *Serve it in salads with lettuce mixed with it, if you object to its slightly bitter taste.*

FENNEL or FINOCCHIO

Foeniculum vulgare. *Umbelliferæ.* Looks like celery, but the feathered leaves have a sweet anise-like flavor. Leaf-bases are flattened in the Florence type; are swollen and rounded in the Sicilian type. Served as a vegetable, raw or cooked, while the seeds are used for flavoring. Supposed to impart physical strength and to cure obesity. Treat as an annual; it grows 2 feet high.

FENNEL. *This is the preferred Sicilian type.*

GARLIC

Allium sativum. *Liliaceæ.* You buy ordinary garlic; best get it from a seed store, because then you can be sure it will grow. Strip the skin and pull off the fleshy scales or cloves, discarding the center stem. Plant the scales 6 inches apart.

Some regard it as a useful flavoring, used sparingly; others that it is a wonderful health-giving plant, and should be eaten generously. So take your choice; believe it or not, it is claimed to sweeten the breath.

The giant garlic or rocambole, Allium scorodoprasum, is a 3-foot plant rarely seen in America.

WEST INDIA GHERKIN or BUR GHERKIN

Cucumis anguria. *Cucurbitaceæ.* Cultivated in the same manner as the cucumber. The spiny fruits are gathered when only 2 inches long and are much used for small pickles.

GUMBO. See Okra.

HORSERADISH

Armoracia rusticana. *Cruciferæ.* Mature roots are grated to furnish the pungent sauce served with meat, oysters and fish. Grown from sections or cuttings of the root branches, which are set in rich soil with the top of the cutting 3 inches underground. Roots are dug any time as needed.

HORSERADISH. *A little goes a long way. You can dig one or two roots of this any time; cut off and replant larger branches.*

KALE or BORECOLE

Brassica oleracea acephala. *Cruciferæ.* The densely curled Scotch kale is at its best after November frosts. Sow in June or July; when large enough, transplant into deep, rich soil, allowing 24 inches between the plants, of which one ounce of seed produces 3000. A 25-ft. row will yield 8 bushels of healthful food, possibly much more, that has a pleasing flavor. Ready in 12 weeks after setting out.

The Siberian variety, known as German greens, is not so densely curled, but is very hardy and yields heavily.

SCOTCH KALE. *Densely curled, this is best after first frosts.*

SIBERIAN KALE. *Less densely curled, but equally resistant to cold.*

KOHLRABI

Turnip-rooted-Cabbage or Stem Turnip

Brassica caulorapa. *Cruciferæ.* Sow in early spring in rows 2 feet apart, and thin away the plants to 4-inch spacing. Sow again in summer for an autumn crop. Delicious when about 2 inches in diameter; larger roots become woody. One ounce will sow about 200 feet of row, and yield over 200 pounds. Ready in 8 or 9 weeks. An excellent source of vitamin C, a fair one of G. Also contains phosphorus, copper and calcium. There are two types, white and purple.

KOHLRABI. *Actually a type of cabbage with a swollen stem. Varieties with either green or purple skin may be grown.*

111

LEEK

Allium porrum. *Liliaceæ.* Mild onion-like plants, served boiled. Sow in early spring outdoors, and thin to 6 inches, or transplant them, at the bottom of trenches 6 inches deep, in rich soil. Gradually fill the trenches as the plants grow, and later draw additional soil up to them. You will have fine, large blanched leeks a half-foot long, which may be stored all winter in sand.

LYON LEEK
The long slender type.

One ounce of seed will sow about 100 feet of row or yield over 1000 seedlings for transplanting. About 18 weeks from seed to the edible stage. A fair source of vitamin B_1; an outstanding one of copper.

There are two main varieties; the lyon, which is long and slender, and the broad London, or Musselburgh, which is stocky.

MUSSELBURGH LEEK.
Stocky and more tolerant of frost.

LETTUCE

Lactuca sativa. *Compositæ.* Lettuce contains the vitamins carotene and riboflavin. The outer leaves are better for one than the heart.

Sow indoors the first week in March. When seedlings are about 3 inches tall, transplant them to the garden, 1 foot apart. These should give you well-developed heads by Decoration Day.

As soon as the ground can be worked outdoors, sow early sorts. Gradually thin until the plants stand a foot apart. After mid-May sow sorts like salamander and Imperial No. 456. Make repeated sowings to have lettuce always available. In August sow Thanksgiving Day. Easiest lettuce to grow are the non-heading types: the Salad bowl, bronze beauty, grand rapids, simpson or slobolt. Almost as easy is oakleaf, a semi-heading kind with leaves shaped as the name indicates.

Next easiest is the cos or romaine type, Paris white, which is upright-growing. When about a week short of maturity it is usual to draw the outer leaves together and tie them, blanching the inner heart and enhancing its crispness and fine flavor. The crisphead varieties are a little difficult; the group is called Iceberg lettuce in the stores, but the varieties are New York 12 and New York 515 for loamy land, and imperial 456 for hot weather.

SOME LETTUCES. Left, *New York, a crisphead type; Paris White, a cos or romaine kind; Salamander, a butterhead; stem lettuce;* right, *Simpson, an all-leaf kind easiest to grow.*

Chief problem with growing lettuce is in getting the land right; it should drain well, yet contain sufficient organic matter to retain moisture, and be well supplied with plant-food. Hoeing must be continuous.

A type of lettuce not often seen is the stem lettuce or celtuce. The leaves are not so palatable as the thick main stem, which is peeled and eaten raw or cooked, giving us another and different vegetable. As healthful a food as any other lettuce.

CELTUCE. *A type of stem-lettuce.*

LOVAGE or LIEBSTOCK

Levisticum officinale. *Umbelliferæ.* The seeds are used in confectionery, and in French cooking. Leaves are blanched and eaten like celery. It is grown from roots or seeds.

LOVAGE. *A 6 ft. tall perennial ornamental herb.*

POT MARJORAM. *Decorative perennial.*

113

MARJORAM

Origanum. *Labiatæ. Pot Marjoram.* Origanum vulgare. A 20-inch plant that may be used as a decorative edging.

Sweet or Knotted Marjoram. Origanum majorana. A perfumery oil is extracted from it. Grows 2 feet high.

Both these may be used in salads and for seasoning; if you are likely to make potpourri, dried marjoram leaves are a valuable ingredient. Roots may be purchased of both, and seed is sometimes available of sweet marjoram.

Sweet Marjoram. *Not quite so hardy; protect the roots over winter with 4 inches of leaves.*

MARTYNIA PROBOSCIDEA

Unicorn Plant or Proboscis Flower. *Martyniaceæ.* The lilac-purple flowers are followed by curved seed-pods. These are pickled. Sow indoors, and transplant when frost is over to stand 3 feet apart. The plants are very sensitive to cold.

The Unicorn-plant. *These curved seed-pods make good pickles.*

MINTS

Labiatæ. These require moist ground and will tolerate partial shade. The mint pool was a feature of the monastery garden in medieval times. All are perennials; put in plants—none of the following may be produced from seed.

Some of the Better-Known Mints. Left to right: *pennyroyal, peppermint, spearmint, lemon or bergamot mint.*

Anise Mint. **Mentha anisatus.** The aroma of anise combined with mint. For salads and cold drinks. Grows 2 feet high.

Lemon Mint or Bergamot Mint. **Mentha citrata.** The lemon-like scent is unusual.

Peppermint. **Mentha piperita.** This is the variety used for flavoring juleps and candy; a medicinal tea is infused from it, and menthol is made from it. Quite a tall plant, it grows 3 feet high.

Spearmint. **Mentha spicata.** This is the common garden mint. For mint sauce, julep, jelly, etc., and for flavoring vegetables in cooking. Leaves are candied for sweetmeats. Grows 2 feet high.

Pennyroyal. **Mentha pulegium.** An aromatic medicinal herb that is also valuable in the kitchen for seasoning. Grows 12 inches.

MUSHROOMS

Agaricus campestris. *A Higher Fungus.* Invaluable for their zestful flavor. Turn fresh horse-manure every day for four days; then build beds with it, one foot thick when tamped. Test with a hot-bed thermometer; when the internal temperature falls to 75 degrees, plant the spawn broken into walnut-size pieces at 12-inch spacing. This consists of spores from choice mushrooms propagated in sterile bottles, removed, dried, and packed in cartons. Excluded are spores of other fungi; allow one quart for each 35 square feet.

MUSHROOMS. *Difficult to grow mushrooms in the home, but a barn or a root-cellar is suitable.*

The manure mixture may be placed in shelves. Air temperature should be 60 degrees.

Cover with three inches of hay for a week; remove the hay, and in its place spread one inch of soil. Keep the barn at 60 degrees, and moisten the walls and floors daily. This is why the average home cellar is unsuitable for mushroom growing, unless a tent can be improvised around the beds, and the tent kept moist. You gather mushrooms six weeks after planting the spawn.

Inch-size pieces of spawn may be planted one inch deep in a lawn or in a compost-heap during late summer. A crop of mushrooms may be expected in autumn.

Or the manure may be placed on a dirt floor. Walls are sprinkled with water daily.

SOME MELONS
Left, *Montreal, Bender's surprise, casaba;* right, *banana-shape.*

MUSKMELON or CANTALOUPE

Cucumis melo. *Cucurbitaceæ.* These are quite easy to grow. Sow seed in mid-April and protect with hotkaps; sow in the open in May. Hills or groups the size of a dinner-plate may be arranged 5 feet apart each way; sow 6 to 8 seeds in each. When they have produced their rough leaves, thin to three plants per group. Place a spadeful of earth half-way along each stem, to induce the formation of additional roots, and offset attacks of the bores.

As soon as the plants are well above ground, dust them or spray with an insecticide to protect against the squash-bug that sometimes gives trouble. One containing pyrethrum or tobacco is recommended, but one containing sulphur should be avoided.

One ounce of seed will plant about 80 hills. Each should give you five or more perfect melons in from 12 to 16 weeks. Melons are a fair source of vitamins C and G.

The variety Montreal is a large type, Bender's Surprise is much grown. An old type with a queer shape is banana. A long-keeping kind is casaba.

CURLED MUSTARD

Brassica juncea. *Cruciferæ.* Sow in spring, in drills, and thin the plants to stand 6 inches apart. Healthful boiled greens, and the quickest garden crop; gather leaves when they are young and discard the stems. A second seeding in August will give a fair crop in early fall. A good source of vitamin B_1; vitamins C and G are excellent. Calcium and iron are outstanding.

CURLED MUSTARD. A *speedy green-leaf garden vegetable; healthful also.*

116

WHITE LONDON MUSTARD

Brassica alba. *Cruciferæ.* The seedlings are sheared when 2½ inches high, and are excellent for sandwich fillings and for adding to salads. A good crop to have growing in the house all winter; broadcast seed on fine soil and press in lightly—do not cover. Ready in about ten days.

OKRA or GUMBO

Hibiscus esculentus. *Malvaceæ.* Adds a mucilaginous quality and a piquancy to soups and stews, and may be served alone as a pleasing vegetable. Only young pods are used; when old they have no value. A quick crop; ready about 9 weeks after sowing.

OKRA. *A handsome member of the hibiscus family; relative of the cotton-plant.*

Sow in late May in drills 1 inch deep; thin to 12 inches. One ounce of seed is sufficient for about 100 feet of row.

ONION

Allium cepa. *Liliaceæ.* Onions are an aid to buoyant health. One ounce of seed will plant 100 feet of drill and yield 100 to 150 pounds of food. Allow 5 or 6 pounds of seeds for an acre.

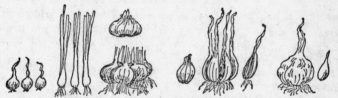

ONIONS

Left, *onion sets, onion seedlings with the tops clipped ready for planting, potato onions, shallots.* Right, *garlic.*

SOME MORE ONIONS

Left, *Bermuda, Prizetaker, Wethersfield, Southport globe, pickling.* Right, *perennial Egyptian onions.*

117

For large onions sow ½ inch deep in a hotbed early in January or February, and transplanted to the open in May, 5 inches apart. For the main supply, sow in rich sandy soil, river-bottom loam or muck-land early in spring, and firm well. Thin to 3 inches apart. Three to four months are needed to produce large mature onions. To hasten maturity, especially if they are slow to form bulbs, bend over and lightly break the tops; some growers roll an empty barrel along their rows.

Small white onions, maturing when the size of marbles, are used for pickling, White pickling is a good variety to ask for. Bunching onions or scallions may be the thinnings from your rows intended for larger onions, or you may buy seed of White bunching or evergreen bunching, which do not develop into larger ones. Evergreen bunching can be sown in late summer and protected over winter with a mulch of leaves in the Middle Atlantic states.

Here are some reliable varieties among onions of the regular type:

Large onions for exhibition. Prizetaker, Valencia, sweet Spanish.

Red onions for longest keeping. Wethersfield, Southport red globe.

White onions for mild flavor. Southport white globe, Portugal or silverskin, Bermuda.

Yellow onions for general purposes. Danvers, southport yellow globe.

Some varieties are not grown from seed but from previously matured bulbs:

Multiplying onions, potato onions, and shallots with purple flesh, all increase in the soil. For every bulb of these three that you plant in spring you dig a cluster of bulbs in the fall. Shallots, by the way, are especially good for pickles.

Egyptian onions are autumn-planted hardy perennials, yielding green pulling onions of fair quality every spring. The plant is remarkable in that no flowers or seeds are produced, but in their stead at the top of the plant are clusters of small bulbs. These are what you buy and plant.

Onion sets, or Dutch sets, are miniature onions grown from seed sown very thickly last year; soon after they started they became overcrowded and ceased to develop. If you plant them in spring they will commence growing again, to produce pulling onions in five to seven weeks; or they may be allowed to develop into full size onions, which they will do in a shorter time than would onions grown from seeds. Put the sets in one inch deep and two inches apart; pull every alternate onion for salads, and allow the remainder to mature into large ones. Depending on the size of the sets, one pound plants from 50 to 100 running feet.

THREE PARSLEYS
Left, *curled; plain; and* right, *turnip-rooted.*

PARSLEY

Petroselinum hortense. *Umbelliferæ.* The kind usually grown and ordinarily sold in the markets is the curly parsley. There are two other useful sorts, however, the Italian or plain parsley, which has a fern-like leaf but is not curled; and the Hamburg or turnip-rooted parsley.

All parsleys should be used freely in salads, soups and sauces. They are good sources of carotene, and of the mineral food elements. Sow early in spring ½ inch deep; thin the young plants to stand inches apart.

One ounce of seed will sow about 150 feet of row, and yield over 150 good bunches, or 100 pounds of Hamburg parsley roots.

PARSNIP

Pastinaca sativa. *Umbelliferæ.* Parsnip is a good source of vitamin C, a fair source of B₁. Gives us phosphorus.

Sow in April or May ½ inch deep, and thin to 4 inches between the plants. The quality of the roots is improved after frost, and they may be allowed to remain in the ground over winter.

THREE PARSNIP TYPES
Left, *round, hollow-crown.* Right, *long. The hollow-crown is the kind usually grown.*

One ounce of seed will take care of 200 feet of row and yield 300 or more pounds of food. Use 5 or 6 pounds of seed per acre. Parsnips need 15 weeks and more from seed to maturity.

119

Although parsnips take all season to grow, you may practice companion cropping by sowing parsnip, beet and radish seed in the same row at the same time. You pull radishes in four weeks, beets in ten, and a full yield of parsnips in the winter.

Get parsnip seed from a reliable source. It must be new-crop, for it loses its vitality in less than a year; note the guaranteed germination on the package and the date the test was made.

PEAS. Left, *round seeded, wrinkled seeded marrowfat;* right, *edible podded. All need to be sown early.*

PEAS

Pisum sativum. *Leguminosæ.* Sow peas early, the round or dimpled seeded kinds as soon as the ground is dry and workable; the wrinkled types a week later. Use several varieties, because most of them vary as to the time taken from seed to crop, and this is the only way we have of getting a continuing supply; in most parts of the American continent we get inferior results from seedings made later than the earliest practical seeding date in spring.

Sow the peas two inches deep and about two inches apart; thin to three or four inches. Tall varieties must have the support of brush or wire to climb upon, and even the dwarf ones are better for this help. Place it on the lighter side of the row, if there is any difference; and if you grow peas in double rows six inches apart, put the brush or wire between the rowlets.

Peas are a valuable protein food, an excellent source of vitamin B_1, a good one of vitamin G, and a fair one of A. Outstanding in their phosphorus content, they also furnish copper.

Some peas are round; they are slightly hardier and may be sown first. Others are wrinkled; in these, some of the starch has changed to sugar, and they are sweeter; you see them referred to as marrowfat peas. Not quite so tolerant of cold, these wrinkled sorts should be sown a week later than the round seed varieties. Midway between round and wrinkled peas in sweetness and hardiness are a few dimpled sorts. All peas seem to benefit from dirty stormy weather after sowing.

Good varieties are:

	Height in inches	Days, seeding to picking
Round-seeded		
first of all	30	55
Alaska	30	60
Dimpled		
early bird	36	62
Wrinkled		
freezonian *	30	63
laxtonian *	24	65
little marvel	24	65
gradus *	36	68
potlach	24	80
telephone *	60	84

* These are kinds suitable for deep freezing.

PEANUT or GOOBER

Arachis hypogæ. *Leguminosæ.* These very-sensitive-to-cold plants may be grown as a novelty; they require a sandy or sandy-loam soil, and temperatures similar to those helpful to garden corn. Remove the outer shell without injuring the kernels, and sow the latter in rows 1½ inches deep around May 25. Allow 3 inches between one nut and the next in the drill, afterwards thinning to 9 inches from plant to plant.

PEANUT. *The flower grows above ground, is pollinated, then enters the soil where the nut matures.*

PEPPER

Capsicum frutescens. *Solanaceæ.* An outstanding source of vitamin C, and a fair one of A and G. All varieties may be used either green or red; green peppers merely are unripe red peppers. An occasional yellow or orange variety is met with.

They should not be set out until settled warm weather has arrived. The seed may be sown in a hotbed, greenhouse, or a box in a sunny window; transplant them 18 inches apart, and protect for the first month against cutworm; and during growth keep the soil constantly hoed. One ounce of seed will produce about 1000 plants. From a 25-ft. row you should gather more than 35 pounds of good peppers. You may begin to pick 9 to 12 weeks after planting out.

SOME PEPPERS
Left, *world beater, Chinese giant, ruby king, red cherry.* Right,
red Cayenne. First three are sweet; last two are hot.

Most peppers grown in gardens are the sweet kinds, like world beater, California wonder, Chinese giant, ruby king, or Neapolitan. But hot types are available in Hungarian wax and red Cayenne, both with long narrow fruits, and red cherry, with small round fruits; the hottest pepper of all is tabasco, from which the sauce for oysters is made.

The powdered black or white pepper that we buy in the stores is from a different plant, Piper nigrum, a vine growing in the tropics.

POTATO

Solanum tuberosum. *Solanaceæ.* Potatoes contribute the vitamin thiamin. The best soil for them is a well-drained fibrous loam. On certain clay soils, where local gardeners claim they cannot readily be grown, attempts at their culture are not recommended. Before planting, it is usual to work under a commercial fertilizer with a high potash content—the last figure in a typical analysis should be 5 or more—at the rate of 1500 pounds to the acre if broadcast, or 750 pounds if applied under the row: respectively 40 and 20 pounds per 1000 square feet, say 50 feet by 20 feet. Always buy certified

POTATO TUBERS. *They grow on the plant underground. Plants should have the soil drawn up to them every week or two.*

seed potatoes; here are some good varieties: chippewa and Irish cobbler, early; katahdin, intermediate; green mountain and sebago, late.

Cut each potato into pieces, each holding at least two good eyes or buds, plant them 10 inches apart and 3 inches deep from April 20 to

May 31. Allow 7 to 10 pounds for each 100 feet of row; 600 pounds will plant an acre. Growing period is around 110 days, by which time the tops will have died down, and the potatoes will be ready to dig. Potatoes are often discussed in terms of pecks and bushels; one peck weighs 15 pounds, one bushel 60 pounds

Spraying with Bordeaux mixture for blights and scab, and with 25 per cent D.D.T. for the potato bug or beetle, which is one-half inch long, yellow with black stripes, are a necessary process with the potato crop. Frequently arsenate of lead is employed for the bug.

Earth should be drawn up to potato plants during growth. One reason is to prevent exposure to light of an occasional tuber; it will develop a green color, and be harmful. Avoid eating green potatoes, or leaves.

SWEET POTATO

Ipomœa batatas. *Convolvulaceæ.* One of our most important food crops; so highly nutritious that in areas where ordinary potatoes cannot be grown profitably everyone should try it. Rooted cuttings are obtainable at most seed establishments; they are set out 2 feet apart each way in June in sandy soil; and dig the crop after first frost. Cultivate around them every week, and

Sweet Potatoes. *These do best in a medium to sandy soil, and need plenty of heat.*

lift the creeping stems at the same time to prevent their taking root.

The tubers keep well if they are thoroughly cured, and are handled with care to prevent bruising. Murff is a good sort recently introduced.

Two Pumpkins
Large cheese at left; *Connecticut field* at right.

PUMPKIN

Cucurbita pepo. *Cucurbitaceæ.* Plant around May 15 in groups or hills 8 to 10 feet apart, and otherwise treat in the same manner as muskmelon, which see. 1½ ounces of seed will take care of 50 groups; the fruits are ripe 15 to 18 weeks after sowing, and 4 or 5 per group may be expected. Sometimes they are grown among corn, putting half a dozen seeds with every third group of corn; thin to three plants. Good sorts are Connecticut field, for pies; large cheese; sweet or sugar; winter luxury, and king of the mammoths. You can grow the last named up to 200 pounds in weight.

RADISH TYPES

Left to right, crimson crisp, cherry belle, French breakfast, icicle. Center *two are summer radishes; two* at right *are winter* sorts.

RADISH

Raphanus sativus. *Cruciferæ.* Refreshing, fresh-pulled radishes are excellent for salads. Only moderate amounts of vitamins are present, but they furnish a fair quantity of copper.

As early in the spring as the ground can be worked, sow sparingly, ½ inch deep, any of the round or olive-shape spring varieties. Thin to one inch apart, but summer and winter sorts need 2½- to 4-inch spacing. Hoe frequently. The round and olive-shape sorts serve until June 15, when icicle and Cincinnati market are at their best. Summer sorts are good until frost from repeated sowings. Winter varieties should be sown from July 15 to August 15, and may be pulled after light frosts.

One ounce will plant about 100 feet of row, and one generous bunch per running foot is a normal yield.

In the average garden, space is too valuable for rows of spring and summer radish alone. Put the seeds in the same row along with carrot, beet, celery, dandelion, leek, onion, parsley, parsnip, salsify, scorzonera and chard. Radish seedlings are vigorous, often breaking the soil crust to let others through; they mark the row so that hoeing can start.

Good varieties include, Round: cherry belle, crimson crisp, sparkler. Olive-shape: French breakfast. These four are ready within a month. Long varieties: icicle, Cincinnati market, both taking 35 days from seed. Summer radish: white Strasburg, 40 days. Winter radish: long black Spanish, round black Spanish, both ready in two months.

RHUBARB or PIE-PLANT

Rheum rhaponticum. *Polygoneæ.* Plant the roots in well-manured land, 3 feet apart in the rows and 3 inches deep. If you wish to grow your roots from seed, sow thinly in spring, thin and transplant so that they stand 6 inches apart; transfer to their permanent bed in the fall. One ounce of seed will produce about 1000 roots. Victoria and McDonald are superior varieties.

RHUBARB OR PIE-PLANT.
This plant needs plenty of room.

Should you have more rhubarb roots than you need, some can be dug up and planted during the winter in boxes of soil in the cellar. They will grow, and the stems will reach for the half-light of the nearest window; they will be long, lighter in color and very sweet.

Here is a special warning: the stalks of rhubarb are good for you, but do not eat the leaves—they are poisonous.

ROMAINE. See Lettuce.

ROSEMARY

Rosmarinus officinalis. *Labiatæ.* Valuable in the kitchen for seasoning. The dried leaves may be added to potpourri. Packed with linen and clothing, they repel moths. You may plant roots or sow seeds.

FRAGRANT ROSEMARY.
Cultivated for ten centuries at least. Subject of the old saying, where rosemary grows woman rules. Should be a favorite with lady gardeners.

RUE

Ruta graveolens. *Rutaceæ.* Leaves are used for seasoning and flavoring beverages. In medieval prisons it was used to keep down typhus. Grows 2½ feet high; you may plant roots or sow seed.

RUTABAGA. See Turnip.

RUE.

SAGE

Salvia officinalis. *Labiatæ.* The dried leaves are employed for stuffings and sauces. Even today, the Chinese are said to prefer sage tea to tea as we know it. Its essential oil is used in perfumery. You may set out plants or sow seeds.

SAGE

SALSIFY

Tragopogon porrifolium. *Compositæ*. Its common name, the vegetable oyster, describes its flavor; grow and serve it as you would parsnip; like the latter, autumn frosts improve it. Sow early in spring one inch deep, thinning out the young plants to 4 inches. The roots will be ready in October, when a supply may be taken up and stored like carrots; the remainder may be left in the ground and dug up in spring.

One ounce of seed will sow 50 feet of row.

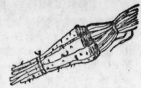

SALSIFY *or* OYSTER PLANT. *Grow it, try it and you'll like it.*

SCORZONERA or BLACK SALSIFY

Scorzonera hispanica. *Compositæ*. A little known vegetable root. Similar to salsify, but the skin is black. Grow it exactly as suggested for salsify above. Leaves of this plant may be added to salads.

SCORZONERA. *Remove the black skin before serving it at table.*

SAVORY

Satureja. *Labiatæ*. *Summer Savory*. S. hortensis. Perhaps better known as Bohnenkraut. Valuable seasoning for all dishes, imparting a meat-like flavor to vegetables. An 18-inch high annual, easily grown from seed.

Winter Savory. S. montana. Valuable seasoning herb, and user for flavoring liqueurs. Said to relieve bee-stings. A perennial that may find a place in the flower garden, for it is a good edging plant, growing one foot high. Purchase roots.

SUMMER SAVORY. *Adds a meat-like flavor to vegetables.*

WINTER SAVORY. *Grows in fairly poor soil.*

SOUTHERNWOOD, OLD-MAN, LAD'S LOVE

Artemisia abrotanum. *Compositæ.* Shrubby plant with divided, fern-like, highly aromatic leaves. Keeps moths from clothing; sprinkled on the stove will dispel kitchen odors. A 3- to 4-ft. high perennial. Purchase roots, then divide them every second year.

SEAKALE

Crambe maritima. *Cruciferæ.* Seed may be sown in spring, and the plants thinned to stand 12 inches apart; two years later they may be dug up, and a forced growth obtained indoors in the dark, as suggested for chicory. Or they may be forced outdoors by planting them in late summer in pairs or threes so that a bushel-basket or half-barrel can be placed over them in the field, bank-

FORCED SEAKALE. *Sprout the roots in the dark to produce this.*

ing first with leaves; then with earth. Sometimes roots can be purchased in winter for forcing right away: you might try the seed-stores.

SORREL or SOURGRASS

Rumex acetosa. *Polygonaceæ.* It has a pleasantly acid flavor, and is good for salads, served boiled like spinach, or in soups. A hardy perennial that should yield for several years from one planting.

Sow seeds in rows, eventually thin to 8 inches. One ounce will sow about 150 feet of row.

SORREL. *Pleasantly acid leaf vegetable. Serve boiled or raw.*

SPINACH

Spinacia inermis. *Chenopodiaceæ.* Its mineral and vitamin content are proverbial. Essentially a cool-weather crop, main sowing should be made early; later sowings are likely to bolt to flower and to seed, unless you choose sorts suited to the season. Your seed catalogue will guide you.

Chief sowing should be made in April in rows ½ inch deep, again in August or September. Thin to three inches between plants. Well prepared, rich land is essential.

SOME VARIETIES OF SPINACH
Left, *bloomsdale savoy-leaved, plain-leaved, prickly or winter.*
Right, *New Zealand spinach.*

One ounce of seed will take care of 100 feet of row and produce over eight bushels of spinach, ready about seven weeks after sowing.

Sometimes the land is made smooth in late autumn, seeds sown in November or December and covered with two inches of manure instead of soil. Growth begins in late winter. Some good spinach varieties are blight-resistant, old dominion, bloomsdale savoy, long-standing savoy. These four are advised for deep-freezing and have crumpled leaves; plain-leaved sorts can be had, and the prickly or winter type is recommended.

NEW ZEALAND SPINACH

Tetragonia expansa. *Aizoaceæ.* Spinach-like plants grow vigorously close to the ground; they do not bolt to seed, and they stand drought quite well. Allow one ounce of the large seeds for 50 feet of row, and push them in about 5 inches apart; no thinning will be necessary. The spinach will be ready for the kitchen in about 10 weeks.

SPINACH BEET. See Swiss Chard.

SQUASH

Cucurbitaceæ. Some types produce running stems and are classed as trailing sorts under **Cucurbita maxima**; others are non-trailing or bush varieties, mostly **Cucurbita melopepo.**

It is not advisable to sow before May 15. Sow bush varieties in groups 5 feet apart, trailing sorts 6 or 8 feet apart; use 6 or more seeds for each group, thinning later to 3 each. One ounce plants about 25 groups, and each should yield from 5 to 10 squashes.

Winter squashes furnish some vitamin G, and are an excellent source of vitamin A; summer squashes are almost as good. The summer ones are ready in 9 to 11 weeks from sowing; winter ones take 13 to 15 weeks. Good winter squashes are hubbard, warted hubbard, Boston marrow,

WINTER SQUASHES
Left, *hubbard, warted hubbard, butternut, acorn.* Right, *delicious.*

SUMMER SQUASHES
Left, *pattypan, crookneck.* Right, *straightneck.*

MORE SQUASHES
Italian snake, cocozelle. Right, *zucchini.*

delicious, acorn, U.-Conn and butternut. Good summer squashes for immediate use: cocozelle, crookneck, straightneck, pattypan, zucchini.

SWISS CHARD or SPINACH BEET

Beta vulgaris cicla. *Chenopodiaceæ.* This delectable vegetable is one you must grow yourself, for it is rarely offered for sale. Leaves are boiled, adding fried chopped bacon if you so desire. The stalks may be served as a distinct dish, cooked like asparagus. Sow early in spring, and thin to nine inches. One ounce of seed will sow about 100 feet of row, and yield more than 10 bushels of produce. Cutting commences in 8 weeks.

CHARD. Left, *green lyon, giant lucullus.* Right, *red or rhubarb chard.*

Among the most healthful of foods. High in vitamin A, vitamin G, and in all minerals, especially iron.

There are two general types of green chard, one represented by lucullus or Fordhook, with blistered wrinkled leaves; the other with smooth leaves and wide stems, represented by green lyon and mammoth New York. A third chard is red or rhubarb chard. Bright crimson stems and green and crimson leaves give this variety a striking appearance; grow and cook it as you would other chards, and you will find it even more delicious. Decorative in the flower garden also.

TARRAGON or ESTRAGON

Artemisia dracunculus. *Compositæ.* For seasoning salads and flavoring vinegar. An essential oil made from it is used in perfumery. This plant cannot be reproduced from seed; so purchase a few plants.

TARRAGON. *The correct ingredient for tartar sauce.*

THYME

Thymus vulgaris. *Labiatæ. English Thyme or Common Thyme.* The half-inch-long leaves are rounded. For seasoning all foods, including salads and wine. Makes an excellent edging plant for the flower garden. Only grows 8 inches high, and may be raised from seeds, or roots can be purchased, as you wish. *French Thyme.* The leaves are even smaller and decidedly narrower. Its seasoning properties are the same as the common thyme, of which it is a sub-variety. A potpourri ingredient; the heathlike plants will stand

COMMON THYME. *Spreads the softest fragrant carpet foot of man can tread. Thymes do not mind being walked upon to a reasonable degree.*

130

walking upon, and will then release their fragrance. Buy roots.

TOBACCO

Nicotiana tabacum. *Solanaceæ*. Sow sparingly indoors in March or April. Press in gently; do not cover with soil. Transplant at 30-inch intervals after May 25. Needs rich but porous, well-drained soil; its suitability influences smoking quality. Curing does also —bulletins from your state college or department of agriculture will give the details. Some available varieties are Connecticut seedleaf, for cigar wrappers and fillers; Kentucky burley, for pipes and chewing; Virginia bright-leaf, for cigarettes. With care, ¼ ounce of seed will provide enough plants to set for one acre.

FRENCH THYME. *This has slightly smaller leaves and is equally sweet scented.*

TOMATO

Lycopersicon esculentum. *Solanaceæ*. Abundant source of the vitamins ascorbic acid and niacin. Although the purchase of plants is established practice with most home gardeners, raising them from seed is economical. Seed should be sown sparingly in a

TOBACCO. *This will grow almost anywhere, but only certain soils, ascertained only by growing it, produce tobacco of smoking quality.*

pot or box indoors, in a hotbed or in a greenhouse, from March 15 to the end of April. When the plants are about three inches high they should be transplanted into other pots or boxes about 4 inches apart, or thinned so that they do not crowd. Around May 15 the plants may be set out in the open ground at 2 by 4 feet spacing. Protect each plant with a card wrapped around the stem and held in place by drawing a little soil up to it; otherwise cutworms may destroy it. For an autumn crop, sow seed in May in the open.

To have clean, disease-free tomatoes provide each plant with a strong stake to which it can be attached with pipe cleaners, and the fruit kept off the ground; many gardeners like to prune off side branches, so that each plant has but one main stem.

If you find the leaves being eaten, search for and destroy the large green tomato horn-worm; there rarely are more than one to a plant. Recommended varieties are beefsteak or crimson cushion, very large

SOME TOMATOES

Left to right, *ponderosa, beefsteak, marglobe, golden jubilee, a good yellow one.* At right, *sunrise.*

SMALL FRUITED TOMATOES

Left to right, *pear, currant, cherry, plum, peach.*

fruits; golden jubilee, orange-yellow fruit on an exceptionally vigorous plant; ponderosa, enormous purple-red fruits, often weighing a pound; Queens, marglobe, Rutgers and scarlet topper, all scarlet globe-shape, wilt- and rust-resistant, Vaughan's early hybrid, a heavy yielding sort. Sunrise is a medium-size tomato produced in bunches of six or eight.

Small-fruiting tomatoes are valuable for pickles, preserves and pepperhash. Their small size, quaint shapes and bright colors make attractive salads. Their flavor is pleasing and sweet. Red or yellow fruits can be grown in various shapes, all small: cherry, pear, plum and peach. Smallest of all is the currant tomato. Italian canner is a plum-shape scarlet small tomato with thick and rather dry flesh; good for preserves, pastes and sauces.

HUSK TOMATO. *Each is inside a protective sheath. Yellow and very sweet. So prolific that only a few plants are needed.*

The strawberry or husk tomato is a variety of Physalis, and close to the Chinese lantern plant; each sweet yellow cherry-size fruit is enclosed in a husk.

TURNIP

Brassica rapa. *Cruciferæ.* Sow as soon as the ground is ready in the spring ½ inch deep; thin to three inches from plant to plant. Sow again for winter use from June 25 to July 25. One ounce of seed is sufficient for a 150-ft. row, from which 150 lbs. or more of turnips will be dug or pulled.

Mostly the flesh is white, but good yellow types can be grown. Try the golden ball variety. A refined white type is white Milan; so is purple-top Milan. Purple-top white globe is popular. A thick carrot-shape turnip is long white or cowhorn, especially suitable for gardens where the topsoil layer is deep.

In addition to serving them boiled and mashed, try some thin slices raw or grated in salads. And serve turnip-tops, the leaves, as spinach, boiled lightly, and you have food of exceptional value; outstanding in vitamins A, C and G, also of calcium; a good source of thiamin and niacin, also of iron. Some who prefer the flavor of the leaves to the turnips themselves grow the variety seven-top, which has no swelling of the stem at the ground level, but produces an abundance of leaves only.

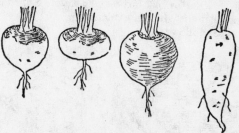

SOME TYPES OF TURNIP
Left, *purple-top white globe, purple-top Milan, golden ball;* right, *long white or cowhorn.*

RUTABAGA or SWEDE

Brassica napobrassica. *Cruciferæ.* Hardier than garden turnips, this is a large yellow-fleshed kind that keeps through winter when stored in a cool frost-free cellar or in a pit in the garden, well-drained, ventilated and lined with hay. The succession of leaf-scars on a characteristic long neck distinguishes rutabagas from yellow garden turnips. Usually sown from June 15 to July 15; thin to 6 inches between the plants.

133

VEGETABLE MARROW

Cucurbita pepo. *Cucurbitaceæ.* A type of summer squash that occupies an important place in European gardens. Cultivation is similar, although it is often grown in a few inches of soil placed on a manure-pile or compost-heap. The marrows are gathered before they are ripe, peeled, divided and the seeds removed; then cut into squares, boiled until tender and served with cream sauce.

One ounce of seed plants 50 groups or hills, and each group should produce 4 to 8 marrows in about 8 weeks. Vegetable marrow is a good source of vitamin A.

Following are types often grown: long green trailing, averaging 20 inches long, 3½ inches diameter, with a mottled light and dark green skin; long white trailing, similar to the foregoing but the smooth skin is white; cocozelle, not unlike the long green trailing but usually gathered when small; caserta, an improved cocozelle also gathered when young, about 7 inches by 1½ inches. The last two are non-trailing or bush types, popular with Italian gardeners.

WATERCRESS follows Cress.

TWO WATERMELONS
Left, *kleckley sweets;* right, *honey cream.*

WATERMELON

Citrullus vulgaris. *Cucurbitaceæ.* These are not grown in water; instead a rich, sandy soil suits them. Their name comes from the large amount of juice they contain. They are as easily grown as pumpkins or squash, and are recommended for the home garden if you have the room. After mid-May sow about 6 seeds to a hill or group, and have the hills 8 feet apart; thin to three plants to a hill.

One ounce of seed is sufficient for about 35 hills, and each hill should yield 3 to 5 watermelons, ready in from 12 to 14 weeks.

Recommended varieties are dixie queen, honey cream, which has yellow flesh, kleckley sweets and Tom Watson. An easily grown, quick type with mottled skin is the citron, which, with sugar, ginger and spices, makes the well-known marrow-jam or "marmalade." This citron is quite different to the crystallized fruit of the same name used in cake, candy and mincemeat: a large citrus fruit grown in Mediterranean countries.

Watermelon cubes, often with the skin attached, are a favorite sweet pickle.

To sum up: Among the nearly 100 vegetables and herbs listed here many are essential; some are less important. Most may be grown very easily; only a few need special care.

CHAPTER 18

Storing Your Crops Over Winter and Other Topics

Any man that walks the mead
In bud, or blade, or bloom, may find
A meaning suited to his mind.

ALFRED TENNYSON, 1809–1892

ONE way to take care of beet, carrot, kohlrabi, potatoes, salsify, scorzonera, shallots, turnip and rutabaga is to dig a hole in a well-drained location; put stones, gravel or sand on the bottom and cover with straw or salt-hay. Put in the vegetables; place one or more drain-tiles upright on the top, cover with straw and then with at least 6 inches of earth. An inverted tomato-can on the exposed top of each drain-tile keeps out rain, but admits air.

Small quantities can be kept in boxes of peatmoss, leaves or sand in a cool part of the cellar; or in an unheated garage, in which case they need extra covering in severe cold. Cabbages may be pulled with their roots entire and stored in the boxes or the outdoor heap upside-down.

For celery dig a trench in land that is gently sloping. If you have no sloping land, grade the bottom of the trench so that water drains down and away; you may have to run it into a blind well or sump. Replant the celery, packed closely, in the trench; the leaves should be several inches lower than the sides of the trench. Build a sloping roof of boards over the celery; pile earth well up to the top of the roof, but leave some cracks for ventilation until heavy freezing weather arrives, when additional earth and salt-hay would be spread.

When setting the celery, roots should be fairly moist, but stalks and leaves good and dry. Trench may be dug extra deep to accommodate cabbages, suspended head down from the roof.

FOOD FROM THE WILD

Many weeds of the countryside can be eaten, and some people find them quite good. Identify these with the aid of a guide to wild flowers, consult local residents, or look them up in your local library; then confirm your identification by consulting your county agent, or by sending specimens to your agricultural college or experiment station. Care is necessary, because some harmful weeds may be confused with them. Some of the better ones:

Skunk Cabbage. SYMPLOCARPUS FOETIDUS. When the evil-smelling plant first pushes its leaves above the swampland in spring, the leaves and white stalks may be collected. Boil them in two changes of water, and serve them buttered and seasoned with pepper and salt. Said to be good eating.

SKUNK CABBAGE. *A wild plant of the swamps.*

Curled Dock. RUMEX CRISPUS. Boiled in two changes of water it is good; leaves are used, and with them some dandelion and curled mustard from the garden can be mixed with advantage.

CURLED DOCK. *A well-known weed.*

Lamb's Quarters or Goosefoot. CHENOPODIUM ALBUM. One of the commonest weeds, which may grow 10 feet high, makes excellent spinach when young if boiled for 20 minutes and served with butter and vinegar.

LAMB'S QUARTERS. *A tall gray-green wild plant that may be found growing almost anywhere.*

Good King Henry or Mercury. CHENOPODIUM BONUS-HENRICUS. Another good spinach. A perennial with 3-inch arrow-shape leaves that sometimes is grown in the herb garden.

GOOD KING HENRY. *Originally a European weed, it is widely-spread in America.*

137

Russian Thistle. SALSOLA PESTIFER. Tender young plants are washed, boiled till tender and served on toast with cream-sauce. Available in spring only.

RUSSIAN THISTLE. *A prickly-leaved weed of Europe, America and Asia.*

Poke, Scoke or Pigeonberry. PHYTOLACCA AMERICANA. The large green and red strong-smelling plant, sometimes 10 feet high, and known as inkberry because of the dark crimson staining juice of the berry, has poisonous roots, but the early spring shoots from these roots are wholesome when served like asparagus.

POKEWEED. *This appears annually as a wild plant in American gardens.*

Purslane or Pussley. PORTULACA OLERACEA. Familiar fleshy prostrate annual weed, sometimes 18 inches high, with reddish stems and shiny 1½ inch leaves that may be served as spinach or used as salad.

PURSLANE. *Sow a lawn, and one of the most troublesome weeds is this one.*

Spanish Lettuce, Miner's Lettuce, Indian Lettuce or Winter Purslane. MONTIA PERFOLIATA. This dwarf annual weed of moist areas was found to be a good vegetable by gold miners in the early days of California. Easily recognized by the leaves on its 10-inch flower-stems: the stems grow through them—hence perfoliata. Use it boiled, or as a salad.

SPANISH LETTUCE. *Found to be edible when pioneers in California were hard put to for food.*

Chickweed. STELLARIA MEDIA. This most common of weeds is an excellent and wholesome spinach.

CHICKWEED. *In a wet season, many lawns are full of it. A good boiled vegetable.*

Marsh Marigold. CALTHA PALUSTRIS. The 2-inch bright yellow flowers of the well-known plant of the swamps and drainage-ditches make it easy to identify. It grows 2 feet high. The leaves and stems are boiled, chopped fine and served with butter, and the buds may be pickled.

MARSH MARIGOLD. *This handsome water-plant can be eaten.*

May-Apple or Pinxter Flower. AZALEA NUDIFLORUM. A one- or two-inch diameter fruit-like growth appears on the stems, in the nature of a gall. May be pickled in spiced vinegar.

MAY-APPLE. *Can be made into pickles.*

Milkweed. ASCLEPIAS CORNUTI. Young plants are collected, washed and boiled in several changes of water. The young tops may be prepared like asparagus.

MILKWEED. *The silk-covered seeds of this weed of the fields were collected in two World Wars as a stuffing for life-jackets.*

Wild Onion or Wild Garlic. ALLIUM CERNUUM. The small onions are 1½ inches long and ½ inch through. They may be boiled and then used in pickles; or some of the bulbs and a few leaves may be added to salads.

WILD ONION or WILD GARLIC. *Hated by farmers, but much enjoyed by the folks who know it.*

New Jersey Tea. CEANOTHUS AMERICANUS. A common shrub of dry sandy soils almost throughout the country. From the dried leaves a tea was brewed during the Revolution; served with cream and sugar, it is not unlike imported tea.

NEW JERSEY TEA. *Our forebears in the War of Independence drank an infusion made from it.*

Labrador Tea. LEDUM GROENLANDICUM. An evergreen shrub with thick, leathery leaves found north from the 40th parallel, reaching 3 feet, with oblong 2-inch leaves, downy on their lower side. A tea is infused from the dried leaves, but because the western type, **Ledum glandulosum,** is claimed to possess poisonous properties, it would be well to drink it sparingly unless you can identify it definitely.

LABRADOR TEA. *Leaves have been used in the North country for tea.*

Wild Mushrooms. Many are edible and good, but the bad actors are so highly poisonous, that all should be under suspicion. Do not gather or prepare them except in the company of an experienced local person, or after showing them to your county agent. Those you plant and grow yourself can be trusted; but from even a mushroom bed do not eat any growths that appear different to the true variety, which will be seen growing where you first planted the pieces of spawn.

HYDROPONICS or GARDENING WITHOUT SOIL

As a botany-class experiment it has long been the practice to grow plants in a weak chemical solution containing the big four plant-food elements, calcium, nitrogen, phosphorus and potassium, along with trace-elements like iron, manganese and magnesium. The experiment demonstrates that plants need these chemicals; if the student omits one of the big four, his plant stops growing at once; if the student omits one of the trace elements, the plant gradually fades away.

Starting from this experiment, so-called chemical gardening or hydroponics became very popular some years ago. Persons interested in it felt that here at last was what they had been looking for; soil, being the home of troublesome insects, fungi and plant diseases, the logical way to avoid them was not to use soil. It was thought that since plants need their important foods in proportions that varied with different varieties, here was a way to control their growth. But successes were few and disappointments were many, the new culture bringing with it new problems.

If you have a greenhouse, try hydroponics. Some florists have grown good roses with chemicals. If you are in a spot where soil is unobtainable, like a Pacific island, but water is plentiful, try it. It is complicated, but has some value as a method of gardening on the roof of an apartment-house.

Sometimes plants are floated or suspended with their roots hanging in the chemical solution, or they may be planted in sterile sand which is kept moist by the solution, which should be circulated or agitated by some means. There are several formulae; one listed in the book "10,000 Garden Questions" being:

> 1 oz. potassium nitrate
> ½ oz. monocalcium phosphate
> ¾ oz. magnesium sulphate
> 1 teaspoon iron sulphate
> 5 gallons water
> To which may be added
> ½ teaspoon Trace-L

Best make up a new solution fresh every time you change it; so lay in a stock of the chemicals, with a set of accurate scales.

But fungi will still give trouble; plants still need as much light as they ever did; coal-gas, illuminating-gas, and over-dry air still make the growing of plants indoors difficult, and chemical gardening is not the help in this regard the first experimenters hoped it would be.

To sum up: To store vegetables, give them ventilation, keep them cool, but protect them against frost. There is much good food by the wayside, available for the gathering. Growing plants in chemical solutions has solved few of the amateurs' problems.

CHAPTER 19

Plants Get Sick Too

Fragrant the fertile earth after soft showers.
JOHN MILTON, 1608–1674

UNDER the names of anthracnose, blast, blight, canker, fire, knot, mildew, mold, mosaic, rhizoctonia, rot, rust, scab, slime, speck, wilt, yellows and others are many illnesses to which plants are subject, due to fungi, bacteria, viruses and protozoa. Some are connected with food deficiencies, soil poisoning, too much or too little water, lack of air circulation, heat, cold, too much or too little light, industrial air poisoning, infected seeds, nematodes or eel-worms. Mostly they are communicable from one plant to another of the same variety. Insects are flagrant spreaders of many plant diseases.

Following are some of the methods by which they are kept under control:

1. Rotating crops
2. Spraying or dusting with insecticides
3. Clean cultivation, leading to the eradication of weeds.
4. Pulling, drying and burning infected plants.
5. Autumn digging
6. Spraying with fungicides. Important with potatoes
7. Avoidance of over-crowding
8. Shaking up cabbage seeds, and dusting cut potatoes, with Semesan
9. Working among plants only when the soil is dry. This applies particularly to beans.

Scientists have helped in recent years by breeding plants which resist some of these infections. However severe the troubles are, the chances are that some few will escape; these that the sickness misses are used as parents to produce a number of rust-resistant, mosaic-resistant, blight-resistant and wilt-resistant varieties. The following are some already available; it is not claimed that they are immune, but they resist them:

Beans, supergreen
" plentiful
" puregold
" Wade
Asparagus, Mary Washington
Cabbage, yellows-resistant
Celery, golden plume

Celery, Cornell no. 19
Corn, honey cross
" Lincoln hybrid
" spancross
" golden cross bantam
" evergreen hybrid
Cucumbers, Vaughan's hybrid

Pea, freezonian
Spinach, blight-resistant
" Old Dominion
Tomato, marglobe
" scarlet topper
" Rutgers

Something new is to breed vegetables to resist insect attacks. Two new corns, flagship and Lincoln hybrid, have ears so tightly wrapped in their husk that the ear-worm cannot enter.

INSECTS WANT THEIR SHARE

An enthusiastic gardener, you have put in a busy evening, planted cabbages and tomatoes. Tired, you happily survey your neat garden. But you get a shock next morning: some of your new plants are lying in the dirt, for they have been neatly nipped at the ground. Scrape the earth away from a broken plant and you may find the culprit—a curled-up, dirt-colored caterpillar, the Cutworm. Replace with new plants, and henceforth you will wrap a stiff card collar around every tomato, cabbage, broccoli and let-

CUTWORM. *He works while you sleep.*

TOMATOES, *collared to protect against cutworm.*

tuce plant that you set out. Ordinary 3 by 5 inch index cards, spindled, will serve, and special collars of asphalt material are obtainable at your seed-store. Also you can get a poisoned bait called Snarol, that you can scatter near the plants as an added precaution, with no risk of harming Fido, or Minnie the cat. This material will also control SLUGS.

APHIDS. *The great plant-suckers. Ants maintain milking herds of them.*

But your troubles may not be over. You may find the growing tips of your bean plants, broccoli, lettuce or tomato wilting; look closely, and you find crowds of small green or black **Plant Lice**, aphis or aphids, sucking the juices of your plants. Bring out your dust-gun or sprayer. With the former you may blow on ¾ per cent rotenone dust, or with the latter you spray a mixture of Black Leaf 40 and soapy water.

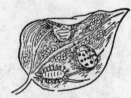

SLUGS. *Slow-moving, they betray their presence by the damage done and their sticky trail.*

Your bean-leaves may be skeletonized by the **Mexican Bean-Beetle** which eats the soft parts of the leaves but ignores the veins. Like a rather large spotted lady-bug; you may find it under the leaf with its yellow spine-covered grub and yellow eggs. This beetle will destroy the crop in a few days, so get after it promptly by blowing ¾ per cent rotenone dust up under the leaves. When the crop has been harvested be sure to dry and burn the plants, otherwise a second brood will appear more deadly than the first.

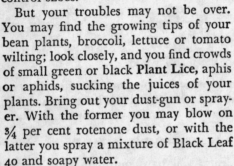

MEXICAN BEAN BEETLE. *He can destroy .your plants in a few nights.*

The same ¾ per cent rotenone dust is blown onto broccoli, cabbage, cauliflower and turnip to control the green **Cabbage-Worm**, resulting from the

CABBAGE-WORM. *He feeds on broccoli, cauliflower and cabbage.*

144

pretty white butterfly which flits in the garden from early spring on.

Hand-pick the savage-looking four-inch **Tomato Horn-Worm,** when sharp eyes find him camouflaged against a stem, which he matches exactly. But when you find little white balloons sticking out from the sides of a hornworm, leave it alone. A parasitic wasp has already taken care of the situation for you; the worm is dying, and the young wasps will emerge from the balloons to continue their good work on other worms.

Tomato Hornworm. *He looks dangerous, but merely is destructive. Look for pellets of excrement.*

Spray or dust **Japanese Beetles** with 25 per cent D.D.T. dust, and knock survivors into a can of water with a film of kerosene on the surface.

Japanese Beetles. *Eat almost any vegetation above ground.*

When digging the garden you may turn up gray-white shiny six-legged creatures about an inch long, but normally curved into a U-shape; probably grubs of the Japanese Beetle, Asiatic Garden Beetle or Oriental Beetle. Those dug up probably all die, hoeing kills a lot more. Nearby lawn areas may well be dusted with lead arsenate, a violent poison, so be careful; use 10 to 15 pounds per 1000 square feet.

A pretty black-banded green and white two-inch creature is the **Celery Caterpillar,** found on carrots and other members of the umbelliferæ. It develops into the handsome swallow-tail butterfly. Easily seen; and when there are only a few, pick them off. Don't be afraid of the red sting-like horn which it erects from its head when disturbed: it's just a bluff, and will not hurt you. If they are numerous, dust or spray with ¾ per cent rotenone.

Droves of brown striped caterpillars may invade your plot from the surrounding fields, eating everything of value in their path. They are **Army-Worms.** The usual remedy is to scatter poisoned bait ahead of them: one tablespoon of Paris green in 2½ lbs. of bran, moistened with one cup of molasses in one pint of water.

Onions may take on a whitened unthrifty look; minute flying

145

insects called **Thrips** are causing the trouble. Spray with Black-leaf 40; be sure to cultivate thoroughly, rotate your crops, clean up in the fall, burning dried onion foliage.

Ants running over plants do not of themselves do much harm, but it is well to get rid of them when you can, because they keep plant-lice and milk them, as we do the cow; and they sometimes establish plant-lice colonies for this purpose. If you can locate the nests, place a Magi-Kil ant trap near by each.

LEAF-MINER. *It lives within the leaf.*

Beet, chard and spinach leaves may develop dead brown patches, which tend to grow bigger. Hold a leaf up to the light, and you may see a tiny caterpillar, or a colony of them between the two surfaces of the leaf, safe from your sprays; so small, you may need a magnifying glass to see the **Leaf-Miner.** When preparing beet greens, chard and spinach in the kitchen eliminate these leaves and burn them; go through your rows, nip off the damaged leaves and burn them also. Keeping the leaves dirty with ¾ per cent rotenone dust will help.

The **Corn-Borer** enters the stem and ear of the corn plant. The **Corn Ear-Worm** enters the ear where the silk emerges. For the borer, ¾ per cent rotenone dust blown into the leaf bases every five days is recommended. For the ear-worm ¼ teaspoon of mineral oil may be squirted inside the tip of the ear just when the silk starts to darken. Under various names, the oil may be pur-

CORN-EARWORM

chased mixed with an insecticide. Another thing you can do, and that is to grow the new varieties Flagship and Lincoln, the husks of which are so heavy and tight that the ear-worm has difficulty in entering.

Dust with ¾ per cent rotenone when you see the little shot-holes made by the **Flea-Beetle** on your plants. When lettuce and cabbage leaves are perforated with ¼ inch irregular holes they are probably being eaten at night by **Slugs**, and their slimy trails will confirm it. Spread some Snarol around.

Striped yellow and black, ½ inch long, the Potato Beetle is easily recognized; look for the egg-clusters and the larvae under the leaves. Spray or dust with 25 per cent D.D.T.

These are the better known insect pests. Consult your county agent in regard to others, and in the meanwhile use ¾ per cent rotenone dust.

Also take up with your county agent the advis-

FLEA-BEETLE
Its damage looks as if someone fired a load of fine shot into the plant.

CORN-BORER *will eat its way through the husk or through any part of the stem. The corn-earworm enters at the tip of the ear. See previous page.*

ability of planting a little earlier or a little later, if you are producing vegetables on a large scale. Some insects come and go, and the methods followed by others in your locality, which your agent will know about, may help you. Large scale Brussels sprouts growers, for example, find they must avoid certain planting periods to escape infestation by aphis.

In the average garden, controlling insect pests with sprays and dusts is not difficult if the gardener goes to work promptly. Delay, and they may well ruin his crops.

To sum up: The diseases of vegetables are not likely to be serious in the home garden; and their insect enemies can readily be combated. Spraying or dusting with fungicides and insecticides, crop rotation and clean cultivation will see the garden through most attacks.

POTATO BEETLE

CHAPTER 20

Hazards in the Garden

Accidents will occur in the best regulated families.
CHARLES DICKENS, 1812–1860

GARDENING is an avocation with little personal danger; you are unlikely to be hit by a golf-ball or an automobile in back of the house; but ordinary caution should be practiced.

Keep weeds in check by continuous hoeing, and you should have no **Poison Ivy**, **Poison Oak**, and certainly no **Poison Sumach**.

POISON IVY. *Stay to windward of a fire in which poison ivy is being destroyed.*

POISON SUMACH. *Note that the berries of poison sumach are white.*

If you are cleaning weeds from among berry-bushes it is just as well to wear gloves and garments with sleeves, to avoid contacts of this nature. If you think you have touched one of these pesky plants, wash at once with plenty of soap; then apply a lotion recommended at the drugstore. Remember, too, that a well-hoed garden has no **Ragweed** to give you hay fever.

In a heavy bramble-patch, sleeves and gloves will protect against the **Black-Widow Spider**, which probably you will never meet; shiny black, its body is ½-inch long and its reach about 1½ inches; the female, which is the more formidable, has a bright hour-glass-shape red spot on the under side, seen through the spider-web, like two triangles with their points together. The male, usually smaller, may have stripes of red and black on its top-side. If bitten, call a doctor; while he is on his way, give the victim hot baths.

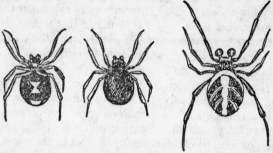

BLACK-WIDOW SPIDERS, *both females.* Left *shows the under side with the* hour-glass *marking. Natural size.*

THE MALE BLACK WIDOW. *Enlarged*

The black widow does not attack unless bothered, or unless it is guarding its eggs, or squeezed when putting on a shoe, or between the sheets of a bed in which it has taken refuge. In the autumn the black widow may enter the house, and the chance of being bitten is greater indoors than out. A kerosene emulsion spray should control any infestation of this creature which may occur, but rarely does, among plants in the garden. Ninety-five per cent of black widow spider victims recover.

If Mosquitoes, Black-Flies, Gnats and No-See-Ums annoy, use a repellent lotion, and wear gloves and sixty-mesh screen-cloth over the head, well tucked into the clothing about the neck; tie sleeves at the wrist.

Wood-Ticks and Spotted-Fever Ticks are flattish, eight-legged blood-sucking bugs which attach themselves to the skin; they may come from weedy underbrush. If they cannot be flicked off, touching them with a drop of turpentine will make them release their hold; they can be pulled off with a steady drag, but the

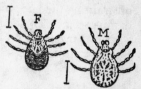

WOOD-TICKS, *female and male. Use patience in getting them off your skin.*

149

mouth-parts may break off and remain in the skin, needing a doctor to take care of the situation.

Yellow-Jacket nests should be avoided in daylight, but at night cyanogas blown into the opening, and then plugging the entrance, will settle them. Their sting is unimportant, though painful, unless they gang up on one, or sting near the eye or in the mouth.

Harmful snakes are rarely encountered in gardens. If you are in Rattlesnake country and hear a rattle, leave the garden to the snake for the time; let an experienced woodsman take over. The writer has seen about one Copperhead a year near rocks in rough country; leave him alone. In this book, emphasis is placed on using the hoe continuously; snakes avoid a constantly cultivated garden as a rule, while the occasional one can be seen at once. In snake territory, wear high leather shoes; here is a good reason for women to wear heavy slacks or dungarees in the garden, tucked into boots. Also, fence the garden with the smallest mesh chicken-wire.

The Gila Monster and Coral Snake of the southwest should be avoided, but they seldom appear.

Should a snake-bite unfortunately happen, send for a doctor. If the tooth marks are like a horseshoe, the snake is probably harmless. If the mark consists of a pair or double pair of punctures commence the first-aid treatment given in the Textbook of the American Red Cross: with a razor blade make a cross-cut at each puncture, like a plus mark or multiplication mark; let each of the two bars be ½ inch long, and let them be about ¼ inch deep; then suck and spit out. While you are cutting get someone to tie a bandage, a belt, tie or shoelace above the bite on the side nearer the heart. Keep the victim quiet and lying down.

More likely than meeting any of these hazards is the possibility of straining the knee-joint or contracting a chill from kneeling on damp ground. These are easily avoided by using a Gardenade or wearing knee pads. A Gardenade (see p. 152) lets a middle-age person get onto his knees in comfort, and handles help him get back on his feet.

BOOK III

Lawns

Index

CHAPTER 1

Renovate Your Old Lawn

"And he gave it for his opinion, that whoever could make two ears of corn, or two blades of grass, to grow upon a spot of ground where only one grew before, would deserve better of mankind, and do more essential service to his country, than the whole race of politicians put together." JONATHAN SWIFT (1667–1745).

A GOOD LAWN may be defined as an area of smooth fertile soil, covered with mown plants of perennial grasses, with both their leaves and roots intertwining. They completely hide the land from view and are emerald-green in spring, summer, and autumn. A lawn makes the proper setting for the home, is the background and foundation of your garden, enhances the value of your property, and is a community asset.

A good permanent living outdoor carpet can be produced, but there is the satisfaction that even a good one can be improved; and a really perfect turf, calling for planning and continued effort, is something of which we can be very proud.

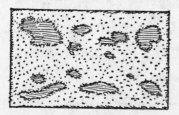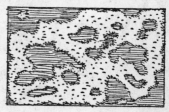

Do we need a new lawn? LEFT: *no, repair what you have, for less than half is bare.* RIGHT: *yes, because more than half is without grass. Make the new one at summer's end.*

11

Let us first consider a problem of the average owner. He has a neglected lawn; it is ragged, has a lot of weeds, is bare in places, and the soil is uneven. What should he do? The extent of the bare or weed-occupied areas will suggest the answer; if in total they represent half the lawn, it is best to make a new one, as described in Chapter 2; if they comprise less than half the area, repair it.

REPAIRING A LAWN. (Directions on following pages.)

Avoid June 15 to August 15 for the work, but do it at any other time of the year when the lawn is bare of snow, with both the grass and soil dry, and free of frost. For lawns of 5000 square feet or less the following would be a good program:

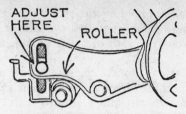

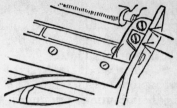

Principle of the average hand-mower design. Machine runs on a rear roller and the pair of forward side wheels. Height of cut is regulated by the rear roller.

When a hand-mower squeezes grass instead of cutting it, turn the machine over and see if the cutting spiral is in close adjustment with the bottom knife.

Moving the spiral slowly by hand (watch your fingers), see if it will cut a few leaves of grass its entire length. On each side of most makes are two screws, one brings the bottom blade closer to the spiral, the other pulls it away. Take plenty of time to make the ideal adjustment, and then leave the screws tight.

1. Mow it to leave the grass one inch long.

The height that a mower cuts is found by placing it on a table and with a ruler measuring the distance between the table surface and the point where the stationary blade or bed-knife is wiped by the revolving spiral. You will note that the cutting action is quite like that of a pair of shears, one spiral being followed by another at so high a speed, obtained by means of cogwheel gearing, that the action is almost continuous. Generally, the more expensive the mower the higher the speed of the spiral in relation to the forward movement of the machine; and the better the machine the more knives there are on the revolving spiral, usually as many as five. A hand-mower with fewer than five knives produces a definite ribbing effect or "corduroy," but cuts long grass easier; a machine with more than five is hard to push unless the grass is cut with it almost daily. The average mower runs on a rear roller and on two side wheels, which are linked to the train of cog gears and are the source of power to rotate the spiral wiper. On the bridge made by the side wheels and the rear roller is the bed-knife. By loosening two nuts, one at each side of the rear-roller assembly, the brackets holding the roller can be pushed *down* to raise the cutting height, or pulled *up* to lower the cutting height. When the desired length of cut is obtained, the nuts are tightened.

2. Wherever there is crabgrass in abundance, spray with a solution of PMAS, following closely the directions in Chapter 12. In the meantime, pry out all dandelions and plantains with a weeding knife or an old chisel. Cut out crabgrass also if there is not overmuch of it; forget the PMAS if the infestation is moderate or if the lawn is small.

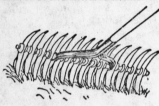

The Cavex rake is a series of self-sharpening knives; one side cuts deep, other side, shallow.

3. Comb the area clean. For this a Cavex rake is recommended; if you cannot get one, use an ordinary iron rake. The Cavex is a series of curved knives; it is self-clearing; push it forward and pull it backward without lifting it, and it will take out a surprising quantity of leaves, rubbish and shriveled grass clippings; occasionally a grass plant will come away, but this is not important. Another thing the rake will do is to make a series of cuts in the land, into which the materials you now add will find their way.

4. Spread a good fertilizer, and not the cheapest you can buy. The reason is that one made with both chemical and organic ingredients is best, for the organic substances which are the remains of dead plants and animal excreta, may consist of refuse from the stockyards, castor pomace, cottonseed meal, bird manure, sheep manure, or bonemeal. All these have to decay before the grass roots can use them, so their effect is slow, and their presence in fertilizers gives them a lasting quality. The chemical elements are usually quick, and a mixture of the two classes is desirable. Organic ingredients are the more expensive.

For your purpose, the analysis of a fertilizer, required by law to be printed on the bag, is relatively unimportant, whether it is 4–8–4, 5–10–5 or 8–6–2, except that the first of the three figures indicates the amount of nitrogen in the mixture. Divide this into

14

100, and the answer is the number of pounds of the compound you may safely spread on each 1000 square feet without burning the grass you have there—25 pounds of 4–8–4, 20 pounds of 5–10–5, or 12½ pounds of 8–6–2, all per 1000 square feet (say, 20 by 50 feet, or 40 by 25 feet). Multiply the length in feet and the width in feet to get the number of square feet in your lawn; estimate curves or irregular shapes as closely as you can.

Divide the fertilizer into two parts, and dress the whole area first with one half and then with the other, to give an even distribution, which is important. Rub the lawn once with the back of a rake to knock the fertilizer off the grass. Turf must be dry.

5. Spread enough topsoil to fill minor depressions when it is leveled off, but do not use so much that the grass is buried; the green color should show through when you have finished. Spread it with a shovel, and draw it to and fro and up and down with the back of a wooden rake until the surface is even, using the rake as a straight-edge. The average quantity is ½ cubic yard to each 1000 square feet, but if you find you have too much, spread the balance later in small amounts. Sifting the topsoil through a ½-inch screen is helpful but you can take out larger stones and pieces of root and other debris when you rub with the back of the rake, if it is more convenient to use unscreened soil.

6. On each 1000 square feet broadcast 5 pounds of a good quality grass-seed mixture, preferably one with a high proportion of the grass variety, fescue, at least 50 per cent by weight; if you cannot find such a mixture, buy an additional quantity of Illahee, F 74, or Chewing's fescue and add it to the mixture. These seeds are somewhat expensive, but they are worth their cost.

7. Carefully brush the area with a house broom, so that many of the new seeds are covered with soil. It would be good to complete the work by rolling, but this is not so important that a roller must be purchased. Better not water, but wait for rain, because watering is likely to dislodge the seeds, washing them from some spots and concentrating them on others.

One such treatment as this may not result in a perfect lawn right away. A second effort may be required some months later, perhaps a third; and making an annual affair of it, preferably late every summer, will be worth while. Also helpful are a winter dressing of lime, unless you are in a limestone region, and a twice yearly application of fertilizer, unless your soil is fertile.

For large lawns, playing fields, or golf fairways the same principles may be followed, except that plantains and dandelions are sprayed with the new chemical 2–4-D, again following exactly the manufacturer's instructions. This is in addition to PMAS. Tractor-drawn implements are used instead of hand tools; a soil-perforating device, and an adjustable disk-harrow, with the disks set straight and made to cut into the land by weighting it with sandbags, will take the place of the Cavex rake; a broadcast fertilizer-spreader; a broadcast seed-sower; a bush-harrow made of tree branches spiked to lumber to be dragged over the seed will serve for the house broom; and a tractor-drawn roller would be employed. Apply fertilizers at the same rate, multiplying the above figures by 40 to give you the allowance per acre, but use seeds more sparingly: 75 pounds per acre over the best spots; up to 150 pounds per acre over the worst.

If you are aiming for a bent turf and are willing to give it the extra care that bent needs, the seeding parts of these programs would be changed. Use 2½ pounds of bent seeds instead of 5 pounds of the fescue-containing mixture—from 40 to 75 pounds per acre on the larger areas. And if your lawn is in the southern states the seeds might well be Bermuda grass in spring and rye grass in autumn.

Should the weeds consist of wild strawberry, sourgrass, or moss, they usually indicate that the land lacks lime. Start the renovating program with a dressing of 100 pounds of pulverized limestone or ground limestone rock per 1000 square feet, or 2 tons per acre, wait for rain, and then, when the land is dry again, go ahead with mowing, weeding, and scarifying as suggested.

Dry soil and dry grass are important when carrying out this program. It might seem a good thing to spread fertilizer or sow seeds during rainy weather, but you will run into difficulties; fertilizer will scald the grass and, since you will not be able to spread seeds fairly, you will waste some. So we suggest that you do this work only when grass and soil are dry.

16

CHAPTER 2

The New Lawn

"Too often reliance is put largely in fertilizers or in seed mixtures without the realization that either of these, however meritorious it may be, is but one of the many factors requisite for success." C. V. PIPER AND R. A. OAKLEY, Turf for Golf Courses, 1917.

THE PROBLEM OF TOPSOIL

YOU HAVE a worn-out lawn and decide it needs remaking, because less than half the area has grass on it. Or you have purchased a new home and are going to make your own lawn. Perhaps you are converting your flower-beds or part of your vegetable plot into turf. Maybe you have acquired some additional land, torn down a building, or eliminated a driveway. Possibly you are a school official and have to convert waste land into a

One reason for poor lawns is that the subsoil excavated for the building may have been spread over the area, burying the topsoil.

playing field; or a highway engineer aiming to have green roadsides; you may be contemplating a golf course or a flying field.

The basic requirement is the same for all—a minimum 6 inches of topsoil. If grading or erosion has robbed the area of the loam that should be there, you should replace it with topsoil from elsewhere. In excavating the cellar for your new home, the builder may have covered the topsoil with subsoil; by digging, you may be able to bring some of it to the surface. The same ap-

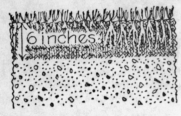

Minimum topsoil thickness for a lawn is 6 inches. Ideally, it should stand on porous subsoil.

Topsoil is often missing in spots on a new lawn through careless grading.

plies if grading has covered a low spot with subsoil; there may be some useful material down under. Should you bring topsoil onto the area, first roughen the surface with a hoe or fork; with a disk-harrow if the area is large. Then spread the new material.

LEFT TO RIGHT: *weeding knife, garden fork, spade, pointed shovel. All useful to the lawn-keeper.*

Where grading has to be done, scoop or bulldoze the topsoil into heaps onto a neutral area, where you have neither to cut nor fill; perform the grading and return the topsoil onto the new surface. In the case of rough land being brought into cultivation, fork out weed roots and young saplings, or drag out larger trees; and cover with topsoil any spots where this work has brought subsoil to the surface.

18

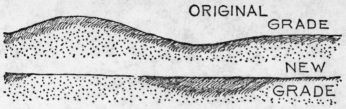

Incorrect grading may result in scraping much topsoil into hollows, removing it entirely from the high land.

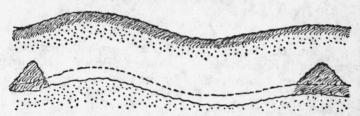

Better way to grade is to scrape topsoil into heaps in spots already at the correct level, where there will be no cutting or filling.

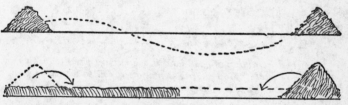

Grading is then carried out in the subsoil, and the topsoil returned in a uniform covering over all.

On very large areas, a tractor-drawn stone-rake will pull rocks and roots into windrows for easy removal off the area.

It usually is not difficult to tell what is topsoil and what is not. It is often darker in color than the subsoil on which it rests; look closely and you will see plant remains in it.

And you can best appraise its quality by looking at it. If you see it before it is dug, the size and luxuriance of the weeds growing on it assure you it is good. After it is dug, if the remains of

*When grading above level near
a tree, build a wall of concrete
blocks or stone to retain the soil.*

dead plants are abundant it is generally good. Do not be de-
ceived by a dark color due to moisture; a spadeful from a heap
of damp screened subsoil can look quite good.

LEFT: *best indication of good land is a luxuriant weed crop. In 1592
Shakespeare wrote, "Most subject is the fattest soil to weeds."* 2 Henry
VI. RIGHT, *sparse weeds show poor land.*

A soil test does not help much. We expect the best topsoil often
to be sour, because decaying vegetation produces organic acids;
and a little limestone easily corrects the condition. An examination may disclose that phosphorus or potassium may be in short
supply, but periodic applications of fertilizer take care of this. The
important thing is: has the soil grown good crops or good weeds,
and are the remains of crops or weeds plentifully distributed
throughout it?

If topsoil is difficult to obtain, and the area is large, you can
get fair results by spreading less than 6 inches, mixing it thoroughly with hoe, fork, rake, or disk with the surface to give you

Good topsoil is full of the remains of past generations of plants. If you looked closely, you should see many decayed leaves, stems, and root fibers. Twigs, branches, and wood shavings are not wanted, however.

a top layer consisting partly of subsoil and partly of topsoil, and adding also from 250 to 500 pounds per 1000 feet of commercial humus, compost, rotted manure, or one large bale of peatmoss. Then add 200 pounds or more of pulverized sheep manure and 100 pounds of bonemeal per 1000 square feet.

If topsoil is impossible to obtain you can still get a passable turf by raking fertilizer under and sowing equal parts of the only three grasses that will grow in subsoil—namely F 74, Chewing's, or Illahee fescue —allowing 7½ pounds of each per 1000 square feet, or 300 pounds of each per acre. The seeds happen to be very large, with comparatively few in a pound, which accounts for the heavy seed allowance. Be sure to work under the organic materials and manures listed above.

An average wheelbarrow load is 10 shovelsful, or ½₀ yard; 100 to 125 pounds of soil.

Having solved the topsoil problem—it is already there, you have brought it onto the property, or you feel you must do without it—the site should be made rough with a cultivator-hoe, or disked if the area is large. Mixing a less than normal amount of topsoil with the subsoil, along with humus, compost, manure or decayed leaves also calls for hoeing or disking. If you are forced to do without soil and are going to sow fescue seeds, the hard surface will similarly have to be broken up. At this hoeing or disk-

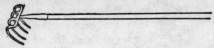

Sharp prongs of the cultivator-hoe are excellent for breaking hard soil.

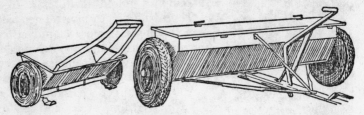

LEFT: *a spreader operated by hand;* RIGHT: *one hauled by a tractor.*

LEFT: *28-tooth wood rake; back makes a useful straight-edge.* CENTER: *steel rake for working soil.* RIGHT: *flat steel brume-rake for trash.*

ing all sticks, stones, and rubbish will be picked up. An even surface is most important; so several rakings should be given.

The next step is to spread 50 pounds of 4–8–4, 40 pounds of 5–10–5, or 25 pounds of 8–6–2 per 1000 square feet. Respectively, these are 2000 pounds, 1600 pounds, and 1000 pounds per acre. Note that these quantities are twice those suggested for renovating in Chapter 1. Rake the surface, or drag a bundle of tree branches over acreage, and you are ready to sow seeds.

SOWING GRASS SEEDS—THE BEST KINDS TO USE

What these seeds should be is often open to debate, and experienced turf-makers sometimes disagree on what is best to use. There are several reasons why they do: some grasses do better in

THE NEW LAWN.

Having made the surface even, spread compost and fertilizer; rake to mix them with the top 3 inches.

Sow larger grass seeds and rake; sow smaller seeds and roll or tamp.

one kind of soil than in another, and only by actually sowing them can one tell which are the more suitable. Some varieties grow better in hot weather, like the bents; others prefer a dry summer, like the fescues. Some varieties, including the bluegrasses, like cold; others like heat. Some are at their best in spring; others in summer. Some need rich soil; others do better in soil that is on the poor side. Some are highly resistant to wear; others are easily injured by traffic. For the home lawn, a combination of several varieties is generally favored; a mixed turf will survive some inattention, yet will improve and respond to care when you can get around to giving it. If you make a lawn of one variety you often invite weeds to come in, and should the lawn be attacked by disease you may find the whole area in trouble; but disease usually confines itself to one kind, and a mixed sward will show less injury. So if you decide to use several varieties, as it is recommended that you do, buy the necessary seeds from your local supplier, and be prepared to pay a fairly heavy price, because the important grass varieties are costly. Buy the best stock mixture you can get if the area is small. If the area is considerable, pick out a combination from the tables on pp. 26–28, purchase the ingredients separately and make two mixtures, the larger seeds in one, the smaller

RYE GRASS   FESCUE

One good way to sow grass seeds: mix larger kinds, sow and rake. These are slightly enlarged: rye grass averages ½ inch long, and 1 pound contains 300,000 grains; fescue, ¼ inch long, and one pound has 600,000.

BLUE GRASS   BENT

One good way to sow grass seeds: mix smaller seeds, broadcast over larger seeds, and roll or tamp without raking. Seeds somewhat enlarged: bluegrass averages ⅛ inch long, with 2½ million to the pound; bent, 1⁄16 inch long, 6 million to the pound.

seeds in the other. Obviously the larger seeds should be deeper in the soil than the smaller ones; sow the large seeds and rake so as to cover them; then sow the smaller seeds and roll without raking. This does not apply to the seeds for a bent lawn, which are all small; mix these together, sow half the mixture over the area, and rake under as shallow as you can; then broadcast the other half and merely roll. Carry out this same procedure when you buy a stock seed mixture for a small area: sow and rake in half the allowance; sow and roll in the other half.

Best sowing period: first choice, early autumn; second choice, late autumn or winter; third choice, very early in spring. Avoid late spring or summer.

If you like clover in your lawn, add 5 per cent of wild white clover, which is preferred, or of white Dutch or Alsike clover. On steep slopes or on very dry land, add 2½ per cent of yarrow.

Three kinds of clover that may be used in lawns. LEFT: *wild white.* CENTER: *alsike has light purple flowers.* RIGHT: *white Dutch clover.*

For white clover or wild white clover, do not be misled into using sweet clover, tall, unsuitable and not permanent.

To encourage clover in your lawn, apply increased amounts of limestone, bonemeal, or superphosphate.

Shortly after sowing, birds may be seen eating your grass seeds. They seldom do serious harm; the larger seeds interest them most, especially ryegrass, the cheapest ingredient in an average seed mixture. This variety is included as a nurse, and the loss of a few plants will have little effect subsequently on the lawn. There seems to be small need for strings of fluttering paper; yet there is no objection to erecting them, along with dummy cats and scarecrows, usually ineffective, if you feel like doing so.

WEIGHT OF GRASS SEED

In the event you are advised to use grass seed by the quart or bushel, 1 bushel contains 32 quarts and weighs 25 pounds on an average. One quart weighs from 12 to 15 ounces, and 1 pound measures from 1⅛ quarts to 1½ quarts.

SEED MIXTURES
Table A

RECOMMENDED LAWN MIXTURES FOR WASHINGTON, D. C.,
NORTH TO THE ARCTIC

(Sow spring or autumn.)

	Sunny lawn within 100 miles of coast	Sunny lawn inland	Shaded or partly shaded lawn	Bent lawn	Playing fields and airports; steep hillsides
PERMANENT VARIETIES *Bent grasses*	Lbs. or ozs.	Lbs. or ozs.	Lbs. or ozs.	Lbs. or ozs.	Lbs. or ozs.
Seaside	5	5	..	25	..
Rhode Island (Colonial)	5	5	..	25	..
Highland	..	..	..	..	5
Astoria	5	5	..	25	..
Velvet	..	..	5	..	..
Bluegrasses					
Kentucky	..	10	..	..	..
Merion B 27	10	10	..	..	..
Shade bluegrass (Bird grass)	..	..	20	..	..
Fescues					
Chewing's, F74, or Illahee	50	40	50	..	40
Smooth brome grass	..	..	..	..	15
Crested wheat grass	..	..	..	..	10
TEMPORARY VARIETIES (Nurse grasses for quick coverage; they disappear in time.)					
Redtop	10	10	10	25	..
Meadow fescue	..	..	..	..	10
Alta fescue	..	..	..	..	10
Perennial rye grass	15	15	15	..	..
Domestic rye grass	..	..	..	..	10
Total	100	100	100	100	100
Amount to sow, per 1000 sq. ft.	5 lbs.	5 lbs.	5 lbs.	2½ lbs.	3 lbs.
per acre	200 lbs.	200 lbs.	200 lbs.	100 lbs.	125 lbs.

Table B

RECOMMENDED SEED MIXTURES FOR THE MID-SOUTH
35TH TO 39TH PARALLEL
(Sow every spring and autumn.)

	Sunny lawn		Shaded or partly shaded lawn		Bent lawn		Playing fields, airports, steep hillsides	
	Spring	Fall	Spring	Fall	Spring	Fall	Spring	Fall
PERMANENT VARIETIES	Lbs. or ozs.	Lbs. or ozs.	Lbs. or ozs.	Lbs. or ozs.	Lbs. or ozs.	Lbs. or ozs.	Lbs. or ozs.	Lbs. or ozs.
Bent grasses								
Highland	5	5	··	··	15	30	··	··
Astoria	··	··	··	··	15	30	··	··
Velvet	··	··	5	5	··	··	··	··
Bluegrasses								
Shade bluegrass (Bird grass)	··	··	15	15	··	··	··	··
Fescues								
Chewing's, F74, or Illahee	45	45	45	40	··	··	20	30
Smooth brome	··	··	··	··	··	··	10	10
Crested wheat	··	··	··	··	··	··	10	10
Bermuda grass	50	··	35	··	50	··	30	··
TEMPORARY VARIETIES (Nurse grasses; they disappear in time.)								
Redtop	··	10	··	10	20	40	··	··
Meadow fescue	··	··	··	··	··	··	··	··
Alta fescue	··	··	··	··	··	··	10	10
Perennial rye grass	··	40	··	30	··	··	10	15
Domestic rye grass	··	··	··	··	··	··	10	25
Total	100	100	100	100	100	100	100	100
Amount to sow, per 1000 sq. ft.	2½ lbs.	2½ lbs.	2½ lbs.	2½ lbs.	2 lbs.	2 lbs.	2½ lbs.	2½ lbs.
per acre	100 lbs.	100 lbs.	100 lbs.	100 lbs.	75 lbs.	75 lbs.	100 lbs.	100 lbs.

Table C

RECOMMENDED FOR SOWING BELOW 35TH PARALLEL (LEVEL LAND)

	Spring	Fall
	Lbs. or ozs.	Lbs. or ozs.
PERMANENT VARIETY		
Bermuda grass, for dry land ⎱	100 *	..
Carpet grass, for moist acid land ⎰		
TEMPORARY VARIETIES		
(They generally disappear in spring.)		
Redtop	..	25
Domestic rye grass	..	75
Total	100	100
Amounts to sow, per 1000 sq. ft.	2½ lbs.	4 lbs.
per acre	100 lbs.	160 lbs.

* Bermuda grass or Carpet grass, depending upon whether the area is normal and reasonably dry, or is marshy.

PURE LIVE SEED

The federal government and most state governments require that only seeds of high *purity* and high vitality or *germination*

LEFT: *a seed-broadcasting device that works well.* RIGHT: *a machine that is suitable for seeding large grounds.*

be offered for sale. These qualities are expressed in percentages: for example, 90 per cent purity means that of every 100 grains, 90 are seeds of the variety needed, the balance being empty husks, stem fragments, or rubbish. Ninety per cent germination would mean that in every 100 seeds, 90 are able to grow. Seeds offered 90–90 have 90 per cent purity and 90 per cent germination. By multiplying the two percentages and dividing by 100 we have the *pure-live-seed* content, a basis on which some large purchases are made; in this case, 81 per cent.

CHAPTER 3

The New Lawn (Continued)

"But plow not an unknown plain:
First you must learn the winds and changeable ways
of its weather,
The land's peculiar cultivation and character,
The different crops that different parts of it yield or
yield not.
A corn-crop here, grapes there will come to the hap-
pier issue:
On another soil it is fruit trees, and grass of its own
sweet will
Grows green."

VIRGIL, Georgics (70–19 B.C.)*

SOIL TESTS

IN THE LAST chapter it was suggested that a test of the soil may be unnecessary. But you might feel on safer ground, in more ways than one, if you had it examined. Soil-testing kits are offered by the supply houses, and you can work on it yourself; or you can get in touch with your county agricultural agent or your agricultural experiment station. Distinguish between a series of tests, which are somewhat rough-and-ready, and an exact soil analysis, which could be furnished you by a chemist but which involves a chain of complicated experiments and a high cost—and in the end the report may mean little to you. The simple tests, however, made by the county agent, the experiment station, or yourself may help you decide which is the better topsoil to buy, whether to take it from this spot or that, and whether through the years

* Translation of C. Day Lewis

the lawn should be dressed with extra amounts of lime or phosphatic or potassic fertilizers. Whether soil has an adequate supply of organic matter is readily judged by its darker color, and whether it contains enough grit in it to drain well can be decided by rubbing it between the fingers.

A soil-testing kit indicates whether or not your soil needs extra amounts of the big-four elements—calcium, nitrogen, phosphorous, or potassium. Sets can also be obtained to show the score regarding the trace elements.

Grass grows more readily, lasts longer, and resists wear better on land that is porous and lets moisture descend freely. A lawn is more satisfactory on a sandy loam than on clay soil. For a small lawn the land can be made suitable; some heavy soil can be taken away and replaced with lighter soil, or gravel screenings, coarse washed sand or screened coke ashes can be dug into it to lighten it. But the quantities needed are large and render the project well-nigh impossible on wide areas. However, the quality of the land may help in determining whether a playing field shall be constructed here or a golf course built there.

INDICATOR WEEDS

When wild plants are present in considerable numbers they give one a good idea of the kind of soil they are growing in.

Wet land. Here we find ferns, the equisetum or horsetail, sedge, rush, cattail, buttercup, pennywort. Sometimes the surface is dry, but they tell you that it is wet underneath. Drainage may be necessary.

LEFT: *equisetum or horsetail.* CENTER: *sedge.* RIGHT: *rush. These weeds indicate that drainage probably is necessary. In early spring the fir-tree-like growth of equisetum is preceded by a pink-brown toadpipe.*

Buttercup tells us that the land is wet; dock, in CENTER, *that it needs lime; devil's paintbrush, at* RIGHT, *that it requires organic matter and plant foods.*

LEFT: *pennywort is a sign of over-wet soil.* CENTER: *chicory indicates a limestone soil; looks like a dandelion in turf, but the flowers are on a 3-foot spike and are blue.* RIGHT: *wild onion grows in deep rich clay soil.*

Sour land. Sorrel, dock, wild strawberry, bramble. Lime is needed.

Poor, dry soil. Devil's paint-brush, spurge. Manure, mushroom soil, and plant foods generally are indicated.

Tight, compressed soil. Knotweed, poa annua. Perforating the soil, and working under coarse sand and peatmoss dust will help.

Deep, clay soil. Self-heal, wild onion.

Limestone. Chicory, teasel.

THE pH FACTOR AND THE NEED FOR LIME

This combination of two letters with a number is a mathematical symbol describing the concentration of the hydrogen ion. Its practical application is that it expresses the degree of acidity in soil. pH 7 is neutral. Figures above 7 show an alkaline condition; those below 7 indicate an acid one, suggesting that lime is needed.

Grass grows well within a range of pH 6 and pH 8. Because minerals other than calcium have an alkaline reaction, the pH is likely to be misleading if 7 or above is shown, when the alkalinity may be due in part to sodium, potassium, magnesium, or other alkaline elements. It is quite possible for land to show a high pH reading owing to the presence of these and yet be deficient in calcium or lime. A more reliable test is to spread hydrated lime over a limited turf area and to watch results. But patience is necessary: six months may elapse before some improvement is observed.

THE LEVELING BOARD

A lawn that is intended to appear level need not be exactly so; it may be graded to a slightly convex surface, having an almost invisible "crown" so that at no time can water remain on it. All water will then either seep into the subsoil or gradually run off. If the center is 2½ per cent above the sides, or raised 30 inches in 100 feet, it will take care of this and yet not be apparent.

One way to obtain a contour of this nature is to make a leveling board with a light plank—say, 6 inches wide, 1 inch thick

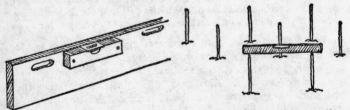

A leveling board helps you drive in stakes of equal height regardless of the contours of the ground.

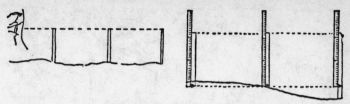

LEFT: *when some stakes are in accurately, many more can be placed speedily merely by sighting.* RIGHT: *with the help of a yardstick and by measuring from the top, mark on each stake the point from which you will take away or add soil to obtain the grade you are seeking.*

and 10 feet long—and accurately attach a spirit level to it. Drive in a number of stakes at 9-foot intervals—4-foot bamboo canes will often serve very well and are obtainable at a garden supply store—and with the aid of the board drive them in so that their tops are level. Measuring from the top, mark where the finished surface should be on each stake; then add soil around some and take away from others, as may be necessary. It will now be easy to make the surface even between each stake. Where you are adding a layer of topsoil onto a subsoil base, drive the stakes into the subsoil, true the sub-grade and roughen the surface. Then add topsoil up to the marks which you will have put on the stakes.

DRAINAGE—THE GRASSY SWALE

Under-drainage of the soil is usually necessary to take care of wet spots, but first make sure they are not due to surface water unable to run off, which simple grading will cure. Wet spots on

Draining a wet area to a stream; ditches have a slight fall.

LEFT: *with no stream available, drainage can be into a blind well.*
RIGHT: *where drain tiles butt, joints are wrapped with waterproof building paper. End of drain is covered with wire mesh to keep out nesting animals.*

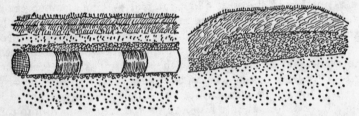

LEFT: *drain pipes are surrounded by gravel or cinders. Subsoil and then topsoil are returned, filling to 15 per cent over grade to allow for sinkages.* RIGHT: *on an incurable wet spot, grade the surface to a slight slope; place a 12-inch layer of ashes or gravel; on this spread topsoil.*

level or slightly sloping land are mostly caused by springs coming to the surface. For these a series of ditches are dug into the subsoil, with a 5 per cent grade on the ditch floor, to a lower point, which may be a stream, a blind well, possibly an open ditch; a blind well, by the way, is merely a hole filled with large rocks. The drainage ditches start 24 inches beneath the surface, and are 15, 20, 25, or 30 feet apart, depending upon the nature of the land; they are closest in heavy clay. Hollow drain tile is laid on the ditch floor, the ends butted and wrapped with roofing paper; rocks, gravel, or ashes are placed around the tile, and the ditches are filled to 15 per cent above level, subsoil being returned first, topsoil last.

You have a wet spot in the lawn. LEFT: *sometimes spreading extra soil will shed surface water and cure it.* CENTER: *try driving in a long pipe, stopping and withdrawing it every few feet. If water starts draining away, you have struck a porous stratum.* RIGHT: *you would be justified in digging a dry well, filling it with rocks.*

There are occasions when a wet spot can be dried by installing a blind well in its center. This works if there happens to be a layer of porous gravel or sand below to carry the water away. Before digging, find out if there is such a layer by driving down a long crowbar or length of iron pipe, first to 5 feet, then to 10 feet, or to deeper levels. Withdraw the boring tool at each 2 feet and see if the patch tends to dry. If it does, you will be justified in digging a shaft down to the porous layer, filling it with rocks, placing smaller stones on the top, and capping with 18 inches of topsoil, which again should be 15 per cent over-grade. This would be 1½ feet over-grade in the case of a dry well 10 feet deep.

Sometimes the situation suggests that a grassy swale will take care of a moist area by providing a ready means of exit for surface water. This swale is a wide, shallow depression with slopes so gradual that grass will grow satisfactorily upon them, and the grading is so little removed from level that it is scarcely apparent. The swale is made by scooping away the topsoil, the grades found by means of the stakes and leveling board, and resoiling and sowing the area.

The filling over-grade referred to above is necessary to allow for sinkages which always will occur when holes are filled or soil is spread. Let a year elapse, and the surface will have dropped to level. Sometimes it will sink below level, when several topdressings with soil will be necessary to bring it to where it should be.

Despite grading, tile drainage, or blind-well digging, some spots may still be over-moist. Should this be the case, strip the topsoil and pile it, grade the subsoil to a slight slope, and lay a bed of steamed ashes or gravel 12 inches thick to make a foundation. On this will be a 12-inch bed of topsoil, the original soil you stripped with some additional amounts from elsewhere. Make your lawn on this.

COMPOST

If the soil is lacking in organic matter, some should be worked in at the time the lawn is made, using from 250 to 500 pounds of commercial humus, compost, or rotted manure per 1000 square feet, or one bale of peatmoss per 1000 square feet; then 200 pounds or more of pulverized sheep manure and 100 pounds or more of bonemeal may be spread and raked under. In other words, proceed as suggested in Chapter 2 where less than the normal allowance of topsoil was considered.

Through the seasons there is a tendency for organic matter to disappear, largely through decomposition, when the decaying materials yield their plant foods to the grass. This disappearance can be delayed or even prevented by (1) occasional surface dressings of compost, humus, manure, or powdered peatmoss, with organic manures, and (2) mowing so frequently that the grass clippings are small and, instead of raking them up, letting them shrivel, decay and become part of the land.

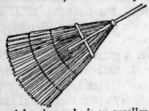

A bamboo rake is an excellent clean-up tool. Its use stimulates the grass, too.

Compost referred to above is a great grass-grower. Merely rake up and put on a heap all the autumn leaves you can save; add to them all weeds, clean vegetable refuse, and any manure you can collect. Find a place for the heap under trees where little of anything can be grown, and at the end of a year your leaves will have decayed into a black mold—sooner if you water the heap in dry weather and add during its building one of the materials offered to hasten decomposition. Compost may be sifted through a ½-inch screen before using it.

SCREENING OR STERILIZING SOIL

Other than this, there is little use for a screen in lawn-keeping, unless you have a small area to sow and feel like sifting a very light dressing of soil onto the seed, just enough to hide it, instead of raking after sowing. There is another occasion when sifting soil is justified: if the surface is particularly stony, some turf-keepers like to screen the top inch to make a "germinating layer." With these exceptions, sifting soil does not appear to be a good thing; stones and particles of various sizes seem to be helpful; remove them, and the land becomes packed and "saddened," to use the lawn men's term. During the making of a lawn, raking out the larger stones will usually be sufficient.

This worker is exposing soil to the flame from a fire-gun prior to sowing. Surface weeds are killed.

And it does not aid the lawn-maker to attempt to sterilize soil to destroy weed seeds, insects, and disease organisms. Some large operators build a bin in which several cubic yards of soil can be subjected to hot steam; and they sometimes inject tear gas or chloropicrin into a heap of soil or compost, but it is debatable if it is worth the effort for the moderate-size lawn. It is not practical to put a heap of soil on a hot stove and bake it, because the all-important organic matter is burned away, and instead of soil we are left with a heap of ash that has no value. However, if you own a gasoline- or kerosene-burning fire-gun you might paint with the flame the finished soil surface before sowing seeds; on a very small area you could use a blowtorch. Heat travels downwards slowly and little damage is done to the soil, and many weed seeds on the surface will be killed.

WEEDS

Weed seeds are always present in good soil, and the better the soil the more weed seeds there are in it. But of the hundreds of wild plants brought in with soil, only some two dozen are serious lawn weeds. Leave a heap of topsoil around for the summer, and you find it clothed with ragweed, goldenrod, thistle, and many another wild plant that you never see in turf because mowing eliminates the taller weeds. Don't be alarmed when weeds come up along with the young grass from newly sown seeds, for nearly all of them will quickly disappear without any effort on your part. Be choosy as to the quality of the topsoil you buy, because good soil will bring few crabgrass plants, as a rule; you may have noticed that crabgrass prefers poor soil. You may also have looked in vain for crabgrass in the woods, because it grows only in full light; for limited quantities of soil, woodland is a good place to scrape for it. This shade-hating habit of crabgrass is one of the means whereby we can fight it. Also fertilizing, eliminating grubs, and setting the mower high so as to shade the surface of the soil, will keep crabgrass plants from developing.

Nearly all the weeds that come up with newly sown grass disappear—eliminated by mowing.

If you need a limited quantity of topsoil, look in the woods for it. You never saw crabgrass growing in the shade.

To sum up: *Neutral soil is pH 7. Higher figures indicate alkalinity; lower figures, acidity. Porous self-draining soil is most helpful. When grading, topsoil must be conserved. Its most valuable ingredient is organic matter. Screening soil is not recommended as a general rule. All good soil contains weed seeds, but mostly kinds that give little trouble.*

CHAPTER 4

The New Lawn (Continued)

"For out of the old fieldes, as men saithe,
Cometh al this new corne fro yere to yere,
And out of old bookes, in good faithe,
Cometh al this new science that men lere."

GEOFFREY CHAUCER (1340–1400)

THE TURF NURSERY

THE LARGE OPERATOR finds a turf nursery valuable. Soil is prepared and seeds are sown just as carefully as for a permanent lawn, and stones are raked out even more thoroughly. It is mown when other lawns are mown, and is weeded as necessary. When a

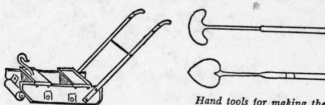

A tractor-drawn sod-cutter; thickness of the turf is regulated by roller in front. Cuts the turf 12 inches wide.

Hand tools for making the horizontal undercut when lifting turf. Kidney-shaped is the American type; ace-of-spades, the English pattern. Vertical cut is often made with a spade.

new lawn is needed speedily or damaged areas have to be patched promptly, the turf is cut into 12-inch squares with an edging knife, working against a board serving as a straight-edge, and the

39

horizontal cut is made with a turf-cutter; for large areas a tractor-drawn sod-lifted is used. Turves are usually cut with 1½ inches of soil; they are placed grass-down in a shallow box and the soil is shaved with a scythe blade to a uniform 1¼-inch thickness.

TO PREPARE TURVES.

LEFT: *grass is mown short, 12-inch squares are cut with 1½ inches of soil. A box is made 13 inches square, with three sides 1¼ inches high, inside measurement; each end of a scythe blade is wrapped with friction tape. RIGHT: turf is laid grass-down in box and the dirt side trimmed. This box is spiked to a stump; if none available, use a bench, table, or sawhorse.*

LAYING TURF.

Soil is prepared carefully; turves are cut to uniform size and thickness, laid, tamped, and watered.

When dry, topdressing is spread, drawn to and fro so that cracks are sealed. Grass seeds are sown.

40

Brushing with a house broom covers seeds with soil, and rolling finishes the work, but be sure turves and soil are dry when doing this.

LAYING TURF

The area to receive the turf is prepared as though seed is to be sown: fertilizer is spread and raked under, and the turves are placed in position, tight against each other. They are set firmly with several light blows of a tamper, or a beetle, if a slope makes the latter more convenient, and the area is given a thorough watering. Next day, when the new grass is reasonably dry, some compost or soil is spread, and drawn up, down and across with the back of a rake until all joints are filled. Broadcast some grass seeds and brush them into the cracks with a house broom. Experienced lawn men like a turfed lawn for speedy results, but they claim that often it looks best at first and never quite so good later.

A kind of tamper called a beetle. Good for laying turf, or when working on a hillside.

A tamper is useful when laying turf and when repairing minor injuries. A type is offered that has a reversible business-head: one side is flat; on the other, which is specially for repair work, there are a number of spikes. Using the spiked side, hundreds of perforations can be made in thin and semi-bare spots, in which soil or compost can lodge along with mixed seeds and soil.

PLANTING STOLONS

Another method of making a lawn is to plant creeping stems or "stolons" of bent. These stems have the ability to develop new

41

PLANTING STOLONS OF CREEPING BENT.

The stolon, or trailing stem, produces a young plant at each joint or "node"; it is cut into pieces, which are spread and covered with a layer of soil. In large operations, a feed cutter may be used to chop the stolons.

plants along their length; if you cut them into short pieces, spread the sections, and cover them with ½ inch of soil, the plantlets are induced to grow. The result is a turf of extreme uniformity, each plant being identical with its neighbor. A bent turf is less rugged than one derived from mixed seeds; it requires constant watering in dry weather, frequent and close mowing, and is

One good method of placing a soil cover on stolon cuttings of creeping bent. LEFT: *laying a flexible steel mat over the cuttings.* CENTER: *about a bushel of soil is deposited on the mat.* RIGHT: *soil is drawn level with the back of a rake.*

very open to attacks of disease. Stolons are given much attention by golf-course superintendents, many of whom have putting greens and turf nurseries produced in this way, but few home owners are prepared to give the constant care that this kind of turf requires. An all-bent turf produced from seeds is almost as uniform, usually costs less, and probably is less temperamental.

Bermuda grass, the invaluable turf plant for the southern

states, can be produced by planting stolons, somewhat as described for bent. However, it is the custom to insert individual stolons into the land at 6- to 10-inch intervals, instead of cutting them in pieces, and this process which has been in use for many years is termed sprigging. A closer, finer, and more level turf can be grown from seeds and at a lower labor cost. Don't be impatient when planting Bermuda turf. Sprigs will not start, nor will seed germinate, until the soil becomes warm.

When making a new lawn the soil must be dry; and for sowing seeds, choose a time when there is little or no wind. Do not sprinkle a newly seeded lawn, for fear your efforts may move organic materials and soil or may uncover some of the seeds; there would be an exception to this if extended dry weather followed your lawn making; but use great care in sprinkling. A new lawn made by laying turf, however, should be watered every second day, and one in which bent stolons have been planted must also be watered often enough to keep it always moist until the grass appears. The use of a revolving sprinkler or one of the ring type is preferable to a hand-held hose, though the latter with a fine rose nozzle, breaking the water into rain-like drops, is satisfactory for small lawns.

WATCH FOR BEETLE GRUBS

During your preparatory work watch for the curled white or gray-white grubs of the Japanese beetle, oriental beetle, or May beetle, all of which feed on the grass roots and cause injury when they become numerous. If you turn up more than three to the square foot, spread and rake under arsenate of lead, allowing 10 pounds per 1000 square feet. Let two weeks elapse and then go ahead with fertilizer and seed. Grubs are treated in detail later in this book.

A TOPSOIL NURSERY

If you have charge of a large area of grass it may pay you to have a topsoil nursery. Smooth the surface, work in fertilizer, and sow a crop for the sole purpose of later digging it under so that it may decay; then you spread more fertilizer and sow another dig-under crop, repeating year after year. When you need soil for grading, dressing poor areas, or filling weed holes, you take off 3 inches and immediately resume cover-cropping. Following are the plants you might grow and the time of year you would sow them; they are not grown to maturity, but only until they are about a foot high, when they are plowed or spaded under, and another crop put in:

	Amount of seeds to sow	
	Per 1000 sq. ft.	*Per acre*
Sow in spring		
Spring rye	2 qts.	2 bu.
Canada field peas *	2 qts.	2 bu.
Sow in summer		
Soy beans *	2 qts.	2 bu.
Buckwheat	2 qts.	2 bu.
Crimson clover *	1 lb.	35 lbs.
Sow in autumn		
Winter rye	2 qts.	2 bu.

* These are legumes; since they take nitrogen from the air, they are especially valuable.

The varieties may be mixed with advantage, using 1 quart each of rye and peas, or 1 quart each of soybeans and buckwheat.

SOIL-IMPROVING CROPS

Occasionally there is no hurry in making a new lawn; and here is the opportunity to improve the soil by growing and digging under one or more soil-improving crops, in addition to adding compost, organic plant foods, and fertilizers. One of the most satisfactory crops for this is crimson clover, an annual plant that is unknown as a turf weed. So there is no danger of trouble arising from the use of crimson clover, which is a legume and markedly improves the quality of the soil in which it grows.

To sum up: *Grow a supply of turf. Grub-proof soil by working under arsenate of lead if beetle grubs are observed. Make your own good topsoil.*

44

CHAPTER 5

The New Lawn (Continued)

"The art of agriculture, when confined to growing plants, is simply adapting the soil, and surrounding circumstances, to the natural demands of the plant; each plant varying somewhat from another, in its requirements." American Text Book of Agriculture, 1854.

SOWING SEEDS ON A SLOPE

THERE IS a critical period between seed sowing and the development of roots large enough to hold the plants and keep the surrounding soil from being washed down a grade. For slopes of 22½ degrees or less, prepare two combinations of seeds and soil. One will contain the larger seeds mixed one part with ten parts of soil; if the slope is from 10 to 22½ degrees, add wheat, oats, or rye grain to the larger seeds in an equal volume—if the larger seeds amount to a quart, add a quart of the grain. The other mixture would consist of the smaller seeds mixed one part to five parts of soil. The seed varieties would be those in tables D or E. and the allowance of both large and small seeds together would be 10 pounds per 1000 square feet, plus the grain if you use it. Ingredients in the seed mixture should be purchased separately.

Leave the seed and soil in the garage for six days, while the final preparation of the surface would be made. Should the slope comprise a large area, provision may be made to prevent the concentration of rain into channels: fix upright boards across the slope or lay sod across it. Either boards or turf would

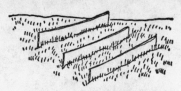

Sowing seeds on a slope. Erosion may be prevented by planting rows of turf across the slope and at a slight angle to the slope.

Boards placed edgewise are sometimes used to prevent soil and seeds from being washed downhill.

be placed at a slight angle to the slope to deflect water rather than to dam it into a pond. Six days after the combinations of soil and seeds are mixed, spread that containing the larger seeds, followed with the mixture of soil and the smaller seeds. Roll with a medium-light roller or firm with a tamper; or on a steep

Cloth tacked on sloping land will also prevent loss of the surface. Slows evaporation also, and the shade hastens germination.

slope use a beetle. Spreading cheesecloth or canvas over the new seed at this stage will help; and a large mesh material for this purpose is obtainable.

The first stages of germination having taken place in the heap, the area that has been dressed with the mixtures will become green in a few days and within another week should be anchored sufficiently to resist average washings.

REPAIRING EROSION

Should some erosion occur, however, make another batch of the seed and soil mixtures, place baffle-boards across the washed-out channels, fill the channels with soil, using the washings carried down to the foot of the slope as much as you can. Get additional soil if you have to, and six days after making the mixtures spread them as before, large seeds first, then small seeds. Before the first mowing remove the baffle-boards.

When grassing a steep slope, holes made with a pick may be filled with mixed soil and grass seeds. The resulting green clumps meet quickly.

SOWING ON A STEEP SLOPE

Any grade more severe than 22½ degrees may be grassed over in the following manner:

Prepare a mixture of seeds and soil six days before you propose to use it; large and small seeds will be together. Two men should do the planting: one, using a pick, opens a hole in the hillside, while the other fills the hole with a handful of the seed-soil mixture, pressing on it with his shoe. Holes may be about 9 inches apart. The first few months the hillside will be a series of clumps of grass, knitting over later. The more often the clumps are cut, the quicker will they join. Another thing you can do to hasten their joining is to broadcast some additional mixed seeds and soil over the slope after the clumps show green.

Even on steep slopes, mowing with a machine is often possible; in this event, select the appropriate seed mixture from table D. Tall nurse grasses are included, and these need weekly mowing.

If the grade is of a character that mowing with a machine will be difficult or impossible; cutting will have to be done with grass-hooks or sickles; possibly with scythes. For this difficult-to-cut turf let the seed mixture be one from table E.

To maintain grass on a severe slope is always a problem. Much of the rain that falls on the slope runs off, and the soil usually is dryer than on level land. The running surface water carries fragments of topsoil, soluble plant foods, and much organic matter with it, tending to impoverish the soil.

TABLE D

Seed Mixtures for Slopes
(Steep grades, but machine-mowing possible.)

Use 10 lbs. per 1000 sq. ft.	Washington, D. C., north to the Arctic	35th to 39th parallel		Below 35th parallel	
	Spring or fall	Spring	Fall	Spring	Fall
	Lbs. or ozs.	Lbs. or ozs.	Lbs. or ozs.	Lbs. or ozs.	Lbs. or ozs.
Seaside bent	5	5	5	..	..
Shade bluegrass	15	10	15	..	..
Chewing's, F 74, or Illahee fescue	30	20	30	..	..
Smooth brome	10	5	10	..	..
Crested wheat	10	5	10	..	..
Domestic rye grass	25	10	25	..	75
Yarrow	2½	2½	2½	..	..
White Dutch clover	2½	2½	2½	..	..
Bermuda grass	..	40	..	100	..
Redtop	..	..	..	..	25
Total	100	100	100	100	100

Amounts to use per 1000 sq. feet 10 lbs., per acre 400 lbs.

Sometimes a drain or a grassy swale along the top of the slope may be justified, carrying water to the sides instead of letting it find its course down the slope. Semi-annual topdressings with soil and fertilizer, and seeds mixed with soil are most important. Knowing that rain will carry your materials down, spread the major part of each dressing towards the top of the slope.

SHADING SEEDS HASTENS THEIR GROWTH

Most grasses need full light in which to develop, though some will tolerate partial shade. But under trees or against a north wall there may be insufficient light to keep grass alive; so we turn to ivy, pachysandra, or other plants to provide a green cover for the soil. Here's a curious fact: although the sun, or bright diffused daylight, is all-important to the grass plants, growth actually slows down as darkness gives place to dawn, the most active growth taking place at night. And seeds germinate in the dark rather than in the light.

TABLE E

Seed Mixtures for Slopes
(Steep grades, machine-mowing impossible.)

Use 10 lbs. per 1000 sq. ft.	Washington, D.C., north to the Arctic	35th to 39th parallel		Below 35th parallel	
	Spring or fall	Spring	Fall	Spring	Fall
	Lbs. or ozs.	Lbs. or ozs.	Lbs. or ozs.	Lbs. or ozs.	Lbs. or ozs.
Seaside bent	5	5	5	..	..
Shade bluegrass	25	10	25	..	..
Chewing's, F 74, or Illahee fescue	60	30	60	..	..
Yarrow	5	2½	5	..	..
White Dutch clover	5	2½	5	..	..
Bermuda grass	..	50	..	100	..
Redtop	..	..	..	..	25
Domestic rye grass	..	..	..	..	75
Total	100	100	100	100	100

Amounts to use per 1000 sq. ft. 10 lbs., per acre 400 lbs.

This is one of the reasons why seed-sowing is rarely successful in the long sunny days of summer. But you can get seeds to grow during this period, provided, first, you keep the soil continually moist and, second, you partially shade the surface. Regarding the first, sprinkling in the evening and allowing the sun to dry the surface next day helps very little. The grasses you want will not grow, but crabgrass, goosegrass, and barnyard grass will.

One way to take care of the moisture requirement is to soak a quantity of peatmoss in water, scatter it in a uniform layer averaging ¼ inch to ½ inch thick, and then keep it moist by occasional sprinkling during the day. The partial shading which encourages the seeds to grow can be taken care of in several ways. Some stretch cheesecloth, tack it in position with large nails, and water through it; others spread small tree branches and brush, preferably without leaves, in a layer 4 to 6 inches thick. Some spread salt hay, fresh meadow hay, or straw in a 2-inch layer, holding it in position with a few branches. These, or the cheesecloth, would be removed when the young grass starts.

CHAPTER 6

The New Lawn (Continued)

"Now 'tis the spring, and weeds are shallow-rooted;
Suffer them now, and they'll o'ergrow the garden,
And choke the herbs for want of husbandry."
SHAKESPEARE, 2 Henry VI.

SNOW—THE POOR MAN'S FERTILIZER

IN ITS DESCENT, snow cleans the atmosphere of soot and dust, materials which are helpful to growth. Snow should remain on the lawn undisturbed, and there is no harm in piling more onto it when shoveling the sidewalk and driveway. It is helpful, too, to lay branches or erect fences on exposed lawns to catch additional snow. This increased thickness will retard spring growth, which is a good thing, and will do much to avoid injury to over-early grass by belated frosts.

MELTING SNOW CAUSES WINTER-KILL

It is not a good thing, however, to walk, slide, or toboggan over a snow-covered lawn. The clods of ice into which snow is compressed by heavy wear is harmful to turf and appears to be one of the causes of snow-mold and winter-kill.

If the grading of the land or wind-blown drifts cause pockets in the snow enclosing spots of bare turf, warm spells may cause water to collect in the pockets; towards the end of winter, alternate freezing by night and thawing by day of this water is likely to cause a dead area of winter-kill by spring. Some lawns suffer from this every year; if yours is one of them, see if a change in grading will help in avoiding water pockets. Then in late autumn place in the spots likely to be affected some materials that will freeze into the ice. A bale or so of tobacco stems is sometimes used, or a quantity of branches, or trash from the garden of a fibrous rather than a leafy character. At the temperature when ice forms it expands slightly, causing our sidewalks to crack and pipes to burst. It has long been known that by floating empty barrels or some timbers in a swimming pool that cannot conveniently be drained, the concrete structure will not be damaged by winter's freeze: the pressure is relieved by the floating wood. Under the same principle the grass plants being frozen into the ice are not damaged because the tobacco stems, branches, or garden trash absorb the pressure at the moment of freezing.

What are tobacco stems? Tobacco leaves are stripped from their stems and larger veins in the manufacture of cigars, cigarettes, smoking tobacco, and snuff. The stems and veins are tough and they decay very slowly. They are spread on turf as a protection against winter-kill and as a shading material to induce summer-sown seeds to germinate. They ward off many insects, most of which dislike tobacco; rain washes out their juices, which are high in potash, resulting in healthier growth.

SOWING ON THE SNOW AND ON FROZEN LAND

Should you have a level area prepared for lawn seeds, intending to sow in late autumn or early spring, you are lucky if you are caught with a snowstorm. Sow right on the snow, and your seeding will be successful; there is no need to cover the seed; merely broadcast it. You are also lucky if you have to sow on bare frozen soil in winter. Freezing and thawing cause the formation of millions of holes; the seeds you sow fall into these holes, to be sealed in by the next thaw and frost.

Actual cold, even when extreme, has no harmful effect on seeds.

TURF IN THE SHADE

You have a good lawn except under the maple tree and along the north side of the house, and you learn from experience that grass is not easy to grow in continual shade.

Of course, you will spread lime every winter. In early spring fork the area in which grass does not grow, dig it about 3 inches deep, and turn it; on the rough surface spread 50 pounds of pulverized sheep manure and 25 pounds of bonemeal (both per 1000 square feet) and then rake smooth. On 1000 square feet also scatter 1¼ pounds each of Illahee, F 74, or Chewing's fescue, and ¾ pound perennial rye grass; rake under; then sow 1 pound shade bluegrass, ½ pound redtop, ¼ pound velvet bent; and roll, but do not rake. The idea is that the smaller seeds will be merely pressed into the surface, while most of the larger seeds are ¼ inch or ½ inch under. Do the same in September.

The following spring, if there is still an area on which there is no turf, you will decide that grass cannot be grown there. Apply your spring plant foods on the turf up to the bare area; beyond this plant one of the ground-cover plants that will tolerate shade.

Three ground covers; plant them where grass cannot be made to grow. LEFT: *English ivy.* CENTER: *pachysandra.* RIGHT: *periwinkle.*

GROUND COVERS

Here are some shade-tolerant plants that may be used to hide otherwise-bare soil under trees; they are obtainable from nurserymen:

Common garden violet. *Viola cucullata.* Plant 10 inches apart.
Japan spurge. *Pachysandra terminalis.* Plant 12 inches apart.
Lily-of-the-valley. *Convallaria majalis.* 12 inches.
Creeping bugle. *Ajuga.* 15 inches.
Periwinkle. *Vinca minor.* 2 feet.
Japanese evergreen ivy. *Euonymus radicans.* 2 feet.
English ivy. *Hedera helix.* 2½ feet.

CHAPTER 7

Caring for the Lawn

"The general management of grass lawns after-wards consists in mowing them once a week * or ten days throughout the summer and autumn, either with the mowing-machine or with the scythe. . . . The mowing machine is better used when the grass is dry; the scythe when it is wet." The New Practical Gardener (1845).

FREQUENT MOWING IS ESSENTIAL

YOUR LAWN should be mown at regular intervals, and much more frequently than is generally supposed. One mowing a week is not enough; make it twice a week at least. If you have a hired man to do the mowing, let him use your mower rather than his, so that you can determine the height of cut. A good length is 1½ inches, but if bad weather causes mowing to be delayed, raise the machine so that it cuts 1¾ inches or higher, bringing it back to its normal 1½ inches in easy stages. A lawn can be gravely injured by suddenly cutting long grass short and exposing to light portions of the plants that hitherto have been protected by upper growth. Your clippings should always be short and well-nigh impossible to rake up. If they are large enough to pick up, still let them lie and realize you have done harm to your turf and markedly encouraged a crabgrass invasion.

One of the worst things you can do is to mow less frequently or not at all in summer, on the theory that grass is protected

---

* This would not be considered often enough nowadays.

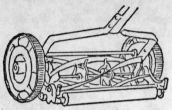

A good hand-mower is the
Great American, and 17 inches
is a suitable cutting width for
the average person. Aim to mow
east-west one time, north-south
another, diagonally also. That is,
if the shape of the lawn allows.

This trimmer and edger
enables you to mow close
to walls, rocks, and trees.

A 30-inch-cut power-mower,
like this, is best if you have
much straight-away cutting, with
the minimum of turning. A
sulky for the operator to ride
can be obtained.

This 21-inch-cut power-
mower lets you into con-
fined places; design your
lawn so that you get out
again without backing.

To mow neatly right up to the edge, lay a 2
by 8 plank on the path for one side of the
machine. Metal curbing (right) defines lawn
and path well, and wickets discourage corner-
cutting.

LEFT: *a power-mower designed to give the ¼-inch cut of a golf putting green. It has seven blades on the spiral knife.* RIGHT: *a tractor-drawn five-unit mower for playing fields and golf fairways; seven, nine, and more units are possible, each cutting 30 inches wide. Frame is flexible to adapt it to undulating land.*

A high quality hand putting-green mower. Seven cutting blades, 18-inch cut; may be adjusted to ¼ inch or shorter. Use of grass-catcher slows spreading of annual bluegrass, seeds of which are frequently in grass clippings.

Improved type of trimming shears; blades cut horizontally, but pressure is vertical.

These trimming shears give you a neat edge with little effort.

against the sun by its longer growth. When you do get around to cutting, you will take off so much that the green color will change to gray and crabgrass will find the opportunity it has been waiting for. Best to start mowing in spring as soon as grass starts to grow on an old lawn, or on a new one as soon as new grass is tall enough to reach the mower; thereafter mow twice weekly right into winter and stop only when growth has ceased. There would be every advantage in raising the adjustment of

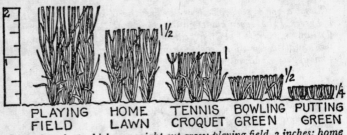

PLAYING FIELD   HOME LAWN   TENNIS CROQUET   BOWLING GREEN   PUTTING GREEN

The length at which you might cut grass: playing field, 2 inches; home lawn 1½ inches; tennis and croquet, 1 inch; bowling green, ½ inch; golf putting green, ¼ inch. Soil under the grass must be made even through top dressing for these lengths.

the mower in hot weather, but please continue to use it twice a week. One of the reasons why a golf putting green is so perfect is that it is mown almost daily.

Your mower should be used frequently enough that grass clippings cannot easily be raked up because they are so small.

MOWING A SLOPE

If the grade is moderate, either a hand-mower or a power-mower may be run across the grade. To cut a severe slope, attach a rope to a hand-mower; let it run down the grade and pull it up. If it is inclined to bounce, wrap some lead pipe around the tie-rods or attach weights to it. But it is possible for a declivity to be so steep that a sickle or scythe is the only practical tool to use.

WATERING

Do not be in a hurry to water your lawn. Grass usually can take care of itself in spring and autumn; if the surface soil is a little dry, roots will go down after moisture. Turf that is watered generously all through the growing season often has shallow roots, which is why some lawns suffer badly in midsummer. You have to watch conditions, however: if you have a dry period and the lawn shows signs of suffering from thirst, one of which is the dry turf showing footprints where you walk on it, set a sprinkler and give it plenty of water. One of the ring type is satisfactory for a small lawn; a revolving or oscillating pattern

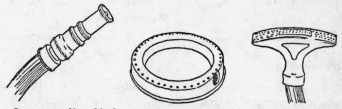

LEFT: *an adjustable hose nozzle; twist it for either a coarse or fine spray.* CENTER: *a ring sprinkler.* RIGHT: *a flaring rose nozzle, which delivers a gentle rain like a watering can.*

SPRINKLERS.
LEFT: *double-rotary.* CENTER: *skinner broadway.* RIGHT: *spray-wave. The first two revolve; the spray-wave oscillates and waters a rectangle.*

is more desirable for a large lawn, possibly several of them. There's a deal of satisfaction in filling a pipe or lighting a cigarette, holding the end of a hose, and sprinkling a lawn by hand. But the average person lacks the patience to do this often enough or long enough; a sprinkler is recommended.

The bent grasses, having shorter roots than others, need water more often than the fescues, and for a bent lawn a system of underground pipes and pop-up surface valves is suitable. But even here do not be tempted to turn on the water until it is definitely needed.

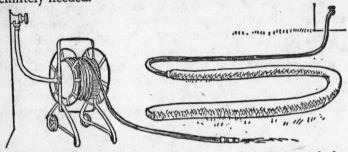

LEFT: *a modern hose reel; water runs through the hose whether coiled or not.* RIGHT: *a porous weeping sock; water seeps gradually from the canvas pipe.*

Some spots on a lawn are found to become dry sooner than others, due perhaps to tree roots taking up moisture or perhaps to rocks or boulders a short way down in the land. Here a "weeping-sock" has value. It is a short length of porous canvas pipe screwed onto the hose and closed at the far end. When water is turned on, it seeps very slowly from the weeping-sock to soak thoroughly the soil.

If you have no water supply you can still have a good lawn by working plenty of organic matter into the soil and making your turf of Illahee, F 74 or Chewing's fescue. Drought will not kill these grasses, though they may take on a brown color during July and August; they recover readily enough with autumn rains.

WEEDING

Weeds are always with us. Their seeds remain in the soil for many years with their germination unimpaired; until some trigger effect of climate or some added plant food starts them growing. Wind, birds, and rain bring them, and earthworms eject them onto the surface from lower levels. They are easily taken out by hand when they are small; but if the work is postponed and they become large and numerous, we have a major problem, needing perhaps the aid of chemicals. Better go after them as soon as they are seen: dig them out with a weeding knife; have a pail containing mixed seeds and soil, one handful of seeds to eight of soil; and plug each weed hole.

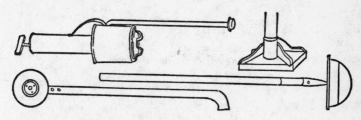

USEFUL LAWN TOOLS.

TOP LEFT: *dusting device for insecticides or weed-killers.* TOP RIGHT: *head of an iron tamper.* LOWER RIGHT: *a half-moon edger for trimming turf.* LOWER LEFT: *a wheel edger; center of knife-wheel may be run on a thin board acting as a straight-edge.*

One important exception to this rule is crabgrass, which in most sections of the U. S. does not have a perennial root. Go after this with a sharp kitchen knife, cutting the plant just below the soil level and rub in a spoonful or so of the mixed seeds and soil. This same mixture may be used to heal over damage caused by a car running over the lawn or the dog's bone-burying project.

WHEN IS MECHANICAL AID NEEDED?

Power-mowers, fertilizer drills, seed-broadcasting devices, and chemical weed-killers are justified if your lawn is 5000 square feet in area or larger. If you suffer from some physical disability you may need them on a smaller lawn. Consult your physician; he may tell you that the gentle exercise is likely to be helpful.

CHAPTER 8

Plant Foods and Further Care of the Lawn

"A common thing is a grass blade small,
Crushed by the feet that pass,
But all the dwarfs and giants tall,
Working till doomsday shadows fall
Can't make a blade of grass."
JULIAN STEARNS CUTLER.

THE NEED FOR PLANT FOODS

LIKE EVERY OTHER living thing, a lawn needs to be fed. In nearly every locality an application of lime late every winter is advantageous: 100 pounds of pulverized limestone or 50 pounds of hydrated lime per 1000 square feet are the usual allowances, 2 tons or 1 ton per acre, respectively. The limestone is slow to act and has no tendency to cement the land; hydrated lime has a slight binding action on the land, but is quicker to show results. Either may be used, but if the land is sandy you will do better with hydrated lime. There are two other forms of lime that are used occasionally: gypsum or lime sulphate is useful on a bent lawn or when trying to eliminate clover; and commercial hardwood ashes, containing lime and potash, are good to use if a soil test indicates that potash is in short supply in the land. Thirty-five pounds of either per 1000 square feet would be a good allowance.

Every lawn, too, should have a spring and fall application of balanced commercial fertilizer—25 pounds of 4–8–4, 20 pounds of 5–10–5, or 12½ pounds of 8–6–2 per 1000 square feet. If some other analysis is offered you, divide the first or nitrogen figure into 100 and the result is the number of pounds of the compound you may use per 1000 square feet without scalding the grass, provided it is dry when you apply it.

The essential plant foods are calcium or lime, nitrates, phosphoric acid, and potash; the last three salts are those indicated in a fertilizer analysis, the 5–10–5 formula above giving the number of pounds of each in a 100-pound bag.

TRACE ELEMENTS

At the same time these are applied, some compost, old manure, spent mushroom soil, or topsoil from some other part of the property may be spread with advantage. One reason is that in addition to the "big four" essential elements, grass and other plants need small quantities of the so-called trace elements, because they are needed only in trace amounts. They include magnesium, sodium, sulphur, iron, manganese, boron, iodine, zinc, copper, molybdenum, cobalt, and chlorine. These are present in most fertile soils, certainly in the organic materials recommended to be spread at the same time as the fertilizer. There are two additional reasons for using these organic substances: their use maintains this important part of the soil's framework. And they are bulky; spreading them and drawing them to an even surface with the back of a rake tends to fill any little hollows and depressions in the soil.

TOPDRESSING

Sometimes quite large amounts of compost and soil are used, especially on a new lawn which may develop minor sinkages in its first few years. A perfect soil surface makes for a perfect mowing job; should a mower wheel drop into a depression it will "scalp" the turf, cutting the grass at that point shorter than elsewhere, perhaps down to the soil surface, cutting long grass short, and definitely injuring the turf. This spreading of sizable quantities of soil-building material is termed topdressing.

In the case of a large depression, skin the turf, fork the undersurface, and add soil or compost to bring it slightly above level;

dust enough fertilizer to whiten the surface, rake and then return the turf. Roll or tamp it into place, and water.

Few soils are ideal mixtures; perhaps a near-satisfactory one for grass would consist of 2 parts clay, 1 part silt, which is made

DEVICES TO PUNCH HOLES IN TURF.
LEFT: *a hand spike-disk.* RIGHT: *a spike-disk hauled by a tractor.*

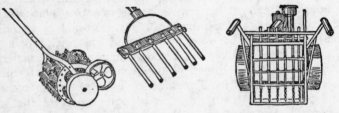

LEFT: *a type of hand-spiker much used on bowling greens or putting greens.* CENTER: *a fork with hollow tines which remove cores of soil.* RIGHT: *terforator, a machine which bores auger holes in the land.*

LEFT: *a power soil-punching machine called the night-crawler.* RIGHT: *aerifier, a power-drawn device with dozens of spoons; they dig out large cigar-like cores.*

up of particles midway between fine sand and clay, 1 part coarse sand, 1 part fine gravel, and 2 parts decaying organic matter—all parts by volume, all formed naturally, and all having stood on the surface for many years—topsoil, in other words. Perfect soil is seldom found in a lawn, and if it was good originally it tends to change; so the process of topdressing is often used to improve the framework of the soil. If organic matter is low, it is added in the topdressing; if clay is in short supply, loamy soil is used, or a sandy topdressing or a silty one, as may be desirable. To get the topdressing down into the soil, the surface is often perforated with thousands of holes into which it can be brushed, by using a device like an aerifier, spike-roller or hollow-tine fork. On small lawns, the turf is sometimes pricked with a garden fork or with a spike-tamper.

ROLLING

Rolling is desirable to complete the job of seed sowing or stolon planting.

It is standard practice to roll the lawn in late spring, after the soil is frost-free and dry. Then roll once only. The roller should be medium-heavy, 100 to 125 pounds per foot in width. If you use a water-ballast roller, fill it half full. Use it only one quarter full during the summer and autumn, if you have to reseed or patch the lawn.

A water-ballast roller. Be sure you let out water before winter.

A roller is a good thing to have, but often is not needed badly enough to warrant the purchase of one. When repairing an old lawn or making a new one it is valuable. In spring in northern climates a roller is used to bring back into contact with the soil the turf which has been loosened by winter and is swollen up into frost blisters. This spring rolling should only be done after the soil has become free of frost and is dry. Much rolling is unfortunately done while the land still is moist; the rolling job will be perfect, but the soil often is made so compact that it is injured for the rest of the year until the following winter's frost makes it porous again.

63

Turf tennis courts at a membership club present a special problem to the lawn-keeper. Players look for fast courts, they like the grass mown too short for reasonable protection against wear, and they want the turf rolled too tight. In the private court near home, counsels of moderation can prevail—fairly short grass and moderate rolling.

Also, take every opportunity to aerify, terforate, or spike-roll, and to work under topdressings of sandy compost. Change the net and lines so that recovery can take place after wear; if room is lacking, provide a reserve of turf that can be used for quick repairing.

HIDEBOUND TURF

Sometimes a lawn on clay or clay-loam soil is subjected to too much wear, is heavily rolled when wet, or is mown with such weighty machinery that the soil is squeezed into a tight mass that permits little water to seep downwards. The grass grows slowly, suffers markedly in hot weather, and the lawn is hard and unyielding.

The remedy is to use a hollow-tined fork, terforator, aerifier, or spike-roller. Should the area be quite small, inserting a garden fork, prying on it until the turf is broken and raised 2 inches, withdrawing the fork and reinserting it 4 inches to the rear, and again prying, will take the place of the first mentioned implements. Then ½ bale of screened peatmoss and ½ cubic yard of coarse sand is spread over 1000 square feet and drawn to and fro with the back of a rake and then with a broom until it disappears. The hidebound condition will improve, though several treatments at intervals of two months may be necessary to cure it entirely.

To sum up: *Lime late every winter is desirable in most sections, fertilizer every spring and fall. Compost or soil from elsewhere are usually good sources of the trace elements. Rolling wet land does much harm, as does an over-heavy roller; injury can be rectified, however, but at much effort.*

64

CHAPTER 9

Some Fertilizers, Plant Foods, Manures, and Soil Ingredients

"And though theyr soyle be not verie frutefull, nor their aier very wholesome, yet againste the eyer they so defende them with temperate diete, and so order and husbande their grounde with diligente travaile, that in no countrey is greater increase, and plenty of corne and cattell, nor mens bodies of longer lyfe, and subject or apte to fewer diseases." SIR THOMAS MORE, Utopia, 1515.

HERE ARE THE MATERIALS COMMONLY USED TO FEED LAWNS

Use these quantities when topdressing; note that 1 pound of nitrogen per 1000 square feet is the maximum allowance.

Use up to three times the amounts given when making a new lawn.

Organic substances maintain the soil's framework; chemical fertilizers leave no helpful residue. Nitrogen develops leaf growth; phosphoric acid will build the plant's roots and stem; potash is a health-giving element.

CHEMICAL FERTILIZERS

There are three classes of these: first, those that are a mixture of chemical salts and an inert material, which may be regarded as a distributing agent, makeweight, or filler. These are lowest in cost and are not recommended, because their effect is quick but transitory; unless used with extreme care they will burn the

65

Apply three times quantities given when making a new lawn

	Nitrogen	Phosphoric acid	Potash	Per 1000 sq. ft.	Per acre
	Typical analyses			*Use to topdress*	
	%	%	%	Lbs.	Lbs.
CHEMICAL FERTILIZERS					
These are three popular analyses	4	8	4	25	1000
	5	10	5	20	750
	8	6	2	12½	500
ORGANIC PLANT FOODS					
Bonemeal	2.4	22	0	40	1500
Castor pomace	4	1	1	25	1000
Cottonseed meal	6	2	1	15	600
Manure, Shredded cattle	1.7	1	1	50	2000
Manure, Pulverized sheep	2	1	2	50	2000
Tankage	7	8	0	14	575
Tobacco scrap	2.5	.5	4	40	1500
Urea	46	0	0	2	100
INORGANIC PLANT FOODS					
Muriate of potash	0	0	48	5	200
Nitrate of soda	15	0	0	6	250
Sulphate of ammonia	20	0	0	5	200
Sulphate of alumina. Acidifying agent; not a fertilizer				5	200
Trace-L. Dissolve one teaspoonful in a gallon of water	8	16	7	Gals. 10	

turf. The second group consists of those mixtures in which part of the inert material is replaced by some valuable organic material, such as castor pomace, cottonseed meal, or tankage. They are readily obtainable. The third group is hard to find; these mixtures have no inert material, but are made up entirely of chemical salts and useful organics.

The more organic ingredients there are in a mixture the more expensive it is, but since they actually improve the land their extra cost is usually justified. Moreover, their feeding effect is sustained over a longer period.

Apply three times quantities given when making a new lawn

	Typical analyses			Use to topdress	
	Nitrogen	Phosphoric acid	Potash	Per 1000 sq. ft.	Per acre
	%	%	%	Lbs.	Tons
SOIL, SOIL INGREDIENTS, AND BULKY MANURES					
Humus	..	..	..	100 to 250	2 to 5
Rotted manure, horse or cow	½	1	½	200	4
					Lbs.
Poultry manure, fresh	3¼	1¾	1	30	1200
Mushroom soil	1	1½	1	100	4000
				Bale	Bales
Peatmoss	..	..	..	½	20
				Cu. yd.	Cu. yds.
Sand	..	..	..	½	20
Topsoil	..	..	..	½	20
LIME AND LIMESTONE SUBSTANCES				Lbs.	Lbs.
Hardwood ashes	1% potash				
Hydrated lime	5% potassium carbonate 60% calcium oxide			50	2000
Pulverized limestone	3.5% magnesium oxide 52% calcium oxide			50	2000
	90% calcium carbonate 10% magnesium oxide			100	4000
Gypsum	95% calcium sulphate			35	1400
Superphosphate	20% phosphoric acid			25	1000

ORGANIC PLANT FOODS

Bonemeal. This stockyard by-product furnishes nitrogen, phosphoric acid, and calcium; it is excellent when preparing land for a new lawn or for topdressing old turf. Coarse ground meal is slow; the finer grinds are quick to act, often showing greener grass when spread on turf within two weeks; a mixture of coarse and fine is advisable. There is a feeling on the part of some professional turf-keepers that the use of bonemeal stimulates clover in a lawn; others question this, however.

Castor Pomace. The ground remains of castor beans after they have had castor oil squeezed from them; castor pomace is an excellent slow-acting plant food but it should be used in combination with others.

Cottonseed Meal. Cottonseed oil is squeezed from the seeds of the cotton plant after the fibers have been removed. Since the squeezed residue, called cottonseed cake, is in demand for feeding cattle, little is available for plant food; slow-acting and good, however, it is an excellent source of nitrogen. It should be used along with other materials, not alone.

Manure, Shredded Cattle. Largely cleanings from stock-yard pens, it is good to work into the soil when preparing it for new lawns. It is valuable, also, when used as a topdressing in efforts to eliminate white clover.

Manure, Pulverized Sheep. The particles are small and powdery, making the manure suitable for mixing with topdressing. As the drying process destroys most weed seeds, you are not likely to have additional weeds as a result of using it.

Tankage. This is a powdery material, made up of urea and blood, manure fragments, and smaller rubbish fragments from the stockyards. Its composition varies, but usually it is very high in nitrogen and phosphoric acid. It is valuable as an ingredient in a topdressing mixture.

Tobacco Scrap. The sweepings from tobacco factories, consisting of stem and leaf fragments. A slow-acting but good organic source of potash.

Urea. Originally the salt that crystalizes when animal urine is evaporated, nowadays it is made synthetically. A potent source of nitrogen, it causes burning of the grass unless used with caution.

INORGANIC PLANT FOODS

Muriate of Potash. Sometimes applied with topdressing materials when brown-patch is being combated. Often a tendency to fungus disease is associated with a deficiency of potash in the soil.

Nitrate of Soda. It is a very quick-acting source of nitrogen and one of the few salts to go directly into the plant without chemical changes in the soil.

Sulphate of Ammonia. Not quite so speedy as nitrate, but quick enough; a much-used source of chemical nitrogen.

Sulphate of Alumina. Not a fertilizer, but occasionally used as an acidifying agent, when one wishes to lower the pH reading of the soil—mostly when trying to eliminate white clover in turf.

Trace-L. A water-soluble mixture of chemicals containing the four essential plant foods, along with twelve of the trace elements needed by most plants in minute amounts. If your lawn is not doing well and its condition can be attributed to a shortage of one or another of the trace elements, it is suggested that one teaspoonful of Trace-L be dissolved in one gallon of water and sprinkled on the turf. Allow 10 spoonfuls in 10 gallons on each 1000 square feet.

SOIL, SOIL INGREDIENTS, AND BULKY MANURES

Humus. In areas that once were shallow ponds, generations of cattails grew, died, and decayed, to be followed by others living on their remains, until the ponds filled to become deposits of muck or black soil. Best grades are from areas that have been ditch-drained, cultivated or planted to a succession of cover-crops, plowed under.

Manure. It may be dug into land for new lawns or added to the compost heap. Horse manure preferably should be rotted; cow manure may be either fresh or rotted. Prior to the automobile age, an over-winter dressing of manure was standard practice for the home lawn, with the remains being raked up in spring; it encouraged the blue-grasses, leading to a thick, matted, though somewhat coarse, turf in spring and autumn.

Poultry Manure, Fresh. It may be used when preparing land for a new lawn or it may be added to the compost-heap. A strong fertilizer; it should not be put onto a lawn as is, for the grass will be burned; composted and decayed, it is helpful. Do not exceed the amounts suggested in the table.

Mushroom Soil. Horse manure and loam, which together have produced a crop of mushrooms; the manure now will be partly rotted. Since mushrooms can only be grown in rich soil and in manure from healthy horses, the product is a material of reliable quality, despite the occasional horseshoe or piece of harness that you find in it. Excellent to put on the compost heap, to screen and use as a topdressing material, or to dig under for a new lawn.

Peatmoss. Instead of cattails in water, sphagnum moss established itself in rather higher areas than those producing humus, but again one generation lived on the remains of previous ones in a peat bog; the mossy material is stripped, dried, and baled. Occasionally this is offered screened to make a specially fine material for mixing with soil or for working into perforations when an effort is being made to correct a hidebound condition; it may be described as PEATMOSS DUST or PEATMOSS SCREENINGS.

Sand. For use on turf it should be coarse and sharp; the grade described as gravel-screenings is especially good; the best is made up of pieces of quartz or silica. Sand should be washed to free it from any soil or loam that may be mixed with it. A month or more in a flat heap, open to the weather, is sufficient; or turn a hose on the heap, allow it to dry, then use it.

Topsoil. Most suitable for lawns is a well-drained sandy loam, with the remains of past generations of plant life plainly visible. There should be no subsoil in it; and the weeds or crops standing on it should be large, lush, and healthy.

LIME AND LIMESTONE SUBSTANCES

Lime, or calcium, is one of the four essential plant foods; if it is absent, plants cannot live. Lime sweetens acid soil and tends to make cohesive soils porous and to bind sandy land. An adequate supply of lime in the land makes it accept water readily, giving it the full benefit of every rainfall.

The convenient forms of lime are as follows; they are discussed in Chapter 8,

Hardwood ashes	Pulverized limestone
Hydrated lime	Gypsum

Superphosphate. Mostly made from phosphate rock, but occasionally from bonemeal. Either material is treated with acid to make the plant foods more readily available, resulting in superphosphate or acid phosphate.

To sum up: *Organic plant foods are preferred over chemical fertilizers. Like humus, manure, and peatmoss they not only encourage good grass but they improve the soil at the same time.*

CHAPTER 10

The Grass Varieties That Make American Lawns

"Grass may be the commonest of weeds; unwanted, it often grows freely. Yet it may be the most difficult to cultivate where it is needed." UNKNOWN AUTHOR.

THE GRASSES comprise the most important family of plants, because they feed the human race. Wheat, barley, and rye, sources of the white man's bread, are grasses; corn or mealies, feeding the African, is a grass; rice, the mainstay of the Asiatic, is a grass; so are oats, sugar cane, and the 60-foot bamboo. Grazing animals feed on grasses, and we eat them indirectly as meat. Without the grasses we probably would starve.

The grass family is large, comprising thousands of members, but only a very few of them are found in lawns. Nearly all lawn grasses are perennials when grown from the 35th parallel north; and the colder the climate the better they grow. Many are used as annuals during the winter months south of this latitude.

BENT VARIETIES

Plants are dwarf and tend to spread; they have small silky leaves, which are flat and come gradually to a fine point. They have parallel veins and show no definite keel or gutter. All do best in moist land, will tolerate slightly acid soil, and are at their best in summer. They cover the ground perfectly, so that you rarely see earth when you look straight down. All the bents have their young leaves rolled in the bud. One pound of seed may contain over five million grains, each capable of producing a plant.

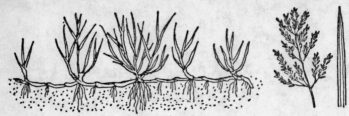

THE LONG STOLON OF CREEPING BENT.

On the right is a typical leaf; flat, it reaches a point gradually. Between is the flower head or panicle on which the seeds develop, but creeping-bent seeds often do not have the power to grow, which is one of the reasons why this variety normally is produced by planting portions of the stolon.

Creeping Bent. *Agrostis stolonifera.* A strongly creeping, medium-coarse grass, often gray-green. This variety can be reproduced only by planting the creeping stems or stolons; seed is rarely developed, and none is available commercially. Ligule is short.

Seaside Bent. *Agrostis palustris.* Flat bluish-green leaves are often scimitar- or sickle-shaped. It is a strongly creeping grass, developing

Seaside bent produces stolons, but its seeds grow and can be used. Leaf also reaches a point gradually and often is curved like a Turkish sword.

stolons or runners, which could be used in lawn-building, like creeping bent; but seeds are produced freely and they reproduce readily with less labor. First collected in Coos county, Oregon, the seed was introduced some 25 years ago under the name of Cocoos bent.

Rhode Island Bent, Colonial Bent. *Agrostis tenuis.* It creeps slowly by means of short stolons. If you separate the stems and leaves which form the dense sod, you will often find the leaf sheaths a reddish-brown, giving a suggestion of this tint to the turf.

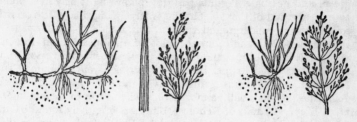

LEFT: *Rhode Island or colonial bent has stolons, but they are short.* RIGHT: *velvet bent is a dwarf plant with flat narrow silky leaves and even shorter stolons.*

Astoria Bent. *Agrostis tenuis.* A desirable narrow- and flat-leaved strain that creeps slowly and is very similar to Rhode Island bent. **Velvet Bent.** *Agrostis canina.* The flat leaves are silky and very small in this dwarfest of the bent grasses. In an established lawn it grows in well-marked patches which cover the ground completely, so you rarely see earth when you look straight down. Long pointed ligule.

THE BLUEGRASSES

These creep very little. They grow best in cool weather. One pound contains about 2,500,000 live seeds. The young leaves are folded in the bud; all leaves have a center furrow, and the stems

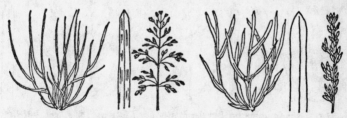

LEFT: *Kentucky bluegrass has a leaf with parallel edges which come suddenly to a point like a boat and with a furrow or keel along its center.* RIGHT: *Canada bluegrass has a keel, too.*

are flattened. The leaves are shaped like a boat, their sides parallel until they come suddenly to a point.

Kentucky Bluegrass, June Grass. *Poa pratensis.* The color is medium green, and not blue. Possibly pastures comprising it may look bluish towards the end of the day, but this is largely imaginary. It likes rich soil, has short underground runners, but frequently is dormant in midsummer. This unfortunate habit of disappearing in the hot weather is a direct invitation to crabgrass, and for this reason some lawnkeepers avoid its use. Run a leaf between your thumbnail and forefinger: *poa pratensis* readily splits at the tip. The ligule is small. As a rule the seeds will germinate only when sown in the autumn.

Merion B 27. A strain of Kentucky Bluegrass originally found on the fairways of the Merion Cricket Club in Philadelphia. Dwarfer than Kentucky, it has a shorter dormant period in summer, making it a more desirable turf grass. Selected and developed by Dr. Fred Grau of the U. S. Department of Agriculture and the United States Golf Association, it is decidedly an acquisition. Only moderate quantities of seed are available at this writing, and the cost is high; larger supplies may be looked for in future years.

Canada Bluegrass. *Poa compressa.* Similar to *poa pratensis,* but a less pleasing gray-green color, and a somewhat coarser plant. Less exacting in its soil preferences, thriving a few hundred miles further south. The leaves feel soft and yielding, the ligule is long, and the stem is markedly flattened, hence *compressa.* It has short underground runners.

Shade Bluegrass. Bird Grass. Rough-Stalked Meadow Grass. *Poa trivialis.* The sheath at the base of each shoot wraps around it com-

LEFT: *shade bluegrass has the boat-shaped leaf with the keel, but the leaf is narrower than in Kentucky bluegrass and it shines.* **RIGHT:** *annual bluegrass or poa annua, is a dwarf weed grass, disliked because it fades away just when the crabgrass growing season starts.*

pletely; in nearly every other grass it is split. The sheath also is rough, but the stems and leaves shine as though varnished; often yellowish-green. The ligule is long. A major ingredient in seed mixtures for shaded lawns. The plants have short above-ground stolons and tend to grow mostly in one direction, often the north-east.

Annual Bluegrass. *Poa annua.* A lime-loving weed grass that is encouraged by hard wear and tight land; rolling when wet sometimes brings it. It is incorrectly named, because it is a biennial. Seeds germinate in late summer, give a fine turf in fall and spring, and die in early summer, leaving the turf open to a crabgrass invasion. Rarely sown intentionally, but a serious weed in established turf. Since it is one of the few grasses able to mature its flowers and seeds under the mower, however closely it is cut, you may see flowers any time from spring to fall. For this reason, your mower is cutting flower stems, while it cuts only leaves of the other grasses: a turf of *poa annua* needs a sharp mower, and even then is hard to cut. The ligule is medium-long.

FESCUES

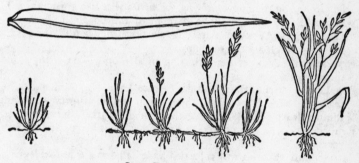

Some Fescue Grasses.

The first two with wire-like bristly leaves. LEFT: *fine-leaved.* Center: *creeping Illahee.* RIGHT: *alta, with wide flat leaves, one of which is shown at the top.*

The first two varieties following are brownish-green, especially in summer. To distinguish between them: Illahee is more strongly creeping, tending to spread; Chewing's is inclined to grow into individual clumps in poor land. The tenacity with which these fescues hold onto life is responsible for this; they persist after the land has lost much of its fertility and is on the way to becoming a desert; the last survivors grow as individuals, which gives them the reputation of growing in clumps. In normal soil, however, and with fair treatment, the crowding plants do not become isolated; instead they make an even, resilient turf. Watering in spring and autumn is harmful to the fescues, though adequate irrigation in midsummer is beneficial. Close cutting does not injure the fescues, but infrequent mowing does.

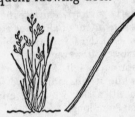

Chewing's red fescue has wiry leaves; it stands drought, heat, and poor soil and has deeper roots than most other grasses.

Chewing's Red Fescue. *Festuca rubra fallax.* The leaves are rolled lengthwise on themselves, giving the turf a wire-like appearance. The plants tolerate heat, drought, hard wear, and poor soil.

Illahee Creeping Fescue. A recent selection from *festuca rubra;* more stoloniferous, less likely to clump.

F 74 Fescue. Another new selection of *f. rubra.* Finer texture, more tolerant of water.

Fine-Leaved Fescue. Hair Fescue. *Festuca tenuifolia.* Similar to Chewing's red fescue, but one-half the size: smaller plants, with shorter and thinner leaves. Plants are sometimes medium-green, sometimes gray-green. The seed is produced in Europe and has been scarce in recent years.

All four varieties will tolerate shade; all have wire-like leaves.

THE TEMPORARY GRASSES

Quick-growing, they are often used as nurses, mixed with the permanent varieties, to furnish a turf as quickly as possible. This quick dense turf discourages the growth of weeds during the formative weeks. Taller than lawn grasses, continued close cutting causes them gradually to disappear, leaving the desirable varieties in possession. Their dead roots add to the supply of organic matter in the land. The first four are used for temporary winter lawns in the southern states; they die in spring.

Italian Rye Grass. *Lolium multiflorum.* An annual variety with wide leaves, living for only one season. Prominent rounded ribs are on the upper leaf surface; their under side is glossy. Young leaves are rolled in the bud; the ligule is a short membrane, and near it are two auricles clasping the stem. In the soil, the base of the leaf is violet-pink.

Perennial Rye Grass, English Rye Grass. *Lolium perenne.* Some of the best seeds are imported. A true perennial; if you use a high-adjusted mower it will remain in the turf into the second season before disappearing. Leaves are less coarse than the Italian, but have the same rounded ribs, and again the under side is glossy. The young leaves are folded in the bud; the ligule is short and blunt, and the underground base of the leaf is red. Has narrow and claw-like auricles.

Domestic Rye Grass. A mixture of the above two, grown in the United States, and largely used as a temporary winter lawn in the South.

Redtop is quick-growing and is a good nurse, but continued mowing kills it within two years, for its normal height is 2½ feet.

Redtop. *Agrostis alba.* A tall plant with underground rootstocks, medium broad and coarsely veined leaves. The ligule is prominent, long, and membranous.

Alta Fescue. *Festuca elatior.* A good nurse on difficult land; deep-rooted, somewhat coarse, and yellow-green.

Kentucky 31 Fescue. A new strain of *f. elatior;* similar to Alta.

DROUGHT-TOLERANT GRASSES USED IN AVIATION AND SPORTS TURF

Smooth Brome Grass. *Bromus inermis.* A useful ingredient in seed mixtures for football, polo, and aviation fields, especially in the Mississippi valley from Arkansas north. Thirty inches high, it has creeping roots, binds soil, and withstands drought. Close cutting eliminates it, so it is rarely met with in lawns.

77

Crested Wheat Grass. *Agropyron cristatum.* A very deep-rooting and coarse grass that has value in a turf intended to stand hard wear. Does well in areas of reduced rainfall and extreme cold. Much used in turf that can be kept at a high cut in the north-western prairie and mountain states. Seldom seen in a lawn.

SUB-TROPICAL GRASSES

Bermuda Grass. *Cynodon dactylon.* This has both white underground rootstocks and overground stolons. Leaves are medium short with parallel edges; they leave the stem at uniform intervals and present their surface to the light to give a ladder-like appearance. Likes much lime in the land. Bermuda remains green all year south of central Florida, but has an increasingly longer winter resting period as we proceed north, until above Wilmington, Del., winter kills it. It is the ideal permanent lawn grass in the southern states. Standard practice is to scarify and topdress Bermuda turf in the autumn, sowing rye grass for a temporary winter turf. When warm weather kills the rye grass another heavy raking and topdressing is given, and the Bermuda comes through. New hardy strains of this grass are being developed which it is hoped will be perennial farther north. The strong growth of Bermuda during the hottest part of the year should help against crabgrass.

Carpet Grass. *Axonopus compressus.* In the southern states this makes a good coarse lawn in moist acid soil, where Bermuda will not do so well.

SOME UNWANTED GRASSES

Sometimes they are intentionally sown; more often they occur as weeds.

Bulbous Bluegrass. *Poa bulbosa.* The plant grows from small bulbs the size of a mustard seed. From Richmond, Va., south, it is a good perennial autumn, winter and spring turf grass. It may be planted along with Bermuda.

Sheep's Fescue. *Festuca ovina.* Like Chewing's fescue, with wiry leaves, but coarser, longer, and thicker; color is a displeasing bluish-gray, and it grows in clumps. Sometimes occurs as a weed accompanying Chewing's fescue seed.

Meadow Fescue. *Festuca pratensis.* Tall, broad, and flat-leaved grass; similar in general appearance to rye grass and, like it, is sometimes used as a nurse grass. Has narrow claw-like auricles.

Couch, Twitch, or Quack. *Agropyron repens.* Well-known noxious farm weed; will often persist in a lawn, forming a cluster of coarse, flat, thin, and dry-feeling leaves. Has long, strong, white underground stems. Young leaves are rolled in the bud, and the upper surface of mature leaves are strongly ribbed. The ligule is a short margin. Two auricles near the ligule are like little scythes. The leaf bases are hairy.

Sweet Vernal. *Anthoxanthum odoratum.* Perennial, with flat leaves, broad at the base and gradually tapering to a point. There are rounded ears or auricles where the leaf leaves the stem. The young leaves are rolled in the bud. When chewed the leaf yields the taste and aroma of new-mown hay. Plants met with in old lawns are often carry-overs from European seed mixtures containing this variety that were sown years ago.

Timothy, Cat's-Tail. *Phleum pratense.* Sometimes used as a nurse grass, but quite unsuitable; often used as a cheapening ingredient in seed mixtures. Perennial, with a small bulbous root. Leaves are flat, coarse, and gray-green; when young, they are rolled in the bud. They narrow gradually to a fine point; the ligule is small and pointed. There are low, flat, inconspicuous ribs on the leaves' upper surface.

Holcus, Velvet Grass, Fog. *Holcus lanatus.* Stoloniferous perennial with flat, medium broad, light gray leaves, covered with fine hairs to produce a cloth-like feel. The ligule is toothed and prominent. The young leaves are rolled in the bud. The leaf bases are white and have red veins.

THREE WEEDS.

LEFT: *barnyard grass, an annual that appears in spring-sown lawns.* CENTER: *quack or twitch. Avoid soil containing pieces of the white underground runners.* RIGHT: *shepherd's purse.*

79

Goose Grass, Yard Grass, Silver Crab. *Eleusine indica.* Annual. The leaves are flat, glossy, and gray-green, with well-marked white leaf bases. The young leaves are folded in the bud. The ligule is a medium-long membrane, and on the outside of the leaf in back of the ligule is a ring of hairs. Grows close to the ground in mown turf in a characteristic star shape or cross formation, appearing after hot weather sets in; turns white and dies at summer's end. The roots are particularly tough.

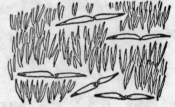

This is what crabgrass looks like when its seeds germinate in a sunny spot in early summer. Few other grasses have horizontal leaves. When you see crabgrass seedlings, hurry and pick them out, or spray with PMAS.

Crabgrass. *Syntherisma sanguinalis.* Perennial in the sub-tropics, but an annual in the north; it develops stolons towards the end of summer. Leaves are broad and flat, not shining, and sometimes slightly hairy. Leaf is semi-transparent and yellowish-green when young. The ligule is a long membrane, and the leaves are rolled in the bud. Grows close to the ground, the stems and leaves mingling through the turf for a radius of a foot or more. Germinates only when warm weather begins, seedlings being readily recognized (see illustration). Turns red in autumn. A serious turf problem.

HOT-WEATHER GRASSES

Two southern varieties that will withstand most northern winters north and east as far as Long Island are:

> **Zoysia matrella or Flawn.** Manila grass.
> **Zoysia japonica.** Japanese or Korean lawn grass.

They are creeping grasses, and are normally reproduced by planting stolons. They grow best in summer heat, and they are logical varieties to use when you are worried about crabgrass. But they go into their resting period in mid-autumn and only become green in mid-spring. During their long resting period the lawn is white; unless the grass has been mown closely, this white turf is likely to be a fire hazard.

SUBSTITUTES FOR GRASS

Mowing grass at short and regular intervals is essential for its well-being; when one is busy and the lawn is large, the cutting may develop into a dreary chore, and it is not surprising that attempts have been made to find a substitute for grass. Plants that have been experimented with and have shown some promise include:

White clover	Turfing daisy
Alsike clover	Selaginella
Suckling clover	Yarrow
Japan clover	Pearlwort
Birdsfoot trefoil	Chamomile

These should all grow little more than ankle-high, which is what most people who are trying to avoid lawn-mowing would accept. But one reason why we mow is to keep tall weeds out of the lawn; stop mowing and the thistles and docks, goldenrod and ragweed will quickly appear and will take over if mowing is continuously omitted.

Perhaps the nearest thing to a solution is to sow a mixture of dwarf grasses and wild white clover; to purchase a power-mower with a cutter that works on the principle of the hay-mower and to use it about once a month. This will not be a lawn in any sense of the word, but it will be green, neat, and satisfactory at a distance.

DWARF GRASSES

The following are 12 inches or less when mature:

Velvet bent	Bird grass
Creeping bent	Chewing's fescue
Canada bluegrass	F 74 fescue
Kentucky bluegrass	Illahee fescue
Merion B 27 bluegrass	Annual bluegrass

To sum up: *The bents and the fescues, and bluegrasses under certain conditions, are the important lawn grasses; quick-growing temporary nurse grasses are usually sown with them. Dwarf substitutes for grass that should need no mowing have been tried with little success because, if mowing stops, weeds take over.*

CHAPTER 11

How to Identify the Grasses in Your Lawn

"Some so-called grasses are not members of the Gramineae; among them are the weeds, knotgrass or knotweed, ribgrass or plantain, grass of parnassus, an adventive of wet land. Another is scorpion-grass, for-get-me-not or myosotis of the flower garden."

FIRST EXAMINE the plant closely. Then refer to the following lists numbered 1 to 7 until you decide that you have identified the plant or that it is one of perhaps two or three varieties. Then read the descriptions of those you think it may be, and you will be able to decide what your plant is.

TO EXAMINE THE PLANT

Provide yourself with a pocket lens; then:

a. Dig up a small section of the turf, roots and all.

b. Separate one of the plants in which you are interested from the remainder, and wash away the earth from the roots.

c. Look at the roots. Are they tough, part of a coarse time-beaten tangle, suggesting a perennial plant? Or are they weak, thin, and obviously young, suggesting an annual? Is there an underground creeping root? Is there a creeping stem or stolon on top of the ground? Does the plant spring from a small bulb?

d. Look at the leaves. Are they flat? Or are they bristly, rounded in section like wire?

e. Look at the base of the leaves, just where they enter the ground. After you remove any rough, dead scales, what color is the base? Is it hairy?

f. Look at the tip of the leaf. It may come to a point gradually, or it may come to a sudden, blunt point.

g. Feel for ribs on the leaf. Look at the veins against the light; whether the ribs and veins are prominent or not is a clue.

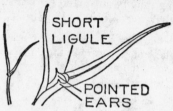

SHORT
LIGULE

POINTED
EARS

Pull a leaf away from the stem and you will see the collar or ligule which prevents rain from getting into the plant's center. Sometimes on both sides of the ligule are ears or auricles. The kind of ligule and auricle helps you identify the grass.

h. Look for the ligule. Pull a leaf away from the stem and notice the point where the leaf clasped the stem. Here you will find a little collar or projection which serves to keep rain falling on the leaf from running down into the plant and causing it to decay. Use your lens and consult List 3.

i. Look for ears, or auricles, near the ligule. Where the leaf leaves the stem there may or may not be a pair of them.

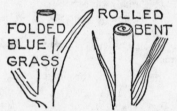

FOLDED
BLUE
GRASS

ROLLED
BENT

Cut a stem; if in section it is triangular, or if it is solid, it is not a grass. The young leaves of a grass are either folded like a fan or rolled around each other like a spiral.

j. Note the internal structure of the growing shoot. Cut a stem across and examine it under your lens. You will find the new leaves wrapped around each other, the younger ones in the center. They will be wrapped in one of two different ways. They may be rolled, or they may fit fanlike over each other.

Watch for plants that are not grasses but that may look like them. Pearlwort occurs in closely mown old turf as patches of bright, emerald-green—brighter than any grass. Under your glass you will find that tiny leaves spring off in pairs, opposite one another, from a central stem, and at the blossoming period the plant has small white flowers like chickweed; no grass has showy flowers like this. Sedges and rushes occur on wet land and look like grasses; their stems, however, are solid and triangular in section, while grass stems are hollow and round or oval in section. Seedlings of knotweed in spring may be mistaken for grass; but washing them discloses that they are individual plantlets.

List 1. The kind of leaf is a clue. Following are flat-leaved grasses, which have the young leaves *rolled* in the bud. They are in the order of the narrowness and smallness of their leaves, the smallest first.

Velvet bent	Bermuda
Colonial bent	Holcus
Creeping bent	Crabgrass
Seaside bent	Meadow fescue
Redtop	Italian rye grass
Sweet vernal	Couch

Timothy

Grasses that have their young leaves *folded* in the bud. They are in the order of their fineness, the finest first.

Shade bluegrass	Kentucky bluegrass
Chewing's fescue	Canada bluegrass
Illahee fescue	Bulbous bluegrass
Sheep's fescue	Goosegrass
Annual bluegrass	Perennial rye grass

Carpet grass

Bristle-leaved grasses in the order of their fineness, the finest first:

Fine-leaved fescue	F 74 fescue
Chewing's fescue	Illahee fescue

Sheep's fescue

Six grasses that have very small leaves:

Velvet bent (silky to the touch)	Fine-leaved fescue (wiry to the touch)
Astoria bent	Chewing's fescue (wiry)
Rhode Island bent	F 74 fescue
Shade bluegrass	Illahee fescue

Five grasses having glossy leaves:

Shade bluegrass	Perennial rye grass
Meadow fescue	Italian rye grass

Goosegrass

List 2. The base of the leaf gives a hint. It may be:

Red	Meadow fescue, perennial rye grass
Violet-pink	Italian ryegrass
White, red veins	Holcus
Dun-colored and parchment-like	Illahee fescue, Chewing's fescue, F 74 fescue
Hairy	Couch, sweet vernal, holcus, crabgrass, Bermuda
Rough	Shade bluegrass

List 3. The ligule will help you name the grass. The ligule is short in:

Perennial rye grass	Meadow fescue
The fescues	Couch
Kentucky bluegrass	Creeping bent
Italian rye grass	Timothy

The ligule is medium-long in:

Goosegrass   Holcus

Annual bluegrass

The ligule is a ring of hairs in:

Carpet grass   Bermuda

The ligule is long in:

Shade bluegrass	Crabgrass
Sweet vernal	Velvet bent
Redtop	Canada bluegrass

List 4. The auricles are narrow and claw-like in:

Perennial rye grass	Meadow fescue
Italian rye grass	Couch

List 5. Look at the general habit of the plant. Varieties with stolons above ground, in the order of their stolon length, longest first:

Bermuda	Rhode Island bent
Carpet grass	Shade bluegrass
Creeping bent	Crabgrass
Seaside bent	Holcus

Varieties producing creeping rootstocks beneath the soil, listed in the order of the length of their rootstocks, the longest first:

Couch
Bermuda
Kentucky bluegrass

Canada bluegrass
Redtop
Illahee fescue

Chewing's and F 74 fescue

Varieties that produce bulbous roots:
Bulbous bluegrass

Timothy

List 6. The color of the grass is helpful in determining the variety. The color, however, changes somewhat in different locations.
Rich dark green grasses:

Perennial rye grass
Kentucky blue grass

Italian rye grass
Meadow fescue

Redtop

A gray grass:

Holcus

Pale gray-green grasses:

Couch
Canada bluegrass
Sweet vernal

Timothy
Goosegrass
Fine-leaved fescue

Brown-green grasses:
Illahee fescue

Chewing's fescue

F 74 fescue
Rhode Island bent

Blue-green grasses:

Sheep's fescue

Creeping bent

Bermuda

Yellowish-green grasses:

Annual bluegrass
Shade bluegrass

Crabgrass
Velvet bent

Bulbous bluegrass

List 7. The peculiar habits of some varieties are a clue. Grass in flower spring, summer, and fall, even when closely cut .... Annual bluegrass

Turf which is difficult to mow .... Annual bluegrass

Grasses that grow strongly in early spring, late fall; even in winter, often under the snow....... Annual bluegrass

      Bulbous bluegrass   Canada bluegrass

      Kentucky bluegrass   Perennial rye grass

Enters its winter sleep early; still dormant when other grasses commence to grow in spring .... Creeping bent, velvet bent

Do not appear until late in the spring .... Crabgrass Goosegrass

Turns red in autumn .... Crabgrass

Patches of silklike grass in old turf .... Velvet bent

Turn white in autumn .... Goosegrass Bermuda

When the hand is drawn lightly over the turf, the grass gives a prickly feel...................... The fescues

Gray patches in turf .... Holcus

Quick-growing grass; upright-growing spears in mown turf at day's end; ½ inch taller than the turf, looking yellow against the setting sun ...... Crabgrass in June

Shiny grass in well-kept lawns, the plants mostly growing in one direction .... Shade bluegrass

Strong, coarse weed grasses growing in patches among seedling grass .... Couch

Hay-like odor and taste of the plant. .... Sweet vernal

TO IDENTIFY SEEDLINGS

Dig the plants carefully and wash soil from the roots; you will usually find the remains of an oat, a rye grain, or a wheat grain adhering to the root. On seedling grasses you can usually find the husk of fescue, bluegrass, and even the tiny bent seeds.

Remains of seeds may usually be found still attached to the roots of a seedling plant; these are shrivelled rye and oat grains. Fescue, bluegrass, and others can be identified, but a pocket lens is needed.

CHAPTER 12

Lawn Troubles

"Everything that grows without being sown or planted, among a Crop that has been sown or planted, is in that Place a Weed. The whole benefit of the Tillage was intended for the Crop, and this robs it of a Part." THOMAS HALE, 1756.

You WILL HAVE fewer weeds if your lawn is growing in well-drained soil; if it is near-neutral, neither too acid nor over-alkaline; if it is raked weekly with a Cavex or other sharp rake; if it receives lime every winter; if it is given chemical plant foods every spring and fall; if all thin or semi-bare spots are perforated, topdressed, and seeded; and if the seeds you use are the cleanest and best you can obtain.

WEEDS AND WEEDING

In a lawn of moderate size you should have no difficulty in keeping weeds under control, by getting after them the moment you see them. Only if you neglect them and they pile up, or if your lawn is large, do weeds become a problem. Kinds that mostly grow individually include dandelions and plantains, shepherd's purse, hawkbit, chicory, and dock; these are best eliminated by prying them out when they are small, and with their roots entire. A weeding knife and a one-inch chisel are equally satisfactory for most weeds: insert the tool near the weed, bear down on the implement, and the earth will crack in the vicinity of the weed; lift it out. Prepare a mixture of one part grass seeds and ten parts soil, fill the weed hole with it, and press with the shoe.

Some weeds have a spreading habit of growth and develop into mats; this group includes chickweed, mouse-ear, and speedwell.

Dandelions should be taken out without breaking the root; but crab-grass may be cut just below the surface. Some mixed seeds and soil should be put into the holes.

If the mats are not numerous they can be eliminated by raking with a Cavex rake or roughening with an old-time curry comb, which you can still find in a country store, or by slashing them in several directions with a kitchen knife down into the soil, and

SEED + SOIL   STORE 6 DAYS

PRE-SOWN SEEDS FOR QUICK TURF.

Seeds and fairly dry soil are mixed; heap stands in the garage while the area outside is being prepared. First stages of germination take place in the heap. Sprouts often appear two days after spreading.

then plucking at the mats. After scratching and plucking, spread a ¼-inch layer of seed and soil mixture and rub it into the rake furrows or knife cuts.

In turf subject to exceptional wear, such as tradesmen taking a short cut or the running of an auto onto the grass, infestations of knotweed or knotgrass are frequent. Groups of the plants merge into the surrounding turf until autumn, when they die and become dark-brown patches. Strongly self-seeding, these brown spots become green again in spring, when the thousands of knotweed seeds germinate. At first they may deceive you into thinking they are new grass plants, but pull some up and you will soon see they are not grasses. Among other signs, the first seed leaves or cotyledons are in twos; no grass plant has a pair of cotyledons. You may find remains of the seeds tangled amid the roots; under a pocket lens you will see they are not tiny oat-shaped grass seeds, but are dark-brown, small, buckwheat-shaped grains.

If you can recognise the brown patches of dead knotweed during winter or the emerald patches of germinating knotweed seeds in spring, your best method is to dig out the trouble spots 2 inches deep with a trowel or narrow hoe, refill the hole with clean soil, and sow grass seeds.

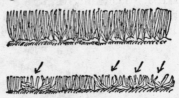

One way to dodge crabgrass, which hates shade, is to feed generously and to mow long, top. To increase crabgrass, which likes poor land, cut short and neglect fertilizer; arrows indicate where crabgrass is starting.

Crabgrass is not difficult to control if the area is small, if the plants are few and far-between, and if they are taken out early. In June the crabgrass seedlings are so easily recognised in bare soil or in young lawns that they can be pulled out with the thumb and finger. (See the illustration of these young plants in Chapter 10.) Few young grasses have horizontal leaves—nearly all are near perpendicular; few other grasses have a purple tint at the extreme ends of the leaves. In mown turf, at the end of the day, you can often see crabgrass plants half an inch higher than the lawn grasses, due to their more rapid growth. The wider leaves are yellow-green against the setting sun. At this time they may be pulled with a knife blade and the thumb, like taking pinfeathers from a chicken.

Later, when they have developed into mature crabgrass plants, raking the turf will disclose their presence and they can be cut out. With crabgrass, actually digging out the roots is unnecessary because it cannot grow another year from the same root. Cutting off the plants just under the surface with a sharp knife is sufficient.

Raking also discloses the sticky latex-filled plants of spurge, whose branches run through turf. Favored by hot, dry weather, this plant has a thin but tough taproot; cut this with a sharp knife and lift out the plant.

Raking also helps remove moss and the scale-like, membrane-like lichen. But these growths are symptoms of lack of lime and topsoil, or of adequate drainage, or both, and these weaknesses should be corrected.

CHEMICAL WEED-KILLING.
Dusting with lead arsenate; spraying with 2–4–D; sprinkling with iron sulphate solution.

But you will have to turn to selective chemical weed control if your lawn is too large for hand-weeding or if, for one reason or another, your weeds have increased to the point that their eradication by other means is too difficult.

The chemical PMAS (see p. 97), applied as a spray, is one

answer to the crabgrass problem, but it has little effect on silver crab or goosegrass, except when the plants are very young.

Most other weeds can be controlled by spraying with the chem-

Spreading sodium arsenate and sand; spooning with calcium arsenate; spotting with sodium chlorate.

ical 2–4–D. The manufacturers' directions should be followed meticulously; too heavy an application will injure your turf. Several chemical houses prepare it.

THREE BAD TURF WEEDS.
LEFT: *crabgrass*. CENTER: *goosegrass*. RIGHT: *knotweed*.

THE MAJOR TURF WEEDS

Crabgrass. *Syntherisma sanguinalis.* A description of this appears above and in Chapter 10. Keeping a thick, healthy turf and mowing at regular intervals, with the machine set to leave the turf long, are the best means of keeping it out. Elimination of beetle grubs and avoiding turf diseases also help. Early recognition and early hand-weeding are important. If these fail, spray with PMAS or a similar preparation.

Crabgrass which has been killed by chemicals or by autumn frost, should be raked out, the area topdressed and sown with grass seeds that same year—early fall, late fall, or winter.

Goosegrass, Silver Crab. *Eleusine indica.* Described in Chapter 10. Selective chemicals have little effect on this weed. Hand-cutting with a sharp knife at the ground level should be practiced.

Quack, Twitch, Switch. *Agropyron repens.* This also is described in Chapter 10. It is rarely met with in any large quantity in lawns, because constant close cutting eventually eliminates it; the few plants that may be found should be dug out by hand and the hole filled with clean soil and dressed with mixed seeds and soil. In building a new lawn or when topdressing, avoid the use of soil containing the white string-like roots of quack.

Barnyard Grass. *Panicum crus-galli.* A quick-growing dwarf annual grass with brush-like flower heads; matures to a white hay by autumn. Commonly seen in a new-seeded lawn, but mowing quickly eliminates it.

Nut Grass. *Cyperus rotundus.* A pest in southern turf. Grass-like plants with coarse leaves and small rounded rootstocks. When building lawns in the South, use soil known to be free of this weed. Continuous routine mowing will be helpful.

Bermuda Grass. *Capriola dactylon.* This valuable southern turf grass may occur as an annual weed in the north. Cutting at the soil surface, like crabgrass, is recommended.

Annual Bluegrass. *Poa annua.* This is described in Chapter 10. It is encouraged by heavy wear, tight land, excess of lime, too much moisture. It is discouraged by spike-rolling, drainage, the application of sandy topdressings. Lead arsenate, used for grub-proofing turf, has a definite but slight effect of keeping it in check.

Dandelion. *Leontodon taraxacum.* When taking it out individually, be sure to get the complete root; otherwise it will branch underground, and several new plants will replace the one you hoped to destroy. A weed-gun can be obtained, filled with a weed-killing chemical; punch the center of the dandelion and a few drops of the liquid will enter the plant. Sulphuric or carbolic acid applied on a skewer will kill it. Or you can spray with 2–4–D.

Dock. *Rumex species.* A large plant with a deep taproot which often appears in newly seeded land. The leaves are large, reddish-green, and shining. Eventually it will disappear under mowing, but the plant takes up so much room and smothers the grass over so wide an area, that it is usual to dig out the root with a garden fork, smooth the surface, and put a 1/4-inch coating of mixed seed and soil over the spot.

Heal-All, Selfheal. *Prunella vulgaris.* Blue-purple flowers and a square-section mint-like stem enable you to identify it. When you see it you may assume that your lawn is growing on deep, heavy, clay-loam soil. Apply sandy topdressings, perforating first; comb often with a Cavex rake, and spray with 2–4–D.

Marsh Pennywort. *Hydrocotyle vulgaris.* A wild plant with creeping stems, rooting at the joints, and with round leaves attached by their center to rather long stems. Grows only in water-logged soil, indicating that drainage is necessary; deep spiking and rubbing coarse sand into the holes will help.

LEFT: *smooth chickweed.* CENTER: *mouse-ear, which has hairy leaves.* RIGHT: *purslane, occurring rarely in established turf, but often seen in a new lawn.*

Mouse-Ear. *Cerastium vulgatum.* **Smooth Chickweed.** *Alsine media.* Two matting weeds that often appear during and after a wet spring. Scarify the mat, pluck out some of the plants, and topdress with mixed seeds and soil. If the mats are numerous and extensive, dust them with calcium arsenate; in a few days the killed mats will be brown.

Pearlwort. *Sagina procumbens.* Beautiful patches of bright green appear in old lawns; they may look like grass at first sight, but small white flowers are occasionally noted, and the base of the stem is brown. Accepted practice is to cut out the weed and replace with grass turf.

Plantains. *Plantago species.* Either hand-digging, taking out the entire tassel-like root, pricking each plant with a weed-gun, or spraying with 2–4–D will rid you of this weed.

Purslane. *Portulaca oleracea.* This weed often appears in lawns that have been recently seeded, especially in the spring. The plant has red stems which run close to the ground and which will produce roots here and there along their length. Evenly placed are rounded oval-shaped leaves about 1 inch long, green and shiny. The small flowers are yellow.

Although 2-4-D will control purslane, frequent raking and routine mowing are usually relied upon to kill this plant, and it seldom trou-

LEFT: *broad-leaved plantain.* CENTER: *narrow-leaved plantain.* RIGHT: *dandelion. Three weeds which 2-4-D will control.*

bles established turf. There is a good excuse for removing it by hand, however, for washed and boiled, it is an excellent culinary vegetable.

Chicory. *Cichorium intybus.*

Shepherd's Purse. *Capsella bursa-pastoris.*

Snakeweed, Hawkbit. *Hieracium species.*

These three would receive the same treatment as dandelion. But snakeweed is an indicator of poor land. Generous feeding is a necessary part of the treatment to get rid of this and many another weed.

LEFT: *the pretty fern leaf of yarrow.* CENTER: *snakeweed or hawkbit.* RIGHT: *heal-all.*

Sorrel. *Rumex acetoscella.* Small plants with halberd-shaped leaves which are pleasantly acid (unwholesome; don't swallow). Produces plants at intervals on creeping stems. It likes acid land, and its presence indicates that an annual application of lime is necessary. 2-4-D will control it.

95

Speedwell. *Veronica species.* Flowers are light blue, but otherwise the matting plants are similar to mouse-ear and should be given similar treatment.

LEFT: *sorrel, a sign that lime is needed.* CENTER: *speedwell.* RIGHT: *spurge, which is often disclosed by raking the turf.*

Spurge. *Euphorbia arvensis.* Small spreading plant with brown-red spots on the grayish leaves. These and the stems exude a white sticky latex when broken. Raking to make the plants stand up, then hand-weeding, is standard practice; also raking prior to mowing will keep the weed in check.

Yarrow. *Achillea millefolium.* There is little need to get rid of this plant, because the fern-like leaves blend so well with lawn grasses. Very deep digging is necessary to take out the entire root; otherwise the weed will promptly return.

IS CLOVER A WEED? HOW TO ELIMINATE IT

If you play golf or lawn tennis you will probably answer yes to this question and will want to get rid of clover. It makes sports turf slippery and sometimes soils clothing and balls.

To get rid of it this is what you do:

Let your annual liming consist of 35 pounds per 1000 square feet of gypsum. Give the spring and fall feeding suggested in Chapter 8, but instead of the materials given there, use 5 pounds sulphate of ammonia and 50 pounds shredded cattle manure per 1000 square feet. Rake the lawn each week with a sharpened rake.

Should this fail to reduce the clover there is one more thing you can do: (1) Loosen the soil in any convenient manner: pry it with garden forks or perforate it along the lines suggested in Chapter 4. (2) Spread 5 pounds of *aluminum* sulphate, mixed with a bushel of compost, per 1000 square feet. Rub it into the holes in the soil. Aluminum sulphate is not a fertilizer, but an acidifying agent; it should not be confused with ammonium sulphate or sulphate of ammonia.

SOME CHEMICAL WEED-KILLERS

PMAS, the letters standing for phenyl-mercuric-acetate-soluble, is the wonder-working chemical that has been used successfully for over five years to kill crabgrass in turf. To apply it, procure a sprayer that will hold 2½ gallons or more of water; mix 1¼ fluid ounces of 10% PMAS with 2½ gallons of water and spray the dilution on 500 square feet. Spray thoroughly and cover equally every part of the 500 square feet; this is best done by walking briskly while spraying and by going over the area at least twice.

Mark each 500 square feet with stakes; spray right up to but not over the margins. Measurement of the lawn must be exact, and the amount of 10% PMAS must be exact also: 1¼ fluid ounces per 500 square feet. Reduce this allowance to 1 ounce for new lawns less than six months old and to ⅗ ounce per 500 square feet for closely cut bowling greens or putting greens. Any time of the day is suitable, and the best time of the year is when crabgrass seeds first germinate, which may be from mid-May on, depending upon the locality. Three sprayings should be given at ten-day intervals.

Within seventy-two hours the turf will show injury, taking on a yellow cast; but the true grasses recover, while crabgrass withers, usually disappearing three or four weeks after the start of the treatment.

The manufacturers also offer 2½% PMAS, which is identical except that it is one-quarter the strength; and four times the amount is needed on a given area: 5 ounces per 500 square feet on an average lawn, 4 ounces on new grass, 2⅖ ounces per 500 square feet on closely mown turf. The water remains the same, 2½ gallons.

PMAS is a dual-purpose chemical; it is also an efficient fungicide and will do much to prevent or cure snow-mold and dollar-spot. As many as nine treatments in a season may be given when used to prevent disease.

Other chemicals that may be used to fight crabgrass include P.C. (Potassium cyanate), Sodium chlorate, Crab-Not, Seltox, Scutl, etc. Like PMAS, directions must be followed precisely: if you apply less than advised your work may be in vain, while if you give too much they probably will damage the grass.

2–4–D will clear a lawn of plantains, dandelions, chicory, and many another unwanted plant. A convenient formulation of it is Tufor, prepared by the U. S. Rubber Co. Add 4 ounces of Tufor to sixteen gallons of water and spray onto each 3250 square feet. One pint dilutes to 64 gallons, enough for 13,000 square feet; between 3¼ and 3½ pints of Tufor will take care of 1 acre. Be prepared to give a second spraying if necessary.

Spring is the best period for chemical weed-killing; early autumn is the next best. Tufor can be obtained in soluble tablets; one, dissolved in 2 quarts of water, will treat 100 square feet.

Weedar 64, Weedone 48, Weed-no-more, Barweed are other good preparations containing 2–4–D. Feedz-an-Weedz is a reliable combination of 2–4–D and fertilizer; Wooster Lawn Bilder is along similar lines.

Sodium arsenite. From 2 to 8 ounces is the allowance of this poisonous chemical per 1000 square feet. Dissolve each ounce in 2 gallons of water and spray. Or mix each ounce with 25 pounds of sand and spread dry.

Sodium chlorate. This is a dangerous chemical because it is inflammable and explosive, but it is good for crabgrass. Allow from ½ pound to 2 pounds per 1000 square feet, mix with two pailfuls of dry sand, and dust on the weeds. Do not dissolve it and spray, as was the original recommendation when the use of this chemical was first advised: but large users would get their clothing moistened with it; next morning the dried clothing would ignite like a match being struck on a match box. Better use another remedy.

Calcium arsenate. Either a dust-gun or a can with a perforated bottom and a wooden handle may be used to dredge mat-forming weeds.

Iron sulphate. For each 1000 square feet dissolve 6½ pounds in 4 gallons of water, and spray. Repeat every two weeks until heal-all, dandelion, plantain, and other weeds disappear.

Lead arsenate. This poison, much used for destroying beetle grubs and earthworms, is found also to have a weed-destroying effect. Used as a dust, it is effective on mouse-ear and chickweed; and it is claimed to reduce annual bluegrass. Rate of application is 10 pounds or more per 1000 square feet.

Sulphuric acid is helpful where we have a limited infestation of dandelion, plantain, or dock. A jar half full of this, standing in a deep bowl, may be on the ground alongside you. Wearing a pair of rubber gloves, dip a skewer into the acid and press the point ½ inch into the center of the weed; withdraw it, dip it into the acid, and sting the next weed. Don't spill or splash; sulphuric acid is a dangerous chemical. Carbolic acid may be used in the same way; almost as effective, it is safer to use.

Sprayers should be thoroughly cleaned after applying any weed-killing chemical—tank, hose, and nozzle. A detergent like sal-soda should be used.

To sum up: *Best way to eliminate weeds is to dig them out. Chemicals are necessary when weeds are too numerous or the lawn is over-large.*

CHAPTER 13

Lawn Troubles (Continued)

"Ill weede growth fast." JOHN HEYWOOD (1497–1580).

WEAR

TURF IN WHICH the fescue grasses predominate and which is growing on well-drained sandy soil, will stand a lot of wear if it is evenly distributed and if rest periods are provided for the recuperation of the turf. But the bents and the bluegrasses will not take hard wear so well.

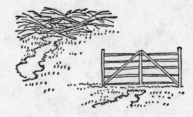

Neighbors, tradespeople, and pets often take short cuts; if they are not discouraged, paths may develop. Divert traffic with a layer of branches or a section of fencing kept in position for a week or so.

Tradespeople will make a definite path on your lawns; even dogs have their regular routes. Place tree branches across these paths to divert the traffic. Let the obstructions stand for a couple of weeks, and then move them to another position astride the traveled route. Some units of iron fencing, or wooden field fencing, may be preferred to the branches.

Urine injury by dogs sometimes occurs; here the remedy is to place a sprinkler as soon as the damage is seen, to wash the poison from the soil. Then dust some nitrate of soda, at the rate of

5 pounds per 1000 square feet, and sprinkle again. Should the grass be killed, dig out the soil to a depth of 2 inches, replace with fresh soil, and sow with pre-sown seeds.

FUEL OIL

The spilling of fuel oil onto the lawn calls for digging out the injured spot. The center of the front lawn is an unfortunate place to put the fuel-oil intake. Either move it to the driveway or dig out the turf and soil around it to a depth of 12 inches and replace with cinders, topped with small-size gravel or bluestone.

A lawn is no place for the fuel-oil intake. If it cannot be moved to the driveway, cut neatly around it 12 inches deep; fill 9 inches with cinders, top 3 inches with small stone or gravel.

SCALD

Scald is a condition met with in hot weather in retentive clay soils or those on which there has been too much rolling. Rain collects and cannot escape into the land before the sun raises its temperature to a point where the grass is killed. Grading to avoid the accumulation of water, under-drainage, and the use of one of the devices for perforating soil to permit sandy compost to be worked in are advised. The killed spots should have the top 2 inches of soil replaced with fresh; the whole would then be dressed with mixed seeds and soil.

We sometimes see a similar condition in a new lawn where more seeds than usual have germinated, causing the plants to overcrowd. If you are sure this is the case, do not be in too great a hurry: in a few weeks' time the condition may possibly cure itself, the surviving grass plants being the fittest. If the reverse happens, and the spots die, take out 2 inches of the surface, replace with new soil, and dress with mixed seeds and soil.

FERTILIZER BURN

In previous pages we suggest that dividing the nitrogen figure of a fertilizer analysis into 100 gives us the quantity of the fertilizer we may spread on each 1000 sq. ft. without burning, providing grass is dry, fertilizer has been spread fairly, and the rake has been used to knock the powder off the grass. If we do cause burning through failure to observe these points, we note that the scalding usually discloses the sweep of the material where it was cast, or a well-marked band appears where a fertilizer drill overlapped and the allowance at that point was doubled. Try to wash away the chemical by letting a sprinkler run for half an hour or longer; if the grass proves to be dead, replace the top 2 inches of soil and dress with mixed seeds and soil.

The sun's rays intensify fertilizer scald, and if we can get a protective covering of brush, garden trash, or tree branches in position quickly, the partial shade will often save the turf. Sprinkling can be done through the protective cover.

This protection against sunlight is all-important when sea water spills over grass, as it has done in some recent hurricanes. Turf in the open died; but anywhere within the shade from trees or buildings, the grass survived. Two essentials are shading and a generous sprinkling.

Grease spots from mowers are best cut out, replaced with soil, and dressed with mixed seeds and soil; or plugged with pieces of turf cut to fit.

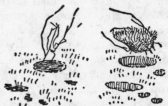

Modern mowing methods mean an occasional spilling of oil or gasoline onto the turf. Cut out the plug of injured grass and 2 inches of soil beneath it; fashion a piece of clean turf to fit the hole, or partly fill with dirt and spread mixed seeds and soil.

MOLES

These animals do not cause much trouble on home lawns as a rule, but the increase of white grubs in the soil in recent years, due to the spread of the Japanese beetle, has placed more food at their disposal; their chief foods are earthworms and grubs. The establishment of moles on your property may well help you in your fight against soil animals. Kill grubs, and grub-proof the

Unwelcome helpers, moles are usually hunting for beetle-grubs when you find their runs in your lawn.

land, and you will have little trouble with moles. To get rid of them:

1. Purchase and place at intervals in the run some poisoned food. Note, however, the mole has an acute sense of smell and he avoids anything touched by your hand. Bury an old pair of gloves for a day, put them on, and only then open the mole bait and place it according to the directions given on the container.

2. Attach a hose to the exhaust of an automobile, tractor, or power-mower. Often a tube that is part of the set of attachments for an electric sweeper will serve. With the engine idling, insert the other end of the hose into a mole run and keep it there for 10 minutes; then move it to another position 15 or 20 feet distant. Moles will be asphyxiated.

3. Buy a couple of mole traps. They are placed straddling the mole run at its end, where the mole is digging.

ANTS

These usually are more numerous in dry soil and in hot weather. They are stubborn, and their eradication is sometimes difficult. Applying ½ pound of 5 per cent chlordane dust per 1000 square feet, mixed with topdressing material, is probably more effective than anything else.

Various poison ant baits, using sugar or grease as the attracting ingredient, will often work. The usual poison is the metal thallium, which acts slowly. Worker ants seek out food, and have a remarkable method of transporting it to the nest: they eat it, then regurgitate it for the queen and other stay-at-homes. Obviously, a material that eventually will be fatal to the queen yet is slow enough for the worker to carry it within itself, is a very slow poison, and thallium is just that.

Normal ant colonies in lawns are small, the average hill being perhaps 1½ inches in diameter. But sometimes a large colony will develop, and a space several feet across will be occupied by nests and tunnels. Cyanogas helps here. Make holes in the area a foot deep and a foot apart. Put in each a teaspoon of cyanogas powder. Spread one or more empty canvas bags or old newspapers over the colony and keep them there for two hours, after which you should see little movement in the nests. However, if the queen has escaped, the ant population will gradually build up again, and the treatment will have to be repeated. Grass may have to be replaced.

CHINCH BUGS

Patches of injured grass, often brick-red, suggest chinch-bug injury. Smaller than the head of a pin, they are speedy and hard to see.

In hot weather you may find your lawn has various odd-shaped patches, not round or oval, of brick-red. Usually this suggests chinch bug. Get down close to the grass and separate the plants; you may get a glimpse of tiny creatures darting to cover. Draw a calling card over the injured grass, and you may catch some rushing across the card—little round individuals, gray, and rather smaller than the head of a pin. They actually are little beetlelike bugs with brown bodies and white wings, giving the general effect of a gray color. Injuring and killing grass by sucking the juices from the plant, they can be killed by spraying or dusting with rotenone or nicotine; or by spreading ½ pound per 1000 square feet of 5 per cent chlordane dust mixed with any convenient quantity of soil, sandy compost, or sand to enable you conveniently to distribute it. When you dust or spray, give two treatments on the same day a few hours apart; many of the bugs are missed by the first.

To sum up: *Fescue turf withstands wear better than bent or bluegrass. The ills that may happen to turf include spilt oil, sun scald, overcrowding, fertilizer burn, and salt water. Moles want to help you eliminate white grubs, ants like you as neighbors, and chinch bugs like your grass. The remedies are suggested here.*

CHAPTER 14

More Lawn Troubles

*"The sixth help of Ground is, by Watring and
Irrigation, which is in two manners; the one is by
Letting in, and Shutting out Waters, at seasonable
times; for Water, at some seasons, and with reasonable stay, doth good; but at some other seasons, and
with too long stay, doth hurt. And this serveth only
for Meadows, which are along some River. The other
way is to bring Water from some hanging Grounds,
where there are Springs, into the lower Ground,
carrying it in some long Furrows; and from those
Furrows, drawing it traverse to spread the Water:
And this maketh an excellent improvement both for
Corn and Grass."* FRANCIS BACON, 1625.

ARMY WORMS, CUTWORMS, SOD
WEBWORMS, GRASSHOPPERS

IN EARLY SUMMER, a large infestation of army worms or caterpillars may be found on the lawn. Mix up a poison bait as
follows:

2½ lbs. bran
1 tablespoon Paris green
1 cup molasses
1 pint water

Scatter on the lawn; keep the cat
in the house and tie up the dog.
Collect the bait after two days and
bury it.

*Army worms sometimes invade a
lawn in large numbers.*

Sometimes you will find a groove in your lawn; it may be 8 inches long, and at one end you may dig out a cutworm, similar to the type that eats one's garden plants. Grooves, sealed over with silken threads to make tunnels, may contain at one end a

LEFT: *cutworms burrow near the surface; investigate if you see an 8-inch line in the grass looking as if the point of a spade has been dragged in the turf; a cutworm may be hiding at one end.* RIGHT: *one of several types of burrowing wasps; females often pack a hefty sting.*

sod webworm, a hairy, spotted caterpillar about ½ inch long. You may be suspicious if you find birds interested in your grass and if you find the light gray moths or millers, which lay the eggs of the webworm, flitting over the turf around sundown.

For cutworms, sod webworms, and for grasshoppers also should they appear in large numbers, the poisoned bait is effective. After you have collected the bait on the second day, spread 10 pounds per 1000 square feet of arsenate of lead, and water it in.

WHITE GRUBS

You may wonder what is the matter with your lawn: you find some holes in it large enough to admit your finger; you may come across some spots where the turf has been pulled away in inch-size pieces; you sense an earthy smell; the turf is yielding and feels like a heavy carpet when you walk. These are warnings of coming trouble; the holes may be where robins and crows have been feeding on white grubs; the torn turf may be where skunks have been digging for them. Better get after the grubs at once; otherwise one day you may find your turf brown and killed, and the surface broken up by these grub-hunters.

Several races of beetles spend part of their lives in the soil. Best known of these is the Japanese, but equally serious are the oriental beetle, the May beetle, and the Asiatic garden beetle. The grubs of all are very much alike, about 1¼ to 1½ inches long if straightened out, but they usually are doubled on themselves. All are gray-white, shining, wet and altogether disgusting; their tail-end is dark-grayish. The evil they do is in eating the roots of the grass plants an inch under the surface; when they are in

NOV. DEC. JAN. FEB. MAR. APR. MAY

THE FACTS OF LIFE OF THE JAPANESE BEETLE.
Grub is dormant in winter, feeds in April, becomes a pupa in May.

JUNE   JUNE THRU. SEPT.   JULY

Pupa produces a beetle in June, which feeds above ground all summer, but revisits the soil in July to lay eggs.

AUG.   SEPT.   OCT.

Eggs hatch in August; grubs eat and grow until November.

108

large numbers the grass is killed, and you find you can lift it up because the grubs have eaten the upper part of the roots and severed the plants' connection with the ground.

The usual corrective measure is to "grub-proof" the lawn by spreading on each 1000 sq. ft. 10 pounds of lead arsenate or $\frac{1}{2}$ pound of technical D.D.T.; the latter means 5 pounds of a 10 per cent D.D.T. compound or 1 pound of a 50 per cent compound. For an even distribution, mix the poison with sand, sifted soil, or compost; the amount of the latter is unimportant; a wheelbarrow-load would be a convenient amount. Put on a respirator, mix and apply, and then wash into the soil by setting a sprinkler, which you would move from time to time—say, every fifteen minutes.

If you care to take the trouble, you might carefully dig out a cube of grass, including the soil under it, that is 12 inches by 12 by 12 inches—in other words, a cubic foot. Carefully pick out, count, and place in a jar every grub you can find, including the very small ones that are newly hatched. Even the smallest will not be difficult to find, for they will be moving. Take your count and a representative group of the grubs to your county agent or agricultural station. An expert will estimate the approximate number of the different kinds, and if the Japanese predominate he may advise you to use the spores of the milky disease, an infection that attacks the Japanese but has no effect on the others. Possibly he will also tell you where the spores of the milky disease can be obtained.

JUNE BEETLE

Similar in appearance, but very much larger, is the 2-inch grub of the green June beetle or fig-eater. It does considerable damage, but lives as an individual, making a deep hole in the turf large enough to admit one's finger, alongside which is a large worm-cast-like heap of excavated soil. The above remedies may be used, the arsenate of lead or D.D.T. But should you have only a few of the grubs make a cone of paper to conduct a teaspoonful of cyanogas into each hole; close the hole with a plug of dirt to keep in the poisonous fumes. You can identify June beetle grubs by their size—almost that of a man's little finger—and also by the remarkable fact that when dug out or caught in the open, the grubs have the habit of crawling on their back, with legs in the air. Normally a pest in the southern states, it comes as far north as Illinois and Long Island.

MOLE CRICKETS

LEFT: *mole cricket; its burrowing habit makes it serious in southern turf, and it sometimes gives trouble as far north as Long Island. Usually 1½ inches long.* RIGHT: *the minute chinch bug (greatly enlarged) sucks the sap from grass.*

Also mostly in the south and extending just about as far north is the mole cricket or ground-puppy, a brown hairy cricket, 1½ inches long, with two front legs which are thick, flat claws adapted to digging. Occurring in wet or sandy land it makes burrows like small mole runs, eats grass roots, and is generally objectionable. Arsenate of lead and D.D.T. are effective remedies. Or prepare and spread a poison bait by mixing 2 tablespoons of Paris green, 2½ pounds cottonseed meal, 2½ pounds bran. Moisten the mixture with 2 cups of molasses stirred into 1 quart of water. Remove the bait after a few days, and in the meanwhile watch that children or pets do not become involved with it.

CRAYFISH

Crayfish or crawfish are little lobster-like creatures which sometimes give trouble in the vicinity of streams and rivers. They build 4-inch piles of mud on the lawn with a hole at the top. They emerge from this hole at night, living on plants as well as insects and small animals. Put two teaspoons of cyanogas powder down the burrow and plug with soil.

CRAYFISH OR CRAWFISH.

Fresh-water lobster-like creatures, usually about 3 inches long, that trouble river-level turf in the South. The crayfish home is a 4-inch mound of mud in your lawn; from a hole on the top it emerges at night to feed.

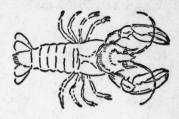

LAND CRABS

Land crabs are a nuisance in southern lawns near the sea; the pudgy little creatures come inland from the beach at night and bore holes 2 inches in diameter in the turf. Pouring 2 teaspoons of cyanogas into the hole and plugging with soil will kill

Land crabs trouble southern lawns near the coast.

the crab, but many more will probably arrive the next night. A barrier consisting of planks set edgewise in the sand, covered with metal or smooth linoleum and supported by stakes on the landward side, will probably keep them out.

WASPS AND YELLOW JACKETS

Two large wasps called the European hornet and the digger or cicada-killer sometimes build their nests in lawns; if disturbed the females will sting savagely, so they are best eliminated. D.D.T. can be sprayed or 5 per cent chlordane dust can be mixed with ten times its bulk of dry soil or sand and scattered where the wasps have their nests. Allow ½ pound of the powder per 1000 square feet. Make the application after sunset.

Yellow-jacket nests in the ground might have two teaspoonfuls of cyanogas powder pushed in the entrance, which is then plugged. Best do this in the evening also.

EARTHWORMS

A morning chore on the average golf putting green is to whip the grass with an 18-foot bamboo. Breaks up worm casts and knocks off the dew; grass dries promptly to permit early mowing.

It is always debatable whether earthworms should be welcome or not. They are helpful in perforating and draining the soil; their ability to bring soil from below to the surface in the form of worm casts amounts in the course of time to a decided turn-over of part of the land. They improve soil. But the lawnmower produces a small spot of dead turf where each worm cast is squeezed flat. Worms make a lawn muddy and render its use for games well-nigh impossible. Grub-proofing soil with 10 pounds of arsenate of lead per 1000 square feet tends to make it earthworm-proof as well. Mowrah meal is also used. Select a rainy period in spring or autumn, when the weather is warm and the worms are close to the surface. Spread ½ pound per 10 square feet and wash it into the soil with an abundance of water from a hose. Mowrah meal varies in its effectiveness: sometimes it works very well, and sometimes not at all. It is the safest material to have around, however, being non-poisonous. The other materials must be kept under lock and key and used with great care.

STINKWORMS

In recent years a strange earthworm has made its appearance —the tropical earthworm or stinkworm. Medium in size, it is very prolific and its presence is indicated by the unusual number of worm casts. Don't handle it, because days of washing will not remove the skunk-like odor—hence stinkworm. Ordinary remedies at usual rates have little effect. Try 5 pounds of 5 per cent chlordane dust per 1000 square feet; mix with ten times its bulk of compost, sand, or soil; and water it in thoroughly.

SOME MATERIALS TO ELIMINATE LAWN PESTS

Arsenate of lead. A much-used poison, especially for grub-proofing soil and eliminating earthworms. It has some weed-killing properties, which are discussed in Chapter 12.

Chlordane. A chemical introduced in recent years that is proving to be an efficient killer of stinkworms, wasps, ants, and chinch bugs. The 5 per cent dust is generally used, and ½ pound per 1000 square feet, mixed with sand, soil, or compost, is the usual dosage—but much more is needed for the stinkworm.

Cyanogas, A dust. Kills hornets, yellow jackets, mole crickets, land crabs, ants, rats, moles, woodchucks, and similar pests. Use outdoors only and do not inhale the fumes, which are lethal.

D.D.T. A highly effective poison for most insects, though there are a few on which it has no effect. It may be used dry, mixed with sand, limestone, or dry screened compost; or it may be stirred into water and sprinkled or sprayed onto the turf.

Paris green. A complex salt containing copper and arsenic; an effective insect poison.

Rotenone. An insecticide that kills by poisoning or contacting almost every insect, but is harmless to man and his household pets.

Keep all poisons locked up. Read the labels carefully, and have recommended antidotes available.

Milky disease. A sickness that one Japanese beetle grub can communicate to another, resulting in the grubs' dying. Nearly all will take the disease, though a small percentage are immune. Small quantities of the spores are placed on the ground, and eventually the area becomes infected, taking possibly two years. It affects Japanese beetle grubs only; other pests, as well as man, are not involved.

Beetle Traps. These were largely used when the Japanese beetle first landed on our shores; but they are not so freely recommended as formerly, as they are accused of attracting as many beetles from elsewhere as they trap. The bait used is geraniol, a fragrant material. Flying to it, the beetles drop into a jar. Empty the jar daily into a paper bag, put a spoonful of cyanogas powder with them, then bury or burn.

To sum up: *Army worms, cutworms, sod webworms, and grasshoppers will take poisoned bait. White grubs can be liquidated. Japanese beetle grubs can be infected with milky disease. Less often seen are the giant grubs of the June beetle, mole crickets, crawfish, and land crabs. Hornets, digger wasps, and yellow jackets sting painfully and are serious when they gang up on one; get rid of them. Earthworms and the loathsome stinkworms are best eliminated also.*

CHAPTER 15

Still More Lawn Troubles

"Who weeding slacketh,
Good husbandry lacketh."
THOMAS TUSSER, 1557.

FUNGUS DISEASES

Brown patch. Your lawn is thriving; you are doing all you can to keep it in good shape. But one day you are disappointed to find something unusual: a hard-to-describe darkening of the grass in one or more patches. If you were to spill some kerosene on your coat sleeve you would see something like the same effect.

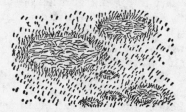

Large brown patch appears suddenly in hot weather; attacked by a fungus, grass sickens and dies in circles. Prompt treatment with a fungicide is necessary.

Return to the patch in a few hours and you will find that it has increased in size. In another short period the center older part is seen to be dying. Next day both the dead portion and the outer rim of darker grass have increased in size. This is large brown patch or mildew. A number of fungicides are available, and all are partially helpful in controlling or warding off the condition, but none are 100 per cent effective. Best known are Semesan, Tersan and Caloclor, obtainable at supply houses.

LEFT: *a knapsack sprayer for fungicides, insecticides, and weed-killers.* CENTER: *use a respirator when spraying, dusting, or spreading arsenate of lead, D.D.T., etc.* RIGHT: *a hand-pressure sprayer for small jobs.*

One application may not stop the development of the fungus; it may take several—at weekly intervals. Because no one may be entirely effective, use at least two of them alternately until the grass is normal. It is most important that this trouble be treated the moment it is seen; for, once the center of the patch has been killed, it is necessary to dig out 2 inches of soil, replacing with fresh soil and sowing with pre-sown seeds—that is, seed and soil mixed together. Or patch with turf.

It is usually necessary, when grass is killed by disease, frost, or insect attack, to replace the old soil with new. Raking off the dead plants, smoothing, and then sowing seeds does not appear to work; the seeds rarely grow unless fresh soil is applied.

Dollar spot. Besides the discoloration, injury, and killing of the grass in circular or oval patches that we call brown patch, there is a rather similar condition known as dollar spot. With this there are hundreds of spots of injured grass, each the size of a silver dollar. Unless immediately treated there will be more of them. Caloclor and a material called 531 are the favorite remedies.

Snow mold. There is another troublesome condition that sometimes appears in very early spring: as snow disappears there may occur perfectly round patches of white dead grass, varying in diameter from 2 to 10 inches. The grass leaves are glued together, and a definite mildew-like growth can sometimes be seen in the circle. Breaking up this glued-together condition by forthright raking and spraying with Tersan or Caloclor causes them quickly to heal. This happens to be one condition where usually the soil does not need to be replaced.

FAIRY RINGS

Toadstools and mushrooms often appear in a lawn in wet weather; they usually originate in pieces of manure or rotting

Fairy rings grow bigger year by year. Caused by mushrooms or toadstools, they do no harm for they are not parasites but saprophytic fungi, feeding on dead organic matter in the soil.

wood in the soil. They do no serious harm, because they are not parasites feeding on living grass, but saprophytic fungi feeding on dead organic matter. They do compete with grass for the plant foods in the soil, however, and on poor land and in dry weather you can notice their effect. Always they grow in circles starting from their point of origin outwards, like the splash of a pebble in a pond. About a foot outside the circle are the mycelia, which is the name given to the roots of a fungus; their presence is indicated by the lighter color of the grass, because for the moment the soil is partly exhausted. The reverse is the case a foot inside the circle; here the grass is a deeper green, where last year's mycelia, now decaying, are furnishing extra plant food for the grass.

Some of these fairy-ring circles are many years old and may enclose thousands of square feet in area. Sometimes only parts of the circle may be seen, and sometimes several of these portions have joined together.

Mowing or rubbing with the back of a rake readily breaks up the surface growth of toadstools and mushrooms, and the presence of fairy rings is usually ignored. But in porous, sandy soil, the difference in the turf is so marked between the grayish outside and the emerald inside, that attempts are sometimes made to clean up the condition. It is not easy, and you may have to work on it for some time. Perforate the turf on the active outside edge of the ring with an aerifier or spike-roller, and dust 6 ounces of Tersan per 1000 square feet; wash it into the soil with much water from a hose.

The fungicides mentioned are readily obtainable; a small quantity of each should be on hand at all times for immediate use when necessary.

CHLOROSIS

This is an anemic condition involving the yellowing of the grass plants which may have a variety of causes: (1) A lack of plant foods, including one or another of the trace elements. (2) Parasite infestation, perhaps a virus, bacterium, fungus, or insect. (3) An excess of soluble salts as found in soils of arid regions or in the neighborhood of alkali, sulphur, or chalybeate springs. (4) Outcrops of subsoil. (5) Overcrowding. (6) Sudden frost.

To sum up: *Brown patch, dollar spot, and snow mold are not serious if fungicides are applied immediately. Neglect them and your lawn may be ruined. Fairy rings are unimportant.*

CHAPTER 16

Lawns in Competitions; Sports Areas, and Some Tables

"Grass is the forgiveness of nature—her constant benediction. Fields trampled with battle, saturated with blood, torn with the ruts of cannon, grow green again with grass, and carnage is forgotten. Forests decay, harvests perish, flowers vanish, but grass is immortal. JOHN JAMES INGALLS.

JUDGING LAWNS IN COMPETITION

YOUR COMMUNITY or your garden club may wish to encourage home-owners to have better lawns, and prizes may be offered for the best. Following is a schedule of points that will enable a committee of judges fairly to appraise the turf. Lawns will look their worst in July and August; September is probably the fairest time to judge them. Highest possible score is 1000.

You may have classes for (a) unassisted owners or families, (b) owners with paid help, (c) lawns cared for by jobbing gardeners. You may also have classes for lawns of less than 2500 square feet, of 2500 to 5000 square feet, and of over 5000 square feet.

Higher numbers in each class should be re-scored independently, and average totals arrived at.

	Points
What is your first impression of the lawn?	
Poor	No score
Fair	5– 25
So-so	25– 50
Good	50– 75
Excellent	75–100

119

Looking down, how does the grass cover the soil?

More than 25 per cent of the area is bare	No score
10 to 25 per cent is bare	25– 50
5 to 10 per cent is bare	50– 75
Less than 5 per cent is bare	75– 95
Soil completely hidden	100

How is the soil surface under the grass?

Very uneven	0– 25
Uneven	25– 50
Pretty good	50– 75
Nearly perfect	75–100

How is it policed? Are twigs, paper, match sticks, et cetera, in evidence?

Some	No score
Few	10– 25
None	25– 50

How is the irrigation?

No water is available	50

Water is available. If judged in spring or autumn:
Has it been over-watered?

Yes	No score
To some extent	25
No	50

Water is available. If judged in July and August:

Soil is dry	No score
Moist 1 inch down	10
Moist 2 inches down	25
Moist 3 inches down	50

How is the mowing?

Poor	No score
Fair	25– 50
Good	50– 75
Very good	75– 90
Perfect	100

Mowing frequency. Collect clippings and measure them.

	Points
Longer than 1 inch	No score
1 in.	25
¾ in.	50
½ in.	75
¼ in.	100

Adjustment of mower.

Height of cut lower one side than the other	No score
Both sides equal	25– 50
Some leaves bruised but not cut	No score
All leaves cut properly	25– 50

Weeds. (For this purpose, clover is not a weed)

Many: 10 or more per 10 sq. ft.	No score
Quite a few: 2½ to 10 per 10 sq. ft.	25 –50
Some: 1 to 2½ per 10 sq. ft.	50– 75
No weeds	100

Disease. Brown patch, dollar spot, etc.

More than 15 per cent of the surface injured	No score
10 to 15 per cent injured	
Condition uncontrolled	15– 25
Disease stopped	25– 50
Less than 10 per cent of the surface injured	
Condition uncontrolled	25– 50
Disease stopped	50– 75
No disease	100

Insects. Grubs, chinch bug, webworm, etc.

More than 15 per cent of the surface injured	No score
10 to 15 per cent affected	
Area not treated	15– 25
Treated with accepted remedies	25– 50
Less than 10 per cent affected	
Area not treated	25– 50
Treated with accepted remedies	50– 75
No insects	100

121

AREAS REQUIRED FOR VARIOUS TURF GAMES

Archery. Golds are from 90 to 300 feet from the archer. Allow an additional 900 feet at back and sides for safety.

Badminton. A doubles court measures 44 feet by 30 feet. Allow 15 feet between courts.

Baseball. Diamond is a square with 90-foot sides and a diagonal 127 feet 3⅜ inches. Average area of field, 3½ acres.

Basketball. Total area, 104 feet, more or less, by 68 feet, more or less.

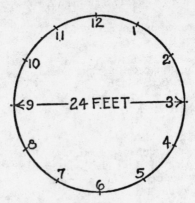

CLOCK-GOLF.

A hole is cut and lined with a 4¼-inch-diameter metal cup, obtainable at supply houses. It may be placed anywhere within the circle and would be changed on occasion. Ball is teed from against each number in succession.

Clock Golf. A circle 20 to 24 feet in diameter, or larger.

Cricket. Field should be 450 feet square; pitch, or distance between wickets, 66 feet.

Croquet. 105 feet by 84 feet.

Football. Between goal posts, 360 feet. Total advisable length, 425 feet. Width recommended, 160 feet.

Golf. Eighteen holes need 100 acres or more; the mown fairways occupy 40 to 50 acres. Nine holes need 50 acres up; mown fairways occupy 20 to 25 acres. Fairways average 150 to 200 feet wide; hence, each 100 yards' distance is 1 acre on a narrow fairway, 1⅓ acres on a wide fairway. Average area of putting greens 4500 to 11,250 square feet each—1/10 to ¼ acre.

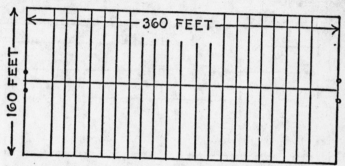

For a football field 425 feet is the advisable length; allow a margin on the sides also.

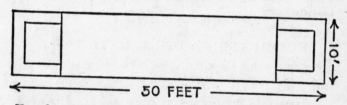

Horseshoe-pitching needs 50 feet by 10 feet. An ideal pastime for the suburban home—no ball-retrieving to annoy the neighbors.

Horseshoes. 50 feet by 10 feet. Pins 40 feet apart.
Lacrosse. 360 to 380 feet by 230 to 300 feet.
Lawn Bowling. 126 feet square or larger. If flooded for curling, 135 feet square; curling tees or marks 114 feet apart.
Lawn Hockey. 330 feet by 150 to 180 feet.
Lawn Tennis. Court markings are 78 feet by 36 feet. Desirable total area per court, 120 feet by 65 feet.

Polo. Boarded field, 900 feet by 480 feet. Field not boarded, 900 feet by 600 feet.

Roque. 60 feet by 30 feet.

Soccer. Between goals 300 to 360 feet; width 165 to 225 feet.

Volleyball. 80 feet, more or less, by 50 feet, more or less.

Orientation. Plan your sports grounds, so far as possible, to run north-south.

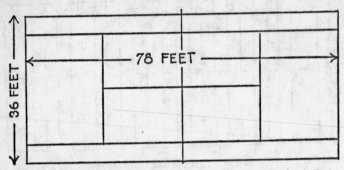

Lawn tennis needs a total outside measurement of 120 by 65 feet. Orient the court north and south, so that you don't have to play into the setting sun.

ROUGH AND READY CAPACITY TABLE

10 medium shovelfuls equal 1 wheelbarrow-load
20 wheelbarrow-loads equal 1 cubic yard.

APPROXIMATE WEIGHT OF SOIL MATERIALS

	Cubic yard Pounds	Cubic foot Pounds		Cubic yard Pounds	Cubic foot Pounds
Humus	940	35	Quartz sand	2435	90
Water	1683	61	Sandy topsoil	2610	97
Clay	1700	63	Heavy subsoil *	2740	101
Medium topsoil	1925	71	Medium subsoil	2760	102
Sticky topsoil			Light * (sandy)		
(heavy) *	2410	89	topsoil	2885	107

* Heavy and light, applied to soil, refer to the work needed to dig it, not to its actual weight.

Thickness of layer	On one square yard	On 1000 square feet	On one acre	Area that one cubic yard will cover	
Inches	Cubic yards	Cubic yards	Cubic yards	Square yards	Square feet
.1	.0028	.31	13.4	360	3240
.25	.0069	.77	33.6	144	1296
.5	.0138	1.54	67.2	72	648
.75	.0207	2.31	100.8	54	486
1.	.0278	3.09	134.4	36	324

Manure is often sold by the cord, or fraction of a cord. A regular cord is 128 cubic feet or 4.74 cubic yards, measuring 4 feet by 4 feet by 8 feet. It can vary, however; it may be:

130 cubic feet: 4 feet by 5 feet by 6½ feet
160 cubic feet: 4 feet by 5 feet by 8 feet

APPROXIMATE DISTRIBUTION TABLE

Per 1000 square feet. Per acre.

Given any number of pounds per 1000 square feet; multiply by 2 and divide by 100 to find tons per acre.

Given pounds per 1000 square feet; multiply by 40 to find pounds per acre.

Given any number of tons per acre; multiply by 50 to find pounds per 1000 square feet.

Given any number of pounds per acre; divide by 40 to find pounds per 1000 square feet.

To sum up: *Measurements suggest that games needing more space than you have available may be unfair to your neighbor; he is entitled to the uninterrupted use of his property, with no trespassers seeking balls.*

BOOK IV
Fruits

Index

Don't Crowd—Fruits Need Adequate Room

"They shall sit every man under his vine and under his fig-tree." MICAH. IV.

TREES, BUSHES, and plants are small when you set them, but in a short while most will expand and eventually dominate your garden, leaving little room for vegetables and flowers. Few plants will grow underneath, or even near, a mature apple or cherry tree, and when you dig in their neighborhood you will find the earth full of roots spreading far beyond their water curtain. This curtain is formed by the rain cascading down from one leaf to another, until the drops combine into a ring of water where they strike the ground. It is under this water curtain that most of the tree's feeding takes place, but many roots will travel beyond it.

So be sure to follow the planting distances recommended in the following pages, and unless you have plenty of available room it is suggested that you grow fruits in moderation. However, there are some kinds that give good returns and yet take little space, and these are the suitable ones for the moderate-size garden.

Here are some favorite fruits. Allow space for flowers and vegetables; then plant those you like best.

Strawberries growing in a barrel. Soil has much weight, so move it on a dolly. Sleeve of wire netting in the center permits drainage.

WHAT YOU CAN GROW IN A TINY GARDEN

Strawberries in a specially designed earthen pot, with holes all around its sides; or in a strong barrel with 2-inch holes cut in its sides. Fill the pot or barrel with good soil and plant the strawberries, one to a hole.

A specially made strawberry pot of glazed ware or clay.

Flat-trained trees. Tie the branches and stems to wires attached to a sunny wall, which means you will avoid the north side of the house; you may use apple, cherry, grape, nectarine, peach, pear, or plum.

Fruit trees in pots. A large pot or a wooden tub may contain a dwarf tree, kept small by careful pruning. Room might be found for several.

Apricots above, peaches beneath, on a multi-variety tree. Plums may be on other branches.

14

WHAT TO PLANT IN A SMALL GARDEN

Under 5000 sq. ft.

Northern half U. S., and Canada

Five-variety apple tree; an apricot-plum-peach tree; grapes; black raspberries; strawberries.

Southern half of the U. S.

Figs; grapes; muskmelons; peaches; peanuts; strawberries.

Two types of fruit trees: standard at left, dwarf at right. Dwarfs are the more suitable for the home garden.

IN A MEDIUM GARDEN

5000 to 10,000 sq. ft.

(Figures suggest minimum worth-while quantities.)

Northern half U. S., and Canada

3 Dwarf apples
6 Blackberries
6 Boysenberries *
2 Dwarf cherries
6 Dewberries
3 Grapes
6 hills Muskmelons
2 Peaches *
2 Dwarf pears
6 Raspberries
50 Strawberries

Southern sections of the U. S.

6 Boysenberries
2 Figs
3 Grapes
2 Kumquats **
6 Loganberries
2 Loquats **
6 hills Muskmelons
2 Peaches
100 feet Peanuts
50 Strawberries

You may not have room for all; select those you prefer.

* These may be excluded north of the border states and the Great Lakes.
** Grow these only in the nearly frost-free areas of the far South.

15

FOR A LARGE GARDEN

Over 10,000 sq. ft.

(Figures suggest minimum worth-while quantities.)

Northern half of the U. S. and Canada

6 Dwarf or standard apples
2 Apricots *
6 Blackberries
6 Blueberries (if you have acid soil, porous, yet with a high water table)
6 Boysenberries *
4 Bush cherries
2 Sour cherries, standard or dwarf
2 Sweet cherries, standard or dwarf
3 Chinese chestnuts *
6 Dewberries *
3 Figs (with winter protection) *
6 Grapes
6 Hazelnuts or Filberts
6 Loganberries *
10 hills Muskmelons
3 Nectarines *
3 Peaches *
3 Pears, dwarf or standard
3 Quince *
6 Raspberries
100 Strawberries
10 hills Watermelons *

Southern sections of the U. S.

3 Almonds
3 Avocados **
6 Boysenberries
3 Cashews **
6 Citrus fruits in variety **
3 Figs
6 Grapes
3 Guavas **
6 Loganberries
3 Loquats **
3 Mangos **
10 hills Muskmelons
3 Nectarines
3 Peaches
200 feet Peanuts
3 Pecans
3 Persimmons
3 Pistachios
3 Plums, dwarf or standard
2 Pomegranates **
100 Strawberries
10 hills Watermelons

* These may be excluded north of the border states and the Great Lakes.
** Grow these only in the nearly frost-free areas of the far South.

16

CHAPTER 2

Planting Trees

"Wholesome berries thrive and ripen best
Neighbour'd by fruit of baser quality."
WILLIAM SHAKESPEARE, Henry V.

YOU PLANT FOR YEARS AHEAD—DO IT CAREFULLY

MOST FRUITS may be set in spring, which experience shows is more advisable in the colder sections of the country; in the middle areas, fall planting is equally satisfactory. Make your purchases from a reliable local nursery, ordering well ahead of planting time. Young trees are usually supplied with their roots bare; older ones, with the ball of soil containing the roots wrapped in burlap. If your trees and bushes arrive too early for spring planting, you heel them in, which means that you plant them temporarily in a shady spot, close together, until you are ready to set them out. Should the land be frozen and no soil be available with which to cover the roots, lay them on the ground outdoors in the shade, sprinkle the roots, and cover them with burlap, boxes, boards, or garden trash. Cold is unlikely to harm them. Get young plants; there is little advantage in buying trees of bearing age: the shock of transplanting will offset any advantage of an extra year or two of growth. Young trees are best to plant because they "take" better.

Plants heeled in until you are ready to set them. If soil is frozen, lay them outdoors, water them, and cover.

Trees and bushes should be plump, and the cambium should be green under the bark when you nick it with your thumbnail. If any look withered when you unpack them, dig a wide trench and bury them entirely; when you dig them up a week later, they should appear normal. If they are still withered, do not plant them.

HOW TO SET YOUR TREES AND PLANTS

When the land is free of frost and has dried, tap in a stake where you expect to set each of your fruits, avoiding areas where the roots of shade trees or hedges are occupying the soil. Use the table in Chapter 12 and be sure to keep them the suggested distance apart; the sparse appearance of your garden at planting time may tempt you to set them too close, but a few years later you may be regretful. Space may be used for small and short-lived kinds between the larger and more permanent ones. The

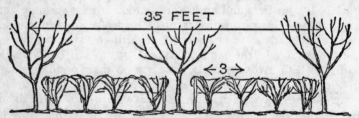

In the opening years, slow-growing apples allow ample room for a quick-maturing peach (center), which in turn lets you get several annual crops from brambles. Gradually the brambles and finally the peach will give way to the apples and turn the entire area over to them.

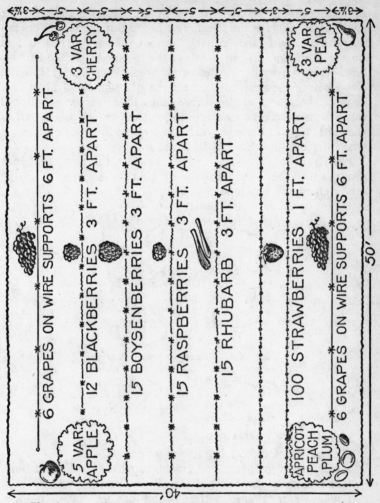

Plan for a small fruit garden 40 by 50 feet. Multi-variety fruit trees will be in the rows along with blackberries, grapes, and strawberries for the first years. As the trees grow, individual plants that gradually come under their influence will be moved elsewhere.

It is assumed that the surrounding area belongs to you. If others own around you, better have only one tree, placed in the center.

following should be planted the proper distance apart: apple, cherry, Chinese chestnut, pear, and plum. But the space between may be set with shorter-lived apricot, nectarine, peach, and quince. Between these in turn put the so-called bramble fruits—blackberry, boysenberry, dewberry, loganberry, and raspberry. Long before the peaches need all the space you will plant new rows of the brambles elsewhere. And as the years pass you will put new apricot, nectarine, and peach trees in some other part of the garden; plant these in good time to have them in full bearing when the old ones have to be discarded.

Finally, as you age along with your plants, this portion of your grounds will be occupied only by your now strongly bearing apple, cherry, chestnut, pear, and plum.

Standard planting mixture A, to go in contact with the roots when planting: two parts by measure of topsoil and one each of grit and organic matter, which may be humus, compost, or rotted stable manure.

Prepare a mixture for planting of:

2 measures of topsoil from your garden.

1 measure of grit: screened gravel, using the smaller portions, or coarse, sharp sand.

1 measure of organic matter: rotted manure, rotted compost, humus, or peatmoss.

(A measure may be a quart milk bottle, a 12-quart pail, or a wheelbarrow- or truck-load.)

Fortified planting mixture B to fill hole after roots are covered with A. To each four pails are added 2 quarts of bonemeal and 4 quarts of pulverized sheep manure.

Pile these in a heap; then make another mixture, but with each 4 pails mix 2 quarts of bonemeal and 4 quarts of pulverized sheep manure, shredded cattle manure, or pulverized poultry manure. Vary the mixture somewhat, as suggested in the discussion of the various fruits in later pages. Where a light soil is indicated, double the grit ingredient; where a clay soil is advised, double the topsoil; where organic matter is stressed, double this ingredient. A quart milk bottle makes a good measure at first; afterwards you can judge the quantity or you can paint a mark inside a pail at 2 quarts, another at 4 quarts. Turn the mixture twice and stir with a hoe until the white bonemeal is seen to be fairly mixed through the heap.

Take a large washtub or similar container; half fill it with water, first glancing under virus infections in Chapter 5; and stir

Planting a tree. Left: cut off damaged roots. Right: stir roots in a mud made of soil, grit, and organic matter.

in enough of the first mixture of soil materials, without the bonemeal and manure, to mix into a watery mud or slurry.

Planting a tree. Left: dig a large hole; put in a pyramid of unfortified soil mixture A. Right: set tree with roots carefully arranged and not crossing; place enough additional soil mixture A to cover the roots; work the tree up and down to get material between the roots. Soil mark should be 1 inch below surrounding level.

Planting a tree. Left: fill to the top with fortified soil mixture B and tread firm. Right: fill depression with water; two days later, when it has drained away, add more mixture B and rake smooth.

Meanwhile dig a hole or pocket, wide and deep enough to allow the roots to be arranged naturally; in the bottom put about half a pail of the mixed soil, grit, and organic matter, without the bonemeal and manure. Take your first young tree or bush and prune off any broken or inconveniently long roots, then stir the roots into the slurry so that they are well coated, and place the plant on the hillock of unfertilized mixture at the bottom of the pocket, arranging the roots so that they all run downwards and outwards. It is important that no two roots are twisted around each other; if they cannot be arranged naturally, prune away one of them. Intertwined roots will grow thicker as the plant develops and are likely to strangle one another, cutting off food and moisture and often resulting in a one-sided and imperfect plant.

Before you stir the roots in the slurry, note the soil mark on your young plant. The portion that was underground in the nursery can be seen clearly, for it will be soiled with dirt. The portion that was aboveground is colored under the influence of light; the bark is clean and often greenish-purple. The soil mark is where the greenish color ends and the root begins; you will have no difficulty in determining it. For most varieties, the tree or bush should be so placed that the soil mark is exactly 1 inch below the soil level when the plant finally is in position in your garden.

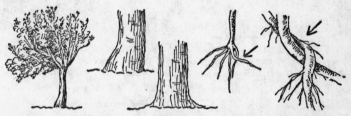

Lack of symmetry in a tree. Left to right: tree developed mostly on one side. It is buttressed only on one side. Normal tree is buttressed on all sides. Probably carelessly planted with crossing roots. Roots expand and strangle each other; pressure interferes with sap movement.

We left our plant standing on the pyramid of unfertilized soil at the bottom of the pocket, its muddy roots carefully arranged outwards and downwards. Holding it upright, place some more of the mixture without the bonemeal and sheep manure on the roots, and jiggle the plant up and down slightly to work the soil between the roots; check the soil mark and spread a final spadeful of the unenriched soil. Now fill up the pocket with enriched soil, containing bonemeal and sheep manure. Tread the new soil around the young plant to firm it. This will leave a depression several inches deep, which you fill with water; next day, the water having disappeared, add more enriched soil and rake the surface level.

Some pruning will be necessary; shear away any branches that have become broken or bruised during the digging, transportation, and planting. It is usual, also, to cut off the top foot or so of the main stem to encourage side branches to develop into the open bowl-shape that is usually desired.

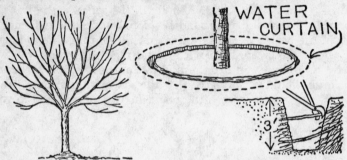

To transplant a tree that is several years old (left). Dig a trench in spring (right) one-third the distance in from the water curtain. cut all roots, fill the trench with new soil, and leave until next spring.

After the wait, dig another trench (left) just beyond the one you dug last year, which is now filled with new roots. At 3 feet, dig under the tree, severing all roots (right).

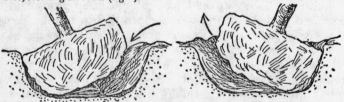

Rock the tree (left) and get a large sheet under it; sheet edges under tree are folded several times. Rock tree and straighten sheet (right).

Left: draw sheet around the ball; tie at trunk with rope. Right: get a stoneboat under. In northern winters, sheet is omitted; ball freezes.

Left: haul it to its new position; or—right: forget the whole thing and plant a new one.

TRANSPLANTING MATURE TREES

If you wish to transplant a mature tree, dig a circular trench around it parallel to the drip-curtain line, but one-third the distance in from the line to the trunk; if the drip curtain makes a circle with a radius 6 feet from the bole, the trench will have a radius of 4 feet. Cut through the roots and dig 3 feet deep; fill the trench with topsoil and leave for a season. The following spring dig just beyond the topsoil-filled circle, which now will be crowded with new roots; then dig underneath the tree on all sides until you have a ball of soil. Rock the tree gently to enable you to get a large sheet of canvas below it, the part going under the tree folded several times, 12 inches wide; again rock the tree until you can unfold the canvas. When it is entirely beneath the tree, gather the corners and tie them with rope.

Rock it to get a stoneboat under the canvas-wrapped ball;

drag it up an incline of planks and to the hole you have prepared for it. Guy it with wires for the first year.

When the tree is large, move it in winter in the north. Dig the first trench, cut the roots, and fill with soil; leave for a season. Take several weeks to dig the second trench, going 6 inches down every few days and putting straw in the bottom of your new trench to prevent its freezing; remove the straw and dig another 6 inches, replacing the straw. Eventually the earth-and-root ball will be frozen solid. Rock it to push boards under it and get it onto a stoneboat.

You will probably need a winch or a stump-puller, and rollers of 2-inch pipe under the stoneboat, possibly a heavy truck. Unless you have a special affection for the tree, you might consider felling it and planting a new one as a better course to take.

FIRST PRUNING

Prune severely when the transplanting is complete; in fact, whenever you move a tree, bush, or vine, follow up with pruning to bring the top growth into balance with the lessened efficiency of the roots. However careful you are you cannot avoid doing unseen damage to the roots; you may save every last rootlet, with all the soil around it, but the delicate root hairs near the ends of the smallest roots, which may only be seen under a microscope, are the absorption organs; the slightest disturbance breaks them, and until the plant has replaced them it can draw little moisture from the soil. So we prune to reduce the leaves, which evaporate water, and bring them more into proportion with the plant's lessened feeding ability. It is a good plan to prevent fruit production the first season by pinching away the blossoms. Plant and transplant only when trees, bushes, and vines are dormant, with no leaves on them.

The site of a strawberry bed should have a wheelbarrow-load of compost, humus, or rotted manure dug into each 100 square feet—say 10 feet by 10 feet—and 20 pounds each of bonemeal and sheep manure deeply raked under, and with these a second wheelbarrow of the organic material. Planting on the smooth surface is best done with a trowel, with a length of twine attached to two pegs to give the professional appearance of a straight line. Your weeding and scuffle-hoeing later will be made easier by so doing.

Seeds of muskmelons and watermelons are sown in groups or hills, six or eight to a hill. Dig out pockets or holes; fill with the mixture of soil, grit and organic matter, bonemeal, and sheep manure. Press a large inverted flowerpot into the surface to make an inch-deep circular groove. Drop the seeds in the groove, rub lightly with your open hand to cover them, then press lightly with the shoe. When the seeds germinate, remove all but three young plants to each hill.

These "hills" are not raised above the ground level unless the area is very wet, when they may be 4 inches above grade; ordinarily they are flat, and "group" is a better word with which to describe them. Seeds are sown only after settled warm weather has arrived, with no danger of frost, but you may get them in about two weeks earlier if you protect each group with a hotkap. Both muskmelons and watermelons need about sixteen weeks of warm weather; so if you are in a short-summer latitude, sow seeds in pots, starting them in the house and transferring them to a cold frame, which may be improvised if necessary with some boards, boxes, and a storm-sash. Or skin some turves from your lawn, turn them over, and sow seeds on the dirt side; at planting-out time, cut pieces with a mason's trowel, each piece containing a young plant. Put three plants in each group.

CHAPTER 3

Pruning

*" 'George,' said his father, 'do you know who killed
that beautiful little cherry tree yonder in the garden?'
. . . Looking at his father with the sweet face of
youth brightened with the inexpressible charm of all-
conquering truth, he bravely cried out, 'I can't tell
a lie. I did cut it with my hatchet.' "* MASON LOCKE
WEEMS, The Life of George Washington.

PRUNING IS A NECESSARY SURGICAL OPERATION

The four chief reasons why we prune are:

1. To reduce competition among buds on the tree, bush, or
vine, enabling it to produce fewer but larger fruit. To prevent a
tree from overloading itself.

2. To train it into shape with well-placed main branches, usually developing an open-bowl design by cutting away part or all
of the main stem or leader when the tree is ten feet high or less—
the open bowl allows the sun's rays to reach all parts of the plant.
To reduce crowding branches and permit free access for spray
materials, and to allow easy fruit-gathering. To eliminate one of
two crossing branches to prevent their rubbing, with possible entrance of virus, bacteria, or fungus spores into the exposed area.
In the case of flat-trained trees, to retain their desired shape.

3. To remove weak, diseased, damaged, or dead twigs and
stems. To remove water sprouts or suckers.

4. To induce the formation of fruit-bearing buds.

Pruning. Left: this apple needs severe pruning. Center: the shape of this pear can be improved. Right: crossing branches need removing.

Left: in spring there will always be many dead peach branches to remove. Center: nick away a small section of the bark; if the branch is living, the cambium will be green, even in mid-winter. Right: on most trees, the fat fruit buds may be distinguished from slender leaf buds.

When we should prune:

General pruning for 1 and 2 is usually best done in late winter; for 3, whenever the need is evident; for 4, for the formation of fruiting spurs, pruning is most effective after the tree has blossomed.

Grapes may be pruned only in winter; if portions are cut off too late and after the sap has started to circulate, they will "bleed." From every cut, long skeins of white jellylike material will drain away, seriously exhausting the vine.

In winter, living branches can usually be distinguished from dead ones by making a nick in the bark with the thumbnail. Under the bark is the cambium, which will be green if the branch is alive and usually brown if it is dead. Also, by early summer buds will not have developed on the dead branches. Some apricot, nectarine, and peach branches die in spring, so pruning for number 3 is likely to be considerable with them.

Most professional growers like to use a sharp knife for pruning; along with the skill they acquire they also develop a horny skin under the thumb. Amateurs are not expected to have this, and for them very sharp pruning shears are advised, for a clean cut is necessary, with no crushing of the stem.

Branch removal. Left: how you may avoid splitting (1, 2). Right: do not leave a stump (3).

Branches that are too large for ordinary pruning shears can be taken off with a pair of lopping shears. Limbs beyond the capacity of these will be cut with a sharp saw. Make an undercut first, until the saw binds through the weight of the limb; then saw from above, and the branch will come away without splitting. Another good idea is to cut off a heavy branch a foot from the tree, and then to saw off the stump. Tree surgeons often leave these stumps for climbing, removing them as they descend from the tree when the job is finished. Pruning shears and saws may be obtained on poles from 10 to 16 feet long, to enable you to handle branches beyond your reach.

Pruning angle. Left: correct. Right: incorrect.

Stems are best cut at an angle rather than straight across, and large branches should be sawed so that the wound is close to and parallel with the trunk; the callus that develops from the cambium, will seal and protect the wound quicker with angle-cutting and flush-cutting. If the wound is larger than one inch, it is a good idea to paint it with thick linseed-oil paint; and it is just as well to make sure of its quality by using the special paint offered by the supply houses. This will keep the wound sanitary until nature closes it over.

On apples, pears, and plums you may often distinguish between buds that will produce flowers to be followed by fruit and those from which only leaves are developed. If you are pruning trees that hitherto have fruited poorly or not at all, you will carefully avoid cutting away any twigs that bear the thicker, stockier fruit buds; on many kinds these appear on short branches close to the stem, termed spurs. Often fruiting spurs may be developed by cutting young thin twigs 2 inches from the parent branch, repeating season after season.

Green, slender, young, obviously quick-growing branches are often seen growing straight upwards from the larger main branches; these are termed water sprouts or suckers. An accumulation of these reduces the production of fruit, and in the late winter dozens of them often have to be pruned close to the branch.

Young apples or pears that crowd, despite the June-drop, should be thinned out.

Many varieties will have their fruits thinned away in the so-called June-drop—Nature's method of avoiding overcrowding; and often the ground beneath a tree is covered by the little fruits, which you put on the compost heap. In addition to this, if large specimens are aimed for, it is sometimes desirable further to reduce overcrowding fruit clusters by snipping off more of the fruit to allow the remainder sufficient room.

ROOTS OCCASIONALLY NEED PRUNING ALSO

If a tree of fruiting age produces many leaves and leaf-bearing twigs but little or no fruit, it may often be brought into bearing by root-pruning. Take off a little of the soil, to expose partly some of the upper roots. It is possible that some husky ones may

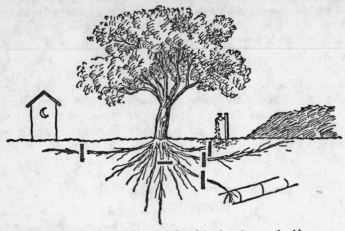

Runaway roots to a manure pile, dripping faucet, backhouse, or sewer line will cause heavy foliage but few fruits. Dig around the water curtain and prune; dig deep to intercept roots to the sewer; dig under and saw the taproot if one is found.

have pushed out to reach a source of food—perhaps to the neighborhood of a compost or a manure heap, perhaps to a lower, wetter spot, perhaps to a leaking water faucet, or to a sewer line. Pruning off some of these wandering roots at the spot where the water curtain hits the soil will sometimes bring the tree into bearing.

Another method is tunneling under the tree, finding a thick taproot going vertically down into the subsoil under the bole of the tree, and sawing through it. This is a difficult process, requiring much time and patience; a narrow transplanting spade, pointed at the tip, a narrow trowel, a kneeling pad, and a sheet on which to lie.

Root-pruning is also a part of tree-planting; if any broken or injured roots are observed, they are carefully cut away.

CHAPTER 4

Insects and Animals—Good and Bad

"The birds, God's poor who cannot wait."
HENRY WADSWORTH LONGFELLOW, Sermon
of St. Francis.

INSECT PESTS

BECAUSE FRUIT TREES, vines, brambles, and bushes occupy one position in the garden for a long while, their insect enemies take up permanent residence in the vicinity; fungus and bacteria that live in the plants take up their abode there also. Rotating crops is not possible with fruit. That is why fruit-growing consists largely of fighting these pests with sprays and dusts.

Here is a partial list of insect troublemakers:

Sucking insects. These take the juices from the plants and carry diseases from sickly to healthy plants. They are controlled by materials that kill on contact. The spray formulas later in this book are designed to take care of them.

Aphids, aphis, or plant lice. Small, they usually crowd on the soft growing parts of all plants, giving partic-
Wrinkled leaves and misshapen apples are the result of uncontrolled aphids.

ular trouble on apple, cherry, currant, and the bramble fruits. Blackleaf-40 or nicotine sulphate (a tobacco by-product), tobacco dust, or powders or sprays containing rotenone are effective.

Leaf hoppers are troublesome on apples and grapes.

Mealy bugs are serious on some tropical plants. They are minute woolly individuals.

Phylloxera or vine-root louse feeds on grape leaves and, later, on the roots where their colonies form galls. Spray programs later in this book have an inhibiting effect, but the best control is to plant vines grafted onto roots of resistant varieties. Phylloxera troubles European varieties especially in the Western states, but usually is not serious in the East or on American varieties.

Psylla. One-tenth inch long, it attacks the pear and quince.

Red spiders are microscopic bugs, $\frac{1}{60}$ inch long, serious in hot climates. They are usually kept in check with sulphur or rotenone sprays or Black-leaf-40.

Scale. There are many varieties of these small creatures. Mostly they become stationary, covering themselves with a horny shell like a tiny limpet, and are difficult to reach with most of the spray preparations, but lime-sulphur controls them, as do the miscible oil-emulsion preparations.

Scale insects. Left: San Jose on apple, with branch. Center: branch with scurfy scale. Right: oyster-shell scale.

Thrips. Pears are subject to infestations of these.

White flies are very small; they cause much concern in the fruit gardens of the South. Oil-emulsion sprays are used, and some of the states distribute cultures of a disease that reduces their numbers.

Chewing Insects. These insects feed on the leaves and fruit. They are killed by spraying a poisonous film on their food.

Apple maggot.

Codling moth. Serious on the apple, pear, cherry, plum, and quince.

Cucumber beetle. Troubles melons and watermelons.

Curculio. Mostly on apricot, cherry, plum, and quince.

Currant worm. Defoliates the gooseberry also.

Fruit flies. Especially bad on cherries.

Grape rootworm. Oriental peach moth.

Japanese beetles. Highly destructive to almost every fruit.

Pear slug and cherry slug. They are not difficult to control with nico-

34

Codling moth, chief cause of wormy apples, is the most serious of the pests that attack them. The gray-brown moth is 1/2 to 3/4 inch long.

Curculio. A small dark brown beetle with its mouth at the end of a snout; its grub seriously attacks the apple, grape, peach, pear, plum, and quince. Excrescences shown on the fruit above are its trade-mark.

tine dust, or lead arsenate mixed with hydrated lime (1 part lead arsenate to 5 of lime). The powder sticks to the slimy slugs.

Pecan case-bearer. Raspberry sawfly.

Squash bug. Feeds on melons and watermelons.

Strawberry weevil.

Tent caterpillars. Especially troublesome on apples and cherries.

Borers. These are the caterpillars of various beetles and moths. They eat their way through the bark into the wood of various fruit trees and down the stems of brambles and bush fruits, where they are immune to sprays. They may be asphyxiated by injecting a nicotine paste into the holes without injury to the tree, but small trees will be injured by injecting average fumigants into the borer holes. Where the borers are close to the ground they may be fumigated with para-dichlorobenzene, as recommended for peaches. But where the borer holes are higher on the trunk, unless nicotine paste is used, a fine wire with a

Borers at the base of a peach tree. The gum and sawdust attract your attention; clean them up, place a ring of para-dichlorobenzene in late summer, and mound with soil up to the limit of the holes in the tree. Remove the mound after three weeks.

tiny hook may be used to draw them out. Progressively wilting leaves indicate a borer in a bramble branch. Prune piece by piece until you no longer see the central channel which it makes.

Nematodes, or eelworms are one-celled creatures. They live in soil and in roots, sometimes enter into and circulate in the plant. Serious in the warmer parts of the country. Usually not overimportant where the soil freezes deeply in winter.

Nematodes or eelworms. These are one-celled microscopic animals that live in the roots and the soil around them. They suck the plants' juices and may cause the plants eventually to die; some types swim in the juices and circulate through the stems and leaves.

Nematodes cause much worry to southern gardeners; but in the central states and the north, winter's frost keeps them down mostly to unimportant numbers. Some varieties of apricot, avocado, cherry, citrus, peach, plum, and pistachio are more or less immune to their attacks.

Where nematodes are numerous, the pocket in which a tree is planted may be wider and deeper than usual, and the soil ingredient in the planting mixture may well be sterilized with steam, chloropicrin, carbon bisulphide, or DD mixture.

36

Wasps. These sometimes sting individual grapes (see page 114) and other fruits.

Wash all fruits in running water before serving, especially if poisonous insecticides and fungicides have been used.

WHAT TO DO IF POISONS ARE TAKEN ACCIDENTALLY

Insecticides and Fungicides May Be Poisonous

Keep all insecticides and fungicides under lock and key, away from children; never in the kitchen where they may be absent-mindedly used in cooking. Keep the labels clean and intact. Make your spray mixtures in the garage with the doors open, for fumes may be irritating and some are harmful. Don't smoke, for some mixtures are inflammable. Pour any of the mixture that is not used down the sewer or on the driveway gravel. Wash thoroughly before serving all fruit that has been sprayed after it has begun to develop.

If a person is overcome by fumes, CALL A DOCTOR, place the victim outdoors in the shade, and apply artificial respiration. If poison is swallowed accidentally, CALL A DOCTOR and meanwhile give the treatment detailed on the container. If you cannot find the container, fill the victim with quarts of soapsuds, salt water, soda water made with baking soda, plain warm water, dish water, or water mixed with milk. These should induce vomiting. If not, tickle the back of the throat.

After the victim has vomited well, fill him with milk or an

egg and milk beaten up together. Keep him warm. Give artificial respiration if breathing stops.

Read about artificial respiration in the American Red Cross First Aid Text-book, and practice it. It's a good thing to know anyway.

If chemicals or lime get into the eyes, immediately wash them with large quantities of water, gently holding them open the while. An ear syringe is helpful for this, or use a cup or a hose with the water rather more than dripping. Don't worry if the clothing gets wet.

Continue long enough to remove all the material—10 minutes or more; then use several fillings of the syringe with milk. Finally put 6 drops of clean olive oil, mineral oil, or castor oil into each eye; lightly put on a sterile bandage, with no pressure on the eye.

Meanwhile, you will have CALLED A DOCTOR, or will take the victim to a hospital.

Conditions that Predispose to Trouble

Overacidity and overalkalinity in the soil bring more insect pests and plant diseases; so does moisture. Overwet land predisposes to disease. Too dry a soil or spells of drought bring an increase in insects. Drainage and irrigation are things to consider.

Frost is generally helpful to those fruits that can stand it; nematodes are usually most numerous in land that does not freeze deeply, and winter kills a lot of grubs in the soil.

HELPFUL INSECTS

The mantis is a great killer of harmful insects. Leave its rough tan-white egg cluster alone when you see it in the hedge (right).

Know the insects you have to fight. Not all small creatures are harmful; some are definitely our friends. Several types of wasps are predatory on harmful insects and help in their control; ladybugs eat thousands of plant lice; the praying mantis lives on other insects. Bees are our busiest carriers of pollen. Preserve them carefully.

Ladybugs which kill aphids, and the honeybee, our busy pollen-carrier. These are beneficent insects which deserve every protection.

OTHER CREATURES WHICH AID THE GARDENER

Great gardeners, earthworms drag autumn leaves into their holes, casting onto the surface soil materials from which they have absorbed their food.

The busy friendly woodpecker helps to keep within bounds the insect population of your apple and other trees.

Robins dig in your garden for beetle grubs and other pests from spring to fall.

The industrious little phoebes work from dawn to dusk to feed their hungry family.

VARIOUS PREDATORS

Although birds take our cherries, grapes, raspberries, and strawberries, they should be welcomed for the insects they kill.

Watch a woodpecker working for you on your apple tree. Go into your garden in early spring and you find the surface perforated by the robins seeking out your beetle grubs; perhaps your lawn will be torn up by skunks or mounded by moles, also seeking beetle grubs.

If deer cause trouble, contact your county agent or State conservation department; they may have some valuable suggestions.

Get in touch also with your State experiment station and your county agent for helpful information if you get serious trouble from insects and diseases that you seem unable to control.

WHEN RABBITS RING YOUR TREES

Palisade-grafting to heal rabbit injury. Left to right: sore is trimmed. Twigs from the same tree are trimmed to shape. They are inserted under the bark—cambium of both twig and tree must be in contact. A light nail holds them; they are bowed to allow the tree to sway.

Palisade-grafting. Left: all cions are in position; cover with grafting wax. Right: twenty years later this is what the job will look like.

During a hard, snowy winter, when their usual food is covered, rabbits may turn to one of the other sources available to them—

gnawing through the bark of young trees to obtain the juicy green cambium between the bark and the wood. Some other animals, from mice to deer, may join the feast. If the damage that they do circles half the circumference, the tree's growth will be given a setback; if the damage goes completely around, the tree will be killed. But there is something you can do about it.

If rabbit injury is observed as the snow disappears, you may save your tree by "palisade-grafting." Purchase some grafting wax and with a sharp knife trim away the gnawed portions of the bark. Cut from the injured tree, or from another fruit tree of the same kind, a number of branches that are young enough to bend easily. These are to form a bridge of branches from the bottom to the top of the trimmed sore. Measure the sore and cut each twig from 1 inch to 2 or 3 inches longer than the open space; cut a long sliver from each end, so each will have the shape of a carpenter's chisel. Push the thin upper end of a cut twig between the bark and the wood at the top of the sore until the green cambium in it is in contact with the cambium of the tree. Fix it with a light nail driven through the bark and twig into the wood. Spring the branch and push the lower end between the bark and wood, contacting the cambium at the bottom of the sore, and tack this end into position. Have some warmed grafting wax ready in a can and with a putty knife smother the junction of the twig and bark to keep out moisture and air. Shape and insert another twig about 2 inches away and continue until the sore is bridged all around.

You may have to pry up the bark a trifle with a chisel to get the twigs into position. When placing the twigs, have a piece of wood ½ inch thick under the center of the twig against the wood; remove it when you have tacked the top and bottom. The object is to make each twig slightly bowed to withstand swaying of the young tree in a heavy wind. Plaster the whole operation with grafting wax and wrap it with canvas.

As the tree ages the twig bridges become covered with callus and partly hidden with bark. But keep your eyes open when you go through an old established orchard, and you may find a tree bearing well-marked vertical corrugations near the ground, showing where palisade-grafting was practiced perhaps many years ago.

Another year, wrap creosoted building paper around the base of the trunk from the ground to above the highest expected accumulation of snow. Or wrap tough paper or strips of canvas around it in a spiral, or enclose it within a sleeve of small-mesh chicken wire. Scatter poisoned grain in mouse runs under the surface, where mice will get it but birds cannot. If rabbits are a serious menace, see if your county agent can suggest additional remedies.

Ringing is sometimes done intentionally in early summer on tree branches to restrain the return flow of sap, thus concentrating it in the branch and often obtaining larger and earlier fruit. A 1/8-inch band of bark is taken out with a gouge; this narrow wound heals itself in a month or so. Constriction with a wire band is sometimes tried, and you may sometimes observe the effect of a wired plant label, identifying the variety when you bought the tree, inadvertently left on the branch. It is claimed that this type of ringing, if not repeated, does no serious harm to a tree, but it does set it back and is not recommended as a general practice.

CHAPTER 5

Plant Diseases

"Remember Johnny Appleseed,
All ye who love the apple;
He served his kind by Word and Deed,
In God's grand greenwood chapel."
WILLIAM HENRY VENABLE.

Like ourselves, plants become sick and sometimes recover, sometimes die; like humans, also, these illnesses may be due to a virus, to bacteria, or to fungus parasites. Some common diseases are listed here, and the cultural practices and spray programs discussed under the various fruits are designed to check them.

VIRUS INFECTIONS

Because there is little one can do to control these fatal diseases, it is fortunate that their numbers are smaller than those in the other groups. They are conveyed from one plant to another by insects, especially aphids, leaf hoppers, and thrips, which is another good reason for spraying. They are also controlled by budding, grafting, and pruning only with carefully sterilized tools, by the selection of healthy plants, and by the painting of all large stumps or scars caused by pruning. The destruction of infected plants and exchanging infected soil are also recommended.

The water in the slurry into which the roots of apples, pears and quince are stirred before planting may well have ⅔ ounce of copper-sulphate dissolved in each gallon. For less hardy apricot, peach, and plum use ⅓ ounce in each gallon.

43

Three fatal virus diseases. Left: peach yellows, with smaller, more numerous, willowlike, and yellowing leaves. Center: little peach, with smaller rectangular fruit; a normal peach is in rear. Right: peach rosette, with bunching leaves.

Most important of the virus diseases are:

Mosaic. Shows itself in paler leaves, stunted plants, excessive branching, and death of the plant, section by section. Leaves have a mottled appearance, with curling and wrinkling; stems show discoloration and cankers appear. Mosaic diseases are frequently seen in raspberries and other brambles; also in apple, cherry, cranberry, currant, grape, and strawberry. They trouble least in weed-free gardens.

Mosaic, a virus disease, occurs in the apple; the type infecting raspberries is particularly serious. First signs are the leaves becoming mottled, like a tabby cat, in various shades of green.

Little Peach. A virus condition affecting the peach. The fruit is smaller and ripens later, often assuming a rectangular shape.

Peach Rosette. The buds develop into tufts of hundreds of small leaves. Even with prompt removal of the affected branches, the tree eventually dies.

Yellows. Another virus peach disease. The leaves become yellow, the shoots are wirelike and sickly, and the fruit matures prematurely.

BACTERIAL ILLNESS

Plants should be guaranteed disease-free when you buy them. Pruning, budding, and grafting should be as antiseptic as a veterinary operation. Accidental wounds on plants should be carefully avoided, especially stinging their stems with a hoe. Galls and tubers should be cut off and the scars painted. Follow

44

the spray programs under the various fruits later in this book, for insects are flagrant carriers of bacterial disease.

Three bacterial diseases of the apple. Left: crown gall. Center: hairy root. Right: fire blight.

Some bacterial diseases are:

Black spot of plum and peach; black knot of the grape; blister spot of apple; brown rot of the plum.

Crown gall, black knot, and hairy root of raspberries, apples, and pears; also plums.

Fire blight. Best-known bacterial disease. When a branch of a pear, apple or quince is affected, the leaves are blasted as though a brush fire had passed through. Overlight soil, high nitrogen fertilizers, and too severe pruning are claimed to predispose toward this condition.

Gummosis of stone fruits.

FUNGUS TROUBLES

Fungus troubles are legion, and the following list of the more important ones represents a mere fraction of the total. Spraying should prevent them; if you spray faithfully and on time you are likely to see none of them. But when a fungus disease does appear, remember that what you see are the effects of the parasite within the plants. Spray of course, but all you can expect to achieve is to prevent the spread of the disease to other plants.

Anthracnose. Disease to which currants, grapes, raspberries and other brambles are subject. Leaves and canes are spotted.

Apple blotch. A serious disease, especially in the Midwest.

Apple rust or red-cedar rust. The fungus uses both plants as hosts and affects each of them.

Apple scab. Causes dark green spots on the leaves, discoloration and distortion of the fruit, and premature dropping of the leaves.

Bitter rot or ripe rot of the apple, grape, pear, and quince.

Black knot or plum wart of stone fruits; cankerous growths appear along the branches.

Black rot of the grape.

Blight or **California** blight of stone fruits.

Blue mold of apples in storage.

Brown rot of apricot, peach, and cherry. The fruits decay into mummies.

Cankers of apple, quince, and pear.

Cherry leaf spot. Foliage is covered with dead spots; leaves often fall away, defoliating the tree.

Apple rust, a deforming and crop-reducing fungus disease. Spores carried from the apple by insects or wind, infect near-by cedar trees, frequently killing them.

Chestnut blight. No cure is known; it has destroyed practically all our wild chestnut trees.

Dead-arm disease of the grape.

Dieback of stone fruits.

Downy mildew of grapes. A spotting and blighting of the leaves and young stems, and rotting of the berries.

Leaf blight of pear and quince.

Leaf curl of cherry and peach.

Leaf spot of cherry and plum.

Leaf spot of the pear.

Leak of strawberries; the berries frequently rot in transit.

Orange rust of blackberries and raspberries.

Peach leaf curl. The foliage thickens, takes on a reddish or yellowish tint, becomes blistered, drops off and the fruit becomes distorted.

Plum pocket. The fruits become inflated.

Powdery mildew of the apple. Leaves develop a light grey felt-like covering. Similar mildews occur on cherry, gooseberry, grape, peach, and strawberry. Familiar to all rose-growers, the black spot is a fungus in this group.

Red stele root rot of the strawberry.

Root rots of various fruit trees. **Rots** of various fruits in storage.

Strawberry leaf spot.

White-pine blister rust of gooseberries and black, white, and red currants; these are the intermediate hosts. The pines eventually die.

Witches' broom of cherry. A crowding of twigs at the ends of the branches is the symptom.

46

CHAPTER 6

Fighting Pests and Diseases

"Let it please thee to keep in order a moderate-sized farm, that so thy garners may be full of fruits in their season." HESIOD, *c.*720 B.C. Translation by J. Banks, M.A.

SPRAYING AND DUSTING ARE A MUST

An average pest- and sickness-fighting schedule for most fruits includes one dormant spray in winter, when the tree or bush is sleeping. Then a second delayed-dormant spray is given when the buds show signs of bursting, but before they actually open; this is to kill the first insect broods, which often hatch out just before their food becomes available to them.

The most sensitive portions of the plant are the leaves, and prior to their appearance in spring, the branches and bud coverings may safely be sprayed with solutions that are stronger and more effective than those used on the leaves a week or so later. Destroying insects, some bacteria, and most fungi would be simple were it not easy to harm the plant also, which is a living thing too; the trick in developing insecticides, bactericides, and fungicides is to compound them weak enough not to injure the plant, but strong enough to kill the troublemakers. Do not use household insecticides on your plants; you will probably harm them.

Dormant, followed by delayed-dormant spraying. The latter is carried out as soon as the earliest bud in the sunniest part of the garden shows signs of opening, as in figure 1. Figure 2 is a little too far advanced for the strong solutions used at this time.

Succeeding the dormant and delayed-dormant treatments, trees and bushes should mostly be sprayed before the flowers appear, and again after the petals fall. They are left alone while the flowers are open, or you may interfere with pollination and with the agents that carry the pollen—bees and other insects—which the spray is likely to kill too. The leaves of the stone fruits are very sensitive to some chemicals, particularly to arsenate of lead. Follow closely the spraying suggestions in later pages where the particular fruits are considered.

A spraying device is an essential part of the fruit-grower's equipment. For a very few small plants, flicking the material on with a clothes whisk is convenient. But a continuous hand-sprayer, holding as little as a quart of solution, is better and is all-sufficient for a few brambles or one or two young dwarf fruit trees. However, secure a hand-sprayer that gives a continuous mist rather than a spurt with each push of the plunger; one made of brass is preferred.

For a larger planting have a sprayer of the type that is filled, pumped while on the ground to build up pressure, and then carried with the aid of a shoulder strap through your rows or up a ladder into your apple, peach, pear, or plum tree. Normally these hold 2 or 4 gallons; the latter will weigh over 32 pounds and are heavy enough for most people. A brass extension pipe

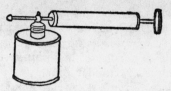

A good continuous sprayer. Made in brass, it holds one quart.

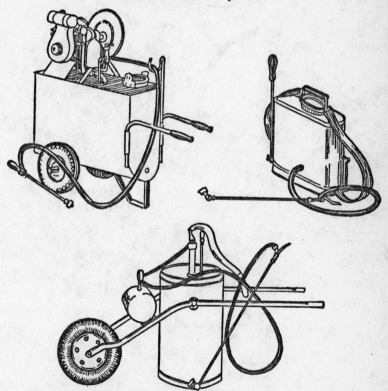

Sprayers. Left: a power-driven type holding about 50 gallons. Right: knapsack sprayer, capacity 4 gallons. Below: a two-man hand-operated barrow kind, carrying 15 gallons.

may be attached to take the spray nozzle as much as 4 feet beyond your extended arm. Or you may prefer a knapsack sprayer which fits your back, your arms going through canvas loops to make carrying much easier. You can maintain a steady 80-pound pressure by working a lever under your arm.

Next in order of size is a type of hand-pushed wheelbarrow which holds a tank carrying 15 gallons and in which a pressure of 200 or 250 pounds can be kept up by a person working a kind

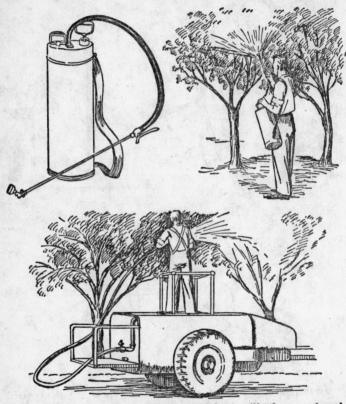

Sprayers. Left: a 4-gallon tank sprayer. Right: it will take care of moderate-size trees. Below: a commercial spray rig.

of pump handle while another worker directs the spray. Similar in principle are the wheelbarrow types where the man working the pump handle is replaced by a gasoline engine. These develop around 250 pounds pressure and may have a capacity of up to 50 gallons.

Commercial fruit-growers have larger outfits mounted on a truck or trailer with capacities of up to several hundred gallons and engines developing such high pressures that tall trees may readily be sprayed from a distance.

The main point in spraying is to deliver the material in a fine cloud; to get it on both the upper and under side of the leaves; to apply the mist everywhere for a long enough period that it drips onto the ground.

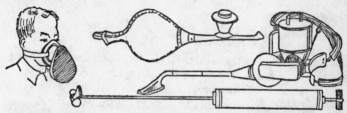

Dusting devices. Left: a respirator is desirable. Right: upper, a bellows-type duster; center, a mechanical duster—weight is carried on shoulder straps, and handle is rotated; bottom, hand duster suitable for the home garden.

When planting fruit trees near your property line, think ahead to the time when they are large and will need to be sprayed with a powerful machine. If your neighbor's dog dies of old age, your spray solution will be charged with poisoning him; if paint on the next-door garage is of poor quality and peels, your spray will be accused of ruining it; so do not plant trees closer than 20 feet from the line or near any buildings not on your property.

Wear goggles while spraying and pruning; solutions may be harmful, and a swinging twig may do grievous injury to an eye. Wear a respirator when dusting with poisonous materials. As soon as trouble is seen, dusting and spraying must have first preference over other work, but arrange to stop spraying early enough to allow you to clean thoroughly your sprayer, its tubing and nozzles. When washed out, place some clean water in it and pump a pint or so through it, leaving the remainder in until the device is next operated, except during freezing weather. Empty the water from the tank when you next use it. Keep the cover on loosely when the sprayer is not in use; but don't leave it off, or some leaves or rubbish may get in to give you clogging trouble at an important moment.

Your sprayer will also be used on vegetables and flowers, when the same types of materials will be in it. But when you use it for killing weeds in lawns or in the driveway, any material remaining in it may kill your plants also. So cleaning must be very thorough, with sal-soda or a similar detergent. Mercuric fungicides also call for thorough after-cleansing because of their corroding effect.

GREASEBANDING TREES

Some insects pass the winter in the land and ascend the trunks in spring. All summer there is traffic in both directions by canker-

A greasebanded tree, using tanglefoot.

worms, gipsy-moth larvae, borers, inchworms, and other creatures. Some do serious damage, and many are guilty of spreading disease. Greasebanding of trees is often desirable: a strip of heavy wrapping paper is placed around the trunk at any convenient height, tied with twine, and then coated with tree-tanglefoot—a sticky substance that captures the insects and should be renewed every two months through spring, summer, and fall; more frequently, if needed.

WHITEWASHING TREES

The painting of the trunks of fruit trees is a long-established practice with a few precise garden owners. Although disparaged as unnecessary by most, it has some merit. It looks neat, may protect to some extent against the scalding effect of the sun in early spring, may kill some insects, and may discourage animal damage.

Here is a good formula if you have the time to undertake this work:

Obtain some quicklime; carefully slake it with a little water, gradually added until it ceases to heat; and then thin to a paste with skim milk. Add 2 ounces of salt to each pail. The inclusion of one-tenth the volume of lime-sulphur will deter some borers from entering the tree. Be sure to protect the eyes when preparing and applying the whitewash.

Neatly   whitewashed fruit trees are evidence of the precise mind, and the work may be worth the effort.

CHAPTER 7

Care of Fruits

"My faith is all a doubtful thing,
Wove in a doubtful loom,—
Until there comes, each showery spring,
A cherry-tree in bloom."

DAVID MORTON.

THE BEST SOIL FOR FRUITS

THE SOIL is discussed in detail when we consider the different varieties of fruit on later pages. Most fruits, but not all, like rich but well-drained porous soil. Most, but not all, do best in one that is slightly on the acid side, around pH6.5, nearly but not quite neutral.

The quality of the earth is relatively unimportant in the average home garden, because your trees and bushes will be planted in pockets or holes, filled with the kind of material that suits them best. The more unsuitable your garden soil, the larger and deeper should be the pocket.

Wherever the land is of average quality, under good cultivation, and dries normally after rain, you may plant apples, cherries, grapes, peaches, pears, plums, quince, and strawberries. In spots that are moist, but not wet, set blackberries, dewberries, boysenberries, and raspberries. If you have an acid soil but good drainage, you may expect annual crops of blueberries. On the whole, most fruits do better on land that is slightly higher than the surrounding terrain: good soil drainage and air circulation are usually better there.

To prepare land for an extensive fruit-planting a good idea is to grow for a season crops of vegetables that need hoeing—beans, corn, parsnips, and the like—digging their remains under after they have yielded. The hoeing kills the weeds and digging in the old plants adds to the organic matter in the earth. Areas that are not producing vegetables may be cover-cropped, which means that plants are grown in them for the sole purpose of plowing or digging them in to increase the organic matter: rye sown in autumn, crimson clover or field peas in spring, soybeans in early summer, or buckwheat in late summer. Gathering and digging under autumn leaves is recommended rather than burning them. You will find that vegetables are satisfactory crops for growing between your fruits for the first few years but, as your orchard, berry- or bramble-patch develops, the area available for the truck crops will grow smaller.

YOU ARE GROWING FRUIT, NOT WEEDS— KEEP THE SOIL RAKED

In the home garden, weeds should be kept under control and a thin powdery layer of soil maintained on the surface at all times by very light raking around your trees and bushes. It is a good rule that cultivation should be as shallow as possible, because most fruits have their important feeding roots close to the top. Pull all the weeds you can by hand; those you cannot reach, cut with a scuffle-hoe at the ground level. Rake up their remains and all trash with a flat-tined, springy lawn rake.

Weeding strawberries is always a chore. A good scheme is to use the scuffle-hoe up to within 6 inches of the plants and to go on your knees and pull out all weeds nearer your plants than 6 inches. You can construct a good kneeling pad for this work out of an old flour or seed bag; cut a piece of 12-inch wide linoleum as long as the width of the bag; put it into the bag with a large quantity of straw, hay, or discarded rags on top of it; close the bag with a row of large safety pins against the linoleum and padding; wrap the rest of the bag around it and fix the end with more safety pins; put a mark on the soft side to indicate where you should kneel.

FRUITS NEED FOOD

Though blueberries must have an acid soil, most other fruits prefer a near-neutral one. So for most fruits an application of powdered limestone on the surface every winter is desirable—often 10 pounds per 100 square feet. Lime is helpful, too, in a soil that is either too heavy or too sandy, for lime has a tendency to lighten the one and bind the other. For improving the soil's texture hydrated lime is often preferred to limestone and is applied several times in a season—at 5 pounds to 100 square feet on each occasion.

Feeding your fruits. In most areas, broadcasting limestone in winter is advisable. Not for blueberries, however.

Feeding your fruits. In spring, balanced fertilizer like 5–10–5 or 8–6–2 may be scattered. Also spread superphosphate if a soil examination shows a dearth of phosphorus; apply scrap tobacco if potassium is in short supply.

In spring 5 pounds per 100 square feet of a good balanced fertilizer—say, a high grade 5–10–5—may be very lightly raked under, and the dressing may well be repeated in midsummer. Your soil may be checked with a soil-testing kit, and if phosphorus is found to be in short supply, 5 pounds of superphosphate may be given in addition every spring and summer; if potash is found to be low, some scrap tobacco or commercial hardwood ashes may also be spread at the same rate. But do not work under any great abundance of commercial fertilizer or manure, for your plants may produce more leaves and branches than fruit if they are too well fed.

It is good insurance, too, to give several applications in a season of one of the combinations of the trace elements that are offered, in the event that some one or other of these vital substances may be absent. Needed in trace amounts and usually abundantly present, especially if rotted manure, compost, and other organic substances are used, the commercial mixture will correct any deficiency.

The fertilizer should be raked in.

Trees and bushes in sandy land are helped by a "mulch" or blanket of organic matter in the hot months, two inches thick and added to as it disappears. This will keep weeds down, prevent loss of moisture by evaporation, slow the run-off of water during heavy rain, and liberate plant foods as the mulch decays. You may use peatmoss, humus, compost, garden trash, leaf mold, straw, salt hay, and certain factory waste products. Try small amounts of the latter around some vegetable plants to find if they have any harmful effect before spreading something that neighbors do not use; among safe materials are spent malt and hops from a brewery, spent tea leaves from a caffeine factory, or sweepings from a cigar factory. Maintain the mulch on certain semi-hardy subjects during winter, but rake it 18 inches away from the base of a tree to keep mice from injuring it.

A good insurance is to water your plants with a solution containing the trace elements.

Feeding your fruits. In summer again dress with fertilizer, adding superphosphate and scrap tobacco if needed. Keep fertilizer off leaves.

If an old tree appears to be suffering from malnutrition, the crowbar method of feeding may be tried. Around the water-curtain circle shed by the leaves during rain, make a series of crowbar

Again follow the fertilizer with a light raking.

The water curtain, caused by rain dropping from one leaf to the next until a ring of water surrounds the tree. Most feeding takes place at the water curtain.

Crowbar feeding is sometimes desirable. Holes are made at the water curtain three feet apart.

Each hole receives about a quart of 5–10–5 or 8–6–2 fertilizer. Obtain a good-quality one, with a high organic content.

holes about 3 feet apart; drive the bar down 2 feet, rotating the top to make the hole a narrow funnel. Place in each hole about a quart of an 8–6–2 or similar high-nitrogen fertilizer.

Unlike vegetables, which must be grown quickly, most fruits are best when they develop slowly, and excessive amounts of fertilizer are likely to give you handsome trees and bushes with large leaves but a small yield. If some of your plants are not doing well, it probably is not because they are getting insufficient or improper fertilizer; more likely the cause is to be found in the plant's location, drafts perhaps, too much shade, late frosts, insect attacks, virus, bacterial, or fungus troubles, lack of a compatible neighboring plant for the transfer of pollen, too close pruning, or varieties unsuited to your conditions.

TRANSFER OF POLLEN NECESSARY FOR FRUITS

Fruits cannot develop unless the pollen or male element from one flower reaches the stigma or female element of another, carried by bees, other insects, or the wind. Varieties differ in their behavior in this process. Some have the ability to pollinate themselves, the pollen from one flower being able to fertilize other flowers on the same tree; these are termed self-pollinators. Many apples, most European plums, some peaches, cherries, and European, and Japanese plums will not pollinate themselves. This "incompatibility" extends to the hybrids in which these varieties have a share in the parentage.

If you are planting one tree, for instance, be sure to purchase a self-pollinating kind (see pages 84 to 140 for suitable ones). When you are planting several trees of a kind, either buy self-pollinating ones or include a good pollinator in the group. Chinese chestnuts pollinate their neighbors, but not themselves, so at least two are set close to each other. If your space is limited, see if you can arrange with a friend near by to plant varieties that will be helpful to both of you. A sweet cherry cannot pollinate itself, but two sweet cherries will pollinate each other; if you have room for only one, graft a young branch of another variety of sweet cherry onto an upper branch of your tree.

Fruit trees are not sprayed when they are in flower and the bees are gathering nectar and, as a by-product of their labors, are transferring pollen from one flower to another.

CHAPTER 8

Propagation

"Grafting and budding are two different operations.
Where buds push out from the bark
And burst their delicate sheaths, you should make
*   a narow slit*
In the actual knot: it's here that you enclose a bud
From another tree and train it to grow in the sappy
*   rind.*
Grafting's different—it's done by cutting a smooth
*   trunk,*
Splitting the wood deeply with wedges, and then
*   inserting*
The fertile scion . . ."

VIRGIL, Georgics (70–19 B.C.).*

HOW TO HAVE MORE FRUIT TREES AND BUSHES

YOU HAD BEST start by purchasing plants from a reliable nursery, which is near by so that you may be guided as to the varieties that yield best in your neighborhood and are most likely to thrive. Once your first plants are growing you may engage in the fascinating process of increasing your stock.

Cuttings. Grapes will develop roots at the base of cuttings, slips, or cions. These are 10-inch long pieces of the young branches which you cut and save during your winter pruning. They will have grown the previous summer and will be a year old or less. Select vigorous ones, with buds close together. Tie them in bundles and bury 2 inches deep until the soil warms;

* Translated by C. Day Lewis, Oxford University Press, 1947. By permission.

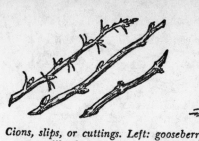

Cions, slips, or cuttings. Left: gooseberry, currant, and grape. Right: more will take root if they are kept damp under a ventilated jar.

then insert them to three-quarters of their length, top end up, and 6 inches apart, in gritty soil in a slightly shaded place: they need light, but strong sun is not very helpful. If your soil is heavy clay, spread an inch-thick band of gravel screenings or coarse sand where you have space; hoe the screenings or sand under, spread another inch-thick band, and rake smooth. This will be your cutting bed.

The slips should be cut with a knife or sharp shears immediately below one of the buds; with the point of your knife, nick out all buds on the portion to go underground. Push the slips into the gritty soil. Most of them will have roots by fall, while others will shrivel and die. You are likely to get a higher proportion of rooted ones if you plant them in groups of three and place a large inverted Mason jar over them, the neck standing on four pebbles to permit ventilation; remove the jar when growth appears. Water the cions if you run into a spell of dry weather; the young living ones may be set out a foot apart in the autumn, and a year later they may be placed in their permanent positions. Quince is also frequently propagated from cuttings.

Layering. If, after full consideration and inquiry, you decide to grow currants in your home garden, your stock of them may be increased in the same way. More often, however, layering is the process employed. A young branch that is close to the ground is gently bent to the soil surface; where it touches, you make a glancing cut half-way through it and slip a toothpick to keep the tongue you have made away from the stem. Fix the cut portion in contact with the earth, using a couple of clothespins or stones,

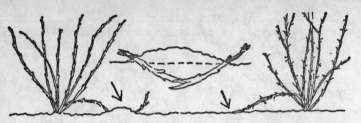

Layering. Left: currant bush. Center: close-up of currant branch; roots form at the notch. Right: gooseberry often layers itself, forming tip roots.

and put a spadeful of dirt over the cut portion. It will develop roots, and by autumn you may separate it from the parent plant and plant it elsewhere. Instead of cutting a tongue you may cut away an inch-wide band of bark completely around the stem; the ringed portion goes underground with the spadeful of soil over it. Gooseberries, also rarely planted, may be reproduced in the same manner, but usually it is not necessary. They are prone to root at the branch tips, and when you are cleaning up the garden in the autumn you can usually get all the self-rooted plants you need. Blueberries are sometimes increased by layering.

Tip-rooting, division, root cuttings. Dewberries, boysenberries, raspberries, and some blackberries also need little of your help; their stem tips root themselves where they bend over to the ground. The chief work in caring for the bramble patch is to take out these newly formed plants. If you have the room you can plant them elsewhere; but if you have no space, they are readily saleable at planting time if you know the variety and it is a good one. If you wish to multiply a particular individual, dig up a large plant in late winter, wash the soil from the roots, divide the clump into several pieces, cutting from top to bottom, and plant the pieces. If you need a larger number of plants, cut off all the roots that are $\frac{1}{4}$ to $\frac{3}{4}$ inch thick and keep them in damp peatmoss until spring in an unheated place. Then trim them into 4-inch lengths and plant them 2 inches deep at a slight angle, thin end down; if there is no difference in thickness, place them horizontally.

Strawberry runners. Strawberry care is largely a matter of weeding and taking care of the runners that develop around midsummer. If you are growing them in the bed system, however, they make weeding more difficult by overcrowding. In the hill system, the runners that appear after fruiting are snipped off with shears. When you want additional plants, you let some runners develop, however, and each runner will make one, two, three, or more baby plants. When the baby farthest from the parent is rooted in the soil, clip the runners and next spring dig up the juveniles and plant them elsewhere. But in summer, if you care to bury a small soil-filled flowerpot under each little plant when you first see it, steadying each side of the runner with a small stone, you will have pot-grown plants, the pots filled with roots. Sever the runners connecting these baby plants with the parent and each other as soon as they are growing merrily. Pot-grown strawberries are better for autumn planting; feed them well, for the more leaves each plant develops the larger the crop of berries you are likely to have the following spring. The usual system of growing strawberries is to set a new row every season and to dig up the older rows as soon as they begin to have smaller berries or fewer of them, usually after three years.

Melons from seeds. Muskmelons and watermelons are grown in "hills" from seeds sown every year. Rhubarb may also be raised from seeds if you need a lot of roots and have some patience. Rhubarb seeds are sown in rows, and the resulting plants are set out in the autumn. More often a few large roots are dug in late winter, cut from top to bottom with a sharp spade into four or five sections, and each section planted four feet from its neighbor in well-enriched soil.

GRAFTING

Apples, apricots, cherries, nectarines, pears, and plums are invariably grafted onto other husky plants of a near variety, sometimes onto seedlings of the same kinds or onto special ones that are known by experience to be good hosts, or "stocks" as the orchardist calls them. Mostly the stocks are heavy feeders with extensive root development and proven resistance to tem-

Grafting cions onto an apple. Cion and stock cut this shape will be very stable with maximum cambium contact. Bind, and seal with grafting wax.

The art of budding. Left to right: the stock or host plant. Crosscuts down to the wood are made in it near the roots. A leaf of the tame variety, with a good bud in its angle, is selected. Its stem serves as a handle; it is cut from the tame variety with the bark in the form of a shield.

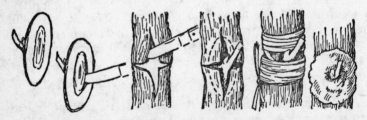

The art of budding. Left to right: the shield-shaped sliver containing the bud. The small wooden shaving is nicked away. The crosscuts in the stock are opened. Tame bud is inserted; cambium of bud and stock must be in contact. Cuts are tied back into place. Operation is sealed with grafting wax.

perature extremes or to disease. Some are known to be dwarfing stocks: they cause the varieties joined to them to grow short and are used for producing dwarf fruit trees. The type of grafting known as "budding" is invariably used.

BUDDING

In the budding process a new plant is obtained by inserting one bud of the wanted sort under the bark of a one- or two-year-old stock plant, mostly near the ground. Both the bud and the host grow, but within the year the stock or host tree is cut off just above the bud you inserted. Growth from the stock may appear below your bud; unwittingly you may preserve this and get a tree of two qualities—perhaps a worthless crab-apple from the stock along with the good apple from the bud. Sometimes the wanted variety will die and the stock

Result of budding. If your work was carefully done and the variety a compatible one, bud will start to grow. Stock is pruned above it. New shoot bends upward and becomes the vertical main stem.

flourish, giving rise to the fiction that varieties may deteriorate in cultivation, which rarely happens.

The green cambium of both the new bud and the stock must be in close contact. Occasionally an entire cion will be inserted onto the stock plant, its several buds giving several branches, each starting from a bud on the cion. This would be true grafting, but the budding process has the advantage because each bud produces a new tree, which obviously is more economical and the care and training of the new plant is simpler. Budding is standard practice for nearly all fruit plants in the nursery. The varieties used as stocks are mentioned under the various fruits on pages 84 to 140. Budding may be carried out in early summer, while true grafting is usually performed in early spring when the growth of both cion and stock is commencing.

It is recommended that you grow neither peach or plum trees from pits nor apple or pear trees from pips, because the resulting fruit is almost certain to be inferior to that of the trees from which they came—though sometimes these seedlings make good stocks. If you have a large garden and lots of time you may grow them along in the hope of accidentally getting a superior tree. The commercial grower does this, but he usually isolates his plants from vagrant pollen and carefully allows pollen from plants he likes to reach them; he knows their ancestry also and painfully through the years he develops new and superior types.

Budding may not be as simple as it sounds. One handicap is that sometimes the tame variety does not want to attach itself to the stock customarily used. Dwarf pears, for example, are budded onto quince seedlings as a rule. A few, however, will not grow on quince. These are "double-worked": a sort that will grow on quince is first budded, and a year later the stubborn variety is budded onto the new tree. To "work" plants is a gardener's term for multiplying plants from cuttings, grafts, or buds. If you have a storm-damaged tree, and an important

Cleft-grafting to repair a storm-damaged branch. The stump is trimmed and split, and cions are inserted in the cut. Trimmed to shape, they are placed cambium to cambium. Cover with grafting wax. Next winter, prune away the weaker and retain the stronger.

branch is fractured, you may replace the branch by trimming the stump and grafting a cion onto it. Better insert several and cut away all but the strongest.

MULTI-VARIETY TREES

If you want to make a multi-variety tree you can insert buds or cions of other close varieties onto your own tree, which should be young; or you may attach them to young branches on an older tree. You may read up on the subject, which is complicated by the fact that some kinds are readily budded onto others or readily accepted by them, while some are not. Conceivably you may own a tree onto which a dozen or a score of other varieties have been worked. Five-variety apples and three-variety pears or cherries are in general commerce, as well as apricot, peach, and plum on one tree; all are advised for the small garden.

In making your own you must keep within the same type of plant—pears onto other pears, cherries onto other cherries. Don't attempt to bud an apple onto a pear. During flowering and fruiting time put a dab of different color paint on the branches to guide you in your next pruning to insure that you do not cut away an entire variety. You bud in summer, but graft in spring.

Save good cions at pruning time by tying them in bunches, attaching a wooden tag to them, wrapping the bases in damp peatmoss and waterproof paper, and keeping them in an unheated garage. Place the bundles in water when growth is seen outdoors, and their buds will begin to swell at the same time as the trees onto which you propose to graft them. For budding, leave them longer for the leaves to start, or take buds directly from trees in summer; cut the leaf but leave its stem to form a convenient handle for placing the bud.

CHAPTER 9

Flat-trained Trees and Fruit Trees in Tubs

"By their fruits ye shall know them." MATTHEW. VI.

FLAT-TRAINED TREES

FOR CENTURIES, skilled European gardeners, wise in the ways of fruit-growing, have produced trees that are pruned and trained to certain shapes. Many are called "espaliers"—flat plants designed to grow attached to a wall. Invariably they are suitable varieties budded onto dwarfing stocks. They are especially valuable for localities where some fruits may be grown only with difficulty because of low temperatures or early spring hot sun. Under the more favorable climate of the U. S. they are not so important from this angle, but they do solve the problem of growing fruit in a limited space. They also are decorative and interesting. Their usual support is a series of stout horizontal or vertical wires attached to 6-inch brackets or big lag screws fastened to the wall. A red brick wall is ideal; the reflected light from a white wall may cause the plants to be overheated in summer.

A frequently used design is a flat upright one with horizontal branches, called "cordons," leaving the main stem at right angles. But U-shaped trees are to be seen, as well as fan-trained styles, where five or more branches leave the plant at one point, radiating to the left, upwards, and to the right. A lot of patience enters into their production, part of the training being to splint curved but pliable branches to stakes so that they mature and stiffen into the shape and direction wanted. Trees with only two cordons, one on each side, are used to edge a walk; the two horizontal branches need but one supporting wire which is carried on short stakes and is hard to find when the curious little trees are in leaf.

Flat-trained trees. Left: single-cordon. Right: double-cordon.

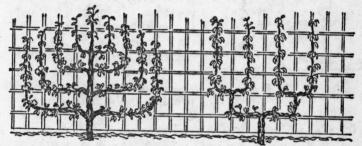

Flat-trained trees. Left: palmette-verrier. Right: double-U.

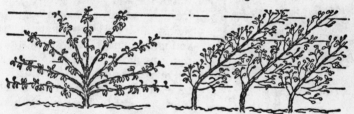

Flat-trained trees. Left: fan-shaped. Right: oblique cordons.

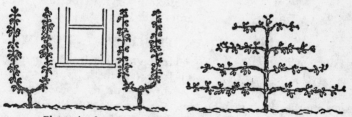

Flat-trained trees. Left: U-form. Right: four-tier T-shape.

Other uses for flat-trained trees would be in the garden to separate one section from another: the vegetables from the flowers, perhaps; the cut flowers from the roses. But they are chiefly used growing against a wall to save space in the small garden or to take the place of a creeper. Their possibilities are intriguing. Imagine a wall covered with several of them, over, under, and between casement windows; the blossoms just outside one's room in spring, the roosting birds in summer, the apples, pears, or plums within easy reach in autumn.

Flat-trained trees are preferable to a creeper on the residence.

Their care is a matter of constant pruning and training throughout the year to maintain the shape and direction wanted: removing unnecessary branches ruthlessly, including all those that want to grow directly away from or towards the wall; cutting to develop fruiting spurs evenly along the stems; and patiently shaping the young branches. Meanwhile, spraying must go on as usual.

For permanent fruit production, an east or a west wall is usually more favorable than a southerly aspect, which may induce too early blossoming with possible injury from late frosts.

FRUIT TREES IN TUBS

Here is another interesting phase of fruit culture.

Apple fruiting in a tub.

Apples, pears, peaches, and many another fruit may be grown in large pots or tubs, pruning being necessary to keep the plants dwarf. They are helpful where space is limited and they make interesting subjects on a terrace or patio, especially when you have a meal outdoors, and your guests have the opportunity to gather their own fruits. Better avoid poisonous sprays, using rotenone or pyrethrum instead of arsenate of lead, as the fruits swell.

Because the roots are confined in a limited space rake fertilizer into the soil surface each spring and late summer. Also see that they have adequate moisture.

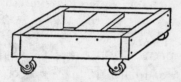

A dolly, strongly made and on caster wheels, enables you to move heavy fruit trees in tubs.

Since the containers and soil are necessarily heavy, a wooden frame with four caster wheels is helpful in moving the plants from one spot to another. Furniture movers use such a device and call it a "dolly." To wheel a laden dolly over a lawn or uneven terrace, four planks are helpful; adze one end of each of two of them to a slope up which the dolly may be rolled.

CHAPTER 10

Protecting Your Trees

"Nuts!" ANTHONY CLEMENT MCAULIFFE.*

Section through a tree branch; annual rings indicate it is six years old. Sap circulates in the cambium, and adds to the wood; to the bark also, but weathering keeps latter from becoming thicker.

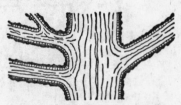

Exaggerated diagram of a tree. Wood is sheathed by cambium, which adds a layer to the wood annually. Cambium is protected by bark, which stretches, splits, and heals as the diameter increases.

HOW A TREE GROWS

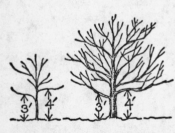

Trees grow taller, branches larger, but they do not move upwards. Left: two-year-old tree. Right: same five years later.

AT PLANTING TIME it is well to remember that a tree grows by increasing its height, by lengthening its branches, by adding to its branches, and by increasing in girth, but not by hoisting itself upwards. Take a young tree with three whippy branches, respectively 3, 4, and 5 feet from the ground. Unless they die or are pruned off, they will increase in size but they always will be 3, 4,

* Reply (December 23, 1944) to German major and captain who brought an ultimatum from their commander, demanding the surrender of 101st Airborne Division men trapped for seven days at Bastogne, Belgium.

and 5 feet from the ground; many more will develop above them, but they do not *move* upwards. If you have to stoop to get under a branch when you set a tree, you will still be stooping twenty years later.

KEEP BRANCHES OFF THE GROUND

Many tree branches stretch outwards gracefully in spring. As the years go by you had better shorten these by one-third in your winter pruning; otherwise, when they are heavily loaded with fruit in autumn they may reach to the ground. Also, heavy winds may cause the laden branches to split. Preserve for supports any stout, straight, long tree branches you lop off. Or go into the woods for them, selecting where possible those with a convenient fork, to serve as props. If they are long, drive the bottom end into the soil and, if their length is just right, place a flat stone or a shingle under their base. For a whippy branch make a bipod or two-legged prop by wiring together two stakes six inches from their ends; open the bipod to form an inverted V, and lay the branch in the crotch.

Fruit-laden branches should be propped when necessary to keep the fruit off the ground.

THE TRESPASSER IS A TRIAL

Lot-crossing is often a problem in suburban gardens. Many a respectable citizen, short on brains but proud of his thievery, will boast of the time when, as a boy, he would raid the neighbor's melon patch—then, as now, unappreciative of the labor, expense, and longings that go into the average garden. Parents are responsible more than their children or the youngsters who play with them. The suburbanite who encourages baseball, archery, or tennis in a space far too small or who installs basketball equipment near the property line, has little thought for his neighbors. Unless you are firm, boys, and girls too, in cowboy regalia and with a brace of toy pistols in their belts, may regard your compost heap as a good outlaws' hangout to attack and defend, or will stalk each other around your garage or through your brambles. As your berries ripen, the temptation to pick them must be overwhelming.

A good plan is to erect a fence—do not use barbed wire—and plant a hedge inside it; keep it trimmed and fertilized and enforce your no-trespassing rule, possibly erecting a sign or two. In a kindly manner, talk it over with the young offenders; tell them to phone you and you'll be glad to go down into the garden and toss over their balls. In the same reasonable spirit, speak to the parents if it seems necessary, but only after you find the youngsters will not cooperate. It helps if neighbors will join in discouraging lot-crossing. Only as a last resort seek help from the school principal and police department; both have more important things to do. But adolescents prowling after dark are definitely a police problem; when an arrest is made, sign a complaint and go through with it; don't tie the hands of the officials by failing to prosecute; this in the interest of your neighbors as well as yourself.

A few signs may discourage ball hunters crashing your hedge.

CHAPTER 11

Wild Fruits and Fruit Storage

"The kindly fruits of the earth." THE LITANY, Book
of Common Prayer.

HINTS ON PICKING FRUITS FROM THE WILD

ON YOUR SUMMER auto trips there will be many occasions when
you may supplement your home-grown fruit by gathering wild
fruits like beach plums of the sandy seashore, blueberries, blackberries, juneberries, raspberries, saskatoons, cranberries, dewberries, wild grapes, nuts, wild cherries, elderberries for wine, pies,
and jelly, and wild strawberries. And in the rough woodlands
that are abandoned farms and are now grown into weed timber, many an accidental apple tree will be found—sometimes a
seedling from an apple discarded many years ago, and sometimes
a crab apple also. Gathering the dwarfer fruits has a slimming
effect on the picker.

Stick to public lands, including the margins of the highway,
and do not enter what looks like waste land without inquiring
for the owner and getting his permission. A piece of rough-look-
ing country may turn out to be a valuable blueberry field, with
the owner sitting in a parked car with his shotgun; another un-
kempt area may be a cranberry bog. A near-by gas station or the
general store are possible sources of information. To avoid argu-
ment, better even leave highway margins alone in cultivated
blueberry territory.

Fruits from the wild. Left: beach plums. Right: low-bush and high-bush blueberries.

Fruits from the wild. Hazelnuts.

Fruits from the wild. Left: elderberries for wine. Right: crab apples for jelly.

Fruits from the wild. Grape and wild strawberry.

Fruits from the wild. Left: blackberries, which have a core. Right: red and black raspberries, which leave their core on the plant.

Poisonous plants to leave alone. Left: jack-in-the-pulpit. Right: monks-hood—its white root has on occasion been mistaken for a vegetable.

Poisonous plants to leave alone. Left: woody nightshade. Center: deadly nightshade. Right: poison hemlock or winter fern.

Some harmful fruits may be gathered in mistake for harmless ones. Get local advice before eating what look to be beach plums, blueberries, cranberries, and elderberries. Study illustrations of poison ivy, poison oak, and poison sumac, and leave the fruit near them for others to pick. Retire to another spot if you hear a rattle or see a snake.

Poisonous plants. Left: water hemlock or musquash root. Right: Jimson weed or stramonium.

Poisonous plants. Left: locoweed. Right: pokeweed or inkberry.

Avoid these when berry-picking. Left: the climbing, three-leaved, drooping, shiny poison ivy. Center: the 6- to 10-foot poison sumach; berries are white and pea-sized. Right: 18-inch poison oak.

Suspend a Mason jar from your neck and steady it with a belt. Wear clothing that will not readily tear, like a leather windbreaker. Wear a leather glove on one hand and pick with the other. Don't pick where shade trees have been sprayed. Don't pick after August 10 amid ragweed if you are subject to hay fever. Retire from the scene if you hear hunters around; their dogs are often more intelligent, but they cannot stop some owners from letting off at anything that moves. Discourage the life-of-the-party with his high boots treading a patch to make your picking easier, but ruining the take for the next group that comes along.

For storage, apples may be placed in shallow baskets, separated by strips of torn paper (left). Both apples and pears are sometimes lightly wrapped in special oiled paper. They should be inspected every week.

STORING YOUR FRUIT

Peaches, nectarines, cherries, grapes, apricots, berries, plums, quince, raspberries, and strawberries are gathered when ripe; so are a few early apples and pears. But late and winter apples and pears are gathered in autumn when a few have dropped to the ground, to ripen in storage.

A storage room in the coolest part of a frost-free cellar, well ventilated, is worth building. Air should circulate: run a fan for an occasional half hour if necessary. Narrow shelves with an inch-high fillet will retain a bed of peatmoss, excelsior, or paper, on which the fruit may be placed carefully. Avoid bruising at all costs. Your stock should be inspected weekly: fruit showing signs of ripening may be used and any beginning to decay should be removed at once.

Ideal temperature would be 34° F. and humidity 85 per cent. Spray the walls or shelves occasionally with water if apples show a tendency to shrivel. Extra good specimens may each be placed in small open cellophane bags or wrapped in special oil-impregnated paper, which prevents a withering condition termed "scald." Air circulation helps to avoid scald, as does the growing of varieties that are resistant to scalding in storage.

CHAPTER 12

The Popular Garden Fruits

"The ripest fruit first falls."
WILLIAM SHAKESPEARE, Richard II.

Precipitation of 24 inches per year or more is essential for most fruits. If you are in an area that normally receives less rain, consult your county agent, your nearest agricultural experiment station or college, or your near-by nurseryman; get their advice as to what to plant. In a home garden of limited extent, too, you will be able to irrigate your fruits.

EDITOR'S NOTE: *On the next two pages you will find tables showing the 48 most popular garden fruits with distance between plants and other instructions for most effective planting.*

How Far Apart to Plant Them. When First Crops Are Expected. Subject to Much

	Diameter of circle occupied by each mature tree or bush eventually FEET	Brambles, bushes, and vines. Average setting distance; one plant to the next FEET	After planting, expect first fruits in— YEARS
Apple, dwarf	20	—	4 to 8
Apple, standard	30	—	4 to 8
Apricot *	20	—	3
Avocado **	20 to 30	—	2 to 3
Banana **	10 to 15	—	1
Blackberry	—	6	2
Blueberry	—	6	3 to 4
Boysenberry *	—	6	2
Cashew **	30	—	4
Cherry, bush	8	—	2
Cherry, sour	25	—	3 to 4
Cherry, sweet	30	—	4 to 5
Chestnut, Chinese *	30	—	2 to 3
Citrus fruits: **			
Calamondin	15	—	
Citrange	15	—	
Citrangedin	15	—	
Citrangequat	15	—	
Citron	25	—	In most
Grapefruit	30	—	varieties, a
Kumquat	20	—	token crop of
Lemon	30	—	a few fruit
Lime	20	—	the third year
Limequat	25	—	
Orange	30	—	
Tangelo	25	—	
Tangerine	15	—	
Cranberry	—	1	3
Currant	—	4	2
Dewberry *	—	4 by 5	2
Fig *	15 to 20	—	3

GARDEN FRUITS

Variation Due to Variety, Latitude, Soil, Aspect, and Care.

	Diameter of circle occupied by each mature tree or bush eventually	Brambles, bushes, and vines. Average setting distance; one plant to the next	After planting expect first fruits in—
	FEET	FEET	YEARS
Gooseberry	—	4	2
Grape	—	6	3
Guava, common **	30	—	3
Guava, Strawberry **	20	—	3
Guava, Pineapple **	15	—	4
Hazelnut, Cobnut, and Filbert	—	10	4
Loganberry *	—	6	2
Loquat **	20	—	2
Mango **	35	—	3
Mulberry	30	—	3
Muskmelon	—	Hills 5	Same year
Nectarine *	20	—	3
Peach *	20	—	3
Peanut *	—	2½ by ¾	Same year
Pear, dwarf	20	—	3
Pear, standard	25	—	3
Pecan *	55	—	6
Persimmon, dwarf types *	20	—	3
Pineapple **	—	3 by 2	2
Pistachio *	20	—	4
Plum	20	—	3
Pomegranate **	15	—	4
Quince *	15	—	3
Raspberry	—	6	2
Rhubarb	—	3	1
Strawberry	—	{ Hills 1 by 2 } { Matted rows } { 2 by 3 }	1
Watermelon *	—	Hills 8	Same year

* These are sensitive to heavy frost and should not be planted in the extreme north.

** These may only be grown in frost-free or near-frost-free areas; read the individual descriptions on the following pages.

CHAPTER 13

Fruits for the Home Garden

"Cherry ripe, ripe, ripe, I cry,
Full and fair ones,—come and buy!"
ROBERT HERRICK.

LIST OF FRUITS FOR THE HOME GARDEN

Types of apples. From left to right: Baldwin, Delicious, McIntosh.

APPLES

You MAY PLANT 6-feet tall, 1- or 2-year-old "standard" trees, which eventually reach 40 feet, or dwarfs. The former let you rake the soil up close and are easier to protect against rabbit damage; the clear 4-foot bole protects the tops against many other browsing animals, and the large orchardist often prefers them. But the dwarf types are also recommended for the home garden, for they need less room and are easier to prune, spray, and pick because the tree is close to the ground. Set apples in early spring in the northern states; either spring or fall elsewhere.

Many varieties in both shapes should produce fruit the fourth year after planting and continue to do so for 50 to 75 years. They

84

are easily grown in any good, well-drained soil. It is quite usual for some kinds to bear a good crop one year and a poor one the next; there is little one can do about it.

The average dwarf apple covers a circle about 20 feet in diameter; the average standard tree spreads about 30 feet. This is when they are fully grown, so they should be set at least these distances apart, and eventually they should have this space available to them on all sides. But shorter-lived peaches, brambles, and bush fruits may be planted closer to them until they need their full room. The table in Chapter 12 will help you make a selection of sorts to grow alongside them for the first few years.

If your new tree is a year old, it will probably have one main stem; after planting it, cut the stem 4 feet from the ground. If it is a two-year-old tree, this will have been done at the nursery and some branches will have developed. Cut these branches all off except for one growing upward to make the leader and from one to three others, spaced as far apart as possible, which will become the main branches. The leader will also be shortened eventually. The branches you leave will be pruned back by one third their length. Once you have three main branches, pruning through the years will be a matter of eliminating dead or broken branches, quick upright-growing suckers, or water sprouts, and reducing the number of secondary branches to admit light through the tree. Pruning is carried out any time the tree is dormant, customarily in late winter.

Apple trees are occasionally produced by grafting, but more often by budding wanted sorts in summer onto stocks of one-year-old apple seedlings. Dwarf apples are budded onto stocks that develop short trees, branching close to the ground and maturing at 12 to 15 feet. A stock used for dwarfing for years was known as the "paradise," but more recently at the East Malling research station in England all possible host stocks have been collected and tested, and then distributed to nurserymen. When a tree is offered to you on a Malling stock, it means that one of these modern proven stocks was used, probably one that produces dwarf upper growth. These smaller types may be planted closer together—15 or 20 feet. Good apples for use on dwarfing stocks include Cortland, Delicious, Greening, Northern Spy, McIntosh, and Yellow Delicious.

If your tree bears flowers, but few or no fruits, it probably needs the companionship of a variety that will furnish it with pollen. To insure pollination, several apple varieties should be planted together. Although most varieties are satisfactory sources of pollen, Baldwin, Gravenstein, Greening, Winesap, and some others cannot be relied upon to pollinate others. But good pollinators include Cortland, Delicious, Grimes, and McIntosh.

For plant sorts that are customarily grown in your area, consult your county agent or nurseryman. Among the hundreds of apples available, here are some of the kinds they are likely to recommend:

Astrachan. Usually bears in alternate years. A hardy and accommodating cooking variety that is good for the northern states, the Pacific coast, and Midwest. Grows in the Gulf states also.

Baldwin. The fruit matures late. A good all-purpose apple, large and flushed with red. Not a good pollinator of other varieties.

Cortland. An improvement of the older McIntosh variety and a good pollinator of other sorts. The fruit has bright red skin and firm flesh. A late apple that keeps well: good for dessert and cooking.

Delicious. A dark red, late, eating apple, ribbed at the blossom end; excellent flavor. Delicious is a good pollinator of other apples, but a poor self-pollinator. Hardy and accommodating, it does well in the northern states, the Midwest, the Gulf states, and the Pacific coast.

Golden Delicious. Yellow skin. Often bears the fourth year after planting. Popular in the Pacific northwest.

Gravenstein. Medium-size early apple with a striped red skin; flesh is yellowish, juicy, and aromatic; excellent for eating or cooking. Hardy, it is good for the northern states; grows well on the Pacific coast also. It is not a good pollinator of other sorts.

Greening. The large yellow-green apples mature in winter. It is not a good pollinator of other varieties.

Grimes. Pollinates other varieties well. The medium-size fruit has a yellow skin with russet dots, and the flesh is yellowish. Grows well on the eastern shore of Maryland, the Midwest, and the Pacific coast. Good eating apple.

86

Hyslop. One of the most satisfactory of the crab apples for jellies and jams. The handsome apple is striped red and yellow.

Jonathan. A late-ripening crisp, hard, juicy, slightly acid, aromatic eating apple, medium in size. Lively red skin, with white or yellowish flesh. Does well in the Shenandoah Valley, the Midwest, and Pacific coastal states.

King, Tompkins King, or King of Tompkins County. A very large, round apple, flushed red on yellow and dotted with white or russet. Aromatic and of good quality. Popular in the western states.

McIntosh. An extra quality, large, dark red apple with white flesh. Sweet when ripe; it is then an excellent eating apple. A good pollinator of other apples. Hardy; good for the northern states and Canada.

Northern Spy. A slow-growing sort that will not come into bearing until 10 or perhaps 15 years after planting. A good, very large, all-purpose winter apple. Hardy, it is much used in the northern states.

Rome Beauty. It blossoms later than most others, making it suitable for areas subject to late spring frost. It also matures its fruits later in storage; they are large, yellow-red. A good cooking apple.

Stayman. A good brittle, slightly acid juicy dessert fruit, ripening late.

Wealthy. A medium-early variety that is quick to bear, often yielding a fair crop the fifth year after planting of bright red, hard, crisp, juicy, and slightly acid apples. Hardy, it is suitable for the Midwest, the northern states, and Canada. Good for both eating and cooking.

Williams Early Red. A medium-size early apple of good quality for dessert and cooking: desirable for the home garden.

Winesap. A medium-size, late, all-purpose apple, conical in shape and dark red; flesh is firm and very juicy. Grows well in the southeastern and Gulf states; the Pacific coast also. Not a good pollinator of other varieties.

Yellow Transparent. The medium-size fruit is ready in late summer. It has a yellow waxy skin, pure white flesh, and is slightly acid when fully mature. Hardy, it is good for the northern states, yet does well in the Shenandoah Valley and the Midwest.

June-drop. Under your tree are hundreds of small apples. A natural phenomenon by which nature avoids overcrowding.

Crab apples are close relatives of the regular apple and are largely grown for the decorative effect of their blossoms and fruit. Mostly small, the fruits are made into preserves.

Multiple-variety apples are valuable where one has room for only one tree; find out the kinds on any offered to you to be satisfied that at least one good pollinator is among them.

Apples must be protected from their enemies, mostly by routine spraying, the worst of them include:

Aphids or plant lice.

Apple blotch. Brown star-shaped marks on the fruit.

Apple scab, which causes dropping of the fruit and disfigurement of the leaves and surviving fruits, with dark gray spots on the latter.

Borers, which burrow into the wood. Watch for sawdust.

Caterpillars of various kinds.

Tent caterpillars on the apple. Spray; don't burn.

A looper caterpillar defoliating an apple branch.

Codling moth, which causes most of the wormy apples.

Fire blight. Similar to blight of the pear, this trouble is met with in the apple also. Amputate infected limbs, sterilizing your tools by dipping them in an antiseptic solution.

Leaf hoppers, seen just after the tree blooms. Attack them as soon as seen with Black-leaf-40; they are more difficult to control later.

Red-cedar rust, of which the cedar tree and the apple are alternate hosts; it causes orange-yellow spots on apple leaves. It is useless to spray, but possibly you can get rid of the cedars.

San José scale, small sucking insects which protect themselves with closely sealed coverings like limpet shells, and in consequence are very difficult to reach with a spray. A dormant spray such as lime-sulphur, Scalex, or Scalecide is the remedy.

Tent caterpillars. Spray with arsenate of lead. Do not burn them or you may injure your tree.

SPRAY PROGRAM FOR APPLES

For one or two trees buy a ready-mixed preparation at your seed or hardware store, and use it as directed on the container. If you own a small orchard and prefer to mix your own, the following is a good schedule:

1. In late winter, while the tree is still dormant, strong solutions are possible. Spray with 1 pint of lime-sulphur mixed with 8 pints of water.

2. Give a delayed-dormant spray when the buds begin to swell, just before they open. Since the first insect broods hatch out a few days before their food is ready, this treatment kills most of them. See below.

3. Calyx spray, given just after the blossoms have fallen. See below.

4. Final spray, given three weeks later. See below.

For sprays 2, 3, and 4, mix:

> 1 pint lime-sulphur
> 1 oz. lead arsenate
> 1 oz. Black-leaf-40
> 40 pints water

For picking apples a special bag may be used, with the weight carried on the shoulders. If the first stem does not part readily from the spur, wait a week and try again. A ladder will be necessary for a tall tree.

Apple-picking. Give the fruit a slight twist; support the spur on which it grows with your thumb; a slight further twist and it comes away. If the spur is broken (lower left), you get no more apples at that point; keep it uninjured (lower right).

APRICOTS

With a superior flavor all their own, apricots ripen a week or two earlier than peaches. Requiring about the same temperature as peaches and a rich, deep, well-drained soil, they deserve a space in your garden. Wet subsoil kills them, but ordinarily they are as easy as peaches, and the trees often live longer. The stocks on which apricots are budded affect this longer life: those whose host tree is a myrobalan plum stand heavy soils better; those on seedling peach and apricot stocks are best for hungry overporous land.

One drawback to apricot culture is that the flower buds, which open very early, risk being injured by late spring frosts. To overcome this, select a cool and not over-sunny spot, planting in a northern or western exposure to delay the opening of the buds, but avoid shade. An eastern aspect is objectionable, because the morning sun does not allow frost-bitten buds gradually to recover, as they may if sunlight does not get on them immediately.

Two-year-old 6-foot whips are good for planting. The average apricot tree covers a circle about 20 feet in diameter when fully grown; this means that apricots should be set at least this distance apart, and eventually they will need this space available to them on all sides. But shorter-lived brambles and bush fruits may be planted closer to them until they need their full room. The table in Chapter 12 will help you make a selection of sorts to grow alongside them for the first few years.

Good varieties are:

Alexander. A cold-resistant Russian variety, with small freestone fruits.
Blenheim, Moorpark, and Scout. The last-named being non-self-pollinating.
Early Golden, which has large fruits, almost as big as peaches. An old-time reliable sort.

Some modern kinds, introduced from North China in the past 25 years, include such sorts as Chow, Manchu, Mandarin, and others, which are extra hardy, claimed to withstand temperatures down to 40° below in their native land.

Apricots are subject to the brown-rot disease and to attacks of curculio, among other pests. The spray program may well be the same as that for cherries (see page 98). Young fruits should be rigorously thinned; otherwise lean years may alternate with fruiting years. Important: when they are half-grown, snip out one of every two fruits that touch.

Borers sometimes get into the lower parts of the trunk; proceed as advised under peaches (see page 122).

Multi-variety trees may be obtained: apricot, peach, and plum on one tree. They are recommended for the garden that is limited in area.

Left: apricot. Right: avocado or alligator-pear.

AVOCADO

Grown in Florida and the warmer parts of Arizona, New Mexico, and California, the pear-shaped or oblong alligator pear is mostly served as salad. The ripe buttery fruit is halved, the seeds are removed, and it is flavored with lemon juice and eaten with a spoon; or the flesh may be sweetened with sugar.

Quality of the soil is relatively unimportant provided it is well supplied with organic matter and drains well. An annual wide, thick mulch of old manure or compost is desirable on the soil above the roots, which travel far beyond the plant. The roots also are shallow, and any cultivation more drastic than a light raking is likely to injure them.

Ultimately reaching a height of around 30 feet, year-old plants are usually purchased and carefully planted in spring, without disturbing the soil supplied along with the roots and bound to them in burlap. Trees budded on avocados grown from seed should always be procured, because they are superior and usually stocky, while the seedlings may grow to immense proportions. They are thirsty plants so water must be supplied in dry seasons for the first half of the year, then withheld to permit them to ripen their wood. Avocados usually bear two or three years after planting and, when mature, they cover a circle of soil 20 to 30 feet in diameter.

Pruning is designed to maintain low, open bushes with all possible air and sunshine admitted to the tree; it is done in winter. As the trees are easily injured, fruit-gathering is done with shears or a sharp hook with an open canvas bag attached under it. Ladders should not be placed against the tree. The fruits are green when harvested, one or two weeks before ripening, and they must be used within a few days of maturity.

There are several dozen varieties available under three general headings: West Indian, often the largest fruits and needing the most heat; Mexican types with many small fruits, thin skins, and good flavor, considered the best; and Guatemalan types, the hardiest but with fruits midway in size and quality. By selecting suitable kinds you may get avocados every month in the year. Take your local nurseryman into your confidence, tell him the months you want avocados, those with little or much oil in them —for they vary quite a lot in this respect—and be guided by his suggestions. Among the sorts he may offer are Fuerte, fruiting during winter, and Taft, Nabal, or Queen for summer and autumn production. An established tree may yield from 125 to 150 pounds of avocados.

BANANA

A banana plant may be seen occasionally in home gardens in the extreme south, dwarf Chinese being a variety often

Dwarf Chinese is a good banana for gardens in central Florida.

planted. Frost destroys the fruit and may injure the crown from which the shoots arise. The shoots usually die after bearing fruit. Give the plants a mulch in winter if cold is expected and take other precautions against frost (see page 101). Bananas are propagated by suckers dug from around the crown, and the plants need a free space around them of 10 to 15 feet. Plant them this distance apart.

BLACKBERRY

Two-year-old clumps are advisable for setting out and they may be planted along a wire fence in rows 7 feet apart, the plants 3 feet or more from each other in the line. The stems or "canes" may be coiled along the wires with an occasional tie to hold them. Some are grown against strong 6-foot stakes 6 feet apart, canes being tied to the stake. They like rather heavy, loamy soil.

They cannot be grown in some areas north of the Canadian border or the northwestern plains, because of extreme winter cold, while the heat and drought of the Southwest is against them. They are usually increased by digging up and transplanting the suckers that arise from the clumps, and occasionally by planting 3-inch sections of the roots taken in the autumn, buried all winter, and planted in spring. Some varieties root at the stem tips where branches touch the ground; these may be severed and transplanted. Take away all branches over four from each clump.

After the fruit is picked, the fruiting cane is cut away and younger canes are fastened to the wire or pole. Canes produced this season yield their fruit the next. As the new canes grow they are sometimes pinched at 3 feet; they will then branch. Next spring the branches are cut back to 18 inches.

Some good varieties are:

Alfred. Very hardy, with sweet berries, large, early, and good.
Blowers and Brewer. Two good kinds.
Brainerd Evergreen. A strongly trailing sort. Plant twice the normal distance apart or attach the canes to bean poles.
Eldorado. Large, long black fruits. Very early and very sweet. The most popular, yielding heavily and resistant to disease. Ripens gradually over a long season, which is an advantage in the home garden. A hardy sort.

Hedrick. A new variety of great promise, recently developed by the N. Y. State Experiment Station.

Oregon Evergreen or Black Diamond. For Washington, D. C., and south. A thornless, strongly trailing sort, needing more than the usual amount of room.

If the leaves become yellow with the spores of orange rust and drop off, dig up and burn the plants; they will die anyway, and there is no known control. Mosaic disease may strike as described under raspberries and should be treated in the same way (see page 135).

Loganberry or Phenomenal (see page 116) may be regarded as a large red blackberry and its culture is similar. It is winter-hardy south of Louisville or Wichita and on the West Coast.

BLUEBERRY

Blueberries like a moist, self-draining, sour garden. To aid land add quantities of peatmoss and sand, and plant the bushes six feet apart. Have two or more together, of different varieties, for pollinating. Two-, three-, or four-year-old plants are usually available. They are shallow rooted subjects, so cultivation must consist of pulling weeds by hand and the lightest of raking.

Pruning is carried out during the winter and consists mostly of removing injured, dead, or weak branches and shortening long twigs that are well covered with flower buds, each of which will produce a cluster of berries. Reducing the number of these buds makes for larger but fewer berries. Named varieties of blueberries often are as large as grapes. The bushes are handsome and may well find a place in shrubbery along with acid-loving evergreens such as azaleas and rhododendrons. Like the evergreens, blueberries like a moisture table within 3 feet of the surface, and the pH rating of the land should be around 5. When finding a place for them in the garden, remember that blueberries need full sun, and maintaining a straw or peatmoss mulch over the roots during summer will be helpful.

Propagation is mostly done by setting pieces of year-old branches in a mixture of half peatmoss and half sand. Take these cions in early spring; they should be without flower buds and are set with ⅔ their length in the mixture at an angle of 45°; they need slight shade. They also may be increased by dividing the clumps or by layering. (See under propagation, Chapter 8.)

Among good varieties, mostly 6 to 8 feet high when mature, are:

Burlington (late). Mammoth berries; among the newest and best.
Concord (mid-season). A tall bush that will bear a heavy crop of best-quality large berries in July.
Grover. Recognize it by its light yellow-green leaves.
Jersey (late). The tall attractive bush produces large good-quality berries.
June (early). Recommended.
Rancocas (second-early). A tall, vigorous, and productive hybrid variety.
Rubel (late). A variety that ripens its berries in August. Large fruit of fine color.
Stanley (mid-season). Tall strong plants, producing large, delicious, aromatic berries.

Blueberries usually commence to bear fruit 3 or 4 years after planting. Acid plant foods like cottonseed meal, sulphate of ammonia, acid phosphate, and muriate of potash should be used on them in moderate amounts; and, if the pH exceeds 5.5, an occasional application of aluminum sulphate or hardwood sawdust may be used to bring it down. If you have to water your plants and your normal water supply contains lime, catch and store rain from the roof.

To find the pH of your soil, get in touch with your county agent or your state agricultural experiment station; a soil-testing kit for your own use would be a good investment.

BOYSENBERRY

Dark wine-red berries, much larger than dewberries, are produced in quantity. Seeds are few, while the canes have few and small thorns. Less hardy than other brambles, the roots should be covered with a mulch of leaves over the winter north of Philadelphia after the ground freezes; remove the mulch in spring. Some growers lay next season's fruiting canes on the ground and cover them with straw over winter in cold climates. Plant boysenberries 6 feet apart and tie them to either tall strong stakes or a wire fence.

The stems or canes are biennial and those that have borne a crop will be dead by spring; prune them down to the ground level. Canes that grow this year bear a crop the next.

Boysenberries are delicious and should find a place in every home fruit garden, where the climate is not too severe.

Youngberries are somewhat similar and may receive the same care. Thorny and thornless types are seen; growers seem to prefer the former.

Cashew nuts grow on the end of the "cashew-apple."

CASHEW

These tropical nuts may be grown only in southern California, Florida, and the Gulf states. They are borne on 40-foot evergreen trees, each at the tip of a bright, yellow-red, pear-shaped fruit called the cashew apple, which is also edible. The nuts are the seeds and they have to be roasted to remove the caustic juice found beneath the skin enveloping the nuts. Cashew trees eventually occupy a circle 30 feet in diameter.

CHERRY

Sweet cherries do well on rather light sandy loam, where peaches also thrive, and they eventually develop into larger trees than the sour variety, which does best in heavier land and is more resistant to temperature extremes.

Sour cherries will eventually occupy a 25-foot circle; sweet

Some good cherries. From left to right: sweet black windsor, sour red montmorency, sweet yellow napoleon.

cherries, a 30-foot one. One- or two-year-old trees, 4 to 6 feet tall, are recommended for planting. Plant them in spring in the extreme north; in spring or autumn further south. Other than developing a shapely tree and removing crossing and dead branches, cherries require little pruning after main branches have been developed. Cherries are budded onto nearly related wild-cherry stocks: sweet varieties usually unto Mazzard, sour onto Mahaleb.
Some good varieties follow:

Bing. A mid-season, sweet kind. Very hardy with almost black crisp fruit. It needs a sweet cherry of another variety near by as a pollinator.

Black Tartarian. Early and sweet. Long purple-black fruit of the best quality, juicy, with a rich flavor. Soft flesh. Heavy cropping; vigorous, ripening about June 20. A good pollinator for other sweet cherries.

Governor Wood. A large sweet yellow cherry with a red cheek; early. Soft flesh.

Montmorency. Attractive bright clear red fruit with firm flesh; the best mid-season sour cherry. Ready about July 15.

Napoleon or White Oxheart. A choice, productive, yellow, sweet variety; has a bright red cheek. Firm flesh, rich flavor, and early; it is ready to pick July 7 to 10. Should have another sweet cherry near for pollination.

Sweet September. Plant patent No. 94. Fine quality dark red, crisp, sweet fruit; late, it is ready to pick in early autumn.

Windsor. A black oxheart variety with pink flesh. Large, juicy, firm, and delicious. Vigorous, ripening around July 20 to 28. A good pollinator for other sweet cherries.

Yellow Spanish. An early, sweet variety. The amber-yellow cherries are flushed with red, and the flesh is firm and sweet.

97

Some other good sweet cherries are Coe, Elephant Heart, and Wood. If you have room for only one sweet cherry tree, and your neighbors have none, procure a cion of another variety of sweet cherry and graft it onto your tree. Sweet cherries are not self-pollinating, but usually they will pollinate each other. A sour cherry needs no help; it will take care of itself along these lines.

Forty, fifty, or more quarts per established tree is an average yield for sweet cherries, which are more prolific than the sour ones. But plant cherries only if you are big-hearted and like to feed the wild birds; in the home garden their share of the crop from a tall tree is likely to be larger than yours.

Sweet cherries are subject to:

Aphis. They suck the juices of the young growth.
Brown rot, causing the fruit to shrivel away.
Curculio. A small beetle that, with its grub, destroys the fruit.

Sour cherries are subject to:

Fruit fly and its maggot; the latter found in what appear to be sound fruits.
Leaf spot, a disease which, starting with shot-holes, may defoliate the trees in late summer.

A SPRAY PROGRAM FOR CHERRIES

For one or two trees buy a spray ready-mixed at your seed or hardware store. Use it as directed on the container. If you have a small orchard and prefer to mix your own, the following would be good:

While the trees are dormant:
        1 pint lime-sulphur
        8 pints water
When the flowers fall:
        1 pint lime-sulphur
        1 oz. Black-leaf-40 (nicotine sulphate)
        3 ozs. arsenate of lead
        50 pints water

When fruit flies appear—usually the first week in June:

      6 ozs. arsenate of lead
      ½ cup molasses
      50 pints water
      Wash cherries thoroughly before using them.

After picking the fruit:

      1 pint lime-sulphur
      50 pints water

One month after picking:

      1 pint lime-sulphur
      50 pints water

THE HANSEN VARIETIES OF THE SAND CHERRY

Professor Hansen of South Dakota originated a number of hybrids and selections made from the wild western sand cherry, a prostrate shrub of the plains region. Grown as a many-branched bush, rarely over 5 feet tall, they often start to fruit the second year. The cherries, resembling small plums, are borne in clusters and cover the plant. Their flavor is good and they are excellent for eating as dessert and for making jams and jellies. These bushes occupy a circle 8 feet in diameter.

CHINESE CHESTNUT

This chestnut is a low, spreading, fast-growing tree, producing nuts of excellent roasting or stuffing quality, which are slightly larger than the oldtime American chestnuts, though considerably smaller than the imported Spanish nuts. This tree seems to be the answer to the bark disease or blight, which has killed native chestnuts in the northeast; it is definitely resistant to this trouble.

Any good loamy, well-drained, and slightly acid soil will grow these chestnuts, but they are not advised for our most northern areas. Trees are best planted in twos or threes, with neighbors cooperating by planting one where necessary to insure pollination, which a tree cannot perform on itself but does readily to another. Two-year saplings, 4 feet high, are a good age to plant and they should commence to yield two or three years later. Chinese chestnuts will eventually occupy a circle 30 feet in diameter.

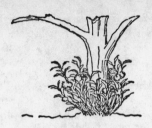

Chinese chestnut. Resistant to blight; needs at least one companion near-by for pollinating. A handsome moderate-size shade-tree that bears edible nuts in 2 or 3 years after planting.

Forests in the north and east contain many a gaunt dead chestnut, killed by blight. Later growth sometimes develops to the point where a few nuts may be gathered before it, too, dies.

CITRUS FRUITS

The commercial growth of grapefruit, lemons, oranges, and tangerines is confined to central and southern Florida, southern California, favored parts of the Gulf states, Arizona, and New Mexico. As garden subjects, however, where the trees are limited in number, arrangements may be made to give emergency protection during sudden unusual drops in the thermometer, and with this aid they may be planted considerably farther north.

Their soil needs are simple in the home garden, because they will be set in pockets in which the soil mixture can be made to fit their requirements. They all want good drainage, but plenty of moisture, so an abundance of organic matter is placed in the pocket, and during growth they appreciate a mulch of compost, hay, straw, or leaves on the surface.

Planting in winter or spring is usual, and the nurseryman commonly supplies them balled and burlapped. Set the ball in the pocket with the burlap binding the roots, slash it just before filling in the hole, and it will soon decay. The position of the soil mark is important; set it exactly at the soil level. When the hole is half filled, pour in plenty of water, waiting until it has drained away before completely filling the pocket.

Base of a grapefruit tree. Grow it only where frost does not occur.

Kumquat, a desirable member of the citrus group.

Citrus trees need comparatively little room. The average circle occupied by them when they are mature is approximately as follows: 15 feet diameter: calamondin, citrange, tangerine, cintangedin, and citrangequat; 20 feet diameter: kumquat and lime; 25 feet diameter: tangelo, limequat, and citron; 30 feet diameter: orange, grapefruit, and lemon.

Pruning is largely a matter of developing several important limbs and having a well-lighted, well-ventilated tree with an open top.

Sudden frosts are the bane of the citrus-grower, and the thaw that follows is equally harmful. Smudge pots will protect against a few degrees—cans containing greasy rags, ignited and allowed to smolder. Smoky fires of damp straw may be used. Playing a hose in the neighborhood of your trees will help, the nozzle adjusted to break the stream into a cloud of small droplets. Hoeing or cultivating the soil will also raise the surrounding temperature a degree or so. Finally, if you have only one or two trees you may even devise a sort of tent of canvas or cheap light cloth.

If the tree has been slightly hit by frost, let it thaw without the sun's rays shining on it. Erect a screen of some kind. Rush to paint the trunk and limbs white to reflect light and, with it, heat. If the frost has split the trunk or branches, hurry and bind them tightly back into position with strong wide tape, soaked in liquid wax or melted grafting wax, to keep out moisture and air until the cambium has healed the damage, which it will do in about half a year. The only pruning advised during the twelve months following the freeze is removal of dead wood.

Here are the best-known citrus fruits arranged in the order of their resistance to light frost, the hardiest first:

Calamondin. The inch-and-a-half acid fruits are used in flavoring and in marmalade-making. Probably the most cold-resistant citrus fruit.

Citrange. A hybrid between the true orange and the Japanese or trifoliate orange. Its fruits may be preserved.

Tangerine. Satsuma or kid-glove orange. A dwarf spreading shrub that will stand a degree or two of frost. The ease with which the fruit may be peeled is the reason for its third name. A good early variety is Silver Hill; a mid-season one, Algerian; late sorts, King and Temple.

Citrangedin. A hybrid between the citrange and calamondin. The small fruits are like the calamondin.

Citrangequat. A hybrid between the citrange, the true orange, and kumquat. The fruits are used for juice and preserving.

Kumquat. The 15-foot trees are kept pruned to small shrubs. Marumi and Nagami are two varieties.

Orange. Louisiana sweet is a popular variety. Navels and Valencia are among the California sorts.

Tangelo. A hybrid between the grapefruit and tangerine. Practically a small grapefruit with the easy peeling of the tangerine.

Grapefruit or pomelo. Grown in Florida, southern Texas, and Arizona. The enormous fruits are borne in clusters, like grapes—hence the American name; very similar to the fruit known elsewhere in the world as the shaddock. Royal is a good mid-season kind; Thompson is late and has pink flesh; Marsh is a late seedless variety. The use of grapefruit as a breakfast opener is almost exclusively American.

Limequat. A hybrid between the lime and kumquat. The small trees are quick-growing.

Lemons are particularly sensitive to cold. Picked green when about 2½ inches in diameter, the fruit is washed and the skin allowed to dry and ripen to yellow, when they are ready for sale.

Lime. The trees are small and are often planted as close as 20 feet. Harvesting is similar to that of lemons, but they are sold green.

Citron. Most frost-sensitive of the citrus group. Trees are small, but the fruits are as large as grapefruit; their peel is candied for Christmas cooking of cakes and mincemeat.

In the dryer areas, insects are troublesome; in the moister regions, fungus gives more trouble. Usual spray materials are lime-sulphur and bordo-mixture. Consult your experiment station or county agent for guidance in this.

Left: the cranberry. Right: juneberry or shadbush, a native wild fruit gathered from Canada to the central U. S.

CRANBERRY

Not one garden in a thousand has the conditions suitable for this fruit; but in the exceptional one where there is a stream with some marsh suitable for a bog garden, a miniature cranberry bog may be an interesting feature.

Banks must be built and flood gates installed so that the bog may be flooded at short notice to make a pond, and so it may be emptied quickly. Government leaflets will give the details. Roughly, they call for the clear space between the banks to be coated with 4 inches of sand. Plant cuttings of the 3-foot vines through the sand covering into the soil beneath 12 to 15 inches apart, placing them in holes made with a sharpened dowel stick. Weeds must be pulled by hand, and when frost is expected or insects are giving trouble the bed is flooded, to be emptied next morning. And the bed is kept flooded from December to mid-April, largely to prevent frost-heaving. Some water would be let in during the dry summer months for irrigation; the plants are not covered, but merely given water-covered soil for half a day. For actual flooding at other times have about a foot of water over the plants.

At the outset the bog is sometimes flooded for a season to kill wild growth in preparation for the bed, the dead vegetation being raked out and surface tillage, sanding, and planting started. Every second year a half-inch dressing of sand is spread over the bed, and not until the third year after planting can a crop be expected.

The currant worm will quickly defoliate gooseberry and currant bushes. It is green.

CURRANT

If your garden is well away from northern pine forests, if your neighbors have no five-needle pines amid their shrubbery, and if their possession is not banned in your locality, these husky, frost-resistant plants are desirable for the home garden. Currants make good jelly, jam, and wine.

Two-year-old bushes may be set 4 feet apart in autumn or very early spring. Their feeding roots are close to the surface, so weeds should be pulled by hand and cultivation limited to brushing away leaves and rubbish with a flat-tine spring rake. Several dustings on the soil around the bushes of 5–10–5 or a similar balanced fertilizer each spring are desirable; and a winter dressing of powdered limestone on the surface is recommended if your land has a marked tendency to acidity.

At the most each bush should carry from nine to fourteen branches, consisting equally of one-, two- and three-year-old ones, which means that late summer pruning is a matter of taking away all four-year-old stems as soon as they have yielded. In early spring pruning, all but the four strongest of last year's new branches are pruned away. Stems that over-top the others may be shortened. Prunings of young branches may be set in gritty soil to root and form new plants.

The following are good varieties, red ones being the most commonly grown:

Fay's Prolific. Vigorous and productive, with clusters of dark red, juicy berries.
Red Lake. One of the newer sorts.
Wilder. An upright bush. Fine large, bright red berries, firm and juicy.

Among very similar white currants, the Imperial is a reliable variety; and of the very different black currants, Boskoop Giant is often preferred. Whites are less popular than the reds, and the blacks are rarely seen. Black currant jam—two spoons stirred into hot water to be taken at bedtime—is an old and often effective remedy for colds.

It is too bad that black, white, and red currants, along with gooseberries, are winter hosts for the white-pine blister rust. They *may not* be planted in certain areas and they *should not* be planted if you or your neighbors have white pines or other five-needle varieties in the garden (the five-needle group, including our valuable forest tree, is sometimes planted for decoration).

CURRANT SPRAY PROGRAM

For a few bushes, buy a ready-mixed spray at your seed or hardware store and use it as directed on the container. If you have a large planting you may prefer to mix your own. The following sprays are recommended:

During winter, use 1 pint lime-sulphur in 8 pints of water.
Early spring. Just before the flower buds open, spray with bordo-mixture, adding 1¼ tablespoons of lead arsenate to each gallon of the dilution.
Late spring. Repeat the bordo-lead-arsenate spray when the fruit is well formed, but still green.
After picking. Spray with 2 tablespoons of lead arsenate to 1 gallon of water.

Without adequate spraying, scale will possibly give trouble. If the leaves show wrinkling and blistering, look for aphis on the under sides of the foliage. If found, spray with Black-leaf-40, both under and over the leaves.

Despite this program, you may discover small green currant worms defoliating your bushes: spray with a mixture containing ¾ per cent rotenone. If you are in a hurry to catch your morning train, dust with a powder containing the same insecticide.

Be sure to wash currants before using them to remove any possible trace of lead arsenate.

DEWBERRY

A popular description of this plant would be of a low-bush trailing blackberry. It bears a week or two earlier than the blackberry, with large berries having a less-pronounced flavor. The branches may be tied to upright posts or along wire; usual planting distances are 4 feet by 5 feet. They do best in a sandy soil. Roots should be mulched over winter in areas north of Philadelphia; and in the far north, unfasten the canes from the posts or wires, lay them on the ground, and cover them with soil.

Dewberries begin to bear when the last spring strawberries are being picked. If you plant only one variety you may run into difficulties through lack of pollination; so, split your order among the following two sorts and set them alternately:

Lucretia, the more popular, and Mayes, a good pollinator.

For maintaining or increasing one's stock they practically do the work for you: the tips of the longer branches will curve onto the ground and take root there. Sever the stem and transplant in autumn or spring.

(See under raspberries for other cultural notes and the insects and diseases affecting the bramble fruits, along with a suitable spray program.)

FIG

These may be grown with little trouble in sheltered spots south of Illinois; while north to Long Island individual specimens may be found producing, but at the cost of troublesome winter protection. The usual method is to tie the soft pliable branches fairly close to the main stem, pack with straw, and, starting from the bottom, wrap with burlap; cover with pieces of linoleum, often obtained from vacant lots and the town dump. A cap of linoleum at the top keeps water and snow out of this undecorative structure. Another method is to prune the tree so that its branches are close to the ground, press them to the surface, and cover them with soil over winter, mounding to a hill at the center of the plant.

Figs need watering in dry weather and a mulch over the roots during the hot months; also elaborate protection during winter in the north.

A neutral, rather heavy soil suits figs best, organic matter must be worked under, and the trees are planted in spring. They should be watered during dry spells, and a straw or compost mulch is maintained over the roots in hot weather. A 15- to 20-foot circle is required by the fig. The usual design in a suitable climate is a bush or semi-standard with four or five main branches open to the sun and air. Cultivation of these shallow-rooted subjects should be confined to hand-weeding and the lightest possible raking, dusting the soil before raking with limestone, and 5–10–5 fertilizer alternately.

After the first year, pruning in spring consists mainly of shortening the branches to half their length and cutting completely away any that mar the shape of the bush, that crowd, or that are dead or injured; as well as unwanted suckers.

Propagation is performed by rooting cuttings or, where only a few plants are needed, by layering: a notch, kept open with a small sliver of wood, is made in a low branch; cover the notched portion with soil and keep moist in dry weather; detach and plant the rooted portion in early autumn.

These eyesores in a northern garden are figs, heavily wrapped against winter's cold.

Good varieties for the home garden include **Ischia, Celeste, Kadota, Magnolia, Mission,** and **Brown Turkey.** All these are self-pollinating, but Smyrna, a type grown commercially in California, must have companion sorts near by to pollinate it.

GOOSEBERRY

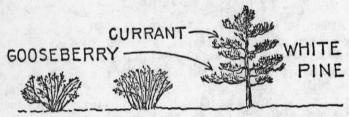

Gooseberries and currants are winter hosts of the white-pine blister rust. Do not grow them near any five-needle pine.

Along with currants (see page 105), these are carriers of the white-pine blister rust and should not be grown near them. In a suitable area set 2-year-old plants 4 feet or more apart in spring or fall. Their roots are close to the surface, so cultivation must be shallow, along the lines suggested for currants. Give them heavy rich land. As they are resistant to northern cold, the limits of Canadian civilization is the boundary for most of the older types, though some of the newer ones may be somewhat sensitive to cold. Gooseberries are regarded as unsuitable for southern gardens. But they are useful in the central and northern states in being one of the few fruits that will withstand partial shade. The pruning schedule is similar to that of currants.

Good proven varieties are:

Downing, a prolific sort with large pale green berries, full flavored and superior.
Houghton, medium-sized red berries.
Poorman, also a reddish fruit.

GOOSEBERRY SPRAY PROGRAM

For a few bushes, buy a ready-mixed spray at your local seed or hardware store, and use it as directed on the container. If you have an extensive planting you may prefer to mix your own. The following are recommended:

In winter, with the plants dormant, spray with 1 pint lime-sulphur in 8 pints of water.
Early spring. Just before the flower buds open, spray with 1 pint lime-sulphur in 40 pints of water, adding 2 teaspoons of arsenate of lead to each quart of the dilution.
Late spring. Repeat the lime-sulphur-lead-arsenate spray when the fruits are formed.
After picking, repeat the lime-sulphur-lead-arsenate spray.

Currant worms bother gooseberries also (see page 104).

Cuttings of young stems take root readily in gritty soil; long branches sometimes develop roots on their tips in contact with the soil. A favorite method of increasing one's stock is to cut off all stems from a good-yielding bush and to mound a pyramid of soil around it. Shoots appear and they send out roots. Dig up the plant, divide the root, and plant the shoots.

GRAPE

Grapes may be grown in almost every part of the country where there is adequate rainfall and the soil is of average fertility and well drained. Rotted manure and coarse bonemeal forked under at planting time, and light dustings of bonemeal raked in several times a year should keep your vines healthy and productive; compost may be used instead of rotted manure if more convenient. A position in full sun is best for them, although they will thrive reasonably well where they get sun half the day. Unlike most other fruits, grapes will color even when the leaves shield them entirely from the sun. A medium-loam soil with a pH rating of 6, which is slightly acid, is considered the most favorable for them; they prefer slightly sloping upland soils and are not planted in muckland.

Two-year-old vines are good to plant and may be set 6 feet apart in either spring or fall. Very long-lived, they stand neglect yet respond markedly to average attention, proper pruning, and suitable spraying. Their roots are close to the surface, and the lightest of shallow raking to keep the area tidy is the most they should receive. Weeds are best controlled by hand-pulling.

In most parts of the U. S. the wonderful European wine grapes cannot be grown unless they are grafted onto American-variety roots; but in favored sections of California they do well, and wine-making with them is a major industry.

PRUNING GRAPES

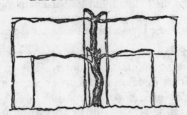

Pruning grapes too late in winter may result in the vine's losing much of its sap.

Pruning must be done in late winter, before the sap starts to rise; if you leave it too late, the jellylike fluid will drain from the cuts and will seriously exhaust the plant—the vine is said to "bleed." But if you are only a little late, slight bleeding may be stopped if you hasten to a supply house for a bottle of vine styptic, which will partly control the situation. Failing this, see what your local drugstore has to suggest.

The pruning principle is mostly a matter of allowing each plant to produce a limited number of large, perfect bunches—eighty for each established vine is the most under any circumstance; far fewer for young vines. About two bunches from each bud left at pruning time is the average production; pruning is also designed to afford as much sunlight as possible on all sides and perfect air circulation. The most popular system of training is known as the Kniffen, which is applicable to the home garden. A slight change in the system will adapt the grapes for growing on a trellis, arbor, pergola, or arch.

Vines are set in a straight line, a 6-foot stake is driven in 6 inches from the plant, and the first year's growth is fastened to it. Sometime during the summer a fence may be erected along the row, with two horizontal parallel rails. Main posts may be of 4 inches by 4 inches, in a long-lasting wood, placed 12 to 18 feet apart, and the rails may be 1 by 2 inch lattice. Post bottoms should be tarred or charred, and the upper portions and lattice should be painted several coats, usually white. Paint heavily where the lattice is nailed or screwed to the posts. If preferred, you may use two parallel lines of No. 9 or 11 galvanized wire on strong cedar posts. The two rails or wires should be 30 and 60 inches from the ground, respectively.

Remove the stake you put in at planting time and attach the main stem to the rails or wires, cutting it at the upper rail to 5 feet above the ground the following winter. If it does not reach the top rail or wire, cut it at the first rail and tie its uppermost branch, or "cane," to the wire or rail above to continue as the main stem. Working in winter, select two canes near each rail or wire and extend them right and left, tying them to the rail. Against each extended cane cut another near-by cane short, leaving only two buds—which we call a spur. The growth from the spur makes the renewal arm at next winter's pruning. All other branches you cut off close to the main stem; so, depending upon the age and size of the vine, you have a main stem with two or four arms spreading right and left, and two or four spurs close to them. During summer you rub off all shoots that start from the main stem; other than this you do nothing in the way of prun-

111

ing in summer, cutting only in winter. But you shorten each arm at your winter pruning, cutting away a part to leave only six or seven buds on each upper arm, four or five on each lower; as the vine ages you may leave a few more buds. From 35 to 45 buds remaining at pruning time is the total for the average established vine.

Repeat this pruning every winter, cutting away all growth but two or four canes and two or four spurs. Canes should be fastened to the wires or slats with tape, raffia, soft thick twine, or by twisting a pipecleaner around them here and there. The green shoots which develop from the buds will attach themselves with their own tendrils.

The main stem is not permitted to grow beyond the upper wire; but if you are training grapes over an arch, arbor, or pergola, you would let it grow as far as you want it, after which it is stopped by cutting its top. There may be occasions when you wish to develop a branch of permanent wood, which you do merely by preserving the most convenient of the canes. The large yellow-green Scuppernong muscadine grape is much used for this purpose in Virginia and the south. The usual training principle is to lead the main stem to the center of the top of the arbor and let eight arms grow from the end, radiating like wheel spokes.

Where you have a choice, the canes you preserve should be vigorous, stocky, with short distances between fat buds, and about the thickness of a lead pencil. The kind you get rid of are the long fast-growing ones, sometimes trailing 20 feet, with long intervals between buds.

Grapes are sometimes thinned in this way (left) to give you perfect bunches of large grapes (center) instead of mediocre bunches (right).

When bunches are overthick, a type of pruning is sometimes practiced. With long-pointed shears you snip away about one-quarter of the little grapes in each bunch; this enables perfect grapes to grow to their proper size, with no cracks due to crowding.

If you wish to reproduce a favorite vine, merely peg down onto the soil some of the arms, cover each with a spadeful or more of soil, and cut and dig up the rooted canes during your winter pruning. Plant these rooted layers in early spring. The Scuppernong muscadine variety is reproduced in this way.

Grapes are suitable for growing against a wall, preferably attached to wires fastened to brackets projecting 8 to 12 inches.

Some good grapes include:

Caco. Large, sweet, wine-red berries. Mid-season.

Catawba. Dark purple-red berries that keep well and are of extra quality. Use it south of Pennsylvania because of its long growing season. Late.

Concord. The leading dark blue grape. Large bunches of large berries. A mid-season variety that makes good grape juice and is hardy enough for the north.

Concord Seedless. Smaller than the above, with only small seeds, which you probably will not notice.

Delaware. Hardy for the north; good also for the south. Red mid-season variety.

Diamond. Good for the south. An early white grape.

Fredonia. An early blue-black type.

Golden Muscat. Small golden-yellow grapes have the aroma of the European muscat. Mid-season.

Niagara. Whitish-green grapes; mid-season and hardy.

Ontario. A good early white.

Portland. An early green-white variety of the highest quality.

Seneca. Early white. The tender skins are readily eaten. Keeps well.

Sheridan. An improved Concord, than which it is about a fortnight later. The blue-black grapes keep well.

Worden. Large clusters of blue-black berries. Early and hardy; good for New England.

If birds take more than a reasonable share, cover the vines with cheesecloth or enclose each perfect bunch in a grape bag.

Grapes wrapped in transparent bags:
protected against birds and wasps.

If you have room, plant a few mulberry bushes, which the birds may prefer to the grapes; they often do.

Phylloxera or vine-root louse, a serious pest of the grape in the middle and far west. It forms galls on the roots; sometimes kills the vine.

Grapes are attacked by the phylloxera or root louse in certain areas; in these particular localities grapes are usually grafted onto varieties that are resistant to these pests. Elsewhere, grapes are normally propagated from slips, which take very freely. Or they maye be reproduced by layering as noted on page 113.

Among other troubles, grapes are hosts to downy mildew and black rot, which shrivels the grapes into mummies. Since wasps and bees sometimes eat cracked fruit, cut off the bunches containing injured individuals and let them mature indoors; cut a long piece of cane with them and stand it in a Mason jar with its end in water.

If wasps are eating your grapes, choice bunches may be ripened indoors in water.

The grape rootworm is usually controlled by the arsenate of lead in the spray mixture. Grape leaf hoppers are sucking insects that make the leaves yellow, then brown; and they finally drop off. Spray with Black-leaf-40 (nicotine sulphate) mixed with soapy water.

SPRAY PROGRAM FOR GRAPES

In winter, with the vines dormant: Spray vines, posts, lattice, and the ground with a saturated solution of iron sulphate.

When the third leaf appears: Spray with bordo-mixture, adding 1½ tablespoons of lead arsenate to each gallon of dilution.

Just before the flowers open: Repeat the bordo-lead-arsenate.

When blossoms fall: Repeat the bordo-lead-arsenate.

Two weeks later: Repeat the bordo-lead-arsenate.

After the leaves have fallen: Again use the saturated solution of iron sulphate.

If Japanese beetles are in force in your locality and if they appear on your vines despite this program, use a rotenone spray in addition.

GUAVA

The guava may be planted only in southern California, the Gulf areas, and south from mid-Florida.

This is grown mostly in southern California and Florida; in the Gulf states it may be cut down by frost, to recover and bear fruit eighteen months later. Two types are popular—the 30-foot common type and the milder-flavored 20-foot Strawberry guava. They may be planted in any type of soil that drains well, but if the land is over-rich, much foliage with fewer and inferior fruits is produced. The common guava occupies a 30-foot circle; the Strawberry, about a 20-foot one. They need watering in dry weather, also mulching the first year. Pruning is largely unnecessary.

Seedlings or budded plants may be obtained, the superior

budded ones bearing in two years, the seedlings in three or four. Fruit matures during the summer, but the main supply is from August to October. The fruits, containing many small seeds like grape pips, vary greatly in shape, size, and color of the flesh; they furnish the well-known paste or jelly. Meaty kinds, possessing a sharp subacid flavor, may be eaten uncooked like a pear or as a dessert with cream. Acid varieties are used for cooking, either alone or with other fruits in jams, pies, preserves, and sweetmeats.

The Pineapple guava or feijoa, spreading in a 15-foot circle, is an allied shrub slightly less sensitive to cold, and may be grown in the Gulf states. The delicious fruit may be eaten out of hand or made into jellies, jams, and candies.

HAZELNUT, COBNUT, AND FILBERT

Tolerant of winter cold, American hazelnuts thrive in rich, well-drained land that is slightly acid. They are round, with thick shells, and the hazelnuts extend beyond the husks; Rush is an accepted variety. European hazelnuts or filberts are hardy from Washington, D. C., south and in the Pacific northwest; Barcelona and Italian Red are popular kinds. Filberts have a husk much longer than the nut. Cobnuts are similar, but angular in section, and are partly covered by their shucks.

Bushes are placed 10 feet apart. Pruning is best done after flowering, shortening strong branches to encourage the formation of spurs and taking out some of the older branches that are no longer producing nuts.

The nuts are gathered as soon as the husks are seen to be turning brown. Let them dry on the garage floor, when they may readily be removed from the husks.

Since excellent nuts may be found when gathering wild fruits in the autumn, there is little point in planting them in any but a large garden.

LOGANBERRY OR PHENOMENAL

This hybrid between a California wild blackberry and a red raspberry, trails like a dewberry and has enormous reddish-purple fruits which are good for canning and jelly-making. It grows on practically any type of soil, but not in the extreme north; zero temperatures usually kill it. Roots are produced where the tips of its long canes reach the ground and are used for planting, preferably in spring.

A good way to grow it is to fasten the canes to stout 6-foot stakes set 6 feet apart—like raspberries. Or you may install a 3-wire fence, the wires respectively 4, 5, and 6 feet above the ground. Parallel fences should be at least 7 feet apart, and the plants set 4 feet or more apart along the fence. Long canes are coiled around the top wire with an occasional tie; shorter ones are fastened along the lower wires. When planted closely, the canes are shortened so they tangle less with those of neighboring plants.

After bearing, the old canes are pruned to the ground, and the newly formed ones are fastened along the wires in their place.

LOQUAT

The loquat may be grown in gardens in the warmer belt across the country from California to Florida.

This attractive evergreen tree from China and Japan is a favorite for the home garden in Florida, the Gulf states, and California. Its 3-inch plumlike fruits, containing pips (it's a relative of the apple) are used raw for dessert or cooked in pies, jams, preserves, and jellies. It may grow 20 feet high and occupies a 20-foot circle.

Plants budded onto seedling stocks are preferable to seedlings. They will thrive in almost any soil that drains well. The trees like liberal fertilizing, but for the best fruit the flower clusters that appear in autumn should be thinned by nipping off some flowers at the end of the cluster. Ten days after the fruit colors in spring it will be ripe and may be gathered.

Pruning is best done after picking, to shape the tree, to remove inferior and dying branches, and to cut off the remains of the fruit clusters—which will induce new clusters to develop at the base of the old.

MANGO

Mango has about the same intolerance to cold as the more tender varieties of citrus, older trees bearing it better than the younger ones. Mid-Florida and south, and southern California are about the only areas where its growth is possible.

This tree from the tropics of Asia is generally grown only from mid-Florida south and in southern California. The juicy plumlike fruits are globular or elongated and weigh from a few ounces to several pounds; they have one large flat stone. Unripe fruits and inferior sorts often grown from seed are not at all pleasing, but good grafted varieties, fully ripe, are fragrant and delicious. So are the kernels good eating when removed from the stones and roasted. The mango is used as a dessert fruit; half-ripe fruits are cooked into preserves, jams, marmalade, and the well-known mango chutney of India.

Most of the abundant flowers of spring drop off, but the few that remain are usually sufficient to furnish a good crop. The large trees are not particular as to soil, provided it is well-drained, but they need watering in dry climates. They occupy a

35-foot circle; if untended they may grow 75 feet high, but are normally pruned to more moderate heights.

Consult your local nurseryman as to the best varieties to plant. Purchase budded or grafted trees, not seedlings.

MULBERRY

The chief reason for planting the mulberry in the home fruit garden is to feed the wild birds and take their attention from your cherries, grapes, raspberries, and everbearing strawberries. The trees make good shade for the poultry yard, and the hens enjoy the berries.

Normally the enormous blackberrylike fruits have little appeal, but you may plant named sorts: Monarch, which is white; Gorgeous, Trowbridge, and New American—all very hardy for the north; Downing for the mid-south; Townsend, Hicks, or Stubbs for the south. All these yield fair-quality fruit. Mulberries are just about the easiest fruit to gather: spread a sheet under the tree and then shake it, as you would a chokecherry.

Mulberries grow in any well-drained soil and need no attention other than pruning out dead branches. The sexes are sometimes on separate trees, so it is necessary to have one male for several females. Otherwise, pollination will not take place and fruits will not develop.

Should your son be interested in sericulture, or the production of silk by raising silkworms, mulberry leaves are the preferred diet of his pets.

Mulberries grow into trees with a 30-foot spread.

MUSKMELON or CANTALOUPE

These delicious fruits are not difficult to grow. Sow seeds in late April under hotkaps, or in the open when all danger of frost has passed, in hills or groups the size of a dinner plate and 5 feet apart each way. Use 8 to 10 seeds in each group. One ounce of seed will plant 80 hills, and each hill should yield 6 or more perfect melons 12 to 16 weeks after sowing. When the plants have developed their rough leaves, remove crowding plants and leave three per hill. From the time they make their appearance above

Growing muskmelons and watermelons. Left to right: fill a foot-deep hole with fortified soil mixture B, with one inch of standard planting mixture A on top. Press in a large flower pot to make a circular groove. Sow seeds and rub to cover. Press lightly with the shoe.

ground, keep the leaves dusty with ¾ per cent rotenone; see that the mixture you use contains no sulphur, or the plants may be injured.

The dusting controls cucumber beetles, which are a quarter of an inch long with three black stripes or six black spots, and squash bugs, which are brown and a half-inch long. Wilting leaves indicate borers. To get rid of them, slit the stem with a razor blade longitudinally just below the wilting, take out the worm, and cover the section of the stem with a spadeful of earth to induce the formation of roots at that point.

Good varieties include Honeydew, Honey-gold, Rockyford, all with green flesh; and the following orange-flesh kinds: **Bender's Surprise, Emerald Gem** and **Golden Delicious.**

NECTARINE

The nectarine is grown along the same lines as the peach (see below), has the same insect enemies, is slightly less resistant to cold, and has a rather smaller fruit. But it is even more delicious, richer, and more aromatic; it may be regarded as a peach with a smooth skin, with none of the fuzz of the peach. The nectarine makes an excellent flat-trained tree for growing against a wall in a small garden.

PEACH

One-year-old peach trees are good for planting in nearly every section where the winter temperature goes no lower than ten de-

Left: the nectarine is smooth, while peaches are fuzzy. Two good free-stone peaches: center, Elberta; right: Hale.

grees below zero, though they are not recommended for the extreme south. Spring is the preferred planting season, except in the mid-south states where either spring or fall is suitable. They give their first small crop the third year and should continue to yield for twenty years in the home garden. The usual practice is to put in one or more new trees every few years. Expect the trees each to cover a 20-foot circle. They prefer a medium loam, but will do quite well in sandy soil if well supplied with organic matter, plant foods, and moisture.

Propagation is carried out in summer by budding good varieties onto young trees grown from pits. Sometimes the stock used is the Damson plum, the resulting plants being preferred for clay land.

Pruning at first is designed to produce 3 or 4 frame branches and to develop an open center. Mature trees in the garden are heavily pruned in late winter to maintain vigor; and in spring dead and crossing branches are taken away. Fruit is gathered when ripe. If your tree is crowded with young fruit, better snip off some of it with pointed shears to give the remainder sufficient room.

Some popular varieties include:

Crawford early, Crawford late. Popular on the Pacific coast. Freestone.
Belle of Georgia. A late white-flesh freestone variety; juicy and of fine flavor. Advised for the Midwest and coastal areas.
Elberta. A hardy yellow freestone; mid-season; attractive and of excellent quality. Our most popular peach, good for the Midwest and the Pacific coast. It suffers little from late spring frosts. The fruit has a pleasing red cheek; it is usually ripe around September 15.

Golden Jubilee. A new early variety unequalled as a large yellow freestone. Ready around August 20.

Hale. A hardy and early yellow freestone, suitable for the north as well as the coastal sections of the Atlantic and Pacific. Large atttractive fruit of extra quality. Self-sterile, it needs another peach in the vicinity, while most others in this list are self-pollinating.

Hiley. An early dependable all-purpose variety for the Atlantic coastal area; white freestone.

Redhaven. Bright red before it is fully ripe. An early fine-flavored freestone that is self-pollinating and a prolific yielder. Ready around August 20.

Southaven. An early and hardy yellow-fleshed freestone.

SPRAY PROGRAM FOR PEACHES

For one or two trees, buy a ready-mixed spray at your seed or hardware store and use it as directed on the container. If you have a small orchard and prefer to mix your own, the following are good:

Late winter; tree is dormant. Spray with 1 pint lime-sulphur in 8 pints of water.

When the husks and old calyx rings are dropping off, the flowers having already fallen, use

> 5 tablespoons bordo-mixture powder
> 1¼   "   lead arsenate
> 2½   "   hydrated lime
> 1 teaspoon Black-leaf-40
> 1 gallon water

Repeat three weeks later.

Gum exudations and sawdust suggest borers at the base of the tree; dig them out with a wire. In early September remove the gum and make a ring of paradichlorobenzene on the ground two inches from the trunk. Cover with a half-inch of soil and mound the soil around the trunk above the topmost borer hole. Remove the mound three weeks later. Allow 1 ounce of the chemical for a 6-year-old tree, ½ ounce for younger trees.

Eggs of the oriental peach moth hatch into small pink worms within the fruit. Under routine spraying they should not appear, but, if they do, there is no satisfactory control.

PEANUT OR GOOBER

This is not a nut but a bean, borne by a plant of the clover family growing about a foot high; after its flowers are pollinated they find their way into the soil, where the pods mature their kernels underground. Preferring sandy soil, the peanut requires the same conditions as garden corn. Temperatures are too low and seasons too short in most areas north and west of Richmond, Virginia. Remove the outer shells without injuring the kernels, and sow the latter in drills 2½ feet apart and 1½ inches deep. Sow about three to the foot and thin to allow 8 inches between one plant and the next in the row.

Varieties include, among others:

Improved Spanish. Though small, this is fairly quick-growing and suitable for the northern edge of peanut territory.

California Long Red. Larger, but slower to mature. Plant it south of Washington, D. C., where the longer summers allow it to mature a heavy crop.

Goobers are dug with a fork when the foliage withers and may be placed on the garage floor to dry.

PEAR

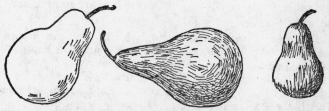

Three good pears. Left to right: Bartlett, the russet-skinned Bosc, the small and very sweet Seckel.

Pears grow on any good, well-drained, loamy soil, preferably one on the heavy side, where the temperature is moderate. Areas in the extreme northern states are often too cold, and they do not thrive in the humid heat of the south. Two-year-old trees are

Branches of a pear affected with fire blight must be promptly amputated with sterile tools.

recommended, and standards or dwarf types may be put in, the latter being most suitable for planting in the moderate-size garden. Keep dwarf trees 20 feet apart, standards 25 feet. Planting in spring is preferred, and they should begin to yield the second or third season after being set out.

Pears are invariably budded; the most popular host stocks are one-year seedling quince or French pear seedlings for some varieties; in California, Japanese pear seedlings. Dwarf trees are produced by budding suitable varieties on certain stocks of quince that have a dwarfing effect.

Pruning is mostly a matter of shaping the tree to an open, well-ventilated design, shortening the main stem at planting time, reducing the length of upright-growing branches, and removing crowding twigs. After the fruit has commenced to increase in size, long lower branches will need the support of props to keep the fruit off the ground; cut away a part of these longer branches when pruning in winter.

Pears are generally self-pollinating, but they produce better when other pears are in the vicinity. Here are some much-used varieties:

Anjou. Large yellow fruit ready in late fall; the pears have a red blush. A good pollinator, and hardy for the northern limits of pear culture. Resistant to fire blight, which is important.

Bartlett. Medium size yellow fruit with a reddish blush on the sunny side. Tender, juicy flesh with a musky aroma; ready in late summer. This is the leading commercial and canning pear, much grown in California. Picked the first week in September and ripe three weeks later.

Bosc. A long tapering fruit on a long stem is able to sway in heavy winds without dropping. The skin is rough, brownish-yellow, or russet-colored; flesh is tender, buttery, very juicy, and sweet. A slow-growing but very productive tree. You pick around September 25, and the fruit is ready to eat from October to December. A good pollinating sort for other kinds. A favorite in California gardens and elsewhere.

Clapp's Favorite. Resembles Bartlett; the skin is yellow with brown dots. Early, juicy, and sweet. Usually ready to gather in late August, and to eat shortly after.

Dana's Hovey. Fruit is ready in December.

Diel. Ready from November to January. Specially fine.

Duchess (Angoulème). Ready from October to November. A self-pollinating sort, but producing a better crop if other pears are near by.

Easter. Ready December to February.

Kieffer. Not held in such high esteem as others by many growers, though it resists the fire blight and is one of the recognized types for lighter land. Suitable for the southern limits of pear culture.

Seckel. Small juicy pears that are very sweet. Pick them in September, and they are ready to eat a month later. Seckel does not often take blight. It is a good pollinator and is resistant to cold.

Winter Nelis. December to January is the period in which it becomes ready to eat.

Gather pears when a few begin to fall by lifting them, when the stem will part from the branch; they are not pulled. Except the very early sorts, pears ripen some time after picking them.

Of the above varieties, these are recommended as standards:

Bartlett, Seckel

Best as dwarfs:

Diel, Easter

Good both as standards and dwarfs:

Clapp's Favorite, Dana's Hovey

The following also are good as dwarfs when they have been "double-worked," which means that any other good variety is budded onto quince and grown for one year; the wanted sort is then budded onto the resulting plant:

Bosc, Winter Nelis

If young pears are crowded, clip off some to allow room for the remainder.

Pears are attacked by San José scale, codling moth, borers, and pear psylla. The spray program may be the same as for apples (see page 89). They are also subject to fire blight, a bacterial disease that enters mostly through insect punctures; the blackened leaves appear to have been near a burning building. Immediate surgery is the only remedy: remove and burn the branch, and disinfect the stub with 1 part mercury cyanide and 1 part mercury bichloride in 500 parts of water. Carry a can of this with you when you're pruning, swab your saw with it, and dip your shears in it between each cut. Over-fertilized trees are more likely to take fire blight than those growing normally; those too severely pruned are also likely to be affected by the disease. As the trees grow older they acquire a partial immunity to it.

Cankers, which are boils or other excrescences on the trunk or stems, should be cut away and the sore disinfected.

A few pears on the ground tell you that it is now time to pick, even if the variety is one that ripens in storage months later.

PECAN

A variety of hickory, this nut is hardy enough to stand the climate of Long Island, Iowa, and Indiana, but mostly only the hard-shell sorts. The more popular paper-shell pecans are grown from Richmond, Virginia, south and west to Texas and southern California; some even in southern New Jersey.

The trees are not exacting in their soil requirements providing the land is well-drained. They may attain a height of 125 feet in their life span of eighty or more years and eventually cover a circle of ground 55 feet in diameter.

In commercial practice the nuts are soaked in water for a day and kept moist for several days longer—they crack more readily. The kernels are then allowed to dry.

Pecans are occasionally subject to scab, for which bordo-mixture is used. Also young plants may be attacked by the pecan case-bearer, for which a spray of 1 pound arsenate of lead in 20 gallons of water is recommended.

PERSIMMON

Persimmons may be grown from Kentucky south. Good varieties are delicious when fully ripe.

There are two types of persimmon: the native American tree, which may be found growing wild from Connecticut to Kansas and the Gulf, often reaching 75 feet or more; and the smaller oriental types, which mature at half the height and are sensitive to cold, mostly grown south of Pennsylvania on the coast, south of Kentucky inland. Customary pruning methods keep these trees much dwarfer, and they are seldom met higher than 30 feet. Some of the Japanese kinds are normally of dwarf stature and are pruned to keep them at 6 feet or so. Persimmons will grow on almost any well-drained soil; they need adequate moisture, however. The dwarfer types occupy a circle 20 feet in diameter.

Persimmons have a remarkable sex life. Occasionally a tree will have perfect flowers, both stamens and pistil in the same blossom, and will be self-pollinating. More often one tree will be entirely male and another entirely female; and from one year to another the sex may change; this year a tree could be male, next year female. So it is important that groups and not single trees be planted. One known to be male at the time is set with from four to six known to be female at the moment. Occasionally, however, a tree will set perfect fruits except that they contain no seeds.

Properly grown nursery plants will be furnished balled and burlapped; they will have been root-pruned to sever the taproot which invariably seeks lower levels. Heavy watering is necessary until the persimmons are established, and at planting time the top should be severely cut back to offset the loss of the taproot.

Good named varieties are obtainable at local nurseries, early, mid-season, and late. The fruits are yellow, orange, or red. Persimmons are astringent to the point of being inedible when immature; but good kinds are delicious when they are ripe, and they are at their best when matured to a soft condition in storage. They bruise so easily that their gathering and handling must be done with great care, and their packing and shipping are not easy.

Persimmons are attacked by white fly, mealy bug, and various scales, for all of which a miscible-oil spray is used. The flatheaded borer also gives trouble; when found, cut or dig it out and use a good tree paint at the site of the injury.

PINEAPPLE

This tropical fruit can decorate the home garden in the extreme south. The crown of leaves above the fruit may be planted, but normally suckers from the base of the plant are quicker. Portions of the stem will also root. Set these cuttings just deep enough to stay upright, 24 to 36 inches apart in any well-drained garden soil; but rotate them to a different part of the garden to escape the nematodes which often appear and multiply in long-established rows. The shallowest scuffle-hoeing and flat-tined raking are necessary, for the roots are close to the surface.

Pineapples may be grown in the extreme south. Change their location when you plant new cuttings, for eelworms, or nematodes, often multiply in the soil where they are grown.

A mixture of 8 parts fine dusting sulphur and 2 parts nicotine sulphate powder is dowsed over the plants if red spider gives trouble or mealy bug attacks the base of the plants.

PISTACHIO

Native to the Near East, the pistachio is now grown in Texas and southern California. As home-garden subjects a group of them may be planted as far north as Washington, D. C., with a fair chance of success. They reach about 20 feet in height, need well-drained soil, and are slow-growing. The nuts are in loose clusters inside a leathery sheath, and their kernels are green, as will be noted in the well-liked pistachio ice cream. Pistachio trees spread in a circle about 20 feet across.

PLUM

Plums do best on rather heavy clay soils, but will give good results almost anywhere, for varieties may be selected to suit almost every climate. Most are not good self-pollinators, requiring other plum trees near by. Two-year-old saplings, 6 or 7 feet high, are

Types of plums. Left to right: Burbank, prune, lombard, damson.

best to plant, and they should begin to bear in three years. They occupy a circle 20 feet in diameter.

Pruning is aimed at producing a bowl-shaped tree with the development of four or five scaffold branches, after which it is mostly a matter of cutting out superfluous, broken, or diseased branches late every winter. Summer pruning is desirable also to retain the open character of the tree.

Plums are of three types. The European includes prunes, damsons, bullaces, and most of the well-known dessert and culinary kinds. Damsons are small and bullaces very small. Prunes have very firm flesh with much sugar, which becomes evident when they are dried. European kinds are mostly grown in the central parts of the plum-growing region. The second group are the Japanese, grown south of the European sorts, with some important exceptions. The third are developed from American wild types and are often used for both the plains region and the south. Like peaches some are clingstone and some are freestone.

Since certain varieties do best in a particular locality, be guided by your local nurseryman and county agent. Those recommended to you may be in the following list:

Abundance. A Japanese red variety with yellow flesh. Grown in New England, the Hudson Valley, and the Great Lakes region. Suitable also for southern planting. A very sweet early kind, good for cooking.

Bradshaw. A reliable variety of domestic origin.

Burbank. Derived from Japanese varieties. Large reddish-purple fruit, ripening around August 25. Suitable for New England, the valley of the Hudson River, the Great Lakes region; and much planted on the Pacific coast. Good for cooking.

Chabot. Developed from the Japanese and suitable for southern planting.

Forest Garden. A fairly recent hybrid derived from native sorts and suitable for southern planting. A good, late, red cooking variety.

Green Gage or Bavay. A European plum, grown in New England, the Hudson Valley, and the region of the Great Lakes. Green when ripe.

Italian Prune. A large late purplish-blue-black European variety. Suitable for New England, the Hudson Valley, and California. Good for both dessert and cooking.

Kelsey. A Japanese hybrid that is suitable for southern planting and for the Pacific coast. A green dessert kind.

Lombard. A European sort grown in New England, the valley of the Hudson River, and the Great Lakes.

Miner. A fairly recent hybrid from American sorts. Suitable for southern planting. A late, red cooking sort.

Red June. A red variety of Japanese origin. A good cooking early sort.

Reine Claude. A good European self-pollinating sort grown in New England, the Hudson Valley, the Great Lakes area, and the Pacific coast. Green when ripe.

Satsuma. Japanese; recommended for southern planting. A good red cooking variety.

Shropshire Damson. European; produces clusters of small purple fruit; an ideal home-garden sort for jams, jellies, and preserves. Grows in New England, the Hudson Valley, and the Great Lakes region. A late sort.

Stanley. European kind, giving splendid large dark blue-purple sweet prunes. Mid-season, the fruit is ripe around September 20.

Washington. Of U. S. origin and suitable for New England, the valley of the Hudson River, and the Great Lakes. A yellow dessert variety; mid-season.

Wayland. A fairly recent American hybrid suitable for the south.

Wild Goose. Another of the newer American hybrids adapted to southern conditions. Red fruits are ripe early. Culinary.

You can obtain multi-variety plums or you can bud them yourself with early, mid-season, and late sorts on one tree; or have a single tree carrying an apricot, a plum, and a peach.

Plums are attacked by the plum curculio and brown rot. If during winter you observe mysterious knotty swellings, better prune away and burn the affected branches, for the trouble is probably black knot, a fungus disease to which plums are subject. Otherwise, follow the spray program for cherry (see page 98).

POMEGRANATE

A long-lived, handsome, and vigorous 20-foot evergreen shrub, with waxy pink flowers and bearing the not-too-well-known "apple with many seeds." Not an apple, but something like a large dull orange on the outside, 3 to 5 inches in diameter and filled with seeds, each surrounded by juicy pink or red pulp. It prefers moist, well-drained inland soils and will thrive where the thermometer goes no lower than 15° above zero. Pomegranate occupies a circle 15 feet in diameter.

Pruning is designed to develop a bushlike plant by shortening the leader at 2 feet above ground, developing 3 to 5 frame limbs, which are shortened a little more than half their length the second season to insure fruit the fourth year. Dead wood and interfering branches are removed, and suckers are ruthlessly cut out below the soil surface.

The fruits, which follow showy orange-red flowers, are gathered before they are quite ripe to avoid splitting. Storage for two months in a cool building improves their quality. They are eaten out of hand, or the juice is used in the preparation of drinks and syrup: grenadine is made from pomegranate juice.

QUINCE

The large yellow pearlike fruits are useless until they are cooked, but they are delicious in jellies and jams, especially when

Left: pomegranate, from the juice of which grenadine is made. Right: quince, good for jams and jellies.

combined with apples and pears. Reaching 20 feet high, the trees occupy a 15-foot circle. Plant in fairly heavy, moist, but well-drained soil. Two-year-old, 5-to-6-foot whips are mostly used, preferably those produced from layers or cuttings rather than by budding.

Pruning in late winter is a matter of removing surplus interior branches to develop an open top and to shorten the branches to develop shoots; at the tips of these shoots a single flower appears. Cultivation must be shallow, for the feeding roots are close to the surface. Propagation is readily done by rooting cuttings.

Perhaps the most-used varieties are:

Meech. Resistant to blight and producing large pear-shaped golden-yellow fruits.

Orange. Excellent for preserving; has deep orange skin and tender flesh. An early variety that is good for northern states.

The quince has many enemies; it is subject to fire blight like pears (see page 126); immediate amputation of the affected branches is necessary. Since borers may attack, protect against them by wrapping the stems of young trees with burlap and painting older ones with whitewash containing 10 per cent lime-sulphur. Cut and pry up sections of discolored bark; if borer tunnels are found, remove each grub with a wire. Codling moth and curculio may be controlled by spraying with 2 ounces arsenate of lead in 3 gallons of water, applied when the petals fall and repeated three weeks later.

RASPBERRY

Raspberries amply repay high cultivation. Plant red varieties in the temperature belt where the wild raspberry grows—from Virginia to Alaska. Black raspberries are less hardy, their northern limit being the Great Lakes. Place them in rows 6 feet apart and 6 feet from each other. Plant red sorts spring or fall, blackcap varieties in spring only. Drive in strong 6-foot stakes for each plant; young branches which appear during the season may be tied to them to keep them off the ground.

In the usual one-crop varieties, stems or canes that develop this

Left: black, purple, and yellow raspberries root at their branch tips without your help. Center: washed root of a red raspberry; take 4-inch cuttings from ¼ to ¾ inch-thick roots. Right: plant them 2 inches deep, in rich soil.

year produce berries the next; when they have yielded their berries they are pruned away down to the ground. Everbearing or two-crop kinds give berries in September on their canes that grew this year, with a second crop in the following July, when they die. The easiest course is to prune away only dead canes of everbearing varieties as soon as they are seen to be dry.

Two-year-old transplanted stock is often available, but one-year-old plants are almost as good. They do best in a rather heavy soil. Some reliable varieties follow:

Bristol. A heavy-yielding superior blackcap kind. Early.

Chief. A mid-season red variety that yields generously.

Columbian. A reliable purple variety that makes good jam.

Cumberland. A heavy-yielding, mid-season, blackcap kind. Good.

Cuthbert. A popular mid-season variety, but one that is subject to mosaic disease; get from your supplier an assurance that his plants have been examined from time to time to keep out this trouble. Red.

Indian Summer. Perhaps the best everbearing red sort. Hardy and vigorous, giving a good crop in July and another equally good one in September and October.

Latham. A full crop of high-quality red berries usually around July 10. Large, firm, and sweet. The leading one-crop variety.

Newburgh. Another good red berry. Early.

Potomac. An improved Cumberland, which is an older blackcap sort.

Sodus. A purple fruit, excellent for jam-making. Perhaps the best variety in this class. Early.

St. Regis or Ranere. Delicious crimson berries. An everbearing or two-crop kind.

Sunrise. A fine red variety that bears early.

Taylor. Another good early red.

Yellow Queen. Unusual amber-colored berry of excellent eating quality.

Blackcaps or thimbleberries, purple and yellow raspberries take root at the tips of their branches where they arch over and touch the ground; these can be cut off and planted elsewhere. Red raspberries produce suckers near their parents: those needed to sell or plant elsewhere may be saved; others should be destroyed. It is a good plan to keep your raspberry patch only a few years; then plant another one elsewhere; when this is bearing destroy the old. This is because troubles are likely to multiply through the years.

If pale green caterpillars with white spiny tubercules of the raspberry saw fly appear, spray or dust with ¾ per cent rotenone.

Wilting leaves, progressing from above downward, suggest the raspberry cane borer. Prune below the damage and, if its hole is in the center of the stub, prune again lower down until you come to the solid stem. Burn the prunings.

Dig up and destroy sickly and wiry plants with the beginnings of an orange color on the under side of the leaves, those with yellow leaves and mummied berries, and those with knots or swellings near the ground. Exchange the soil in which they grew.

In hot weather, drying of the plants suggests red spider. If these minute creatures are found, spray with a dilution of Black-leaf-40.

If birds raid your patch, cover the plants with cheesecloth or plant mulberries (see page 119).

Mosaic is a very fatal disease thought to be caused by a virus carried from one plant to another by insects, aphids especially; so kill aphis, as soon as they are seen, with Black-leaf-40. Every part of a diseased plant should be dug up and burned. It is usually dwarfer than its companions, sickly, stunted, with crowding branches and mottled markings of light and medium green on the leaves. Exchange all surrounding soil. It is a good plan to grow red and black raspberries as far apart as your space allows, since the reds are carriers of mosaic but are little injured by it, while the blackcaps take it readily from them and are quickly injured.

Crown gall causes a hard, woody knot on the canes at the ground level: dig up and burn the plant and exchange the soil.

Gray patches on the canes of blackcaps are usually due to anthracnose. The bordo-mixture in the spray program below should control it. Prune away and burn old fruiting canes as soon as the crop is gathered.

SPRAY PROGRAM FOR RASPBERRIES

When new shoots are 6 inches high, spray with bordo-mixture, adding 1 half pint of molasses to each 3 gallons. Repeat (1) when flower buds have formed but are not yet open, (2) after the flowers have fallen, and (3) after autumn pruning. If beetles or grubs are seen, add 1½ tablespoons of arsenate of lead to each gallon of the solution.

RHUBARB

Propagating rhubarb. Cut an old root or crown with a sharp spade. Pieces, which must be complete with leaf buds and roots, are planted.

Plant the roots 3 feet apart and 3 inches deep in well-enriched land. Remove flower buds if they appear. You may also grow rhubarb from seed if you have the patience. Sow in spring in drills a foot apart, thin to 6 inches, and plant out the following spring. Look for 1000 roots from 1 ounce of seed.

For winter forcing or for growing rhubarb out of season, large roots can be dug up; they may be grown in boxes or half-barrels

*Don't cook and eat the leafy portion
of rhubarb. It is poisonous.*

of soil in a basement. The small amount of light admitted by the average window is sufficient; long thin and sweet stalks will grow towards it.

Two good varieties are:

Victoria.   An old-time reliable and productive variety.
McDonald.   Originating in Canada and exceptionally hardy; thick, sturdy, deep crimson stalks are abundant; tender and delicious.

It is well to remember that, although the stalks of rhubarb are health-giving, the green leaves are poisonous. So never cook and serve them as spinach.

STRAWBERRY

Developing a pot-grown strawberry plant. Center: a strawberry set correctly. Right: incorrect setting—too shallow and too deep.

Rich soil, kept firm and with a plentiful supply of moisture, is desirable; a sandy loam is preferable. It should be pH 5.5 or over. If it is below this, limestone dusted on the surface around the plants will be helpful. Space the plants 12 inches apart in rows 2 feet from each other for the hill system; set them 24 inches apart in rows 3 feet apart for the matted-row system.

Strawberries vary in shape and size. Among the easiest of fruits to manage, provided you keep them free of weeds.

It is a good plan to snip off some of the flowers the first year so that the young plants will not exhaust themselves. Keep the rows well weeded at all times, and your scuffle-hoeing must be very shallow, because the feeding roots are all close to the surface. Whiten the soil around them with 5–10–5 fertilizer in September and April. Spread some twigs on the soil around the plants, and on the twigs a 3-inch mulch of straw, pine needles, leaves, or salt hay over the plants and soil, after the land freezes in the fall; this you remove from on top of the plants in April and from the adjacent soil after fruiting.

Look up the section in Chapter 8 headed "Strawberry Runners." Daughter plants are produced around the parents, and as care of the bed develops into routine, it is usual to retain those daughters that are 8 inches apart in what is called the matter-row system, but to eliminate all the runners in the hill system, restricting the original clump to each hill. In early autumn or spring, plant new rows with the daughters and discard the oldest rows. When the daughters are being retained, the connecting runner between them is cut as soon as the plantlet farthest from the parent has four leaves.

If your garden is very small, strawberries may be grown peeping from holes in a special barrel or a strawberry-pot, as shown in Chapter 1.

Strawberry yield should average rather less than a quart from each large plant; in one crop for early, mid-season, and late varieties; the accumulation of pickings in the case of everbearing kinds through the summer will be approximately the same. Following are good varieties:

SPRING-BEARING STRAWBERRIES

These yield one large crop and then are finished until next year.

Early

* Dorsett. Vigorous variety with large berries. Self-pollinating.

Fairfax. A favorite for quality and productiveness; large, firm, superior, and very sweet berries. Plant it north from Missouri.

Pathfinder. Resistant to the red-stele root rot.

Premier (Howard 17). Produces an abundance of medium-size slightly acid fruit, flame-colored. Has a long bearing season; does well north or south.

Mid-season

* Catskill. Extremely large, irregular, round-conical berries. Heavy cropper; sub-acid. Grow it north from Richmond, Virginia.

Late

Big Joe. Very productive, with large berries, and one of the popular mildly acid sorts. A leading variety; good for the northern states.

Chesapeake. Extra-large berries, round-conical to short wedge-shape; bright crimson. Good for cold climates.

Fairpeake. Medium-large, mildly acid berries, borne in heavy quantity.

Red Star. Large solid berry, red clear through. Slightly acid and of excellent quality. Very late.

* Sparkle. High-quality, medium-size berries that are good for freezing. Vigorous, producing runners freely, and an excellent cropper; resistant to the red-stele root rot.

Temple. Very productive; berries medium to large. Medium red.

EVERBEARING KINDS

The following produce flowers and berries sparingly all year. Some gardeners keep the flowers pinched off until August 1 to build up reserve strength in the plant for a fair crop of autumn

* Varieties commonly used for deep-freezing.

fruit. They also find it profitable to plant a new bed every year, discarding two-year-old plants.

Gem. Produces berries of medium size and full sub-acid flavor all season.

Mastodon. A large round-conical berry, dark scarlet-red, mildly acid, and of fair quality.

Streamliner. A sensational new variety. Very sweet and jumbo in size. Normally bears from August to October, plus a good spring crop.

Wayzata or Rockhill. Produces few runners or none at all, the plant being propagated by separating the two or three clumps it develops. Round-conic, rich red berries, slightly acid and of excellent quality. Good for the north and New England, where strawberries grow especially well.

ALPINE STRAWBERRIES

These may be grown in the flower garden, for they are charming and produce all summer. Berries are sweet, but small; quite similar to our wild strawberry. They are readily grown from seeds.

Ordinary types of strawberries also may be grown amid your flowers if you are pressed for space; both they and the alpines are an effective edging for the perennial border.

STRAWBERRY PROBLEMS

The plants may be attacked by the strawberry weevil, which lays its egg in the bud, causing the bud to drop. Standard control is dusting with 5 parts fine powdered sulphur and 1 part arsenate of lead. This also will control the small leaf-rolling caterpillar. Thorough washing of the berries in running water before serving is important after using poison.

It is a good idea to purchase several varieties and not one only. The reason is that some strawberries, and in some areas, have flowers with poorly developed stamens; termed "pistillate," these sorts are of little use as pollinators, and if your planting were confined to one such variety your crop would most likely be very small.

WATERMELON

Watermelons are grown from seeds and are as easy as pumpkins or squash. They are recommended only if you have plenty of room, for they trail some distance. After mid-May sow about 8 seeds to a hill or group and have the hills 8 feet apart, thinning to 3 plants to a hill. One ounce of seeds will plant about 35 hills, and each hill should yield 3 to 5 watermelons in 12 or 13 weeks after sowing.

Interesting varieties include:

Dixie Queen. Oval.
Honey Cream. A yellow-flesh sort.
Kleckley Sweets. Long type.
Tom Watson. Long.
Citron. Globular variety, speckled in two shades of green like a tabby cat. Used for making the old-time marrow jam: a syrup is compounded and boiled up with assorted spices, and the citron sections are boiled in the syrup. Rind of ordinary watermelons is also prepared as a sweetmeat along similar lines.

Pests may be controlled as recommended under muskmelon (see page 120).

ADDITIONAL INFORMATION

Obtain all the bulletins you can from the U. S. Department of Agriculture and your State experiment stations. Nursery catalogues are also useful, especially for the varieties most suitable for your locality.

BOOK V

Landscaping

Index

CHAPTER 1

Fixed Rules Are Few

*"This rule in gardening ne'er forget,
To sow dry and set wet."*
JOHN RAY, English Proverbs.

IT IS IMPORTANT that you use shrubs and trees likely to grow in your part of the country. This book will help you and you will also get information by reading catalogues issued by nurserymen in your locality, and by inviting suggestions from them when you order. Your State agricultural college will doubtless send you on request bulletins along these lines, and your county agent is ready to assist you. The garden editors of your local newspapers will be other sources of information.

RULE NO. 1 is: *Use varieties that will thrive.*

RULE NO. 2 is: *Purchase plants from a reliable source.* There is much misinformation around us. If your eye catches an attractive little evergreen by the roadside and you ask its name, you may be told it is a dwarf arborvitae. "How tall does it grow?" you inquire. The reply you may get is "Not much taller than it is now, but it will fill out." Fifteen years later your shrub has developed into a tree, maybe as high as your home, and is still growing. A skilled nurseryman might have advised you to plant a Ware arborvitae, which grows no higher than 8 feet, while the cheaper Western arborvitae doesn't stop growing much short of 60 feet.

Your nurseryman, too, will prune the roots of his plants from time to time, which means that the one you buy from him will establish itself quicker. A corollary to Rule No. 2 is: don't buy the cheapest; you may live with your plants for the rest of your life, so buy the best.

1

RULE No. 3 is: *Make your planting look natural.*

It is difficult to improve upon nature. If you plant a shrubbery or wood lot you usually make it appear to have developed without your assistance, avoiding straight lines, regular geometric curves, and uniform distances between plants. Your curves will be bold; the rock garden will be made to resemble a rocky slope, a natural moraine deposited in ages past, or a weather-worn cliff. Your pond garden will appear to be the product of time; your perennial border will have the appearance of happenstance rather than a thought-out design.

On the other hand, you may prefer, and circumstances may call for, a formal design: trees and shrubs in straight lines an equal distance apart; flower beds in perfect rectangles, ovals or circles; the pool neatly enclosed in brick, concrete or finished stone. So be it. A combination may be desirable, and there is much charm in a mixed design, combining the formal with the informal—an artificial rose garden, a rectangular cutting garden, or vegetable patch, surrounded by informal planting.

RULE No. 4 is: *Keep the center open.* Usually this means that the chief feature of your property will be a pond or an area of grass turf surrounded by shrubs and flowers.

RULE No. 5 is: *Plant in masses.* Hesitate to have one each of many kinds of shrubs and flowers; too complete a mixture has an amateur look. An exception is with specimen trees planted on a large expanse of lawn: a flowering cherry here, a horse chestnut there, a clump of birches elsewhere.

RULE No. 6 is: *Avoid crowding.* Plant for maximum effectiveness some years from now. In the meanwhile, annual flowers will give a filled look.

RULE No. 7 is: *Don't hide dwarf subjects behind taller ones.*

RULE No. 8 is: *Observe the plants' requirements.* Refrain from mixing acid-loving with neutral-soil subjects, shade-tolerant with sun-loving ones, moist-land with dry-land kinds.

RULE No. 9 is: *Display good taste and exercise restraint.*

CHAPTER 2

Plans for the Small, Medium or Large Property

"Believe one who knows: you will find something more in woods than in books. Trees and stones will teach you that which you can never learn from masters. ST. BERNARD OF CLAIRVAUX, Epistles.

ONE WAY TO START landscaping is to hire an architect, who will prepare plans for you and supervise their carrying out. The larger the area the more you need him. The smaller the area the more readily can you be your own designer. This book is intended to help you who have a moderate-sized plot and wish to think through your own problems without the assistance of an architect.

The first step is to make a plan of the property as it is at the moment, showing distances. You may get some measurements to start with from your deed. If the area is fairly large, the grades severe or complicated, if you have muddy spots, water that needs draining away, hollows to be filled in, or hills to be leveled, you had best work on a plan of the area prepared by a surveyor showing distances and designating slopes by contour lines. To make your own starting plan, use a tape measure or pace the area, allowing 120 paces for each 100 yards, which is approximately accurate for an average-height adult walking briskly.

Obtain some large sheets of square-ruled paper. Let each square represent one foot. On this paper transfer the plan of your property. The symbols often used by architects to indicate various landscape subjects are shown on page viii.

The second step is to enter on your plan the features you propose to retain: some large trees or rocks, perhaps. Next, enter the

3

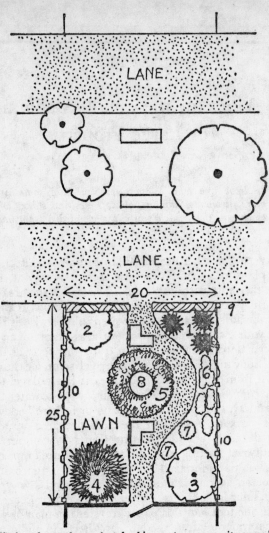

Small city plot 20 by 25 feet backing onto community-owned center park. (1) Mugho pine. (2) Forsythia. (3) Nettletree. (4) White fir. (5) English ivy. (6) Barberry. (7) Ninebark. (8) Statue of St. Fiacre, patron saint of gardening. (9) Privet hedge. Note benches against center.

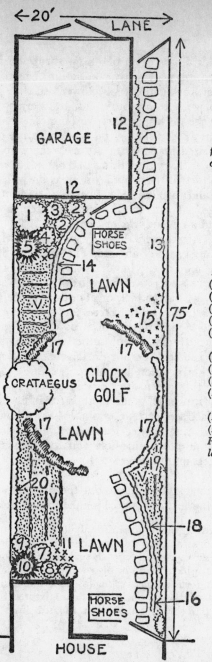

Modest city backyard, fenced, with garage opening onto a lane.

(1) Dogwood.
(2) Forsythia.
(3) Rose of Sharon.
(4) Lilac.
(5) Mugho pine.
(6) Madonna lilies.
(7) Spiraea.
(8) Snowberry.
(9) Cranberry bush.
(10) Colorado spruce.
(11) Regal lilies.
(12) Wisterias.
(13) Red salvias.
(14) Tulips; marigolds planted over them in spring.
(15) Crocus dibbled in turf.
(16) Lilies-of-the-valley.
(17) Barberries.
(18) Daffodils; petunias planted over them in spring.
(19) Snapdragons.
(20) Zinnias. (V) Vegetables. Path of steppingstones is in lawn.

things you wish to add: foundation planting, shrub borders, shade trees, patio garden, play area, lily pool, tennis court, rose garden, perennial border, rock garden, and flower beds.

The third step is to work from your plan, transferring the features to the land. Do the work speedily if you prefer, and complete it promptly; or carry it out slowly and economically.

An average moderate-sized house lot measures perhaps 40 feet in width by 100 feet in depth, or something like one tenth of an acre. All we have room for will be some lawn areas on which to place garden furniture and to picnic, shrubbery to screen much of the neighbor's garage, a flower bed, vegetable patch, a bird bath, feeding station and a nesting box or two.

Many suburban properties have a frontage of 50 feet with a depth of 125 feet, or one seventh of an acre. The increased space can mean more flowers, more of the important vegetables, and a play area, which may serve also as a drying yard.

With a deeper lot, say 55 by 150 feet, or about one fifth of an acre, more can be done: a few dwarf fruit trees and some bramble fruits, a patio garden, rock garden, perennial border, clock golf or horseshoes on the lawn, frames, a tool house.

Graduating to 70 by 200 feet, or one-third acre, a lily pool, sundial, barbecue stove, herb garden, badminton, croquet, roque, volleyball, or a golf putting green are possible on the lawn. A narrow swimming pool or a small greenhouse is feasible.

With an acre, larger facilities become available—lawn bowling among others, the green being flooded for skating in the winter. With several acres an interesting nine-hole golf feature may be considered, with three tees and three greens for nine holes of golf on about eight acres.

Giving rein to your imagination in all but the smallest areas, see which of the following features you can make room for:

Trees and Shrubs. Trees on the boulevard, individuals or groups on the lawn. Two or more oaks or elms fronting the house, perhaps, to shield against the hottest summer sun. Forget these, however, if you are in a part of the country in which storms or high winds are frequent or if your soil is always moist, for it encourages shallow roots and increases the storm hazard. Shrubs—evergreen, deciduous, or a mixture of both —for foundation planting, in shrub borders, or in isolated shrub beds.

6

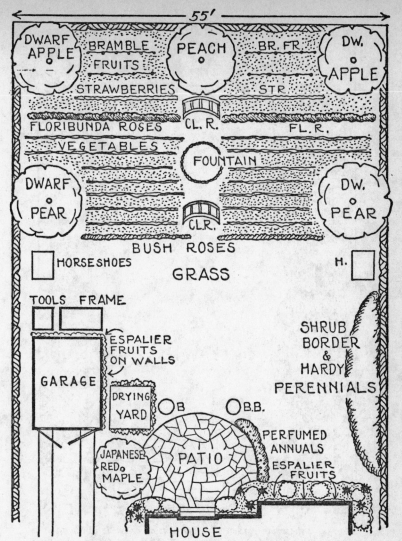

Proposed garden 55 by 70 feet. Bird bath (BB) and feeding station (B) are near patio. Bush roses divide grass from vegetables. Floribunda roses separate vegetables from fruits. Path goes under two arches carrying climbing roses. Espalier fruits are on walls of garage and house. It will be necessary to construct a strong wooden cover for frame to put in place while pitching horseshoes.

7

Plan for a suburban garden 60 by 40 feet; an example of open-center design. (*1*) Bird bath. (*1a*) Sundial. (*1b*) Bird-feeding station. (*2*) Koster spruce. (*3*) Chinese juniper. (*4*) Pfitzer's juniper. (*5*) Golden arborvitae. (*6*) Andorra juniper. (*7*) Small-leaved cotoneaster. (*8*) Ghent azalea. (*9*) Flame azalea. (*10*) Azalea hinodegiri. (*11*) Flowering quince. (*12*) Dogwood. (*13*) Maythorn. (*14*) Cork-bark burning bush. (*15*) Forsythia. (*16*) Rose of Sharon. (*17*) Blue hydrangea. (*18*) Beauty bush. (*19*) Amur privet. (*20*) Japan flowering cherry. (*21*) Lilac. (*22*) Wisteria on building.

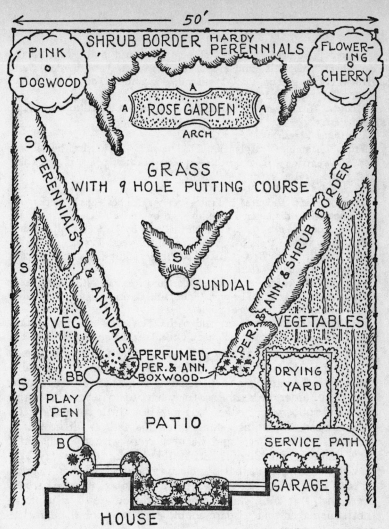

Garden on the outskirts of town measuring 50 by 60 feet, featuring a pair of semi-allées; viewpoint is on patio; accents are a dogwood and flowering cherry. Property is fenced, with shrub border (S) on left, shrubs and perennials at rear. Along right fence is a clipped hedge. Rose garden is entered under four arches (A); allées are bounded by flowers and shrubs (S). Feeding station (B) is at patio near house; bird bath (BB) is at patio corner. Foundation planting between rear steps; deciduous shrubs in rear of garage. Near patio are boxwood and perfumed perennials.

Flowers. Borders and beds of perennials and bulbs, of annuals. Rose beds, rose walks and arches. Rock garden. Patio garden. Fern garden. Cactus garden. Pool. Waterfall. Bog garden. Fountain. Cutting garden. Dry-wall garden.

Hedges. Evergreen, deciduous, or flowering. A fence to discourage trespassers.

Climbing Vines.

Fruit. Brambles—raspberries, blackberries, blueberries, boysenberries. Strawberries. Orchard fruits—apples, peaches, pears, plums, cherries, grapes.

Vegetables and Herbs.

Lawn Games. (Figures indicate necessary dimensions.) Clock golf, circle 20 feet in diameter. Horseshoes, 50 by 10 feet. Badminton, 44 by 30 feet. Roque, 60 by 30 feet. Volleyball, 80 by 50 feet. Golf putting green, 5000 square feet. Basketball, 104 by 68 feet. Tennis, 120 by 65 feet. Croquet, 105 by 84 feet. Lawn bowling, 126 by 126 feet; if flooded for curling, 135 by 135 feet.

Attractive Features. Arches, pergolas, and rose fans. Bird bath, feeders and nesting boxes. Flagpole. Fountain. Gazing globe. Picnic area and barbecue stove. Statue. Sundial.

Utility Features. Driveway and paths. Play area and drying yard. Tool house or potting shed. Frames. Greenhouse. Watering system.

Delete from the foregoing lists the features which you do not want or for which you have too little room. You may have to dispense with the cutting garden, deciding to gather your cut bloom from your borders or beds. Roses may have to go in your perennial border, shrubbery, or hedges. You may have little space for trees.

Fruit needs defending against birds and thieves with constant spraying against insects and sickness every winter, spring, and early summer, and you may decide it is not worth the worry. You may convince yourself that it is cheaper to buy food than to grow it, which is not true, by the way; and vegetables may be thrown overboard. But mint, chives, sage, and thyme are so valuable to the homemaker that a space should be found for them in the perennial border at least.

The water-lily pool may be postponed for the time; the need for a greenhouse and frames may develop later. Some may see little advantage in a hedge or fence at first.

But most owners will want to plan for shrubs, flowers, a patio garden, climbing vines, and lawns.

CHAPTER 3

Crowding, Accent and the Illusion of Distance

"And he spake of trees, from the cedar tree that is in Lebanon even unto the hyssop that springeth out of the wall." 1 Kings. IV. 33.

DON'T CROWD YOUR PLANTS

YOUR GARDEN is to be a place where you may relax, and you cannot relax if shrubs and trees hem you in. Give your property a professional look by allowing yourself plenty of space.

You will be planting trees, shrubs, and roots, which will increase in size year by year until they crowd. Although you will confine your planting to varieties that will not grow to an excessive size, for the first five years or so your garden should be sparse, the plants comparatively few and far between. The second five years, the garden should be mature and look full. When the third five years roll around, you will begin thinning out here and there, getting rid of the plants that please you least. Between shrubs you will put in a decreasing number of annual flowers every spring for a few years, to give a complete look to the planting.

When your shrubs close in as they get older, they will lose some of their leaves where they touch each other. Prune away branches that become bare because of this and transplant the shrubs to wider spacings when occasion permits.

ACCENT

It will be restful to preserve an uninterrupted view of any pleasing object that may be within sight but off the property: a line of distant hills perhaps, a pond, a quiet valley, a wood lot, a pleasing building.

Should there be no point of interest off the property, some larger accent tree or shrub within your own lines may be used, or a statue erected as far away as the area permits. A clump of birches or Japanese cherries in the North; palmettos, palms or bamboos in the South; an arch, pergola, sundial, bird bath, flagpole, gazing globe, a tree with a white seat around the bole—all are desirable accent pieces.

Decide on the best viewpoint and have only grass in a direct line to the object. Let your fence go below the surface in a ha-ha if desirable (*see* Chapter 14). Then plant a double row of shrubs or young trees from the viewpoint towards the accent piece to guide the eye to the accent. Practically a pair of hedges, this double row is termed an *allée*. If both sides of the *allée* develop into tall trees that meet overhead, which they may be permitted to do, you will have a "pleached" *allée*.

In a shrubbery border planting, the taller types, or those that eventually will grow taller, are placed with much thought because they will capture the attention and be the accent shrubs in the group. In a foundation planting, accent shrubs are placed at the corners of the building on the inverted-T line, or to hide rainwater pipes, or at some point towards the center of the building if windows are not obstructed.

THE ILLUSION OF DISTANCE

If you have blue flowers in your borders and beds—hardy asters, campanulas, cynoglossum, delphinium, linum, myosotis, iris and the like; ageratum, lobelia, torenia, and verbena; buddleia, elsholtsia, lilac, hydrangea, and vitex—you foster the illusion that your property is larger than it actually is. Blues add distance, while red and yellow flowers make the area look smaller and have an intimate and homey look.

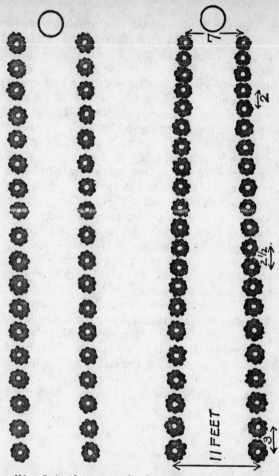

Two allées. Left, the perspective is true; this is desirable for most plantings. Right, the perspective is false; it gives the illusion of greater distance on a limited area. Rows are not parallel, but are slightly closer at the farther end.

Another way to make a garden look larger is to avoid straight lines and straight paths, installing curved driveways if you can handle winter's snow. Many an estate has been designed with sharp bends in the road, well banked with rhododendrons and other shrubs; your car will seem to travel miles before it draws up at the door, yet you may be only a short distance from the entrance gate.

Your curved paths will normally require more steps to get from one point to another, but you will provide short cuts through shrubbery of which you alone will be the chief user.

An exception to the use of curved lines will be when you plant an *allée* giving you a view of an accent object. But here there is something you can do. Ordinarily the two hedges or rows of trees are parallel, the plants equal in height and the same distance apart; but you create an illusion of distance by bringing the rows slightly closer at the farther end of the *allée,* by placing the bushes or trees forming it a little nearer to each other, and by harder pruning keeping them slightly shorter than those at the viewer's end—an exaggerated perspective, in fact.

This must be done with much finesse. Purchase a number of white plant stakes or lengths of 1′ x 1′ lumber. Set them in rows that at first are accurately parallel, with the stakes equal distances apart; now make one of the rows a trifle out of parallel, the two rows slightly nearer at the distant end, and note the point where the *allée* still looks correct. Drive each stake in progressively a mite closer. By trial and error you can arrive at the ideal error, which will not be evident for the stakes will still look parallel. Replace the stakes with plants and attend to the dwarfing to keep the plants progressively smaller by pruning through the seasons.

CHAPTER 4

The Nurseryman's Job

"There is no ancient gentlemen but gardeners." SHAKESPEARE, Hamlet.

THE NURSERYMAN first tries to produce plants; second, he tries to sell them. Plants are produced or propagated in various ways:

Seedage. He grows some trees, shrubs, and perennial plants by sowing seeds. Sometimes "stratified" seeds are employed. These are not sown in the usual manner but, when gathered, are spread in a layer or stratum on a raked surface and covered thinly with soil, several more layers of seeds, and soil on top of them. They pass the winter outdoors in this way, being subjected to freezing in the North, and are sifted and sown in the spring. Occasionally they have to be stratified for two years. If the seeds are too small to separate, small amounts of the mixed seeds and soil are spread on the surface and pressed in.

Division. He breaks up large old clumps of some plants into smaller pieces, and plants and cares for the pieces until they are large enough to plant elsewhere. Clumps often contain stout new shoots, termed "suckers," which are valuable for dividing and usually grow promptly. Roots sometimes form underground branches and develop subterranean buds or "offsets," which may be used to produce new individuals.

Layering. The stems of some plants the nurseryman cuts halfway through, bends the cut stem to the ground, and covers the tongue with earth; roots form at the cut, and when, in a few months, the partly cut stem is strong enough to live alone it is severed from the parent.

Cuttage. He cuts off pieces of stem, which are called cuttings or scions, and inserts them in sandy soil or sand, where many of them develop roots to become new individuals. He is said to "strike" them. He also strikes cuttings made from tubers, roots, and leaves. Usually this has to be carried out in a greenhouse, the cuttings being subjected to bottom warmth—often in a cutting box placed over heating pipes.

15

The skilled grower uses one or other of the plant hormones offered nowadays to encourage the formation of roots and to encourage more vigorous growth—such as Hormodin, Transplantone, Rootone, or Rosetone.

Graftage. Some cuttings he fastens to shaven portions of stems of nearly related plants, covering them with wax where they unite, provided the green bands of cambium, which is immediately under the bark of most plants, are in contact. When the cutting consists only of a bud, this form of grafting is termed "budding."

Differences in color, size, and shape of many plants may not be transmitted through seeds. That is why a peach tree grown from a pit is usually inferior to the tree on which the pit grew, why mint grown from seed lacks the mint flavor and aroma. Some seeds germinate with difficulty, some with ease; some plants may readily be divided and some may not. Some plants graft readily, while others do not. Budding is simple in most cases, though next to impossible in others, yet it is the most popular method of propagation.

Sometimes a variety has to be budded onto one kind, and when new growth has commenced the whole combination—the new bud growing on a portion of host A—has to be grafted onto host B. This is termed "double working."

When the nurseryman has obtained his new plants he must keep them pruned to a suitable shape and he almost always has to root-prune them. At least once a year main roots are sheared off to encourage a dense thick growth of fibrous roots at the base of the plants. When you purchase well-grown specimens, these heavy root systems will take hold quickly, and the plant is almost certain to grow vigorously. But if you go out into the wilds and see a plant, shrub, or young tree you would like to dig up and take home, it is difficult to obtain enough of the root system to enable it to grow, and often it will faii. It is therefore recommended that you purchase nursery-grown plants rather than risk disappointment and loss of time by getting plants from the wild. Further, some choice wild things like mountain laurel are protected in various states, where you would be subject to penalty for taking them.

PLANTS THRIVE IN SOME PLACES, FAIL ELSEWHERE

This applies to all parts of the United States. It is not always a matter of temperature, elevation, latitude or moisture supply. Your nurseryman will help you or your State experiment station, county agent, or near-by agricultural college may send you bulletins which name the plants that do well in your State. Make your plan and list the plants that you propose to use; submit the list to a near-by producing nurseryman for prices and ask him to eliminate any that in his opinion you should not have; ask him also to suggest any others that he thinks you should have.

Not only will your plants have less distance to travel, but they will be out of the ground a shorter period of time. A further reason for using locally produced plants is that there is less chance of introducing new pests.

CHAPTER 5

Some Planting Do's and Don'ts

*"Jock, when ye hae naething else to do, ye may be
aye sticking in a tree; it will be growing, Jock, when
ye're sleeping."* SCOTT, The Heart of Midlothian.

MAKE YOUR plans ahead and in great detail. Particularly, purchase
well in advance. Trees and shrubs are planted for the years to
come, and the process should not be hurried. It would seem that
forward-looking gardeners are in the minority, and every nurseryman knows the person who orders on the spur of the moment and
must have his trees tomorrow because men are coming to set them
in. Living plants should be dug properly and transported carefully, and the producer should be allowed sufficient time to furnish competent service.

B.&B. shrubs may safely be set out at any time of the year
provided they are watered well and shaded during the hot weeks.
B.&B. is the accepted trade abbreviation for "Balled and burlapped." Plants are delivered to you with the original soil around
their roots, held in position with a sheet of burlap tied in a ball.
Costing more than shrubs with bare roots, they suffer less in transportation and planting. Most evergreens are best ordered B.&B.
Some planters put these shrubs in the ground as they are, especially in the Southern States where more rapid decomposition
causes the burlap to decay speedily, but usually they like at least
to cut the cord holding the canvas in position and to slash and
fold down the wrapping at the top when planting.

Trees and shrubs should have their roots, if delivered bare,
carefully spread outwards and downwards and set with the dirt
mark, which shows the depth at which they stood in the nursery,

1 inch under the surface in their new position. It is a good plan to plunge the roots in a thin mud or slurry, made of a mixture of equal parts of compost and topsoil with a cupful of sheep manure to each gallon of mud. Bounce the dirtied roots up and down in the hole to insure that the soil you return works its way between them. To allow you to arrange the roots, all holes should be deep and wide.

If your land is poor, the hole should be extra large and the soil used to refill it should be the best that can be obtained. Mix with this soil 3 pounds of a good-quality fertilizer with a 5–10–5 analysis for each small shrub—5 to 10 pounds for large ones or trees —along with an equal weight of pulverized sheep manure.

Soil around the shrub or tree should be pressed firm with the shoe; then fill the resulting depression with water and refill it with water the next day and again the day after. When the land has dried somewhat, bring in additional earth to make the surface level. Continue watering if the season is a dry one.

WHEN TO PLANT

In spring, shrubs and trees that drop their leaves and have their roots bare are best put in after frost has left the land in the North and the ground has dried. You have about four weeks in which to do the work. Wait two weeks after frost is over before starting to plant evergreens; complete the evergreen planting in four weeks. In autumn, shrub planting takes place from October 1 to November 15 in most sections of the center and North.

During February sow indoors seeds of impatiens, lobelia, salvia, and verbena; in March sow indoors ageratum, alyssum, aster, carnation, cosmos, bedding dahlia, heliotrope, marigold, petunia, snapdragon, and zinnia. Set out the seedlings when danger of frost has passed. In April sow outdoors seeds of other hardy annuals. In May sow other tender annuals outdoors. In June sow most biennials and perennials outdoors. If you do not have facilities for raising plants—greenhouse, frames, or a warm room well lighted by several windows—you had better buy seedlings at planting time. Flower roots are set out in spring or fall: canna and gladiolus bulbs in spring; daffodil, hyacinth and tulip bulbs in autumn; lilies in spring or fall.

Sow eggplant, pepper, and tomato seeds indoors in March for setting out later. Cold-resistant vegetable seeds are sown from April on; cold-sensitive kinds—beans, corn, cucumbers and muskmelon—from May on; with successive sowings of many kinds to mid-August. Lawns are best made or repaired in early fall; next best time is late fall, for the seeds to remain in the ground over winter and start to grow in early spring; it is equally good to broadcast seed on the snow during winter; the third best time to work on the lawn is very early in spring.

The notes above apply to the northern two thirds of the United States. Below the latitude of killing frosts, plant from October 15 to April 15.

Check these dates with your county agent and local nurseryman.

IF SHRUBS ARRIVE TOO SOON, HEEL THEM IN

Dig a ditch, stand the shrubs upright in it close together, and shovel dirt onto the roots; water them if it does not rain. They will keep for several weeks and may grow better than if you had planted them on arrival. If you are not ready, stand B.&B. evergreens in the shade, preferably sheltered against a north wall; keep the roots moist.

Should roses or shrubs arrive looking too dry to grow, return them. But if you cannot do this, dig a hole and completely bury them in it, covering them all over with earth—roots and tops. Dig them up and plant them after two weeks; they will have become swollen to a normal condition, will probably take root, and thrive when you plant them.

CHAPTER 6

Trees for Street, Boulevard and Lawn

*"Rest is not idleness, and to lie sometimes on the grass under
the trees on a summer's day, listening to the murmur of the
water, or watching the clouds float across the blue sky,
is by no means a waste of time."*
LORD AVEBURY, Ease of Life.

IN A LARGE GARDEN, you may plant for effect one or more trees that
will appear from a distance to be near the building, yet on closer
inspection prove to be a good space from it. Placing them too near
the house is objectionable for storms may send them crashing onto
the dwelling or squirrels may use them as a means of entering the
attic. If spraying is necessary, spray materials may harm the finish
of the building.

Street-planting is a worthy community effort. If you put in Norway maples, sugar maples, lindens, elms, pin oaks, ginkgos or
similar trees on the street in front of your home, you may in a few
years have the only shaded parking spot on the street; you will
have the satisfaction of seeing your neighbor's car in the shade in
front of your home, while you have to park near-by in the sun.

If your trees escape the hazards of the automobile when they
are young, they may eventually reach a size that will protect you.
Joy riders may pile up against the sidewalk trees instead of your
porch.

Probably your section of the street does not belong to you, but
to the community. It is always possible for the trees that you
bought and paid for to be trimmed to allow power wires to go

through the street, or the road may need widening and your trees may be taken down with no "by your leave." Do not be too concerned if they are sacrificed on the altar of progress. See if you cannot find room for more.

Watch your sewer line when planting trees, and keep them at least 20 feet away. Settlement through the years may loosen a joint into which roots will find their way and clogging of the sewer may follow. Quicker growth of some trees will make you suspicious. By clearing the pipe with a plumber's snake and dissolving the roots with powerful lye or a solution of copper sulphate, you may stave off the inevitable for a year or two, but eventually you will need an excavation job, in which sections of the sewer are cleaned out and reset, and the joints are properly sheathed in new cement. The various poplars are especially bad actors in this regard.

FRUITS CAN BE DECORATIVE

There is every reason why you should use dwarf apples, cherries, peaches, plums, and other fruits in your landscaping efforts, unless you are fearful of being robbed at ripening time. Fruits must be sprayed in late winter with lime-sulphur or scalecide, also several times in spring and early summer with an all-purpose fruit-tree spray; otherwise a crop of fruit is unlikely. Your bushes and shade trees should similarly be sprayed for best results.

Even in a very small garden you can find room for espalier fruit trees supported flat against your walls, or sharply pruned dwarf trees in tubs or large pots, which may also be placed on your patio. Espalier apples, cherries, pears or plums are sometimes used as edgings. Have single cordon bushes, with the two horizontal branches or "cordons"; set them 10 feet apart, the cordons, running right and left, attached to a single support wire. When they meet they may be grafted one plant to the next to make a continuous foot-high fence.

In spring, all edible fruits are charming when in flower; the non-edible fruits are equally beautiful. Among the latter are some of our most important flowering shrubs—Japanese cherries, crab apples, Japan quince, hawthorns and others.

SOME SATISFACTORY TREES FOR STREET AND BOULEVARD

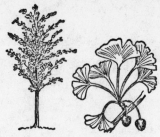

Ginkgo biloba (maidenhair tree).

In the North

Deciduous
Elm, Chinese (*Ulmus pumila*)
Indian bean (*Catalpa speciosa*)
Maidenhair tree (*Ginkgo biloba*)
Maple, Norway (*Acer platanoides*)
Pin oak (*Quercus palustris*)
Plane, Oriental (*Platanus orientalis*)
Tree of Heaven (*Ailanthus glandulosa*)

Evergreen
Arborvitae (*Thuja occidentalis*)
Cedar, red (*Juniperus virginiana*)
Pine, Austrian (*Pinus austriaca*)
Spruce, Koster blue (*Picea pungens glauca Kosteri*)
Norway (*P. excelsa*)

In the Mid-South
Ash (*Fraxinus americana*)
Chinaberry (*Melia azedarach*)
Cucumber tree (*Magnolia acuminata*)
Elm, Chinese (*Ulmus pumila*)
Linden (*Tilia platyphylos*)
Maple, Norway (*Acer platanoides*)
Oak, pin (*Quercus palustris*)
  scarlet (*Q. coccinea*)
  water (*Q. nigra*)
  willow (*Q. phellos*)
Plane, Oriental (*Platanus orientalis*)
Tulip tree (*Liriodendron tulipifera*)

The pin oak.

In the Lower South
Camphor tree (*Cinnamomum camphora*)
Oak, laurel (*Quercus laurifolia*)
  live (*Q. virginiana*)
Palmettos and Palms

Quercus virginiana (live oak).

23

CHAPTER 7

Foundation Planting

"They live 'neath the curtain
Of fir woods and heather,
And never take hurt in
The wildest of weather."
PATRICK R. CHALMERS, Puk-Wudjies.

FIRST CONSIDERATION with most home-owners is to plant a strip
around their house with dwarf conifers or cone-bearing evergreens
like:

arborvitae   mugho pines
cypress   Pfitzer spruces
junipers   yews

Along with them would go other evergreens such as:

andromedas   kalmias
azaleas   leucothoes
boxwood   rhododendrons
cotoneasters

These are kinds mostly used in the northern and central latitudes
of the United States. Refer to the descriptions of individual varieties which follow for additions to this partial list and for
changes in it for the South and Far West.

You may desire to make your planting entirely of evergreens,
as above, for they are effective the year round and are most
friendly in a snowy winter. But you may wish to mix some deciduous or leaf-shedding shrubs with them like:

24

buddleias	hibiscus	prunus
calycanthus	hydrangeas	pyrus
chaenomeles	kerrias	rhus
cornus	kolkwitzias	rosa
cratægus	laburnums	spiraeas
deutzias	loniceras	viburnums
euonymus	magnolias	vitex
forsythias	philadelphus	weigelas

Others in the list of deciduous shrubs later in this book may appeal to you.

Some evergreens are brilliant when they are in bloom, such as rhododendrons, kalmias and azaleas; but many more have only their pleasing shape and year-long foliage to interest you. Mostly they are slow-growing; often they cost more. Deciduous shrubs include a number of flowering kinds, and you can select them to be effective at the time you most need flowers; usually they grow quickly. The autumn leaf color is striking in many; some have colored stems and berries in winter and often attract birds.

The idea behind planting this strip of green is to "tie" the building to the ground as far as appearance is concerned and, since this is partly done by hiding the lower walls, it is natural for it to be termed foundation planting.

The closest average distance between a shrub and the wall is 3 feet, and the same minimum distance is allowed between one average shrub and the next. Shrubs may well be planted in two rows, but try to have them three-deep where the corners of the building meet the ground. At the corners a group of fairly tall-growing plants is set; often you may have matching groups. Among others, neatly sheared arborvitae are helpful in such groups.

Away from the corners the foundation planting may be two lines deep, if room is available. If necessary, the required 6-foot width may be reduced to 5 feet by placing the row in front opposite the spaces in the row to the rear. But avoid symmetry where you can: make the distance between the shrubs approximate; bring narrow shrubs closer together, bushier ones farther apart, than the uniform 3 feet.

A good idea is to set plants of English or Boston ivy 1 foot from the building and 6 feet apart to climb the walls and clothe

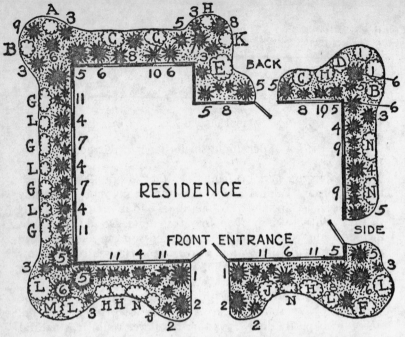

A foundation planting of evergreen and deciduous shrubs. Plants match at entrances. **Evergreen.** *(1) Chinese juniper. (2) Andorra juniper. (3) Savin. (4) Dwarf Alberta spruce. (5) Irish yew. (6) Pyramidal arborvitae. (7) Mugho pine. (8) Pfitzer's juniper. (9) Chinese azalea. (10) Ghent azalea. (11) Hinodegiri azalea.*

Deciduous. *(A) Barberry. (B) Buddleia. (C) Flowering quince. (D) Spindle tree. (E) Forsythia. (F) Blue hydrangea. (G) Kerria. (H) Beautybush. (I) Harison's rose. (J) Spiraea. (K) Lilac. (L) Tamarisk. (M) Blueberry. (N) Viburnum carlesii.*

them with green. A final touch is to hide the soil at the base of the shrubs with a planting of pachysandra or another ground cover (*see Chapters 12 and 13*).

Arrange to clip or shear fast-growing evergreens every spring and autumn to keep them within bounds and, when picking out your varieties, note the heights they may eventually attain. Better use only dwarf kinds, but if some taller ones get into the scheme, shear them four times a year instead of twice and perform your cutting severely. Especially plant only dwarf types beneath win-

26

dows. Set your plants so the effect will be thin and sparse for the first few seasons to allow for a close-knit appearance in later years.

Here are some don'ts: Don't crowd. Don't use plants that quickly develop into tall trees, like some spruces and pines. Don't plant too mixed an assortment, for it will lack the professional look; better have groups of three or more of a kind together. Don't plant shade-loving shrubs in the sun; set rhododendrons and kalmias along the north walls of the building.

Have your shrubs of various heights. Low-growing trailing or horizontal shrubs may go on the lawn side of the border. Tall-growing upright shrubs would be near the building.

When you are planting broad-leaved evergreens, blueberries, and other acid-loving subjects, send a sample quart of your soil to a near-by agricultural college or your county agent for a report on its acidity or alkalinity. You may have to make it acid by raking under aluminum sulphate—10 pounds per 1000 square feet—or hardwood sawdust—50 pounds per 1000 square feet—at least three times a year, spring, summer and autumn. Privet, red-leaved barberry, and viburnum also require an acid soil.

THE SHRUB BORDER

This is an assortment of shrubs similar to the foundation planting except that they are in the open. It is best to allow more than the minimum 3 feet between shrubs; 4½ feet would be better. In a large garden the shrub border may serve to divide one section from another—the lawns from the flowers perhaps—to provide a screen for the playpen or swimming pool, to block out an objectionable building, wall or service entrance, or to be an adjunct to your hedge for additional privacy. The shrub border may serve to make the lawn curve into bays or to make the driveway meander.

If the border is to be viewed from one side and if it backs to a wall or wood lot, the taller shrubs would be in the rear, medium-sized ones in the middle distance, dwarf and trailing ones in front. If it is to be viewed from two sides, the highest shrubs would be in the center and dwarfer ones on both sides.

You can be a collector of shrubs and plants through the years, purchasing three or four each of new or unusual specimens as the occasion arises, and your border will house your collection. You might have a golden section of both evergreen and deciduous

A shrub border 60 by 8 to 12 feet. Evergreen. (1) Chinese juniper. (2) Pfitzer's juniper. (3) Common juniper. (4) Andorra juniper. (5) Red cedar canaertii. (6) Norway spruce. (7) Red pine. (8) Irish yew. (9) Pyramidal arborvitae. (10) Mountain rosebay. (11) Flame azalea. (12) Ghent azalea. (13) Small-leaf cotoneaster. (14) Daphne cneorum. (15) Big-leaf wintercreeper. (16) Perennial candytuft. (17) American holly.
Deciduous. (A) Barberry. (B) Buddleia. (C) Flowering quince. (D) Dogwood. (E) Crataegus. (F) Maythorn. (G) Spindle tree. (H) Forsythia. (I) Ginkgo. (J) Witch hazel. (K) Rose of Sharon. (L) Kerria. (M) Blue hydrangea. (N) Beauty bush. (O) Laburnum. (P) Magnolia. (Q) Bechtel's crab. (R) Harison's rose.

shrubs with yellow leaves and shrubs with yellow flowers. In front of the shrub border is a likely place for the perennial border; in front of the yellow shrubs the perennials could be yellow, orange, or golden. Between and in front of them could be yellow annuals.

In another section of the shrub border the dominant leafage would be red; reddish-leaved evergreens, red maples, red barberry, red-flowered perennials and annuals.

Other shrubs might be included for their attractive autumn color, perfume, or the bird-attracting properties of their berries.

SHRUB BEDS

Sentinel or isolated shrubs look best in the lawn when they are mature, but a group of several of them in a bed is attractive, even if they are young. Entrances to the property, an elbow curve in the driveway, or in front of the refuse cans, are good locations.

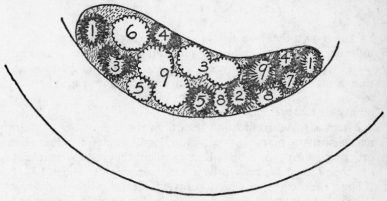

Shrub bed guarding the bend in a driveway. (1) Pfitzer's juniper. (2) Savin. (3) Dwarf Alberta spruce. (4) Globe arborvitae. (5) Hinodegiri azalea. (6) Chinese azalea. (7) Small-leaved cotoneaster. (8) Daphne cneorum. (9) Mountain laurel.

They may well be combined with attractive perennial flowers. Daffodils in variety give a fine effect with shrubs in April and May; iris, peony, delphinium, phlox and chrysanthemum for the summer and autumn; *Lilium candidum, regale,* and *speciosum* and the coral lily if the situation is not overexposed.

CHAPTER 8

Narrow-Leaved Evergreens—
The Conifers

"Then here's to the oak, the brave old oak,
Who stands in his pride alone!
And still flourish he, a hale green tree,
When a hundred years are gone!"
H. F. CHORLEY, "The Brave Old Oak."

IN THE EVENT that you wish to reproduce your own plants, we indicate in this and following chapters the methods commonly used by plantsmen to grow each variety. However, the propagation of plants frequently calls for much experience and is best left to the skilled nurseryman. For the subsequent care of juvenile plants, see Chapter 25.

There is some duplication regarding the common or popular names of many plants. By using the botanical classification when ordering, much confusion will be avoided; they are so listed here, but the popular names will be found readily in the index.

Note the height to which many of the following will grow. When they are young they are attractive bushes, and you set them in your foundation planting or shrub border. But in a few years they may grow out of hand, may overtop other varieties unduly, may even grow higher than your home. They may darken your windows, or at least make it easier for squirrels to enter your attic.

The place for trees is in woodland areas, as accent plants, singly on the lawn, or for boulevard planting.

Some few of the cone-bearers are not evergreen, like the larch or the maidenhair tree, but they are included in this listing because they are true conifers. Among the conifers are many of our stately forest trees and timber producers. Their leaves or needles are narrow; their length and grouping serves to identify them.

THE FIRS

Abies   Pseudotsuga

They are grown from seeds sown in spring, from cuttings, or by grafting onto seedlings of Norway spruce.

Abies balsamea. *Balsam fir.* Attractive, medium-sized, slender tree, with narrow, flat, inch-long leaves, fragrant with resin, matures at around 50 feet. Occurs wild from Labrador to West Virginia and Iowa. The source of Canada balsam, it is one of the conifers cut for Christmas trees.

A. brachyphylla (*Homolepis*). *Nikko fir.* A hardy type that does well in the Middle West. Flat needles are 1 inch long. The tree attains a height of 120 feet in its native Japan.

A. concolor. *White fir.* Hardy throughout the central States and east. Leaves are 2 inches long and flat, and the bark of the younger branches is yellow. Native of California, growing to 100 feet. Stands city conditions.

A. Veitchi. Very hardy type, good for the Midwest. Reaches 100 feet in Japan, its home. Inch-long leaves are flat.

* **Pseudotsuga douglasi** (*taxifolia*). **Abies douglasi.** *The Douglas fir.* Stately 75-foot tree with 12- to 18-foot branches; hardy in the North and suitable for the Middle West. A major timber tree on the Pacific coast. Foliage dark green. Makes a good lawn tree.

Pseudotsuga douglasi (Douglas fir). Majestic tall evergreen that grows wild on both sides of the Pacific—China on one coast, British Columbia on the other.

THE CEDARS

Cedrus

Grown from seed.

Cedrus atlantica. *Atlas cedar.* Tall handsome pyramidal tree.

* Reliable for planting within their climate range. Recommended because they are widely used and most nurseries can supply them.

C. deodara. *Deodar cedar.* Romantic evergreen from the slopes of the Himalaya Mountains. Grows well in the South and in California.

Both the above serve as good lawn and accent trees; they may be seen in sheltered old plantings south and west from southern New England.

C. libanotica. *Cedar of Lebanon.* Long-lived, drought- and heat-resistant tree found in Asia Minor. May be planted on hilly ground in the southern states.

THE CYPRESSES

Chamaecyparis   Cupressus

Grown from seeds, layers or cuttings.

Chamaecyparis lawsoniana. Branches are drooping and the branchlets frondlike. Much planted in the South and California. Hardy south of Philadelphia. In its range it should be included in your foundation planting if you have room for a large subject; it eventually may reach 75 feet, but it stands shearing well.

C. pisifera filifera. *Threadlike cypress; Sawara.* Graceful tree, maturing at 75 feet. Desirable accent plant in a foundation or shrubbery planting; taller than its fellows, it may well go between windows, in front of water pipes, or at the building's corners; or a matched pair may go in front of the entrance. Suitable for landscaping in the South as well as the North.

C. squarrosa. *Moss retinospora.* Another good shrub that stands shearing and is suitable for most parts of the United States, including the North, Midwest and South. Have it in your foundation planting.

C. thyoides ericoides. *White cedar.* A dense shrub with spreading leaves, popular for foundation planting in the southern States, yet is hardy in the North. The younger foliage in the sub-variety **aurea** is golden-yellow.

Cupressus arizonica. Evergreen cone-bearing tree growing to 40 feet high. Good only for the southern States and California.

C. sempervirens. *Italian cypress.* The tree may ultimately reach 80 feet; has dark green leaves. Much used in the warmer sections of California; unlikely to thrive elsewhere in the United States.

Cryptomeria japonica. *Japan cedar.* Evergreen tree which may eventually attain a height of 125 feet or more; much planted in the South. Among the sub-varieties available is **compacta**, a dwarfer type. It is grown from seeds or cuttings.

32

*Ginkgo (*Salisburia*) **biloba.** *Maidenhair tree.* A deciduous conifer; the leaves turn yellow in late fall, then drop. Effective street or boulevard tree, shedding its leaves overnight, simplifying the work of the street-cleaning department. A good specimen tree to set on the lawn. The sexes are in different trees, the male being generally preferred. Highly ornamental and of slender upright growth, but with peculiar spreading branches. The leaves are fan-shaped with a notch, like those of a mammoth maidenhair fern, of deep green color and turning yellow in fall. Valuable in that it is immune to ordinary attacks of insects and it withstands well the smoke and general unnatural conditions of our cities. Propagated by stratified seeds, layers, or cuttings.

THE JUNIPERS AND RED CEDARS
Juniperus

Grown from seeds, which sometimes take a year to germinate, or from cuttings.

Juniperus chinensis. *Chinese juniper.* Typically a large pyramidal tree growing to 60 feet, but in a garden rarely grows higher than 20 feet. Hardy west and south from central New England; stands well in the Midwest. The sexes are distinct in this subject, the male being generally preferred. A good accent plant. Tolerates hot, dry situations.

J. chinensis japonica. *Japanese juniper.* A prostrate widespreading plant that will endure severe cold; hardy from central New York to the Gulf. Covers an area 6 to 8 feet in diameter, but grows only 12 inches high. Stands sun or partial shade. If your rock garden is large, find a place in it for this. Plant it to overhang your pool or use it as a ground cover for terraces and sandy banks.

* J. chinensis pfitzeriana. *Pfitzer's juniper.* Broad low bushy growth, 5 to 6 feet high with a 10- to 12-foot spread if unpruned, with deep green foliage and nodding branchlets. Adaptable to most sections of the United States, it stands shade and does well on the north side of a building; also tolerates dry, hot situations. Valuable for foundation planting and shrub borders. If your rock garden is large, find a space for it at the edge; plant several near the pool.

Pfitzer's juniper.

* Reliable for planting within their climate range. Recommended because they are widely used and most nurseries can supply them.

*J. chinensis pyramidalis. A very narrow shrub, growing to 20 feet high; dislikes too dense shade. Splendid accent plant, or a good entrance or sentinel subject. Two leaf colors are available—blue-green and green.

J. chinensis sargenti. *Sargent's juniper.* A prostrate mat, 8 to 10 feet across, which may be kept smaller by trimming. Height is but a few inches, with bluish foliage. Have it in the front of your foundation planting; in your rock garden if it is large. A good hardy ground cover for poor soil if crowded by planting as close as 2½ feet apart.

* J. communis. *Common juniper.* Shrub or small tree with sharp-pointed leaves, reaching 25 feet in height.

* J. communis aurea. *Golden juniper.* A type which has its young leaves golden-yellow, the color being most marked when planted in full sun. Good for foundation planting and the shrub border. Grows to 20 feet.

J. communis depressa (*canadensis*). Vigorous low-spreading plant, occupying a diameter of 7 or 8 feet. When mature, rarely 4 feet high. A fast-growing gray-green shrub. Use it to clothe terraces or banks.

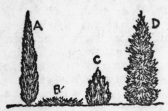

Four useful junipers: (A) Irish. (B) Andorra. (C) Greek. (D) Juniperus scopulorum (Colorado red cedar).

J. communis depressa plumosa. *Andorra juniper.* Spreading dwarf bush, 18 inches high at most. Rapidly spreads to cover a diameter of 6 feet. Grows in shade, but slowly; does best in the sun. Have it in your list of shrubs for foundation planting; put it in your rock garden if it is a large one. Trim it from time to time. Leaves are silvery green in spring and summer, silvery purple in autumn and winter.

J. communis hibernica. *Irish juniper.* A column-shaped tree and a desirable accent plant in shrubbery. Taller than its fellows, it is good for planting at corners and to hide rain pipes when used in foundation work. Somewhat sensitive to cold, it should be planted south and west from Connecticut. The most handsome juniper.

J. communis suecica. *Swedish juniper.* Narrow tree, growing 10 or 12 feet high with a diameter of 12 to 18 inches. Valuable to set in the center or the ends of a shrub planting, where its height will catch the eye.

* Reliable for planting within their climate range. Recommended because they are widely used and most nurseries can supply them.

34

J. excelsa stricta. *Greek juniper.* A column-shaped tree growing to 40 feet, with bluish leaves. Hardy and stands well in the Midwest. Include this where you have room for a tall narrow subject.

J. horizontalis douglasi. *Waukegan juniper.* Trailing, with steel-blue leaves that are pinkish-purple in winter. Plant the little bushes 3 feet apart each way for a ground cover on a terrace or bank. Good for a large rock garden or with its branches growing over a pool. Tolerant of hot, dry situations, including those in the southern States.

*** J. horizontalis plumosa.** *Creeping or Andorra juniper.* A prostrate trailing plant, shade-tolerant and growing in all parts of the United States. Foliage is bright green in summer, changing to reddish-purple over winter. Recommended for the front of a foundation planting.

*** J. sabina Von Ehron.** *Savin.* Spreading or procumbent shrub with very dark green foliage. Keeps at 2 to 3 feet for many years. Stands smoke. Hardy, recommended for the Midwest and South. Valuable for large rock gardens and foundation planting.

J. sabina tamariscifolia. Similar to the foregoing, but more compact. Does well in the southern States.

J. scopulorum. *Colorado red cedar.* Grows to 20 feet and has yellowish-green leaves. Hardy in the eastern and midwestern States. Grows wild in British Columbia and California. Desirable accent shrub.

J. squamata meyeri. *Meyer juniper.* A dense-leaved upright shrub of medium height; light blue-green.

*** J. virginiana.** *Red cedar.* Majestic tree growing from Maine to Florida, eventually reaching 100 feet. Narrow pyramid shape and slow-growing. In its younger years, a good entrance and corner shrub. Likes poor sandy soil. Will attract birds to your property. Stands extreme cold, dust, smoke, and city fumes. Wood used for cedar chests, fence rails, and pencils.

J. virginiana burki. *Silver-leaf red cedar.*

*** J. virginiana canaertii.** Narrow pyramidal tree with dark green tufted foliage, reaching 20 feet when mature. Shearing will keep it within bounds

Juniperus virginiana (Red cedar).

* Reliable for planting within their climate range. Recommended because they are widely used and most nurseries can supply them.

for many years and develop a thick growth. Include it in your planting if you have room for a large subject.

J. virginiana elegantissima. Maturing at 10 to 15 feet, it has slightly drooping branches and a loose pyramidal habit. Branches have cream-colored tips, the color being most marked in spring.

J. virginiana glauca. *Silver red cedar.* Has attractive blue-tinged leaves and does well in most parts of the South; the North also. Rapidly grows to 20 feet, but it may be kept smaller by trimming.

J. virginiana kosteri. *Koster juniper.* Semi-dwarf, handsome, horizontal-growing bush with bluish-green foliage. Good for the front of a shrub planting, overhanging your pool, or in a large rock garden, for the plants are half-erect. Recommended for terraces or sandy banks.

J. virginiana schottii. *Schott red cedar.* Columnar tree with scalelike, bright green and yellow leaves. Splendid accent shrub for planting at corners and to hide water pipes. Matures at 15 or 20 feet, but you may keep it trimmed.

All the red cedars above are good for Midwest planting.

Larix laricina. *Larch; Tamarack; Hackmatack.* Unusual in that it is a coniferous tree that loses its leaves over winter. Looks like a fresh light green pine tree in summer. Adaptable as to soil, thrives even in boggy land. Quick-growing, maturing at 55 feet. Valuable for the ends or center of a shrub planting. Propagated from spring-sown seed.

Larix laricina (larch, tamarack, hackmatack).

THE SPRUCES

Picea

Grown from seeds, layers, or cuttings. Shade young plants the first year.

Picea bicolor. *Alcock spruce.* Hardy and recommended for Midwest planting. Stately tree which grows to 100 feet in its native Japan.

P. canadensis albertiana. *Black Hills spruce.* Very hardy. May grow up to 40 feet in a garden, with 10 to 12 feet branch spread. A compact tree that needs sun part of the day.

P. conica glauca. *White spruce.* Forest tree found across **Canada** and the northern United States. The major spruce of the Maine woods.

* **P. conica glauca albertiana.** *Dwarf white spruce.* Narrow conical growth, covered with short, close-set, twiggy branches; leaves are grass-green. Slow-growing, only ½ inch to 1 inch a year. Maximum height about 8 feet. Very cold-resistant. Plant it in a moist and partly shaded situation, and protect it from winter sun by erecting a burlap screen on the south side of the bush. Recommended for foundation planting north of Philadelphia.

Have your own living Christmas tree. Plant *P. conica glauca* (*above*) or *P. excelsa* (*below*) within view of a main window, near a convenient outlet for colored bulbs or floodlights. Both make good specimen trees.

P. engelmanni. *Engelmann's spruce.* Fine tall tree, native from British Columbia to New Mexico. Hardy and recommended for the Midwest.

* **P. excelsa.** *Norway spruce; Burgundy pitch tree.* Typically a tall tree, widely planted. Some dwarf types are obtainable for shrubbery planting, with variegated or golden foliage. Accepts poor, shallow soil. A hardy quick-growing conifer, successfully planted in the Midwest. Cone is 7 inches long.

Picea excelsa or Norway spruce.

P. omorika. *Servian spruce.* Hardy throughout the northern states, but shelter it from winter winds.

P. pungens. *Colorado spruce.* A hardy tree native to Wyoming, Utah, New Mexico, and Colorado.

* **P. pungens glauca.** *Colorado blue spruce.* Handsome pyramidal tree with bluish-white leaves. A good subject to set in the lawn visible from all sides, or as a specimen at the end of an *allée.* Will endure extreme cold and tolerate city conditions. The * Koster blue spruce, with rich silver-green foliage, is a well-known variety.

Picea pungens glauca (Colorado blue spruce).

* Reliable for planting within their climate range. Recommended because they are widely used and most nurseries can supply them.

THE PINES

Pinus   Sciadopitys

The arrangement of their long and narrow needles or leaves identifies many of them. Grown from spring-sown seeds. Shade young plants the first year

Pinus banksiana. *Jack pine.* For northern planting only. Medium-sized tree with twisted needles, 1 inch long, in pairs.

P. cembra. *Swiss stone pine.* Slow-growing moderate-sized tree. Stands well the conditions of the Midwest. Five-inch needles in clusters of five.

P. densiflora umbraculifera. *Tanyosho; Japanese table pine.* A dwarf form of the Japanese red pine with an umbrellalike head 3 feet from the ground. Has 5-inch needles, which have a pleasing fragrance, in clusters of two. The sub-variety globosa is a rounded, even dwarfer type, 2 feet high. Include both in your foundation planting.

P. monticola. *Western white pine.* Leaves in clusters of five, bluish-green and 4 inches long. Cones 11 inches. Grows from British Columbia to California. Hardy in the North.

The mugho pine at left is an old plant when 6 feet high, while the Austrian pine at right reaches 75 feet when mature.

* **P. mugho.** *Swiss mountain pine.* Desirable for planting in the North and Midwest. A dwarf, very hardy shrub, tolerant of hot, dry situations and of city smoke; much used in foundation planting. Two-inch bright green needles are in clusters of two. Grows to 6 feet, spreading to a diameter of 6 or 8 feet. Likes light, but will tolerate some shade; may be used on the north side of a building.

P. nigra austriaca. *Austrian pine; Corsican pine; black pine.* Hardy, deep green; a good tree for the Midwest. Has 6½-inch needles in clusters of two. Reaches 75 feet and makes an attractive specimen subject. The sub-variety pygmaea is a dwarf shrub. Both austriaca and pygmaea are tolerant of smoke.

P. ponderosa. *Western yellow pine.* Occupant of forests from British Columbia to Mexico. Leaves are 11 inches long in clusters of three. Cones are 6 inches.

* Reliable for planting within their climate range. Recommended because they are widely used and most nurseries can supply them.

38

*P. resinosa. *Red pine.* Hardy, suitable for Midwest planting. Native, growing from Newfoundland to Pennsylvania and west to Minnesota. Leaves are 6 inches long in clusters of two. A good sentinel tree to place on the lawn and be visible on all sides. Globosa is a dwarf, rounded sub-variety.

Pinus resinosa (red pine).

P. rigida. *Pitch pine.* Five-inch needles in groups of three. Cones are 2½ inches long. Abundant in eastern forests from Newfoundland to Pennsylvania and west to Minnesota.

*P. strobus. *White pine; Weymouth pine.* A valuable forest tree, hardy and characteristic of the New England woods. May be planted in the Midwest. Matures at 120 feet. Five-inch needles are in clusters of five. This takes the white-pine blister rust, slow to develop but eventually fatal, so that its value is limited; elimination of the alternate hosts of fungus, currants, gooseberries, and wild barberries from the neighborhood is the only protection.

The white pine (Pinus strobus).

* P. sylvestris. *Scots pine; deal wood.* A hardy specimen tree or good for woodland planting; tolerant of shallow rocky soil and city smoke. Suitable for the Midwest. Has 3-inch needles in clusters of two. Grows quickly. Nana is a low dense variety suitable for landscaping.

Pinus sylvestris (Scots pine).

P. taeda. *Loblolly.* Nine-inch needles in threes; 5-inch cones. A major pine of the Atlantic coastal woodlands.

Sciadopitys verticillata. *Umbrella pine; parasol fir.* Hardy south from New England, suitable for the Midwest. A slow-growing tree reaching a height of 100 feet in its home in Japan. Set at the ends or center of a large shrubbery border.

* Reliable for planting within their climate range. Recommended because they are widely used and most nurseries can supply them.

THE SEQUOIAS OR REDWOODS

Sequoia

Grown from seeds, layers, or cuttings.

Sequoia gigantea. *Giant sequoia; Wellingtonia.*
S. sempervirens. *Redwood.*
These big trees of California are unlikely to interest you for landscaping, because of their 300-foot height and slow growth. The giant
sequoia will live in a stunted form in the central States, the redwood
only in the South.

Taxodium distichum. *Bald cypress.* A deciduous conifer, good for
planting in the southern States. Grown from seeds, layers, or cuttings,
it will stand overwet soil.

THE YEWS

Taxus

Grown from seeds, layers, or cuttings.

The English yew (Taxus bac-cata).

* **Taxus baccata.** *English yew.*
Lives to a great age. Much planted in
medieval Britain to maintain a supply
of bow wood for English archers;
gnarled specimens in churchyards
there survive from this period. Eventually reaching 60 feet, slow-growing,
and a desirable specimen to set in the
lawn. Young plants make satisfactory
hedges also.

* **T. baccata fastigiata.** *Irish yew.*
A columnar type good for planting at
corners, between windows, or to hide rain pipes in foundation planting.

T. baccata repandens. *Prostrate English yew.* A hardy horizontal
type. Recommended for the Midwest. If your rock garden is large, find
a place in it for this. Keep it small by trimming.

T. brevifolia. *Western yew.* A large, hardy, rounded tree reaching
45 feet. Valuable to set in the ends or center of a shrubbery.

T. canadensis. *Ground hemlock.* A straggling shrub growing up to
6 feet; thrives in peaty soil.

* Reliable for planting within their climate range. Recommended because
they are widely used and most nurseries can supply them.

* T. cuspidata. *Japanese yew.* An upright pyramidal yew with glossy, deep green foliage. Tolerant of city smoke, and hardy. Recommended for the Midwest; stands shade. Include in your foundation planting.

Japanese yew (taxus cuspidata).

T. cuspidata nana. A dwarf shrubby form, 3 feet high and spreading 3 feet. A slow-growing and long-lived bush. Good in a large rock garden.

* T. media hicksii. *Hicks' yew.* A distinct hybrid of columnar form with rich deep green foliage. Hardy and suitable for the Midwest.

* T. media kelseyi. *Kelsey's yew.* Of upright bushy habit. Produces an abundance of red yew berries. A good hedge plant.

THE ARBORVITAES

Thuja

Grown from seeds, layers, and cuttings.

Thuja occidentalis. *American arborvitae.* Makes a good hedge and a good specimen tree on the lawn. Foliage is flat, arranged in sprays of lacy, dark green, scalelike leaves. Adaptable as to soil, including bog land. Slow-growing trees, mostly maturing around 60 feet, but they may be kept within bounds for many years by shearing.

T. occidentalis douglasi. *Douglas arborvitae.* A dense pyramid with fernlike foliage, glossy green. Tips are like cockscombs. Slender, it grows to 15 feet.

* T. occidentalis douglasi aurea. *Douglas golden arborvitae.* A broad bushy pyramid with golden foliage which is brightest in spring.

* T. occidentalis globosa. *Globe arborvitae.* Dwarf rounded form, deep green. Good for foundation planting; thrives in the cooler parts of the South on clay soil, north to Canada.

* T. occidentalis pyramidalis. *Pyramidal arborvitae.* A compact, narrow, bright green shrub suitable for placing at entrance corners. Especially valuable for the Midwest. Grows rap-

Thuja occidentalis pyramidalis.

* Reliable for planting within their climate range. Recommended because they are widely used and most nurseries can supply them.

idly to 20 feet with a diameter of 4 feet. Can be kept within bounds by shearing. Plicata is a similar shape with flattened branches.

T. occidentalis rosenthali. *Rosenthal's arborvitae.* Columnar shape; dark green.

T. occidentalis vervæneana. Small and dense; the branchlets are bronzy in winter.

T. occidentalis wareana. *Ware arborvitae.* Symmetrical, compact, conical shrub, very long-lived, matures at 6 to 8 feet. Fine deep green winter color. Good for foundation planting, the shrub border, and hedges.

T. occidentalis woodwardii. *Woodward arborvitae.* Dense, globe-shaped, deep green foliage. Three feet high and 3 feet in diameter. Ideal for foundation planting; set it in your rock garden if it is large. Keep the plant small by shearing.

T. orientalis aurea. This golden-foliage type is recommended for foundation planting. For California; the North also.

T. orientalis bakeri. *Baker's arborvitae.* The leaves are pale green; plants are cone-shaped and exceptionally resistant to heat and drought. Hardy north to Long Island, yet it does well in the southern States.

T. orientalis compacta. Dwarf and compact. For North and South.

T. orientalis flagelliformis. Pendent and threadlike branches.

T. orientalis gracilis. Slender and pyramidal in shape.

T. orientalis pyramidalis. *Chinese arborvitae.* Planted as a low py-

THE HEMLOCKS

Tsuga

Hemlock (Tsuga canadensis)

* **Tsuga canadensis.** A tall forest tree, but maturing at 30 feet under garden conditions when it is retarded by the competition of neighboring shrubs and if it is trimmed occasionally to prevent its growing out of hand. A good place to plant it is toward the north side of the building. It is too large for inclusion in the average foundation planting; it is a good specimen tree to set in the lawn,

* Reliable for planting within their climate range. Recommended because they are widely used and most nurseries can supply them.

however. Prefers a moist situation to a dry one, but is tolerant of shallow soil; stands shade. Young plants make excellent hedges. Ranges from Nova Scotia to Alabama.

T. caroliniana compacta. A dense round-topped dwarf type of the American hemlock.

Both the above grow well in the northern sections of the United States, including the Midwest; they may be planted as far south as the highlands of Georgia.

The hemlock makes an efficient windbreak. Pruned and clipped, it is a good hedge.

CHAPTER 9

Broad-Leaved Evergreens—
Rhododendrons and Azaleas

"And in the woods a fragrance rare
Of wild azaleas fills the air,
And richly tangled overhead
We see their blossoms sweet and red."
DORA READ GOODALE,
"Spring Scatters Far and Wide."

RHODODENDRONS AND AZALEAS are propagated by spring-sown seeds, layers, or cuttings, and are slow to germinate or root. Limestone soils and heavy clays do not suit these broad-leaved evergreens.[1] Plant in soil containing by measure one third each of loam, sand, and compost or peat moss; soil should be acid; it may be made and kept so by occasional dressings of hardwood sawdust and aluminum sulphate. These evergreens also require partial shade; the north side of a building is generally a desirable location as well as open woodland areas.

RHODODENDRONS

Some are very large subjects; **catawbiense** reaches a height of 20 feet; **maximum** may grow to 35 feet. Select only dwarf types where space is limited. They are ideal for foundation planting, for the shrub border, and for screening objectionable areas.

[1] Note that a few azaleas are deciduous.

Rhododendron arbutifolium. A hybrid variety growing 4 feet high; it has pink bell-shaped flowers in June and July.

R. azaleoides (*R. odoratum*). A semi-evergreen hybrid with pale rose-purple flowers.

*** R. carolinianum.** Six feet high with rose-purple flowers, occasionally white, in May and June. Found in open woodland in the higher sections of North Carolina.

Three native rhododendrons. LEFT TO RIGHT: *1 and 2, Maximum. 3, Catawbiense or mountain rosebay. 4, Carolinianum.*

*** R. catawbiense.** *Mountain rosebay.* Reaching 20 feet when fully mature. It is a native of light forest lands of our eastern highlands from Virginia to Georgia. Flowers are lilac-purple, but white specimens are found.

R. ferrugineum. A dwarf evergreen, it has pink to carmine flowers in July and August. It is found wild in the mountains of Central Europe.

R. hirsutum. An exceptional variety which tolerates lime. Three feet high, it bears pink to carmine flowers in June. Native of the uplands of Central Europe.

*** R. indicum** (*Azalea indicum*). Six feet high with striking red or pink flowers, trumpet-shaped and 3 inches across. Native of Japan, it thrives in the southern States.

R. maximum. One of our native plants, found in open woods from Nova Scotia to Georgia and Alabama. White, purple, and pink are the colors. Large plants growing to 35 feet and suitable only for landscaping work on large areas.

R. myrtifolium. Growing to 5 feet, it has pink funnel-shaped flowers, 1 inch across, in June and July.

R. smirnovi. Reaching 18 feet in height, it has narrow bell-shaped flowers, 3 inches in diameter and rose-colored, in May. Large subjects, suitable for planting in wide areas.

*** Reliable for planting within their climate range. Recommended because they are widely used and most nurseries can supply them.

AZALEAS

Recommended for foundation planting and for a shrub border. They are called rhododendrons in many books of reference. The differences are slight, but some azaleas are deciduous and most have funnel-shaped flowers; rhododendron flowers are more often bell-shaped.

Azaleas with lawn stepping-stones, and a statue up against rhododendrons for accent.

* Azalea amœna (*Obtusa*). An evergreen type, the leaves becoming bronzy in winter. Grows to 3 feet. Flowers are rose-purple and are effective in April; mostly they are 'hose-in-hose," a type of double bloom where one bloom is neatly surrounded by another.

A. arborescens. Growing to 10 feet, deciduous, with white or pink funnel-shaped flowers, 2 inches long and fragrant, appearing in June and July. Stamens are very prominent and curved. Native, found from Pennsylvania to Georgia and Alabama.

Three native American azaleas. LEFT: *Azalea canadense or Rhodora, with rose-purple blooms.* CENTER: *A. canescens, pink or white flowers.* RIGHT: *A. nudiflorum or Pinxter flower. Light pink.*

* A. calendulacea. *Flame azalea.* Two-inch flowers are orange-scarlet, appearing in May and June. The deciduous plant may eventually reach 10 feet in height. Wild from Pennsylvania to Georgia and Kentucky.

A. canadense. *Rhodora.* Growing to 3 feet, it has rose-purple flowers in April and May. Deciduous native, found from Newfoundland to Pennsylvania.

* Reliable for planting within their climate range. Recommended because they are widely used and most nurseries can supply them.

46

A. canescens. Deciduous and growing to 15 feet. The funnel-shaped flowers are pink or white and they appear in April. A native plant found from North Carolina to Florida and Texas.

A. dauricum. *Dahurian azalea.* Growing to 6 feet, this semi-evergreen shrub has solitary rose-purple flowers in early spring, which are broad, bell-shaped, and 1½ inches across. It is a native of eastern Asia.

* **A. gandavensis.** *Ghent azalea.* A series of hybrids in various brilliant colors, averaging 8 feet in height.

* **A. hinodegiri.** Grows to 3 feet. Japanese hybrids, much branched and spreading. The purple, brilliant crimson, or scarlet flowers appear in April and May. Thrives in most parts of the United States including the central southern States.

A. ledifolia. Grows 6 feet high and is evergreen. Fragrant white flowers are funnel-shaped and 2 inches across; they are borne in May. Native of China.

A. lutea. Growing to 12 feet; deciduous. Highly fragrant flowers are yellow and 2 inches in diameter; they appear in May. A desirable accent shrub that is found wild in the Caucasus.

* **A. mollis.** *Chinese azalea.* Deciduous, maturing at 5 feet. Funnel-shaped flowers are golden-yellow and 2 inches in diameter.

A. nudiflorum. *Pinxter flower.* Growing 6 feet or more; deciduous. Flowers are light pink, funnel-shaped, and 1½ inches across, appearing in May. Stamens are curved and very prominent. Native plant found from Maine to Florida and Texas.

A. schlippenbachii. Growing to 15 feet, deciduous, with 3-inch pink flowers spotted brown, fragrant, and broadly funnel-shaped.

A. vaseyi. Growing to 15 feet; deciduous. Flowers are rose, spotted with brown, borne in April and May. Stamens are curved and very prominent. Occurs wild in North Carolina.

A. viscosa. *White swamp honeysuckle.* Growing to 10 feet; deciduous. Fragrant flowers are white or pink, fragrant, funnel-shaped and 2 inches long, borne in June and July. Found in swamps from Maine to South Carolina.

* Reliable for planting within their climate range. Recommended because they are widely used and most nurseries can supply them.

CHAPTER 10

Broad-Leaved and Other Evergreens— General List

"Beauty has no relation to price, rarity, or age."
JOHN COTTON DANA, Libraries.

PRUNE OR SHEAR evergreens during the latter part of May and repeat in September. This will improve their shape and develop a bushy habit. Never prune evergreens in winter.

When reducing the length of a branch it is a good plan to do it gradually, always leaving at least one green branchlet on the remaining stub. This is unlike the practice with most deciduous shrubs, which may be pruned at any point, the maximum growth then arising immediately below where you have cut if the branch is living.

* **Andromeda polifolia.** *Bog rosemary.* A dwarf shrub, 12 inches high and creeping. Pinkish urn-shaped flowers are in nodding clusters. Very hardy. Include it in your plantings as a desirable evergreen ground cover. It is grown from seeds or layers.

Other andromedas are described in this list under chamædaphne, leucothoe, pieris and zenobia.

Arctostaphylos uva-ursi. *Bearberry; manzanita.* Prostrate and trailing evergreen, suitable for a ground cover. Bears white or pinkish flowers in clusters. Grown from seed.

Aspidium (*Polystichum*) **acrostichoides.** *Christmas fern; dagger fern; shield fern.* Hardy evergreen plant, occurring wild from Nova Scotia to Texas. Grows 2 feet high. Increased by division of the clumps.

* Reliable for planting within their climate range. Recommended because they are widely used and most nurseries can supply them.

Aubrieta deltoidea. Dwarf, evergreen, mat-forming perennial, with purple or lilac flowers in spring. Good for the front of the hardy border or for planting in the rock garden or in dry walls. Does not thrive in shade. Grown from spring-sown seeds, divisions, or cuttings.

Aubrieta deltoidea.

Aucuba japonica. Evergreen shrub that may reach 15 feet; has 7-inch-long smooth leathery leaves and red berries in the fall. Grows south from Washington, D. C.

A. variegata. *Gold-dust tree.* This has leaves spotted with gold. Aucubas are grown from spring-sown seeds or cuttings.

Bambusa. *Bamboo.* Striking members of the grass family. Most of the taller kinds grow only in the extreme southern parts of the United States. **B. arundinacea** may reach 100 feet. **B. nana,** only 10 feet, sometimes stands as far north as Philadelphia. Grown from divisions or layers.

Bauhinia variegata. *Orchid tree; mountain ebony.* Small tree growing to 25 feet, with red flowers marked with white and yellow. Suitable only for the South and California. Grown from seeds or cuttings.

THE EVERGREEN BARBERRIES

Berberis

Their berries attract many birds. Grown from stratified seeds, divisions, layers, or cuttings.

Berberis julianæ. *Juliana barberry; wintergreen barberry.* An evergreen shrub growing to 6 feet; yellow flowers and blue-black fruits; spiny.

B. sargentiana. Evergreen 6-foot shrub, with small yellow flowers in clusters in spring. Hardy in the North; much used in the South.

B. verruculosa. *Evergreen barberry.* Growing 3 feet high, with yellow flowers and black fruits. Spiny.

Bouvardia humboldti. A medium-sized shrub bearing fragrant white flowers. May only be used in sub-tropical areas; much planted in California. Grown from stem and root cuttings.

Brachychiton acerifolium. *Australian flame tree.* Sixty-foot tree with large maplelike leaves and bright scarlet fruits. Much planted in California and the southern States. Grown from seeds and cuttings.

Brunfelsia calycina. Medium-sized shrub with large, dark purple flower clusters. Grown only in California and Florida. Raised from cuttings.

THE BOXWOODS

Buxus

Slow-growing and strongly aromatic, they will stand most winters in the vicinity of New York. South of this area they are much planted. Propagated from seeds, divisions, layers, and cuttings.

Buxus microphylla koreana. *Korean little-leaf box.* Desirable evergreen shrub growing to 2 feet.

B. sempervirens. *Common box.* Slow-growing bush or tree, maturing at 25 feet. North of the Middle Atlantic States it requires winter protection: erect light burlap screens around the bushes; edging may be covered with peat moss, salt hay or sawdust, to be brushed away in the spring. Rake under a side dressing of limestone every spring. Prefers a light, well-drained soil. Makes a good hedge.

* **B. sempervirens myrtifolia.** A dwarf boxwood with narrow leaves. Hardier than most others.

* **B. sempervirens suffruticosa.** *Dwarf box.* Has smaller leaves; a good type for dwarf hedges.

Calluna vulgaris. *Scotch heather.* Small evergreen shrub with purple flowers; hardy in the North. Grows in poor sandy and peaty soil. Raised from cuttings.

Camellia. This shrub is a close relative of the tea plant, growing up to 40 feet high and bearing striking stemless flowers which are white, red, or white and red, sometimes 5 inches in diameter. Hardy outdoors south and west from Georgia; a popular skilled gardener's conservatory subject in the North. Grown from cuttings or layers.

Carissa arduina. *Hedge thorn.* This 10-foot spiny evergreen shrub may only be grown in the extreme South, where it is a popular hedge plant. Flowers are white, and the half-inch bright red fruits are edible.

Casuarina equisetifolia. *Horsetail tree; beefwood; Australian pine—* but it is not a pine. Will grow to 70 feet in height and is much planted in Florida as a street tree. Grown from seeds or cuttings.

Ceratonia siliqua. *Carab tree; St. John's bread.* Evergreen, reaching 50 feet, with clusters of small red flowers followed by foot-long edible pods. Grown in Florida and California. Raised from seeds or cuttings.

Cercocarpus montanus. *Mountain mahogany.* Evergreen shrub growing to 8 feet. May be planted in dry soil from South Dakota to New Mexico. Limited to the western States. Raised from seeds or cuttings.

* Reliable for planting within their climate range. Recommended because they are widely used and most nurseries can supply them.

Cestrum parqui. *Willow-leaf jessamine.* Six-foot shrub with green-white or green-yellow flowers that are fragrant at night. Plant it only in the southern States; popular in California. Grown from cuttings.

* **Chamædaphne calyculata.** *Leather-leaf; Andromeda.* Shrub eventually reaching 5 feet. Native of northern bogs in Europe, Asia, and America. Clusters of nodding urn-shaped flowers appear from April to June. Plant in a mixture of peat moss, soil and sand. Include it in your foundation planting. Propagated from seeds, cuttings, layers, or suckers.

Chimaphila maculata. *Pipsissewa.* Less than a foot high, this evergreen woods plant has white or pinkish flowers in June. Good for a shaded part of the rock garden. Leaves are spotted.

C. umbellata. Similar to the above, but the leaves are without spots. Pipsissewas are raised by dividing the creeping stems.

Chiogenes hispidula. *Creeping snowberry.* Little plant with white flowers in May and June. Grown from seeds, divisions, or cuttings.

Cinnamomum camphora. Reaching 40 feet, it bears clusters of yellow flowers. Thrives only in the southern States and in California. It supplies the camphor of commerce. Grown from seeds or cuttings.

THE COTONEASTERS

Plant them in sun in well-drained soil. They do well both south and north. Raised from spring-sown seeds, by layers or cuttings in autumn, or by grafting onto quince or hawthorn.

Cotoneaster adpressa. Semi-evergreen prostrate plant, with small pink flowers in pairs.

C. horizontalis. Semi-evergreen spreading plant with small pinkish flowers. Makes a good ground cover for partial shade.

* **C. microphylla.** *Small-leaved cotoneaster.* Spreading 3-foot evergreen with white flowers. Will climb several feet up a bare stone wall, where its scarlet fruits look good during winter. Include it in your foundation planting.

(For deciduous cotoneasters, see Chapter 11.)

Cowania stansburiana. *Cliff rose; quinine bush.* Evergreen shrub reaching 12 feet, native of the southwestern United States. Cream-white flowers are borne from July to fall. Tolerates medium-dry soil.

Cytisus canariensis. *Broom; Genista.* Sparse evergreen shrub, growing to 6 feet and bearing fragrant yellow flowers in spring and summer. Plant it in the mid-South. Raised from seeds, layers, or cuttings.

* Reliable for planting within their climate range. Recommended because they are widely used and most nurseries can supply them.

THE DAPHNES

Grown from seeds or cuttings.

Daphne blagayana. Evergreen growing 1 foot high, with creamy-white fragrant flowers in early spring, borne in clusters.

The garland flower (Daphne cneorum).

* D. cneorum. *Garland flower*. Sub-shrub with trailing branches. Height around 12 inches. Bears fragrant pink flowers in clusters during early spring and again in September.

D. odora. Evergreen shrub growing 4 feet high, with clusters of highly scented white or purple flowers. Plant in the South and California.

Delonix regia. *Royal ponciana; peacock flower; flamboyant.* Growing to 50 feet, this magnificent subject from Madagascar is much planted as a boulevard tree in frost-free regions of the southern States. Flowers are 3 to 4 inches across and flaming red, followed by 2-foot-long pods.

Diosma (*Coleonema***) alba.** *Breath of Heaven.* Dwarf heathlike plant grows to 12 inches; white flowers. Bruised leaves emit a pleasing perfume. Will thrive only in the South and California. Grown from cuttings.

Elægnus pungens. *Oleaster.* A spiny evergreen growing to 15 feet with small inconspicuous, but fragrant flowers. Does well in southern plantings. Grown from seeds stratified one year, cuttings, or layers.

Empetrum nigrum. *Crowberry.* Spreading heathlike evergreen shrublet about 10 inches high. Small pink flowers are followed by small, oval, brownish-black, edible berries. Good ground-cover or rock plant.

* Epigæa repens. *Trailing arbutus; ground laurel; mayflower.* Perennial with creeping stems, bright green leaves, and clusters of white or pinkish flowers in May. Good for a shaded portion of the rock garden or as a ground cover under evergreens; needs acid soil. Wild from Newfoundland to Florida and Kentucky. Grown with difficulty from seeds or cuttings.

Epigæa repens (trailing arbutus).

Eucalyptus ficifolia. *Scarlet-flowering gum.* Australian evergreen; reaches 30 feet; bears white, pink, or scarlet flowers in long clusters.

* Reliable for planting within their climate range. Recommended because they are widely used and most nurseries can supply them.

E. globulus. *Blue gum.* Enormous tree growing to 300 feet in its native Australia. Source of eucalyptus oil.

The gum trees are so called because of the gum that issues from the trunk. The two above are limited to cultivation in the southern States and California. They are grown from seeds or cuttings.

Eugenia. Semi-tropical shrubs that may be grown in southern Florida and California.

E. aromatica. *Clove tree.* Grows to 30 feet in its native Moluccas; has purple flowers. The dried buds are the cloves of commerce.

E. cauliflora. *Jaboticaba.* Tree growing to 40 feet. The small flowers are white and the fruits are edible.

E. jambos. *Rose apple.* Growing to 30 feet, it has greenish white flowers and edible fruit.

E. paniculata myrtifolia. Small evergreen Australian tree with white flowers followed by ¾-inch rose-purple berries which may be preserved.

Eugenias are readily propagated from seeds or cuttings.

THE SPINDLE TREES

Euonymus

Birds are attracted by their berries. They are grown from stratified seeds or cuttings or by grafting.

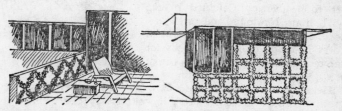

Euonymus may be used decoratively with formal modern architecture.

Euonymus patens. Ten-foot evergreen shrub, bearing attractive orange-red fruits in autumn. Much planted in southern gardens.

E. radicans carrierei. Low spreading shrub, slightly climbing.

* E. radicans coloratus. *Purple-leaf winter creeper.* Leaves are red in autumn.

* E. radicans vegetus. *Big-leaf winter creeper.* This hardy evergreen trailing shrub has round leaves and is sometimes called the evergreen

* Reliable for planting within their climate range. Recommended because they are widely used and most nurseries can supply them.

bittersweet on account of its red berries, which are effective all winter. (For deciduous types of euonymus, see Chapter 11.)

Makes an excellent ground cover or will climb on brick or stone.

Galax aphylla.

Galax aphylla. Evergreen wild perennial herb found from Virginia to Georgia. Leaves are shining, turning to bronze in autumn; they are collected for sale by florists. The small flowers in July are white. Galax makes a good ground cover; it is sometimes planted in rock gardens in damp woodsy soil. Plant in a northern exposure only. Propagated by division.

Gardenia jasminoides. *Cape jasmine.* Evergreen shrub growing to 6 feet with leathery leaves and 3-inch waxy-white extremely fragrant flowers. Good for the lower southern States. Tender in the North where the flowers are produced commercially in greenhouses. Sometimes grown as a house plant, mostly with indifferent success. Raised from cuttings.

Gaultheria procumbens. *Wintergreen; checkerberry; teaberry.* Small creeping plants with shining leaves and small white flowers from May to September. They are followed by scarlet edible berries. Collected in the wild from Newfoundland to Manitoba, south to Georgia. Good ground cover in sandy or peaty soils, or for the rock garden in shade. Grown from seeds, layers, divisions, or cuttings.

Wintergreen (Gaultheria procumbens).

Helianthemum chamaecistus. *Sun rose.* A semi-evergreen perennial growing 1 foot high with 1-inch yellow flowers. Likes dry limestone soil. Grown from seeds, layers, or cuttings.

Helleborus niger.

Helleborus niger. *Christmas rose.* Grows to 1½ feet. Leaves are hand-shaped with seven or more fingers. Flowers, 2½ inches across, are greenish-white or light purple, appearing in the earliest spring or in the winter in mild climates. Grown from seeds or divisions. A useful plant but in no way does it resemble the rose.

Holmskioldia sanguinea. *Chinese hat plant.* Evergreen shrub that may reach 30 feet; orange and red flowers. Suitable for California gardens.

ST. JOHN'S WORT

Hypericum

Grown from seeds, cuttings, or divisions.

Hypericum aureum. *St. John's wort.* Semi-evergreen shrub growing 4 feet high, with bluish-green leaves and 2-inch-diameter yellow flowers.

H. calycinum. *Aaron's beard.* Dwarf evergreen growing 12 inches high and suitable for use as a ground cover in the shade. Yellow blooms are 2 inches across. Hardy south from New York.

Iberis sempervirens.

* Iberis sempervirens. *Perennial candytuft.* Low-growing compact plant, evergreen, 12 inches high; flowers are white. Useful for edging the shrub border or the perennial border and for planting in pockets of soil between the rocks of a dry wall. Grown from seeds or divisions.

THE HOLLIES

Ilex opaca (American holly).

Ilex

They transplant with difficulty; set them in early spring or early fall, stripping off some of the leaves when doing so to reduce evaporation from the plant until the roots have recovered from the shock. Holly berries attract many birds. The plants are grown from seeds stratified one year or from cuttings.

Ilex aquifolium. *English holly.* Grows to 40 feet. Many forms are obtainable, including the sub-variety I. ferox or hedgehog holly, which has stouter, sharper, and more numerous spines, many of them along the veins on the leaf surface. Valuable to set at the center or at the ends of

* Reliable for planting within their climate range. Recommended because they are widely used and most nurseries can supply them.

a shrub planting for accent. Some types of English holly neglect to develop spines at all once they grow beyond the limit of browsing animals.

I. cornuta. Evergreen shrub with shiny strong-spined leaves and white flowers, followed by red berries. Fairly hardy north, but much grown in California.

I. crenata convexa. *Japanese holly.* Grows to 20 feet; leaves are oval and berries are black. Grows both in northern and southern States.

I. crenata latifolia. *Round-leaf holly.* Grows to 5 feet; leaves are elliptic and berries are black.

I. glabra. *Inkberry; winterberry.* A native plant growing from southern New England to Florida and Mississippi, and reaching 8 feet in height. Leaves are usually without spines except at the apex. Berries are black. Good in foundation planting and desirable for shade.

* I. opaca. *American holly.* Evergreen tree growing to 50 feet, with sharp spines on the edges of the leaves; white flowers, followed by dull red berries—sometimes yellow. Grows wild in woods from New England to Florida and Texas.

(A deciduous Ilex is listed in Chapter 11.)

Jacaranda mimosifolia. Grows to 50 feet, with fernlike leaves and nodding blue flowers. Grown only in the South and California.

THE MOUNTAIN LAURELS

Kalmia

Increased with difficulty from seeds, cuttings, or layers.

Kalmia angustifolia. *Lambkill; sheep laurel.* Grows to 3 feet; purple or crimson flowers in July. It and *K. latifolia* grow well in peaty soil.

* K. latifolia. *Mountain laurel; calico bush.* May grow to 10 feet. Bears rose-white flowers marked with purple in May and June; an all-white type can be procured. Does well in the North, the central States and the elevated sections of the South. Include it in your foundation and shrub-border plantings.

K. polifolia. *Bog Kalmia.* Two-foot evergreen with clusters of rose-purple flowers in June.

Laurus nobilis. *Laurel; sweet bay.* Evergreen tree with yellow flowers and dark purple berries. It may grow to 40 feet. Needs rich soil and adequate moisture; grows in the mid-southern and southern States. Increased by seeds, layers, and stem and root cuttings.

* Reliable for planting within their climate range. Recommended because they are widely used and most nurseries can supply them.

56

Ledum grœnlandicum. *Labrador tea.* Low evergreen shrub, growing to 3 feet, with small white flowers in clusters. Native of the northern sections of our continent. A passable tea has been made from it. Will grow in peaty soil. Propagated by layers, divisions, and seeds.

Ledum grœnlandicum.

L. palustre. *Crystal tea; wild rosemary.* Growing to 3 feet, it has small white flowers in clusters.

Leiophyllum buxifolium. *Sand myrtle.* Low compact evergreen shrub with small pink or white flowers in clusters in May and June. Suitable for borders and rock gardens in peaty or sandy soil. Increased by seeds and layers. A native American plant found from New Jersey to Florida.

Leptospermum lævigatum. *Australian pea tree.* Growing to 25 feet, it has small white flowers. Planted in the southern States and California, especially to hold soil against erosion by wind or rain. Grown from seeds or cuttings.

Several evergreens with pendent greenish flowers are known as Andromedas. This is one of them, best known by its botanical name, Leucothoe catesbæi.

* Leucothoe catesbæi. *Drooping leucothoe; Andromeda.* One of the broad-leaved evergreens, with shining oval leaves, it bears racemes of white flowers in May. Native from Virginia to Georgia and Tennessee. Needs protection over winter north of New York City. Desirable accent plant in foundation shrubbery. Taller than its fellows, 6 feet, it may well go between windows, in front of rain pipes, or at the building's corners. Increased by seeds, divisions, or layers.

THE EVERGREEN PRIVETS

Ligustrum

These are reproduced from stratified seeds, divisions, or cuttings.

* Reliable for planting within their climate range. Recommended because they are widely used and most nurseries can supply them.

57

Ligustrum japonicum. *Evergreen Japanese privet.* Growing to 10 feet or more, it makes a fine hedge or specimen bush in the southern States. Not hardy in the North.

L. lucidum. *Glossy privet.* Growing to 30 feet, it is usable only in the southern States; for foundation plantings, shrub borders, specimen groups, or hedges.

Lycopodium obscurum. *Ground pine.* A trailing club moss met with in the woods of New England. Much used for decoration bound into long thin skeins for Christmas roping. Before picking it, obtain the owner's permission and inquire if it is protected by the State; better, buy it at a nursery. Reproduced from spores, like ferns, and cuttings.

Magnolia grandiflora. *Bull bay.* Noble evergreen tree reaching a height of 100 feet, with large white fragrant flowers. Hardy in North Carolina to Florida, Texas, and California. Reproduced from seeds, cuttings, or layers.

(Deciduous types of magnolia are listed in Chapter 11.)

THE EVERGREEN BARBERRIES

Mahonia

Grown from stratified seeds, suckers, layers, and cuttings.

Mahonia bealei (*Berberis japonica*). Evergreen shrub eventually reaching 12 feet, with yellow flowers in 6-inch racemes. Much used in foundation planting in the South; not hardy in the North.

M. pinnata wagneri. Grows to 12 feet, with 3-inch racemes of yellow flowers. Adapted to California and warmer parts of the South; not recommended for the North.

M. repens (*Berberis repens*). Foot-high creeping evergreen with 3-inch racemes of yellow flowers. Native from British Columbia to California. Hardy south from southern New England. A good ground cover.

(Deciduous types of barberry [*Berberis*] are listed in Chapter 11.)

Mitchella repens. *Partridge berry.* Trailing evergreen with rooting stems and shining dark green leaves. White flowers in pairs are followed by vivid scarlet berries ⅓ inch in diameter. Good for a partly shaded portion of the rock garden or for planting under the taller subjects in a foundation planting. Reproduced by division of the roots.

Myrtus communis. *Myrtle.* A sweetly scented evergreen shrub, growing 10 feet high. Not hardy north of Richmond, Virginia, but popular in the South and on the west coast. Grown from cuttings or seeds.

Nandina domestica. *Heavenly bamboo.* Shrub reaching 8 feet, recommended for the southern States and California. Its leaves turn red-purple in fall. Has small white flowers in foot-long panicles, followed by bright red berries. It grows in sun or semi-shade, but must be well watered. Root-hardy in the north; completely hardy south of the 34th parallel. Propagated by seeds.

Nerium oleander. *Oleander*. Evergreen shrub reaching 20 feet; hardy outdoors only in the southern States and California. Flowers are 3 inches in diameter and are purple, red, pink, or white.

N. odorum. A dwarfer plant, reaching only 8 feet with pink or white fragrant flowers. Restricted to the warmer parts of the country.

The two plants above are reproduced by cuttings.

Olea europæa. The olive of commerce. Reaching 25 feet, it has silvery foliage and small white flowers followed by the small plumlike fruits, which are the source of olive oil and are usually gathered for pickling while still green, sometimes when ripe and black. Grown for ornament or for olives in California and the South. Propagated from seeds or cuttings.

* Pachysandra terminalis. *Japanese spurge*. Ideal ground cover for shade. Evergreen herbs 12 inches high, with unimportant white flowers. Increased easily from cuttings.

Photina serrulata. Shrub growing to 40 feet with panicles of white flowers, followed by small red berries. Not hardy in the North. Increased by seeds, cuttings, and layers, and by grafting onto quince or hawthorn.

* Pieris floribunda. *Mountain fetterbush; Andromeda*. One of the broad-leaved evergreens growing to 6 feet. Pure white, urn-shaped flowers in terminal panicles in April and May. Leaves turn bronze in the late fall. Will grow in peaty soil. Important for foundation planting.

P. japonica. A taller type from Japan. The nodding panicles of greenish-white flowers are 6 inches long.

The plants above are increased by seeds, layers, or cuttings.

Pittosporum tobira. Japanese shrub growing to 10 feet; not hardy in the North, but much planted in California and the southern States The fragrant flowers are greenish-white.

P. undulatum. *Victorian box*. Attractive Australian evergreen tree maturing at 40 feet. The fragrant flowers in long clusters are white. Grown in southern California, where it makes a good hedge.

Pittosporums are increased from seeds, cuttings, or by grafting.

Plumbago capensis. *Leadwort*. Small, spreading and partly climbing shrub that may be grown in the South. Flowers are azure-blue. Much

* Reliable for planting within their climate range. Recommended because they are widely used and most nurseries can supply them.

planted in California. Increased by seeds, divisions, and cuttings.

Polygala chamæbuxus. *Milkwort.* Creeping evergreen shrub growing to 12 inches, with yellow flowers. A good ground cover, hardy south of Connecticut. Increased by seeds or cuttings.

Potentilla tridentata. *Blood-root.* Growing to 12 inches with shining leaves and small white flowers in loose clusters. Grows wild from Greenland to Georgia and Minnesota. May be used as a ground cover. Grown from seeds or divisions.

Prunus ilicifolia. *Islay; Catalina cherry.* Small evergreen tree growing to 30 feet with spiny hollylike leaves. Flowers are white, followed by ¾-inch dark red or near-black fruits.

P. laurocerasus. *Cherry laurel.* Small evergreen tree with half-inch flowers that are sweetly perfumed. Much planted in the southern States and California; not winter-hardy in the North.

P. lusitanica. *Portugal laurel.* Similar to *P. laurocerasus,* but larger, growing to 25 feet. Not hardy in the North.

These three are grown from seeds (stratified) or cuttings.

(Deciduous types of Prunus are included in Chapter 11.)

Pyracantha coccinea or firethorn.

Pyracantha coccinea. *Firethorn.* Thorny shrub, sometimes reaching 20 feet, with white flowers in corymbs in May, followed by showy red fruits. Good hedge plants, hardy only mid-South and South. In its climate range, an important foundation subject. Propagated by seeds, cuttings, or layers.

P. formosana and **yunnanensis.** Two evergreen, white-flowered, red-berried firethorns much planted in California. Reproduced by cuttings, layers, and rarely by seeds.

Pyxidanthera barbulata. *Pixie; flowering moss; Pine-Barren beauty.* Creeping evergreen sub-shrub, forming cushions in the Pine-Barrens of New Jersey; may be planted in the rock garden. The tiny white flowers are borne from March to May. Propagated by root divisions and seeds.

Quercus virginiana. *Live oak.* Evergreen tree reaching 60 feet, with shining green leaves. Much planted as an individual specimen tree in the southern States. Reproduced by cuttings or seed.

Roystonea oleracea. *Barbados royal palm.* Growing up to 100 feet, this handsome tropical tree is much planted in southern Florida.

R. regia. *Cuba royal palm.* Seventy feet high, the trunk is swollen at the center, slightly tapering above and below. For the far South only.

Sabal minor. *Dwarf palmetto.* A stemless palm, native to moist land in South Carolina, Georgia, and Florida. This and other varieties are often planted along boulevards in the southern States.

Sapium sebiferum. *Chinese tallow tree.* Evergreen growing 40 feet high; the seed-covering yields a wax which may be made into candles, and latex in the stems and leaves furnishes rubber. An ornamental shade tree planted in the South. Propagated from cuttings or seeds.

Shortia galacifolia. *Oconee bells.* May be planted in woodsy soil in a sheltered portion of the rock garden or at the foot of broad-leaved evergreens. Growing only 8 inches high, it makes an attractive ground cover. Propagated by division and runners.

Shortia galacifolia.

Sterculia diversifolia. *Kurrajong* (*Brachychiton*); *bottle tree.* An Australian native reaching 60 feet, bearing yellowish-white and red flowers. May be grown in the southern States and California. Reproduced by cuttings or seeds.

Tecomaria (*Tecoma*) **capensis.** *Cape honeysuckle.* Climbing shrub, native of South Africa; much planted in the South and California. Orange-scarlet flowers are 2 inches long. Grown from cuttings or seeds.

Creeping thyme, mother-of-thyme, or Thymus serpyllum.

* **Thymus serpyllum lanuginosus.** *Mother-of-thyme; creeping thyme; brotherwort.* Prostrate sub-shrub with hairy gray leaves, stem-rooting, with small purple flowers from June to September. Set it in the rock garden, in the front of the perennial border, or in spaces between stones of the patio garden or garden steps where it will stand considerable wear. When walked upon, it exudes its thyme fragrance. Propagated by seeds or root division.

Vauquelinia californica. *Arizona rosewood.* A broad-leaved evergreen shrub, growing 7 feet high and bearing small whitish blooms in flat panicles. Its range is from southwestern New Mexico to southern California. Somewhat experimental, its planting even in this area might at first be confined to one or two specimens.

* Reliable for planting within their climate range. Recommended because they are widely used and most nurseries can supply them.

THE CRANBERRY BUSHES OR HAWS

Viburnum

These are propagated by seeds, cuttings, layers or grafting.

Viburnum rhytidophyllum. Evergreen, growing 10 feet high with shining leaves and yellowish-white flowers in 8-inch clusters. Valuable accent shrub in a foundation planting.

V. suspensum. Evergreen shrub growing to 6 feet, with pinkish flowers in dense clusters in June and July, followed by red haws or fruits. Suitable for the South and California.

V. tinus. *Laurestinus.* Shrub reaching 10 feet; white or light pink flowers in 3-inch clusters, followed by black fruits. Good for the South. Birds are attracted by viburnum haws.

* **Vinca minor.** *Periwinkle; running myrtle.* Trailing evergreen with lilac-blue flowers, sometimes purple or white. Forms with variegated leaves are obtainable. Popular ground cover for shade; or plant in the rock garden or hanging baskets. Grown from divisions or cuttings.

Washingtonia filifera. A tall palm reaching over 80 feet, much planted for tropical effect in central and southern California. Does best inland.

W. robusta. Even taller than the above and more suitable for the coastal areas of the extreme South.

Palms are reproduced from seeds and suckers.

Yucca filamentosa.

* **Yucca filamentosa.** *Adam's needle.* Good to plant along with shrubs: from a cluster of sharp-pointed narrow leaves, with long curly threads along the margins, in summer a flower spike arises, which may well be 12 feet tall, bearing a number of 2-inch-long white flowers. Increased by seeds, division, or root cuttings.

Zenobia pulverulenta (*Andromeda pulverulenta*). One of the broad-leaved evergreens; a shrub growing to 6 feet, bearing small, white, bell-shaped flowers in May and June. Needs sandy or peaty soil. Does well in the South; not hardy north of New York City. Include it in your plantings within its climate range. Increased by seeds, layers, or cuttings.

* Reliable for planting within their climate range. Recommended because they are widely used and most nurseries can supply them.

CHAPTER 11

Deciduous Trees, Shrubs and Herbs

"Warble me now for the joy of lilac-time."
WALT WHITMAN, "Warble for Lilac-Time."

DECIDUOUS PLANTS are those that lose their leaves in fall, as distinguished from evergreens. But a few semi-evergreens are included in this list; often these are nearly deciduous in the North, nearly evergreen in their southern range.

Notice how tall some of the deciduous trees grow. Refrain from planting types that may eventually cover windows, or overshade or overtop the building. Keep trees 20 feet or more distant from house drains or sewage systems to avoid trouble from roots blocking them.

Abelia grandiflora (*chinensis*). Attractive half-evergreen shrub, growing to 7 feet, with small single pink flowers during summer and fall, yellow tinted. Propagated by layers and cuttings.

Aberia engleriana (*dovyalis*). Deciduous sub-tropical shrub growing to 6 feet, with rose-purple flowers less than 1 inch long, in clusters. Fairly hardy in the North, but mostly planted in the southern States. Both male and female plants must be used to obtain the berries, which are edible. Reproduced by seeds and layers.

Acacia baileyana. A brilliant wattle from New South Wales with the customary yellow flowers. May be grown outdoors only in the South and California. Favorable temperature limits are 18° F. to 50° F.

A. floribunda. *Sydney golden wattle.* Has whitish-yellow flowers. Similarly sensitive to cold and heat.

Acacias are grown from seeds or cuttings.

Acanthopanax pentaphyllum (*Sieboldianum*). A desirable hardy shrub growing to 10 feet. Its flowers are greenish-white. Include it in your foundation planting if you have room for a large subject. It is propagated by root or stem cuttings.

THE MAPLES

Acer

Mostly grown from stratified seeds; sometimes from layers and cuttings.

Acer ginnala. *Amur maple.* Graceful shrub growing to 20 feet. Set it in the center or at the ends of a shrub border, so its height will catch the eye.

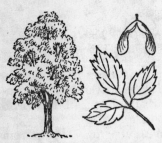

Acer negundo (box elder).

A. negundo. *Box elder.* A 70-foot tree found wild from Ontario to Florida and Texas. Grows quickly; tolerates city smoke and auto fumes. Leaves turn yellow in the autumn.

*** A. palmatum.** *Japanese maple.* Slowly maturing to a height of 25 feet. Many horticultural varieties have colored leaves; if not already colored, most turn red in autumn. Have this in your list of shrubs for foundation planting.

*** A. platanoides.** *Norway maple.* Large and handsome tree with spreading branches and a compact round head. Leaves turn to a pastel hue of green and gold in fall; much planted as a boulevard tree or as a specimen on the lawn. Various horticultural forms are available, including **Crimson King** (Patent No. 735), a new purple-leaved sort that holds its rich dark color through the summer. The subvariety **columnare** is upright.

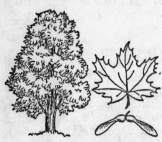

Norway maple (Acer platanoides).

A. rubrum. *Red maple; scarlet maple; swamp maple.* Leaves turn scarlet in early fall. Native tree found from Newfoundland to Florida and Texas. Grows to 100 feet and higher.

A. saccharum. *Sugar or rock maple; silver maple.* Over 100 feet, with leaves that color red after first frosts. A fast-growing native tree, found from Quebec to the Gulf of Mexico. A good specimen tree to

---

* Reliable for planting within their climate range. Recommended because they are widely used and most nurseries can supply them.

set on the lawn or at the end of an *allée*. Sap starts to flow in the late winter while there is still snow on the ground. It is collected and boiled to make maple syrup; further boiling produces maple sugar.

* *Æsculus hippocastanum*. *Horse chestnut* or *buckeye*. A much-planted tree, stately native of Europe. Has foot-long spikes of white flowers spotted with red, followed by handsome polished nuts in blunt-spiked capsules. The nuts are not edible. Good for giving shade on large parklike estates. The tree is attractive to Japanese beetles, which may partly defoliate it every summer. Tolerating smoke and auto fumes, it is good for city planting, but its roots sometimes search out and clog sewer lines if within 20 feet of them. The red-flowered variety is a smaller tree. Propagated by stratified seeds, layering, budding, or grafting.

* *Ailanthus glandulosa*. *Tree of heaven*. Native of China, it is a successful immigrant, appearing in vacant lots of eastern cities. It is rapid-growing, largely immune to insect attacks, and eventually reaching 60 feet. It is smoke-tolerant and will stand alkali soil. Use as a street and boulevard tree in difficult situations. Reproduced from root cuttings, seeds, or suckers.

Alnus glutinosa (*vulgaris*). *Black alder*. Deciduous; grows to 80 feet.

A. incana. *Speckled alder*. A. rugosa. *Smooth alder*.

All these alders are adapted to boggy land. They are usually reproduced from seeds.

The sugar maple (Acer saccharum).

Æsculus hippocastanum (horse chestnut or buckeye).

The tree of heaven (Ailanthus glandulosa).

* Reliable for planting within their climate range. Recommended because they are widely used and most nurseries can supply them.

Amelanchier canadensis (shadbush).

Amelanchier canadensis. *Shadbush, serviceberry,* or *Juneberry.* Eventually growing to 30 feet, it is covered with racemes of white flowers ahead of the leaves, which turn bright yellow in autumn. Grown from seeds, layers, or cuttings.

Amorpha canescens. *Lead plant; false indigo.* Native of the central United States from the Canadian border to the Gulf of Mexico. Grows up to 4 feet, and in July and August has 6-inch racemes of blue pea flowers. Will tolerate the reduced rainfall of the southern Great Plains. Reproduced from seeds, occasionally from layers or cuttings.

A. fruticosa. *Bastard indigo.* Growing to 20 feet, it has purple, blue, or white flowers in May or June.

A. nana. *Dwarf indigo.* Grows 15 inches at most: a good ground cover. Purple flowers in summer. Native south and west from Minnesota.

Anisacanthus wrightii. In the warm climate of Texas and New Mexico this shrub will grow to 4 feet; less than half this in Kansas. Suitable for the South. Slender orange-red flowers from July to fall.

Aralia spinosa. *Hercules club; devil's walking-cane.* Small, spiny, deciduous tree growing to 30 feet, with long leaves and tiny white flowers in 4-foot panicles. A curiosity when planted as a lawn specimen. Hardy in rich soil from southern New York to Texas. Propagated by seeds, and root and stem cuttings.

Aronia arbutifolia. *Red chokeberry.* Reaching 10 feet, this showy densely branched shrub has white or pinkish flowers in early spring, followed by red fruits. Grows in moist soil from Massachusetts to Florida and Texas. Raised from seeds, suckers, layers, and cuttings.

Aster fruticosa. A shrub bearing blue flowers in spring. Needs good light and a porous soil. Much planted in California.

Benzoin aestivale. *Spice bush; lindera.* Aromatic deciduous shrub growing to 15 feet. Small greenish flowers appear before the leaves; they are followed by scarlet fruits which attract many birds. A native, growing in moist places from Maine to Florida and west to Texas. Produced from stratified seeds, divisions, or cuttings.

THE BARBERRIES

Berberis

Their fruits are attractive to birds. Barberries are reproduced by stratified seeds, suckers, layers, or cuttings.

Berberis koreana. *Korean barberry.* A 6-foot spiny shrub with small yellow flowers, followed by scarlet berries in autumn. Include this in your foundation planting.

* **B. mentorensis.** *Mentor barberry* (Patent No. 99). Matures at 3 feet. Foliage is heavy and thick; withstands heat and drought.

* **B. thunbergii.** *Japanese green-leaved barberry.* Matures at 4 feet. A popular hedge plant for both North and South. Normally trimmed to 24 inches high. Withstands smoke and fumes of the city streets. Leaves turn scarlet in autumn, and over the winter the plant has scarlet berries which attract birds. Minute thorns which are difficult to extract from the skin make the plant hard to handle—wear leather gloves.

* **B. thunbergii atropurpurea.** *Red-leaved barberry.* Maturing at 4 feet, the foliage is rich bronzy-red all summer. Plant it both north and south, and in the sunlight to develop its full color.

B. thunbergii erecta. *Truehedge columnberry* (Patent No. 110). Thrives in the southern States.

(Evergreen Berberis will be found in Chapter 10.)

THE BIRCHES

Betula

Betula alba. *European white birch.* A graceful tree, maturing at 30 to 40 feet. Upright, with beautiful white bark. Leaves are small and finely toothed.

B. lutea. *Yellow birch.* A tall native tree, found from Newfoundland to Tennessee and growing to 90 feet. The leaves turn yellow in autumn.

B. papyrifera. *Paper birch; canoe birch.* Tree growing up to 100 feet with white, self-shedding bark.

European white birch (Betula alba).

Grows wild in the northern sections of the United States in poor sandy soil. Better plant this and allow your youngsters to use the bark sections; dissuade them from peeling bark from other birches in the woods, which will injure and may kill the trees.

* **B. pendula gracilis.** Cut-leaved weeping birch, 30 to 40 feet. Graceful, with drooping branches, finely cut leaves and silver-white bark.

* Reliable for planting within their climate range. Recommended because they are widely used and most nurseries can supply them.

Birches make splendid groups on the lawn. If the leaves appear partly shriveled they may have been attacked by the leaf-miner, tiny worms which burrow into the leaf and live between its upper and lower surface. Spray at once with Black-leaf-40 or Lindane; repeat in July and again in August. Next year start spraying two weeks ahead of the date when the injury was first seen. There are three broods a year of the sawfly causing the trouble in most parts of the country.

Birches may be reproduced by seeds.

Buddleia or butterfly bush is a herbaceous perennial in its first years and in the North; becomes a tall woody shrub in the mid-South.

* Buddleia variabilis. *Butterfly bush; summer lilac.* The long tapering spikes of bloom are crowded with small tubular flowers that are pleasingly fragrant and attractive to butterflies; starting in July, they continue till frost. During the first few winters in the north the plants act as herbaceous perennials, dying to the ground; later they often continue as deciduous shrubs. Some modern varieties include:

Charming. Lavender-pink.

Dubonnet. The color matches that of Dubonnet wine, glowing red in the sun; 4 feet.

Fascinating. Orchid-pink.

Orchid Beauty. Cattleya lilac with an orange center. The florets are fringed.

Peace. Rich shining purple; each floret has an orange-red center.

Royal Purple. Glowing red-purple; 3 to 4 feet.

Royal Red. A brilliant flower.

Be sure to include buddleias in your foundation or shrubbery plantings south from New York to the Gulf. They are reproduced from seeds or cuttings.

Callicarpa americana. *French mulberry.* A 6-foot shrub with bluish flowers from May to July, followed by violet fruits. It grows from Virginia to Texas and is not hardy north.

C. dichotoma (*C. purpurea*). *Beauty berry.* Grows to 4 feet, and bears pink verbenalike flowers in August. Berries are blue-violet and showy. Good in both North and South.

* Reliable for planting within their climate range. Recommended because they are widely used and most nurseries can supply them.

Callicarpas are propagated by seeds, divisions, or cuttings.

Calycanthus floridus. *Carolina allspice; sweet shrub; strawberry shrub.* Grows 6 to 8 feet high and bears 2-inch, chocolate-colored, and fragrant blooms. Include it in your shrub plantings wherever you have space for a large subject. Grown from seeds, divisions, or layers.

Calycanthus floridus (strawberry shrub, Carolina allspice).

Caragana arborescens. *Siberian pea tree.* Growing to 15 feet, it has yellow flowers in May and June. Valuable to set in the center or at the ends of a shrub border where its height will catch the eye. It makes a good hedge. This plant is readily grown from seeds.

Carpinus caroliniana. *American hornbeam; blue beech.* The leaves turn orange in autumn. Grows to 40 feet, but usually is only half this height in the woods from Quebec to Florida and Texas. It makes a good hedge. Propagated by seeds which germinate slowly and irregularly.

Carpinus caroliniana (American hornbeam or blue beech).

Hickory or mockernut (Carya alba).

THE HICKORIES

Carya

Propagated by sowing the nuts after they have been stratified for six months.

Carya alba. *Hickory; mockernut.* A native from Massachusetts to Florida and Texas. Grows eventually to 90 feet. The leaves turn brown in autumn.

C. ovata. *Shagbark; shellbark.* An even taller hickory, native over the same range. Has flaking bark in large, rough, scaly slabs.

Either is a good specimen tree to set in the lawn, or will make a good accent at the end of an *allée,* especially if a white seat is constructed around the bole.

Caryopteris incana. *Bluebeard; blue spiraea.* Growing to 5 feet, it has small violet-blue flowers from August to frost. Usually planted in the southern States and of doubtful hardiness north of Baltimore, Maryland. The foliage is fragrant. Caryopteris is increased by cuttings.

Chinese chestnut.

* Castanea mollissima. *Hybrid Chinese chestnut.* A low spreading tree, 50 feet high, yielding edible nuts a year or two after planting. Appears immune to the chestnut blight which has killed nearly all American chestnuts. Best planted in threes to insure pollination; neighbors might cooperate where space is limited. If you have room plant three on your lawn for an effective group. Can be grown from stratified seeds, but resistance to disease may be doubtful with seedlings; best method is probably to graft or bud onto these seedlings from proven blight-free trees.

Catalpa bungei. Small tree with 6-inch leaves and white flowers, spotted with purple. Plant it in Georgia and south, also in California. Propagated by cuttings.

* **C. speciosa.** *Indian bean.* Big-leaved boulevard tree; brown-spotted white bell-flowers in May in 6-inch skeins, followed in autumn by 12-inch flat pods. Fast-growing, it may eventually reach 100 feet. Hardy north. Grown from seeds or cuttings.

Ceanothus pallidus. Deciduous shrub 2½ feet high, bearing light blue flowers. A hybrid much planted on the West Coast. Usually winter-kills to the ground in the North and East, acting as a herbaceous perennial. The sub-variety roseus has flesh-colored flowers. Propagated by layers, cuttings, or stratified seeds.

Celtis occidentalis. *Hackberry; nettletree.* One of our natives, found from Quebec to North Carolina and in Alabama. Grows to 75 feet. The hackberry attracts many birds to the property. Stands city conditions in the North. Increased by seeds, layers, or cuttings.

The hackberry or nettletree (Celtis occidentalis).

* Reliable for planting within their climate range. Recommended because they are widely used and most nurseries can supply them.

Cephalanthus occidentalis. *Buttonbush.* It needs moist land, when it may grow to 15 feet, bearing cream-white flowers from July to September. Its value is in mass plantings, especially in the mid-South. Hardy to the middle Atlantic States. Increased by seeds, layers, or cuttings.

Cercidiphyllum japonicum. *Katsura tree.* Grows to 100 feet in its native Japan; hardy south from New York and Massachusetts. Its leaves turn yellow to crimson in early fall. Grown from cuttings.

* **Cercis canadensis.** *Redbud; Judas tree.* Deep rosy-pink flowers are borne ahead of the leaves, which turn yellow in early fall. Grows to 35 feet but, if the leading stem is kept pruned back, it may be developed into a useful shrub 10 to 12 feet high. Native and a picturesque feature of our woodlands from New Jersey to Florida and Texas, where it is a sure sign of spring. Have it in your shrub border if you have room. It stands the smoke and auto fumes of city streets. Propagated from soft cuttings in summer.

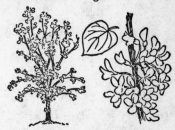

Redbud or Judas tree (Cercis canadensis).

Chænomeles lagenaria (flowering quince).

* **Chænomeles lagenaria.** *Flowering quince.* Frequently listed as *Cydonia japonica.* Handsome bush, maturing at 10 feet, it has spiny branches and brilliant orange-scarlet-red flowers in March and April. The greenish-yellow fragrant fruits are not usable. By all means include it in your list of shrubs for foundation planting; it grows well in the South as well as the North. Propagation is by stratified seeds, root or branch cuttings, or layers.

Chilopsis linearis. *Flore de Mimbre; desert willow; willow catalpa; flowering willow.* Bears lilac and yellow flowers; may grow to 20 feet. Native shrub of California and Texas, found near springs and streams in dry regions; of doubtful value north of New Mexico and Oklahoma. Increased by seeds or cuttings.

* Reliable for planting within their climate range. Recommended because they are widely used and most nurseries can supply them.

Fringe tree (Chionanthus virginica).

Cladrastis lutea (Dyer's yellow-wood).

Chionanthus virginica. *Fringe tree.* The flowers in May and June are white and scented; the leaves turn yellow in early fall. Grows to 30 feet. Native from Pennsylvania to Florida and Texas. Needs moist soil and full sun. Hardy north in a sheltered position. Grown from seeds, layers or cuttings, grafting or budding onto the ash.

Cladrastis lutea (*tinctoria*). *Dyer's yellowwood.* Has fragrant white flowers and the leaves turn yellow in late fall. Reaches 50 feet. Suitable for the southeastern United States; of doubtful value elsewhere. Raised from seeds or root cuttings.

Clethra alnifolia rosea. *Sweet pepperbush; summer sweet.* Native shrub growing to 5 feet, with fragrant pink flowers in August. Requires damp land, but thrives either in sun or shade. Found from Maine to Florida. Grown from seeds, divisions, or layers.

Clivia miniata. *Kafir lily (Imantophyllum).* Leaves are 18 inches long and 2 inches wide, topped by large heads of scarlet and yellow flowers. Familiar conservatory plant in the North, and outdoors in shady places in California. Raised from seeds or divisions.

Colutea arborescens. *Bladder senna.* May reach 12 feet. Yellow pea-shaped flowers are followed by inflated pods. Does well in the South and is hardy in the North. Grown from seeds or autumn-planted cuttings.

THE DOGWOODS
Cornus

Straight tough twigs of some varieties were used for skewers in colonial days, for daggers in medieval times. Thought to have originally been called "dag-wood," corrupted later to "dogwood." Birds are attracted by the berries. Most varieties may be raised from seeds, suckers, layers, or cuttings.

* **Cornus alba.** *Tatarian dogwood; red osier.* Speedily growing to 10 feet. White flowers are small and in clusters. Twigs are blood-red.

C. amomum *(Sericea). Silky dogwood.* The branches of this 10-foot bush are purplish. White flowers in June and July are followed by globular blue berries.

* **C. florida.** *White dogwood.* Growing to 35 feet, the flowers are white, beautifying American spring woodlands from Maine to Florida and Texas. Leaves turn scarlet in late autumn.

The chief attraction of Cornus alba (Tatarian or Siberian dogwood) is in its blood-red branches. The flower clusters are quite unlike one's usual idea of the dogwood.

* **C. florida rubra.** The more rare pink-flowering dogwood. Dwarfer, maturing at 20 feet.

The two above are valuable to set as accent plants in the center or ends of a shrub planting. Or place them just within a woodlot. These two thrive in both North and South; all the dogwoods stand city conditions.

C. stolonifera flaviramea. *Osier.*

Cornus florida (dogwood).

Growing to 10 feet. Small flowers are in clusters; branches are yellow.

THE COTONEASTERS

Grown from spring-sown seeds, by layers or cuttings in autumn.

* **Cotoneaster acutifolia.** *Pekin cotoneaster.* Matures at 10 feet. Small leathery leaves are rich glossy green, turning red in autumn. Berries in fall are black. It makes a good hedge, trimmed like privet, and is tolerant of shade. Does well in the southern States and in the North.

C. divaricata. *Spreading cotoneaster.* Growing 6 feet high; flowers are pinkish, in clusters, followed by bright red fruits. Grows in the southern States and is hardy north.

C. multiflora. *Many-flowered cotoneaster.* Growing to 6 feet, it has many white flowers in April and May. For planting in the southern and southwestern States.

* Reliable for planting within their climate range. Recommended because they are widely used and most nurseries can supply them.

C. racimeflora (*C. nummularia*). Deciduous shrub growing to 6 feet with clusters of white flowers, followed by coral-red berries.

(See Chapter 10 for evergreen cotoneasters.)

THE THORNS
Cratægus

Include them in your foundation plantings where you have space for large subjects: carrierei, crus-galli, oxyacantha stand clipping and make excellent hedges. They are mostly raised from seeds, stratified for two years. All stand city conditions.

Cratægus carrierei (*lavallei*). Shrub growing to 20 feet, with savage 2-inch spines and red flowers.

Cratægus crus-galli (cockspur thorn).

C. coccinea (*intricata*) *Scarlet-fruited thorn.* Shrub growing to 10 feet; has few spines.

C. crus-galli. *Cockspur thorn.* Growing to 25 feet, it has spines several inches long.

C. mollis. Tree growing to 30 feet, with red flowers and 2-inch spines. Hardy north.

Cratægus oxyacantha (English hawthorn).

* **C. oxyacantha.** *English hawthorn; thornapple; maythorn.* Grows to 15 feet, with fierce 1-inch spines and bright red flowers. Leaves turn orange-red in autumn. * Paul's Scarlet, a cultivated form, bears clusters of double red flowers. Makes a good hedge.

C. phaenopyrum. *Washington thorn.* Deciduous shrub or small tree growing to 30 feet, with 3-inch spines and bright red fruits. Hardy south from Delaware.

All varieties of *Cratægus* attract birds to the garden.

Cytisus scoparius. *Scotch broom.* Reaches 10 feet and bears yellow flowers. It may be planted south from Connecticut. Easily grown from seeds, layers or cuttings.

* Reliable for planting within their climate range. Recommended because they are widely used and most nurseries can supply them.

Dalea frutescens. *Black dalea; pea bush.* Small shrub reaching 2 feet, native of dry sandy areas from Texas to Mexico. Covered with violet flowers several times in the season. Severe pruning aids it. Of value as an edging plant in the Southwest.

Daphne genkwa. Growing to 3 feet, this deciduous shrub from China has lilac-blue flowers in clusters, appearing before the leaves in early spring. Good for foundation planting or the rear of a large rock garden. Hardy south from New York. Grown from seeds, layers, or cuttings.

Deutzia gracilis. Deciduous shrub growing to 6 feet. Flowers are white in spreading clusters. Does well from New England to the mid-South.

* D. scabra. *Pride of Rochester.* This quick-growing shrub, maturing at 8 feet, has fine double white flowers, individually small but in upright skeins. Good for foundation planting, north or south.

Deutzias are propagated from cuttings.

Deutzia scabra (Pride of Rochester).

Diervilla lonicera. *Bush honeysuckle.* Deciduous 4-foot shrub, native in Canada and occurring south to the Carolinas. The clusters of small flowers in spring and summer are yellow, shaded reddish-brown.

D. rivularis. Growing to 6 feet. Yellow flowers.

D. sessilifolia. Grows to 4 or 5 feet. Yellow flowers.

These three are much planted in the mid-South. They are propagated by suckers or cuttings.

(See also *Lonicera tatarica* on page 85.)

Echium fastuosum. *Tower of jewels.* Huge dense spikes of brilliant blue flowers in spring and summer. A 6-foot shrub for California gardens. Propagated by cuttings or layers.

Elaeagnus umbellata. Ornamental decorative shrub growing to 18 feet and bearing fragrant flowers in early summer. Hardy north. Grown from seeds stratified one year, cuttings, or layers.

Elsholtzia stauntoni. *Heathermist.* Aromatic shrub growing to 5 feet with lilac-purple flowers. Give it a sunny position in your shrub border or foundation planting. Grown from cuttings or seeds.

Enkianthus campanulatus. A shrub that eventually reaches 20 feet. Has small, orange and red, bell-shaped, pendulous, heatherlike flowers ½ inch long. Raised from seeds, cuttings, or layers.

* Reliable for planting within their climate range. Recommended because they are widely used and most nurseries can supply them.

THE SPINDLE TREES

Euonymus

Birds are attracted by their berries. Propagation is by spring-sown stratified seeds, cuttings, or layers.

* Euonymus alatus. *Cork-bark; spindle tree.* Bark is corklike and curiously winged. Leaves turn scarlet in late autumn. Fruits are red. The plant tolerates shade and grows to 6 feet. Good subject for foundation planting or shrubbery.

E. americanus. *Strawberry bush.* Deciduous shrub growing to 8 feet and bearing pink fruits. Hardy from New York to Florida and Texas.

E. atropurpureus. *Burning bush; wahoo.* Growing up to 25 feet, this is a native plant, found from Ontario to Florida and Montana. The leaves turn red in late fall. Desirable accent subject.

E. bungeanus. *Winterberry.* Growing to 15 feet, very hardy and drought-resistant. The fruit capsule splits in the autumn to disclose the bright red seeds. May be planted in the South; in the North also.

E. europaeus. *European spindle tree.* Bears greenish-white flowers, followed by pink berries. The leaves turn red in late fall. Grows up to 25 feet, is tolerant of shade, and makes a good hedge.

(See Chapter 10 for evergreen types of Euonymus.)

Euphorbia pulcherrima. *Poinsettia.* This well-known Christmas pot plant is a 10-foot shrub in the tropics. It can be planted outdoors only in California and the southernmost tip of Florida. The yellow or white flowers are small and insignificant, but the upper leaves or bracts surrounding them are brilliant and take the place of flowers. Propagated by cuttings taken in early summer, forming well-colored pot plants by the following Christmas.

Exochorda racemosa. *Pearl bush.* Growing to 10 feet, it has 2-inch white blooms in early spring. Looks like spiraea or mock orange. Plant it in the southern States; it is hardy in the North also. Propagated from seeds, layers, cuttings, and suckers.

* Fagus americana. *American beech.* Stately tall forest tree with smooth gray bark, furnishing valuable timber and edible nuts. Grows 75 feet high. The leaves turn yellow in late fall. Occurs from New Brunswick to Florida and Texas. Prefers a limy sweet soil. Groups in American woodlands are ascribed to birds who have cached stores of nuts under the soil surface and have failed to return for them. A good specimen tree to set on the lawn to be visible on all sides; or at the

---

* Reliable for planting within their climate range. Recommended because they are widely used and most nurseries can supply them.

end of an *allée,* where a white seat around the bole will be effective. Can be pruned to make a good hedge. Propagated from spring-sown, previously stratified nuts.

Fallugia paradoxa. *Apache plume.* Semi-evergreen, growing 6 to 8 feet high. Plant it in the southwestern States. Bears white blooms that look like apple blossoms in spring, with a few later flowers till fall.

American beech (Fagus americana).

Ficus carica. *Edible fig.* Deciduous tree to 30 feet, grown for its fruit south from the latitude of New York, with winter protection in cold latitudes and as an orchard crop in Louisiana, Texas and California, where sometimes it also is planted for decoration.

F. benghalensis. The famous banyan tree of India.

F. elastica. The familiar rubber plant of northern greenhouses.

F. pumila. Self-clinging climbing fig of the deep South.

Figs are readily grown from seeds or cuttings.

Fontanesia fortunei. Privetlike shrub growing to 12 feet; small white flowers in May and June. Does well in dry soil. A good sheared hedge. Plant in the southwest; hardy north. Raised from layers or cuttings.

Forestiera neomexicana. *Adelia; tanglebush; wild olive; false privet.* Grows up to 10 feet from Texas westward; not hardy in the North. Has clusters of small yellow flowers before the leaves. Needs moist soil. Grown from seeds or layers.

GOLDEN BELL

Forsythia

They are tolerant of city conditions. Propagated from cuttings.

* **Forsythia suspensa.** *Golden bell.* Universally planted, handsome suburban shrub, maturing at 10 feet. Easily grown, the bush is a mass of brilliant yellow bloom in April and May before the leaves appear.

A flowering branch of Forsythia.

* Reliable for planting within their climate range. Recommended because they are widely used and most nurseries can supply them.

77

F. viridissima. *Dark green golden bell.* Growing also to 10 feet, the leaves turn purple in late fall.

* Spring Glory. A new and improved golden variety.

The three above grow in the South as well as in the North.

Fothergilla major. An American deciduous shrub with dense clusters of white flowers, appearing early with the leaves. Grows to 6 feet. Native of Georgia and hardy north. Grown from seeds or layers.

White ash (Fraxinus americana).

Fraxinus americana. *White ash.* A valuable timber tree reaching 100 feet when mature. The foliage turns yellow in autumn. Good specimen tree to set in the lawn or to plant at the end of an *allée.* Stands city conditions and boggy land. Raised from seeds that have been stratified for one year.

Fuchsia magellanica. A handsome shrub that may reach 15 feet under favorable conditions, bearing red and blue flowers. Makes an effective shrub and even a hedge in mild climates; much planted in California. In the north small types of Fuchsia hybrida are taken from the greenhouse in spring and set in flowerbeds. Propagation is by cuttings.

Gleditsia triacanthos. *Honey locust; sweet locust.* A large vigorous tree with spreading branches and handsome feathery, fernlike leaves. Has savage 4-inch spines. Good for lawn and street planting, and will withstand the dust and smoke of the city; but branches are likely to break off in strong winds. Grows to 50 or 75 feet. Hardy from the Middle Atlantic States south and west. Fairly tolerant of alkaline soils. The * Moraine Locust

Gleditsia triacanthos (honey locust).

(Patent No. 836) is a selection from the honey locust that is without thorns. Grows rapidly.

* Reliable for planting within their climate range. Recommended because they are widely used and most nurseries can supply them.

Gordonia (*Franklinia*) alatamaha. Deciduous and growing to 18 feet, this has leaves that turn red in autumn, at which time it is in flower. White blooms are 3 inches across. Much planted in the South, but hardy north to Massachusetts. Grown from seeds, layers, or cuttings.

Halesia tetraptera. *Great silverbell; snowdrop tree.* Maturing at 25 feet. The striking flowers are white. Makes a good lawn specimen. Propagated by layers, root cuttings, or seeds stratified for one year. Native of the southeast and Texas, it is winter-hardy north to Long Island.

Halesia tetraptera (great silverbell, snowdrop tree).

Halimodendron halodendron. *Salt tree.* A 6-foot deciduous shrub from the salty plains of central Asia. Purple sweetpealike flowers. Tolerates alkali. Hardy north. Increased by seeds, layers, and cuttings.

THE WITCH HAZELS

Hamamelis virginiana (witch hazel).

Hamamelis

*Hamamelis virginiana. *Witch hazel.* Growing to 20 feet, the leaves turn yellow in the fall. Valuable to set at the ends or in the center of a shrubbery border, where its height will catch the eye.

H. vernalis. A dwarfer and neater plant; grows only to 10 feet.

These both produce yellow and reddish flowers in autumn or very early in spring; south of Washington, D. C., they may carry them all winter. Both are increased by layers.

Helianthemum ocymoides. Bush growing to 3 feet, bearing yellow and purple 1-inch flowers. Plant it only in the South.

*Hibiscus syriacus. *Rose of Sharon; shrub althaea.* Maturing at 12 feet, this is an upright shrub blooming from July to October, with a preference for heavy rather than sandy soils and tolerant of city condi-

* Reliable for planting within their climate range. Recommended because they are widely used and most nurseries can supply them.

79

Rose of Sharon.

tions. Flowers resemble those of the hollyhock and are very showy; white, purple or pink, single or double, are the forms obtainable. Can be trimmed to form a good flowering hedge. Grows equally well in the North and South. Include it in your foundation planting if you have room.

Hippophae rhamnoides. *Sea buckthorn.* Grows to 30 feet. A spiny shrub with yellow flowers in May, followed by bright orange berries. Desirable for planting near the seashore. Reproduced by seeds, suckers, layers, and cuttings.

THE HYDRANGEAS

Multiplied by cuttings or layers; *H. quercifolia* by root buds.

* **Hydrangea arborescens.** *Snowball hydrangea; hills of snow.* Large flattened heads of white flowers in June and July. Matures at 10 feet. Place it in your shrub border if you have room. Grows north and south.

* **H. macrophylla caerulea.** *The blue hydrangea.* To maintain a deep color the soil should be made and kept on the acid side by occasional light applications of aluminum sulphate. Iron filings or alum are also sometimes added to the ground. Do not allow the plant to lack water. Needs slight winter protection north and east of the Middle Atlantic States. Have it in your list for foundation planting. The flowers become pink in an alkaline soil.

H. otaksa. A 6-foot shrub bearing clusters of blue, pink, or white flowers in June and July. Grown under glass in the North and outdoors in California and the South.

Two white hydrangeas. LEFT: *a standard plant and flower head of H. paniculata.* RIGHT: *flower cluster and shrub of H. arborescens.*

* Reliable for planting within their climate range. Recommended because they are widely used and most nurseries can supply them.

* H. paniculata grandiflora. *P-G or peegee hydrangea.* Grows to 8 or 10 feet. Immense panicles of bloom 1 foot long appear in August; they fade to a rose color as autumn approaches. Plant this wherever you have room in the North and mountainous districts of the South.

H. quercifolia. *Oak-leaf hydrangea.* Growing to 6 feet, the leaves of this shrub turn yellow in autumn. An American plant, native to Georgia, Florida, and Mississippi, but hardy well north.

Hypericum, Hidcote variety. Dwarf shrub, 2½ to 3½ feet high. Most of the summer it bears bright yellow, fragrant flowers. Hardy north or south. Readily grown from root or stem cuttings or seeds.

Ilex verticillata. *Winterberry; black alder.* Deciduous shrub reaching 10 feet with bright red berries. Does well in boggy land. Usually grown from stratified seeds. (See Chapter 10 for evergreen types of Ilex.)

Indigofera kirilowii. *Indigo.* Shrub growing to 4 feet, with pealike pink flowers in May. Hardy in the North. Grown from cuttings or seeds.

Itea virginica. *Sweet spire; Virginian willow.* Shrub growing to 10 feet, with fragrant white flowers. The leaves turn brilliant red in autumn. Grows in sun or shade and in any soil, including boggy land. Raised from layers in autumn, seeds or suckers in spring.

THE JASMINES

Jasminum beesianum. Bush growing to 3 feet and partly climbing. The fragrant flowers are pink.

J. nudiflorum. Loosely branched shrub growing to 15 feet, with yellow flowers in early spring.

Plant both these in the latitude of Baltimore and south; also in California. Reproduced from cuttings or layers; sometimes from seed.

WALNUTS
Juglans

Juglans nigra (black walnut).

* Juglans nigra. *Black walnut.* The * Thomas hybrid is recommended. Growing eventually 75 to 100 feet high, grafted trees grow quickly and bear nuts when quite young. They pollinate themselves and make beautiful shade trees, as well as produce an abundance of nuts that are large and easy to crack into halves and quarters.

* Reliable for planting within their climate range. Recommended because they are widely used and most nurseries can supply them.

81

J. regia. *English walnut.* Hundred-foot trees, much grown on the West Coast for the nut crop. May also be planted in the East, but unlikely to mature nuts north of Philadelphia.

Either walnut is a good specimen tree to set on the lawn visible from all sides, or at the end of an *allée.* Walnuts are increased by sowing stratified seeds; special varieties by grafting or budding onto seedlings.

Kerria japonica.

* Kerria japonica pleniflora. *Double kerria.* Growing up to 5 feet, this dainty green-twigged shrub has double golden-yellow flowers, 2 inches across, in June. Useful for foundation planting both north and south. Increased by cuttings, layers, and root division.

Kœlreuteria paniculata (varnish tree or golden-rain tree).

Kœlreuteria paniculata. *Varnish tree; golden-rain tree.* Growing up to 30 feet, it bears panicles of yellow flowers. The leaves turn yellow in early fall. Prefers a sunny position. Native of China and Japan, it is hardy in the northern portions of the United States and will live in some black alkali soils. A good accent shrub, it is effective in the center or at the ends of a planting. Produced from root cuttings or seeds.

Kolkwitzia amabilis (beauty bush).

* Kolkwitzia amabilis. *Beauty bush.* Well named, it is a graceful shrub reaching 6 feet in height. It makes a wonderful showing in June, when its long arching branches are covered with pink snapdragonlike flowers. Include it in all shrub plantings for North and South alike. Increased by cuttings.

* Reliable for planting within their climate range. Recommended because they are widely used and most nurseries can supply them.

Laburnum vossii. *Golden chain; bean tree.* An improved hybrid with skeins of yellow pea flowers. Reaches a height of 15 to 20 feet. Discourage children from eating the beans and pods, which are poisonous. Will stand partial shade. Include in all shrub plantings where you have space for a tall subject. Laburnum grows readily from seed, but this one should be increased by budding or grafting onto the seedlings to obtain large blooms.

Laburnum vossii (golden chain or bean tree).

THE CRAPE MYRTLES
Lagerstroemia

Lagerstroemia indica. Deciduous shrub or small tree growing to 25 feet, with showy pink, purple or white flowers from July to fall, which are soft and crepelike. Widely planted where the winter is mild.

L. speciosa. *Queen crape myrtle.* Tree growing to 60 feet. The 3-inch flowers are mauve to purple. May be planted in southern California or the south of Florida.

Lespedeza bicolor. *Shrub lespedeza.* Bush growing to 8 feet, with rosy-purple pea flowers from July to October. Of limited usefulness as an occasional shrub in mass plantings in the Great Plains area, but hardy north.

Leucophyllum texanum. *Texas silver leaf; barometer bush.* Shrub growing to 8 feet; gray-green leaves and 1-inch purple flowers in midsummer. Planted in Texas and southern California as a hedge or decorative subject in a mass planting. Multiplied by division or cuttings.

THE PRIVETS
Ligustrum

Ligustrum amurense. *Amur privet.* Normally used as a clipped hedge, it will grow to 15 feet as a single shapely bush.

L. obtusifolium (*Ibota*) **regelianum.** *Regel's privet.* Grows to 10 feet; many of the branches are nearly horizontal.

L. vulgare aureum. *Yellow-leaved common privet.* This golden type makes an attractive hedge, either planted alone or with the green **Ligustrum vulgare.**

Privets are quick-growing and tolerant of smoke and gases of city streets. They are propagated by division, cuttings, or stratified seeds.

(For evergreen types of Ligustrum, see Chapter 10.)

Liquidambar styraciflua (sweet gum).

Liquidambar styraciflua. *Sweet gum.* Source of styrax gum, this balsam-bearing American plant is found from Connecticut to Florida and Mexico. Grows to 140 feet. The leaves turn scarlet in early fall. Reproduced from stratified seeds which may take over a year to germinate.

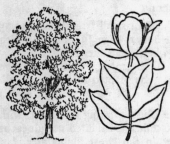

Liriodendron tulipifera (tulip tree, whitewood).

* **Liriodendron tulipifera.** *Tulip tree; whitewood.* Attains 100 feet. Flowers are fragrant, large, colored green and orange; the leaves have an unusual truncated apex and turn yellow in early fall. Transplant it only in the spring. Grows wild from Massachusetts to Florida and Mississippi. It tolerates smoke and auto fumes and is recommended for planting in cities. A good specimen tree to set on a large lawn. Grown from stratified seeds, but many will fail to germinate.

HONEYSUCKLES

Lonicera

Lonicera korolkowii (blue-leaf honeysuckle).

Lonicera fragrantissima. *Fragrant honeysuckle.* A semi-evergreen trailing shrub growing 8 feet high. Cream-white flowers are in pairs, appearing in March and April. Thrives in the southern States.

* **L. korolkowii.** *Blue-leaf honeysuckle.* Reaching 12 feet, this quick-growing shrub is useful for screen-planting. Small pink, red, or white flowers in May, followed by scarlet currantlike berries, which birds like.

* Reliable for planting within their climate range. Recommended because they are widely used and most nurseries can supply them.

L. korolkowii zabeli. The flowers are larger than those of the above, and they are dark red.

L. morrowi. *Morrow honeysuckle.* Small, sweetly perfumed, waxy flowers appear in spring before the leaves; the plant is covered with brilliant red berries in autumn. Growing from 6 to 8 feet. Much planted on the West Coast.

L. tatarica. *Tatarian bush honeysuckle.* Quick-growing 10-foot shrub, with white or pink flowers in spring, followed by currantlike red berries of which birds are very fond. Very hardy and quick-growing.

The loniceras may be grown from cuttings, layers, or stratified seed.

Lyonia ligustrina. *He-huckleberry; Male berry.* Deciduous shrub reaching 12 feet. Wild from Maine to Florida and Texas. Has skeins of pinkish flowers from May to July. Increased by cuttings or layers.

Maclura pomifera. *Osage orange.* Spiny native tree found in the mid-South, hardy north to southern New England. Quickly grows to 60 feet, needing but poor soil. The striking nonedible fruit looks like a large grapefruit. Makes an efficient hedge. Reproduced very easily from spring-sown seed previously soaked in water for three days.

THE MAGNOLIAS

Grown from cuttings, layers, or seeds.

Magnolia acuminata. *Cucumber tree.* Reaches 100 feet. Hardy south and west from New York. Has wide, 10-inch-long leaves and yellow flowers in early spring.

M. denudata (*M. conspicua*). Large deciduous tree from China which may grow to 50 feet. The large white fragrant flowers appear in April before the leaves and are 6 inches across.

M. parviflora. Attractive 30-foot tree with 4-inch white semi-double flowers appearing with the leaves; scented.

*** M. soulangeana.** *Saucer magnolia.* Matures at 20 feet; cup-shaped flowers appear in spring before the leaves, are 3 to 5 inches across, and in the usual variety are rosy-pink when in bud. Other colors are available; also pure white. Valuable to set at the ends or center of a shrubbery border to catch the eye.

M. soulangeana lennei. *Lenne magnolia.* Leaves are broader, and the flowers are rosy purple outside.

*** M. stellata.** *Star magnolia.* Matures at 15 feet. The flowers are white and star-shaped. A splendid accent shrub.

* Reliable for planting within their climate range. Recommended because they are widely used and most nurseries can supply them.

M. stellata rosea. The flowers are pink outside.

M. virginiana. *Sweet bay.* Reaching 60 feet, it bears white flowers along with the leaves. Grows from Massachusetts to Florida and Texas. Semi-evergreen, with fragrant leaves and scented white 3-inch flowers. (The evergreen magnolia, *M. grandiflora,* is described in Chapter 10.)

LEFT: *blossoms of the saucer magnolia.* RIGHT: *those of the star magnolia.*

THE MAHONIAS

Grown from stratified seed, suckers, layers, or cuttings. May take a year or more to start.

Mahonia aquifolium (*Berberis aquifolium*). *Oregon grape; holly mahonia; holly barberry.* Grows to 3 feet and bears glossy, dark green, holly-shaped leaves, with racemes of yellow flowers. Leaves turn bronze in late fall. Native plant found in British Columbia to Oregon; hardy from southern New England. Plant it in sheltered spots and protect against hot sun and strong wind. Have this among your shrubs for foundation planting; always buy it B.&B.—it transplants with difficulty. (See also Berberis in chapters 10 and 11, Mahonia in Chapter 10.)

Melia azedarach. *Chinaberry; pride of India; Indian lilac.* Deciduous garden shrub, maturing into a 60-foot tree. Fragrant purple flowers are followed by yellow ¾-inch berries.

M. umbraculiformis. *Texas umbrella tree.* Similar to the above, but with drooping foliage. Both these Melias are planted south from Virginia. They may be produced from cuttings or seeds.

Mondo jaburan. *Lily-turf.* Sod-forming plant growing south of the latitude of New York and much planted in California. Leaves are 12 inches long. Bears small lilac-blue flowers in loose racemes, followed by blue berries the size of a pea. Increased by division.

Montanoa grandiflora. *Mexican tree daisy.* Tropical shrub growing to 10 feet, covered with white 3-inch daisies with yellow eyes and a heliotropelike perfume. It needs sun; plant it in California. Propagated by cuttings or by seed.

Morus alba. *White Chinese mulberry.* Quick-growing tree that may eventually reach 50 feet. Can be planted as a lawn specimen, and the weeping type on a 5-foot straight upright stem is attractive. The 2-inch pink fruit, shaped like a large raspberry, is edible; birds are very fond of it, so the mulberry may be planted in an orchard to lure birds away from cherries and bramble fruits. The variety tartarica, or Russian mulberry, is smaller and so hardy it is sometimes grown as a screen or windbreak, the plants set 8 to 10 feet apart; they may be clipped.

M. nigra. *Black mulberry.* The fruits are dark purple.

M. rubra. *Red mulberry.* Berries are similar in color and size. A native American plant found from Massachusetts to Florida and Texas.

Mulberry leaves are the correct food for silkworms; they may be planted from the Great Lakes to the Gulf. If you enjoy the company of birds, mulberries will bring them. Propagate them from cuttings or seed.

Myrica cerifera. *Bayberry; wax myrtle; myrtle-wax.* Reaching 35 feet and semi-evergreen; the leaves turn bronze in fall. Source of the vegetable wax used in colonial times to make bayberry candles. Reproduced from layers, divisions, or stratified seed.

Myrica cerifera (bayberry).

Neillia sinensis. Six feet high, this attractive shrub has waxy, pinkish, tubular flowers 2 inches long in May and June. Hardy in the north-central States and the South. Grown from cuttings and seeds.

Nyssa sylvatica.

* **Nyssa sylvatica.** *Tupelo; pepperidge; black gum.* American native tree found from Maine to Florida, and growing up to 75 feet. The leaves turn red in autumn. A good subject to plant to attract birds; grows in any soil of fair quality, even boggy land. Propagated from layers or stratified seed, which often takes a year to start.

* Reliable for planting within their climate range. Recommended because they are widely used and most nurseries can supply them.

*Ostrya virginiana (hop horn-
beam, ironwood).*

*Oxydendrum arboreum (sour-
wood or sorrel tree).*

Ostrya virginiana. *Hop hornbeam; ironwood.* Small native tree found from Ontario to Florida and Texas. Reaching 35 feet, the leaves turn yellow in late fall. A good accent shrub to give emphasis to a group. Reproduced from seeds.

Oxydendrum arboreum. *Sourwood; sorrel tree.* This beautiful hardy tree grows to 50 feet. Bears white flowers in drooping 10-inch panicles in July and August. Leaves turn scarlet in early fall. Reproduction is difficult; try layers and seeds.

Paliurus spina-Christi (*Aculeatus*). *Christ thorn; garland thorn.* Recommended only for planting from Washington, D. C., south. It grows to 10 feet. Flowers are greenish-yellow, and the 1-inch fruit, resembling a head wearing a broad-brimmed hat, is brownish-yellow. Increased by seeds, layers, or root cuttings.

Perovskia atriplicifolia. *Russian sage; silver sage.* A small shrub growing to 5 feet, bearing long spikes of blue flowers from July to fall. The plant has a mint fragrance. Likes full sun and good loam in which to grow. Adapted to the southern districts, but hardy north to the Middle Atlantic States. Grown from cuttings.

Phellodendron amurense. *Chinese cork tree.* A quick-growing subject from China and Japan; hardy in the North. Eventually grows to 50 feet. Flowers are greenish and insignificant, followed by black berries. The bark is corklike. Raised from root and stem cuttings or seeds.

THE MOCK ORANGES

Philadelphus

Reproduction may be from cuttings, suckers, layers, or seeds.

* **Philadelphus coronarius.** *Mock orange.* The bushes grow from 7 to 10 feet high and have fragrant white flowers in late spring. * **Minne-**

* Reliable for planting within their climate range. Recommended because they are widely used and most nurseries can supply them.

sota Snowflake (Patent No. 538), growing 8 feet high, is a new double-flowering type.

P. lemoinei. *Mont Blanc.* Graceful
dwarf shrub growing to no more than
3 feet, covered in early summer with
dazzling white blooms.

P. virginalis. A hybrid growing 8
feet high, and one of our most beauti-

*Philadelphus coronarius or
mock orange.*

ful shrubs. In June the bushes are covered with single and semi-double,
pure white, sweet-scented flowers.

The three above should be in your list of shrubs for foundation
planting; water them thoroughly in dry weather. They grow quickly
and well both north and south.

Photina villosa. *Christmas berry.* Growing 15 feet high and hardy
north, this shrub has 2-inch clusters of white flowers in June. The glossy
foliage turns red at the end of summer.

Physocarpus opulifolius. *Common ninebark.* A 10-foot shrub that
makes a good individual specimen: a desirable hedge also when sheared.
Thrives in either sun or shade, country or city; has white or pinkish
flowers. A quick-growing native. The **Golden Ninebark** and **Dwarf
Ninebark** are also recommended.

THE PLANES

Platanus

They shed their bark every year, making them good city trees,
tolerant of smoke. Propagation is by cuttings, layers, or seed.

Platanus acerifolia. A desirable hybrid between the following two
varieties.

P. occidentalis. *Buttonwood; buttonball; Western plane; sycamore.*
Native of the United States. A large tree growing to 80 feet. Sections of
its bole were hollowed out in colonial times to serve as barrels.

* P. orientalis. *Oriental plane.* Native of southern Europe, rarely
seen in the United States. Reaches 80 feet. The leaves turn yellow in
early fall. Will tolerate alkali soils.

* Reliable for planting within their climate range. Recommended because
they are widely used and most nurseries can supply them.

Poinciana gilliesii. *Bird of Paradise.* Straggling 3-foot shrub bearing light yellow flowers with bright red stamens. For the warmer parts of the southern States. Grown from seed.

Poncirus trifoliata. *Trifoliate orange.* Spiny deciduous tree. Hardy in protected spots as far north as Wilmington, Delaware. Has small white flowers and aromatic fruits 2 inches in diameter, which are inedible but may be used to flavor marmalade and preserves. Grows 10 feet high. Used as a stock for other citrus fruits to be budded upon, to develop a resistance to cold. Handsome plant for the shrubbery, as a specimen subject, or a hedge. Grown from seed.

THE POPLARS

Populus

Do not plant them within 30 feet of house drains or septic systems. Not recommended for street planting because of their propensity to lift sidewalks. They are grown from cuttings, suckers, or seed.

Fruit trees used as an allée, with statue backed by Lombardy poplars.

Populus balsamifera. *Balm of Gilead; cottonwood.* Growing to 90 feet, it is found west from Quebec and south to Florida. Sexes are in different trees; the male fills the air with cotton at pollination time.

P. canadensis. *Carolina poplar.* A smoke-tolerant tree, reaching 90 feet.

P. nigra pyramidalis. *Lombardy poplar.* Quickly reaching 90 feet; comparatively short-lived. This narrow tree is found in Holland, Belgium, and northern France, planted in straight lines along canals. Has some value where a speedy screen is required.

P. tremula. *European aspen.* Reaching 90 feet; long flexible leaf stalks permit the leaves to quiver in the slightest breeze.

Populus canadensis (Carolina poplar).

THE STONE FRUITS

Prunus

Here are some of the types planted for decoration:

Prunus besseyi. *Sand cherry; bush cherry.* Maturing at 5 feet, this hardy plant bears edible fruit resembling a small plum from the ground up. The fruit is preceded by fragrant white flowers, and the silver-green foliage turns red and gold in fall. Good for foundation planting. May be raised from stratified pits.

P. blireana (*Cerasifera*). *Blirana plum* or *Myrobalan.* Much used as a stock on which stone fruits for the orchard are budded, but decorative in its own right. The small slender tree bears white cherry-blossomlike flowers in spring. May be raised from stratified pits.

Prunus glandulosa sinensis. A double-flowering cherry, but frequently called a flowering almond.

* P. glandulosa sinensis. *Double pink-flowering cherry.* Up to 6 feet high when mature, these bushy shrubs produce in early spring, before the leaves appear, a profusion of small, double, pink, roselike flowers, closely set along the branches. Include this among your shrubs for foundation and group planting, either north or south. Raise this type from cuttings, or bud onto plum or peach seedlings.

P. maritima. *Beach plum.* Straggling bush or small tree. Tiny white flowers are followed by small red or yellow edible plums. Reproduced from cuttings.

P. persica. *Double-flowering peach.* Charming and graceful tree all year, but in spring it is a mass of large, double, rose-pink flowers. Raise from cuttings or bud onto peach seedlings.

* P. pissardi rosea. *Purple-leaved flowering plum.* Clouds of single white flowers are borne in spring. Its dark foliage all season makes it

* Reliable for planting within their climate range. Recommended because they are widely used and most nurseries can supply them.

an outstanding subject. Matures at 10 feet. **Prunus pissardi Veitchi is a** hardier type and useful for difficult locations. Flowers of this sub-variety are double and pink. Matures at 15 feet. Valuable to set at the center **or** the ends of a shrub planting. Raise from cuttings or bud onto peach seedlings.

Prunus spinosa (sloe or black-thorn).

P. spinosa. *Sloe; blackthorn.* A thorny bush growing to 10 feet, making a good hedge. Produces the small sloe plum, used for flavoring liqueurs. Stems are straightened, cut and polished to make the Irish shillelagh. Reproduced from suckers, layers, or cuttings.

*P. triloba.** One of the several plants known as flowering almond. A bush, sometimes treelike and reaching 10 feet or more. Fragrant flowers appear on slender branches ahead of the leaves in early May. Can be planted north or south. Raise from cuttings or bud onto plum seedlings.

OTHER JAPAN FLOWERING CHERRIES

Groups of three or more of any of the following may be set on the lawn; good for the end of an *allée.*

* **Kwanzan.** *Rosy-red.* Bushy upright growth. Large double flowers on long stems. Foliage in spring has a coppery hue.

* **Subhirtella.** *Rosebud cherry.* Beautiful weeping tree with a profusion of light pink flowers.

Bud the two above onto seedling cherries. (For some evergreen types of Prunus, see Chapter 10.)

A Japanese flowering cherry of the type famous in Washington, D. C.

* Reliable for planting within their climate range. Recommended because they are widely used and most nurseries can supply them.

Punica granatum. *Pomegranate*. Handsome tropical tree growing to 20 feet, with handsome orange-red flowers followed by orange-shaped fruits. Adaptable only to southern California, Arizona, the Gulf States, and southern Florida. May be grown from cuttings, layers, or seeds.

THE CRAB APPLES

Pyrus malus

Sow seeds; bud or graft the named variety onto the seedlings.

* **Bechtel's Crab.** Maturing at 15 feet, these medium-sized trees are covered in early spring with large, beautiful, double, fragrant flowers resembling small pink roses.

Eley Crab. Maturing at 15 feet, the green spring foliage turns later to bronze-green. Clusters of wine-red flowers followed by dark red showy fruits.

* **Rose-Flowering Crab** (*Hopa*). Fifteen feet high and very hardy; one of the best flowering trees, with quantities of large, bright pink, fragrant flowers in spring, followed by large red-fleshed fruits valuable for jelly-making. An outstanding Japanese variety.

THE OAKS

Quercus

Good for planting as specimens on the lawn.

Quercus alba. *American white oak.* Reaches 75 feet, the leaves turning purple in late fall. A native, found from Maine to Florida and Texas.

Q. coccinea. *Scarlet oak.* Reaches 75 feet when mature. The foliage turns scarlet in autumn.

The oaks above are good street and boulevard trees and will grow in almost any soil. They may be reproduced from seed.

Q. laurifolia. *Laurel oak.* A 60-foot semi-evergreen native from Virginia to Florida and Louisiana. Good street tree in the South.

Quercus alba (white oak).

* Reliable for planting within their climate range. Recommended because they are widely used and most nurseries can supply them.

Q. nigra. *Water oak.* Maturing at 80 feet, a deciduous native found from Delaware south. Much planted below the Mason and Dixon Line.

* Q. palustris. *Pin oak.* Growing to 65 feet. A symmetrical, quick-growing, medium-sized tree popular for street and avenue planting. Stands dust, smoke, and soot, as well as overwet soil. The foliage is bright green.

Q. phellos. *Willow oak.* Native deciduous tree, reaching a height of 60 feet, with light green leaves. Ranges from New York to Florida and Texas. Good street tree for the mid-South.

Q. rubra. *Red oak.* Growing to 80 feet, the leaves turn scarlet in autumn. Grows from New Jersey to Florida and Texas.

Q. velutina. *Black oak.* Mammoth tree growing to 100 feet. The leaves turn orange-red in fall. A native, growing from Maine to Florida and Texas.

Q. virginiana. *Live oak.* This is described under evergreens in the preceding chapter.

Rhamnus cathartica. *Common buckthorn.* Fine 12-foot tree with spines at the end of the branchlets. Valued cover plant to attract and protect quail. Grows in the southern States and is hardy far north.

Rhamnus frangula (glossy buckthorn). The red berries ripen to black.

R. frangula. *Berried alder; black dogwood; glossy buckthorn.* Shrub growing up to 10 feet with small greenish flowers in clusters. Made into charcoal, the wood was preferred for making gunpowder in Europe in Napoleonic times. Makes a good hedge and withstands city conditions. Grow rhamnus from layers or seeds.

Rhodotypos kerrioides (*Tetrapetala*). *Jetbead.* A fine 6-foot Japanese shrub with 2-inch white flowers in May and June, followed by 1/4-inch black beadlike berries. Hardy in New England and thriving in the southern States, where it is much planted. Propagation is by cuttings, layers, or root divisions.

THE SUMACS

Rhus

Their berries attract many birds; propagation is by suckers, layers, root and stem cuttings, or seed.

* Reliable for planting within their climate range. Recommended because they are widely used and most nurseries can supply them.

Rhus canadensis. *Fragrant sumac.* Reaching 8 feet, the bush has remarkably colored leaves in autumn—brilliant red. A native, growing in rather dry soil from Ontario to Florida and Louisiana.

R. copallina. *Flameleaf; shining sumac.* Fifteen feet high, it has greenish flowers in terminal panicles during July and August, followed by hairy red berries. Grows from Maine to Minnesota, south to Florida and Texas.

R. cotinus. *Smoke tree.* Bush growing to 15 feet, with clouds of tiny flowers in June and July, so small and numerous that their appearance is suggestive of smoke. Grows well in the southern States; tolerant of dry conditions, and hardy in the North. This sumac is easily grown from seed.

R. typhina. *Staghorn sumac; vinegar tree.* Growing to 30 feet; a native, growing south from Quebec to Georgia, west to Iowa. The leaves turn scarlet in early fall. Greenish flowers are followed by crimson berries.

Rhus typhina (staghorn sumac, vinegar tree).

(Read about the poison sumac in Chapter 19, and avoid it.)

Ribes aureum. *Golden flowering currant; buffalo currant.* Native plant growing from Washington to Montana and California. Has yellow fragrant flowers followed by yellow fruits. The leaves turn yellow in autumn. Reproduced by cuttings, layers, or stratified seed. Better not plant it near white pines; may convey the blister rust.

Ribes aureum (Buffalo currant, flowering golden currant).

THE SHRUB ROSES

Rosa

All are suitable for foundation planting. Reproduced from cuttings or by budding onto rose seedlings or manetti rose plants (*Rosa chinensis*).

* **Rosa harisonii.** *Harison's yellow rose.* A bush growing 5 feet high, with double yellow blooms; makes a spectacular show in June.

R. hugonis. *Hugo rose.* Grows to 8 feet; branches droop. Flowers are yellow, 2 inches in diameter, appearing in May and June.

LEFT: *Harison's yellow rose.* CENTER TWO: *rosa multiflora, single and double; parent of many of our garden varieties.* RIGHT: *rosa rugosa.*

* **R. multiflora.** *The fence rose.* Growing 6 to 8 feet, the white or light pink flowers mature into bright red haws or berries which attract game and song birds. Armed with sharp thorns, it makes a tight hedge.

R. rugosa. *The Japanese rose.* Often planted with other shrubs. It grows 6 feet high and you may obtain pink, red, white, or purple single flowers, or double white ones, sometimes 4 inches across.

* **R. rugosa hybrids.** These are excellent to include in a shrub planting: Hansa. Five to six feet, with double reddish-violet flowers, large and freely produced; very fragrant. F. J. Grootendorst. Five to six feet. Flowers are bright red, fringed, and produced in clusters. Blooms from June to frost. **Pink Grootendorst.** Clear pink blooms.

R. wichuriana. *Memorial rose.* It is a trailing shrub useful for covering banks. It has single white blooms which are sweet-scented.

THE WILLOWS   Salix

All are quick-growing; propagate from cuttings.

* **Salix babylonica.** *Weeping willow.* Tree grows to 30 feet, has long drooping branches and narrow leaves. Tolerant of city smoke and wet land. If you have a large pond or stream, plant it to droop over the water.

Salix babylonica.

* **Reliable** for planting within their climate range. Recommended because they are widely used and most nurseries can supply them.

* S. discolor. *Pussy willow.* Bushes 10 to 15 feet high bear handsome furry catkins in early spring before the leaves; plant in wet soil.

S. nigra. *Black willow.* A 25-foot tree that is tolerant of smoke and auto fumes; grows in wet land.

Salix discolor, the pussy willow.

Salvia greggii. *Autumn sage.* A desirable shrub growing 3 feet high, with red or purple-red flowers in late summer. Native of southern Texas and Mexico. Give it full sun, but plant it only in the Southland. Produced from cuttings.

Sambucus canadensis. *American elderberry; sweet elderberry.* Quick-growing bush to 12 feet, with white flowers in large flat clusters during June and July, followed by purple-black edible berries. Grows from Nova Scotia to Florida and west to Texas. It needs moist, acid soil. Grown from seed.

S. pubens. *American red elder.* Ten-foot shrub bearing white flower clusters in June followed by scarlet fruit, which is not edible. Grows from New Brunswick to Georgia and west to Colorado.

Sassafras officinale.

* Sassafras officinale. *Common sassafras.* Native aromatic tree which grows to 50 feet, occurring from Maine to Florida and Texas. Leaves turn orange and red in early fall. A good specimen tree to set on the lawn or at the end of an *allée.* Increased by root cuttings, suckers, and seed. Attracts the Japanese beetle.

Shepherdia argentea. *Buffaloberry.* Shrub growing to 18 feet, thorny, with grayish-green foliage and edible red berries. Extremely hardy, it is a good shrubbery and hedge plant. Grows in dry rocky soil from Manitoba to Minnesota and Kansas. Raised from fall-sown seed; stratified if sown in the spring.

Sophora japonica. *Pagoda tree; Chinese scholar tree.* Deciduous, growing to 80 feet, with light yellow sweetpealike flowers in 15-inch panicles, followed by 3-inch pods. Hardy in the North. Grown from cuttings, layers, or seed.

* Reliable for planting within their climate range. Recommended because they are widely used and most nurseries can supply them.

Sorbaria aitchisonii. *Spiraea. False Spiraea.* Eight feet high, this shrub has 10-inch panicles of white flowers in July and August. Needs moist, rich soil. Reproduced from suckers, stem or root cuttings, or seed.

Sorbus aucuparia. *Mountain ash; rowan.* Easily grown deciduous tree reaching 50 feet, with gray-green pinnate leaves and white flowers, followed by orange-colored rowanberries,

Sorbus aucuparia.

which may be made into preserves. Birds like them also. Propagated from seed sown when ripe in autumn or stratified in spring.

THE MEADOWSWEETS

Spiraea

All are valuable for foundation or border planting. Tolerant of soot, dust, and city fumes. Propagated by seed sown as soon as ripe or stratified, by layers or cuttings.

* Spiraea arguta multiflora. *Snow garland.* Grows 4 to 5 feet. Small, pure white flowers borne in such profusion in May that the whole shrub appears laden with snow. Planted throughout the United States.

* S. bumalda. *Anthony Waterer.* A 2½-foot bush bearing flat clusters of rosy crimson flowers in June and July. Hardy as far north as the latitude of New York City.

S. douglasii. *Douglas spiraea.* Shrub growing to 8 feet bearing deep rose flowers in long panicles during July and August. Grows from British Columbia south to California. Hardy north and much planted in the South.

Spiraea, Anthony Waterer.

* S. froebeli. One of our best low-growing shrubs for general use and flowering hedges. Three feet high; round flat clusters of rose-pink flowers from June to October. Hardy north; much planted in the South.

S. prunifolia. *Bridal wreath.* Shrub grows to 6 feet and bears pure white flowers very early in spring, which are small, buttonlike, and in long clusters. Good for southern planting, yet hardy north.

* Reliable for planting within their climate range. Recommended because they are widely used and most nurseries can supply them.

S. thunbergii. Shrub grows 5 feet high and bears white flowers in April and May. Somewhat sensitive to cold; grow it south of New England.

S. trichocarpa. *Korean bridal wreath.* A 6-foot shrub with white flowers in clusters in June, which is two weeks later than some other spiraeas, enabling it to escape many a late frost in exposed areas.

* **S. Vanhouttei.** *Bridal wreath.* Maturing at 5 to 6 feet, it is one of our most beautiful shrubs. Flowers are white in many-blossom clusters. Grows from New England to the Gulf.

Strelitzia reginae. *Bird-of-Paradise flower.* Three-foot perennial herb. The flowers are a combination of yellow, blue, and purple. Conservatory plant in the North; grown outdoors in southern California. Increased by division, suckers or seed.

THE SNOWBERRIES

Symphoricarpos

They are reproduced from suckers, cuttings, or seeds.

Symphoricarpos chenaultii. *Chenault coralberry.* Shrub growing to 8 feet, with showy fruits that are red with white spots. Plant it south and west of Long Island.

S. mollis. *Spreading snowberry.* A procumbent shrub with pink or white flowers, followed by yellowish-white fruits. Ranges from British Columbia to California. It prefers moist land.

Symphoricarpos racemosus (snowberry, waxberry).

S. occidentalis. *Wolfberry; Western snowberry.* Shrub growing 5 feet high, bearing pinkish flowers in June and July, followed by white berries. Its range is from British Columbia to Kansas and Michigan.

S. orbiculatus. *Indian currant; coralberry; buckbrush.* Shrub growing to 7 feet, bearing white flowers in June, followed by purple-red fruits. Plant it anywhere south of Connecticut and the Canadian-border States except in mountain country. Enjoys shade or full sun.

* **S. racemosus.** *Snowberry; waxberry.* A 3-foot shrub with pink bell-shaped flowers from June to September, followed by snow-white globular berries. Excellent for foundation planting in the northern and central States; do not use it south. It tolerates shade and the city.

* Reliable for planting within their climate range. Recommended because they are widely used and most nurseries can supply them.

THE LILACS

Syringa

Propagated from stem or root cuttings, layers, suckers or seeds.

Robin nesting in lilac. Probably you are unaware of her presence until fall discloses the empty nest.

Syringa amurensis. *Amur lilac.* Shrub growing to 10 feet, bearing loose panicles of yellow-white flowers in June and July. An occasional specimen may be planted in the border for good effect.

S. amurensis japonica. *Japanese tree lilac.* Treelike shrub growing to 25 feet and bearing its small cream-white flowers in clusters 12 to 18 inches long in May and June. Does well in the mid-South.

S. chinensis. *Chinese lilac.* Symmetrical shrub growing 15 feet high. Somewhat small purple flowers are in 6-inch panicles. The best variety for the mid-South.

S. microphylla. *Littleleaf lilac.* Small shrubs; purple-blue flowers.

S. persica. *Persian lilac.* The flower clusters are looser and more decorative; either purple or white. The shrub matures at 8 feet. Striking in a group of other shrubs. Does well in the West and mid-South.

S. persica villosa. *Late lilac.* Flowers are purple or pinkish white. The bush matures at 10 feet. Plant if you have room.

* S. vulgaris. *Common lilac.* Growing up to 15 feet high this hardy and vigorous shrub is tolerant of soot, dust, and city fumes; clusters of fragrant flowers are borne in May; colors are blue, purple, violet, and white. Some forms are double. Plant them in your shrub border, both north and south. French hybrids are especially fine, with extra heavy flower spikes; they generally are dwarfer. Some good French varieties are:

Belle de Nancy. Double; satiny pink with white eye.
Charles Joly. Double; wine-red.
Charles X. Single; violet-purple.
Madame Lemoine. Double white.
Marie Legraye. Single; cream-white.
Michel Buchner. Double; lilac-pink.
President Grevy. Double; soft blue.

* Reliable for planting within their climate range. Recommended because they are widely used and most nurseries can supply them.

* Tamarix hispida aestivalis. *Tamarisk.* Magnificent shrub growing to 8 feet, with pink flower spikes all summer. Soft feathery gray-green foliage that withstands fresh- or salt-water spray. To get best results, cut to the ground when transplanting. Grows in most of the United States except the extreme north. Good subject for the western plains. Propagated by cuttings.

Tamarix hispida (tamarisk).

Tecoma stans. *Yellow elder; trumpet bush.* Treelike shrub growing to 10 feet, bearing bright yellow trumpet flowers, 2 inches long, most of the summer. Plant from Florida to southern California, as it stands only a few degrees of frost. Propagated from seed, layers, stem and root cuttings.

Teucrium chamaedrys. *Germander.* Procumbent shrub 12 inches high, with flower spikes of red-purple or bright rose. Makes a satisfactory ground cover. Grown from cuttings, root division, or seeds.

THE LIMES OR LINDENS

Tilia

All are good street and boulevard trees and desirable lawn specimens. Reproduced from cuttings, layers, or stratified seed.

Tilia americana (American linden, basswood).

* Tilia americana. *American linden; basswood.* Grows to 120 feet. Will live in almost any soil, including boggy land. Stately tree with fragrant, small, yellow flowers.

T. cordata. *Littleleaf European linden.* Tree grows to 100 feet, with small yellowish fragrant flowers that are attractive to bees.

T. platyphyllos pyramidalis. *Pyramidal large-leaved linden.* European variety that grows to 100 feet.

T. tomentosa. *White* or *silver linden.* A stately 100-foot tree that grows well in the southern States.

* Reliable for planting within their climate range. Recommended because they are widely used and most nurseries can supply them.

THE ELMS

Ulmus

Effective street and boulevard trees. The following are fairly tolerant of alkali soil. Grown from seed sown in spring.

Ulmus americana (American elm). Many fine specimens in New England today were planted by the American colonists.

*Ulmus americana. *American elm.* Majestic tree with arching branches, growing to 120 feet. Native, growing wild from Newfoundland to Florida, west to the Rockies. Leaves turn yellow in autumn. Stands difficult soil, including boggy land.

*U. americana molineri. *Moline elm.* Similar to the above, but the leaves are larger. Grows to 100 feet.

Either of the elms above will make an excellent individual tree planted on the lawn.

U. fulva. *Slippery elm.* Well-known hard-to-climb tree, medium in size and native from Canada to Florida.

U. parvifolia. *Chinese elm.* Medium-sized tree which will grow throughout the United States and is much planted in California and the South.

*U. pumila. *Chinese or Siberian elm.* Growing to 60 feet. On account of its rapid growth and ability to thrive in almost any situation, this is one of the most popular subjects in America. Effective street and boulevard tree. Pruning can keep it low-growing, so that it forms a dense impenetrable hedge with small dark green foliage. For this obtain seedlings, 2 to 3 feet tall, and plant them 12 to 18 inches apart.

U. serotina. *September elm.* Medium-sized tree, suitable for planting in Kentucky, south and west.

THE BLUEBERRIES

Vaccinum

They tolerate boggy land. Increased by division, root cuttings, layers, and seed. The latter may take up to a year to germinate.

* Reliable for planting within their climate range. Recommended because they are widely used and most nurseries can supply them.

* Vaccinum corymbosum. *High-bush blueberry; tall cranberry.*
Growing to 8 feet, this shrub is decorative, deep green all summer with
the leaves turning to red in autumn; in winter the twigs are red. This
source of fruit is excellent for planting along with broad-leaved evergreens, because both need an acid soil, vaccinum a very acid one. One
plant is not enough: set them in groups of three, so that they may cross-
pollinate. Include in your foundation or border if you have room.

V. pennsylvanicum. *Low-bush blueberry.* Growing 2 feet high, this
native plant grows from Newfoundland to Virginia, and westward to
Wisconsin. Makes an attractive ground cover if set 1 foot apart; include
it in your foundation and border plantings.

LEFT: *the high-bush blueberry.* RIGHT: *low-bush blueberry.*

THE WAYFARING TREES
Viburnum

Propagated by stratified seed, which may take a year to germinate; also by layers and cuttings. They thrive under city conditions, but some varieties need frequent spraying to combat aphis
or plant lice. Birds are attracted by their berries.

Viburnum acerifolium. *Ma-*
ple-leaved viburnum; Dock-
mackie. Growing to 6 feet, it has
white flowers in 3-inch clusters
in May and June; the leaves
turn purple in autumn. A native, found from New Brunswick to North Carolina, west to
Minnesota.

Viburnum Carlesii. One of the plants
known as "snowball."

* V. carlesii. *Fragrant viburnum.* Handsome 5-foot shrub, native of
Korea, with large, fragrant, waxy, white flowers, 3 inches across, in April
and May. Should be included in all plantings within its climate range.

* Reliable for planting within their climate range. Recommended because
they are widely used and most nurseries can supply them.

V. dentatum. *Arrowwood.* Fifteen-foot shrub, this native of North America is found from New Brunswick to Georgia and west to Minnesota. The leaves turn red in autumn.

V. fragrans. Ten-foot shrub. The scented blooms are white or pinkish and borne in 2-inch panicles in April and May.

V. lantana. *Wayfaring tree.* Shrub grows to 15 feet and has white flowers in clusters 4 inches across in May and June.

V. lentago. *Nannyberry; sheepberry.* Trees up to 30 feet high bear clusters of white flowers, 5 inches in diameter, in May and June.

* V. opulus. *Snowball; European cranberry bush.* Maturing at 10 feet, it bears large balls of white flowers in May, followed by showy cranberrylike berries in fall and early winter. Be sure to plant it if you have room for a tall subject.

V. tomentosum. Deciduous shrub growing to 10 feet, with white flowers in 10-inch clusters in late spring, followed by small red berries which turn to blue-black. Does well in the South.

Vitex agnus-castus.

(For evergreen types of viburnum, see Chapter 10.)

Vitex agnus-castus. *Chaste tree; hemp tree; monk's pepper tree.* Matures at 10 feet. Unusual subject with flowers of lavender-blue. Roots should be given a 3-inch winter mulch in the North; good for the mid-South and West.

V. negundo. *Cutleaf chaste tree.* Slightly more winter-hardy than the above.

Vitex are raised from cuttings, layers, suckers, or seed.

THE WEIGELAS

Weigela rosea. Shrub maturing at 6 feet, with quantities of large, showy, trumpet-shaped pink flowers in June. Becomes effective quickly.

* Eva Rathke. A garden hybrid with ruby-carmine flowers, in bloom all summer. Grows to 5 feet.

* Bristol Ruby (Patent No. 492). A 6-foot shrub and a new garden hybrid that blooms profusely in June and early July, with scattered flowers later in the season. The color is ruby-red, shading to garnet-crimson. Vigorous grower, forming a nice compact bush.

These three weigelas are valuable for foundation and border planting. They are multiplied by suckers or cuttings.

* Reliable for planting within their climate range. Recommended because they are widely used and most nurseries can supply them.

CHAPTER 12

Climbing Plants

"In green old gardens, hidden away
From sight of revel and sound of strife,
Here may I live what life I please,
Married and buried out of sight."
VIOLET FANE, "In Green Old Gardens."

IF THE WALL of the house is of brick, Boston ivy or English ivy may be planted to climb upon it; Boston ivy will even climb on wood. Bignonia or trumpet creeper also clings to brick and often to wood, as does the climbing hydrangea. A trellis tacked to the wall or horizontal wires 12 inches apart attached to the wall will accommodate wisteria, silver lace vine, groups of bittersweet, clematis, Dutchman's pipe, honeysuckle, or kudzu vine.

SOME WOODY PERENNIAL CLIMBERS

Akebia quinata. *Five-leaf akebia.* Needs sun and well-drained soil. The flowers are fragrant. Hardy in the North and much planted in California. Increased by division, cuttings, or seed.

Ampelopsis aconitifolia. *Monkshood vine.* The leaf is made up of 3 or 5 leaflets, or has 3 or 5 lobes. Fruits are like tiny grapes, orange or yellow in color, sometimes bluish. Grows freely and is comparatively immune to insect injury. An American native plant, reproduced from layers or cuttings.

A. cordata. *Heartleaf ivy.* Leaves are heart-shaped, and the berries are blue. Its range includes New Mexico, Oklahoma, and Texas. Grown from layers or cuttings.

(See also *Parthenocissus* in this chapter.)

Antigonon leptopus. *Coral vine; pink vine; corallita; Confederate vine; Rosa de Montana.* Climbing by tendrils and reaching 40 feet, with arrow-shaped leaves and skeins of bright pink flowers. For the warmer parts of the South and California. Propagated by cuttings and seed.

* **Aristolochia sipho.** *Dutchman's pipe; birthwort.* A vigorously growing climber with brownish flowers, each in the shape of a small curved pipe. Its large, dark green, heart-shaped leaves give a tropical-foliage effect and afford complete privacy when it is used to screen a porch. Thrives either in sun or semi-shadow, from Canada to the mid-South, but needs a fence or series of cords on which to climb. Propagated by seeds, layers, and cuttings—difficult with any of them.

THE TRUMPET VINES

Bignonia or Campsis

Bignonia capreolata. *Trumpet flower; cross-vine.* Climbing to 50 feet, it has 2-inch yellow-red trumpet flowers. An effective evergreen south of Richmond, Virginia. The top dies but the root lives north to Long Island when given a winter mulch.

B. cherere. Showy Mexican evergreen climber. The red or purplish trumpets are 4 inches long and grow in clusters. For the warmest parts of the country only.

B. grandiflora. *Chinese trumpet creeper.* Does well in the southern States and is hardy north to southern New England. The 3-inch blooms are scarlet.

* **B. radicans.** *Trumpet vine; trumpet creeper.* A robust tall climber with large leathery trumpet flowers of brilliant orange-scarlet, lasting well into summer. Will cling to a rough surface of stucco, stone, or coarse brick. Because it grows so strongly it can become a pest, but chemical weed killers may be used. It is worth while to stem-root it on slopes to prevent erosion. The sub-variety Mme. Galen is a stocky form, but still climbing, with immense flower clusters often exceeding 15 inches in length. The most adaptable of the named sorts, Yellow Trumpet, has pure chrome-yellow blooms, 2½ to 3 inches across; it is a good one to plant in partial shade.

These bignonias are grown from root cuttings, stem cuttings, layers and occasionally from seed.

* **Celastrus scandens.** *False bittersweet; waxwork.* A well-known twining plant that grows wild in woodland shade. The blooms are frequently offered for sale along the roadside for winter decoration. Give it a trellis to climb or plant it near a fence; in its wild state it gains

* Reliable for planting within their climate range. Recommended because they are widely used and most nurseries can supply them.

support from other plants. The flowers are everlasting. Celastrus may be grown from suckers, layers, cuttings, or seed. Do not confuse it with the true bittersweet, *Solanum dulcamara,* with violet flowers and red berries, which is poisonous.

Cissus incisa (*Vitis incisa*). *Marine ivy; treebine.* The fleshy leaves are made up of three leaflets. A tall climber which may be used as a ground cover. Grows from Missouri to Florida, Texas, and Arizona. Reproduced from cuttings.

VIRGIN'S BOWER

Clematis

Perennial woody climbers that are covered with showy flowers in summer; *C. paniculata* blooms in autumn. Grown from stem and root cuttings or from stratified seed.

Clematis jackmani. Large, deep violet-purple, velvety blooms.
C. lawsoniana henryi. Large white flowers often 8 inches across.

* Clematis hybrids

Crimson King. Large red blooms.
Lord Neville. Velvety dark purple.
Mme. Edward Andre. Bright velvety red.
Nelly Moser. Pale mauve, striped red.
Prins Hendrik. Azure blue.
Ramona. Light lavender.
 * **C. paniculata.** *Sweet-autumn clematis.* Flowers are white, small, very fragrant and produced in abundance in September.

Cotoneaster microphylla. See evergreens, Chapter 10.
Euonymus radicans vegetus, radicans carrierei and radicans coloratus are trailing ground covers and slow climbers. They are described among the evergreen shrubs in Chapter 10.
Ficus pumila. *Climbing fig.* See Chapter 11.
Gelsemium sempervirens. *Carolina yellow jessamine.* Evergreen twiner with yellow flowers 1½ inches long. A native subject found from Virginia south; much planted in California. Reproduced from cuttings.
 * **Hedera helix.** *English ivy.* A graceful semi-evergreen vine that has dark green foliage. Succeeds in shady places and makes an excellent ground cover. Will support itself as a strong climber on rough stone, stucco, or brick.

 * Reliable for planting within their climate range. Recommended because they are widely used and most nurseries can supply them.

H. helix baltica. *Baltic ivy.* Has smaller leaves and is hardier. Climbs like English ivy.

H. helix caenwoodiana. Small black-green leaves striped white.

H. helix gracilis. Smaller leaves which take on a bronze tint.

English ivies may be grown from cuttings, layers, pieces of stem rooted in water, or seed.

Hydrangea petiolaris. *Climbing hydrangea.* Produces 6- to 8-inch loose clusters of white four-petal flowers in July. Will cling to brick and stone walls, but becomes a straggling partly decumbent bush if it has nothing to climb upon. Good ground cover for a steep slope, because roots are developed on the stems when they come into contact with the ground. Propagated from cuttings or pieces of rooted stem.

Jasminum beesianum. See Chapter 11.

HONEYSUCKLES

Lonicera

Many are semi-evergreen. They are propagated from cuttings.

Lonicera demissa. A species from Japan with cream-white flowers. Trails 12 feet.

L. fragrantissima and korolkowii. See Chapter 11.

* **L. heckrottii.** *Everblooming honeysuckle.* Remarkable for the abundance and large size of its fragrant flowers, which are crimson outside, apricot within. Blooms from June to frost.

L. henryi. *Henry's honeysuckle.* Prostrate twining evergreen with yellow-red or purple-red flowers from June to August.

* **L. japonica halliana.** Almost evergreen, with very fragrant white flowers which change to yellow in late summer. Much planted in California.

L. japonica. *Goldflame.* Scarlet trumpets, lined with gold.

L. korolkowii zabeli. *Red honeysuckle.* Flowers are rose, appearing in May and June.

L. ruprechtiana. *Manchurian honeysuckle.* Growing to 12 feet, it bears cream-white flowers in May and June.

L. sempervirens. *Trumpet honeysuckle.* Two-inch flowers are orange-scarlet, yellow inside. Grows from Connecticut to Florida and Texas; evergreen in the southern part of its range.

L. tatarica. *Tatarian honeysuckle.* Climbs to 10 feet, deciduous. White, pink, and red-flowering sorts may be purchased.

* Reliable for planting within their climate range. Recommended because they are widely used and most nurseries can supply them.

Lycium chinense. *Matrimony vine; Chinese wolfberry.* Climbing bush with small purple flowers, followed by orange-scarlet berries. Good small-game cover and bird-sanctuary shrub. Suitable for the mid-southern States on unfavorable land where other vines cannot thrive. Grown from cuttings, layers, suckers, and seed.

* **Parthenocissus quinquefolia.** *Virginia creeper; American ivy; five-leaved ivy.* Climbs by tendrils like a grape; the leaves are made up of five leaflets or lobes. The tendrils have no disks. Grows everywhere in the United States.

P. quinquefolia engelmannii. *Engelman ivy.* Leaves are smaller than the above; they also have five leaflets or lobes, and their tendrils similarly have no disks.

* **P. tricuspidata.** *Boston ivy; Japanese ivy.* The leaves have 3 leaflets or lobes, and are up to 8 inches apart. The tendrils have clinging disks at their tips, enabling the plant to attach itself to almost anything. Plant it anywhere in the United States except the northern and eastern border States. In the sub-variety **tricuspidata lowii,** or miniature Boston ivy, the leaves are smaller and are purplish at first.

The three above may be raised from cuttings, layers, or seed.

Periploca graeca. *Silk vine.* Climbing to 40 feet, the 1-inch flowers are greenish and brown-purple inside. Plant it south from Baltimore. Grown from layers or stem cuttings, root cuttings or seed.

P. sepium. Leaves are narrower and smaller than those of the above. Hardy to Long Island.

* **Polygonum auberti.** *Chinese fleece vine; silver lace vine.* A twiner growing to 25 feet. In late summer it is covered with foamy sprays of greenish-white fragrant flowers which turn pinkish before they fade. Increased by cuttings.

Schizophragma hydrangeoides. *Japanese hydrangea vine.* Climbing to 30 feet. White flowers are in 9-inch clusters. Hardy throughout the United States. Propagated from cuttings, layers, and seed.

Tecomaria capensis. See evergreens, Chapter 10.

Vitis. The domestic grape serves as a satisfactory climber provided it has a trellis or fence on which to climb. Any sort that is popular may be selected for the North; the scuppernong grape, a variety of *Vitis rotundifolia,* is good for the southern States. Grapes are propagated from cuttings, layers, or seed.

Wisteria floribunda. *Japanese wisteria.* A vigorous twining plant with 18-inch-long racemes of single violet, white, or pink flowers, or double violet ones.

* Reliable for planting within their climate range. Recommended because they are widely used and most nurseries can supply them.

W. floribunda macrobotrys. A sub-variety with enormous 3-foot racemes.

W. multijuga rosea. Vigorous variety with pink flowers.

* **W. sinensis.** *Chinese wisteria.* Strong-growing perennial twiner, blooming profusely in early summer, with an occasional flower cluster the rest of the year. Flowers are sweetpealike and blue.

* **W. sinensis alba.** Pure white blooms; very fragrant.

Do not allow the young shoots to work around rain pipes; although weak at first, in two years they may pull the pipes away from the building. Reproduced by division, stem cuttings, root cuttings, or seed.

CLIMBING HERBACEOUS PERENNIALS

Their tops die down in autumn to reappear in spring.

Boussingaultia baselloides. *Madeira vine.* Fleshy leaves, and clusters of fragrant white flowers in summer and autumn. Protect the roots with litter over winter north and east of Long Island. Grown from tubercules on the stems, root cuttings, or seed.

Cymbalaria muralis. *Kenilworth ivy; mother-of-thousands; creeping sailor.* Good for trailing over and holding a bank because it develops roots on its stems. Its small flowers are blue, white, or pink. Propagation is by division or seed.

Lathyrus latifolius. *Perennial sweet pea.* A hardy plant climbing to 9 feet, with pink, purple, white, or red flowers. Grown from seed or cuttings.

Passiflora caerulea. *Passion vine.* A curious and charming flower; the petals are creamy white, with a fringed crown or halo of blue and purple around the mystic center. Here the hammer, nails, and crown of thorns of the Crucifixion story may be recognised. This is a perennial only in the southern States; treat it as an annual in the North.

Pueraria thunbergiana. *Kudzu vine; Jack-and-the-beanstalk.* Grows slowly at first, afterwards very rapidly; in rich soil it will reach 70 feet in a season. Flowers are sweetpealike, purple, and fragrant. Grown by root division, cuttings, or seed.

CLIMBING ANNUALS

Sow seeds every spring.

Calonyction aculeatum (*Ipomoea bona-nox*). *Moonflower.* Growing 10 feet, it has white flowers.

* Reliable for planting within their climate range. Recommended because they are widely used and most nurseries can supply them.

Cardiospermum helicacabum. *Heart seed; love-in-a-puff.* Small white flowers are followed by curious seed pods. Ten feet.

Cobaea scandens. *Cup-and-saucer vine.* Flowers are like large canterbury bells and violet-purple. Grows 25 feet.

Dolichos lablab. *Hyacinth bean.* Purple or white flowers followed by colored pods. Grows 8 feet.

Echinocystis lobata. *Wild cucumber.* Small white flowers; grows 20 feet. Do not allow it to escape from your garden; it may become a bad farm weed.

Humulus japonica. *Oriental hop.* Grown for its foliage; the flowers are without interest; grows 25 feet.

Ipomoea. *Morning glory.* Blue, red, or white flowers. They are open the first half of the day, closed in the afternoon. Grows 7 feet.

Lathyrus odoratus. *Sweet pea.* White, pink, red, or lavender flowers. Needs rich land and the cold nights of the northern and New England States; may be disappointing elsewhere.

Ornamental Gourds. Curious fruits, mostly inedible, but they may be dried, varnished, or shellacked for home decoration.

Phaseolus coccineus. *Scarlet runner.* Red flowers, edible beans, though stringy. Grows 7 feet.

Quamoclit pennata. *Cypress vine.* Scarlet or white flowers. Grows 20 feet.

Q. sloteri. *Cardinal climber.* Crimson and white flowers. Grows 15 feet.

Thunbergia alata. *Black-eyed Susan; clock vine.* Cream, white, and buff flowers. Grows 4 feet.

Tropaeolum canariensis. *Canary bird vine.* Yellow flowers. Grows 5 feet.

T. majus. *Climbing nasturtium.* Yellow, orange, or red flowers. Grows 6 feet.

CHAPTER 13

Ground Covers

"Which May had painted with his softe showers
This garden full of leaves and of flowers."
CHAUCER, *The Frankeleyns Tale.*

GROUND COVERS are planted to form a carpet of vegetation and are used in place of grass where turf cannot be grown because of shade, soil exhaustion, tree roots, or water dripping from tree branches or roofs. They are useful also for hiding the soil in a foundation planting or shrub border. Sometimes they serve to clothe steep sunny banks.

Here are some ground covers widely used in the temperate northern three quarters of the United States.

The following are used for shady places:

(Plant 9 inches apart.)
Pachysandra terminalis. Japanese spurge. Evergreen.
Violas or tufted pansies

(Plant 12 inches apart.)
Lily-of-the-valley
Perennial candytuft
Plumbago larpentae
Vinca
Sweet violets

Three ground covers; they will live where grass cannot grow, such as under a maple tree. LEFT: *vinca; blue flowers.* CENTER: *pachysandra.* RIGHT: *English ivy. The last two are planted for their leaves only.*

(Plant 18 inches apart.)
Creeping Jenny
Funkia
Mazus reptans

(Set 3 feet apart.)
English ivy
Euonymus radicans
Ground ivy

The following are useful for sunny spots:

(Plant 12 inches apart.)
Chrysogonum or golden star
Mother-of-thyme

(Plant 2 to 3 feet apart.)
Honeysuckle
Mountain pink

Three flowering ground covers that will stand shade. LEFT: *violet.* CENTER: *funkia, with either blue or white flowers; variegated leaves if you wish.* RIGHT: *lily-of-the-valley.*

You may wish to try some of the following for ground covers:

Arbutus, trailing
Bearberry
Blood-root
Blueberry, low-bush
Bog rosemary
Cotoneaster, horizontal
Crowberry

Junipers, prostrate evergreen:
Andorra
Bar Harbor
Japanese
Sargent's
Waukegan

Milkwort
Oconee bells
Wintergreen

More useful ground covers. LEFT: *honeysuckle; will hide the soil on a slope and prevent erosion.* CENTER: *crowberry; has black fruits.* RIGHT: *bearberry; has white or pinkish fruits.*

CHAPTER 14

Hedges Restrain the Average Person ·

"Some people talk of morality, and some of religion, but give me a little snug property."
MARIA EDGEWORTH, The Absentee.

The Washington thorn makes an effective screen through which dogs hesitate to walk. The plant is hardy south from Wilmington, Del.

MUCH OF THE VALUE of your property is in the privacy it affords you. Your planning and planting are based on the assurance that only you, your family, and friends may use it; and that your shrubs, flowers, fruits, and vegetables will be respected in your absence. This is likely to be so if your home is in a long-settled conservative part of the country; with considerate neighbors and cooperative youngsters, you may have no need for a fence. But one mean-acting dog, one rabid fox, or one "So what?" family may be a menace even in rural areas; and lot-crossing, trespassing, vandalism, night-prowling and petty thievery, not to forget rabbit damage, occur in suburban sections that appear to be respectable.

It is wise to eliminate these worries at the outset by erecting a fence well inside your line, 3½ feet or higher with 2-inch spacings or less—½-inch spacings in snake country—and well-fitting, spring-closing gates. Plant a single hedge along one side of the

Boxwood hedge around a formal fountain spot. Short-clipped California privet and dwarf perennials are within the square.

fence, but a pair of hedges, one on each side of it, will be better; and you will have little to be concerned about, for your fence soon will be hidden by the hedges. Weeding will be no more of a problem with the double hedge than with a single one, for your plants will be set at a minimum of 12 inches apart—twice or even thrice this distance with some of the evergreens. Frequent scuffle-hoeing will take care of unwanted plants.

Frequently hedges are undernourished. At planting time dig a trench 1 foot wide and 15 inches deep, which should be large enough to enable you to arrange the roots in a natural untangled manner. Place a 1-inch layer of rotted manure, humus or compost on the bottom; spread ⅛-inch layer of Groganic, sheep manure or bonemeal and the same amount of 5–10–5 or 8–6–2 fertilizer. With a hoe or small rake mix these materials with the soil at the bottom of the trench. Place your plants in position in a straight line with the soil mark 1 inch lower than it was in the nursery; cover the roots with unfertilized soil, tread firmly with the shoe, and water generously. At planting time prune away any damaged roots and branches. Whiten the soil with 5–10–5 or 8–6–2 every spring and early fall, and rake under.

You allow one plant of privet or barberry per running foot for a single hedge, two to the foot when you plant a double hedge. With other plants, take into consideration their size when they mature, which means you will set them from 18 inches to 3 feet apart in the row. To avoid discussions with neighbors in future years, keep hedges 2 or more feet back from the property line; also keep them well in from sidewalks and garden paths.

Privet, caragana, crataegus, lilac, osage orange, Siberian elm, and others may be "plashed"; that is, planted not upright but with the main stems directed at an angle of 45 degrees, pointing in any direction. Young branches may be wired together where they cross. This is ordinary plashing and results in a nearly impenetrable hedge. Further, if the hedge is but a few feet long and if you have the time, you can make a hedge that can only be broken through with an axe or machete; this is termed "inarching" or "grafting by approach." Shave the crossing branches one third of their thickness—leaving two thirds—for a length of 2 inches to expose the green cambium; then wire them so that the cambium of one branch is in contact with that of the other, and cover the joint with grafting wax. (Twistems, which are stocked by your garden supply house, are convenient for wiring as are pipe-cleaners.) The best time for plashing is when the plants are in full active growth, which is in spring for most plants. A plashed and grafted hedge of spiny plants is a savage thing, but an effective protection.

The American beech may be planted as a hedge.

Decide early the permanent height at which you desire to keep your hedge at maturity, and at your first pruning cut 9 inches lower than this height; in each of the next two prunings leave it 3 inches higher, and you should have a dense hedge from the ground up.

Pruning should be carried out in spring and autumn; light trimming can be done at any time except in July and August. Any flowering shrubs in your hedges will be an exception: you give them their major pruning immediately after they have, or should have, flowered.

Hedge-trimming calls for hedge shears and pruning shears or secateurs. An electric hedge-cutter does much of the work of these two, enabling you to do a better job more quickly. But see that no fence wire is hidden in your hedge and know exactly where your flexible electric cord is: the first will cause you to send the

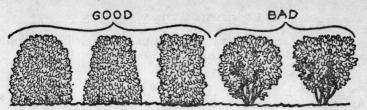

When clipping a hedge, do not aim for a broad top and narrow bottom. The reverse is better for the hedge.

device away for repair; the second, if you chance to sever the cable, will call for a wire-splicing and fuse replacement. With an older hedge one will need in addition a pair of tree-lopping shears and a pruning saw to take care of heavy branches and steps that are too large for the lopping shears.

Hidden fence or ha-ha; it protects the property without obstructing the view.

To thicken a hedge that has grown overtall, cut it down to within 6 inches of the soil either in spring or early autumn, removing any dead wood.

If your property is large you may have use for a ha-ha, which is a sunken fence or a fence-and-hedge at the bottom of a trench or ravine. A valley or an old water course may be available for part of this, aided by man-made excavation where needed. The land is fenced, cattle are kept away from the home grounds, and the fence is not seen—much like the modern zoological park where the animals appear to be dangerously free, but actually are behind well-concealed efficient fences and moats. If deer are to be kept out, find out the necessary fence height from your game warden.

SOME GOOD HEDGE PLANTS

These may serve as windbreaks too, in which case larger shrubs and trees are usually planted.

Evergreens

Arborvitae, American (*Thuja occidentalis*)
Ware (*T. wareana*)
Barberry, evergreen (*Berberis verruculosa*). Spiny.
Juliana (*B. julianae*). Spiny.
Boxwood (*Buxus sempervirens*)
dwarf (*B. suffruticosa*)
Cedar, red (*Juniperus virginiana*)
Cypress, Hynoki (*Chamaecyperis obtusa*)
Firethorn (*Pyracantha coccinea*). Thorny; for the mid-South.
Hedge thorn (*Carissa arduina*). Spiny; for the South only.
Hemlock, American (*Tsuga canadensis*)
Holly, American (*Ilex opaca*)
Japanese (*I. crenata*)
Juniper, in variety
Pfitzer's (*J. chinensis pfitzeriana*)

A pair of pruned and clipped arborvitae stand guard at the entrance gate.

Laurel, cherry (*Prunus laurocerasus*)
Portugal (*P. lusitanica*)
Moss retinospora (*Chamaecyperis squarrosa*)
Myrtle (*Myrtus communis*). Plant south of Richmond, Virginia.
Pine, red (*Pinus resinosa*)
Privet, evergreen (*Ligustrum lucidum*)
Spruce, dwarf white (*Picea conica glauca*)
Norway (*P. excelsa*)
Serbian (*P. omorika*)
Yew, English (*Taxus baccata*)
Kelsey's (*T. media kelseyi*)

Deciduous

Abelia, glossy (*A. grandiflora*)
Acanthopanax pentaphyllum
Alder, berried (*Rhamnus frangula*)
Barberry, green-leaf (*Berberis thunbergi*). Prickly.
Red-leaf (*B. atropurpurea*)
Beech (*Fagus americana*)

Blackthorn (*Prunus spinosa*). Spiny.
Buckthorn (*Rhamnus cathartica*). Spiny.
glossy (*R. frangula*)
Buffaloberry (*Shepherdia argentea*). Thorny.
Cockspur thorn (*Crataegus crusgalli*). Spiny.

118

Hills of snow (*Hydrangea arborescens*)
Honey locust (*Gleditsia triacanthos*). Spiny.
Honeysuckle, bush (*Lonicera korolkowii*)
Hornbeam, American (*Carpinus caroliniana*)
Corkbark, winged (*Euonymus alatus*)
Cotoneaster, Pekin (*C. acutifolia*)
Crataegus carrierei. Spiny.
Deutzia gracilis.
Elm, Chinese or Siberian (*Ulmus pumila*)
Golden bell (*Forsythia suspensa*)
Lilac (*Syringa vulgaris*)
Maple, Japanese (*Acer palmatum*)
Maythorn (*Crataegus oxyacantha*). Spiny.
Ninebark (*Physocarpus opulifolius*)
Orange, hardy trifoliate (*Citrus trifoliata*). Spiny.
Osage (*Maclura pomifera*). Spiny.
Pea tree, Siberian (*Caragana arborescens*). Spiny.
Privet, Amur (*Ligustrum amurense*)
Golden-leaf (*L. vulgare aureum*)

Regel's Ibota (*L. obtusifolium*)
Quince, flowering (*Chaenomeles lagenaria*). Spiny.
Rose, fence (*Rosa multiflora*). Prickly.
Floribunda. Prickly.
Hugo (*R. hugonis*). Prickly.
Japanese (*R. rugosa*). Prickly.
Polyantha. Prickly.
Rose of Sharon (*Hibiscus syriacus*)
Sloe (*Prunus spinosa*). Spiny.
Snowball (*Viburnum opulus*)
Spindle tree (*Euonymus alatus*)
Spiraea, Anthony Waterer
 S. *Vanhouttei*
Weigela rosea
Willow, black (*Salix nigra*)

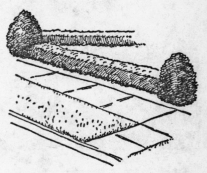

Japanese barberries and junipers; both trimmed to make a well-defined boundary.

Consider a mixed hedge. Try planting golden privet with green, forsythia with lilacs, Japanese maples with rose of Sharon—a number of interesting combinations may be worked out.

CHAPTER 15

The Patio Garden

"Let others tell of storms and showers,
I'll only mark your sunny hours."
Motto on a Sundial, AUTHOR UNKNOWN.

Enclosed formal garden with fountain,
suggesting quiet and seclusion.

THE PATIO GARDEN is a paved area which can be an ideal extension of the home and may be considered an open-air sitting room or outdoor study. It is the logical spot for your garden furniture.

Some shrubs with perennial and annual flowers may well be planted in a border around the patio, and perfumed subjects should be included. Between the stone or concrete slabs forming the floor, occasional 2-inch gaps may be left; fill these with soil and plant in them mother-of-thyme, mazus, or various sedums. But if the primary use of the floor is to be for dancing, the slabs or stones should fit closely in the center and should be tightly cemented there, with planted gaps only around the edges.

A tent roof may be erected over one corner for a few months in summer to enable you to picnic in bad weather; or to read,

Barbecue stove can be the main feature of the patio garden. An antique millstone serves as a table.

write, or sew. Get from your supply store a suitable spray or dust to control mosquitos and flies.

In planning your garden you may assume that your principal vistas will start at the patio; *allées* will radiate from it; a wading pool may lead off from it. The whole should be adequately lighted to permit its use after dark.

LEFT: *novel treatment for the patio floor: Italian pebble paving with colored stones set in cement.* RIGHT: *mother-of-thyme and other herbs may be planted between flagstones; they emit a pleasing fragrance when walked upon.*

Formal patio pool, with clipped taxus hedge and pachysandra. Evergreens in pots.

If your property is extensive and hilly, and your location is in the northern section of the country, consider a snow slide for winter, starting from the patio with easy and safe curves, with steps to take you to a higher level for a return run to the patio. A type of power-mower with a snow-scraper attachment will be useful on the patio, on paths, sidewalks and driveway, and on the snow slide.

CHAPTER 16

Gather Roses from June to November

"Poor Peggy hawks nosegays from street to street
Till—think of that who find life so sweet!—
She hates the smell of roses."
THOMAS HOOD, "Miss Kilmansegg."

OF COURSE you will make provision for a rose garden in your plans. The area should be fully open to the sun, or have sunshine for most of the daylight hours; trees should not overhang it. Any shape and any design will be suitable that allows you to set your everblooming roses 3 feet apart each way.

The soil should be topsoil and level, or only slightly sloping. It need not be clay; a clay loam or even a medium sandy loam will

Formal rose garden. Each corner bed contains one standard rose, several bush roses; edges are of miniature roses. Note the secluded arbor.

give you good roses. The important thing is that it should drain thoroughly: a continuously damp spot is no good. You can divert excess moisture through land drains to a lower spot or to a dry well, which is a 6-foot-deep hole or cesspool, which you keep from collapsing by lining the sides with rocks, filling with more rocks, and then placing a layer of stones, one of ashes, and finally soil on the top.

Slightly moist areas, which remain damp overlong after rain, will often make a good rose garden provided you first remove the soil 1½ feet deep, keeping topsoil and subsoil separate. Excavate a further 12 inches and replace the subsoil you have removed with 12 inches of rocks; place smaller stones on the upper layer to prevent earth washing between them. Fill in the 1½ feet with topsoil, some of which you will scrape from other parts of the garden. Thus on a foundation of a foot of rocks you have 1½ feet of topsoil.

A practical design for a rose garden is to have one or more long beds 5 feet wide, with a well-raked 3-foot path between them. The whole rose area may be surrounded by 7-foot cedar posts—5 feet being out of the ground—set 6 feet apart. Against each post two climbing roses may be planted. Chains or wire cable may be festooned from post to post, and half the "canes" or stems of each rose fastened to them; the remaining canes will be wired to the cedar post.

Dig holes for your roses, 1 foot square and 1 foot deep; mix with the earth at the bottom of each pocket 3 trowelsful of sheep manure or other organic plant food, 1½ trowelsful of bonemeal, and a small pailful of compost, humus, or rotted manure. Stir thoroughly with a small rake, hoe, or trowel. Then plant your rose, taking care that the roots are arranged outwards and downwards, with none twisting. If the hole is too small for some roots that may be overlong, shorten them with pruning shears. Prune away also branches that may be damaged. Surround the roots with plain unfertilized soil, tread firm, and water copiously.

Do your planting in spring in northern New England and the border States; in spring or fall elsewhere. When your roses have been set out, prune them. Successful growers have various pruning methods, but a good one that will produce large roses is to:

1. Cut away all but four main stems, the strongest.
2. Remove side branches.
3. Cut the top of each stem to just beyond a bud that points away from the center of the plant, leaving on the stem one, two, three or more buds. The number you leave depends upon the position of the buds, the nearer to three on each stem the better.

A climbing rose may be allowed up to five main stems: prune out the oldest stems and cut those you take out to the ground level. When any stems grow much beyond the height of the support, prune the particular stem to a level with the top of the support; when another gets too tall, prune *it* to 1 foot below the support, the next one 1 foot below the last. Additional side stems will grow below where you have pruned; cut these to 9 inches and, if they are very numerous, cut some of them to 3 inches from the main stem.

Keep the rosebeds free of weeds and hoe the surface with a scuffle-hoe to keep a soil mulch around the plants; let your scuffling be very shallow, because the important roots are close to the surface.

You may very well have a hedge of floribunda roses around the rose garden, with a rose arch entering and leaving it. In the center a circular space with seats and a fountain, bird bath, or sundial would be in order.

When late autumn arrives to the latitude of Philadelphia and north and the bushes have lost their leaves, a quantity of soil is borrowed from another part of the garden. Wheel enough of this to make a foot-high pyramid around each bush, with the bush in the center. In New England and the border States the soil pyramid may be 18 inches high and reinforced with a covering of hay, straw, or shingles, the whole kept intact with a large rock or two. In spring when other plants in the garden burst their buds, the covering is taken away from the roses, the soil being wheeled back to the garden. Probably all the exposed portions of the bush that were above the pyramid will be killed, but you prune the tops of branches to below the frost-killed portion. Note that in building the pyramids, earth is not hoed up to the bushes, for doing so would expose and injure the roots.

There are seven types of roses you may wish to use:

Bushes of everblooming or hybrid-tea varieties. Every year many new introductions appear, which should be included if you have the room, such as: Peace (591), with changing colors from ivory through canary-yellow to cerise and pink. Fred Howard (1006), rich yellow, penciled with soft pink. Capistrano (922), rose-pink. New Yorker (823), brilliant red. Forty-niner (792), a two-color rose, yellow and red. Katherine T. Marshall (607), coral-pink. Mirandy (632), deep, rich, dark red, with black shadings, and many another modern sort which you can pick out from an up-to-date nursery catalogue.

The numbers throughout this chapter are those of the patents issued by the U. S. Government to raisers of meritorious kinds to protect the introducer against commercial interests exploiting the new kinds. But equally beautiful in the opinion of many people are the old-line sorts which have been extensively planted through the years and whose popularity has stood the test of time, such as: Etoile de Hollande, brilliant dark red. McCredy's Yellow. Radiance, rosy carmine with pink shading. Snowbird, very fragrant white. Talisman, combination of gold and pink. These were introduced before the patenting of new plants came into effect; they are splendid nevertheless and with many others they can be selected from the catalogues.

Everblooming roses give crops of blooms from June to frost.

Tree or standard roses. Most bush roses are reproduced by budding a new variety onto the lower part of the stem of a wild rose, which usually is a stronger feeder than the new kind. With the tree or standard rose the choice bud is attached to the wildling 3 feet from the ground. The wild stem is kept bare of leaves and branches on top, so the new plant is brought right up to you for enjoying conveniently its color and perfume.

Standards add accent to your rose garden and should be included in your plantings. Put them also into your perennial borders or shrub borders, but not too many in sections of the country where winter temperatures may drop to 15° F. In cold latitudes you dig them up and bury them completely for the winter. Or you place straw through the rosebush on top of the standard stem, and bind the whole plant in burlap. South of the 15° F. limit, however, they should stand an average winter.

Pruning standard roses is carried out just the same as with a bush rose, but remember that your bush starts 3 feet above ground and any suggestion that roses be pruned within 12 inches of the ground—although it may be good in some cases—does not apply to tree roses. With these the ground is represented by the point where the bush is attached to the 3-foot stem. Many hybrid-tea or everblooming sorts are obtainable in the standard form, as also are some of the hybrid-perpetual kinds.

Hybrid-perpetual, ramontant or cabbage roses. These roses do not flower perpetually, as their name would imply. They bloom once a year only, in June, with the possibility of an additional sparse crop later on. But the blooms mostly are larger and the crop is heavier than with the everblooming ones. Some old-time favorites are in this grouping, such as: **Frau Karl Druschki,** non-fragrant white. **Paul Neyron,** dark rose-pink. **Magna Charta,** very fragrant large pink. **General Jacquemont,** fragrant brilliant crimson.

Floribunda roses. These are shrubs and are a comparatively new group of extremely hardy, continuous-blooming types; some kinds have large blooms, but most are of moderate size, semi-double, and produced in clusters. All color combinations are found in this class. Among the best are: **Anne Vanderbilt** (504), coppery-orange and semi-double. **Curly Pink** (842), two tones of pink. **Fashion** (789), semi-double blooms of coral-pink and gold. **Goldilocks** (672), rich gold and very double. **Pinocchio** (484), gold, salmon and pink. **Summer Snow** (416), white. **Vogue** (926), cherry-coral. **World's Fair** (362), large, rich velvety black-scarlet, and semi-double Floribundas are the best kind to choose if you set roses in your foundation planting or shrub border. They are excellent for lining driveways, and a hedge of them, blooming all summer and fall, is something of great beauty.

Polyantha roses. Everblooming, they have smaller flowers in clusters and the plants are dwarfer. They are recommended for edgings. Include in your planting the following: **Dick Koster,** dwarf bushy plants with clusters of rose-red flowers. **Gloria Mundi,** fully double, brilliant orange-scarlet. **Margo Koster,** like Dick Koster, but the flowers are vivid orange, flushed coral. **Triomphe Orleanais,** brilliant cherry orange-scarlet.

Miniature roses. These midgets are excellent for planting in a mass. The plants are only 6 to 8 inches high when mature. The following are everblooming: **Pixie** (408), double white. **Red Elf** (973), rich deep velvet-red. **Rouletti,** the fairy rose, semi-double, pink. **Sweet Fairy** (748), apple-blossom pink, and very double. **Tom Thumb** (169), semi-double carmine flowers with white centers, dime-size.

Climbing roses. For growing on a trellis, rose fan, fence post, or festooning from one post to another.

Everblooming Climbers

These are newer but generally less hardy; they may not bloom persistently in all parts of the country. In the North, lay the canes down over winter, blanketing them with straw, hay, or canvas.

Aloha (948). Rose-pink blooms in long-stemmed clusters.

Climbing Crimson Glory (736). An abundance of perfect crimson blooms.

Climbing Peace (932). Large ivory blooms, tinged pink and cerise.

Dr. J. H. Nicholas (457). Deep rose-pink; very fragrant.

Thor (387). Scarlet red blooms 4 to 5 inches across, and double.

Older Climbing Roses

In addition to planting roses to climb a fence or post, as suggested above, they may be planted on steep slopes and pegged down to hold the soil against erosion.

Blaze. Scarlet-red double flowers, 4 inches across. Gives a fine display in June. May flower again sparingly in the fall.

Climbing American Beauty. Rose-carmine blooms, 3 to 4 inches in diameter, are produced freely in June.

City of York. Heavy blooms of lovely, long-lasting, 3-inch semi-double, cream-white flowers.

New Dawn. A sort from Dr. Van Fleet, with charming flesh-pink flowers in June and some scattered blooms the rest of the season.

Paul's Scarlet Climber. Vivid scarlet large and double flowers in June.

CHAPTER 17

Borders and Beds

"So great is their love of flowers." VIRGIL, Georgics.

PERENNIAL.BORDERS

The perennial border needs little attention other than weeding and hoeing; choose plants so that some will bloom in spring, others in summer, others in fall. Few perennials are effective all season.

IN AREAS 3 feet or more wide and of any convenient shape or size, hardy perennials are usually planted with little regard for symmetrical arrangement or regular spacing. The important point is that each plant has sufficient room in which to grow, which means a plant to each 1 to 3 square feet, depending upon the size of the variety; taller kinds are placed in the rear of dwarfer ones. Plants are often set in groups of five or more of a kind, and the groups are so placed that the sorts flowering early will be set against others flowering during midsummer, which again may be near a group that blooms at the end of summer.

Other planters like to have one whole section of a border in flower at once, and as this goes out of color another section will come into bloom.

Perennials and a brick walk for informal charm.

Some valuable lists showing color, height, and flowering season of perennial, biennial, and annual flowers will be found in *Better Flowers for Your Home Garden* (Melady Garden Books, Grosset & Dunlap, Inc., pages 93–105). With these lists you can make up color schemes and have your borders at the greatest effectiveness when you need them. Here is a partial list which will be sufficient for most planters; it includes the important hardy perennials that should be in every garden.

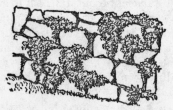

To define your property, to terrace land, or to hold a bank, a wall of fieldstone is often built. Plants may be set in pockets of soil between the stones. Use types offered for rock gardens.

SIX BEST FROST-RESISTANT BULBS

Varieties marked * are suitable also for the rock garden. Plant them in autumn; no need to dig them in spring.

	Average height in inches	Colors							Blooming period					
		White; near white	Pink	Red	Orange and yellow	Lavender, mauve, or purple	Blue	Multi-colored flowers	Apr.	May	June	July	Aug.	Sept.
* Crocus	6	x				x	x		x	x				
* Daffodils, dwarf kinds	10	x			x	x			x	x				
* Daffodils, normal varieties	15	x			x			x	x	x				
* Hyacinths, Dutch	12	x	x	x		x	x		x					
* Hyacinths, grape	10	x					x		x					
Tulips, Darwin and breeder	30	x	x	x	x	x		x	x	x				
* Tulips, early flowering	12	x	x	x	x	x		x	x					

SIX IMPORTANT HARDY LILIES

Plant bulbs in autumn or spring. There is one exception: set L. candidum in September. Once planted, let all these lilies remain in the ground through the years. *L. tenuifolium may be planted in the rock garden also.

	Average height in inches	Colors							Blooming period					
		White; near white	Pink	Red	Orange and yellow	Lavender, mauve, or purple	Blue	Multi-colored flowers	Apr.	May	June	July	Aug.	Sept.
Auratum (Goldband lily)	40	x						x					x	x
Candidum (Madonna lily)	40	x									x			
Regale (Regal lily)	48	x						x			x	x		
Speciosum (Oriental orchid)	48	x											x	x
* Tenuifolium (Coral lily)	24			x							x			
Tigrinum (Tiger lily)	70			x								x	x	

YOUR HARDY BORDER

The following are the most popular biennial and perennial flowers, with their height, color, and blooming period.

Twenty Leading Herbaceous Perennials

Varieties marked * are also suitable for the rock garden. Roots are planted in spring or fall. Seeds are obtainable of some; sow them June to August. Mostly they bloom the following year, but a few take longer.

	Average height in inches	Colors							Blooming period					
		White; near white	Pink	Red	Orange and yellow	Lavender, mauve, or purple	Blue	Multi-colored flowers	Apr.	May	June	July	Aug.	Sept.
* Alyssum saxatile (Madwort; golden rain)	12				X				X	X				
* Aquilegia (Columbine)	30	X			X	X	X	X	X	X				
Chrysanthemum ("mums")	24	X	X	X	X	X		X					X	X
Dicentra spectabilis (Bleeding heart)	30		X							X				
Funkia (Plantain lily)	30	X				X						X	X	
* Geum (Avens)	24			X	X							X	X	X
Gypsophila paniculata (Baby's breath)	36	X										X		
Hemerocallis (Day lily)	36	X	X	X	X						X	X	
Iris kaempferi (Japan iris)	30	X	X	X		X		X			X	X	
Iris vulgaris (Bearded iris; flag)	24	X	X		X	X		X		X	X			
Monarda didyma (Bee-balm)	36	X	X	X								X	X	
* Myosotis palustris (Forget-me-not)	10						X		X	X	X			
* Papaver nudicaule (Iceland poppy)	12	X		X	X			X		X	X	X		
Papaver orientale (Oriental poppy)	48	X		X				X		X	X			

	Average height in inches	White; near white	Pink	Red	Orange and yellow	Lavender, mauve, or purple	Blue	Multi-colored flowers	Apr.	May	June	July	Aug.	Sept.
Peony	36	x	x	x						x				
Phlox decussata (Garden phlox)	36	x	x	x								x	x	
*Phlox subulata (Moss or mountain pink)	4	x	x	x		x				x				
*Pyrethrum (Painted daisy)	24	x	x	x		x					x			
Tritoma (Red-hot-poker)	36			x	x			x					x	x	x
Yucca filamentosa (Adam's needle)	100	x						x				x	x	x

Six Best Hardy Biennials

Varieties marked * are suitable also for the rock garden. Roots are planted in spring or fall. Seeds are obtainable; sow them June to August, to bloom the following year.

	Average height in inches	White; near white	Pink	Red	Orange and yellow	Lavender, mauve, or purple	Blue	Multi-colored flowers	Apr.	May	June	July	Aug.	Sept.
Althaea rosea (Hollyhock)	100	x	x	x	x							x	x	
*Bellis perennis (English daisy)	6	x	x	x					x	x				
Campanula calycanthema (Canterbury bell)	48	x					x				x			
*Dianthus barbatus (Sweet William)	24	x	x	x		x					x			
Digitalis purpurea (Foxglove)	48	x			x	x					x			
*Viola tricolor (Pansy)	10	x			x	x	x	x	x	x				

ANNUAL BORDERS

Border of annual flowers. Plants are set according to your color preference; and they are placed in reference to their height, the tallest in back. Begonias, callas, cannas and gladioli may be grown with them, because they have to be dug in the fall.

Plantings of annual flowers along the same lines as the perennial border are much used. Seeds may be sown directly into the border and the seedlings thinned to stand 9, 12, 15 or 18 inches apart, according to the size of the mature plants. A better scheme is to sow seeds ahead of time in the home or in a frame or greenhouse and transfer the plantlets out of pots or flats.

Annual borders have the disadvantage of having to be replanted every spring; this can be a good thing, however, because new colors may be planted each year. Annuals are often more colorful than perennials, and most of them are effective from the time they begin to bloom until frost stops them.

FLOWER BEDS

An all-red flower bed of cannas and salvias. Cannas are dug in fall and replanted in spring. Salvias are replaced every spring.

These usually are designed more formally than borders and are often circles, ovals, or rectangles. The plants set in them are usually arranged formally also: with an edging of a dwarf variety paralleling the sides, perhaps with a second edging of a less dwarf kind, a taller kind yet within the edgings, and the center occupied by kinds 3 to 6 feet high. Bright colors are preferred.

Greenhouse subjects and house plants from within the home may be used in the center of the beds, to be returned indoors at the end of summer. Through the years skilled gardeners have exercised their ingenuity in developing combinations that are highly attractive, from a simple joining of scarlet geraniums and blue lobelias to highly complicated schemes.

Competent plantsmen of a past decade were aided by foremen, journeymen, and apprentices, all learning the horticultural art and willing to work for very little while they were acquiring their trade; now this type of labor is rarely seen. It costs real money to dig, hoe, or rake and mechanical methods are used wherever possible. We mow with power and have the fewest possible flower beds in the lawn, because island beds are costly to trim while borders coming to the edge of the lawn are less so. An occasional large flower bed is sometimes seen, but many small ones rarely.

Multicolor flower bed using the national colors: red salvias in center, white petunias around them, an edging of blue ageratum. All are annuals; replace with new plants in spring.

From the following partial list of the subjects for flower beds it will be seen that the possible combinations are almost endless:

Dwarf plants for edging a flower bed

Ageratum	Carnation, annual	Phacelia
Alyssum, white carpet	Cuphea	Pinks, annual
Brachycome	* Eschscholtzia	* Portulaca
Candytuft	Lobelia	Violas and Pansies
	Matricaria	Virginian stock, etc.

* These are difficult to transplant. Sow seeds in small groups where they are to flower and thin to one plant. Better to sow earlier indoors in small pots; thin to one plant per pot; set the plant with the ball of soil intact.

Tall plants suitable for the center of beds

Cannas	*Sundry house or*	*Sundry perennials*
Castor-beans	*greenhouse plants:*	*transplanted from*
Cleome	Acacia	*the border:*
Cosmos	Araucaria	Aconitum
Gladiolus	Croton	Coneflower
Kochia	Dracena	Delphinium
* Larkspur	Ficus (rubber plant)	Geum
Lilies in variety	Fuchsia	Lupinus
Marigold, tall	Genista	Phlox
Nicotiana	Hydrangea	Salvia farinacea
Salpiglossis	Pandanus	Stokesia
Tithonia, etc.	Strelitzia, etc.	Tritoma, etc.

Medium-height plants for main part of the bed

Antirrhinum	Four o'clock	* Mignonette
Arctotis	Gaillardia	Myosotis
Aster	Gerbera	Nasturtium, dwarf
Balsam, bush type	Gomphrena	Nemesia
Begonia, fibrous	* Gypsophila elegans	Nierembergia
tuberous	Helichrysum	Pelargonium (gera-
Caladium, fancy-leaf	Heliotrope	nium)
Calendula	Impatiens	Petunia
Calliopsis	Kalanchoe	* Poppy, annual
Celosia, cockscomb	Lantana	Salvia, scarlet
* Centaurea	Linaria	Scabiosa
Coleus	Linum	Schizanthus
* Cornflower	Lupin, annual	Snow-in-summer
* Dimorphotheca	Marigold, dwarf	Stock
Euphorbia, annual	Mathiola bicornis	Verbena
poinsettia	Matricaria	Zinnia, etc.

All these may be sown outdoors in spring, or started earlier indoors and transplanted; or you may buy plants from a florist. Plants are necessary for violas and pansies.

Roots, corms, tubers, or bulbs of the following may be set out in the beds when danger of killing spring frosts is over:

Caladium	Canna	Gladiolus	Lilies	Begonias

* These are difficult to transplant. Sow seeds in small groups where they are to flower and thin to one plant. Better to sow earlier indoors in small pots; thin to one plant per pot; set the plant with the ball of soil intact.

Or they may be planted indoors in pots or flats six weeks earlier, and transferred outdoors with soil around them in a started condition when warm weather has arrived. Lilies may be left in the ground for years, but the four others should be lifted in the fall when the first frosts arrive; let them dry on the garage floor, then store them in a frost-free but cool place.

CARPET BEDS

A formal lily pool combined with carpet-bedding.

These old-time supreme examples of the landscaper's patience and art are rarely seen nowadays. Set in closely mown, well-fertilized, and well-rolled lawns were geometric designs, quite like those of a Persian carpet. The colors were obtained from flowers, or more often from the colored leaves of red and golden alternanthera, golden feather, and many another set 1½ to 2 inches apart —while in normal flower beds, plants are set so that they only grow to touch toward the end of summer.

The artist would draw his plan to scale, mark in white sand the lines where his plants were to go, set them with great precision, and by weekly shearing keep them from growing out of hand. Under glass he would be occupied all the previous winter with producing plants from divisions, cuttings, or occasionally from seed; when May arrived he would plant his carpet beds with the contents of his glasshouses and frames. All summer long he would remove weeds by hand.

Large carpet beds are suitable for parks, memorial areas or the grounds around City Hall. As yet they seem to have been little taken up for commercial advertising.

Some Carpet-bedding Plants

Grown from cuttings and used mostly for their leaves:

Acalypha wilkesiana. Copper-leaf.
Alternathera bettzickiana. Yellow or red leaves.
A. versicolor. Copper or blood-red leaves.
Centaurea cineraria. Dusty Miller.
C. gymnocarpa. Dusty Miller.
Chrysanthemum parthenum aureum. Golden Feather. Feverfew.
C. parthenum glaucum.
Coleus verschaffelti.
Echeveria (Cotyledon) atropurpurea.
E. (Cotyledon) fulgens.
E. (Cotyledon) glauca.
E. (Cotyledon) secunda.
Iresine herbsti. Blood-leaf.
I. lindeni. Blood-leaf.
Oxalis corniculata. Wood Sorrel.
Pelargonium hortorum. Succulent Geranium.
Piqueria trinerva. Stevia.
Santolina chamaecyparissus. Lavender Cotton.
Sempervivum arachnoideum. Cobweb Houseleek.
S. calcareum. Hen-and-chickens.
S. tectorium. Common Houseleek.
Senecio cineraria. Dusty Miller.
Thymus serpyllum. Mother of Thyme.

Grown from seed or cuttings, and used mostly for their flowers:

Ageratum, dwarf types. Blue or white.
Begonia rex
B. semperflorens
Brachycome iberidifolia. Swan River Daisy.
Cuphea. Cigar Plant.
Heliotrope
Iberis amara. Rocket Candytuft.
I. umbellata. Candytuft.
Lantana

Lobelia, blue or white.
Lobularia maritima. White Sweet Alyssum.
L. maritima. Violet Queen.
Petunia, miniature types.
Phlox drummondi, dwarf.
Portulaca, single or double.
Salvia, scarlet dwarf.
Salvia, Clary.
Torenia flava, yellow.
T. fourneiri, blue.
Verbena, dwarf.

Many other dwarf annuals or perennials may be used for this purpose. Carpet-bedding is a highly skilled effort and is not generally recommended for the amateur. But it has possibilities if one has time and patience and wishes to make the most of a limited area.

CHAPTER 18

A Section Especially for Cut Flowers

"Who loves a garden still his Eden keeps,
Perennial pleasures plants, and wholesome harvests reaps."
AMOS BRONSON ALCOTT, Tablets: The Garden.

FLOWERS FOR CUTTING are grown as a crop, with no attempt at decorative arrangement. Seeds are best sown, or bulbs and roots are best planted, in straight lines 24 inches apart; 1 foot or more spacing is allowed between plants in the line. The soil should be topsoil, but need not be given fertilizer beforehand unless it is of poor quality. The space between the plants is hoed every ten days and the soil alongside them is given an occasional side dressing of fertilizer. To save space in turning your wheel-cultivator you had better run the rows the longer direction of the cutting garden, regardless of whether north-south or east-west is the more favorable direction. Buds are snipped out here and there with shears so that the remaining buds grow into larger and more shapely flowers.

Most blooms are gathered just as the bud is opening, immediately plunged the entire length of the stems in water, which you carry into the garden with you, and kept overnight in a cool cellar or shed. Next morning the flowers are water-gorged and have that perfect look which may not be seen in most home-grown flowers.

Most flowers continue to produce for a longer period if they are sheared off before they fade. To allow plants to mature their seed is one way to stop further flower production. This is a worthwhile weekly chore.

A separate cutting garden is desirable in plots over 10,000 square feet; for smaller areas take flowers sparingly from your annual and perennial borders. And in late winter cut branches of spring-flowering shrubs, forsythia especially, to bloom in the home.

Here are some good subjects for the cutting garden. In small gardens merely be sure to include them in your borders and beds.

ANNUALS

Sow seeds and thin so that individuals stand the proper distance apart. For earlier results purchase seedlings or produce seedlings in your greenhouse, frame, or sunroom and plant them out when frost has gone.

Alyssum, purple
Asters
Baby's breath. Sow in April, again in June.
Calendula
Carnation
Centaurea americana
C. cyanus
Cosmos
Dahlia
Globe amaranth, an everlasting
Helichrysum, everlasting
Lantana
Larkspur
Marigold
Mignonette (Sow outdoors in April, May, and June. Do not transplant.)
Nasturtium, Gleam
    Globe
Phlox, Annual
Pinks (dianthus)
Queen Anne's Lace
Salpiglossis
Salvia, Clary
    farinacea
Scabious, annual
Schizanthus
Spider-flower
Stock
Sweet Peas
Tithonia
Verbena
Zinnia, midget varieties
    Fantasy
    giant varieties

BIENNIALS

Sow in late spring or early summer to bloom the following year.

Daisy, English
Honesty, everlasting
Pansies (Sow August 1.)
Sweet William
Wallflower

PERENNIALS

Plant roots in spring or autumn; sow seeds of some in spring or summer. Most will bloom the following year; a few, one or two years later.

Alyssum saxatile
Aquilegia
Aster novae-angliae
   nova-belgii
Chrysanthemum
Delphinium grandi-
   florum
Gaillardia
Gerbera

Geum
Gypsophila panicu-
   lata
Heuchera sanguinea
Iris cristata
I. kaempferi
I. siberica
I. vulgaris
Myosotis palustris

Peony
Phlox divaricata
P. suffruticosa
Physostegia virgini-
   ana
Plumbago larpentae
Pyrethrum
Scabiosa caucasica
Tritoma uvaria

AUTUMN-PLANTED BULBS

These flower the following spring. Hardy perennials; let them remain through the years.

Daffodils
Tulips, April-flower-
   ing

Tulips, Darwin,
   breeder and
   parrot

Hyacinths, Dutch
   grape

SPRING-PLANTING BULBS AND ROOTS

Perennials; those marked * are sensitive to frost; lift and store them over winter. Lilium and lily-of-the-valley remain in the ground.

* Calla, golden
* Dahlia
* Gladiolus
* Glory lily
* Tuberose

Lilium auratum
L. candidum. Plant
   in late summer
L. henryi
L. philippinense

L. regale
L. speciosum rubrum
L. tenuifolium
L. tigrinum
Lily-of-the-valley

Depending upon the area available for a cutting garden, you will need only some of these. Nearly all should be included in a large plot intended for a hotel, where cut flowers are needed all season. Paths through the garden may make it a source of great interest to the guests; here large stick labels will enable them to identify the varieties.

CHAPTER 19

Wild Flowers and Poisonous Plants

"Meadows trim with daisies pied,
Shallow brooks and rivers wide."
MILTON, L'Allegro.

A WILD-FLOWER GARDEN

OUR NATIVE PLANTS have a charm that many cultivated types lack, despite the large size and brilliant colors of many of the latter. To go through the woods, along the back roads, or in the open fields and endeavor to identify the various flowers as they develop in the succeeding weeks of spring, summer and autumn, is an interesting occupation. One good method is to purchase a "vasculum," which is a convenient flat tin box carried on a shoulder strap. Gather and put into the vasculum a specimen spray of each plant found in bloom. Though they are sad-looking when you empty the vasculum at day's end, most of the specimens will revive when you stand them in water overnight.

Make a list of the wild flowers you have collected, using one of the several books that have been published for the purpose of naming them. One of the most complete, though expensive, is Britton and Brown's *Illustrated Flora of the Northern United States and Canada* (New York Botanical Garden). Difficult at first, wild-flower identification will become progressively easier.

You will discover some wild plants that you would like to bring into your own informal wild garden because of their beauty or interest. Buy at the supply store a box of 6-inch wooden pot labels; stick a label half its length into the ground alongside the plant you want; write its name if you know it. In late autumn, which will be a favorable time of the year, take a trowel and dig up the entire plant; set it on your property in a situation like the one from which you have taken it—in shade if from the woods, in the sun if from the open country. Remember two important rules, however: Find out what plants may legally be taken from the wild; mountain laurel, bloodroot, and gentian are among those protected in some States. Secondly, be sure to obtain the owner's permission if you wish to dig in a field or other private place.

Mixed seeds of American wild flowers may be purchased at the larger seed stores—your agricultural college may suggest a source. Mix 1 teaspoon of these seeds with 10 spoons of sifted earth; broadcast the mixture in spring and again in fall. To prevent weeds from choking the wild flowers, scythe the area or cut unwanted growth with a grass whip. Be sure to get seeds of actual American wild plants, not "mixed flower seeds," which usually consist of garden types.

Recognise these two contact-poisonous plants. LEFT: *poison ivy.* CENTER: *poison ivy creeping over the ground.* RIGHT: *poison oak.*

These look like poisonous plants, but they are innocent. LEFT: *Virginia creeper.* CENTER: *Engelman's ivy.* RIGHT: *Boston ivy.*

Recognise the Contact-Poison Plants

Poison Ivy. *Rhus toxicodendron.* It trails over the ground, climbs tree trunks to 15 feet, goes over rocks, fences, and stone walls. *Leaves are in threes;* they usually are not toothed; their edges are entire. Often they are shiny and mid-green; sometimes without luster and light green. They mostly hang down; on a tree trunk they are often arranged like shingles. It has clusters of pea-sized lusterless berries in August. Common both in the open and in woods; often found in full sun. Abundant in New England and the East; distributed more sparingly throughout the rest of the United States.

Poison Oak. *Rhus quercifolia.* Erect small shrub growing up to 20 inches. Leaves, also in groups of three, are shaped like wide, coarse oak leaves and are light green, first covered with light hairs, later smooth. Has dull whitish berries rather smaller than a pea, in clusters; each has a nipple at the end. Found in light woods and barren tracts, mostly near the coast from Virginia south and westward.

Poison Sumac. *Rhus vernix.* A small tree growing from 5 to 15 feet, sometimes with a 6-inch-diameter trunk, branching near the ground like a dwarf fruit tree, with a round-topped head. Bark is gray, smooth when young, with raised *horizontal markings* when old. Leaves have 7 to 13 pale green leaflets, each abruptly pointed; they turn red in autumn. Berries the size of a small pea are green at first, then ivory or dull white; they hang in long slender clusters on female trees, persisting into winter. There are separate male and female trees of this variety; male trees have no berries. Occurs in swampy ground in the rectangle from southwest Maine, through southern Canada to Minnesota and Arkansas, south to Louisiana, east to northern Florida.

We may not touch any of these poison plants, wear clothing that has been in contact with them, or stand near a patch of them on a hot day. Individuals vary as to their sensitivity to the poison. For years you may have considered yourself immune but may suddenly find you have taken the poison and develop a rash of itching blisters. Falling against a tree covered with the leaves or stumbling into a patch of them may affect your face and cause temporary blindness, your eyes being closed by swollen cheeks;

this will happen also if you rub your face with a hand carrying the poison, or even if you scratch a blistered ankle and then rub your face.

What to do. 1. Wash thoroughly using lots of soap; use old-time yellow laundry soap if you have it; or clean with alcohol. 2. Consult a physician. 3. Spray the plants with a weed-killing chemical like Ammate or Weedone. Do not burn the killed plants; allow time to cause them to decay. 4. If you burn garden rubbish, keep well to windward of the fire. Inhalation of the smoke may be serious; the physician may have to use oxygen.

Don't Eat Strange Berries or Chew Unknown Plants

Many plants are poisonous, but there is little danger from them if the following precautions are taken.

1. Discourage the younger members of your family from indiscriminate eating of strange berries and seeds. Jack-in-the-pulpit, deadly nightshade, woody nightshade, or bittersweet are typical poisonous berries. Laburnum and castor-oil plant are among those having harmful beans.

2. Only eat mushrooms that have been bought in stores, grown in your own beds, or gathered from the fields by experienced people.

3. Do not chew listlessly on stems or leaves of plants, despite the fascination in doing so. The garden flowers, snow-in-summer or annual poinsettia, will cause inflammation of the bronchial tubes with alarming symptoms. Leaves of the wild black cherry, garden poppy, and foxglove are poisonous, as are the seeds of *Daphne mezerium.*

4. Do not grow or eat horseradish or parsnip if an old perennial border is near by—the deadly *Aconitum napellus,* or monkshood, may be growing in it, and its roots may be mistaken for those of the vegetables.

Some insecticides, fungicides, and weed killers are usually poisonous; they should be kept under lock and key, and the labels bearing the antidotes kept undamaged.

In the event of poisoning act promptly. *Call a doctor.* With chemicals give the antidote listed on the container. If you cannot find it and in the case of accidental vegetable poisoning, fill the victim with quarts of soapsuds, salty water, plain warm water, or water mixed with milk. These should induce vomiting; if they do not, tickle the back of the throat. After the victim has vomited well, fill him with milk or eggs and milk beaten up together. Keep him warm and give artificial respiration if breathing stops.

Obtain the American Red Cross First-Aid Text Book and practice artificial respiration.

CHAPTER 20

A Water Garden

"On every thorn delightful wisdom grows,
In every rill a sweet instruction flows."
YOUNG, Love of Fame.

A square pool is the easiest to construct.

THIS MAY BE of formal design, circular or oval in shape; or, preferably, an attempt may be made to attain a natural appearance. Such an attempt to imitate nature may form an extension of your rock garden. Around 9 to 12 inches of water is shallow enough to be safe should small children tumble in.

A pleasing design would be a narrow winding pond to suggest a stream. The illusion could be furthered by including a small waterfall, with water piped from the house or produced by circulating a few gallons of water with a small pump. The "stream" would be crossed by a bridge or some wide flat steppingstones at one or more places.

If your soil is sandy and too porous to hold water, try puddling the bottom with 6 inches of clay; or you may have to cement the bottom and sides.

If you intend to imitate nature when building your pond, it is a good idea to let the pond's edge consist of boulders or flat rocks too high to allow cats to be interested in your pets underneath—schools of fish may hide from sun and from fish-hunting birds, which are often a source of loss, especially near the Great Lakes or

Irregularly shaped pool. Fish are protected by overhanging sides.

the oceans. You need fish to destroy mosquito larvae. Consult a dealer as to the kinds you should have; find out if they should be transferred to an indoor aquarium or may remain in the pond all winter in your locality. One fine late-winter day you will happily hear that the peepers or tree frogs have moved in as residents of your pool area.

PLANTS FOR YOUR POOL

Most effective are water lilies or nymphaeas, and you may buy either hardy or tropical types; the former will stand frost, the tropical ones will not. The hardy ones remain with their roots in the bottom all year, while the tropical types, which you plant in tubs or pots, have to be taken up in the autumn if you are in a section where ice forms in winter. The tropical kinds are then allowed to dry and the containers are placed in a cool but frost-free cellar or barn.

You may drain your pond if you wish, and the hardy lilies planted in the bottom will be unharmed, especially if you put a foot of leaves over them. Even if the pond is made of cement, you need not drain it unless you want to: merely float some heavy timbers or barrels to absorb the expansion that occurs when ice is formed, and the cement will not crack.

Part of a rock garden planting; informal pool with waterfall.

You can procure named hardy nymphaeas—red, amber, orange, white or pink—and allow one for each 25 square feet of the pond area. Roots are set in the mud; in a concrete pond, flower pots containing them stand on the bottom. Along with the nymphaeas an occasional plant of *Sagittaria* (arrowhead), *Typha* (cattail), and *Nelumbium* (hardy American lotus) could be set; stand them on the cement bottom or plant them in the mud.

A formal pool with a natural look.

Tropical nymphaeas have larger flowers and their colors are more brilliant; among them are blue, pink, red or white. You may have day-blooming sorts which open in the sun or night-blooming ones which are effective in the evening or on an overcast day. With these tropical sorts you might set a plant or two of *Nelumbium nucifera* (sacred lotus), *Nelumbium albo pleno* (Shiroman lotus), and *Nelumbium pekinensis* (Chinese lotus), *Cyperus papyrus* (Egyptian paper plant), and *Cyperus alternifolius* (Umbrella palm). These spend the winter indoors along with the tropical nymphaeas away from frost.

The ideal water depth for these plants is 1½ feet, but if you need less water for young children, get some pots one size larger than those containing your plants; when cementing your pond leave holes in the cement to hold the larger pots and put the pot containing the plant inside the larger one. Two years hence when the plants have outgrown the original pots replant them into the larger pots. In a mud-bottom pond, merely bury the double pot in the bottom. Your pond may now be from 9 to 12 inches deep and less of a hazard to the small fry.

Watercress seed may be mixed with sifted soil—1 spoonful to 10 of the soil—and the mixture rolled into marbles to be pushed into the mud at the water line. If you have to cement the pond, watercress may be grown in pots; place flat stones here and there on the sides to serve as under-water shelves for the pots; let the pot rims stand 1 inch under the surface. Let some plants of water hyacinth with blue flowers and of water lettuce float on the surface. These two must be taken indoors over winter and placed in a frost-free barn, garage, or cellar and packed in damp peat moss.

If you have a section of the pond extended to make a muddy section, which also should be furnished with steppingstones, you might plant in the wetter portion: *Acorus calamus* (sweet flag), *Iris pseudacorus* (yellow flag), *Iris versicolor* (marsh iris), and *Zizania aquatica* (wild rice).

In the drier but still marshy part you may have *Alisma plantago* (water plantain), *Pontederia cordata* (pickerel rush), and *Sagittaria latifolia* (arrowhead), which are obtainable from specialist nurserymen. Also, you may collect interesting plants around a lake and bring them home.

Wall fountain with Pfitzer's juniper and wisteria.

On a higher level, but where the land is still wet, you may grow *Lobelia cardinalis* (cardinal flower), *Iris kaempferi* (Japan iris), various hardy primulas, and *Sarracenia purpurea,* an interesting insectiverous plant.

CHAPTER 21

Lawns for Appearance and Home Sports

"We say of the oak, 'How grand of girth!'
Of the willow we say, 'How slender!'
And yet to the soft grass clothing the earth
How slight is the praise we render."
EDGAR FAWCETT, "The Grass."

TURF is considered by many property owners to be the most important part of their plantings. A minimum 4 inches of topsoil is most desirable, but in locations where topsoil is missing or additional supplies are impossible to obtain, a turf of fair quality is possible on subsoil if plant foods are used liberally and often, and if fescue varieties of grass are employed north of the Mason and Dixon line to the Arctic. Before sowing seed, incorporate 50 pounds per 1000 square feet of a 5–10–5 fertilizer mixture and almost any quantity of humus, peat moss, rotted manure or seaweed. And from time to time, spread 20 pounds per 1000 square feet of the 5–10–5 mixed with five times its bulk of peat moss as a topdressing.

Divide the first figure of the analysis of any fertilizer into 100, and the answer is the number of pounds of the fertilizer per 1000 square feet you may safely spread on turf with no danger of burning the grass, provided the application is made when the grass is dry. This figure represents the percentage of nitrogen in the material.

Use the same plant foods in the same amounts when making the lawn on topsoil. The turf will be greener, thicker, and more weed-free than where there is no topsoil.

Here are some general principles in lawn-making and care that may well be followed:

Arrange that all surface water runs off the turf onto the garden; grades should be so slight as to be difficult to detect. Wet areas should be drained or not used as part of the lawn; plant a clump of pussy willows in them.

Have few flower beds or none at all cut into the lawn; better have flowers in borders edging the lawn. Do not run gravel walks through the lawn. Both present mowing problems. Some straight lines to the lawn are admissible, but generally the boundaries should be wavy.

Even if you mow by hand at present, design your lawn for the motor age; some power mowers are hard to back or to make sharp turns. So make your lawn wide, and always mow every bay in your shrubbery or perennial border by going forward.

Do not water the lawn in spring and autumn unless you encounter an exceptionally dry spell, but water freely in July and August. Grass roots will go deep after food and moisture if they have to, and witholding water when the roots do not need it desperately makes them better able to withstand the hot weather.

Mow your lawn often—at least once a week, and twice a week is better. One inch is a good height at which to cut the home lawn. Do not rake up clippings; let them remain to shrivel and become a part of the soil.

The best time to make a new lawn is early autumn; next best is early spring, or in winter on level land. A turf of mixed grasses is preferable to a single-variety one. In the central and northern sections of the United States, mixtures of Merion bluegrass, Chewing's, illahee or creeping fescues, with highland, seaside, Astoria or colonial bents, are recommended. Use the amounts advised by the concern compounding the mixture. When the lawn is three months old, weeds may be controlled by spraying with 2-4-D, PMAS or potassium cyanite. Fungus troubles usually may be kept in check by fungicides advertised in lawn and golf magazines. Most lawn insects may be taken care of with applications of chlordane.

In the southern States, Bermuda grass is the popular lawn variety; shoots or runners may be planted at 12-inch intervals— a method known as "sprigging." If preferred, seed of Bermuda grass may be sown instead in late spring.

In the mid- and upper-southern States, Bermuda grass has a long dormant period in winter. Here it is usual to sow a temporary winter turf on the Bermuda, first spreading soil; rye grass or redtop and rye grass are much used for this. This turf is mown regularly all winter and disappears in spring. Except for this temporary turf, do not experiment with northern grasses in the South or southern grasses in the North; it has been tried many times before and always with very mediocre results.

A steeply sloping lawn is difficult to use and the turf is hard to maintain. It is better to terrace it. A hundred or so 6-foot bamboo canes, ordinarily sold for supporting dahlias, will be useful for this.

Attach a spirit level to a 12-foot board and test its accuracy. Strip the topsoil. Drive the canes in the stripped area 9 feet apart; tops must be level as shown by the level board. Measuring from the top of each cane, note on each the thickness from which subsoil has to be taken or to which it has to be added. A wall of field-stone or a 22½-degree slope may be built and another level may be started. When the level is satisfactory, the topsoil is returned.

Steps with very wide treads may be grassed if little traffic is expected; crushed stone may be spread for heavy wear. Trunks of young cedars from 3 to 6 inches in diameter may be spiked in to strengthen the treads. At each side of the steps an occasional dwarf perennial may be planted against the risers. If the retaining walls are made of fieldstone or if stones are used to maintain the 22½-degree slopes, similar rock-garden plants may be set between them, and we have a typical dry-wall garden.

When truing-up the edges of a lawn, which has to be done once a month, avoid removing soil to leave a gutter at the lawn's edge. Instead, return the soil on the bare side to the same level as the turf side. One mower wheel can then run in the dirt and a few strokes of the rake can be used to obliterate the tracks. If you prefer a steel edging to hold the grass, or one of brick or concrete, and there is a difference of level, place a piece of 2' x 6' lumber for the mower wheel to run upon.

CHAPTER 22

Some Useful Lists

> " 'Thou wert not, Solomon! in all thy glory
> Array'd,' " the lilies cry, " 'in robes like ours;
> How vain your grandeur! Ah, how transitory
> Are human flowers!' "
>
> HORACE SMITH, Hymn to the Flowers.

BUSHES, SHRUBS AND TREES THAT WILL STAND SHADE

Arrowwood
Azaleas in variety
Carolina allspice
Dogwood
Hemlock, American
  ground
Honeysuckle, bush
  Tatarian
Hydrangea, oak-leaved
Jetbead
Mock orange
Mountain laurel

Nannyberry
Pepperbush
Privet in variety
Rhododendron in variety
Snowball (*Viburnum opulus*)
  (*Hydrangea arborescens*)
Snowberry
Spice bush
Viburnum, maple-leaved
White spruce
Witch hazel

FLOWERS FOR SHADE

Here is a list of annuals, perennials and climbers that will tolerate day-long shade in woodland or against a north wall:

Aconitum
Begonia
Cardinal flower
Digitalis

English ivy
Forget-me-not
Hardy ferns
Lady's-slipper

Lily-of-the-valley
Primula
Vinca
Viola and Violets

FLOWERS FOR SEMI-SHADE

The following need sun for half the day:

Ajuga	Cornflower	Lupinus
Aster	Cynoglossum	Nicotiana
Balsam	Fuchsia	Pansy
Christmas Rose	Gentian	Petunia
Clarkia	Godetia	Snapdragon

FLOWERS FOR SUN

Most other flowers like full sun all day, the following especially:

Armeria	Gladiolus
Calendula	Helianthus
Coreopsis	Marigold
Cosmos	Nasturtium
Dahlia	Portulaca
Eschscholtzia	Zinnia

PERFUMED PLANTS

For the most intimate part of your garden, the areas where you place the garden furniture, in borders surrounding a patio. These are the spots where perfume is as important as color when considering your plantings. Following are some of the subjects you may use to create the perfumed living room:

Annuals

Alyssum	Datura	Mignonette	Pinks
Carnation	Heliotrope	Nasturtium	Snapdragon
Centaurea	Marigold	Nicotiana	Stock
Cynoglossum	*Mathiola bicornis*	Petunia	Sweet Peas
	Wallflower, biennial		

Spring-planting Bulbs

Lilies: auratum, philippinense, regale; Lily-of-the-valley, lycoris, Madeira vine, tuberose.

Fall-planting Bulbs

Pheasant's eye daffodils, Dutch hyacinths, jonquils, *Lilium candidum.*

Hardy Perennials

Arabis albida	Dianthus	Mother of thyme	Valerian
Bee-balm	Dictamnus	Old man	Violets
Daphne	Lavender	Phlox	Yucca
		Sagebrush	

Herbs

Costmary	Lemon verbena	Rosemary
Geraniums, scented	Marjoram	Woodruff
Lavender-cotton	Mints, various	
	Climbing Perennial Kudzu vine	

Woody Perennial Climbers

Clematis paniculata, honeysuckle, silver lace vine.

Shrubs and Trees

Boxwood	Heathermist	*Rosa rugosa*, hybrids
Broom	Jasmine	*wichuriana*
Butterfly bush	Juniper in variety	Roses, everblooming
Carolina allspice	Lilac	Star magnolia
Daphne	Linden	Sweet bay
Dyer's yellow-wood	Myrtle	Sweet pepperbush
Fragrant sumac	Philadelphus	*Viburnum carlesi*
Fringe Tree	*Rosa multiflora*	fragrans

Before planting a subject with which you are not acquainted, refer to Chapters 8, 9, 10 and 11 to ascertain its suitability for your part of the country.

EVERLASTING FLOWERS

Most blooms will wilt or fall apart in a few days after they are gathered, but not so the following; these may be dried and will retain their shape and color for months, making excellent floral decorations in the home over the winter. Cut them and hang the bunches in the garage for a week or two, or until you are ready to use them.

Annuals

Acroclinium	Catananche	Globe amaranth	Sea lavender
Ammobium	*Celosia plumosa*	Helichrysum	Xeranthemum

	Hardy Perennials		Biennial
Echinops	False Bittersweet	Physalis	Honesty
Edelweiss	Lavender	Statice	

Shrubs

Hydrangea paniculata   Holly

Note: Some of the annuals, biennials, and perennials listed in this chapter are not described in this book. Consult the larger seed and nursery catalogues; a reference to them, also, will be found in *Better Flowers for Your Home Garden* (Melady Garden Books, Grosset & Dunlap, Inc., New York).

AUTUMN LEAVES

Trees and Shrubs That Give Color in Fall

Arrowwood	Red	Maple, Japanese	Red
Barberry, Japanese	Red	red	Scarlet
Bayberry	Bronze	sugar	Red
Beech	Yellow	Oak, red	Red
Blueberry, high-bush	Crimson	scarlet	Scarlet
Boston ivy	Red	white	Purple
Burning bush	Scarlet	Oregon grape	Bronze
Cotoneaster	Red	Oriental plane	Yellow
Crataegus in variety	Yellow, red	Redbud	Yellow
Currant, golden	Yellow	Sassafras, common	Yellow-red
Dogwood	Scarlet	Shadbush	Yellow
Dyer's yellow-wood	Yellow	Sourwood	Scarlet
Elder, box	Yellow	Spindle tree	Red
Elm, American	Yellow	Sumac, fragrant	Red
Forsythia viridissima	Purple	staghorn	Scarlet
Fringe tree	Yellow	Tulip tree	Yellow
Gum, sweet	Scarlet	Tupelo	Red
Hickory	Brown	Varnish tree	Yellow
Hornbeam	Yellow	Viburnum	Purple
Hop Hornbeam	Orange	Virginia creeper	Red
Hydrangea, oak-		Wahoo	Red
leaved	Yellow	White ash	Yellow
Katsura tree	Orange	Witch hazel	Yellow
	to red	Yellow birch	Yellow
Maidenhair tree	Yellow		

FOR PLANTING AT THE SEASHORE

Trees and Shrubs that Withstand Spray and High Wind

Alder, speckled
Arrowwood
Barberry, Japanese
Bayberry
Beach plum
Buffaloberry
Buttonball
Chinese matrimony vine
Cockspur thorn
Cottonwood
Currant, Indian
Elderberry
False acacia
Flameleaf
Hackberry
He-huckleberry
Honey locust
Honeysuckle, Tatarian
Hydrangea in variety
Jetbead
Larch
Lombardy poplar
Maple, Amur
   red

Maythorn, English
Oak, red
Pepperbush
Pine, Austrian
   Scots
Privet, common
   Regel's
Red cedar
Rosa rugosa hybrids
Rose, fence
Rose of Sharon
Savin
Thorn, scarlet-fruited
   Washington
Scotch broom
Scotch heather
Sea buckthorn
Shadbush
Spruce, Colorado blue
Staghorn sumac
Swect spire
Tanyosho
Winterberry

CHAPTER 23

Tool House, Frames, and Greenhouse

"Who loves a garden loves a greenhouse too." COW-
PER, The Task.

TOOL HOUSE

UNLESS you have a very large garage in which spreaders, other
wheel tools, and even a tractor may be kept, a separate small
building should be erected, not too far from the residence. Two
wide doors will be desirable to permit mowers to be driven in,
through, and out again without turning. A work bench and electric lighting will be useful as well as a water faucet and sink,
designed to allow the pipes to be drained for the winter in the
North, if you do not propose to heat it.

*A tidy garden is a good garden, and the tool shed helps keep it so;
this is a lean-to against the garage.*

The age in which we are living suggests the desirability of combining the tool house with an air-raid shelter. Your local Civilian Defense authorities will furnish you with plans for an approved shelter which you can make serve.

FRAMES

To extend your garden activity, have two or more frames, which normally are 6 feet square, each accommodating two "lights,"—another name for sash or window—each about 6 feet by 3 feet.

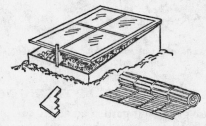

An amateur's cold frame. A storm sash is taken down before winter's end to form the light; the sloping top frame is constructed to accommodate it. Sash is raised a few inches in warm weather, is covered with mats or boards when the thermometer is low.

Cold frames have no artificial heat; they afford protection from March to May and from October to December.

Hotbeds are frames with electric heating wires laid in the soil under them. Or they are placed on a thick layer of fresh stable manure mixed with leaves; some soil is spread and the frames placed on top. A genial warmth is generated by the decaying manure—but manure is scarce in most sections.

With a heated greenhouse the frames could be placed against the greenhouse foundation, where there would be little need to heat them at all. Their use then would be as a temporary storage for plants after they have been produced, to inure them to the change from the heated greenhouse to the outdoor chill. This period of transition is referred to as "hardening-off."

Frames are useful in the growing of bulbs in pots, in sowing delphinium seeds in autumn for flowering the following summer, for sowing pansies on August 1 to be in flower as winter goes and spring arrives, and for many another project.

This small greenhouse can stand alone or be built against the home; some heat will be conserved.

GREENHOUSE AND POTTING SHED

A greenhouse gives your garden an added interest in the colder parts of the year; it may well connect with the tool house, which will then become a potting shed also. The latter will need bins for loam, sand, humus, leaf mold, fertilizer; racks for pots, plant sticks; also shelves for tying materials, plant labels, insecticides and fungicides.

Better let the sink empty outside onto a gravel area instead of into the sewers, which would be likely to clog with the soil accumulated from pot washing. A small heating plant to take care of both the greenhouse and potting shed will be necessary.

The greenhouse will be used to produce your flower and vegetable plants for spring gardening outdoors, to enable you to "strike" cuttings of hundreds of plants, and to enable you to practise your avocation and supply the home with flowers during winter.

The several business concerns specialising in greenhouse construction may be called upon for recommendations as to the efficient arrangement of the greenhouse, frames, and potting shed.

CHAPTER 24

Some Notes and Helpful Hints

"Many a tree is found in the wood,
And every tree for its use is good;
Some for the strength of the gnarled root,
Some for the sweetness of flower or fruit."
HENRY VAN DYKE, Salute the Trees.

EVERGREENS IN WINDOW BOXES

THESE are attractive during the winter months. Dig, trim and root-prune them in spring, planting them in a sheltered spot for the summer. Replant them in the boxes when frost destroys the geraniums, petunias or lobelias which made them effective during the summer.

If the box is 8 inches wide or narrower, have one row of evergreens, and allow one to a foot. Have two rows if the box is wider than 8 inches. Purchase 8-inch- to 18-inch-high young plants of pyramidal arborvitae, Woodward ball-shaped arborvitae, mugho pine, white spruce, small junipers, perhaps, boxwoods or taxus. It is best to have one variety only in a row, but if you are in a part of the country where English ivy is green all winter, put a row of it, with the plants 1 foot apart, just inside the front edge. Transplant these also to the garden in spring.

If your boxes are wide enough for two rows, have two kinds of evergreens and plant the taller row on the inside against the window. The size of the plants that are available will determine which goes where; if they are of equal height, put arborvitaes against the window.

Order your little evergreens "Matched for window boxes." Your nursery will be glad to furnish uniform plants.

OTHER PLANTS IN WINDOW BOXES

Some of the flowering and colored-leaved plants that may be used include:

Outside in Summer: Sunny Position

Alyssum, lobelia, gleam nasturtiums, Kenilworth ivy, balcony petunia, and ice plant. These would be planted along the outside edge of the boxes. In the center you may use geraniums, tuberous begonias, marigolds, or heliotrope.

Shady Position

Tradescantia, sedum, vinca, or again Kenilworth ivy—these along the edge. In the center, dracaena, ferns, coleus, or calla.

Inside in Winter

Daffodils, narcissi, hyacinths, tulips, geranium, fuchsia, or lobelia.

Plants for outside window boxes may be planted directly in the soil. Inside boxes look well if the plants are kept in their pots and placed in the boxes, with some standing on blocks or stones to bring their tops level. Put moist peat moss between them and over the earth in the pots.

You have an opportunity for landscape design in planting even a window box. With a little thought and some effort you can achieve a professional effect instead of an amateurish one. Note the heights the plants eventually attain; change them frequently; select colors with care; don't crowd; plant at the correct depth; shear off fading flowers, dead leaves, or dead branches; pull weeds and keep the soil stirred.

JUVENILE PLANTS

If you propose gradually to landscape your property through the years and you have time to spare, you may wish to develop some of your own plants; you will find it interesting and economical and you may even earn a little money. Send to your nursery for a list of two-year-old seedlings or grafted plants. Purchase those you will want to use; they will cost surprisingly little.

Prepare a plot of level ground and plant the baby plants in straight lines 12 inches apart. Leave a 30-inch-wide bare area for a path between each three rows. Drive in stakes 3 feet apart along the first and third rows of plants; nail 2′ x 2′ lumber to form rails. Attach 4-foot laths crosswise of the plant rows, leaving a space equal to the width of a lath between each. The semi-shade from the laths will encourage the young plants to take hold and grow for the first two years, after which you may transplant them 2 feet apart in parallel rows 3 feet apart without shading. Trim them as necessary and cultivate between the plants, until you are ready to set them in their permanent places. You will probably find yourself with more evergreens than you need, so you will have some for sale to neighbors, seed stores, and garden centers. Better offer them balled and burlaped.

Varieties may well be those listed in this book, so far as baby plants are available. When you come across a State forestry nursery in your travels, stop off and inspect the methods that are being used.

SHRUBS IN TUBS

These are good for placing at the entrance of your home—outside or just within if you wish. Several standing at the corners of your patio will be effective. Good kinds to purchase would be: Pyramidal arborvitae, 3 to 4 feet; Woodward arborvitae, 15 to 18 inches; mugho pines, 15 to 18 inches. Order them "Matched for tubs." *Picea conica glauca* and *Picea excelsa* may be grown in tubs to bring into the house as living Christmas trees.

You can procure suitable tubs from your seed store; measure the ball in "B.&B." plants for size. Replant every spring if you can, every second spring at least, taking the opportunity to wash, dry, and repaint the tubs.

SPECIMEN PLANTS

Sometimes referred to as a sentinel plant, this is one standing by itself, to be viewed from all sides—not grouped with others. Some good evergreen sentinel trees include the Koster blue spruce, *thuja occidentalis, pseudotsuga douglasi, pinus strobus, pinus sylvestris* and *chaemaecyperis*.

Deciduous sentinel trees may be selected from any of the maples, horse chestnut, a group of several birches, hickory, redbud, a group of dogwoods, beech, tulip tree, magnolia, plane tree, Japan cherry, any of the oaks, sassafras, mountain ash, Chinese or Siberian elm.

The nurseryman sometimes calls an extra-fine bush or tree of any variety a "specimen," in the sense that it is a good specimen, near-perfect and shapely, and has not been taken haphazard from the fields.

TOPIARY WORK

The age we live in is more practical than the times of our grandparents. Prior to the advent of the automobile it was usual for a craftsman to spend much of his life perfecting some work to interest his patron or employer—something like the urge that prompted the artist to paint a picture or to perfect a magnificent piece of jewelry for a royal personage.

Old-fashioned topiary work. This is the result of many seasons' painstaking work.

There were thoughts of this nature behind the topiary work of the nineteenth century in Europe. Branches on crataegus, boxwood, holly, cypress or taxus were permitted to mature and harden into suitable curves or straight lines, twisted and pruned to produce the shape of fantastic animals, birds, or merely the more restrained trimming into neat formal designs.

Topiary work is little seen nowadays, but horticulture develops in circles, and it is not unlikely that this quaint effort may be revived.

166

CACTI

These curious plants, mostly natives of the drier sections of North America, provide an unusual feature for a sunny position. Many are hardy only in the southern States, while a few withstand our winters almost anywhere south of the Canadian border. Books on the culture of the more than 1500 known varieties are available, and specialist growers will advise as to which may be desirable for you to plant.

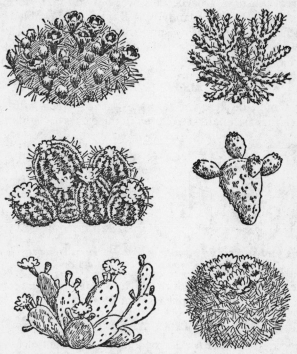

Some hardy cacti. UPPER LEFT: *Echinocereus gonocanthus (the king's crown).* UPPER RIGHT: *Echinocereus viridiflorus; flowers are greenish.* CENTER LEFT: *Opuntia rafinesquei (prickly pear); flowers are yellow with a reddish center.* CENTER RIGHT: *Opuntia rutila.* LOWER LEFT: *Opuntia ficus-indica; flowers yellow; the least hardy of this group.* LOWER RIGHT: *Pediocactus simpsonii, the snowball cactus; pinkish flowers are massed in whitish wool.*

Another way to find suitable hardy sorts is to purchase mixed cactus seeds. Sow them in pots or flats in a greenhouse or indoors against a light window. Transplant them into other pots or boxes, which you set in a sheltered sunny spot indoors; the kinds that survive may be planted later in the outdoor rock garden or in pockets in a dry wall.

PICNIC IN THE GARDEN

For real fun have a barbecue stove; but you need not build a fire every time. In your plan have as few steps as possible between the kitchen and your eating spot, with no steps, so that you can wheel a tea wagon onto the patio amid your outdoor furniture—table, chairs, a chaise longue.

DRYING YARD

This should be near the house. A lattice screen is usual, for drying clothes are unattractive even in these days of highly colored

Drying yard screened by roses or grapes. On a small property it may double as a depository for the trash cans.

lingerie. It is the logical spot in which to hide the refuse cans, too, for it is convenient to the driveway and street.

PLAY AREA

A fenced-in area with a latched gate is an essential feature of the garden if you have children or expect to have them. Since it should be in full view of the most-used rooms in the house, it is well to shade it by locating it under a tall tree or planting a fast-growing one near by to be effective during the heat of the day.

The larger toy stores may be canvassed for the necessary furnishings, like a sandbox, teeter, slide, wading pool and shower. If space is limited, combining the play area with the drying yard may be a possibility, but is not recommended. Within the fence is the place for a playhouse for wet-weather operations.

A SUNDIAL

There should be a space on your lawn that is unshaded, for you will recall that we suggested that you keep the center open—here is the spot for a sundial. Place it on an interesting pedestal, perhaps the balustrade from an old bridge, a timber from a ship, a beam from a mill, or a cairn of cemented fieldstones.

If the angle made by the gnomon with the dial equals the degree of latitude, your apparatus will cast a reasonably accurate shadow to indicate the hour in standard time.

An old wall dial may be obtained, or even the more complicated types may be fabricated in one's own workshop.

An interesting type is a Coast Guard flagpole. A spar guyed at the correct angle and pointing north is an efficient gnomon. Facsimile life-savers or small white-painted anchors may be placed to mark the hours on the grass.

Or the points of the compass may be hammered out of thin brass and set in concrete in your patio.

SWIMMING POOL

For the larger garden a swimming pool 18 by 36 feet or larger may be considered. In the suburbs a fence wall will be necessary, so that it may be locked against transients. Its use only when supervised is important, for there is danger otherwise.

A swimming pool is the high point of design in a large garden.

If you have the room and the finances, a pool may occupy the center of a greenhouse with benches along the sides and glass shelves above them; hang baskets containing plants in the center.

Formal pool with a pleasing wall fountain. Have it a foot deep along the sides, which should overhang to protect fish both against sun and hunting cats.

HAVE A FOUNTAIN

The sound and sight of falling water is always fascinating, and a fountain is a good feature in the layout of a garden. In the nature of a waterfall it may fit in with the pool garden or rock garden, as suggested in Chapter 20, or it may form part of the shower for the play area. As part of the planting scheme the area around a waterfall may have some large hardy ferns or fernlike plants.

If you install a spotlight to show the fountain at night you will have something unusual. Colored lighting is not advised.

Aspidium acrostichoides (Christmas fern, dagger fern). Plant it in damp soil around a waterfall or pool.

HARDY FERNS

For a moist part of a shaded rock garden, for a bog garden, for the neighborhood of the splash from a waterfall or fountain, ferns will provide a picturesque addition to the garden.

Good hardy fern plants may be purchased from specialist growers, and one method of adding to one's stock is to dig promising roots from the wild when on your rambles. If you own a greenhouse you may try the interesting process of growing them from the dust-small spores which are offered by some horticultural houses. Expect to need a year, however, to produce small ferns from spores. They like ordinary good topsoil mixed with coarse sand, enriched with fragments of peat moss and leaf mold.

ENCOURAGE THE BIRDS

Feed the birds, have several seed stations and install suet cakes in protective covers. Erect several bird baths so designed that the domestic cat cannot reach the bathers.

Bird baths. LEFT: *bath with a section for feed; birds don't complain if feed is splashed.* CENTER: *a rustic design.* RIGHT: *bath of wrought iron.*

If you can spare a small patch of ground you may sow or plant subjects that birds like; and if you own large acreage, *allées* may meander through woodlands planted to these same crops. Or grow them in fence corners. Some of the favorite foods are buckwheat, sunflower, canary grass, hawthorn, *Rosa rugosa,* bittersweet, grapes, bush honeysuckle, Virginia creeper, raspberry, blackberry, box elder, hackberry, mountain ash, wild cherry, mulberry and trailing honeysuckle. Do not hesitate to attract birds with these; even birds that live exclusively on seeds pay for their keep by collecting weed seeds.

Bird-feeding stations. LEFT: *on window sill for watching the diners.* CENTER: *away from the house for nervous birds; two are suspended, one is attached to fence.* RIGHT: *a multiple feeder.*

171

Bird houses. LEFT: *robin.* LEFT-CENTER: *apartment house for martins.* CENTER: *a blue jay's home.* RIGHT-CENTER: *a woodpecker feeding near her family.* RIGHT: *wren house; tiny entrance admits only small breeds.*

If you are a large property-owner in the mid-South and wish to attract quail, sow a mixture of bene, lespedeza and sesbania; Egyptian wheat and sorghum are also good. These are field crops much used in the locality, and seeds are readily available. Browntop millet is a southern crop much used to attract doves.

YOUR TREE SURGEON CAN HELP YOU

The longer you own them the more valuable do your trees become. When trees or shrubs become sick, are blown over or broken by storms, are attacked by insects or diseases you cannot control, consult a reliable tree surgeon.

LEFT: *burning tent caterpillars is not advised; spraying with lead arsenate is preferred.* RIGHT: *consult a tree surgeon when trees are sick; he will tell you how to prune broken trees or how to graft new branches onto them.*

His experienced eye will detect borers where the layman would not; he recognises flocks of young scale insects where the owner might find only a few adults. He will warn early of the Dutch elm disease, will look for evidence of gipsy moth, brown-tail moth, or other trouble-makers; he will explain why you should not grow currants or gooseberries if you or your neighbors have white pines, or why cedars and apple trees are mutual enemies. He is a master in efficient spraying and has the necessary equipment.

AUTUMN LEAVES—COMPOST

Do Not Destroy Them

Unfortunately it is standard practice to rake autumn leaves into heaps and burn them. But it is not the best thing to do. Rarely does our soil contain too much organic matter, and there is always a tendency to lose what little we have through the years.

LEFT: *A compost heap dished to hold rain, partly hidden in a fence corner. A receptacle of brick or concrete blocks is permanently helpful.* RIGHT: *the heap screened in by creepers.*

Recommended procedure is to assign an area hidden from view by bushes, in which raked-up leaves, lawn clippings, weeds and clean vegetable rubbish are deposited for the purpose of decaying, which they ordinarily will do in about a year. They will decompose more quickly in warm weather and in the warmer sections of the country; more quickly also if the heap is turned occasionally and wetted down; again more quickly if some soil or sand is added as the heap accumulates; most quickly of all if one of the decay hasteners is used, like Adco or Compo.

Decayed vegetable matter, which the gardener calls compost, acts and looks much like rotted stable manure or leaf mold and is a good substitute for either. Screened through a 1-inch-mesh sieve, it may be used as a mulch around shrubs and roses. A 2-inch blanket of it will retain moisture, hasten growth, and keep many weeds under control.

WATERING

After you have transplanted annuals or perennials they should be watered for several days; the soil around shrubs needs to be kept wet for several weeks after planting; trees for a month or two. But once they are established they should take care of themselves in normal weather.

During spring and autumn, flowers, lawns and shrubs usually need little water, but during July and August the land becomes very dry in some sections. Usually moisture can be retained in the land by continually stirring the surface. Should plants show signs of exhaustion before this, however—if their leaves droop and wilt —water them, and give them plenty—sufficient to bring their leaves upright again by morning.

It pays to let most plants struggle for moisture, up to the point of letting them begin to droop, because deep rooting is encouraged thereby. An exception to this concerns evergreens: in the summer a light sprinkling of their leaves and branches with plain water under forceful pressure will help keep them clean of soot from the oil burner and do much to fight red-spider mites.

At the end of a dry autumn, saturate the soil around all shrubs, using a soil-soaker or weeping sock, a device which allows water to run slowly onto a given area; repeat this for several days. Shrubs which go into winter with well-soaked roots are less likely to be winter-killed.

ENCOURAGE A HEALTHY DISCONTENT

You have made your plan, you have worked on it, and you are generally pleased with the results, except perhaps in one or two sections. Too crowded here, perhaps? The plants too tall there? Over-shaded? The colors not entirely pleasing? The path too narrow?

Work out a solution to these minor problems on paper; then get busy. It will be difficult to discard things you have planted yourself, to get rid of some features that to you seemed important, chiefly because you own them. But it will pay to be ruthless.

> *"Ever charming, ever new,*
> *When will the landscape tire the view?"*
> JOHN DYER, Grongar Hill.